W9-APF-127

Marketing Strategy

Planning and Implementation

The Irwin/McGraw-Hill Series in Marketing

Alreck & Settle
The Survey Research Handbook
Second Edition

Anderson, Hair & Bush
Professional Sales Management
Second Edition

Arens
Contemporary Advertising
Seventh Edition

Bearden, Ingram & LaForge
Marketing: Principles & Perspectives
Second Edition

Belch & Belch
**Introduction to Advertising and Promotion:
An Integrated Marketing Communications
Approach**
Fourth Edition

Bernhardt & Kinnear
Cases in Marketing Management
Seventh Edition

Berkowitz, Kerin, Hartley & Rudelius
Marketing
Fifth Edition

Bowersox & Closs
Logistical Management
First Edition

Bowersox & Cooper
Strategic Marketing Channel Management
First Edition

Boyd, Walker & Larreche
**Marketing Management: A Strategic Approach
with a Global Orientation**
Third Edition

Cateora & Graham
International Marketing
Tenth Edition

Churchill, Ford & Walker
Sales Force Management
Fifth Edition

Churchill & Peter
Marketing
Second Edition

Cole & Mishler
Consumer and Business Credit Management
Eleventh Edition

Cravens
Strategic Marketing
Fifth Edition

Cravens, Lamb & Crittenden
Strategic Marketing Management Cases
Sixth Edition

Crawford
New Products Management
Fifth Edition

Dillon, Madden & Firtle
Essentials of Marketing Research
First Edition

Dillon, Madden & Firtle
**Marketing Research in a Marketing
Environment**
Third Edition

Dobler, Burt, & Lee
**Purchasing and Materials Management: Text
and Cases**
Sixth Edition

Douglas & Craig
Global Marketing Strategy
First Edition

Dwyer & Tanner
Business Marketing
First Edition

Etzel, Walker & Stanton
Marketing
Eleventh Edition

Futrell
ABC's of Relationship Selling
Fifth Edition

Futrell
Fundamentals of Selling
Sixth Edition

Gretz, Drozdeck & Weisenhutter
Professional Selling: A Consultative Approach
First Edition

Guiltinan & Paul
Cases in Marketing Management
First Edition

Guiltinan, Paul & Madden
**Marketing Management Strategies and
Programs**
Sixth Edition

Hasty & Reardon
Retail Management
First Edition

Hawkins, Best & Coney
Consumer Behavior
Seventh Edition

Hayes, Jenster & Aaby
Business to Business Marketing
First Edition

Johansson
Global Marketing
First Edition

Johnson, Kurtz & Scheuing
**Sales Management: Concepts, Practices &
Cases**
Second Edition

Kinnear & Taylor
Marketing Research: An Applied Approach
Fifth Edition

Lambert & Stock
Strategic Logistics Management
Third Edition

Lambert, Stock & Ellram
Fundamentals of Logistics Management
First Edition

Lehmann & Winer
Analysis for Marketing Planning
Fourth Edition

Lehmann & Winer
Product Management
Second Edition

Levy & Weitz
Retailing Management
Third Edition

Levy & Weitz
Essentials of Retailing
First Edition

Loudon & Della Bitta
**Consumer Behavior: Concepts
& Applications**
Fourth Edition

Mason, Mayer & Ezell
Retailing
Fifth Edition

Mason & Perreault
The Marketing Game!
Second Edition

McDonald
Direct Marketing: An Integrated Approach
First Edition

Meloan & Graham
**International and Global Marketing Concepts
and Cases**
Second Edition

Monroe
Pricing
Second Edition

Moore & Pessemier
**Product Planning and Management:
Designing and Delivering Value**
First Edition

Oliver
**Satisfaction: A Behavioral Perspective on
the Consumer**
First Edition

Patton
**Sales Force: A Sales Management
Simulation Game**
First Edition

Pelton, Strutton & Lumpkin
**Marketing Channels: A Relationship
Management Approach**
First Edition

Perreault & McCarthy
**Basic Marketing: A Global Managerial
Approach**
Thirteenth Edition

Perreault & McCarthy
**Essentials of Marketing: A Global
Managerial Approach**
Seventh Edition

Peter & Donnelly
A Preface to Marketing Management
Seventh Edition

Peter & Donnelly
Marketing Management: Knowledge and Skills
Fifth Edition

Peter & Olson
Consumer Behavior and Marketing Strategy
Fifth Edition

Peter & Olson
Understanding Consumer Behavior
First Edition

Quelch
Cases in Product Management
First Edition

Quelch, Dolan & Kosnik
Marketing Management: Text & Cases
First Edition

Quelch & Farris
**Cases in Advertising and Promotion
Management**
Fourth Edition

Quelch, Kashani & Vandermerwe
European Cases in Marketing Management
First Edition

Rangan
**Business Marketing Strategy: Cases,
Concepts & Applications**
First Edition

Rangan, Shapiro & Moriarty
**Business Marketing Strategy:
Concepts & Applications**
First Edition

Rossiter & Percy
**Advertising Communications and
Promotion Management**
Second Edition

Stanton, Spiro, & Buskirk
Management of a Sales Force
Tenth Edition

Sudman & Blair
**Marketing Research:
A Problem-solving Approach**
First Edition

Thompson & Stappenbeck
The Marketing Strategy Game
First Edition

Ulrich & Eppinger
Product Design and Development
First Edition

Walker, Boyd & Larreche
**Marketing Strategy: Planning and
Implementation**
Third Edition

Weitz, Castleberry & Tanner
Selling: Building Partnerships
Third Edition

Zeithaml & Bitner
Services Marketing
First Edition

Marketing Strategy

Planning and Implementation

Third Edition

Orville C. Walker, Jr.
James D. Watkins Professor of Marketing
University of Minnesota

Harper W. Boyd, Jr.
Donaghey Distinguished Professor of Marketing
University of Arkansas—Little Rock

Jean-Claude Larréché
Alfred H. Heineken Professor of Marketing
European Institute of Business Administration
INSEAD

Boston   Burr Ridge, IL   Dubuque, IA   Madison, WI   New York   San Francisco   St. Louis
Bangkok   Bogotá   Caracas   Lisbon   London   Madrid
Mexico City   Milan   New Delhi   Seoul   Singapore   Sydney   Taipei   Toronto

Irwin/McGraw-Hill

A Division of The **McGraw·Hill** *Companies*

MARKETING STRATEGY: PLANNING AND IMPLEMENTATION

Copyright © 1999 by The McGraw-Hill Companies, Inc. All rights reserved. Previous editions © 1992 and 1996 by Richard D. Irwin, a Times Mirror Higher Education Group, Inc. company. Printed in the United States of America. Except as permitted under the United States Copyright Act of 1976, no part of this publication may be reproduced or distributed in any form or by any means, or stored in a data base or retrieval system, without the prior written permission of the publisher.

This book is printed on acid-free paper.

1 2 3 4 5 6 7 8 9 0 QPD/QPD 9 3 2 1 0 9 8

ISBN 0-256-26118-0

Vice president and editorial director: *Michael W. Junior*
Publisher: *Gary Burke*
Executive editor: *Stephen M. Patterson*
Editorial coordinator: *Andrea Hlavacek-Rhoads*
Senior marketing manager: *Colleen J. Suljic*
Project manager: *Karen J. Nelson*
Senior production supervisor: *Madelyn S. Underwood*
Senior designer: *Crispin Prebys*
Supplement coordinator: *Carol Loreth*
Compositor: *GAC Shepard Poorman Communications*
Typeface: *10/12 Times Roman*
Printer: *Quebecor Printing Book Group/Dubuque*

Walker, Orville C.
    Marketing strategy : planning and implementation / Orville C.
Walker, Jr., Harper Boyd, Jr., Jean-Claude Larréché. — 3rd ed.
      p. cm.
    Includes bibliographical references and indexes.
    ISBN 0-256-26118-0
    1. Marketing—Management.   I. Boyd, Harper W.   II. Larréché, Jean
-Claude.   III. Title.
HF5415.13.W249   1998
658.8'02—dc21   98-8631
                                              CIP

http://www.mhhe.com

Preface

At the top of many executives' "things-to-do" list as we move into the 21st Century is the objective of making their organizations more market-oriented, more attuned to customer needs and competitive threats, and quicker to respond to changing market conditions. The question is, How can that goal be achieved? Recent studies conclude that the activities essential for achieving a market orientation are too important and pervasive to be left solely to marketers. Employees in every functional area must be trained and motivated to pay attention to and direct their efforts toward satisfying customer needs and desires.

But even when the day-to-day responsibility for marketing activities is diffused across employees in every part of the organization, someone still has to plan, coordinate, and control those activities for each product or service the firm offers the market. Someone must devise a marketing strategy aimed at providing value to customers and gaining an advantage over competitors, and someone must ensure that the various functional activities necessary to implement that strategy are effectively carried out. That "someone" might be a traditional product or marketing manager, a vice president of marketing, a general manager of a business unit, or even a team of managers drawn from a variety of functional areas. Regardless of who bears the responsibility, that process of formulating and managing the marketing strategy for a given market entry is the central focus of this book.

It is also important to recognize, however, that marketing strategies are not formulated or implemented in a vacuum. Most organizations have corporate and business-level strategies that establish guidelines concerning objectives to be attained, directions for future growth, and how the organization will compete and seek to gain a sustainable advantage in the marketplace. These guidelines impose constraints on the range of marketing strategies a marketing manager can pursue within the larger strategic context of his or her organization. But on the other hand, marketing managers are also uniquely positioned to provide information and insights for the development of corporate and business strategies because they straddle the boundary between the external environment and the inner workings of the firm. Thus as organizations strive to become more customer-oriented and face ever more hostile and rapidly changing competitive environments, the marketer's role in strategy formulation is likely to increase.

Similarly, while marketing managers play a crucial role in translating the firm's broad objectives into strategic marketing programs designed to win customer acceptance and competitive advantage in specific markets, they do not implement those programs by themselves. Effective execution requires cooperative and coordinated efforts across many functional areas. Thus the range of viable marketing strategies available to a manager is constrained by the resources and functional competencies available within his or her organization. And the successful implementation of a chosen strategy depends on the marketer's ability to win the cooperation and support of people in other functional areas.

WHY WE WROTE THIS BOOK

As the discussion so far suggests, the process of formulating and implementing marketing strategy is intimately linked with strategic decisions made at higher organizational levels and with the operational decisions and actions taken in a variety of functional departments. It is these internal linkages—together with their direct links to the external market and competitive environment—that make the management of strategic marketing programs such a challenging and interesting endeavor.

Unfortunately, most of the existing marketing management and strategy textbooks do not provide a very complete picture of the complexities involved in managing marketing strategies. Some examine strategic decisions that are made at the corporate or business level but devote relatively little attention to how those decisions might best be translated into strategic marketing programs for individual products or services. Others tend to treat marketing management as a stand-alone business function. While they do a good job of describing the concepts, analytical tools, and planning techniques that are useful for formulating marketing strategies, they pay only scant attention to the web of internal strategic and operational relationships that surround that formulation process. Consequently, our major motivation for writing this book was a desire to provide a broader, more complete, and realistic view of marketing's strategic and operational roles and relationships within today's organizations.

A FOCUS ON THE STRATEGIC PLANNING PROCESS

As a basis for understanding the strategic role of marketing, one must first understand how strategies are formulated: the planning processes and the analytical tools and techniques managers might use when developing strategies. Thus this book is structured around the analytical and decision-making processes involved in formulating, implementing, and controlling a strategic marketing program for a given product-market entry. It includes discussions of customer, competitor, and environmental analysis; market segmentation and targeting; competitive positioning; implementation; and control. Because we assume that the reader is already familiar with many of the concepts and analytical tools relevant to these topics, however, we go beyond a simple review of definitions and procedures to examine strategic implications. In our discussion of positioning decisions in Chapter 8, for instance, we not only review the techniques a manager might use to analyze a product's competitive position in the marketplace, we also discuss various positioning strategies and the conditions under which each is likely to be most appropriate.

A UNIQUE CONCERN FOR STRATEGIC AND INTERFUNCTIONAL RELATIONSHIPS

This book differs from other marketing management and strategy texts in that it examines in detail how marketing interacts with other levels of strategy and with other functional departments within an organization. Specifically, it includes an examination of three sets of relationships that are given little or no attention in other texts.

1. *The relationships between corporate, business-level, and marketing strategies.* As mentioned, managers responsible for developing and implementing marketing strategies for specific products and target markets are also uniquely qualified to provide insights and information needed to formulate competitive strategies at the business and corporate levels of the organization. And as organizations strive to become more customer-oriented, the marketing manager's role in strategic planning is likely to increase. At the same time, those higher-level strategic decisions often impose guidelines and constraints on the marketing manager's freedom of action in designing marketing strategies and programs for individual products or services.

   This book examines this complex set of relationships between the different levels of strategy in several ways. First, Chapter 1 presents a general discussion of the hierarchy of strategies found in most multiproduct organizations, their interrelationships, and the marketer's role in helping to formulate strategies at different organizational levels. Chapter 3 provides a more specific and unique discussion of business-level competitive strategies and their implications for marketing strategies and actions appropriate for individual products or services within the business unit. Finally, each of the chapters discussing alternative strategic marketing programs appropriate for specific market conditions (Chapters 9-11) examines how those programs should fit the firm's higher-level strategies.

2. *Relationships between the content of marketing strategies and the strategic environment.* Most texts talk in general terms about how the marketing strategy for a given product or service should fit the characteristics of the market and competitive environment. But they usually do not provide much detail concerning the specific kinds of strategic marketing programs that are best suited to different environmental contexts. Nor do they discuss the specific tactical decisions and actions necessary to effectively carry out each strategy.

   In contrast, this book provides an entire section of three chapters that discuss the marketing strategies and tactics best suited to specific environmental situations. Those situations are defined both in terms of market characteristics as defined by the stage in the product life cycle and by the product's relative competitive position. Thus Chapter 9 discusses marketing strategies for new market entries. Chapter 10 examines strategies for growth markets, both share-maintenance strategies for market leaders and growth strategies for low-share followers. Finally, strategies for mature and declining markets are described in Chapter 11.

3. *Relationships between marketing and other functional areas.* A marketing manager's ability to effectively implement a strategic marketing program depends in large measure on the cooperation and competence of other functional areas within the organization. Consequently, we devote substantial attention to the interfunctional implications of specific marketing strategies. Each of the marketing strategies appropriate for the particular circumstances described in Chapters 9 through 11 is also examined in terms of the requirements it imposes on other functional departments such as product and process R&D, production, quality control, logistics, and finance. In addition, Chapter 12 provides an overview of the functional competencies required to effectively implement different competitive and marketing strategies. It also discusses organizational mechanisms appropriate for coordinating efforts and resolving conflicts across functional areas.

THE TARGET AUDIENCE FOR THIS BOOK

Most MBA programs offer at least one course on marketing strategy. While they carry many different names—such as "Marketing Policy," "Strategic Marketing," or "Advanced Marketing Management"—they are usually positioned as capstone courses whose primary purpose is to help students integrate what they have learned about the analytical tools and the four Ps of marketing within a broader framework of competitive strategy. Such courses are often required of all marketing majors toward the end of their academic programs. And similar capstone courses are usually either required or offered as electives in many of the better undergraduate marketing programs as well. We designed this book primarily to serve the needs of students in these kinds of courses.

FEATURES APPROPRIATE FOR A CAPSTONE MARKETING STRATEGY COURSE

We think this book's organization structure and its unique content make it particularly well suited for use in integrative capstone courses at either the graduate or advanced undergraduate level. Some particularly relevant features include the following:

- Because the book is organized around the analytical and decision-making processes involved in formulating and implementing marketing strategies, it provides the opportunity for students to review and integrate many of the concepts and techniques they encountered in earlier courses. But rather than simply rehash basic definitions and descriptions, this text emphasizes the strategic implications of such topics as market segmentation, competitor analysis, target market selection, and positioning.

- The book also provides a sound review of the tactical elements—the four Ps—of marketing. But rather than forcing students to wade through yet another set of chapters on product, pricing, promotion, and distribution decisions, each of these program elements is discussed within the context of a variety of alternative marketing strategies, the objectives they are designed to accomplish, and the situations where their use is most appropriate.

- This book pays a great deal of attention to the role of marketing managers in the formulation and implementation of higher-level strategies within the firm and to the influences and constraints those higher-level strategies subsequently impose on the range of marketing actions appropriate for individual products or services. This helps students more fully understand and appreciate the linkages and interactions among an organization's corporate, business, and marketing strategies.

- We also provide unusually extensive discussions of the various functional competencies and resources required by different types of marketing strategies and the kinds of interfunctional coordination necessary to implement those strategies effectively. Thus this book provides a good framework for reviewing and integrating the material that students have been exposed to in courses in other functional areas as well as in previous marketing courses.

- The ultimate objective of any capstone course is to prepare students to make a smooth transition from their academic program into the business world. All of the features described above should help prepare students to better understand and deal with the kinds of activities and decisions they will soon face on the job. But in addition, we have attempted to write the book in a way that reflects both the excitement and the practical realities of marketing management as it happens in a variety of real world settings. The book incorporates hundreds of up-to-date examples that demonstrate marketing strategies and practices as they are applied to industrial as well as consumer products, services as well as goods, not-for-profit organizations as well as business firms, and foreign as well as domestic markets.

And to further enhance student interest and understanding, every chapter begins with a minicase example that introduces and illustrates the major concepts or strategies discussed in that chapter. These introductory examples are referred to at appropriate places throughout each chapter to further help the student see the relationships among concepts and their relevance to real problems.

MAJOR CHANGES IN THIS REVISION

This revision incorporates some new features and changes in emphasis from the second edition. These changes were based on information obtained from both users and nonusers of the second edition, academic associates and industry friends, and our own experiences both in the classroom and in the real world. We think they reflect some of the important developments occurring in the rapidly changing global marketplace.

- We have increased—and more thoroughly integrated—our coverage of *global marketing.* Rather than assign global topics to a separate chapter as we did in the second edition, we have integrated detailed examinations of global marketing actions, programs, and examples throughout every chapter, and particularly within chapters 9-11 which examine marketing strategies appropriate for specific market situations.

- We have added a new chapter (chapter 5) which examines the many advances in *information technology* that are impacting the kinds and amounts of environmental, competitive, and customer information marketers are able to collect and analyze as a basis for their strategies. Our new chapter examines the kinds of marketing information available and some of the tools and procedures used to gather and evaluate it, including the rapidly increasing role of the Internet in market opportunity analysis.

- We have expanded our coverage of *marketing relationships and alliances.* Many organizations are trying to develop and nurture long-term relationships and alliances with customers, channel partners, and suppliers involving greater amounts of trust and cooperation between the parties. Therefore, we have incorporated discussions and examples throughout nearly every chapter which illustrate how such relationships develop and how they can be managed effectively.

- We have included more material on the development and marketing of *services.* We discuss strategic marketing actions and programs appropriate for service firms, and we examine the important role of customer service as a basis for building customer relationships and sustaining a competitive advantage.

- We have expanded our coverage of functional integration and the *new organization structures* that encourage such integration; particularly the use of cross-functional management teams. This material receives particular emphasis in the implementation chapter (chapter 12), but examples are discussed throughout the book.

- We have added a *new computerized international case,* CONGOLIA, plus the GAMAR3 Simulation software to implement it, developed by Jean-Claude Larréché (who developed the highly regarded MARKSTRAT, GAMAR, and INDUSTRAT simulations). CONGOLIA is designed to provide students with flexibility in deciding how best to allocate resources across a portfolio consisting of both countries (five European countries) and product categories. It can also be adapted to a variety of teaching approaches, as discussed next.

FEATURES APPROPRIATE FOR DIFFERENT TEACHING APPROACHES

Capstone courses dealing with marketing strategy not only parade under a variety of different titles, they are also taught in a variety of different ways. Consequently, this book and its package of supporting materials were designed to fit a variety of teaching approaches. While we have tried to avoid excessive repetition and thereby keep the book relatively short and succinct, instructors who prefer a lecture-discussion approach will find ample material for either a quarter or semester course. For those who prefer case-oriented instruction, the book provides a solid foundation of concepts, techniques, and examples to prepare students for effective case analysis and discussion.

The CONGOLIA case and supporting GAMAR3 Simulation software also provide an exciting and realistic way to expose students to the dynamics of resource allocation problems in a global setting. Students can manage a firm over a period of time, analyze situations, make decisions, receive rapid feedback, and adjust their strategies and tactics. It is a highly flexible teaching instrument because it can be used either as a team project with varying degrees of complexity or as an integrated part of the course requiring a limited number of class sessions. The teaching note in the instructor's manual suggests a variety of ways it can be integrated with material in various parts of the text and with different course structures, including those for executive programs.

We also note the following with respect to the book's adaptability to various teaching approaches:

· For those instructors wanting a second—and somewhat simpler—resource allocation case we have included Jean-Claude Larréché's SAMAR case along with detailed teaching notes in the instructor's manual.

· While no cases other than the CONGOLIA and SAMAR simulations are included in the text, the instructor's manual includes detailed information about how to locate both domestic and global cases relevant to a variety of marketing topics.

· A set of discussion questions on each chapter is also included in the instructor's manual. These questions are designed to provide a vehicle for meaningful student exercises or class discussions. Rather than simple review questions that ask students to regurgitate material found in the chapter, these questions are more application-oriented and often take the form of minicases that reflect actual company problems.

ACKNOWLEDGMENTS

A book like this is never solely the work of the authors. Many people aided this enterprise, and we gratefully acknowledge their contributions.

First, we thank our faculty colleagues in our respective schools for their wise counsel and advice. We are also grateful to our friends in industry. Our conversations with them over the years, both informally and within various executive programs, have contributed much to our understanding of how marketing strategy works in the real world.

We have tried to be customer-oriented in preparing a revision that meets the needs of both instructors and students. We are, therefore, most grateful to our many undergraduate, graduate, and executive program students for their constructive criticism of the first two editions and useful suggestions for making this revision a better book. We also appreciate the help of the following colleagues who provided detailed and constructive suggestions for the revision: Jerry Jones, Oklahoma City University; Pradeep Chintagunta, University of Chicago; Subodh Bhat, San Francisco State University; Richard Leventhal, Metropolitan State College; John Coppett, University of Houston-Clear Lake; Shaheen Borna, Ball State University; Daniel Flood, Hawaii Pacific University; and Richard Celsi, California State University-Long Beach.

We owe a debt of gratitude to Roberta Moore for the many different tasks she performed in preparing this manuscript. We also thank the staff at Irwin/McGraw-Hill for their ability to convert a rough manuscript into an attractive and readable book. We would especially like to thank our editor, Steve Patterson, for guidance both before and during the manuscript preparation, editorial assistant Andrea Hlavacek, for manuscript support coordination, and project manager Karen Nelson for her help in finalizing the project.

Finally we salute our wives for their patience and support throughout the many months during which we focused on this revision. Orville Walker thanks Linda, Harper Boyd thanks Virginia, and Jean-Claude Larréché thanks Denyse.

Orville C. Walker, Jr.
Harper W. Boyd
Jean-Claude Larréché

Contents in Brief

Contents

1 SECTION

Introduction to Strategy

CHAPTER

The Strategic Role of Marketing

COMPAQ SWITCHES STRATEGIES[1]

From the beginning Compaq built its reputation—and a substantial market share in the personal computer (PC) industry—on superior technology. The company's competitive strategy was to match industry leader IBM's prices but to offer more innovative PCs for the money. That strategy worked like a charm for nearly a decade, but then the market environment changed.

Changing customer demands and competitor actions lead to a shift in strategy

The earliest buyers of personal computers were either large organizations with professional information managers or technically sophisticated consumers. As the industry developed, however, later buyers were more price conscious, more interested in buying equipment that was easy to use, and more concerned with receiving good postpurchase assistance and service. By the late 1980s a number of firms—most notably Dell Computer— were appealing to this new breed of customer by offering not only mail order delivery at very low prices, but also impressive service and support programs. At the same time new technologies and applications continued to evolve at a rapid pace within the computer industry, such as new generations of computer chips and new hardware and software for network and Internet applications.

For a time Compaq stuck with its traditional competitive strategy and marketing program. It continued to invest heavily in technical research and

[1]This case example is based on material from David Kirkpatrick, "The Revolution at Compaq Computer," *Fortune*, December 14, 1992, pp. 80–88; R. Lee Sullivan, "The Office That Never Closes," *Forbes*, May 23, 1994, pp. 212–13; Garry McWilliams, "Compaq at the 'Crossroads,'" *Business Week*, July 22, 1996, pp. 70–72; Garry McWilliams, "Battle Stations! Battle Stations!" *Business Week*, August 11, 1997, pp. 34–35; Stephanie A. Forest and Peter Burrows, "Give Me an Extra-Fast Modem with That, Please," *Business Week*, September 29, 1997, pp. 38–39; and Compaq's Website at www.compaq.com.

development (R&D), distribute its products only through specialty computer dealers, devote little attention to customer problems or complaints, and tie its prices to those of IBM. But as one Compaq executive pointed out, "When IBM lost touch with the . . . realities of the marketplace, we walked off the cliff with them." By 1991 the firm's market share, revenues, and earnings had all begun to plunge and it had little choice but to shift strategic direction.

New corporate and competitive strategies

The day after announcing Compaq's first-ever quarterly loss, the firm's board of directors replaced the CEO. Incoming president Eckard Pfeiffer established an aggressive new corporate goal: to become a major competitor in the worldwide computer industry while regaining historical levels of profitability and returns to shareholders. Recently, Pfeiffer laid out more specific objectives for the firm to reach on its way toward that overall goal. These include (1) continued annual revenue growth at 20 percent to 25 percent so that by the year 2000 Compaq will be a $40 billion firm and the number three computer maker in the world behind IBM and Fujitsu; and (2) each division of the company will achieve best-in-class return on assets by the turn of the century. Thus, Compaq's PC division will have to exceed Gateway 2000 Inc.'s 21 percent return on assets, the networking business must surpass 3Com Corp.'s 18 percent return, and so forth.

To achieve those objectives, Pfeiffer charted several changes in Compaq's corporate strategy for attaining future growth and profitability: (1) win an increased share of the domestic PC market by developing more user-friendly machines and more customer services at lower prices; (2) use the new low-price, high-value product offerings to expand Compaq's presence in global PC markets, (3) use the

firm's technical R&D competencies, and acquisitions where necessary, to develop new product lines and services—such as powerful workstations and servers, and software used to manage information on computer networks—aimed at fast-growing business markets, and (4) outsource more manufacturing and inventory management activities and form more alliances with suppliers and channel partners to reduce costs and improve return on assets.

Compaq's new growth objectives also required major changes in competitive strategy in many of its different divisions or business units. The PC division, for example, switched from a strategy of competing primarily on technical superiority and a constant parade of new products to a competitive strategy appealing to larger but less sophisticated customer segments by developing simpler and easy-to-use product lines, offering improved customer support, and charging dramatically lower prices.

Of course, Compaq's PC division had to revamp many of its internal policies and procedures in order to effectively implement its new price-oriented competitive strategy and still reach its revenue and profit objectives. As mentioned, the firm developed more cooperative long-term relationships with many of its suppliers. As a result, the cost of the components used in its PCs dropped nearly 30 percent. Similarly, the firm sought ways to make more efficient use of the capital invested in its plants and equipment. By adding second and third shifts at its three plants, for instance, it doubled the output of PCs from its existing factory space and reduced unit costs by more than half.

New strategic marketing programs

The PC division's new competitive strategy also required adjustments in its strategic marketing programs. For instance, the division had to expand its product offerings to appeal to broader and more price-sensitive target segments. It added several new computer lines, including the low-priced ProLinea line and the user-friendly Presario line of preprogrammed PCs. Of course, the division continued to develop new, technically sophisticated consumer products, but at a slower pace than in the past. Instead, the corporation shifted much of its R&D effort to new divisions developing powerful servers and workstations, network software, and Internet applications for faster growing and higher margin business markets.

To increase awareness of Compaq's revamped policies and products among its new target segments of consumers, the PC division expanded its advertising budget by 60 percent to $90 million. It also changed the content of its ads. Where they used to emphasize computer terminology, they are now more reader-friendly and stress customer benefits, such as why a Compaq notebook is easy to use on an airplane.

To make Compaq computers easier for potential customers to find, and to improve the availability of service and customer support, the company more than doubled its worldwide retail outlets to over 9,000. It added office supply discounters like Office Depot, and even mass-merchants like Wal-Mart, to its distribution channel to supplement the traditional computer stores. Recently, the firm has begun accepting direct orders for customized PCs in order to match some of the competitive advantages of Gateway 2000 and Dell. However, most of Compaq's built-to-order machines will be sold in cooperation with computer retailers like CompUSA.

The firm has also relied on new computer and communications technologies to improve its own marketing productivity and efficiency. Telemarketers, a toll-free customer help-line, and a web page help field routine inquiries about products, pricing, and operating problems, thereby freeing field salespeople to focus on servicing larger accounts and developing new

business. A computerized sales support system includes an on-line database where Compaq staffers from all divisions and functional departments record and coordinate their contacts with each customer and prospect. These new systems enabled the firm's PC salesforce to more than triple its revenue per person.

The bottom line

So far Compaq's new competitive and marketing strategies have performed very well on some dimensions, less well on others. The firm's total revenues more than quadrupled from about $4 billion in 1991 to over $18 billion in 1996. Those results reflect growing success in global markets and in some high-margin commercial sectors of the domestic market, such as engineering workstations and network servers and software. Similarly, the firm produced nearly $800 million in economic value added in 1996. **Economic value added (EVA)** is the amount of return a strategy or operating program generates in excess of the cost of capital. (We will discuss EVA in Chapter 2.) On the other hand, the firm's profits have grown more slowly, so that improvements will be necessary for the firm to make its net income and return-on-assets objectives for the year 2000. For an update on how well Compaq is doing on various performance dimensions, visit the company's website (www.compaq.com) and click on "Inside Compaq."

To some extent Compaq's continued success will depend on the company's ability to maintain productive alliances with its major suppliers, retailers, and corporate customers to hold down costs and improve customer service. Unfortunately, Compaq's new low-price strategy in the consumer market has strained some of those relationships, particularly its long-standing relationship with Intel, the firm's primary supplier of microprocessor chips.

Under its previous strategy, Compaq acted as Intel's close technical partner.

The company spent more on engineering than most of its rivals and was always among the first to bring out new models with the latest Intel chip. But its new strategy motivated the firm to court Intel's rivals—the makers of copycat chips—hoping to foster the development of a commodity market for microprocessors. That would enable Compaq to spread its purchases over several competing suppliers and thereby attain lower component costs. Of course, it also would cut into Intel's margins—margins that are as much as five times higher for its newest state-of-the-art chips than for its older "commodity" chips. Therefore, Intel fought back with an extensive advertising campaign (e.g., the "Intel Inside" campaign extolling the superiority of the firm's Pentium chip) to promote the advantages of PCs—including those offered by Compaq's competitors—carrying the company's most advanced microprocessor. Intel also threatened to integrate forward, and start producing its own competing line of PCs. Thus, Compaq's new strategy is not only influencing its own sales and profit performance in the global PC market, but also it may shake up established alliances and even change the competitive structure of the industry. The firm's future success will depend on how well it continues to adapt to the ongoing changes in technology, competition, and customer desires that characterize the computer industry.

CORPORATE, BUSINESS, AND MARKETING STRATEGIES: DIFFERENT ISSUES AT DIFFERENT ORGANIZATIONAL LEVELS

The experiences of Compaq in the PC industry illustrate some important points about strategy that will recur as themes throughout this book. First, most firms, particularly larger corporations with multiple divisions or business units, pursue a hierarchy of interdependent strategies. Each strategy is formulated at different levels in the organization and deals with different sets of issues. For example, Compaq's goal of capturing market share leadership in the PC industry and its decision to seek future growth primarily by increasing its penetration of global consumer markets and developing new products for corporate networks reflect its new **corporate strategy.** This level of strategy provides direction on the company's mission, the kinds of businesses it should be in, and its growth policies.

On the other hand, attempts to differentiate Compaq's offerings from those of IBM and other competitors by providing greater customer value through lower prices, improved customer services, and the development of more user-friendly products reflect the firm's **business-level strategy** in the consumer market. This level of strategy primarily addresses the way a business will compete within its industry.

Finally, interrelated functional decisions about how to divide the market into customer segments, which segments to target, what products and service enhancements to offer each segment, what promotional appeals and media to employ, and what prices to charge all reflect the **marketing strategies** for each of Compaq's various product-market entries. Each marketing strategy provides a plan for pursuing the company's objectives within a specific market segment.

Because the different levels of strategy are all closely interrelated, individual marketing strategies and programs are not created in a vacuum. Instead, the marketing objectives and strategy for a particular product-market entry should be consistent with the direction and resources provided by the firm's corporate and business-level strategies. Thus, a marketing manager's freedom of action is constrained by strategic decisions made at higher levels within the firm. For instance, the manager responsible for the firm's Prolinea line of PCs has little freedom to increase prices without higher approval because such a move would be inconsistent with the competitive strategy of providing superior value to price-sensitive customers.

On the other hand, a major part of the marketing manager's job is to monitor and analyze the needs and wants of customers and potential customers and to identify emerging opportunities and threats posed by competitors and trends in the external environment. Marketers thus often play a major role in providing input to and influencing the development of corporate and business-level strategies. For instance, when the need for new corporate and competitive strategies at Compaq became obvious due to declining sales and profits, decisions about the content of those new strategies were strongly influenced by customer and competitor information and analyses provided by the firm's sales and marketing personnel. Indeed, the new CEO appointed to lead the firm back to financial health rose through the firm's marketing ranks.

Regardless of who is involved in formulating the various levels of strategy or how appropriate those strategies are for addressing the market and competitive circumstances faced by a firm, they will not lead to successful outcomes unless they are implemented effectively. As Compaq's experience exemplifies, sound implementation requires a clear vision, specific goals, and solid support from top management. And the organization's structure, policies, and processes must also be designed to enable and encourage employees at all levels to take the actions necessary to make the strategy work. As one authority argues, "success comes by aligning the strategy and capabilities of the organization with the market, thereby delivering superior customer value."[2]

Strategy: a definition

Although strategy first became a popular business buzzword during the 1960s, it continues to be the subject of widely differing definitions and interpretations. The following definition, however, captures the essence of the term as it is most commonly used.

> A **strategy** is a fundamental pattern of present and planned objectives, resource deployments, and interactions of an organization with markets, competitors, and other environmental factors.[3]

As this definition suggests, a good strategy should specify (1) *what* is to be accomplished, (2) *where* (on which industries or product-markets it will focus), and (3) *how* (which resources and activities will be allocated to each product-market to meet environmental opportunities and threats and to gain a competitive advantage).

---

[2]George S. Day, "Aligning the Organization to the Market," in Donald R. Lehmann and Katherine E. Jocz, eds., *Reflections on the Futures of Marketing* (Cambridge, Mass.: Marketing Science Institute, 1997), p. 68.

[3]For a summary of the definitions offered by a number of other authors, see Roger A. Kerin, Vijay Mahajan, and P. Rajan Varadarajan, *Contemporary Perspectives on Strategic Market Planning* (Boston: Allyn and Bacon, 1990), pp. 8–9. Our definition differs from some others, however, in that we view the setting of objectives as an integral part of strategy formulation, whereas they see objective setting as a separate process. Because a firm's objectives are influenced and constrained by many of the same environmental and competitive factors as the other elements of strategy, it seems logical to treat both the setting of objectives and the allocation of resources aimed at reaching those objectives as two parts of the same strategic planning process.

The components of strategy

More specifically, there are five components—or sets of issues—within a well-developed strategy.

1. *Scope.* The scope of an organization refers to the breadth of its strategic domain: the number and types of industries, product lines, and market segments it competes in or plans to enter. Decisions about an organization's strategic scope should reflect management's view of the firm's mission or strategic intent. This common thread between its various activities and product-markets defines the essential nature of what its business is and what it should be in the future. Thus, the CEO's vision of Compaq as one of the top three computer firms in the world has motivated the company to aggressively expand its presence in global markets and to expand its product offerings for the high-tech segments of the commercial market.

2. *Goals and objectives.* Strategies also should specify desired levels of accomplishment on one of more dimensions of performance—such as volume growth, profit contribution or return on investment—over specified time periods for each of the firm's businesses and product-markets and for the organization as a whole. The objective for each product division at Compaq is to achieve a return on assets that meets or beats that of the best competitor in the division's market, while the company as a whole continues to achieve 20 percent to 25 percent annual revenue growth.

3. *Resource deployments.* Every organization has limited financial and human resources. Thus, a strategy should specify how such resources are to be obtained and allocated across businesses, product-markets, functional departments or management teams, and activities within each business or product-market.

4. *Identification of a sustainable competitive advantage.* Perhaps the most important part of any strategy is a specification of how the organization will compete in each business and product-market within its domain. How can it position itself to develop and sustain a differential advantage over current and potential competitors? To answer such questions, managers must examine the market opportunities in each business and product-market and the company's core competencies or strengths relative to its competitors. For example, since Compaq is one of the most efficient firms in its industry, aggressive pricing aimed at delivering superior customer value is a primary component of its competitive strategy in the consumer PC market.

5. *Synergy.* Synergy exists when the firm's businesses, product-markets, resource deployments, and competencies complement and reinforce one another. Synergy enables the total performance of the related businesses to be greater than it would otherwise be: The whole becomes greater than the sum of its parts. Consequently, strategies should be designed to exploit potential sources of synergy across the firm's businesses and product-markets as a means of improving the organization's overall efficiency and effectiveness. Thus, Compaq expects that its R&D and product development efforts aimed at the high-tech commercial market will eventually lead to performance improvements for its lower-priced consumer products as well.

The hierarchy of strategies

Explicitly or implicitly, these five basic dimensions are part of all strategies. However, instead of a single comprehensive strategy, most organizations pursue a hierarchy of interrelated strategies, each formulated at a different level of the firm. The three major levels of strategy in most large, multiproduct organizations are (1) corporate strategy, (2) business-level strategy, and (3) functional strategies focused on a particular product-market entry. These three types of strategy are diagrammed in Exhibit 1-1.

While our primary focus is on the development of marketing strategies and programs for individual product-market entries, Exhibit 1-1 shows that other functional departments, such as R&D and production, also have strategies and plans. Thus, the organization's success in a given product-market depends on the effective coordination of strategies and activities across functions. Throughout this book, then, we will pay attention to the inter-functional implications of marketing strategies, the potential conflicts across functional areas, and the mechanisms that firms use to resolve those conflicts.

Strategies at all three levels contain the five components outlined above, but because each strategy serves a different purpose within the organization, each emphasizes different sets of issues. Exhibit 1-2 summarizes the specific focus and issues dealt with at each level of strategy, and they are discussed in the next sections.

Corporate strategy

At the corporate level managers must coordinate the activities of multiple business units and (in the case of conglomerates) even separate legal business entities. Thus, decisions about the organization's scope and appropriate resource deployments across its various divisions or businesses are the primary focus of corporate strategy. The essential questions to be answered at this level are, What business(es) are we in? What business(es) should we be in? and What portion of our total resources should we devote to each of those businesses to achieve the organization's overall goals and objectives? For instance, the highest managerial levels at Compaq made the decisions to provide the resources necessary to pursue market share leadership in both domestic and global PC markets and to invest in developing new businesses focused on printers, servers, and other peripheral equipment.

Attempts to develop and maintain distinctive competencies at the corporate level tend to focus on generating superior financial, capital, and human resources; designing effective organizational structures and processes; and seeking synergy among the firm's various businesses. Synergy can become a major competitive advantage in firms where related businesses reinforce one another by sharing corporate staff, R&D, financial resources, production technologies, distribution channels, or marketing programs.

Business-level strategy

The question of how a business unit will compete within its industry is the critical focus of business-level strategy. Thus, a major issue addressed in a business strategy is how to achieve and sustain a competitive advantage. What distinctive competencies can give the business unit a competitive advantage? And which of those competencies best match the needs and wants of the customers in the business's target segment(s)? For example, a business with low-cost sources of supply and efficient, modern plants might adopt a "low cost" competitive strategy, while one with a strong marketing department and a competent salesforce might compete by offering superior customer service.[4]

---

[4]C. K. Prahalad and Gary Hamel, "The Core Competencies of the Corporation," *Harvard Business Review* 68 (May–June 1990), pp. 79–91. See also Michael Treacy and Fred Wiersema, *The Discipline of Market Leaders* (Reading, Mass.: Addison-Wesley, 1995).

E X H I B I T   1 – 1

The Hierarchy of Strategies

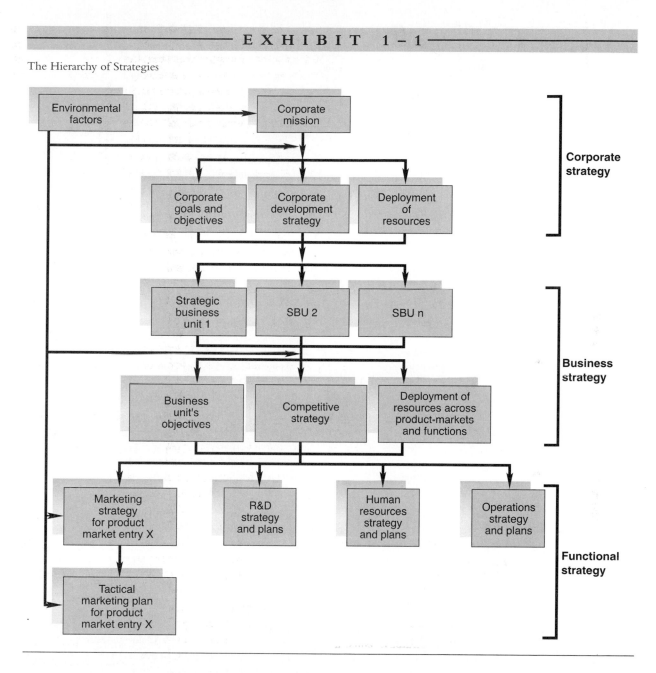

Because different customer segments may want different benefits from the same category of products, a business unit may not have the competencies needed to compete effectively in all market segments. Therefore, another important issue that a business-level strategy must deal with is that of appropriate scope: how many and which market segments to compete in, and the breadth of product offerings and marketing programs needed to appeal to these segments.

Finally, synergy should be sought across product-markets and across functional departments within the business. Thus, Compaq uses some of the same salespeople and distribution channels that handle its PCs to also sell its new servers.

E X H I B I T   1 - 2

Key Components of Corporate, Business, and Marketing Strategies

Strategy components	Corporate strategy	Business strategy	Marketing strategy
Scope	• Corporate domain— "Which businesses should we be in?" • Corporate development strategy 　　Conglomerate diversification (expansion into unrelated businesses) 　　Vertical integration 　　Acquisition and divestiture policies	• Business domain— "Which product-markets should we be in within this business or industry?" • Business development strategy 　　Concentric diversification (new products for existing customers or new customers for existing products)	• Target market definition • Product-line depth and breadth • Branding policies • Product-market development plan • Line extension and product elimination plans
Goals and objectives	• Overall corporate objectives aggregated across businesses 　　Revenue growth 　　Profitability 　　ROI (return on investment) 　　Earnings per share 　　Contributions to other stakeholders	• Constrained by corporate goals • Objectives aggregated across product-market entries in the business unit 　　Sales growth 　　New product or market growth 　　Profitability 　　ROI 　　Cash flow 　　Strengthening bases of competitive advantage	• Constrained by corporate and business goals • Objectives for a specific product-market entry 　　Sales 　　Market share 　　Contribution margin 　　Customer satisfaction
Allocation of resources	• Allocation among businesses in the corporate portfolio • Allocation across functions shared by multiple businesses (corporate R&D, MIS)	• Allocation among product-market entries in the business unit • Allocation across functional departments within the business unit	• Allocation across components of the marketing plan (elements of the marketing mix) for a specific product-market entry
Sources of competitive advantage	• Primarily through superior corporate financial or human resources; more corporate R&D; better organizational processes or synergies relative to competitors across all industries in which the firm operates	• Primarily through competitive strategy; business unit's competencies relative to competitors in its industry	• Primarily through effective product positioning; superiority on one or more components of the marketing mix relative to competitors within a specific product-market
Sources of synergy	• Shared resources, technologies, or functional competencies across businesses within the firm	• Shared resources (including favorable customer image) or functional competencies across product-markets within an industry	• Shared marketing resources, competencies, or activities across product-market entries

Marketing strategy

The primary purpose of a marketing strategy is to effectively allocate and coordinate marketing resources and activities to accomplish the firm's objectives within a specific product-market. Therefore, decisions about the scope of a marketing strategy involve specifying the target market segment or segments to be pursued and the breadth of the product line to be offered. Next, firms seek a competitive advantage and synergy through a well-integrated program of marketing mix elements—primarily the "Four Ps" of product, price, promotion, and place or distribution channels—tailored to the needs and wants of customers in the target segments. For example, user-friendly features, low prices, extensive distribution, and heavy media advertising aimed at buyers seeking PCs for household use are all elements of Compaq's new marketing strategy in the domestic consumer market.

STRATEGIC PLANNING SYSTEMS

Compaq is an example of a company that has well-developed, integrated strategies at all three levels. Unfortunately, this is not the case with all companies, in part because of the wide variations across firms in the extensiveness of strategic planning and the procedures followed in formulating strategies.

The value of formal planning systems

At one extreme, some companies—particularly smaller, entrepreneurial firms—employ few, if any, formal strategic planning procedures. Of course, this does not necessarily mean that they have no strategy. The owner or top executive may have had a clear strategic vision in the beginning. And he or she may give some sporadic thought to strategic issues as the firm and its industry evolve over time. Nevertheless, evidence suggests that such piecemeal, informal approaches to strategic planning are not as effective as more formal systems for formulating strategy. For example, one review of 15 studies comparing firms with formal planning systems to firms without such systems found that the formal planners outperformed the informal planners in two-thirds of the cases examined.[5]

The obvious question, of course, is whether such research findings are still valid in today's more volatile economy. Do firms that engage in formal strategic planning continue to outperform those that don't, even in the face of the rapidly changing market and competitive conditions? Most experts would answer the question with a resounding "Yes!" Even though strategic plans may have to be revised or adapted more frequently than in the past, most organizations still benefit from the process of developing them.[6]

For one thing, a formal planning process forces managers to take time from daily activities to consider strategic issues that might otherwise be overlooked. It also helps structure and operationalize the otherwise daunting task of responding to a dynamic environment and strategically managing a complex organization with limited resources. Thus, research

---

[5]J. Scott Armstrong, "The Value of Formal Planning for Strategic Decisions: Review of Empirical Research," *Strategic Management Journal* 3 (1982), pp. 197–212.

[6]Hal Goetsch, "Are Marketing Plans Passé?" *Marketing News*, December 5, 1994, pp. 4–5.

suggests that formal planning is even more useful under conditions of major change in the firm or its environment, when uncertainty is high, and when complex decisions must be reached. When explaining why United Parcel Service was expanding its formal strategic planning efforts, its CEO said, "Because we're making bigger bets on investments in technology, we can't afford to spend a whole lot of money in one direction and then find out five years later that it was the wrong direction."[7]

Finally, a formal plan can help prevent firms from making too many erratic changes in response to short-lived environmental disruptions, which only confuses employees and customers. As one author suggests, a formal plan is like the rudder on a ship. The plan may be disrupted by changing conditions, just as a ship's rudder may not be very useful during heavy seas. Yet a plan, like a rudder, is essential for providing direction and holding the firm on course when the storm is over.

Evolution of planning systems

Even among firms that do employ formal planning systems, there are great differences in who participates, the procedures followed, and the content of the strategic plans ultimately produced. In spite of this diversity, some attempts have been made to categorize broad types of planning systems. In one of the best-known studies, Gluck, Kaufman, and Walleck of the McKinsey consulting firm examined the planning procedures followed by 120 firms in seven different countries.[8] They identified four types of planning systems: financial planning, long-range planning, strategic planning, and strategic management.

Gluck and his colleagues argue that these four systems reflect an evolutionary process; each type appeared at a different time during the 20th century and each subsequent system added to, rather than replaced, earlier systems. They also found that planning systems within individual companies tend to develop along a similar evolutionary path, with new start-ups concentrating on financial planning but then moving toward strategic management as they grow and the strategic issues they face become more complex. As we shall see, though, many firms have not yet developed the most sophisticated types of planning systems. Major characteristics of each type are summarized in Exhibit 1-3 and are discussed below.

Financial planning systems

This type of planning consists mainly of an annual budgeting process that focuses on forecasting revenue, costs, and capital requirements. Annual budgets are then set for the firm's various businesses and departments, and careful attention is paid to deviations from those budgets to find explanations and determine whether remedial actions are required.

The assumption underlying financial planning systems is that the past will repeat itself, that the market and competitive environment a business will face next year will be largely the same as this year. Thus, detailed strategies are seldom formalized, although implicit strategies often are reflected in the resource allocation decisions made by top management when they approve or adjust budgets for their various businesses. As a result, the planning

---

[7]John A. Byrne, "Strategic Planning," *Business Week*, August 26, 1996, p. 46.

[8]Frederick W. Gluck, Stephen P. Kaufman, and A. Steven Walleck, "The Four Phases of Strategic Management," *Journal of Business Strategy* 3 (1982), pp. 9–21.

—————————————— E X H I B I T   1 – 3 ——————————————

Characteristics of Alternative Planning Systems

Characteristic	Type of planning system			
	Financial planning	Long-range planning	Strategic planning	Strategic management
Management emphasis	Control budget deviations	Anticipate growth and manage complexity	Creative response to changing environment by changing strategic thrust and capabilities	Cope with strategic surprises and fast-developing opportunities or threats
Major assumptions	The past repeats	Past trends will continue	New trends and discontinuities are predictable	Planning cycles are inadequate to deal with rapid changes
Direction of strategic decision making	Top-down	Bottom-up	Mixed (leaning toward top-down)	Mixed (leaning toward bottom-up)
Planning time frame	Periodic	Periodic	Periodic	Real time
Underlying value system	Meet the budget	Predict the future	Think strategically	Create the future
Time period when first developed	Early 1900s	1950s	1960s	Mid-1970s

SOURCE: Adapted from F. Gluck, S. Kaufman, and A. Walleck. "The Four Phases of Strategic Management," *Journal of Business Strategy*, Winter 1982, pp. 9–21; D. Aaker, *Strategic Market Management*, 2nd ed. (New York: John Wiley & Sons, 1988), p. 10; and R. Kerin, V. Mahajan, and P. Varadarajan, *Contemporary Perspectives on Strategic Market Planning* (Boston: Allyn and Bacon, 1990), p. 18.

process, such as it is, under this kind of system is highly centralized at the top levels of corporate management.

Financial planning systems were first widely adopted by firms during the first half of the 20th century. Yet over half the businesses Gluck and colleagues surveyed in the early 1980s, including some very successful firms, still followed this kind of "meeting-the-numbers" approach.

Long-range planning systems

Relative to financial planning and its emphasis on annual budgets, long-range planning systems cover longer time frames (5 or 10 years) and are more future-oriented. Focusing on anticipating growth and managing increasing complexity, they attempt to project future sales, costs, technological changes, and the like. Any gaps between projected sales and profits and the organization's goals are analyzed to determine what operational changes—such as a new plant or a larger salesforce—might be necessary to achieve long-term objectives.

A major assumption underlying long-range planning systems is that past trends can be extrapolated into the future. Unfortunately, this means that little consideration is given to anticipating new opportunities or initiating new directions. Resources tend to be allocated across businesses and product-markets already in the firm's portfolio.

Because many of the projections and forecasts that serve as the foundation for long-range planning are produced by the managers of individual businesses within the firm, such systems tend to be relatively decentralized. While top management makes major resource allocation decisions and monitors the short-term performance of each business, objectives are often set from the bottom up, with each business bearing the responsibility for determining its own goals and strategies.

In spite of its shortcomings, most planning systems in use during the 1980s did not go much beyond this kind of planning by extrapolation according to Gluck and his colleagues. Indeed, observation suggests that such long-range planning systems are still in use at some firms.

Strategic planning systems

Increasingly rapid and disruptive changes in the market environment—such as the energy crisis, high inflation, and increased foreign competition—helped precipitate the development of strategic planning during the 1960s and early 1970s. Because such changes caused discontinuities and shifts in past trends, simply extrapolating such trends into the future was no longer an adequate basis for planning in many industries.

Consequently, strategic planning systems attempt to achieve a more in-depth understanding of the firm's market environment, particularly its customers and competitors. The objective is to anticipate changes and shifts that might have strategic implications. Thus, strategic planning is more dynamic than earlier systems. It focuses on identifying possible opportunities or threats in the environment, evaluating alternative responses, and, when necessary, changing the strategic direction and capabilities of the firm. Current business units and their strengths and weaknesses are not assumed as given; they can change according to market conditions. Thus, a firm's various businesses are not all expected to perform in the same way, and each may pursue its own competitive strategy and objectives.

Like earlier systems, though, strategic planning is a periodic, usually annual, process. Most organizations employing these systems update their strategic plans in the spring or summer. Then, during the fall, those plans provide a foundation for developing annual operating plans and budgets for the individual businesses and products within the firm.

While marketing and business-unit managers often have some input into annual strategic planning processes, top corporate executives usually make final decisions concerning strategic directions and the allocation of company resources. Corporate management hands down strategy and budget guidelines to the business units at the beginning of the planning process, and it reviews and approves each unit's final plan and budget. Thus, while most strategic planning systems involve elements of both bottom-up and top-down planning, corporate management tends to play the dominant role.

One advantage of annual strategic planning is that it forces managers to address strategic issues at scheduled times. Without such a formal process, managers might become absorbed in day-to-day problems and lose sight of the bigger strategic picture. On the other hand, competitive threats and market opportunities can arise so quickly in today's global economy that rigidly tying managers to an annual planning process can severely reduce a firm's flexibility and lead to disastrous outcomes.

Strategic management systems: tools for creating market-driven strategies.

By the late-1970s some firms, particularly diversified manufacturing companies in dynamic industries such as electronics, recognized that an annual formal planning cycle was inadequate to respond in a timely way to rapid changes occurring in their global environments. Consequently, they began developing strategic management systems to

---
EXHIBIT 1 – 4

A Team Approach to Strategic Management at J. M. Smucker Company

> J. M. Smucker Co., the Ohio-based maker of jams and jellies, recently enlisted a team of 140 employees—7% of its workforce—who devoted nearly 50% of their time to reevaluating the firm's strategies for more than six months. "Instead of having just 12 minds working on it, we really used the team of 140 as ambassadors to solicit input from all 2,000 employees," says President Richard K. Smucker. "It gave us a broader perspective. . . ." The company, which has struggled to grow in a mature market, now has a dozen viable initiatives that could double its $635 million revenues over the next five years. One of them is an alliance with Brach & Brock Confections Inc. to make Smucker's jellybeans, the first of several co-branded products to be developed under the pact. The idea came from team members who would not have had much to say about the company's strategy in the past.

SOURCE: John A. Byrne, "Strategic Planning," *Business Week*, August 26, 1996, p. 52. Reprinted with special permission. Copyright 1996 by McGraw-Hill Companies.

supplement, or even replace, the formal planning process with procedures and structures designed to enable the organization to identify and respond quickly to fast-changing customer needs, global market opportunities, and competitive threats. Such systems, in other words, aimed to make the firm a more market oriented, learning organization and to facilitate the rapid development and implementation of market-driven strategies. Efforts to develop and fine-tune these kinds of strategic management systems continue in a growing number of firms to this day.

Firms pursuing this new form of strategic management have developed a variety of new procedures and structures to improve the responsiveness of their decision making, including more detailed environmental scanning; continuous, real-time information systems; seeking frequent feedback from and coordinating plans with cutting-edge customers and major suppliers; decentralization of strategic decisions; encouragement of entrepreneurial thinking among lower-level managers; and the use of interfunctional management teams to analyze issues and initiate strategic actions outside the formal planning process.[9] The J. M. Smucker Company provides one example of a decentralized strategic management system at work (see Exhibit 1-4).

As we mentioned in the case example at the beginning of this chapter, Compaq also has developed some strategic management structures and procedures to help make it more responsive to the market. For instance, it formed a multifunctional management team to assess market conditions and develop its new line of low-priced PCs. The firm has also formed close relationships with retail chains such as Office Depot to expand distribution and (with the possible exception of Intel) has worked closely with suppliers to improve quality and reduce the cost of components for its new machines. These and other actions recommended to make the strategic planning efforts of organizations more market-driven and flexible are summarized in Exhibit 1-5.

Because strategic management systems emphasize staying in close and constant touch with the environment and decentralized decision processes, lower-level managers tend to play a more crucial role in formulating strategy. Of course, top management is still

---

[9]For more detailed discussions of the rationale for and procedures involved in such systems see, George S. Day, *Market-Driven Strategy: Processes for Creating Value* (New York: Free Press, 1990), chaps. 3 and 4; Frederick E. Webster, Jr., *Market-Driven Management: Using the New Marketing Concept to Create a Customer-Oriented Company* (New York: John Wiley & Sons, 1994): and John A. Byrne, "Strategic Planning," *Business Week*, August 26, 1996, pp. 46–52.

E X H I B I T   1 – 5

Guidelines for Market-Driven Strategic Management

1. Create customer focus throughout the business.
2. Listen to the customer.
3. Define and nurture your distinctive competence.
4. Define marketing as market intelligence.
5. Target customers precisely.
6. Manage for profitability, not sales volume.
7. Make customer value the guiding star.
8. Let the customer define quality.
9. Measure and manage customer expectations.
10. Build customer relationships and loyalty.
11. Define the business as a service business.
12. Commit to continuous improvement and innovation.
13. Manage culture along with strategy and structure.
14. Grow with partners and alliances.
15. Destroy marketing bureaucracy.

SOURCE: Frederick E. Webster, Jr., "Executing the New Marketing Concept," *Marketing Management* 3, no. 1 (1994), p. 10. Reprinted by permission from the American Marketing Association.

responsible for defining the organization's basic strategic thrust and has the final authority to approve or reject new strategic initiatives emanating from the lower ranks. Thus, strategic management systems also involve elements of both bottom-up and top-down planning. However, lower-level managers tend to be more active and influential participants in such systems than in firms that rely on more formal, periodic strategic planning.

Characteristics of effective planning systems

As planning systems have evolved over the years, each new type has added features to, rather than replaced, earlier systems. But the fact that the newer systems represent attempts to improve upon and overcome the weaknesses of earlier ones should not be interpreted as meaning that the newest planning approach—strategic management—is the most appropriate and effective for all organizations. Research suggests that any type of planning system can be effective if tailored to the firm's environment, the nature of its businesses, and the organizational context.[10] Thus, for a firm engaged in commodity businesses that competes primarily on price in relatively predictable market and competitive environments, a financial or long-range planning system might be adequate. For example, Cargill—one of the nation's largest dealers in agricultural products like wheat and soybeans—reaches many of its strategic decisions through long-range planning based on projections of future grain production and global demand.

Regardless of the type of system used, firms effective at strategic planning have three things in common.[11] First, there is little resistance to the planning process within the firm. Managers strongly believe that planning is essential for the organization's continued success. Consequently, they are active, willing participants in the planning process; and they are committed to successfully implementing the strategies that are developed.

A second and closely related characteristic is strong support from top management. Clearly, other employees are more likely to take planning seriously when top executives are

[10]Balaji Chakravarthy, "On Tailoring a Strategic Planning System to Its Context: Some Empirical Evidence," *Strategic Management Journal*, November–December 1987, pp. 517–34.

[11]V. Ramanujam, N. Venkatraman, and John C. Camillus, "Multi-Objective Assessment of the Effectiveness of Strategic Planning: A Discriminant Analysis Approach," *Academy of Management Journal* (June 1986), pp. 347–72.

strongly committed to the planning process and its outcomes. This is particularly true for decentralized strategic management systems. When lower-level managers are given more responsibility for making strategic decisions, they should also be given commensurate authority and support, including resources for environmental scanning, market analysis, and other systems needed to provide adequate information for planning and effective implementation of the plans that are developed.

Finally, effective planning systems strike a balance between creativity and control. That is, they encompass elements of both top-down and bottom-up planning. Top management must formulate a clear strategic vision for the firm, guard against the various business and product-market strategies straying too far from that vision, and make sure that strategies at different levels are coordinated with one another. At the same time, lower-level managers must be encouraged to stay in close touch with the market environment, identify emerging threats and opportunities, and initiate strategic responses when necessary.

While all four types of planning systems are in use today, many analysts argue that most companies will need to move toward the more adaptive strategic management–type systems to remain competitive. Increasingly dramatic and rapid environmental changes, brought about by advancing technology, fragmenting markets, global competition, and the like, will require firms to become more market-oriented and more strategically responsive. But the changing business environment not only necessitates changes in how companies formulate and implement their strategies; it is also likely to affect the role that marketing and marketing managers play in those processes.

THE ROLE OF MARKETING IN FORMULATING AND IMPLEMENTING STRATEGIES

Marketing managers bear the primary responsibility for formulating and implementing strategic marketing plans for individual product-market entries. As mentioned earlier, though, their freedom of action in designing such plans is often constrained by their firm's corporate and business-level strategies. The marketing manager for Heinz tomato ketchup, for instance, probably could not gain approval for an aggressive promotional campaign aimed at increasing Heinz's already commanding share of its market. Such a marketing strategy would be inconsistent with a corporate growth strategy that allocates the bulk of the firm's marketing resources to newer, more rapidly growing product categories (such as pet foods and the Weight Watchers' line of entrees) and with a business strategy dedicated to competing in basic food categories by maintaining the lowest-cost position in the industry.[12]

On the other hand, the essence of strategic planning at all levels is identifying threats to avoid and opportunities to pursue. The primary strategic responsibility of any manager is to look outward continuously to keep the firm or business in step with changes in the environment. Because they occupy positions at the boundary between the firm and its customers, distributors, and competitors, marketing managers are usually most familiar with conditions and trends in the market environment. Consequently, they not only are responsible for developing strategic plans for their own product-market entries but also are often primary participants and contributors to the planning process at the business and corporate level as well. As an example, see the wide-ranging influence of marketing managers on

---

[12]Bill Saporito, "Heinz Pushes to Be the Low-Cost Producer," *Fortune* (June 24, 1985), pp. 44–54; and Andrew E. Serwer, "How to Escape a Price War," *Fortune* (June 13, 1994), pp. 84–85.

EXHIBIT 1 – 6

Influence and Participation in Strategic Management by Marketing Managers at General Electric

Strategic planning activity	Marketing's role
Determination of SBU's objectives and scope	Key participant along with SBU's general manager
Environmental assessment (customers; economic, political, regulatory trends)	Primary contributor and a major beneficiary of the results
Competitive assessment (actual and potential competitors)	Primary contributor, working with other functional managers and staff planners
Situation assessment (input to portfolio analysis; industry and market attractiveness; firm and product position)	Primary contributor, working with staff planners and general manager
Objectives and goals	Key participant with other functional managers, including responsibility for measuring several performance indicators
Strategies	Major contributor to determination of SBU's competitive strategy; responsible for marketing strategy and for coordinating plans with other functional strategies
Key program elements	**Marketing's role**
Product-market development	Leadership role
Product quality	Leading responsibility for quality
Distribution	Primary responsibility
Technology	Varies according to the importance of technology to the product or service
Human resources	Responsible for functional area
Business development*	Key supporting role with strategic planning and manufacturing responsible for implementation
Manufacturing facilities	Typically, only limited involvement

*Decisions to expand, improve, or contract the business.

SOURCE: Adapted from a speech presented by Stephen G. Harrell (then of the General Electric Company) at the American Marketing Association Educator's Conference, Chicago, August 5, 1980. Mr. Harrell is currently a Partner in Megamark Partners, a consulting firm specializing in marketing and new product development. Reprinted by permission of the American Marketing Association.

strategic planning within strategic business units (SBUs) at General Electric, as outlined in Exhibit 1-6. GE's marketing managers have primary responsibility for, or are among the key participants in, formulating nearly all aspects of an SBU's business strategy, as well as planning and implementing many functional program elements within the business unit.

Factors that mediate marketing's role in strategic planning

Unfortunately, marketing managers do not always play so extensive a strategic role as they do at General Electric because not all firms are as market-oriented as GE. Not surprisingly, marketers tend to have a greater influence on strategy at all levels in organizations that embrace a market-oriented philosophy of business.

Market-oriented management

Market-oriented organizations tend to operate according to the business philosophy known as the marketing concept. As originally stated by General Electric four decades ago, the **marketing concept** holds that the planning and coordination of all company activities around the primary goal of satisfying customer needs is the most effective means to attain and sustain a competitive advantage and achieve company objectives over time.

Thus, market-oriented firms are characterized by a consistent focus by personnel in all departments and at all levels on customers' needs and competitive circumstances in the market environment. They are also willing and able to quickly adapt products and functional programs to fit changes in that environment. Such firms pay a great deal of attention to customer research *before* products are designed and produced. They embrace the concept of market segmentation by adapting product offerings and marketing programs to the special needs of different target markets. Finally, their organizational structures and procedures reflect a market orientation. Marketing managers or product teams play an active role in planning strategies, developing products, and coordinating activities across functional departments to ensure that they are all consistent with the desires of target customers. Thus, the market-oriented firm keeps its businesses focused on well-defined market segments and continually seeks to enhance its competitive advantages.[13]

Does being market-oriented pay off? Recent evidence suggests that it does, at least in a highly developed economy like the United States. Several studies involving a total of more than 400 business units in a variety of industries indicate that a market orientation has a significant positive effect on various dimensions of performance, including return on assets, sales growth, and new product success.[14]

Nevertheless, many companies around the world are not particularly market-oriented. The reasons why firms are not always in close touch with their market environments include the following:

- Competitive conditions may enable a company to be successful in the short run without being particularly sensitive to customer desires.

- Different levels of economic development across industries or countries may favor different business philosophies.

- Firms can suffer from strategic inertia—the automatic continuation of strategies successful in the past, even though current market conditions are changing.

Competitive factors affecting a firm's market orientation

The competitive conditions some firms face enable them to be successful in the short term without paying much attention to their customers, suppliers, distributors, or other organizations in their market environment. Early entrants into newly emerging industries—particularly industries based on new technologies—are especially likely to be internally

[13]Ajay K. Kohli and Bernard J. Jaworski, "Market Orientation: The Construct, Research Propositions, and Managerial Implications," *Journal of Marketing* 54, April 1990, pp. 1–18.

[14]John C. Narver and Stanley F. Slater, "The Effect of a Market Orientation on Business Profitability," *Journal of Marketing*, 54, April 1990, pp. 1–18; Bernard J. Jaworski and Ajay K. Kohli, "Market Orientation: Antecedents and Consequences," *Journal of Marketing* 57, July 1993, pp. 53–70; and Stanley F. Slater and John C. Narver, "Market Orientation, Performance, and the Moderating Influence of Competitive Environment," *Journal of Marketing*, 58, January 1994, pp. 46–55.

E X H I B I T   1 – 7

Differences between Production-Oriented and Market-Oriented Firms

Business activity or function	Production orientation	Marketing orientation
Product offering	Company sells what it can make; primary focus on functional performance and cost	Company makes what it can sell; primary focus on customers' needs and market opportunities
Product line	Narrow	Broad
Pricing	Based on production and distribution costs	Based on perceived benefits provided
Research	Technical research; focus on product improvement and cost cutting in the production process	Market research; focus on identifying new opportunities and applying new technology to satisfy customer needs
Packaging	Protection for the product; minimize costs	Designed for customer convenience: a promotional tool
Credit	A necessary evil; minimize bad debt losses	A customer service; a tool to attract customers
Promotion	Emphasis on product features, quality, and price	Emphasis on product benefits and ability to satisfy customers' needs or solve problems

focused and not very market-oriented, because there are likely to be relatively few strong competitors during the formative years of a new industry; customer demand for the new product is likely to grow rapidly and outstrip available supply; and production problems and resource constraints tend to represent more immediate threats to the survival of such new businesses.

Businesses facing such market and competitive conditions are often **product-oriented** or **production-oriented.** They focus most of their attention and resources on such functions as product and process engineering, production, and finance in order to acquire and manage the resources necessary to keep pace with growing demand. The business is primarily concerned with producing more of what it wants to make, and marketing generally plays a secondary role in formulating and implementing strategy.[15] Indeed, such firms commonly rely on financial or long-range planning systems and base their strategies on extrapolations of the current situation. Some other functional differences between production-oriented and market-oriented firms are summarized in Exhibit 1-7.

As industries grow, they become more competitive. New entrants are attracted and existing producers attempt to differentiate themselves through improved products and more efficient production processes. As a result, industry capacity often grows faster than demand and the environment shifts from a seller's market to a buyer's market. Firms often respond to such changes with aggressive promotional activities—such as hiring more salespeople, increasing their advertising budgets, or offering frequent price promotions—to maintain market share and hold down unit costs.

---

[15]Slater and Narver, "Market Orientation, Performance, and the Moderating Influence of Competitive Environment"; and John P. Workman, Jr., "When Marketing Should Follow Instead of Lead," *Marketing Management* 2, No. 2, 1993, pp. 8–19.

Unfortunately, this kind of **sales-oriented** response to increasing competition still focuses on selling what the firm wants to make rather than on customer needs. Worse, competitors can easily match such aggressive sales tactics. In other words, simply spending more on selling efforts usually does not create a sustainable competitive advantage.

As industries mature, sales volume levels off and technological differences among brands tend to disappear as manufacturers copy the best features of each other's products. Consequently, a firm must seek new market segments or steal share from competitors by offering lower prices, superior services, or intangible benefits other firms cannot match. At this stage, managers can most readily appreciate the benefits of a market orientation, and marketers are often given a bigger role in developing competitive strategies.[16] It is not surprising, then, that many of America's most market-oriented firms—and those working hardest to become market-oriented—are well-established competitors in relatively mature industries.

The influence of different stages of development across industries and global markets

The previous discussion suggests that the degree of adoption of a market orientation varies not only across firms but across entire industries. Industries that are in earlier stages of their life cycles, or that benefit from barriers to entry or other factors reducing the intensity of competition, are likely to have relatively fewer market-oriented firms. For instance, due in part to government regulations that restricted competition, many service industries—including banks, airlines, physicians, lawyers, accountants, and insurance companies—were slow to adopt the marketing concept. But with the trend toward deregulation during the past decade and the increasingly intense global competition in such industries, many service organizations are working much harder to understand and satisfy their customers.[17]

The manufacturing sector has some mature, "capacity-dominated" industries in which competitors must make relatively large investments in the fixed capacity of their plants. Such industries—including basic fibers and chemicals, steel, and pulp and paper—have high ratios of assets to sales, often exceeding two to one. Because capacity utilization and operational efficiency are so critical, and because the standardized processes necessary to achieve high efficiency result in relatively undifferentiated products, competition in these industries tends to emphasize price. Only when all players are operating close to their capacity limits do price pressures abate. Occasionally a competitor such as Nucor, which pioneered minimills for steel making, will develop a new manufacturing process that reduces costs markedly, but in general the emphasis is on incremental improvements in process efficiency. Consequently, firms in these industries typically spend rather small proportions of sales on marketing or R&D.[18]

Given that entire economies are in different stages of development around the world, the popularity and even the appropriateness of different business philosophies may also vary across countries. A production orientation was the dominant business philosophy in the United States, for instance, during the period of industrialization that occurred from the

---

[16]*Ibid.*

[17]For examples, see "Banks Discover the Consumer," *Fortune*, February 12, 1990, pp. 96–104, and Peter Galuszka, Gail DeGeorge, A. T. Palmer, and Jessica McCann, "See the Doctor, Get a Toaster," *Business Week*, December 8, 1997, pp. 86–7. For a more general discussion, see Valarie A. Zeithaml and Mary Jo Bitner, *Services Marketing* (New York: McGraw-Hill, 1996).

[18]Grant Miles, Charles C. Snow, and Mark Sharfman, "Industry Variety and Performance," *Strategic Management Journal* 15, March 1993, pp. 163–77.

mid-1800s through World War I.[19] Similarly, a primary focus on developing product and production technology may still be appropriate in developing nations that are in the midst of industrialization.

International differences in business philosophies can cause some problems for the globalization of a firm's strategic marketing programs, but it can create some opportunities as well, especially for alliances or joint ventures. Consider, for example, General Electric's joint venture with the Mexican appliance manufacturer Organization Mabe. The arrangement benefits GE by providing direct access to Mexico's rapidly growing market for household appliances and its low-cost supply of labor. But it also benefits Mabe—and the Mexican economy—by giving the firm access to cutting-edge R&D and production technology and the capital necessary to take advantage of its newfound know-how.[20]

Strategic inertia

In some cases a firm that achieved success by being in tune with its environment loses touch with its market because managers become reluctant to tamper with strategies and marketing programs that worked in the past. They begin to believe there is one best way to satisfy their customers. Such strategic inertia is dangerous for the simple reason that customers' needs and competitive offerings change over time. Staying successful requires constant analysis of and adjustments to changes in what customers want and competitors offer. Thus, in environments where such changes happen frequently, the strategic planning process needs to be ongoing and adaptive, and marketers need to provide detailed information about what is happening with their customers and competitors.

Recent developments affecting the strategic role of marketing

In the future, strategic inertia will be even more dangerous in many industries because they are facing increasing magnitudes and rates of change in their environments. These changes are rapidly altering the context in which marketing strategies are formulated and carried out, and the tools that marketers have at their disposal. Such changes include (1) the increased globalization of markets and competition, (2) the growth of the service sector of the economy and the importance of service in maintaining customer satisfaction and loyalty, (3) the rapid development of new information and communications technologies, and (4) the growing importance of relationships as mechanisms for the improved coordination and increased efficiency of strategic marketing programs. Some of the recent impacts of these four developments on marketing management are briefly summarized below. More importantly, however, the impact of these trends on marketing strategy will be continuing themes throughout this book. We will also speculate from time to time about how these ongoing trends may reshape the tasks, tools, and techniques of marketing in the future.

Globalization.   International markets account for a large and growing portion of the sales of many organizations. The 100 largest U.S.-based multinationals generate more than $700 billion in revenues from foreign markets, and many smaller firms rely heavily on international sales as well. For example, Petrofsky's—a St. Louis manufacturer of frozen bagel dough—reformulated its product to fit the preferences of Japanese consumers (a bigger,

---

[19]E. Jerome McCarthy and William D. Perreault, Jr., *Basic Marketing: A Global-Managerial Approach*, 11th ed. (Homewood, IL: Irwin, 1993), chap. 2.

[20]"GE's Brave New World," *Business Week*, November 8, 1993, pp. 64–70.

softer bagel offered in some unique flavors). The results were so successful that the firm recently sold its domestic business to Quaker Oats in order to concentrate on sales to Japan and other Asian markets.

While global markets often represent promising opportunities for additional sales growth and profits, differences in market and competitive conditions across country boundaries might require firms to adapt their competitive strategies and marketing programs to be successful. Even when similar marketing strategies are appropriate for multiple countries, international differences in infrastructure, culture, legal systems, and the like often mean that one or more elements of the marketing program—such as product features, promotional appeals, or distribution channels—must be tailored to local conditions for the strategy to be effective.

Increased importance of service.   A service can be defined as "any activity or benefit that one party can offer another that is essentially intangible and that does not result in the ownership of anything. Its production may or may not be tied to a physical product."[21] Service businesses such as airlines, hotels, restaurants, and consulting firms account for roughly two-thirds of all economic activity in the United States, and services are the fastest-growing sector of most other developed economies world-wide. While many of the decisions and activities involved in marketing services are essentially the same as those for physical goods, the intangible nature of many services can create some unique challenges for marketers. We will discuss these challenges— and the tools and techniques firms have developed to deal with them—throughout this book.

As the above definition points out, however, services such as financing, delivery, installation, user training and assistance, and maintenance are often provided in conjunction with a physical product. Such ancillary services have become more critical to firms' continued sales and financial success in many product-markets. As those markets get crowded with global competitors offering similar products at ever-lower prices, the creative design and effective delivery of supplemental services become a crucial means for a company to differentiate its offering and to generate additional benefits and value for customers. Those additional benefits in turn can justify higher prices and margins in the short term, and help improve customer satisfaction, retention, and loyalty over time, particularly in industrial markets.[22]

Information technology.   The computer revolution and related technological developments are changing the nature of strategic marketing management in two important ways. First, new technologies are making it possible for firms to collect and analyze more detailed information about potential customers and their needs, preferences, and buying habits. For instance, Fingerhut—the $2 billion catalog retailer—stores more than 500 pieces of information about personal characteristics, past purchases, and payment patterns for each of its 50 million active and potential customers. It uses that information to tailor personalized catalogs and mail them to customers when they are most likely to buy. The firm's database has also helped uncover opportunities for new products and services, such as a credit card designed for Fingerhut's mostly low-income customers.[23] Thus, information technology is making it possible for many firms to identify and target smaller and more precisely defined

---

[21]Philip Kotler and Gary Armstrong, *Principles of Marketing* (Englewood Cliffs, N.J.: Prentice Hall, 1989), p. 575.

[22]For examples, see Terry G. Vavra, *Aftermarketing* (Burr Ridge, IL: Richard D. Irwin, 1995).

[23]Susan Chandler, "Data is Power. Just Ask Fingerhut," *Business Week*, June 3, 1996, p. 69.

market segments—sometimes segments consisting of only one or a few customers—and to customize product features, promotional appeals, prices, and financing arrangements to fit such segments.[24]

A second impact of information technology has been to open new avenues for communicating and transacting exchanges with a firm's customers. Obviously, the proliferation of cable TV channels, the rapid expansion of the Internet, and similar technological developments have increased marketers' options for delivering targeted promotional messages, product information, and assistance to individual customers or small market segments. More important, such technologies have also improved the speed and efficiency of many firms' order processing and delivery services. For example, firms like Procter & Gamble and 3M have formed alliances with major retailers—such as Kroger and Wal-Mart—to develop automatic restocking systems. Sales information from the retailer's checkout scanners is sent directly to the supplier's computers, which figure out automatically when to replenish each product and schedule deliveries directly to each of the retailer's stores. Such paperless exchanges reduce mistakes and billbacks, minimize inventory levels, improve cash flow, and increase customer (i.e., the retailer) satisfaction and loyalty.[25]

Relationships across functions and firms.   As the previous example implies, the emergence of new information technologies and the ongoing search for greater marketing efficiency and customer value in the face of increasing competition are changing the nature of exchange between companies. Instead of engaging in a discrete series of arm's-length, adversarial exchanges with customers, channel members, and suppliers on the open market, more firms are trying to develop and nurture long-term relationships and alliances—such as that between 3M and Wal-Mart—involving greater amounts of trust and cooperation between the parties. Such cooperative relationships are thought to improve each partner's ability to adapt quickly to environmental changes or threats, and to gain greater benefits at lower costs from its exchanges.[26]

Similar kinds of cooperative relationships are emerging inside companies as firms seek mechanisms for coordinating more effectively and efficiently across functional departments the various activities necessary to identify, attract, service, and satisfy customers. In many firms, the strategic planning and executional activities that used to be the responsibility of a product or marketing manager are now coordinated and carried out by cross-functional teams.

The future role of marketing

In light of such changes, it is apparent that firms in most, if not all, industries will have to be market-oriented, tightly focused on customer needs and desires, and highly adaptive to succeed and prosper in the future. In turn, this suggests that the effective performance of marketing activities—particularly those associated with tracking, analyzing, and satisfying

---

[24]Sometimes the costs and other implementation problems involved in such "mass customization" can offset the advantages. For a discussion of such problems, see Joseph Pine II, Bart Victor, and Andrew C. Boynton, "Making Mass Customization Work," *Harvard Business Review*, September–October 1993, pp. 108–19.

[25]Bill Saporito, "Behind the Tumult at P&G," *Fortune*, March 7, 1994, pp. 74–82. For other examples involving industrial goods, see Joseph B. Fuller, James O'Conor, and Richard Rawlinson, "Tailored Logistics: The Next Advantage," *Harvard Business Review*, May–June 1993, pp. 87–98.

[26]Robert Morgan and Shelby D. Hunt, "The Commitment-Trust Theory of Relationship Marketing," *Journal of Marketing*, 58 (July 1994), pp. 20–38.

customers' needs—will become even more critical for the successful formulation and implementation of strategies at all organizational levels.

It is important to note, however, that such marketing activities may not always be carried out by marketing managers located in separate functional departments. As more firms embrace the use of multifunctional teams or network structures, the boundaries between functions are likely to blur and the performance of marketing tasks will become everybody's business. Similarly, as organizations become more focused and specialized in developing unique core competencies, they will rely more heavily on suppliers, distributors, dealers, and other partners to perform activities—including marketing and sales tasks—that fall outside those areas of competence. All of this suggests that the ability to create, manage, and sustain exchange relationships with customers, vendors, distributors, and others will become a key strategic competence for firms in the future—and that is what marketing is all about.

THE PROCESS OF FORMULATING AND IMPLEMENTING MARKETING STRATEGY

The primary focus of this book is on the development and implementation of marketing strategies for individual product-market entries. Exhibit 1-8 briefly diagrams the activities involved in this process, and it also serves as the organizational framework for the rest of this book.

Interrelationships between different levels of strategy

Before we can discuss the development of a marketing strategy for a specific product, however, we must first examine corporate and business-level strategies in more detail. As we have seen, marketers often play a major role in formulating such strategies, and that role is likely to expand in the future. At the same time, strategic decisions at the corporate and SBU level often influence or constrain the range of options a marketing manager can realistically consider when designing a marketing strategy for his or her product. After all, the marketing program for an individual product must be consistent with the strategic direction, competitive thrust, and resource allocations decided on at higher management levels. Therefore, Chapters 2 and 3 examine the components of corporate and business-level strategies and their implications for the design and implementation of marketing strategies at the product-market level.

Market opportunity analysis

A major factor in the success or failure of a strategy at any level is whether it fits the realities of the firm's external environment. Thus, in developing a marketing strategy for a product, the marketing manager must first monitor and analyze the opportunities and threats posed by factors outside the organization.

Environmental, industry, and competitor analysis

To understand potential opportunities and threats over the long term, marketers must first attempt to identify and predict the impact of broad trends in the economic and social environment. In some situations a firm might even try to influence the direction of such trends. Chapter 4 discusses a number of macroenvironmental factors to which marketing managers

EXHIBIT   1 – 8

The Process of Formulating and Implementing Marketing Strategy

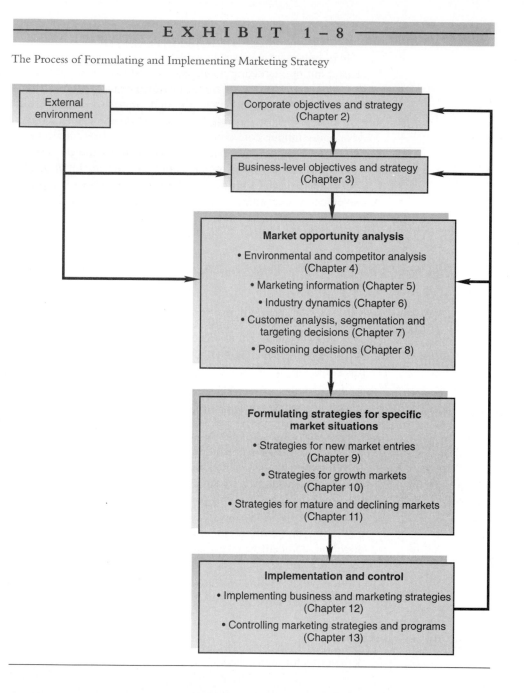

should pay attention, along with some methods for monitoring, analyzing, and perhaps influencing the impact of those factors on the future performance of their product-market entries.

One of the most critical aspects of the external environment for marketers to keep tabs on is the competition. What are the strengths and weaknesses of existing and potential competitors relative to those of the firm? How might the firm gain a sustainable competitive advantage in a given product-market? How might those competitors react to changes in the environment and to the firm's marketing actions in the future? Chapter 4 presents some methods for attempting to answer such questions.

As mentioned, advances in information technology have had a major impact on the kinds and amounts of environmental, competitive, and customer information marketers are able to collect and analyze as a basis for their strategies. Therefore, Chapter 5 examines the kinds of marketing information available to managers and some of the tools and procedures used to gather and evaluate it, including the rapidly increasing role of the Internet in market opportunity analysis.

Of course, the competitive environment of an industry is not static but can change dramatically over time. For example, the aggressive pricing of the clone manufacturers and the threat of potential new entrants such as Intel motivated Compaq to revamp its product line, slash its costs and prices, change its distribution and customer service policies, and increase its advertising budget to strengthen its competitive position in the global PC market. Chapter 6 explores the competitive dynamics of an industry, emphasizing particularly how competition and customer buying patterns are likely to change as the industry or product-market moves through various life-cycle stages.

Customer analysis: segmentation, targeting, and positioning

The primary purpose of any marketing strategy is to facilitate and encourage exchange transactions with potential customers. One of a marketing manager's major responsibilities, then, is to analyze the motivations and behaviors of present and potential customers. Of course, it is unlikely that every potential customer will have the same needs, seek the same product benefits, or be influenced in the same way by the same marketing program. Thus, marketing managers must also determine whether there are multiple market segments that will respond differently to their products and marketing programs and how to best define, identify, and appeal to those segments. Chapter 7, therefore, examines dimensions and techniques that can be used to analyze customers and to define and identify market segments in both consumer and organizational markets.

But not every segment of a market is likely to be equally attractive to a firm. Some may be too small to be profitable, and others may desire benefits the firm cannot provide as efficiently or effectively as some competitors. Therefore, after examining customer needs and competitive strengths and weaknesses, a marketing manager must decide which market segment or segments to target and how to position the product in the target segment relative to competitive offerings. Chapter 7 examines some considerations in selecting target segments, and Chapter 8 discusses various methods for choosing a competitive position for the product within those markets.

Formulating strategies for specific market situations

The strategic marketing program for a particular product-market entry should reflect market demand and the competitive situation within the target market. As demand and competitive conditions change over time, the marketing strategy also should be adjusted. During the 1970s, for instance, American Express's successful "Do you know me?" promotional campaign was aimed at building primary demand by emphasizing the convenience and prestige of carrying a credit card. But as competing bankcards proliferated, American Express switched to a "Membership has its privileges" campaign designed to differentiate the green card from its competitors by promoting superior customer service.

Because demand and competitive conditions change as product-markets grow and mature, the third section of this book discusses a variety of different marketing strategies appropriate for different stages in a market's life cycle. Chapter 9 examines some marketing strategies for introducing new products or services to the market. Chapter 10 discusses strategies appropriate for building or maintaining a product's share of a growing market in the face of increasing competition. Chapter 11 considers the strategies a marketing manager might adopt in mature or declining product-markets.

Implementation and control

A final critical determinant of a strategy's success is the firm's ability to implement it effectively. And this, in turn, depends on whether the strategy is consistent with the firm's resources, organizational structure, coordination and control systems, and the skills and experience of company personnel. In other words, managers must design a strategy that fits existing company resources, competencies, and procedures—or try to construct new structures and systems to fit the chosen strategy.[27] Therefore, Chapter 12 discusses the structural variables, planning and coordination processes, and personnel and corporate culture characteristics related to the successful implementation of different marketing strategies.

Finally, the marketing manager must determine whether the marketing program is achieving its objectives and adjust the strategy when performance is disappointing. This evaluation and control process provides feedback to managers and serves as the basis for a subsequent market opportunity analysis. Chapter 13 examines ways to evaluate marketing performance and develop contingency plans for when things go wrong.

SUMMARY

This chapter argues that a strategy should specify *what* is to be accomplished, *where* it is to be accomplished (which industries and product-markets to focus on), and *how* it is to be accomplished (the resources and activities to be allocated to each product-market to meet environmental opportunities and threats and gain a competitive advantage). Consequently, a well-developed strategy contains five components: (1) scope, or the desired breadth of the organization's strategic domain, (2) goals and objectives, (3) resource deployments, indicating how financial and human resources are to be distributed across businesses, product-markets, and/or functional departments and activities, (4) identification of a source of sustainable competitive advantage, and (5) specification of potential sources of synergy across businesses and/or functional departments.

Most firms—especially those with multiple businesses or divisions—have no single comprehensive strategy but a hierarchy of corporate strategy, business-level strategies, and functional strategies focused on individual product-market entries. A marketing manager's strategy for a specific product-market entry is constrained by the strategic decisions made at the corporate and business-unit levels. On the other hand, marketing managers often play a crucial role in providing necessary information and analyses to the strategic planning process at higher levels of the organization.

The extent of the marketer's role in strategic planning is mediated by the type of planning system the firm uses. As firms grow and mature, their planning systems tend to evolve from the simplest kind of financial planning to long-range and strategic planning. In some cases, firms ultimately embrace the most adaptive, ongoing type of strategic market

---

[27]N. Venkatraman and John C. Camillus, "Exploring the Concept of 'Fit' in Strategic Management," *Academy of Management Review* 9 (1984), pp. 513–25.

management planning system. As this evolution occurs, the role of marketing managers in the strategic planning process tends to increase in importance.

The marketer's role in formulating and implementing strategy is also influenced by the market orientation of the firm and its top managers. Some firms are not very market-oriented because competitive conditions may enable the firm to be successful without being particularly sensitive to customer desires; the firm may be committed to past policies that are no longer appropriate in view of changing conditions in the market; or market and competitive concerns may be outweighed by short-term financial imperatives. However, a clearer focus on customer needs and competitive responses is likely to become more crucial for the future strategic success of most firms because of the increasing rate and magnitude of changes occurring in the domestic and global market environments. And this suggests that marketers will play an even more important strategic role in the years to come.

2 CHAPTER

Corporate Strategy Decisions

GILLETTE: AN INNOVATIVE GLOBAL COMPETITOR[1]

Every working day at a Gillette plant in Boston, 200 men lather up their faces and scrape away the 15/1000ths of an inch of beard hair that grew on their faces over the previous 24 hours. In an adjacent shower room, women are performing a similar exercise on their legs and underarms. These volunteers are evaluating razors of the future for sharpness of blade, smoothness of glide, and ease of handling. When finished, each volunteer punches into a computer his or her judgments of the prototype each used.

It may seem a bit silly in this high-tech age for a company to expend so much effort studying customers' perceptions and preferences in an attempt to develop the next generation of a product as archaic as the wet razor. But paying close attention to shavers' preferences—and spending heavily on R&D to find new ways to satisfy them—has helped Gillette become

one of the world's premier corporate innovators. More than 40 percent of the firm's 1996 revenues of $7 billion came from products introduced within the previous five years.

Gillette's Corporate Mission and Strategic Scope

Of course, not all of Gillette's products are directly related to shaving. While 40 percent of the firm's revenues and two-thirds of its profits come from its razor-and-blade business, the company also makes Braun electrical appliances, Gillette toiletries (Right Guard, Soft & Dri), stationery products (Parker, Paper Mate and Waterman pens), and Oral-B toothbrushes. But all these products share some common traits. For one thing, they are all fast growing, number one worldwide in their markets, and profitable. More critically,

---

[1]This case example is based largely on material found in Betsy Morris, "The Brand's the Thing," *Fortune*, March 4, 1996, pp. 72–86; and Linda Grant, "Gillette Knows Shaving—And How to Turn Out Hot New Products," *Fortune*, October 14, 1996, pp. 207–10. At this writing, the company's website—www.2gillette.com—is still under construction and does not include sales or financial information, but it does describe the firm's history, mission, and product divisions.

they are all consumer package goods that are sold through similar retail outlets and distribution channels, and involve similar marketing programs. As Alfred Zeien, Gillette's CEO, points out, "The products are small and point-of-purchase driven. We have a powerful impact at checkout counters." The products all have a techno logical base which enables the firm to add value and maintain a competitive advantage by means of a continual stream of new products and improvements flowing from its R&D and product development efforts.

These commonalities across Gillette's various product lines did not occur by accident. They reflect the firm's strategic mission and intent, which is formally stated as follows:

> The Gillette Company is a globally focused consumer products company which seeks competitive advantage in quality, value-added personal care and personal use products. We compete in three large, worldwide businesses: personal grooming products, stationery products and small electrical appliances. As a company, we share skills and resources among business units to optimize performance. We are committed to a plan of sustained sales and profit growth which recognizes and balances both short-and long-term objectives.

The statement goes on to say that one of the firm's long-term objectives is to achieve or enhance market leadership, worldwide, in the consumer product categories in which it competes. This mission, together with an additional statement of the company's core values concerning such things as customer focus, personnel policies, and good corporate citizenship are discussed in more detail at the firm's Website (www.2gillette.com).

Gillette's Corporate Objectives and Development Strategy

As the above statement of strategic mission and intent suggests, Gillette has several different though complimentary perfor-

mance objectives, including sustained annual increases in sales volume, profits, and return to shareholders. But given the firm's outstanding performance over the past decade, such annual increases are likely to become harder to sustain. Earnings since 1990 have climbed at an annual rate of 17 percent, return on equity is nearly 33 percent, and profit margins are about 12 percent. Among consumer products companies, Gillette's return on sales is second only to Coca-Cola's. All of this has created a great deal of wealth for the firm's shareholders and pumped up the company's stock price. Indeed, with only about $7 billion in annual revenues, Gillette ranked 10th among the Fortune 500 companies in total return to investors over the past decade.

To continue reaching its goals of annual increases in sales, profits, and return to shareholders, Gillette obviously must continue to grow. Its corporate development strategy emphasizes several different avenues to growth. First, as mentioned, the firm aggressively pursues the development of new products for its existing markets through heavy investments in R&D and customer research. To achieve its objective of generating 40 percent of sales from products introduced within the last five years, the firm must introduce approximately 20 successful new products every year. And to facilitate the development of those new products, the firm spends over $150 million—nearly 2.5 percent of annual sales—on R&D. For instance, the firm's Sensor family of razors and blades, introduced in 1990, cost $275 million to develop and required new technologies which eventually resulted in 29 patents. But this huge investment of money and effort proved worthwhile because Sensor helped Gillette capture 68 percent of the U.S. market in wet shaving, 73 percent of Europe, and 91 percent of Latin America.

As these market share percentages suggest, a second avenue to growth that Gillette has pursued is geographic expansion into new markets around the world. More than 70 percent of the firm's sales and profits come from overseas operations in more than 200 countries. Global markets will probably continue to be a major source of future growth, particularly for Gillette's nonshaving products. Having won the loyalty of 700 million shavers around the world, the company can pour a steady stream of its other products through the same distribution pipelines.

Finally, the firm has pursued growth through concentric diversification into other consumer package goods businesses. Recently, it acquired Duracell—the battery manufacturer—for $7 billion in stock.

CEO Zeien envisions sizzling synergies as Gillette begins marketing Duracell batteries through its far-flung global distribution network.

So far, all of the various avenues by which Gillette has pursued growth seem to have produced substantial volume increases without sacrificing profitability or returns to shareholders. While the firm's recent performance may be a tough act to follow, it is already working on the development of the next great shaving innovation, one that will likely cannibalize Sensor but which Gillette hopes will lay the foundation for continued growth well into the next century.

STRATEGIC DECISIONS AT THE CORPORATE LEVEL

The corporate strategy crafted over the years by Alfred Zeien and his top lieutenants provides a clear sense of direction and useful guidance for all of Gillette's manager because it speaks to all five dimensions of strategy that we discussed in Chapter 1. First, it defines the overall scope and mission of the company by targeting three closely related consumer package goods product-markets where the firm will focus its efforts and attempt to add value for customers.

Gillette's corporate strategy also sets challenging objectives for future growth in new product development, sales volume, earnings, and shareholder wealth. These in turn indicate how the firm intends to allocate its resources and leverage its core competencies to build and maintain a competitive advantage. The firm has dedicated substantial money and know-how to (1) R&D and market research aimed at developing a constant stream of product improvements and innovations for its existing customers, (2) building distribution and market share for its products in new geographic markets around the world, and (3) diversifying into new consumer product categories either through internal development or acquisition. Finally, the firm's development strategy seeks to achieve synergies across product categories by leveraging the marketing and distribution strengths of its very successful wet razor product line.

It should be obvious that Gillette's well-defined corporate strategy both facilitates and constrains the decisions that the firm's marketing managers make when designing and implementing marketing strategies for individual products. For example, the firm backs up its product development strategy by putting substantial marketing resources behind each new offering. CEO Zeien is convinced that fledgling products require adequate advertising and promotion to thrive—a conviction that makes the lives of those products' marketing managers a bit easier. On the other hand, Gillette's strategy of focusing on value-added products with high margins, and its objective of annual increases in profits and shareholder returns, limits the ability of its marketers to rely on some tactics, such as aggressive price promotions.

——————————— **E X H I B I T   2 – 1** ———————————

Corporate Strategy Components and Issues

Strategy component	Key issues
Scope, mission, and intent	• What business(es) should the firm be in? • What customer needs, market segments, and/or technologies should be focused on? • What is the firm's enduring strategic purpose or intent?
Objectives	• What performance dimensions should the firm's business units and employees focus on? • What is the target level of performance to be achieved on each dimension? • What is the time frame in which each target should be attained?
Development strategy	• How can the firm achieve a desired level of growth over time? • Can the desired growth be attained by expanding the firm's current businesses? • Will the company have to diversify into new businesses or product-markets to achieve its future growth objectives?
Resource allocation	• How should the firm's limited financial resources be allocated across its businesses to produce the highest returns? • Of the alternative strategies that each business might pursue, which will produce the greatest returns for the dollars invested?
Sources of synergy	• What competencies, knowledge, and customer-based intangibles (e.g., brand recognition, reputation) might be developed and shared across the firm's businesses? • What operational resources, facilities, or functions (e.g., plants, R&D, salesforce) might the firm's businesses share to increase their efficiency?

In view of the influence of corporate-level decisions making on strategic programs for individual product-market entries, the remaining sections of this chapter discuss the five components of a well-defined corporate strategy in more detail. Exhibit 2-1 summarizes some of the crucial questions about each of these strategy components.

CORPORATE SCOPE: DEFINING THE FIRM'S MISSION AND INTENT

A well-thought-out mission statement guides the managers of an organization about which market opportunities to pursue and which fall outside the firm's strategic domain. A clearly stated mission can help instill a shared sense of direction, relevance, and achievement among employees and a positive image of the firm among customers, investors, and other corporate stakeholders.

To provide a useful sense of direction, a corporate mission statement must clearly define the organization's strategic scope. It should answer fundamental questions such as, What is our business? Who are our customers? What kinds of value can we provide to these customers? and What should our business be in the future? For example, PepsiCo, the manufacturer of Pepsi-Cola, for many years defined its mission as "marketing superior quality food and beverage products for households and consumers dining out." Consequently, the firm pursued growth by both building a line of beverage products such as Pepsi, Diet Pepsi, and Slice, and by acquiring several food manufacturers and restaurant chains such as

Pizza Hut and Taco Bell. More recently, however, the firm narrowed its mission to "the worldwide marketing of superior beverage products" in order to focus its resources more specifically on its worldwide battle with Coca-Cola for market share and customer loyalty in the beverage market. Consequently, PepsiCo has spun off its fast-food operations and devoted additional resources to redesigning the corporate logo and packaging for its beverage products, to more aggressive advertising and trade promotion, and to building a stronger market presence in developing markets like India and Indonesia.[2]

Factors that influence the corporate mission

Like any other component of strategy, an organization's mission should fit its internal characteristics, resources, and competencies and its external opportunities and threats. Thus, while defining the firm's mission is usually a first step in developing corporate strategy, it should be intertwined with analyses of the organization's strengths and weaknesses and of its environment.

Social values and ethical principles.   A firm's mission statement should reflect internal characteristics such as the historical accomplishments, top management preferences, and shared values, myths, and symbols that, taken together, make up the company's culture. An increasing number of organizations are developing mission statements that also attempt to define the social and ethical boundaries of their strategic domain. The annual reports of firms like Borden and 3M, for example, often include sections on social responsibility that outline the ethical principles the firms try to follow in dealings with customers, suppliers, channel partners, and employees, and its policies concerning social issues such as charitable contributions and environmental protection. Indeed, a recent survey by the Ethics Resource Center found that 60 percent of U.S. firms have formal codes of ethics governing how they do business at home and abroad.[3]

One might ask why a corporation should take responsibility for providing moral guidance to its managers and employees. While such a question may be a good topic for philosophical debate, there is a compelling, practical reason for a firm to impose ethical standards to guide employees, particularly when those employees are engaged in marketing activities that involve dealings with the firm's customers, suppliers, or other outside stakeholders. There is a growing body of evidence that unethical practices can damage the trust between a firm and its suppliers or customers, thereby disrupting the development of long-term exchange relationships and resulting in the likely loss of sales and profits over time. For example, one survey of 135 purchasing managers from a variety of industries found that the more unethical a supplier's sales and marketing practices were perceived to be, the less eager the purchasing managers were to buy from that supplier.[4]

Unfortunately, not all customers or competing suppliers adhere to the same ethical standards. As a result, marketers sometimes feel pressure to engage in actions that are inconsistent with what they believe to be right—either in terms of personal values or formal company standards—in order to close a sale or stay even with the competition. This point was illustrated by a survey of 59 top marketing and sales executives concerning commercial bribery—attempts to influence a potential customer by giving gifts or kickbacks.

---

[2]Patricia Sellers, "Pepsi Keeps on Going after No.1," *Fortune*, March 11, 1991, pp. 62–70; and Nicole Harris, "If You Can't Beat 'Em, Copy 'Em," *Business Week*, November 17, 1997, p. 50.

[3] "Good Grief," *The Economist*, April 8, 1995, p. 57.

[4]I. Fredrick Trawick, John E. Swan, Gail W. McGee, and David R. Rink, "Influence of Buyer Ethics and Salesperson Behavior on Intention to Choose a Supplier," *Journal of the Academy of Marketing Science* 19 (Winter 1991), pp. 17–23.

=========== E X H I B I T   2 – 2 ===========

Issues Addressed by Company Ethics Statements

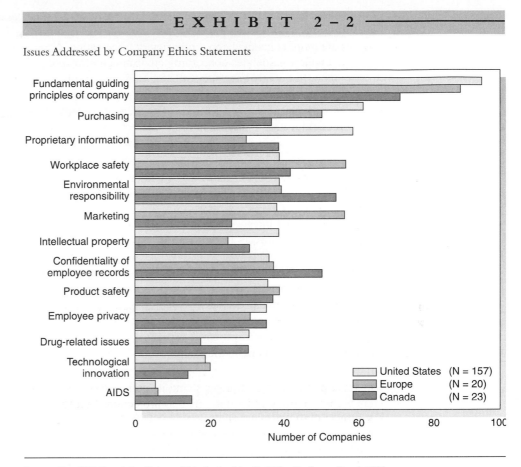

SOURCE: Ronald E. Berenbeim, *Corporate Ethics Practices* (New York: The Conference Board, 1992).

While nearly two-thirds of the executives considered bribes unethical and did not want to pay them, 88 percent also felt that *not* paying bribes might put their firms at a competitive disadvantage.[5] Such dilemmas are particularly likely to arise as a company moves into global markets involving different cultures and levels of economic development where economic exigencies and ethical standards may be quite different.

Such inconsistencies in external expectations and demands across countries and markets can lead to high levels of job stress and inconsistent behavior among marketing and sales personnel, which in turn can risk damaging long-term relationships with suppliers, channel partners, and customers. One way for a company to reduce such problems is to spell out formal social policies and ethical standards in its corporate mission statement and to effectively communicate and enforce those standards. Unfortunately, it is not always easy to decide what those policies and standards should be. There are multiple philosophical traditions or frameworks that managers might use to evaluate the ethics of a given action. Consequently, different firms or managers can pursue somewhat different ethical standards, particularly across national cultures. Exhibit 2-2 displays a comparison of the proportion of company ethical statements that address a set of specific issues. Note that a larger number

[5]Dawn Bryan, "Using Gifts to Make the Sale," *Sales and Marketing Management*, September 1989, pp. 48–53; see also "The Destructive Cost of Greasing Palms," *Business Week*, December 6, 1993, pp. 133–38.

of companies in the United States and Europe appear to be more concerned with the ethics of their purchasing practices than those of their marketing activities. In general, U.S. companies are more concerned about proprietary information, Canadian firms are more likely to have explicit guidelines concerning environmental responsibility, and European companies more frequently have standards focused on workplace safety.

Internal resources and competencies.   The mission statement also should be compatible with the firm's more tangible internal characteristics: its resources, distinctive competencies, and possible synergies across its various businesses. Thus, Gillette's mission focuses on value-added consumer package goods to take advantage of the firm's R&D, product development, and marketing competencies, and to leverage its established relationships with distributors and retailers around the world.

Opportunities and threats.   Finally, a firm's mission statement should take into account opportunities and threats in the external environment. It should guide the organization toward product-markets where customer needs and competitive conditions offer attractive growth possibilities; at the same time, it should steer the company away from industries where stagnant demand, strong competitors, or emerging new technologies might make it difficult for the firm to establish a competitive advantage and achieve corporate objectives. In this sense, a mission statement represents both a response to environmental conditions and an attempt to control them by spelling out which markets and competitors a firm should avoid confronting in the future.

Dimensions for defining the corporate mission

A number of dimensions can be used to define an organization's strategic scope or mission. Some firms specify their domain in physical terms, focusing on products or services the company will produce or technologies it will use. Such mission statements, however, can lead to confusion and slow reaction times if technologies or customer demands change. Nearly 40 years ago, for example, Theodore Leavitt argued that the Penn Central Railroad's view of its mission as being "the railroad business" helped cause the firm's failure. Penn Central did not respond to major changes in transportation technology, such as the rapid growth of air travel and the increased efficiency of long-haul trucking. Nor did it react to changes in customer preferences, such as a growing willingness to pay higher prices for the speed and convenience of air travel. Leavitt argued that it is better to define a firm's mission in terms of what customer needs are to be satisfied and the functions that must be performed to do so.[6] Products and technologies change over time, but basic customer needs tend to endure. Thus, if Penn Central had defined its mission as satisfying its customers' transportation needs rather than simply being a railroad, it might have been more willing to expand its domain to incorporate newer technologies.

One problem with Leavitt's advice, though, is that a mission statement focusing only on basic customer needs can be too broad to provide clear guidance and can fail to take into account the firm's specific competencies. If Penn Central had defined itself as a transportation company, should it have diversified into the trucking business? Started an airline? Considered manufacturing cars? The Burlington Northern, unlike the Penn Central, did have an effective corporate mission statement. As the upper-right quadrant of Exhibit 2-3 suggests, the most useful mission statements focus on *both* the customer need to be

---

[6]Theodore Leavitt, "Marketing Myopia," *Harvard Business Review*, July–August 1960, pp. 45-56.

================= E X H I B I T   2 – 3 =================

The Burlington Northern: Characteristics of an Effective Corporate Mission Statement

	Broad	**Specific**
Functional Based on customer needs	Transportation business	Long-distance transportation for large-volume producers of low-value, low-density products
Physical Based on existing products or technology	Railroad business	Long-haul, coal-carrying railroad

SOURCE: Reprinted by permission from p. 43 of *Strategy Formulation: Analytical Concepts* by C. W. Hofer and D. Schendel. Copyright © 1978 by West Publishing Company. All rights reserved.

satisfied and how the firm will attempt to satisfy that need. They are specific as to the customer groups and the kinds of products or technologies on which the firm will concentrate its efforts.[7] Thus, instead of thinking of itself as being in the railroad business or as satisfying the transportation needs of all potential customers, Burlington Northern's mission is to provide long-distance transportation for large-volume producers of low-value, low-density products, such as coal and grain.

Strategic intent or vision: A motivational view of corporate mission

Recently some writers have argued that mission statements stated in terms of specific customer needs, target markets, technologies, and/or products (e.g., Burlington Northern) may also have some shortcomings as a foundation for a corporate strategy.[8] For one thing, it can be hard to get company employees fired up over something as mundane as "providing long-distance transportation," no matter how necessary or desirable the task. Also, while such specific mission statements may accurately reflect the market situation and the firm's strengths and weaknesses at present, they could prove too rigid as conditions change. Employees may overlook some new market opportunities or new ways of building on the company's strengths or overcoming its weaknesses because the firm's stated mission doesn't explicitly recognize those approaches.

These authors suggest that a firm's basic scope and focus might be more effectively defined by a more general but personally motivating statement of **strategic intent** or **vision**. Consider, for instance, the difference between Burlington Northern's mission statement and the rallying cry that expresses the strategic intent of one Japanese auto manufacturer: "Beat

---

[7]Derek Abell, *Defining the Business: The Starting Point of Strategic Planning* (Englewood Cliffs, N.J.: Prentice Hall, 1980), Chap. 3.

[8]For a more detailed discussion of strategic intent and its implications for formulating corporate strategy, see Gary Hamel and C. K. Prahalad, "Strategic Intent," *Harvard Business Review*, May–June 1989, pp. 63–76; Gary Hamel and C. K. Prahalad, *Competing for the Future* (Cambridge, Mass.: Harvard Business School Press, 1994); and James C. Collins and Jerry I. Porras, "Building Your Company's Vision," *Harvard Business Review*, September–October 1996, pp. 65–77.

Benz!" The first accurately describes the scope of Burlington Northern's business, but it fails to inspire. "Beat Benz," on the other hand, not only expresses the Japanese firm's ultimate goal of taking over world leadership in the manufacture of luxury cars, it also appeals to every employee's competitive instinct and desire for accomplishment. This is the essence of a good statement of strategic intent or vision. It provides a motivational perspective on the corporate purpose by setting an enduring goal worthy of employee commitment, usually couched in terms of unseating the best, or remaining the best, worldwide.

While an effective statement of strategic intent is clear about the organization's long-term ends, it should be flexible as to means. It must leave room for employee improvisation. Indeed, strategic intent usually implies a sizable stretch for an organization. Whereas the traditional approach to strategic planning seeks a good fit between existing resources and current opportunities, strategic intent creates an extreme misfit between the firm's resources and future ambitions. Current capabilities and resources will not suffice. Instead, top management challenges the organization's employees to make the most of limited resources, to be more inventive, and to develop new capabilities. To increase the probability that such challenges will be met, the firm must first provide its employees with the necessary skills (usually via increased training) and then give them substantial freedom to initiate new procedures or programs aimed at moving the organization toward its goal. Such decentralization of decision making can increase both the amount of worker participation and the creativity brought to the process of defining the corporation's strategy.[9]

The risk inherent in this approach, however, is similar to that which arises when a firm defines its mission in terms of satisfying a generic customer need. Although the ultimate objective is clear, there may be many ways to pursue it. And some of those ways may be inconsistent or compete with one another. Even a clear strategic vision, in other words, may not provide a sufficiently specific direction to focus employee efforts.

One possible solution to this dilemma is for management to combine a statement of strategic intent with a more traditional mission statement: one to stimulate employee commitment and the other to focus efforts on a more clearly defined domain of product-markets. The strategic vision statement of Delta Airlines provides an example of how elements of strategic intent and vision can be effectively combined (see Exhibit 2-4).

Management can also convert a broad statement of strategic intent into a more specific mechanism for focusing the organization's efforts by breaking it down into a sequential series of shorter-term objectives or challenges that must be accomplished for the intent to be realized. In attempting to become the worldwide market share leader in the PC industry, for instance, Compaq's CEO first set a goal of becoming number one in the U.S. market by the year 2000. Once that is accomplished, the firm will seek share leadership in Europe (an objective it has already achieved in Great Britain). Later the firm will set its sights on the number one position in the Pacific Rim and other parts of the world.

While a firm's strategic intent should remain constant over time, its shorter-term objectives may change in response to changing market and competitive circumstances and the firm's own changing competencies and resources as it moves toward its ultimate goal. Also, those shorter-term goals should be challenging and specific about the ends to be accomplished, but flexible about the means employees might use to achieve them. Finally, such goals also should carry specific time frames. Note, for instance, that Compaq specified 2000 as the deadline for achieving share leadership in the domestic market. As we shall see in the next section, the points just discussed illustrate characteristics of useful corporate objectives.

---

[9]Shawn Tully, "Why to Go for Stretch Targets," *Fortune*, November 14, 1994, pp. 145–58.

═══════════════════════ E X H I B I T   2 - 4 ═══════════════════════

Delta Airlines' Strategic Vision

> In late 1993, Ronald W. Allen, Delta's chief executive officer, described the company's vision and business mission in the following way:
>
> . . . we want Delta to be the **Worldwide Airline of Choice**.
>
> **Worldwide,** because we are and intend to remain an innovative, aggressive, ethical, and successful competitor that offers access to the world, at the highest standard of customer service. We will continue to look for opportunities to extend our reach through new routes and creative global alliances.
>
> **Airline,** because we intend to stay in the business we know best—air transportation and related services. We won't stray from our roots. We believe in the long-term prospects for profitable growth in the airline industry, and we will continue to focus time, attention, and investment on enhancing our place in that business environment.
>
> **Of Choice,** because we value the loyalty of our customers, employees, and investors. For passengers and shippers, we will continue to provide the best service and value. For our personnel, we will continue to offer an ever more challenging, rewarding, and result-oriented workplace that recognizes and appreciates their contributions. For our shareholders, we will earn a consistent, superior financial return.

SOURCE: *Sky Magazine*, December 1993, p. 10.

CORPORATE OBJECTIVES

Confucius said, "For one who has no objective, nothing is relevant." Formal objectives provide decision criteria that guide an organization's business units and employees toward specific dimensions and levels of performance. Those same objectives provide the benchmarks for evaluating subsequent outcomes. Thus, Gillette's corporate objective of attaining at least 40 percent of sales from products introduced within the past five years provides a clear goal for each of its division as well as a benchmark for evaluating the product development performance of each division.

To be useful as decision criteria and evaluative benchmarks, corporate objectives must be both specific and measurable. Therefore, each objective should contain four components:

- A *performance dimension* or attribute sought.
- A *measure* or *index* for evaluating progress.
- A *target* or *hurdle level* to be achieved.
- A *time frame* within which the target is to be accomplished.

Enhancing shareholder value: The ultimate objective

In recent years a growing number of executives of publicly held corporations have concluded that the organization's ultimate objective should be to increase its shareholders' economic returns as measured by dividends plus appreciation in the company's stock price.[10] To do so management must balance the interests of various corporate constituencies, including employees, customers, suppliers, debtholders, and stockholders. The

---

[10]Alfred Rappaport, *Creating Shareholder Value: The New Standard for Business Performance* (New York: Free Press, 1986), Chap. 1; and Shawn Tully, "America's Best Wealth Creators," *Fortune*, November 28, 1994, pp. 143–62.

firm's continued existence depends on a financial relationship with each of these parties. Employees want competitive wages. Customers want high quality at a competitive price. Suppliers and debtholders have financial claims that must be satisfied with cash when they fall due. And shareholders, as residual claimants, look for cash dividends and the prospect of future dividends reflected in the stock's market price.

If a company does not satisfy its constituents' financial claims, it ceases to be viable. Thus, a going concern must strive to enhance its ability to generate cash from the operation of its businesses and to obtain any additional funds needed from debt or equity financing.

The firm's ability to attain debt financing (its ability to borrow) depends in turn on projections of how much cash it can generate in the future. Similarly, the market value of its shares, and therefore its ability to attain equity financing, depends on investors' expectations of the firm's future cash-generating abilities. People willingly invest in a firm only when they expect a better return on their funds than they could get from other sources without exposing themselves to any greater risks. Thus, management's primary objective should be to pursue capital investments, acquisitions, and business strategies that will produce sufficient future cash flows to return positive value to shareholders. Failure to do so will not only depress the firm's stock price and inhibit the firm's ability to finance future operations and growth, but also it could make the organization more vulnerable to a takeover by outsiders who promise to increase its value to shareholders.

Given this rationale, many firms set explicit objectives targeted at increasing shareholder value. These are usually stated in terms of a target return on shareholder equity, increase in the stock price, or earnings per share. Recently, though, some executives have begun expressing such corporate objectives in terms of *economic value added* or *market value added (MVA)*. A firm's MVA is calculated by combining its debt and the market value of its stock, then subtracting the capital that has been invested in the company. The result, if positive, shows how much wealth the company has created.[11]

Unfortunately, such broad shareholder-value objectives do not always provide adequate guidance for a firm's lower-level managers or benchmarks for evaluating performance. For one thing, standard accounting measures, such as earnings per share or return on investment, are not always reliably linked to the true value of a company's stock.[12] And as we shall see later in this chapter, tools are available to evaluate the future impact of alternative strategic actions on shareholder value; but those valuation methods have inherent pitfalls and can be difficult to apply at lower levels of strategy such as trying to choose the best marketing strategy for a particular product-market entry.[13]

Finally, there is a danger that a narrow focus on short-term financial, shareholder-value objectives may lead managers to pay too little attention to actions necessary to provide value to the firm's customers and sustain a competitive advantage.[14] In the long term, customer value and shareholder value converge; a firm can continue to provide attractive returns to shareholders only so long as it satisfies and retains its customers. But some managers may overlook this in the face of pressures to achieve aggressive short-term financial objectives, as illustrated by the experience of Schlitz Brewing discussed in Exhibit 2-5.

---

[11]Tully, "America's Best Wealth Creators," p. 143.

[12]Bradley T. Gale and Donald J. Swire, "The Tricky Business of Measuring Wealth," *Planning Review*, March–April 1988, pp. 14–17, 47.

[13]Patrick Barwise, Paul R. Marsh, and Robin Wensley, "Must Finance and Strategy Clash?" *Harvard Business Review*; September–October 1989, pp. 85–90; and George S. Day and Liam Fahey, "Putting Strategy into Shareholder Value Analysis," *Harvard Business Review*, March–April 1990, pp. 156–62.

[14]"Debate: Duking It Out over EVA," *Fortune*, August 4, 1997, p. 232.

─────────────── **E X H I B I T   2 – 5** ───────────────

Schlitz: An Example of Increasing Stock Price at the Expense of Competitive Position

In the early 1970s Schlitz Brewing made the mistake of boosting its share price at the expense of its competitive position. The firm shortened its brewing process by 50 percent, reduced labor cost, and switched to less costly ingredients. As a result, it became the lowest-cost producer in the industry, its profits soared, and its stock price rose to a high of $69 by 1974. Unfortunately, however, Schlitz's aggressive cost cutting campaign also degraded the quality of its beer. By 1976 the firm was receiving constant customer and dealer complaints and its market share was slipping badly. In 1978 a new management team attempted to get product quality back on track, but by then consumers had such a low opinion of Schlitz beer that the company could not recover. By 1981 Schlitz's market share position had slipped from number two to number seven, and its share price had dropped to a mere $5.

SOURCE: George S. Day and Liam Fahey, "Putting Strategy into Shareholder Value Analysis," *Harvard Business Review*, March–April 1990, pp. 156–62. Reprinted with permission. Copyright 1990 by the President and Fellows of Harvard College, all rights reserved.

Most organizations pursue multiple objectives

Given the limitations of a single objective focused on enhancing shareholder value, most companies establish multiple objectives to guide and evaluate their managers' performance. Some of those objectives—such as increasing market share, improving product quality, or reducing operating expenses—relate to specific actions that directly influence the firm's ability to generate future cash flows and greater shareholder value.[15] Others may aim at making specific contributions to the firm's various constituencies, such as improving the skill levels of the workforce or contributing to community charities. Exhibit 2-6 lists some common performance dimensions and measures used in specifying corporate—as well as business-unit and marketing—objectives.

Many firms have more than one objective, as the results of a study of the stated objectives of 82 large corporations clearly demonstrate. While the largest percentage of respondents (89 percent) had explicit profitability objectives, 82 percent reported growth objectives, 66 percent had specific market share goals, more than 60 percent mentioned social responsibility, employee welfare, and customer service objectives, and 54 percent of the companies had R&D/new product development goals.[16] These percentages add up to much more than 100 percent, showing that most firms had several objectives.

In addition, while the most commonly reported corporate objective involved some aspect of profitability or return on investment, more than three-quarters of the respondents also had a growth or market share objective. Many firms thus face potential conflicts in trying to fulfill their objectives: the level of investment and expenditure required to aggressively pursue long-term growth may reduce short-term profitability.[17] Similar trade-offs can occur between social responsibility or employee welfare goals and short-term profit objectives. One way to reconcile such potentially conflicting goals is to rank them in a hierarchy, establishing priorities for action. Another approach is to state one of the conflicting

[15]Alfred Rappaport, "Linking Competitive Strategy and Shareholder Value Analysis," *Journal of Business Strategy*, Spring 1987, pp. 58–67.

[16]Y. K. Shetty, "New Look at Corporate Goals," *California Management Review*, Winter 1979, pp. 71–79.

[17]Gordon Donaldson, *Managing Corporate Wealth* (New York: Praeger, 1984); see also Robert S. Kaplan and David P. Norton, "Using the Balanced Scorecard as a Strategic Management System," *Harvard Business Review*, January–February 1996, pp. 75–85.

E X H I B I T   2 – 6

Common Performance Criteria and Measures that Specify Corporate, Business–Unit, and Marketing Objectives

Performance criteria	Possible measures or indexes
• Growth	$ sales Unit sales Percent change in sales
• Competitive strength	Market share Brand awareness Brand preference
• Innovativeness	$ sales from new products Percentage of sales from product-market entries introduced within past five years Percentage cost savings from new processes
• Profitability	$ profits Profit as percentage of sales Contribution margin* Return on investment (ROI) Return on net assets (RONA) Return on equity (ROE)
• Utilization of resources	Percent capacity utilization Fixed assets as percentage of sales
• Contribution to owners	Earnings per share Price/earnings ratio
• Contribution to customers	Price relative to competitors Product quality Customer satisfaction
• Contribution to employees	Wage rates, benefits Personnel development, promotions Employment stability, turnover
• Contribution to society	$ contributions to charities or community institutions Growth in employment

*Business-unit managers and marketing managers responsible for a product-market entry often have little control over costs associated with corporate overhead, such as the costs of corporate staff or R&D. It can be difficult to allocate those costs to specific strategic business units (SBUs) or products. Consequently, profit objectives at the SBU and product-market level are often stated as a desired *contribution margin* (the gross profit prior to allocating such overhead costs).

goals as a constraint or hurdle. Thus, a firm might attempt to maximize growth subject to the constraint that ROI remain above a specified minimum level each year.

Business–unit and product–market objectives

Once broad corporate objectives have been set, they must be broken down into a consistent set of subobjectives for each of the businesses and product-markets in which the firm competes. In some cases, every business unit is expected to match the corporate objective. The Gillette Company, for instance, expects *each* business division to meet the corporate goal of producing 40 percent of its sales volume from products introduced within the past five years as a means of stimulating innovation and growth. More commonly, however, the businesses and product-markets are assigned objectives that reflect differences in their

——————————— E X H I B I T   2 – 7 ———————————

Alternative Corporate Growth Strategies

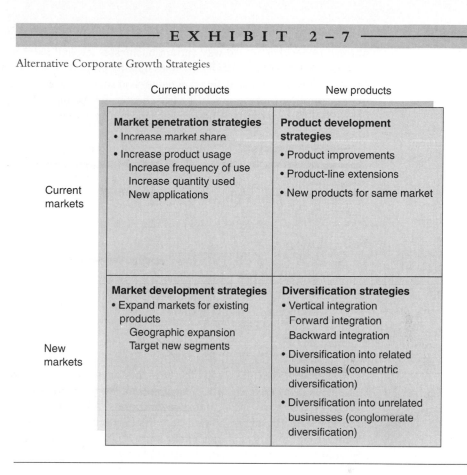

	Current products	New products

Current markets	**Market penetration strategies**
	• Increase market share
	• Increase product usage
	    Increase frequency of use
	    Increase quantity used
	    New applications
		Product development strategies
		• Product improvements
		• Product-line extensions
		• New products for same market

New markets	**Market development strategies**
	• Expand markets for existing products
	    Geographic expansion
	    Target new segments
		Diversification strategies
		• Vertical integration
		    Forward integration
		    Backward integration
		• Diversification into related businesses (concentric diversification)
		• Diversification into unrelated businesses (conglomerate diversification)

competitive positions or the maturity of their markets. A business unit with large market shares in a number of mature product-markets, for example, might be given a lower sales growth objective but a higher profit goal than a unit with a weaker competitive position or more rapidly growing markets.

CORPORATE DEVELOPMENT STRATEGY

Often, the projected combined future sales and profits of a corporation's business units and product-markets fall short of the firm's long-run growth and profitability objectives. There is a gap between what the firm expects to become if it continues on its present course and what it would like to become. This is not surprising because some high-growth markets are likely to mature over time, and some high-profit, mature businesses may decline to insignificance as they get older. Thus, to answer the critical question Where is future growth coming from? management must choose a specific strategy to guide future corporate development.

Essentially, a firm can go in two major directions in seeking future growth: **expansion** of its current businesses and activities or **diversification** into new businesses through either internal business development or acquisition. Exhibit 2-7 outlines some specific options a firm might pursue in seeking growth through each of these directions.

Expansion

Market penetration.   One way current businesses expand is by increasing their share of existing markets. This typically involves making product or service improvements, cutting costs and prices, or outspending competitors on such things as advertising and consumer or trade promotions. As we saw in the last chapter, for example, Compaq is pursuing a combination of these actions to improve customer value and become the market share leader in the worldwide PC market.

A second approach to improving a business's penetration of existing markets encourages current customers to use more of the product, use it more often, or use it in new ways. Packages of Kellogg's Cracklin' Oat Bran cereal, for instance, include recipes such as bran muffins that use the cereal as an ingredient and a coupon good for 50 cents off the purchase of another box.

Product development.   Another way for businesses to grow is to develop product-line extensions or new product offerings aimed at existing customers. For example, Arm & Hammer successfully introduced a laundry detergent, an oven cleaner, and a carpet cleaner. Each capitalized on baking soda's image as an effective deodorizer and on a high level of recognition of the Arm & Hammer brand. Similarly, Gillette is spending millions of dollars on R&D to develop the next wet shaving innovation to replace its current Sensor product line.

Market development.   Perhaps the growth strategy with the greatest potential for most companies is the development of new markets for their existing products or services, particularly through expansion into global markets. As we have seen, global expansion has been an extremely successful thrust of Gillette's growth strategy in recent years. Similarly, General Electric (GE) has announced a growth strategy that will shift the firm's strategic center of gravity from the industrialized West to Asia and Latin America. GE expects much of its growth over the next decade to come from three developing nations: India, China, and Mexico. To compete effectively in such price-sensitive emerging markets, however, the firm is also moving aggressively to improve its manufacturing efficiency and reduce its worldwide distribution and marketing costs.[18]

Diversification

Firms also seek growth by diversifying their operations. This is typically riskier than the various expansion strategies because it involves learning new operations and dealing with unfamiliar customer groups. Nevertheless, the majority of Fortune 500 companies are diversified to one degree or another.

Vertical integration.   Vertical integration is one way for corporations to diversify their operations. **Forward integration** occurs when a firm moves downstream in terms of the product flow, as when a manufacturer integrates by acquiring a wholesaler or retail outlet. **Backward integration** occurs when a firm moves upstream by acquiring a supplier.

Integration gives a firm access to scarce or volatile sources of supply or tighter control over the marketing, distribution, and servicing of its products. But it increases the risks inherent in committing substantial resources to a single industry. Also, the investment

[18]"GE's Brave New World," *Business Week*, November 8, 1993, pp. 64–70; and Aaron Bernstein, Susan Jackson, and John Byrne, "Jack Cracks the Whip Again," *Business Week*, December 15, 1997, pp. 34–35.

necessary for firms to vertically integrate often offsets the additional profitability generated by those integrated operations, resulting in little improvement in return on investment.[19]

Related diversification.   **Related** (or concentric) **diversification** occurs when a firm internally develops or acquires another business that does not have products or customers in common with its current businesses but that might contribute to internal synergy through the sharing of production facilities, brand names, R&D know-how, or marketing and distribution skills. Thus, Gillette acquired Duracell in order to utilize its strong relationships with retailers to market batteries as well as shaving and personal care products.

Unrelated diversification.   The motivations for unrelated (or conglomerate) diversification are primarily financial rather than operational. By definition, an **unrelated diversification** involves two businesses that do not have any commonalities in terms of products, customers, production facilities, or functional areas of expertise. Such diversification is most likely to occur when a disproportionate number of a firm's current businesses face decline due to decreasing demand, increased competition, or product obsolescence; the firm must seek new avenues to provide future growth. More fortunate firms may move into unrelated businesses because they have more cash than they need to expand their current businesses or because they wish to discourage takeover attempts.

Unrelated diversification tends to be the riskiest growth strategy in terms of financial outcomes. Indeed, most empirical studies report that related diversification is more conducive to capital productivity and other dimensions of performance than unrelated diversification.[20] This suggests that the ultimate goal of a corporation's strategy for future growth should be to develop a compatible portfolio of businesses to which the firm can add value through the application of its unique core competencies. The corporation's marketing competencies can be particularly important in this regard.[21] Consequently, it is becoming increasingly common for firms not only to acquire related businesses to expand their portfolio, but also to spin off businesses that no longer fit the company's competencies or growth objectives. For instance, Sprint Communications spun off its cellular phone business, and Hilton Hotels sold its casino operations. Indeed, 27 publicly held U.S. companies spun off operations with a total market value of $22.6 billion in 1994 alone.[22]

Diversification through organizational relationships or networks.   Recently some firms have attempted to gain some of the benefits of market expansion or diversification while simultaneously focusing more intensely on a few core competencies. They try to accomplish this feat by forming relationships or organizational networks with other firms instead of acquiring ownership.

Perhaps the best models of organizational networks are the Japanese *kieretsu* and the Korean *chaebol*—coalitions of financial institutions, distributors, and manufacturing firms in a variety of industries that are often grouped around a large trading company which

[19]Robert D. Buzzell, "Is Vertical Integration Profitable?" *Harvard Business Review*, January–February 1983, pp. 92–102; see also Robert D. Buzzell and Bradley T. Gale, *The PIMS Principles: Linking Strategy to Performance* (New York: Free Press, 1987), Chap. 8.

[20]For example, see P. Rajan Varadarajan, "Product Diversity and Firm Performance: An Empirical Investigation," *Journal of Marketing* 50 (January 1986), pp. 43–57; for a more detailed review of the evidence concerning the effects of diversification on firm performance, see Roger A. Kerin, Vijay Mahajan, and P. Rajan Varadarajan, *Contemporary Perspectives on Strategic Market Planning* (Boston: Allyn and Bacon, 1990), Chap. 6.

[21]George S. Day, "The Capabilities of Market-Driven Organizations," *Journal of Marketing* 58 (October 1994), pp. 37–52.

[22]Stephanie Anderson Forest, "The Whirlwind Breaking Up Companies," *Business Week*, August 14, 1995, p. 44.

helps coordinate the activities of the various coalition members and markets their goods and services around the world. In the United States, Compaq is attempting to develop a similar network of organizational alliances. While Compaq concentrates on its core competencies in marketing and servicing computer hardware and software, it depends increasingly on partnerships with other firms for the performance of other functions and for expertise in new markets and product lines. For instance, Compaq relies heavily on Andersen Consulting for assistance in designing computer networks for its largest customers, and on a number of Asian suppliers and assemblers for the manufacture of its products. These relationships allow Compaq to concentrate on its core competencies while simultaneously expanding its product and service offerings and reducing its costs and assets employed.[23]

ALLOCATING CORPORATE RESOURCES

Diversified organizations have several potential advantages over more narrowly focused firms. They have a broader range of areas in which they can knowledgeably invest, and their growth and profitability rates may be more stable because they can offset declines in one business with gains in another. To exploit the advantages of diversification, though, corporate managers must make intelligent decisions about how to allocate financial and human resources across the firm's various business and product-markets. Two sets of analytical tools have proven especially useful in making such decisions: **portfolio models** and **value-based planning**.

Portfolio models

One of the most significant developments in strategic management during the 1970s and 1980s was the creation and widespread adoption of portfolio models to help managers allocate corporate resources across multiple businesses. These models enable managers to classify and review their current and prospective SBUs by viewing them as a portfolio of investment opportunities and then evaluating each business's competitive strength and the attractiveness of the markets it serves.

The Boston Consulting Group's (BCG) growth–share matrix

One of the first, and best known, portfolio models is the growth-share matrix developed by the Boston Consulting Group (BCG). It analyzes the impact of investing resources in different business units on the corporation's future earnings and cash flows. Each business is positioned within a matrix, as shown in Exhibit 2-8. The vertical axis indicates the industry's growth rate, and the horizontal axis shows the business unit's market share relative to its largest competitor.

The growth-share matrix assumes that a firm must generate sufficient cash from businesses with strong competitive positions in mature markets to fund the investments necessary to build the market shares of other businesses in more rapidly growing industries that represent attractive future opportunities. Thus, the **market growth rate** shown on the vertical axis is a proxy measure for the maturity and attractiveness of an industry. This

[23]Ravi S. Achrol, "Evolution of the Marketing Organization: New Forms for Turbulent Environments," *Journal of Marketing* 55 (October 1991), pp. 77–93; see also Raymond E. Miles and Charles C. Snow, "Causes of Failure in Network Organizations," *California Management Review*, Summer 1992, pp. 53–72.

—— **E X H I B I T   2 – 8** ——

BCG's Market Growth–Relative Share Matrix

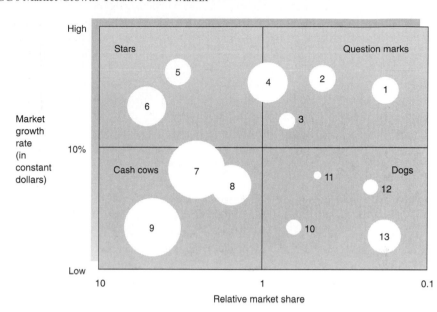

SOURCE: Adapted from Barry Hedley, "Strategy and the Business Portfolio," *Long Range Planning* 10 (February 1977). Reprinted with permission from Elsevier Science.

model views businesses in relatively rapidly growing industries as more attractive investment opportunities for future growth and profitability. In Exhibit 2-8 an annual market growth rate of 10 percent is the cutoff level between fast- and slow-growing industries. This dividing line can vary, however, depending on a corporation's objectives and available opportunities.

Similarly, a business's **relative market share** is a proxy for its competitive strength within its industry. It is computed by dividing the business's absolute market share in dollars or units by that of the leading competitor in the industry. Thus, in Exhibit 2-8 a business unit is in a strong competitive position if its share is equal to, or larger than, that of the next leading competitor (i.e., a relative share of 1.0 or larger). But it is competitively weak if the leading competitor holds a larger share of the market. Finally, the size of the circle representing each business unit is proportional to that unit's sales volume. Thus, businesses 7 and 9 are the largest-volume businesses in this hypothetical company, while business 11 is the smallest.

Resource allocation and strategy implications

Each of the four cells in the growth-share matrix represents a different type of business with different strategy and resource requirements. The implications of each are discussed here and summarized graphically in Exhibit 2-9.

- *Question marks.* Businesses in high-growth industries with low relative market shares (those in the upper-right quadrant of Exhibit 2-9) are called *question marks* or *problem children*. Such businesses require large amounts of cash, not only for

Cash Flows across Businesses in the BCG Portfolio Model

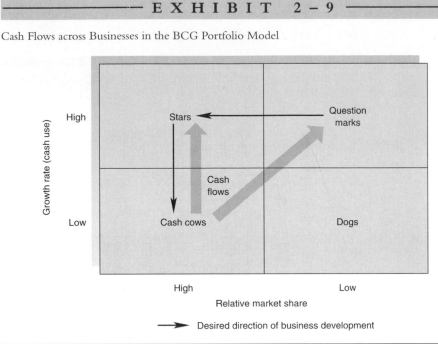

Desired direction of business development

expansion to keep up with the rapidly growing market but also for marketing activities (or reduced margins) to build market share and catch the industry leader. If management can successfully increase the share of a question mark business, it becomes a star. But if they fail, it eventually turns into a "dog" as the industry matures and the market growth rate slows. When this happens it can be difficult for the firm to recoup its past investments in the business. The strategic implication, then, is that management must be careful in selecting which question marks to invest in for future growth. Without sufficient resources and a competitive advantage it can exploit to successfully overtake the market leader, the firm is best advised to divest or harvest the business before its resources are drained.

- *Stars.* A *star* is the market leader in a high-growth industry. Stars are critical to the continued future success of the firm. As their industries mature, they move into the bottom-left quadrant and become cash cows. Paradoxically, while stars are critically important, they often are net users rather than suppliers of cash in the short run (as indicated by the possibility of a negative cash flow shown in Exhibit 2-9). This is because the firm must continue to invest in such businesses to keep up with rapid market growth and to support the R&D and marketing activities necessary to stave off competitors' attacks and maintain a leading market share. Indeed, share maintenance is crucial for star businesses to become cash cows rather than dogs as their industries mature.

- *Cash cows.* Businesses with a high relative share of low-growth markets are called *cash cows* because they are the primary generators of profits and cash in a corporation. Such businesses do not require much additional capital investment. Their markets are stable, and their share leadership position usually means they enjoy economies of scale and relatively high profit margins. Consequently, the corporation can use the cash from these businesses to support its question marks and stars (as shown in Exhibit 2-9). However, this does not mean the firm should necessarily maximize the business's short-term cash flow by cutting R&D and marketing expenditures to the bone—particularly not in industries where the business might continue to generate substantial future sales. When firms attempt to harvest too much cash from such businesses, they risk suffering a premature decline from cash cow to dog status, thus losing profits in the long term.

- *Dogs.* Low-share businesses in low-growth markets are called *dogs* because although they may throw off some cash, they typically generate low profits or losses. Divestiture is one option for such businesses, although it can be difficult to find an interested buyer. Another common strategy is to harvest dog businesses. This involves maximizing short-term cash flow by paring investments and expenditures until the business is gradually phased out. In some cases, though, an argument can be made for continuing to invest in a dog. Such a strategy may make sense, for instance, if the business can be focused on one or a few product-markets where it has some competitive strengths and additional profitable growth can be found.

Limitations of the growth–share matrix

Because the growth-share matrix uses only two variables as a basis for categorizing and analyzing a firm's businesses, it is relatively easy to understand. But while this simplicity helps explain its popularity, it also means that the model has limitations:

- *Market growth rate is an inadequate descriptor of overall industry attractiveness.* For one thing, market growth is not always directly related to profitability or cash flow. Some high-growth industries have never been very profitable because low entry barriers and capital intensity have enabled supply to grow even faster, resulting in intense price competition. Also, rapid growth in one year is no guarantee that growth will continue in the following year.

- *Relative market share is inadequate as a description of overall competitive strength.* It is based on the assumption that an experience curve resulting from a combination of scale economies and other efficiencies gained through learning and technological improvements over time leads to continuing reductions in unit costs as a business's relative market share increases. But a large market share within an industry does not always give a business a significant cost advantage, especially when the product is a low-value-added item, when different products within the business require different production or marketing activities, where different competitors have different capacity and utilization rates, or where some competitors are more vertically integrated or have lower-cost suppliers than others.[24]

  Also, market share is more properly viewed as an outcome of past efforts to formulate and implement effective business-level and marketing strategies rather than as an indicator of enduring competitive strength.[25] If the external environment changes, or the SBU's managers change their strategy, the business's relative market share can shift dramatically.

[24]David B. Montgomery and George S. Day, "Experience Curves: Evidence, Empirical Issues and Applications," in *Strategic Marketing and Strategic Management*, eds. David Gardner and Howard Thomas (New York: John Wiley and Sons, 1984), pp. 213–38.

[25]Robert Jacobson argues that market share and profitability are joint outcomes from successful strategies and, further, that management skills are likely to have the greatest impact on profitability. See "Distinguishing among Competing Theories of the Market Share Effect," *Journal of Marketing* 52 (October 1988), pp. 68–80.

- *The outcomes of a growth-share analysis are highly sensitive to variations in how "growth" and "share" are measured.* Using information from 15 business units within a single firm, one study explored how their positions within a growth-share matrix would vary when different measures of growth and market share were used. The study used four measures of share and four of growth (both past and forecasted future growth). Only 3 of the 15 businesses ended up in the same quadrant of the matrix no matter what measures were used.[26]

  Another measurement problem has to do with how the industry and the SBU's "served market" (i.e., the target market segments being pursued) should be defined. For example, Coke holds about a 40 percent share of the U.S. cola market but less than 8 percent of the market for all liquid beverages. Given that consumers substitute other beverages such as coffee, bottled water, and fruit juice for soft drinks to varying degrees, which is the most appropriate market definition to use?

- *While the matrix specifies appropriate investment strategies for each business, it provides little guidance on how best to implement those strategies.* While the model suggests that a firm should invest cash in its question mark businesses, for instance, it does not consider whether there are any potential sources of competitive advantage that the business can exploit to successfully increase its share. Simply providing a business with more money does not guarantee that it will be able to improve its position within the matrix.

- *The model implicitly assumes that all business units are independent of one another except for the flow of cash.* If this assumption is not accurate, the model can suggest some inappropriate resource allocation decisions. For instance, if other SBUs depend on a dog business as a source of supply—or if they share functional activities, such as a common plant or salesforce, with that business—harvesting the dog might increase the costs or reduce the effectiveness of the other SBUs.

Alternative portfolio models

In view of these limitations, a number of firms have attempted to improve the basic portfolio model. Such improvements have focused primarily on developing more detailed, multifactor measures of industry attractiveness and a business's competitive strength and on making the analysis more future-oriented.

Multifactor portfolio models, typically referred to as *industry attractiveness–business position matrixes* or *directional policy matrixes*, rely on factors other than just market growth to judge the future attractiveness of different industries. Similarly, they use multiple variables in addition to relative market share to judge the competitive strength and position of each of their businesses.

Exhibit 2-10 shows some of the factors that managers might use to evaluate industry attractiveness and a business's competitive position. Corporate managers must first select factors most appropriate for their firm and weight them according to their relative importance. They then rate each business and its industry on the two sets of factors. Next they combine the weighted evaluations into summary measures used to place each business within one of the nine boxes in the matrix shown in Exhibit 2-10. Businesses falling into boxes numbered 1 (where both industry attractiveness and the business's ability to compete

[26]Yoram Wind, Vijay Mahajan, and Donald J. Swire, "An Empirical Comparison of Standardized Portfolio Models," *Journal of Marketing* 47 (Spring 1983), pp. 89–99.

═══════════════ **E X H I B I T   2 - 1 0** ═══════════════

The Industry Attractiveness–Business Position Matrix

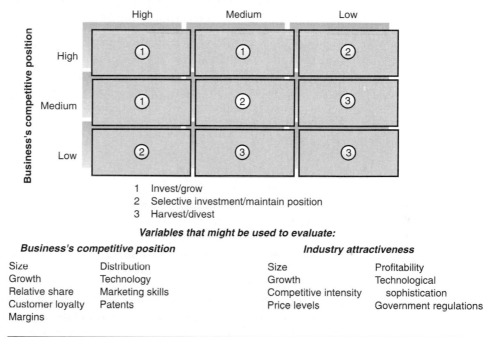

1 Invest/grow
2 Selective investment/maintain position
3 Harvest/divest

Variables that might be used to evaluate:

Business's competitive position		Industry attractiveness	
Size	Distribution	Size	Profitability
Growth	Technology	Growth	Technological
Relative share	Marketing skills	Competitive intensity	sophistication
Customer loyalty	Patents	Price levels	Government regulations
Margins			

SOURCE: The Industry Attractiveness-Business Position Matrix.

are relatively high) are good candidates for further investment for future growth. Businesses in the 2 boxes should receive only selective investment with an objective of maintaining current position. Finally, businesses in the 3 boxes are candidates for harvesting or divestiture.

These multifactor models are richer and more detailed than the simple growth-share model and consequently provide more strategic guidance concerning the appropriate allocation of resources across businesses. They are also more useful for evaluating potential new product-markets. However, the multifactor measures in these models can be subjective and ambiguous, especially when managers must evaluate different industries on the same set of factors. Also, the conclusions drawn from these models still depend on the way industries and product-markets are defined.[27]

Some firms also use portfolio analysis to evaluate how they should allocate resources across the different technologies (as opposed to particular businesses or products) in their asset base. A **technology portfolio matrix** typically categorizes different technologies according to whether the firm is, or will be, an industry leader or follower in the development of the technology, the amount of development needed to commercialize the

---

[27]For a more detailed discussion of the uses and limitations of multifactor portfolio models, see Kerin, Mahajan, and Varadarajan, *Contemporary Perspectives*, chap. 3.

technology, and the likely market potential for products based on the technology.[28] This form of portfolio analysis is particularly useful for high-tech firms or business units that have more potential new technologies and/or applications in the early stages of development than they have the resources to fully commercialize.

Value-based planning

As mentioned, one limitation of portfolio analysis is that it specifies how firms should allocate financial resources across their businesses without considering the competitive strategies those businesses are, or should be, pursuing. Portfolio analysis provides little guidance, for instance, in deciding which of two question mark businesses—each in attractive markets but following different strategies—is worthy of the greatest investment or in choosing which of several alternative competitive strategies a particular business unit should pursue.

Worse, because indicators of past market attractiveness and competitive strength do not always accurately predict the future financial returns a strategic investment will produce, relying on portfolio analysis as a tool for allocating resources across businesses or strategic marketing programs can lead to suboptimal outcomes. In one experiment involving managers from six different countries, for instance, 86 percent of those managers who used a portfolio matrix as a decision-making tool made suboptimal investments in a situation where future profits from two alternative strategic investments were negatively related to market growth and the firm's relative market share. In contrast, only 15 percent of those managers who based their decision on net present value analysis, or other profit-based calculations, made suboptimal decisions in the same situation.[29]

Value-based planning is a resource allocation tool that attempts to overcome the shortcomings and unanswered questions inherent in portfolio analysis by assessing the shareholder value a given strategy is likely to create. Thus, value-based planning provides a basis for comparing the economic returns to be gained from investing in different businesses pursuing different strategies or from alternative strategies that might be adopted by a given business unit.

A number of value-based planning methods are currently in use, but all share three basic features.[30] First, they assess the economic value a strategy is likely to produce by examining the cash flows it will generate rather than relying on distorted accounting measures such as return on investment.[31] Second, they estimate the shareholder value that a strategy will produce by discounting its forecasted cash flows by the business's risk-adjusted cost of capital. Finally, they evaluate strategies based on the likelihood that the investment required by a strategy will deliver returns greater than the cost of capital. The amount of return a strategy or operating program generates in excess of the cost of capital involved is

---

[28]Noel Capon and Rashi Glazer, "Marketing and Technology: A Strategic Coalignment," *Journal of Marketing* 51 (July 1987), pp. 1–14.

[29]J. Scott Armstrong and Roderick J. Brodie, "Effects of Portfolio Planning Methods on Decision-Making: Experimental Results," *International Journal of Research in Marketing* 11 (1994), pp. 73–84.

[30]Two of the most commonly used approaches to value-based planning are the market-to-book ratio model and the discounted cash flow model. The market-to-book ratio model is described in William W. Alberts and James M. McTaggart, "Value-Based Strategic Investment Planning," *Interfaces* 14 (January–February 1984), pp. 138–51; the discounted cash flow model, which is the approach focused on in this chapter, is detailed in Rappaport, *Creating Shareholder Value.*

[31]For a detailed discussion of the shortcomings of accounting data for evaluating the value created by a strategy, see Rappaport, *Creating Shareholder Value,* chap. 2.

Across SBUs. Not w/in SBU's.

commonly referred to as its **economic value added** or EVA.[32] This approach to evaluating alternative strategies is particularly appropriate for use in allocating resources across business units because most capital investments are made at the business unit level, and different business units typically face different risks and therefore have different costs of capital.

Discounted cash flow model

Perhaps the best known and most widely used approach to value-based planning is the discounted cash flow model proposed by Alfred Rappaport and the Alcar Group, Inc. In this model, as Exhibit 2-11 indicates, shareholder value created by a strategy is determined by the cash flow it generates, the business's cost of capital (which is used to discount future cash flows back to their present value), and the market value of the debt assigned to the business. The future cash flows generated by the strategy are, in turn, affected by six factors or "value drivers." They are the rate of sales growth the strategy will produce, the operating profit margin, the income tax rate, investment in working capital, fixed capital investment required by the strategy, and the duration of value growth.

The first five value drivers are self-explanatory, but the sixth requires some elaboration. The duration of value growth represents management's estimate of the number of years over which the strategy can be expected to produce rates of return that exceed the cost of capital. This estimate, in turn, is tied to two other management judgments. First the manager must decide on the length of the planning period (typically three to five years); he or she must then estimate the residual value the strategy will continue to produce after the planning period is over. Such decisions are tricky, for they involve predictions of what will happen in the relatively distant future. Unfortunately, managers must wrestle with several such thorny estimation problems when implementing value-based planning. A detailed discussion of the procedure involved and the kinds of forecasts and predictions a manager must make in using discounted cash flow analysis to evaluate a business strategy is beyond the scope of this chapter, but can be found in one of the specialized books on the subject.[33]

Some limitations of value-based planning.[34] Value-based planning is not a substitute for strategic planning; it is only one tool for evaluating strategy alternatives identified and developed through managers' judgments. It does so by relying on forecasts of many kinds to put a financial value on the hopes, fears, and expectations managers associate with each alternative. Projections of cash inflows rest on forecasts of sales volume, product mix, unit prices, and competitors' actions. Expected cash outflows depend on projections of various cost elements, working capital, and investment requirements.

While good forecasts are notoriously difficult to make, they are critical to the validity of value-based planning. Once someone attaches numbers to judgments about what is likely to happen, people tend to endow those numbers with the concreteness of hard facts.

---

[32]Shawn Tully, "The Real Key to Creating Wealth," *Fortune*, September 30, 1993, pp. 38–50; Tully, "America's Best Wealth Creators"; and Terrence P. Pare, "The New Champ of Wealth Creation," *Fortune*, September 18, 1995, pp. 131–32.

[33]For example, see Rappaport, *Creating Shareholder Value*; or Kerin, Mahajan, and Varadarajan, *Contemporary Perspectives*, chap. 9.

[34]This section summarizes points made in more detail in George S. Day and Liam Fahey, "Putting Strategy into Shareholder Value Analysis," *Harvard Business Review*, March–April 1990, pp. 156–62; see also Alfred Rappaport, "CFOs and Strategists: Forging a Common Framework," *Harvard Business Review*, May–June 1992, pp. 84–91; and "Debate: Duking It Out over EVA," p. 232.

──────────── **E X H I B I T   2 – 1 1** ────────────

Factors Affecting the Creation of Shareholder Value

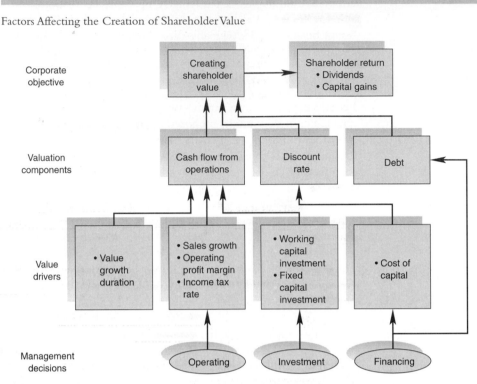

SOURCE: Reprinted with the permission of The Free Press, a Division of Macmillan, Inc., from *Creating Shareholder Value* by Alfred Rappaport. Copyright © 1986 by Alfred Rappaport.

Therefore, the numbers derived from value-based planning can sometimes take on a life of their own, and managers can lose sight of the assumptions underlying them.

Consequently, inaccurate forecasts can create problems in implementing value-based planning. For one thing, there are natural human tendencies to overvalue the financial projections associated with some strategy alternatives and to undervalue others. For instance, managers are likely to overestimate the future returns from a currently successful strategy. Evidence of past success tends to carry more weight than qualitative assessments of future threats. Managers may pay too little attention to how competitive behavior, prices, and returns might change if, for example, the industry were suddenly beset by a slowdown in market growth and the appearance of excess capacity.

On the other hand, some kinds of strategy alternatives are consistently undervalued. Particularly worrisome from a marketing viewpoint is the tendency to underestimate the value of keeping current customers. Putting a figure on the damage to a firm's competitive advantage from *not* making a strategic investment necessary to maintain the status quo is harder than documenting potential cost savings or profit improvements that an investment might generate. For example, a few years ago Cone Drive Operations, a small manufacturer of heavy-duty gears, faced a number of related problems. Profits were declining, inventory costs were climbing, and customers were unhappy because deliveries were often late. Cone's management thought that a $2 million computer-integrated manufacturing system might help solve these problems; but a discounted cash flow analysis indicated the system would be an unwise investment. Because the company had only $26 million in sales, it was hard to justify the $2 million investment in terms of cost savings. However, the financial analysis underestimated intangibles like improved product quality, faster order processing, and improved customer satisfaction. Management decided to install the new system anyway, and new business and nonlabor savings paid back the investment in just one year. More important, Cone retained nearly all of its old customers, many of whom had been seriously considering switching to other suppliers.

Finally, another kind of problem involved in implementing value-based planning occurs when management fails to consider all the appropriate strategy alternatives. Since it is only an analytical tool, value-based planning can evaluate alternatives, but it cannot create them. The best strategy will never emerge from the evaluation process if management fails to identify it.

To realize its full benefits, management must link value-based planning to sound strategic analysis that is rigorous enough to avoid the problems associated with under-valuing certain strategies, overvaluing others, and failing to consider all the options. As Day and Fahey argued:

> Managers must fully consider the competitive context of cash flows and ensure that cash flow projections are directly tied to competitive analysis projections. They must question whether the cash outflows contribute to competitive advantage and to what extent cash inflows are dependent on those advantages. Specifically, they should broaden the range of strategy alternatives, challenge the inherent soundness of each alternative, and test the sensitivity of each alternative to changes in cash inflows and outflows.[35]

In spite of its limitations, when value-based planning is used correctly as an integral part of the broader strategic planning process it can be a useful tool for evaluating, and deciding how to allocate resources among, alternative strategies. An example of a successful appli-cation of value-based planning at the Coca-Cola Company is discussed in Exhibit 2-12.

SOURCES OF SYNERGY

A final strategic concern at the corporate level is to increase synergy across the firm's various businesses and product-markets. As mentioned, synergy exists when two or more businesses or product-markets, and their resources and competencies, complement and reinforce one another so that the total performance of the related businesses is greater than it would be otherwise.

Some potential synergies at the corporate level are knowledge-based. The performance of one business can be enhanced by the transfer of competencies, knowledge, or customer-related intangibles—such as brand-name recognition and reputation—from other units within the firm. For instance, the technical knowledge concerning image processing and the quality reputation that Canon developed in the camera business helped ease the firm's entry into the office copier business.

In part, such knowledge-based synergies are a function of the corporation's scope and mission—or how its managers answer the question, What businesses should we be in? When a firm's portfolio of businesses and product-markets reflects a common mission based on well-defined customer needs, market segments, or technologies, the company is

---

[35]Day and Fahey, "Putting Strategy. . .," pp. 160–61.

EXHIBIT 2-12

A Strategic Application of Value-Based Planning at the Coca-Cola Company

The Coca-Cola Company uses value-based planning to help make decisions about the relative attractiveness of alternative strategies within each of its businesses. An example of the usefulness of the approach is provided by Coke's experience within its soda fountain business. The firm had long considered this business to be very profitable because there were no bottles or cans to fill, transport, or store. But a discounted cash flow analysis revealed that the business was actually destroying shareholder value. Over time, the business had become capital intensive. As a result, the business's return on capital was only 12.6 percent, while its cost of capital was estimated to be 16 percent.

The main culprit turned out to be the expensive, five-gallon, stainless steel containers used to transport the Coke syrup to retail outlets. Therefore, the business changed its distribution and packaging policies. It adopted cheaper, disposable bag-in-a-box containers and sent larger 50-gallon drums to its bigger customers. By thus reducing its investment in containers, the business's return on capital rose to 17 percent. At the same time, by increasing its financial leverage, Coke reduced its cost of capital to 14 percent. Thus, the soda fountain business was turned into a strong contributor to shareholder value.

SOURCE: Bernard C. Reimann, "Managing for the Shareholders: An Overview of Value-Based Planning," *Planning Review*, January–February 1988, pp. 10–22.

more likely to develop core competencies, customer knowledge, and strong brand franchises that can be shared across businesses. However, the firm's organization structure and allocation of resources may also enhance knowledge-based synergy. A centralized corporate R&D department, for example, is often more efficient and effective at discovering new technologies with potential applications across multiple businesses than if each business unit bore the burden of funding its own R&D efforts. Similarly, some experts argue that strong corporate-level coordination and support is necessary to maximize the strength of a firm's brand franchise, and to glean full benefit from accumulated market knowledge, when the firm is competing in global markets.[36]

A second potential source of corporate synergy is inherent in sharing operational resources, facilities, and functions across business units. For instance, two or more businesses might produce products in a common plant or use a single salesforce to contact common customers. When such sharing helps increase economies of scale or experience-curve effects, it can improve the efficiency of each of the businesses involved. However, the sharing of operational facilities and functions may not produce positive synergies for all business units. Such sharing can limit a business's flexibility and reduce its ability to adapt quickly to changing market conditions and opportunities. Thus, a business whose competitive strategy is focused on new-product development and the pursuit of rapidly changing markets may be hindered more than helped when it is forced to share operating resources with other units[37] For instance, when Frito-Lay attempted to enter the packaged cookie market with its Grandma's line of soft cookies, the company relied on its 10,000 salty-snack route salespeople to distribute the new line to grocery stores. The firm thought its huge and well-established snack salesforce would give its cookies a competitive advantage in gaining shelf space and retailer support. But because those salespeople were paid a commission on their total sales revenue, they were reluctant to take time from their salty-snack

---

[36]Hamel and Prahalad, "Strategic Intent," p. 74.

[37]Robert W. Ruekert and Orville C. Walker, Jr., *Shared Marketing Programs and the Performance of Different Business Strategies*, Report 91–100 (Cambridge, Mass.: The Marketing Science Institute, 1991).

products to push the new cookies. The resulting lack of a strong sales effort contributed to Grandma's failure to achieve a sustainable market share.

As we shall see in the next chapter, the type of competitive strategy a business unit chooses to pursue can have a number of implications for corporate-level decisions concerning organizational structure and resource allocation as well as for the marketing strategies and programs employed within the business.

SUMMARY

Decisions about the organization's scope or mission, its overall goals and objectives, avenues for future growth, resource deployments, and potential sources of synergy across business units are the primary components of corporate strategy.

A mission statement provides guidance to an organization's managers about which market opportunities to pursue and which fall outside the firm's strategic domain. Similarly, a statement of strategic intent establishes a long-term direction for the firm and motivates employee effort; but it is flexible in giving employees substantial freedom to decide what means are best for achieving the firm's purpose.

Formal objectives guide a firm's businesses and employees toward specific dimensions and levels of performance by establishing benchmarks against which performance can be compared and evaluated. Increasing shareholder value is the ultimate objective for publicly held companies. But difficulties in determining whether specific actions will create such value lead most firms to set specific objectives for performance outcomes such as sales volume, market share, and return on investment.

The corporate development strategy addresses the question of where the firm's future growth will come from. A company might seek growth either by expanding its current businesses or by diversifying into new businesses.

A firm should allocate its resources across its various businesses to reflect both the relative competitive strength of each business and variations in the attractiveness and growth potential of the markets they serve. Portfolio models help managers make these allocation decisions. Value-based planning is another useful resource allocation tool. It attempts to evaluate potential investments in a firm's businesses, and in the alternative strategies each business might pursue, on the basis of how much value those investments will produce for the firm's shareholders over time.

Finally, corporate synergy can be gained by developing competencies, knowledge, and customer-based intangibles, such as brand-name recognition and reputation, that can be shared across multiple businesses within the company. Similarly, synergy might be sought through the sharing of operational resources and functions, such as a common plant or salesforce, across businesses. Caution is necessary, however, because sharing operational facilities and activities can reduce a business's flexibility and hinder its ability to respond quickly to changing market conditions.

3 CHAPTER

Business Strategies and Their Marketing Implications

BUSINESS STRATEGIES AND MARKETING PROGRAMS AT 3M[1]

The Minnesota Mining and Manufacturing Company, better known as 3M, began manufacturing sandpaper nearly a century ago. Today it is the leader in dozens of technical areas from fluorochemistry to optical recording. The firm makes more than 60,000 different products that generated $14.2 billion in global sales in 1996. The company produced $1.5 billion in net income—more than a 24 percent return on shareholders' equity. For an update on 3M's performance, go to the company's website (www.3m.com), and click on "financial and shareholder information."

As you might expect of a firm with so many products, 3M is organized into a large number of strategic business units (SBUs). The company contains more than 40 SBUs or product divisions organized into two sectors: the Industrial and Consumer Sector, making such things as industrial tapes, abrasives, adhesives, and consumer products like Post-it brand repositionable notes and Scotch brand Magic Transparent Tape; and the Life Sciences Sector, consisting of such diverse businesses as pharmaceuticals, medical equipment, and reflective highway materials, all designed to enhance health and safety. A third sector concerned with magnetic media—such as disks for personal computers—and imaging systems was spun off as a separate company in 1995.

---

[1]Material for this example was drawn from The 3MCompany *1996 Annual Report* (St. Paul, Minn.: 3M Company, 1997); information obtained from the company's website (www.3m.com); and Shawn Tully, "Why to Go for Stretch Targets," *Fortune*, November 14, 1994, pp. 145–58.

While 3M has acquired many smaller firms over the years, its growth strategy has focused primarily on internal new product development, emphasizing both improved products for existing customers and new products for new markets. Indeed, one of the formal objectives assigned to every business unit is to obtain at least 30 percent of annual sales from products introduced within the last four years. The company supports its growth strategy with an R&D budget of $947 million, almost 7 percent of total revenues.

3M also pursues growth through the aggressive development of foreign markets for its many products. Indeed, a fourth organizational sector is responsible for coordinating the firm's marketing efforts across countries. In 1996, 3M attained $7.6 billion in sales—54 percent of its total revenue—from outside the United States.

Differences in customer needs, and life-cycle stages across industries, however, lead 3M's various business units to pursue their growth objectives in different ways. The Industrial Tape group, for example, operates in an industry where both the product technologies and the customer segments are relatively mature and stable. Growth in this group results from extending the scope of adhesive technology (e.g., attaching weather stripping to auto doors), product improvements and line extensions targeted at existing customers, and expansion into global markets.

In contrast, the firm's Medical Products unit develops new medical applications for emerging technologies developed in 3M's many R&D labs. It sells a broad range of innovative medical devices, such as blood gas monitors and an electric bone stapler. Most of the unit's growth, therefore, comes from developing totally new products aimed at new markets.

The competitive strategies of 3M's various business units also differ. For instance, the Industrial Tape unit is primarily concerned with maintaining its commanding market share in existing markets while preserving or even improving its profitability. Its competitive strategy is to differentiate itself from competitors on the basis of product quality and excellent customer service.

On the other hand, the Medical Products unit's strategy is to avoid head-to-head competitive battles by being the technological leader in the industry and introducing a constant stream of unique products. To be successful, though, the unit must devote substantial resources to R&D and to the stimulation of primary demand. Thus, its main objective is volume growth, and it must sometimes sacrifice short-run profitability to fund the product development and marketing efforts needed to accomplish that goal.

These differences in competitive strategy in turn influence the strategic marketing programs within the various business units. For instance, the firm spends little on advertising or sales promotion for its mature industrial tape products. However, it does maintain a large, well-trained technical salesforce that provides valuable problem-solving assistance and other services to customers, and informed feedback to the firm's R&D personnel about potential new applications and product improvements.

In contrast, the pioneering nature of many of the Medical Products Group's goods and services calls for more extensive promotion programs to develop customer awareness and stimulate primary demand. Consequently, the unit devotes a relatively large portion of its revenues to advertising in technical journals aimed at physicians and other medical professionals. It also supports a well-trained salesforce, but those salespeople spend much of their time demonstrating new products and prospecting for new accounts in addition to servicing existing customers. Finally, the unit conducts substantial marketing research to test new product concepts and forecast their demand potential.

THE CONCEPT OF STRATEGIC FIT

The situation at 3M again illustrates that firms with multiple businesses usually have a hierarchy of strategies extending from the corporate level down to the individual product-market entry. As we saw in the last chapter, corporate strategy addresses such issues as the firm's mission and scope and the directions it will pursue for future growth. Thus, 3M's corporate growth strategy focuses primarily on developing new products and new applications for emerging technologies.

The major strategic question addressed at the business-unit level is, How should we compete in this business? For instance, 3M's Industrial Tape unit attempts to maintain its commanding market share and high profitability by differentiating itself on the basis of high quality and good customer service. On the other hand, the Medical Products unit seeks high growth through aggressive new product and market development.

Finally, the strategic marketing program for each product-market entry within a business unit attempts to allocate marketing resources and activities in a manner appropriate for accomplishing the business unit's objectives. Thus, most of the strategic marketing programs within 3M's Medical Products SBU involve relatively large expenditures for marketing research and introductory advertising and promotion campaigns aimed at achieving sales growth.

One key reason for 3M's continuing success is that all three levels of strategy within the company have usually been characterized by good internal and external consistency, or **strategic fit**. 3M's managers have done a good job of monitoring and adapting their strategies to the market opportunities, technological advances, and competitive threats in the company's external environment. The firm's marketing and sales managers play critical roles both in developing market-oriented strategies for individual products and in influencing and helping to formulate corporate and business-level strategies that are responsive to environmental conditions. At the same time, those strategies are usually internally compatible. Each strategy fits with those at other levels as well as with the unique competitive strengths and competencies of the relevant business unit and the company as a whole.[2]

These interdependencies among strategies—particularly those at the business and product-market levels—are the major focus of the rest of this chapter. First, we briefly examine the strategic decisions that must be made at the business level, paying particular attention to a number of generic competitive strategies a business unit might choose to pursue and the environmental circumstances in which each type is most appropriate. We then examine the implications those strategies have for the marketing activities and programs that are most appropriate for businesses pursuing each type.

STRATEGIC DECISIONS AT THE BUSINESS-UNIT LEVEL

When a firm is involved in multiple businesses, it is typically organized in separate components responsible for each business. While these organizational components go by many different names, they are most commonly called **strategic business units** or **SBUs.** Managers of each unit must decide what objectives and strategies to pursue within their specific business, subject to the approval of corporate management.

---

[2]For a more detailed discussion of the concept of strategic fit and of the role of various external and internal variables in influencing the effectiveness of a firm's strategies, see N. Venkatraman and James Camillus, "The Concept of 'Fit' in Strategic Management," *Academy of Management Review* 9 (1984), pp. 513–25.

The first step in developing business-level strategies, then, is for the firm to decide how to divide itself into SBUs. The managers of each business unit then must make recommendations about the SBU's objectives and scope, how resources should be allocated across its product-market entries and functional departments, and which competitive strategy to pursue to build a sustainable advantage in its product-markets.

Defining strategic business units

Ideally, a strategic business unit should be designed to incorporate a unique set of products aimed at a homogeneous set of markets. It should also have responsibility for its own performance and control over the resources that affect that performance.

As Exhibit 3-1 indicates, there is a rationale for each of these desired business-unit characteristics. As might be expected, however, firms do not always meet all of these ideals when designing their SBUs. There are usually trade-offs between having many small homogeneous business units versus fewer but larger and more diverse SBUs that top management can more easily supervise.

The crucial question, then, is, What criteria should be used to cluster product-markets into a business unit? The three dimensions suggested earlier as criteria for defining the scope and mission of the entire corporation can also serve as the basis for defining individual SBUs:

- *Technical compatibility*, particularly with respect to product technologies and operational requirements, such as the use of similar production facilities and engineering skills.
- Similarity in the *customer needs* to be satisfied or the product benefits sought by customers in the target markets.
- Similarity in the *personal characteristics* or behavior patterns of customers in the target markets.

In practice, it is often impossible to meet all three criteria. Instead, the choice is often between technical/operational compatibility and customer homogeneity. Management commonly defines SBUs on the basis of technical and operational interdependence, clustering product-market entries that require similar technologies, production facilities, and employee skills to minimize the coordination problems involved in administering the unit. In some firms, however, the marketing synergies gained from coordinating technically different products aimed at the same customer need or market segment outweigh operational considerations. In these firms, managers group product-market entries into SBUs based on similarities across customers or distribution systems. For instance, 3M's Medical Products unit includes a wide range of products involving very different technologies and production processes. They are grouped within the same business unit, though, because all address health needs, are marketed to physicians and other health professionals, and can be sold through a common salesforce and distribution system.

Business–unit objectives

Companies break down corporate objectives into subobjectives for each SBU. In most cases, those subobjectives vary across SBUs according to the attractiveness of their industries, the strength of their competitive positions within those industries, and resource allocation decisions by corporate management. For example, managers may assign an SBU in

---

E X H I B I T   3 – 1

Characteristics of the Ideal Strategic Business Unit

Characteristic	Rationale
• Serves a homogeneous set of markets with a limited number of related technologies	Minimizing the diversity of a business unit's product-market entries enables the unit's manager to do a better job of formulating and implementing a coherent and internally consistent business strategy.
• Serves a unique set of product-markets	No other SBU within the firm should compete for the same set of customers with similar products. This enables the firm to avoid duplication of effort and helps maximize economies of scale within its SBUs.
• Has control over the factors necessary for successful performance, such as R&D, production, marketing, and distribution	This is not to say that an SBU should never share resources, such as a manufacturing plant or a salesforce, with one or more business units; but the SBU should have authority to determine how its share of the joint resource will be used to effectively carry out its strategy.
• Has responsibility for its own profitability	Because top management cannot keep an eye on every decision and action taken by all its SBUs, the success of an SBU and its managers must be judged by monitoring its performance over time. Thus, the SBU's managers should have control over the factors that affect performance and then be held accountable for the outcomes.

a rapidly growing industry relatively high volume and share-growth objectives but lower ROI objectives than an SBU with a large share in a mature industry.

A similar process of breaking down overall SBU objectives into a set of subobjectives should occur for each product-market entry within the unit. Those subobjectives obviously must reflect the SBU's overall objectives; but once again they may vary across product-market entries according to the attractiveness and growth potential of individual market segments and the competitive strengths of the company's product in each market. For example, when 3M's consumer products group first introduced its Scotch-Brite Never Rust soap pads—a new form of scouring pad that will never rust or splinter because it is made from recycled plastic beverage bottles—its objective was to capture a major share of the $100 million soap pad market from well-entrenched competitive brands like SOS and Brillo. 3M wanted to maximize Never Rust's volume growth and market share even if the new line did not break even for several years. Consequently, the firm's top managers approved a major investment in a new plant and a substantial introductory advertising budget. At the same time, though, the consumer group maintained high profitability goals for its other established products—like Scotch brand Magic Transparent Tape and Post-it brand notes—to provide the cash required for Never Rust's introduction and preserve the group's overall profit level.[3]

---

[3]Tully, "Why to Go for Stretch Targets," p. 150.

Allocating resources within the business unit

Once an SBU's objectives and budget have been approved at the corporate level, its managers must decide how the available resources should be allocated across the unit's various product-market entries. Because this allocation process is quite similar to allocating corporate resources across SBUs, many firms use similar economic value, value-based planning, or portfolio analysis tools for both.[4] Of course, at the SBU level managers must determine the attractiveness of individual target markets, the competitive position of their products within those markets, and the cash flows each product entry will likely generate rather than analyzing industry attractiveness and the overall competitive strengths of the firm.

Unfortunately, value-based planning is not as useful a tool for evaluating alternative resource allocations across product-market entries as it is for evaluating allocations across SBUs. This is because the product-market entries within a business unit often share the benefits of common investments and the costs of functional activities, as when multiple products are produced in the same plant or sold by the same salesforce. The difficulty of deciding what portion of such common investments and shared costs should be assigned to specific products increases the difficulty of applying a discounted cash flow analysis at the product-market level. As we shall see in Chapter 13, some firms have adopted activity-based costing systems in an attempt to resolve such problems,[5] but many difficulties remain.

The business unit's competitive strategy

The essential question to be answered in formulating a business strategy is, How will the business unit compete to gain a sustainable competitive advantage within its industry? Achieving a competitive advantage requires a business unit to make two choices:

- What is the SBU's *competitive domain or scope*? What market segments should it target, and what customer needs will the unit attempt to satisfy? This decision provides guidelines for the desired breadth and complexity of the unit's product line and a foundation for the formulation of marketing strategies for each product-market entry.

- How will the business unit *distinguish itself from competitors* in its target market(s)? What distinctive competencies can it rely on to achieve a unique position relative to its competitors?

Even though a business unit may contain a number of different product-market entries, most analysts argue that the unit should pursue the same overall source of competitive advantage in all of them. In this way the SBU can take full advantage of its particular strengths and downplay its weaknesses. As Michael E. Porter argued in his book on competitive advantage:

> If a [business] is to attain a competitive advantage, it must make a choice about the type of competitive advantage it seeks to attain and the scope within which it will attain it. Being "all

---

[4]Phillipe Haspeslagh, "Portfolio Planning: Uses and Limits," *Harvard Business Review*, January–February 1982, pp. 59–73; and Shawn Tully, "The Real Key to Creating Wealth," *Fortune*, September 30, 1993, pp. 38–50.

[5]For example, see Robin Cooper and Robert S. Kaplan, "Measure Costs Right: Make the Right Decisions," *Harvard Business Review*, September–October 1988, pp. 96–103; and Terrence P. Pare, "A New Tool for Managing Costs," *Fortune*, June 14, 1993, p. 124.

E X H I B I T 3 – 2

Porter's Four Business Strategies

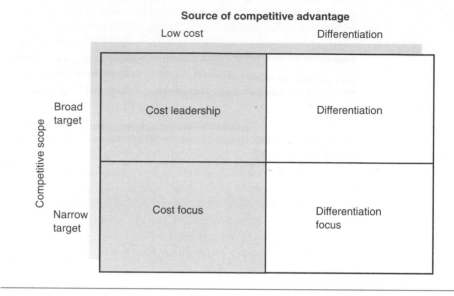

SOURCE: Adapted with permission of The Free Press, A Division of Macmillan, Inc., from *Competitive Advantage: Creating and Sustaining Superior Performance* by Michael E. Porter. Copyright © 1985 by Michael E. Porter.

things to all people" is a recipe for strategic mediocrity and below-average performance, because it often means that a [business] has no competitive advantage at all.[6]

Porter argued that a business might seek a competitive advantage on two broad dimensions: It can try to be the low-cost producer within its target markets, or it can differentiate itself from the competition through its product offerings or marketing programs. It might achieve differentiation, for example, by offering a higher-quality or more technically advanced product, more extensive promotion, broader distribution, or better customer service. Indeed, some businesses attempt to differentiate their various product offerings on multiple dimensions by developing an entire set of competencies.

For instance, Compaq attempts to market PCs that offer lower prices, superior customer service, and more user-friendly features than competing machines. This multidimensional approach to developing a differentiated competitive strategy is sometimes labeled with the buzzwords "total quality management."[7]

Also, a business unit's strategic scope might be defined either broadly or narrowly. That is, it might pursue a wide range of market segments within its industry or focus on only one or a few target segments. As Exhibit 3-2 indicates, Porter suggested that a business unit might adopt one of four basic or "generic" competitive strategies: (1) **cost leadership** across a broad range of product market entries, (2) cost leadership focusing on a narrow

---

[6]Michael E. Porter, *Competitive Advantage: Creating and Sustaining Superior Performance* (New York: Free Press, 1985), p. 12.

[7]Frank Rose, "Now Quality Means Service Too," *Fortune,* April 22, 1991, pp. 97–111; and Rahul Jacob, "Beyond Quality and Value," *Fortune*, Special Issue, Autumn–Winter 1993, pp. 8–11.

═══════════════════ E X H I B I T   3 – 3 ═══════════════════

Summary Definitions of Miles and Snow's Four Business Strategies

[handwritten left margin: Building Demand]

Prospector *[handwritten: Δ'ng Technology / Customer Segments. Early Lifecycle.]*
- Operates within a broad product-market domain that undergoes periodic redefinition.
- Values being a "first mover" in new product and market areas, even if not all of these efforts prove to be highly profitable.
- Responds rapidly to early signals concerning areas of opportunity, and these responses often lead to new rounds of competitive actions.
- Competes primarily by stimulating and meeting new market opportunities, but may not maintain strength over time in all markets it enters.

[handwritten left margin: (A) Differentiated Several Products Superior Quality   (B) Low Cost   Product Improvements or Line Extensions]

Defender *[handwritten: Mature Mkts.]*
- Attempts to locate and maintain a secure position in relatively stable product or service areas.
- Offers relatively limited range of products or services compared to competitors.
- Tries to protect its domain by offering lower prices, higher quality, or better service than competitors.
- Usually not at the forefront of technological/new product development in its industry; tends to ignore industry changes not directly related to its area of operation.

Analyzer *[handwritten: Mature Mkts w/ Some Growth.]*
- An intermediate type; makes fewer and slower product-market changes than prospectors but is less committed to stability and efficiency than defenders.
- Attempts to maintain a stable, limited line of products or services, but carefully follows a selected set of promising new developments in its industry.
- Seldom a first mover, but often a second or third entrant in product-markets related to its existing market base—often with a lower cost or higher-quality product or service offering.

Reactor
- Lacks any well-defined competitive strategy.
- Does not have as consistent a product-market orientation as its competitors.
- Not as willing to assume the risks of new product or market development as its competitors.
- Not as aggressive in marketing established products as some competitors.
- Responds primarily when it is forced to by environmental pressures.

SOURCE: Adapted from R. E. Miles and C. C. Snow, *Organizational Strategy, Structure, and Process* (New York: McGraw-Hill, 1978). Reproduced with permission of the McGraw-Hill Company.

group of target segments, (3) **differentiation** across a wide variety of segments, or (4) more narrowly focused differentiation.

Of course, there are other dimensions besides low cost, high quality, or superior service on which a business unit may try to gain a competitive advantage. For example, Robert E. Miles and Charles C. Snow have identified another set of business strategies based on a business's intended rate of product-market development (new product development, penetration of new markets, and so on).[8] They classified business units into four strategic types: **prospectors, analyzers, defenders,** and **reactors**. Exhibit 3-3 describes each of these business strategies briefly. As indicated, businesses pursuing a prospector strategy focus on growth through the development of new products and markets. 3M's Medical Products business unit provides a good example of this. Defender businesses concentrate on maintaining their positions in established product-markets while paying less attention to new-product development, as is the case with 3M's Industrial Tape business unit. The analyzer strategy falls in between these two. An analyzer business attempts to maintain a strong

---

[8]Robert E. Miles and Charles C. Snow, *Organizational Strategy, Structure and Process* (New York: McGraw-Hill, 1978; for a summary of other recent approaches for defining typologies of business-level competitive strategies, see John A. Byrne, "Strategic Planning," *Business Week*, August 26, 1996, pp. 46–52.

E X H I B I T   3 – 4

Combined Typology of Business–Unit Competitive Strategies

Emphasis on new product-market growth

Heavy emphasis ⟵ ⟶ No emphasis

	Prospector	Analyzer	Defender	Reactor
Differentiation	Units primarily concerned with attaining growth through aggressive pursuit of new product-market opportunities	Units with strong core business; actively seeking to expand into related product-markets with differentiated offerings	Units primarily concerned with maintaining a **differentiated** position in mature markets	Units with no clearly defined product-market development or competitive strategy
Cost leadership		Units with strong core business; actively seeking to expand into related product-markets with low-cost offerings	Units primarily concerned with maintaining a **low-cost** position in mature markets	

Competitive strategy

position in its core product-market(s) but also seeks to expand into new, but usually closely related, product-markets. Finally, reactors are businesses with no clearly defined strategy.

Even though both the Porter and the Miles and Snow typologies have received popular acceptance and research support, neither is complete by itself. For example, a defender business unit might pursue either of Porter's sources of competitive advantage—a low-cost position or differentiation—to protect its market position. Thus, we have combined the two typologies in Exhibit 3-4 to provide a more comprehensive overview of possible business strategies. The exhibit classifies business strategies on two primary dimensions: the unit's desired rate of product-market development and the unit's intended method of competing in its established product-markets.[9]

Of course, each strategy in Exhibit 3-4 could be further subdivided according to whether a business applies the strategy across a broadly defined product-market domain or concentrates on a narrowly defined segment where it hopes to avoid direct confrontation with major competitors (in other words, the focus strategy of Porter). While this is a useful distinction to make, it is more relevant to a discussion of the business's choice of a target-market strategy (as examined in Chapter 7) than to its competitive strategy. Most businesses compete in a consistent way (at least in terms of basic dimensions) across all of their product-markets, whether their domain is broad or narrow.

---

[9]For a more detailed discussion of this "hybrid" taxonomy of generic business strategies, see Orville C. Walker, Jr., and Robert W. Ruekert, "Marketing's Role in the Implementation of Business Strategies: A Critical Review and Conceptual Framework," *Journal of Marketing*, July 1987, pp. 15–33; for another taxonomy of competitive strategies that incorporates elements of both the Porter and Miles and Snow frameworks, see Michael Treacy and Fred Wiersema, *The Discipline of Market Leaders* (Reading, Mass.: Addison-Wesley, 1995).

Note too that Exhibit 3-4 describes only six different business strategies rather than the eight that one might expect. One reason for this is that we view reactor and prospector businesses as two homogeneous categories.

Evidence suggests that a substantial number of business fall into the reactor category. One study, for instance, found that 50 out of 232 businesses examined could be classified as reactors.[10] However, these businesses do not have well-defined or consistent approaches either to new product or market development or to ways of competing in their existing product-markets. As a manager of Sheldahl, Inc.—a firm that designs and manufactures flexible circuit boards and other components for the electronics and defense industries— complained in a discussion with one of the authors:

> Our division is a reactor in the sense that we are constantly changing directions and getting into new areas in response to actions taken by our competitors or special requests from large customers. We are like a job-shop; we take on new projects without ever asking whether there will be a viable future market for what we are doing. Consequently, neither our volume growth nor our profitability has been as good as it should have been in recent years.

The first action managers should take to improve the performance of reactors is to develop and implement a clearly defined and coherent competitive strategy—one that corresponds to one of the other generic strategies outlined in Exhibit 3-4. But because most reactors have no consistent competitive strategy, they typically underperform all other strategic types on growth and profitability dimensions.[11] Therefore, we largely ignore reactors in the remainder of this discussion.

Prospectors are also discussed as a single strategic category because the desire for rapid new product or market development is the overriding aspect of their strategy. There is little need for a prospector to consider how it will compete in the various new product-markets it develops. It usually faces little or no competition in those markets—at least not until those markets become established and other firms begin to enter. In 3M's Medical Products SBU, for example, most marketing programs are aimed at generating awareness and stimulating primary demand instead of offering low prices or finding ways to differentiate products because they are unchallenged by any competitors.

Business-level strategies for global competitors

In terms of the strategies described in Exhibit 3-4, businesses that compete in multiple global markets almost always pursue one of the two types of analyzer strategy. They must continue to strengthen and defend their competitive position in their home country—and perhaps in other countries where they are already well established—while simultaneously pursuing expansion and growth in new international markets.

When examined on a country-by-country basis, however, the same business unit might be viewed as pursuing different competitive strategies in different countries. For instance, while 3M's Industrial Tape Group competes like a differentiated defender in the United States, Canada, and some European countries where it has established large market shares, it competes more like a prospector when attempting to open and develop new markets in emerging economies such as China. This suggests that a single SBU may need to engage in

---

[10]Charles C. Snow and Lawrence G. Hrebiniak, "Strategy, Distinctive Competence and Organizational Performance," *Administrative Science Quarterly* 25 (1980), pp. 317–35.

[11]Jeffrey S. Conant, Michael P. Mokwa, and P. Rajan Varadarajan, "Strategic Types, Distinctive Marketing Competencies, and Organizational Performance: A Multiple Measures-Based Study," *Strategic Management Journal* 11 (1990), pp. 365–83.

E X H I B I T   3 – 5

Much of McDonald's Recent Growth Has Come from Outside of America

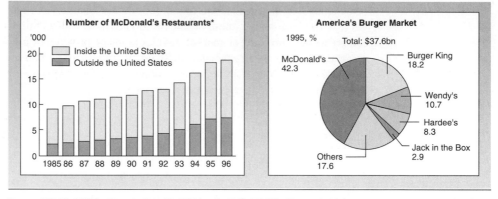

SOURCE: "McWorld," *The Economist*, June 29, 1996, pp. 61–62. © 1996 The Economist Newspaper Group, Inc. Reprinted with permission. Further reproduction prohibited.

different functional activities, including different strategic marketing programs—and perhaps even adopt different organizational structures to implement those activities—across the various countries in which it competes.

McDonald's faces exactly this kind of situation across the 94 countries in which it operates. The firm has nearly 19,000 retail outlets serving 33 million customers around the world every day. As you can see from the left-hand chart in Exhibit 3-5, more than three quarters of all McDonald's restaurants in 1985 were inside the United States, but the proportions have shifted and by the year 2000 more than half will be located outside the country.

Foreign restaurants already account for nearly half of McDonald's $30 billion in sales and 54 percent of the firm's operating profits. This is due in part to the more mature and much more competitive nature of the fast-food market in the United States than in most other nations. Consequently, the firm's competitive strategies—and therefore its prices, marketing costs, and operating margins—tend to be different in other countries than in the United States.

The right-hand chart in Exhibit 3-5 shows that McDonald's holds a commanding 42 percent share of the domestic burger market. The firm's competitive strategy in the United States, then, is that of a differentiated defender intent on preserving its market share position and profitability in the face of slowing demand and increasing competition. Among other things, the company has begun an aggressive campaign to reduce its operating costs by simplifying its restaurant designs, reducing the number of items on the menu, and so forth. Some of those cost savings will be reflected in lower prices, while the rest will be plowed back into advertising and promotion programs. For instance, McDonald's negotiated a deal to sponsor the summer and winter Olympic games in 1998 and 2000—a global agreement that will shut out other fast-food firms. Also, the firm has attempted to move upmarket by introducing new products aimed at generating more sales and profits from older adults, but so far with limited success.

Outside the United States, on the other hand, McDonald's faces little organized competition (Pizza Hut is its nearest rival), but the demand for fast food is just beginning to grow in many countries. Consequently, the firm frequently must pursue a prospector strategy focused on building demand among new customers. This helps explain the rapid rate of new restaurant construction outside the United States. The firm built about 2,000 new outlets in foreign countries in 1996, compared with only about 1,000 in the United States. Unfortunately, infrastructure problems in developing markets such as China and Eastern Europe mean that, on average, new restaurants cost twice as much to build as in the United States. To attract new customers in such markets, McDonald's initially has to price its burgers very low, often below cost. While demand growth and economies of scale usually help individual units turn a profit relatively soon after opening, at the national level McDonald's is often making a rather long-term bet—a bet that can be risky because of the possibility of political or economic upheaval.

To help managers in each country adjust to local market and environmental differences, McDonald's gives them great flexibility and autonomy. In every country the pace of expansion—and the strategy for achieving it—is determined locally. So far those locally developed strategies have been quite successful, as evidenced by growth in the firm's non-U.S. operating profits at a rate of 20 percent a year.[12]

THE UNDERLYING DIMENSIONS OF ALTERNATIVE BUSINESS STRATEGIES

In Chapter 2 we said that all strategies consist of five components or underlying dimensions: scope (or the breadth of the strategic domain), goals and objectives, resource deployments, a basis for achieving a sustainable competitive advantage, and synergy. But the generic business strategies outlined in Exhibit 3–4 are defined largely on the basis of their differences on only one of these dimensions: the nature of the competitive advantage sought. However, each generic strategy also involves some important differences on the other four dimensions. Those differences are summarized in Exhibit 3-6 and discussed below. They provide some useful insights into the conditions under which each strategy is most appropriate and the relative importance of different functional activities, particularly marketing actions, in implementing them effectively.

Differences in scope

Both the breadth and the stability of a business's domain are likely to vary with different strategies. This, in turn, can affect the variables the corporation uses to define its various businesses. At one extreme, defender businesses, whether low cost or differentiated, tend to operate in relatively well-defined, narrow, and stable domains where both the product technology and the customer segments are mature. A company can define and group the related product-market entries into such business units on the basis of the three criteria discussed earlier: technical compatibility, the customer need to be satisfied, and similarity of customer characteristics and behavior patterns. For example, Pillsbury's Prepared Dough Products business unit is a differentiated defender consisting of several product-market entries, such as Hungry Jack Biscuits and Crescent Rolls. All the products in the SBU hold a commanding share of their product category, appeal to traditional households who want fresh-baked breadstuffs, and are based on the same dough-in-a-can technology. Consequently, the SBU is largely self-contained with respect to production facilities, marketing, and distribution.

---

[12]"McWorld," *The Economist*, June 29, 1996, pp. 61–62.

——————————— **E X H I B I T   3 – 6** ———————————

How Business Strategies Differ in Scope, Objectives, Resource Deployments, and Synergy

Dimensions	Low-cost defender	Differentiated defender	Prospector	Analyzer
• Scope	Mature/stable/well-defined domain; mature technology and customer segments	Mature/stable/well-defined domain; mature technology and customer segments	Broad/dynamic domains; technology and customer segments not well established	Mixture of defender and prospector strategies
• Goals and objectives Adaptability (new product success)	Very little	Little	Extensive	Mixture of defender and prospector strategies
Effectiveness (increase in market share)	Little	Little	Large	Mixture of defender and prospector strategies
Efficiency (ROI)	High	High	Low	Mixture of defender and prospector strategies
• Resource deployment	Generate excess cash (cash cows)	Generate excess cash (cash cows)	Need cash for product development (question marks or stars)	Need cash for product development but less so than prospectors
• Synergy	Need to seek operating synergies to achieve efficiencies	Need to seek operating synergies to achieve efficiencies	Danger in sharing operating facilities and programs—better to share technology/marketing skills	Danger in sharing operating facilities and programs—better to share technology/marketing skills

At the other extreme, prospector businesses usually operate in broad and rapidly changing domains where neither the technology nor customer segments are well established. The scope of such businesses often undergoes periodic redefinition. Also, it is usually impossible to organize such units according to all three of the preceding criteria. Thus, prospector businesses are typically organized around either a core technology that might lead to the development of products aimed at a broad range of customer segments or a basic customer need that might be met with products based on different technologies. The latter is the approach taken by 3M's Medical Products SBU. Its mission is to satisfy the health needs of a broad range of patients with new products and services developed from technologies drawn from other business units within the firm. For example, it has developed a variety of innovative drug delivery systems using aerosols, adhesives, and other 3M technologies.

Analyzer businesses, whether low cost or differentiated, fall somewhere in between the two extremes. They usually have a well-established core business to defend, and often their domain is primarily focused on that business. However, businesses pursuing this intermediate strategy are often in industries that are still growing or experiencing technological changes. Consequently, they must pay attention to the emergence of new customer segments or new product types. As a result, managers must review and adjust the domain of such businesses from time to time.

Differences in goals and objectives

Another important difference across generic business-level strategies with particular relevance for the design and implementation of appropriate marketing programs is that different strategies often focus on different objectives. SBU and product-market objectives might be specified on a variety of criteria; but to keep things simple, we focus on only three performance dimensions of major importance to both business-unit and marketing managers:

1. *Effectiveness*—the success of a business's products and programs relative to those of its competitors in the market. Effectiveness is commonly measured by such items as sales growth relative to competitors or changes in market share.

2. *Efficiency*—the outcomes of a business's programs relative to the resources used in implementing them. Common measures of efficiency are profitability as a percentage of sales, and return on investment.

3. *Adaptability*—the business's success in responding over time to changing conditions and opportunities in the environment. Adaptability can be measured in a variety of ways, but the most common ones are the number of successful new products introduced relative to competitors, or the percentage of sales accounted for by products introduced within the last five years.

However, it is very difficult for any SBU, regardless of its competitive strategy, to simultaneously achieve outstanding performance on even this limited number of dimensions because they involve substantial trade-offs. Good performance on one dimension often means sacrificing performance on another.[13] For example, developing successful new products or attaining share growth often involves large marketing budgets, substantial up-front investment, high operating costs, and a shaving of profit margins—all of which reduce ROI. This suggests that managers should choose a competitive strategy with a view toward maximizing performance on one or two dimensions while expecting to sacrifice some level of performance on the others, at least in the short term. Over the longer term, of course, the chosen strategy should promise discounted cash flows that exceed the business's cost of capital and thereby increase shareholder value.

As Exhibit 3-6 indicates, prospector businesses are expected to outperform defenders on both new product development and market share growth. For instance, the Life Sciences sector of 3M, which includes a large proportion of prospector businesses, produced revenue growth of more than 50 percent from 1988 through 1995, and nearly half of that revenue was generated by new products. In contrast, 3M's total revenues grew only about 30 percent during the same period.

On the other hand, both defender strategies should lead to better returns on investment. Differentiated defenders likely produce higher returns than low-cost defenders, assuming that the greater expenses involved in maintaining their differentiated positions can be more than offset by the higher margins gained by avoiding the intense price competition low-cost competitors often face. Once again, both low-cost and differentiated analyzer strategies likely fall between the two extremes.

---

[13]Gordon Donaldson, *Managing Corporate Wealth* (New York: Praeger, 1984); see also Robert S. Kaplan and David P. Norton, "Using the Balanced Scorecard as a Strategic Management System," *Harvard Business Review*, January–February 1996, pp. 75–85.

The validity of the expected performance differences outlined in Exhibit 3-6 is supported by some empirical evidence. One study found that businesses pursuing defender strategies significantly outperformed prospector businesses on return on investment and cash flow on investment regardless of the type of environment they faced, while prospectors generated significantly greater rates of market share growth—particularly in innovative or rapidly growing markets.[14] Similarly, a more recent study found that both prospectors and analyzers outperformed defenders on market share growth and return on equity in markets experiencing steady growth. Surprisingly, the same study found that defenders outperformed all other strategies on both efficiency and effectiveness dimensions in highly volatile markets.[15] This unexpected finding might be attributable to the episodic periods of both growth and contraction that volatile markets experience. Thus, while aggressive prospector and analyzer businesses may outperform the more conservative defenders during growth periods, they also may suffer greater volume and financial losses during periods of market decline.

Differences in resource deployments

Businesses following different strategies also tend to allocate their financial resources differently across product-markets, functional departments, and activities within each functional area. Prospector—and to a lesser degree, analyzer—businesses devote a relatively large proportion of resources to the development of new product-markets. Because such product-markets usually require more cash to develop than they produce in the short term, businesses pursuing these strategies often need infusions of financial resources from other parts of the corporation. In portfolio terms, they are "question marks" or "stars."

Defenders, on the other hand, focus the bulk of their resources on preserving existing positions in established product-markets. These product-markets are usually profitable; therefore, defender businesses typically generate excess cash to support product and market development efforts in other business units within the firm. They are the "cash cows."

Resource allocations among functional departments and activities within the SBU also vary across businesses pursuing different strategies. For instance, marketing budgets tend to be the largest as a percentage of an SBU's revenues when the business is pursuing a prospector strategy; they tend to be the smallest as a percentage of sales under a low-cost defender strategy. We discuss this in more detail later in this chapter.

Differences in sources of synergy

Because different strategies emphasize different methods of competition and different functional activities, a given source of synergy may be more appropriate for some strategies than for others.

At one extreme, sharing operating facilities and programs may be an inappropriate approach to gaining synergy for businesses following a prospector strategy. And to a lesser extent this may also be true for both types of analyzer strategies. Such sharing can reduce an SBU's ability to adapt quickly to changing market demands or competitive threats. Commitments to internally negotiated price structures and materials, as well as the use of

---

[14]Donald C. Hambrick, "Some Tests of the Effectiveness and Functional Attributes of Miles and Snow's Strategic Types," *Academy of Management Journal* 26 (1983), pp. 5–26.

[15]Daryl O. McKee, P. Rajan Varadarajan, and William M. Pride, "Strategic Adaptability and Firm Performance: A Market-Contingent Perspective," *Journal of Marketing*, July 1989, pp. 21–35.

joint resources, facilities, and programs, increase interdependence among SBUs and limit their flexibility. Because prospector and analyzer businesses seek growth through new product and market development, a lack of flexibility makes it difficult for them to successfully implement their chosen strategy. It is more appropriate for such businesses to seek synergy through the sharing of technology, engineering skills, or market knowledge— expertise that can help improve the success rate of their product development efforts.[16] Thus, 3M's Medical Products SBU attempts to find medical applications for new technologies developed in many of the firm's other business units.

At the other extreme, however, low-cost defenders should seek operating synergies that will make them more efficient. Synergies that enable such businesses to increase economies of scale and experience curve effects are particularly desirable. They help reduce unit costs and strengthen the strategy's basis of competitive advantage. The primary means of gaining such operating synergies is through the sharing of resources, facilities, and functional activities across product-market entries within the business unit or across related business units. Emerson Electric, for instance, has formed an "operating group" of several otherwise autonomous business units that make different types of electrical tools. By sharing production facilities, marketing activities, and a common salesforce, the group has been able to reduce per-unit production and marketing costs.

THE FIT BETWEEN BUSINESS STRATEGIES AND THE EXTERNAL ENVIRONMENT

Because different strategies pursue different objectives in different domains with different competitive approaches, they do not all work equally well under the same environmental circumstances. The question is, Which environmental situations are most amenable to the successful pursuit of each type of strategy? Exhibit 3-7 briefly outlines some of the major market, technological, and competitive conditions—plus a business unit's strengths relative to its competitors—that are most favorable for the successful implementation of each generic business strategy. We next discuss the reasons why each strategy fits best with a particular set of environmental conditions.

Appropriate conditions for a prospector strategy

A prospector strategy is particularly well suited to unstable, rapidly changing environments resulting from new technology, shifting customers needs, or both. In either case, such industries tend to be at an early stage in their life cycles and offer many opportunities for new product-market entries. Industry structure is often unstable because few competitors are present and their relative market shares can shift rapidly as new products are introduced and new markets develop. Prospector strategies are common in industries where new applications and customer acceptance of existing technologies are still developing (such as the personal computer, computer software, and information technologies industries) and in industries with rapid technological change (such as biotechnology, medical care, and aerospace).

Because they emphasize the development of new products and/or new markets, the most successful prospectors are usually strong in and devote substantial resources to

---

[16]Stanley F. Slater and John C. Narver, "Market Orientation and the Learning Organization," *Journal of Marketing,* July 1995, pp. 63–74.

=============== E X H I B I T   3 - 7 ===============

Environmental Factors Favorable to Different Business Strategies

External factors	Prospector	Analyzer	Differentiated defender	Low-cost defender
Market characteristics	• Introductory or early growth stage of industry life cycle • Many unidentified or undeveloped customer segments	• Late growth or early maturity stage of industry life cycle • Some segments well established but potential segments or applications remain undeveloped	• Maturity or decline stage of industry life cycle • Most segments well developed; sales primarily due to repeat/ replacement purchases	• Maturity or decline stage of industry life cycle • Most segments well developed; sales primarily due to repeat/ replacement purchases
Technology	• Newly emerging technology	• Basic technology well developed but product improvements/ modifications still possbile	• Basic technology fully developed and stable	• Basic technology fully developed and stable
Competition	• Few established competitors • Industry structure still emerging	• Many competitors • Industry structure still emerging • Changes in relative market shares likely	• Several well established competitors • Industry structure stable but consolidation is possible	• Several well established competitors • Industry structure stable, but consolidation is possible
Business's relative strengths	• R&D • Product engineering • Marketing research • Marketing/sales	• Process engineering • Efficient production • Marketing/sales • Distributor relations • Customer service	• Process engineering • Quality control • Distributor relations • Marketing/sales • Customer service	• Process engineering • Efficient production • Supplier relations • Distributor relations

two broad areas of competence: (1) R&D, product engineering, and other functional areas that identify new technology and convert it into innovative products; and (2) marketing research, marketing, and sales—functions that identify and develop new market opportunities.

In some cases, however, even though a prospector business has strong product development and marketing skills, it may lack the resources to maintain its early lead as product-markets grow and attract new competitors. For example, Minnetonka was the pioneer in several health and beauty-aid product categories with brands like Softsoap liquid soap and Check-Up plaque-fighting toothpaste. However, because competitors like Procter & Gamble and Colgate-Palmolive introduced competing brands with advertising and promotion budgets much larger than Minnetonka could match, the firm was eventually forced to change its strategy and concentrate on manufacturing products under licenses from larger firms.

Appropriate conditions for an analyzer strategy

The analyzer strategy is a hybrid. On one hand, analyzers are concerned with defending (via low costs or differentiation in quality or service) a strong share position in one or more established product-markets. At the same time, the business must pay attention to new product development in order to avoid being leapfrogged by competitors with more technologically advanced products or being left behind in newly developing application segments within the market. This dual focus makes the analyzer strategy appropriate for well-developed industries that are still experiencing some amount of growth and change due to evolving customer needs and desires or continuing technological improvements.

Commercial aircraft manufacturing is an example of such an industry. Both competitors and potential customers are few and well established. But technology continues to improve, the increased competition among airlines since deregulation has changed the attributes those firms look for when buying new planes, and mergers have increased the buying power of some customers. Thus, Boeing's commercial aircraft division has had to work harder to maintain a 50 percent share of worldwide commercial plane sales. Although the firm continues to enjoy a reputation for producing high-quality and reliable planes, it had to make price concessions and increase customer services during the late 1980s and early 1990s to stave off threats from competitors like the European Airbus consortium. At the same time, Boeing's commercial aircraft division had to engage in a $2 billion development effort aimed at producing the next generation of aircraft.[17]

Boeing's experience illustrates one problem with an analyzer strategy. Few businesses have the resources and competencies needed to successfully defend an established core business while simultaneously generating new products. Success on both dimensions requires strengths across virtually every functional area, and few businesses (or their parent companies) have such universal strengths relative to competitors. Therefore, analyzers are often not as innovative in new product development as prospectors. And they may not be as profitable in defending their core businesses as defenders.

Appropriate conditions for a defender strategy

A defender strategy makes sense only when a business has something worth defending. It is most appropriate for units with a profitable share of one or more major segments in a relatively mature, stable industry. A defender may initiate some product improvements or line extensions to protect and strengthen its position in existing segments; but it devotes relatively few resources to basic R&D or the development of innovative new products. Thus, a defender strategy works best in industries where the basic technology is not very complex or where it is well developed and unlikely to change dramatically over the short run. Pillsbury's Prepared Dough Products SBU, for instance, has introduced a number of line extensions over the years; but as noted earlier, most have been reconfigurations of the same basic dough-in-a-can technology, such as Soft Breadsticks.

Differentiated defenders

To effectively defend its position by differentiation, a business must be strong in those functional areas critical for maintaining its particular competitive advantage over time. If a business's differentiation is based on superior product quality, those key functional areas

---

[17]"Booming Boeing," *Business Week*, September 30, 1996, pp. 119–25.

E X H I B I T   3 – 8

The Relationship between Product Quality and Pretax ROI by Business Type

	Quality level				
	Lowest	Below average	Average	Above average	Highest
Consumer durables	16%	18%	18%	26%	32%
Consumer nondurables	15	21	17	23	32
Capital goods	10	8	13	20	21
Raw materials	13	21	21	21	35
Components	12	20	20	22	36
Supplies	16	13	19	25	36

Note: Numbers refer to percent average ROI.

SOURCE: Robert D. Buzzell, "Product Quality," *Pimsletter* no. 4 (Cambridge, Mass.: The Strategic Planning Institute, 1986), p. 5.

include production, process engineering, quality control, and perhaps product engineering to develop product improvements. Interestingly, successful differentiation of its offerings on the quality dimension has a strong impact on a business's return on investment—a critical performance objective for defenders. The positive correlation between quality and ROI holds true even after allowing for the effects of market share and investment intensity. As Exhibit 3-8 shows, the pretax return on investment is higher in all businesses for firms selling above-average- and highest-quality products than for firms selling average- or below-average-quality offerings.

Regardless of the basis for differentiation, marketing is also important for the effective implementation of a differentiated defender strategy. Marketing activities that track changing customer needs and competitive actions, and communicate the product offering's unique advantages through promotional and sales efforts, to maintain customer awareness and loyalty are particularly important. So too are service activities aimed at strengthening customer relationships. In addition, strong relationships with distributors or retailers can be crucial for maintaining the offering's availability in the market.

Low-cost defenders

Successful implementation of a low-cost defender strategy requires the business to be more efficient than its competitors.[18] Thus, the business must establish the groundwork for such a strategy early in the growth stage of the industry. Achieving and maintaining the lowest per-unit cost usually means that the business has to seek large volume from the beginning—through some combination of low prices and promotional efforts—to gain

---

[18]Low-cost defenders are distinguished by the fact that efficiency and competition based on low price are *primary* elements of their business strategy. However, businesses pursuing other competitive strategies also should hold down their costs as much as possible given the functional activities and programs necessary to implement those strategies effectively. Indeed, some of the most successful businesses are those that work aggressively to simultaneously lower costs while improving quality and service. For example, see Ronald Henkoff, "Cost Cutting: How to Do It Right," *Fortune,* April 9, 1990, pp. 40–49; and David Greising, "Quality: How to Make It Pay," *Business Week,* August 8, 1994, pp. 54–59.

economies of scale and experience. At the same time, such businesses must also invest in more plant capacity to anticipate future growth and in state-of-the-art equipment to minimize production costs. This combination of low margins and heavy investment can be prohibitive unless the parent corporation can commit substantial resources to the business or extensive sharing of facilities, technologies, and programs with other business units is possible.

The low-cost defender's need for efficiency also forces the standardization of product offerings and marketing programs across customer segments to achieve scale effects. Thus, such a strategy is usually not so effective in fragmented markets desiring customized offerings as it is in commodity industries such as basic chemicals, steel, or flour, or in industries producing low-technology components such as electric motors or valves. In the future, however, it may become a more widely applicable competitive strategy as computer-assisted design and manufacturing systems make "mass customization" more economically viable.[19]

Changing strategies at different stages in the industry life cycle

A business may have to change its objectives and competitive strategy as the industry and the business's competitive position within it mature and stabilize. Thus, a prospector strategy is most appropriate during the early stages of a product category's life cycle as a business attempts to build a successful product line and increase its market share. As the industry matures and the competitive environment stabilizes, analyzer and ultimately defender strategies become more appropriate as the business turns its attention to maintaining and reaping the higher ROI and cash flows of its hard-won market position.

The problem is that the effective implementation of different business strategies requires not only different functional competencies and resources but also different organizational structures, decision-making and coordination processes, reward systems, and even personnel. Because such internal structures and processes are hard to change quickly, it can be very difficult for an entire SBU to make a successful transition from one basic strategy to another.[20] For example, many of Emerson Electric's SBUs historically were successful low-cost defenders; but accelerating technological change in their industries caused the corporation to try to convert them to low-cost analyzers who would focus more attention on new product and market development. Initially, however, this attempted shift in strategy resulted in some culture shock, conflict, and mixed performance outcomes from within those units.

In view of the implementation problems involved, some firms do not try to make major changes in the basic competitive strategies of their existing business units. Instead, they might form entirely new prospector SBUs to pursue emerging new technologies and industries rather than expecting established units to handle extensive new product development efforts. As individual product-market entries gain successful positions in well-established markets, some firms move them from the prospector unit that developed them to an analyzer or defender unit that is better suited to reaping profits from them as their markets mature. Finally, some firms that are technological leaders in their industries may divest or license individual product-market entries as they mature rather than defend them in the face

---

[19]Gene Bylinsky, "The Digital Factory," *Fortune*, November 14, 1994, pp. 92–110.

[20]Connie J. G. Gersick, "Revolutionary Change Theories: A Multilevel Exploration of the Punctuated Equilibrium Paradigm," *Academy of Management Review* 16 (1991), pp. 10–36; and Michael L. Tushman, William H. Newman, and Elaine Romanelli, "Convergence and Upheaval: Managing the Unsteady Pace of Organizational Evolution," *California Management Review* 29 (1986), pp. 29–44.

of increasing competition and eroding margins. This is an approach commonly taken by such companies as 3M and DuPont.

MARKETING IMPLICATIONS OF DIFFERENT BUSINESS STRATEGIES

Business units typically incorporate a number of distinct product-markets. A given entry's marketing manager monitors and evaluates the product's environmental situation and develops a marketing program suited to it. However, the manager's freedom to design such a program is constrained by the business unit's competitive strategy because different strategies focus on different objectives and seek to gain and maintain a competitive advantage in different ways. As a result, different functions within the SBU—and different activities within a given functional area, such as marketing—are critical for the success of different strategies.

Therefore, different functional key factors for success are inherent in the various generic business strategies. This constrains the individual marketing manager's freedom of action in two basic ways. First, because different functions within the business unit are more important under different strategies, they receive different proportions of the SBU's total resources. Thus, the SBU's strategy influences *the amount of resources committed to marketing* and ultimately the budget available to an individual marketing manager within the business unit. Second, the SBU's choice of strategy influences both the kind of *market and competitive situation* that individual product-market entries are likely to face and the *objectives* they are asked to attain. Both constraints have implications for the design of marketing programs for individual products within an SBU.

Of course, it is somewhat risky to draw broad generalizations about how specific marketing policies and program elements might fit within different business strategies. While a business strategy is a general statement about how an SBU chooses to compete in an industry, that unit may comprise a number of different product-market entries facing different competitive situations in different markets. Thus, plenty of variation is likely in marketing programs, and in the freedom individual marketing managers have in designing them, across products within a given SBU. Still, a business's strategy does set a general direction for the types of target markets it will pursue and how the unit will compete in those markets. And it does have some influence on marketing policies that cut across product-markets. Exhibit 3-9 outlines some differences in marketing policies and program elements that occur across businesses pursuing different strategies, and those differences are discussed next.

Product policies

One set of marketing policies defines the nature of the products the business will concentrate on offering to its target markets. These policies concern the *breadth or diversity of product lines*, their *level of technical sophistication*, and the target *level of product quality* relative to competitors.

Because prospector businesses rely heavily on the continuing development of unique new products and the penetration of new markets as their primary competitive strategy, policies encouraging broader and more technically advanced product lines than those of competitors should be positively related to performance on the critical dimension of share growth. The diverse and technically advanced product offerings of 3M's Medical Products SBU are a good example of this.

============================ **E X H I B I T** 3 – 9 ============================

Differences in Marketing Policies and Program Components across
Businesses Pursuing Different Strategies

Marketing policies and program components	Strategy		
	Prospector	Differentiated defender	Low-cost defender
Product policies			
• Product line breadth relative to competitors	+	+	–
• Technical sophistication of products relative to competitors	+	+	–
• Product quality relative to competitors	?	+	–
• Service quality relative to competitors	?	+	–
Price policies			
• Price levels relative to competitors	+	+	–
Distribution policies			
• Degree of forward vertical integration relative to competitors	–	+	?
• Trade promotion expenses as percentage of sales relative to competitors	+	–	–
Promotion policies			
• Advertising expenses as percentage of sales relative to competitors	+	?	–
• Sales promotion expenses as percentage of sales relative to competitors	+	?	–
• Salesforce expenses as percentage of sales relative to competitors	?	+	–

KEY: Plus sign (+) = greater than the average competitor
  Minus sign (–) = smaller than the average competitor
  Question mark (?) = uncertain relationship between strategy and marketing policy or program component

Whether a prospector's products should be of higher quality than those of competitors is open to question. Quality is hard to define; it can mean different things to different customers. Even so, it is an important determinant of business profitability. Thus, Donald C. Hambrick suggested that in product-markets where technical features or up-to-the-minute styling are key attributes in customers' definitions of quality, high-quality products may play a positive role in determining the success of a prospector strategy. On the other hand, in markets where the critical determinants of quality are reliability or brand familiarity, the maintenance of relatively high product quality is likely to be more strongly related to the successful performance of defender businesses, particularly differentiated defenders.[21]

Differentiated defenders compete by offering more or "better" choices to customers than their competitors. For example, 3M's commercial graphics business, a major supplier of sign material for truck fleets, has strengthened its competitive position in that market by developing products appropriate for custom-designed signs. Until recently, the use of film for individual signs was not economical. But the use of computer-controlled knives and a new

[21]Hambrick, "Some Tests of the Effectiveness and Functional Attributes."

Scotch-brand marking film produce signs of higher quality and at a lower cost than those that are hand-painted. This kind of success in developing relatively broad and technically sophisticated product lines should be positively related to the long-term ROI performance of most differentiated defender businesses. However, such policies are inconsistent with the efficiency requirements of the low-cost defender strategy. Broad and complex product lines lead to short production runs and large inventories. Maintaining technical sophistication in a business's products requires continuing investment in product and process R&D. Consequently, the adoption of such policies is apt to be less common in low-cost defender businesses. As mentioned, however, some of the efficiency problems associated with broader, more customized product lines may disappear with continuing improvements in computer-assisted design and manufacturing, process engineering, and the like.[22]

Instead of, or in addition to, competing on the basis of product characteristics, businesses can distinguish themselves relative to competitors by the *quality of service* they offer. Such service might take many forms, including engineering and design services, alterations, installation, training of customer personnel, or maintenance and repair services. A policy of high service quality is particularly appropriate for differentiated defenders because it offers a way to maintain a competitive advantage in well-established markets.

The appropriateness of an extensive service policy for low-cost defenders, though, is more questionable if higher operating and administrative costs offset customer satisfaction benefits. Those higher costs may detract from the business's ability to maintain the low prices critical to its strategy, as well as lowering ROI—at least in the short term. On the other hand, even low-cost defenders may have difficulty holding their position over the long term without maintaining at least competitive parity with respect to critical service attributes.[23]

Pricing policies

Success in offering low prices relative to competitors should be positively related to the performance of low-cost defender businesses because low price is the primary competitive weapon of such a strategy. However, such a policy is inconsistent with both differentiated defender and prospector strategies. The higher costs involved in differentiating a business's products on either a quality or service basis require higher prices to maintain profitability. Differentiation also provides customers with additional value for which higher prices can be charged. Similarly, the costs and benefits of new product and market development by prospector businesses require and justify relatively high prices. Thus, differentiated defenders and prospectors seldom adhere to a policy of low competitive prices.

Distribution policies

Some observers argue that prospector businesses should show a greater degree of *forward vertical integration* than defender businesses.[24] The rationale for this view is that the prospector's focus on new product and market development requires superior market intelligence and frequent reeducation and motivation of distribution channel members. This can best be accomplished through tight control of company-owned channels. However, these

---

[22]B. Joseph Pine II, Bart Victor, and Andrew C. Boynton, "Making Mass Customization Work," *Harvard Business Review* 71 (September–October 1993), pp. 108–19.

[23]For additional arguments in the debate about the relative costs and competitive benefits of superior customer service, see Rahul Jacob, "Beyond Quality and Value," *Fortune*, Special Issue, Autumn–Winter 1993, pp. 8–11; and Valarie A. Zeithaml and Mary Jo Bitner, *Services Marketing* (New York: McGraw-Hill, 1996), chap. 2.

[24]Miles and Snow, *Organizational Strategy, Structure, and Process*; and Hambrick, "Some Tests of the Effectiveness and Functional Attributes."

arguments seem inconsistent with the prospector's need for flexibility in constructing new channels to distribute new products and reach new markets.

Attempting to maintain tight control over the behavior of channel members is a more appropriate policy for defenders who are trying to maintain strong positions in established markets. This is particularly true for defenders who rely on good customer service to differentiate themselves from competitors. Thus, it seems more likely that a relatively high degree of forward vertical integration is found among defender businesses, particularly differentiated defenders, while prospectors rely more heavily on independent channel members—such as manufacturer's representatives or wholesale distributors—to distribute their products.[25]

Because prospectors focus on new products where success is uncertain and sales volumes are small in the short run, they are likely to devote a larger percentage of sales to *trade promotions* than defender businesses. Prospectors rely on trade promotion tools such as quantity discounts, liberal credit terms, and other incentives to induce cooperation and support from their independent channel members.

Promotion policies

Extensive marketing communications also play an important role in the successful implementation of both prospector and differentiated defender strategies. The form of that communication, however, may differ under the two strategies. Because prospectors must constantly work to generate awareness, stimulate trial, and build primary demand for new and unfamiliar products, high advertising and sales promotion expenditures are likely to bear a positive relationship to the new product and share-growth success of such businesses. 3M's Medical Products SBU, for instance, devotes substantial resources to advertising in professional journals and distributing samples of new products, as well as to maintaining an extensive salesforce.

Differentiated defenders, on the other hand, are primarily concerned with maintaining the loyalty of established customers by adapting to their needs and providing good service. These tasks can best be accomplished—particularly in industrial goods and services industries—by an extensive, well-trained, well-supported salesforce.[26] Therefore, differentiated defenders are likely to have higher salesforce expenditures than competitors.

Finally, low-cost defenders appeal to their customers primarily on price. Thus, high expenditures on advertising, sales promotion, or the salesforce would detract from their basic strategy and may have a negative impact on their ROI performance. Consequently, such businesses are likely to spend relatively little as a percentage of sales on those promotional activities.

DO SERVICE BUSINESSES REQUIRE DIFFERENT STRATEGIES?

The service component of the U.S. economy accounts for roughly two-thirds of all economic activity in this country, and services are the fastest-growing sector of most other developed economies around the world. Expansion in the number of two-wage-earner families and single-person households has made time a more scarce and valuable commodity

---

[25]Although Hambrick argued for the reverse relationship, data from his study of 850 SBUs actually support our contention that defenders have more vertically integrated channels than prospectors; See Hambrick, "Some Tests of the Effectiveness and Functional Attributes,"

[26]Leonard A. Schlesinger and James L. Heskett, "The Service-Driven Service Company," *Harvard Business Review* 69 (September–October 1991), pp. 71–81; and Jaclyn Fierman, "The Death and Rebirth of the Salesman," *Fortune*, July 25, 1994, pp. 80–91.

for many people. This, coupled with increasing household incomes and other factors, suggests that demand for services in the global economy is likely to be robust for the foreseeable future.

But what is a service? Basically, services can be thought of as **intangibles** and goods as **tangibles**. The former can rarely be experienced in advance of the sale, while tangible products can be experienced, even tested, before purchase.[27] Using this distinction, a **service** can be defined as "any activity or benefit that one party can offer to another that is essentially intangible and that does not result in the ownership of anything. Its production may or may not be tied to a physical product."[28]

We typically associate services with nonmanufacturing businesses, even though service is often an indispensable part of a goods producer's offering. Services like applications engineering, system design, delivery, installation, training, and maintenance can be crucial for building long-term relationships between manufacturers and their customers, particularly in consumer durable and industrial products businesses. Thus, almost all businesses are engaged in service to a greater or lesser extent.

On the other hand, many organizations are concerned with producing and marketing a service as their primary offering rather than as an adjunct to a physical product. These organizations include firms providing personal services, such as health care, communications, retailing, and finance companies; commercial service organizations, such as accounting, legal, and consulting firms; public sector services like the military, police and fire departments, and schools; and not-for-profit service organizations, such as churches, hospitals, universities, and arts organizations. The crucial question is whether such organizations must employ different strategies and functional programs than goods manufacturers to be successful.

There are substantial similarities in the strategic issues both goods and service producers face, especially when deciding how to compete at the business level. However, the intangibility, as well as some other special characteristics, of services can cause unique marketing and operational problems for service organizations, as discussed next.

Business-level competitive strategies

The framework we used to classify the business-level competitive strategies pursued by goods producers is equally valid for service businesses. Some service firms, such as Super 8 or Days Inn in the lodging industry, attempt to minimize costs and compete largely with low prices. Other firms, like Marriott, differentiate their offerings on the basis of high service quality or unique benefits. Similarly, some service businesses adopt prospector strategies and aggressively pursue the development of new offerings or markets. For instance, American Express's Travel Related Services division has developed a variety of new services tailored to specific segments of the firm's credit-card holders. Other service businesses focus narrowly on defending established positions in current markets. Still others can best be described as analyzers pursuing both established and new markets. For instance, Cable & Wireless Communications—a long-distance carrier whose competitive strategy is discussed in Exhibit 3-10—might best be described as a differentiated analyzer.

A study of the banking industry provides some empirical evidence that service businesses actually do pursue the same types of competitive strategies as goods producers. The

---

[27]Theodore Leavitt, *The Marketing Imagination* (New York: Free Press, 1986), pp. 94–95.

[28]Philip Kotler and Gary Armstrong, *Principles of Marketing* (Englewood Cliffs, N.J.: Prentice Hall, 1989), p. 575.

═══════ E X H I B I T   3 – 1 0 ═══════

Cable & Wireless Communications: Differentiation through Customer Relationships

Cable & Wireless Communications, the U.S. subsidiary of a British telecommunications firm, competes in the relatively mature and highly competitive business of providing long-distance services to business customers. Company executives knew long ago that their operation could not compete on price with larger competitors such as AT&T, MCI, or Sprint. So they sought to differentiate themselves—and to defend their established customer base—by providing the best customer support in the industry. As a result, Cable & Wireless turned itself from a mundane commodity business into a sophisticated telemanager and partner with its customers.

Part of the success of Cable & Wireless is due to good target market selection. The firm focuses on winning and holding on to small- or medium-sized business clients with monthly billings of $500 to $15,000. In such small businesses, the company's 500 U.S. salespeople, working out of 36 regional offices, can act like telecommunications managers. Corporations too small to hire their own telecom specialists value the advice and expertise that Cable & Wireless people can offer, and top management gives those salespeople substantial autonomy to tailor their offerings and advice to each customer's needs.

Within its target small business segment, however, Cable & Wireless is not content merely to maintain relationships with established customers. The firm also devotes substantial effort and resources to developing and pitching specialized services aimed at attracting new customers from new industry segments. For example, the company has gained substantial business from smaller firms within the legal profession by developing functions that appeal specifically to lawyers, such as innovative ways to track and bill calls linked to specific client accounts.

Cable & Wireless's differentiated analyzer strategy has worked well. The firm not only has remained profitable in the cutthroat long-distance market, but also it has achieved a 20 percent annual growth rate in the number of long-distance customer minutes billed over the past several years.

SOURCE: Michael Treacy and Fred Wiersema, "How Market Leaders Keep Their Edge," *Fortune*, February 6, 1995, pp. 88–98. Reprinted by permission of Addison-Wesley Educational Publishers, Inc.

329 bank CEOs who responded to the survey had little trouble categorizing their institutions' competitive strategies into one of Miles and Snow's four types. Fifty-four of the executives reported that their banks were prospectors, 87 identified their firms as analyzers, 157 as defenders, and 31 as reactors.[29]

The impact of service characteristics on marketing[30]

The business-level competitive strategy pursued by a service business has the same implications for marketing policies and program elements as those discussed earlier for goods producers. For example, a bank pursuing a prospector strategy likely offers a broader range of services, promotes them more extensively, has broader distribution (more branch offices), and charges more for its services than one following a defender strategy. However, services have some characteristics that often give rise to special marketing problems and therefore demand special marketing policies and actions. These characteristics are that services are intangible and perishable, they often require substantial customer contact, and their quality can vary from one transaction to the next.

---

[29]McKee, Varadarajan, and Pride, "Strategic Adaptability and Firm Performance."

[30]For a more detailed discussion of the unique marketing problems faced by service businesses, see Valarie A. Zeithaml, A. Parasuraman, and Leonard L. Berry, "Problems and Strategies in Services Marketing," *Journal of Marketing*, Spring 1985, pp. 33–46; James L. Heskett, Thomas O. Jones, Gary W. Loveman, W. Earl Sasser, Jr., and Leonard A. Schlesinger, "Putting the Service-Profit Chain to Work," *Harvard Business Review*, March–April 1994, pp. 164–74; and Zeithaml and Bitner, *Services Marketing*.

Intangibility

The intangibility of services can make it more difficult to win and hold onto customers. Because prospective customers have difficulty experiencing (seeing, touching, smelling, feeling) the service offering in advance, they are forced to buy promises. But promises are also intangible; hence, metaphors and similes become surrogates for the tangibility that is lacking. This helps explain the solid, reassuring decor of most banks and law offices; the neat, cheerful uniforms worn by employees at McDonald's or Burger King; and the elegant decor and atmosphere of upscale shops and hotels. These things become the tangible symbols of the intangible services being offered.

A further difficulty with intangibility is that customers often don't know what criteria to use in evaluating a service. How do you rate a stockbroker's advice *before* you follow it? Or a doctor's? Typically, customers approach the purchase of services with optimistic expectations. Disappointment is all too easy to come by under these conditions.

One special marketing challenge facing most service businesses, then, is to find ways to make their offerings more tangible to potential customers. Some methods for accomplishing this include the following:

- *Designing facilities and products and training personnel to serve as symbols of service quality.* As mentioned, the firm should attempt to design all aspects of the physical environment surrounding the delivery of its service–including its facilities, advertising, promotional materials, and so forth—to act as tangible symbols of the quality and reliability of its service offering. Such actions are particularly important for prospector businesses attempting to develop new markets for new service offerings. Because new offerings are both intangible and unfamiliar to most customers, potential buyers have a doubly hard time judging whether the benefits they offer justify their cost.

- The service firm's personnel can also be important tangible symbols of service quality. Everyone who comes in contact with customers should be carefully trained to project an appropriate image, as well as to actually provide a high-quality experience for the customer. This is especially true in differentiated defender businesses where superior employee training and performance can provide a premium image and an important advantage over competitors. For instance, American Express devotes much effort to training, measuring, and rewarding the service performance of its employees as a primary element of its strategy for defending its strong position in the highly competitive credit-card industry.

- *Creating a tangible representation of the service.* American Express has done this, for instance, with its prestigious Gold and Platinum Cards.

- *Tying the marketing of services to the marketing of goods.* For example, Midas Muffler shops offer diagnostic and installation services in conjunction with selling mufflers and shock absorbers.

Perishability

Because a service is an experience, it is perishable and cannot be inventoried. Motel rooms and airline seats not occupied, idle telephone capacity, and the unused time of physicians and lawyers cannot be reclaimed. Further, when demand exceeds capacity, customers must be turned away because no backup inventory is available. Thus, service organizations must do everything possible to anticipate peak loads and to fit capacity to demand. Here are some possible approaches to this problem:

- *Smoothing out the variability in demand.* One way firms attempt to accomplish this is by offering lower prices during off-peak periods, as when hotels offer lower rates on the weekends and theaters charge less for tickets to matinee performances. Other firms advertise extensively to get customers to change their habits, as in the case of the U.S. Postal Service's campaign to encourage early mailing of Christmas cards and packages. And some service firms have added additional services or goods to make more complete use of their facilities and personnel during slow periods, as with the addition of breakfast items at fast-food chains.

- *Lowering fixed costs by making capacity more flexible.* Firms have attempted to accomplish this in a variety of ways, such as training employees to handle multiple tasks; substituting machines for labor, such as automatic teller machines (ATMs) at banks; sharing facilities, equipment, or personnel with other similar service organizations, and using part-time or paraprofessional employees.

Customer contact

The physical presence of the customer is another characteristic of many service organizations. Many services are sold, produced, and consumed almost simultaneously. The amount of customer contact during the production process is especially important because it affects service design, production, and delivery decisions. High-contact service systems are more difficult to manage than low-contact systems because the greater involvement of the customer in the process affects the timing of demand and the nature and quality of the service itself.[31]

Exhibit 3-11 shows how a variety of decisions are influenced by high and low levels of customer contact in a service system. Some of the general conclusions suggested by the exhibit follow:

- There is a high degree of uncertainty in the day-to-day operations of high-contact systems because the customer can disrupt the production system in a variety of ways. For instance, an unexpected need for emergency service from a hospital can overload operating room facilities.

- Rarely does the demand for a high-contact service equal capacity at any one time, not only because of the difficulty of making reliable forecasts, but also because of last-minute changes by the customer, as in the case of cancellations of hotel reservations. Low-contact systems can better match supply and demand by structuring a resource-oriented schedule and lengthening delivery times when necessary.

- It is difficult to set up an efficient production schedule for high-contact services because customers cannot be programmed.

- Because employees interact directly with customers in high-contact service systems, their appearance and behavior can directly affect customer satisfaction with the service.

---

[31]Richard B. Chase, "Where Does the Customer Fit into a Service Operation?" *Harvard Business Review*, November–December 1978, pp. 139–73.

═══════════════ E X H I B I T   3 – 1 1 ═══════════════

Major Design Considerations in High- and Low-Contact Service Systems

Decision	High-contact system	Low-contact system
Facility location	Operations must be near the customer.	Operations may be placed near supply, transportation, or labor.
Facility layout	Facility should accommodate the customer's physical and psychological needs and expectations.	Facility should enhance production.
Product design	The environment as well as the physical product define the nature of the service.	Customer is not in the service environment, so the product can be defined by fewer attributes.
Process design	Stages of production process have a direct immediate effect on the customer.	Customer is not involved in majority of processing steps.
Scheduling	Customer is in the production schedule and must be accommodated.	Customer is concerned mainly with completion dates.
Production planning	Orders cannot be stored, so smoothing production flow results in loss of business.	Both backlogging and smoothing are possible.
Worker skills	Direct workforce comprises a major part of the service product and so must be able to interact well with the public.	Direct workforce needs only to have technical skills.
Quality control	Quality standards are often in the eye of the beholder and hence variable.	Quality standards are generally measurable and hence fixed.
Time standards	Service time depends on customer needs, and therefore time standards are inherently loose.	Work is performed on customer surrogates (e.g., forms), and time standards can be tight.
Wage payment	Variable output requires time-based wage systems.	"Fixable" output permits output-based wage systems.
Capacity planning	To avoid lost sales, capacity must be set to match peak demand.	Storable output permits setting capacity at some average demand level.
Forecasting	Forecasts are short term, time-oriented.	Forecasts are long term, output-oriented.

SOURCE: Reprinted by permission of the *Harvard Business Review.* An exhibit from "Where Does the Customer Fit into a Service Operation?" by Richard B. Chase (November–December 1978). Copyright © 1978 by the President and Fellows of Harvard College; all rights reserved.

Variability

A final, closely related characteristic, particularly of high-contact services, has to do with variability, or the difficulty of maintaining quality control. Because of the human element, service quality can vary substantially depending on who provides it and when. In some respects, this can be viewed as a positive opportunity for the service organization. The personal nature of many services enables firms to customize their services and thus attain a better fit with customer needs. For example, travel agencies can prepare special itineraries for individual travelers, and stockbrokers can recommend individualized portfolios for their clients.

On the other hand, variability can lead to inconsistent experiences for the customer and result in dissatisfaction. Variations in quality can be a particularly difficult problem for firms that operate multiple outlets, such as banks, hotels, airlines, and retail chains. Delivering a uniform experience to customers of the Marriott Hotel group is much more difficult than producing and selling Zenith TVs of consistent quality.

To overcome these quality control problems, and to increase supplier productivity, Theodore Leavitt suggested that firms should attempt to "industrialize" their services.[32] Here are some means of accomplishing this:

- *Use of hard technologies.* This involves finding ways to control service production and delivery processes by substituting machinery and/or tools for people where possible. Examples include automatic teller machines, automatic toll collectors, vending machines, and bankcards that enable loans to be preapproved for reliable customers.

- *Use of soft technologies.* This is primarily concerned with improving the quality and consistency of employee performance through the development of standardized job procedures, detailed training, and close supervision. This approach, used by McDonald's, Marriott, H&R Block, and many other firms, helps ensure the delivery of consistently high-quality service regardless of the employee or situation involved.

- *Use of hybrid technologies.* These function by using hard equipment in conjunction with carefully planned job procedures to control service quality and gain efficiency. Leavitt cited as examples specialized, limited-service, fast, low-priced automobile repair businesses such as Midas Muffler and Jiffy-Lube.

On the other hand, James L. Heskett and his colleagues recommended a different approach for improving quality in high-contact service systems. Instead of standardizing or "industrializing" the service, they suggested hiring well-qualified employees, training them extensively, and then giving them substantial *autonomy to customize* the service to the needs and preferences of individual customers. In their view, such an approach both reduces employee turnover and increases customer satisfaction and loyalty, thereby producing greater profitability over the long term even though it may lead to higher wages and other costs in the short run.[33]

Finally, it is important to keep in mind that the marketing programs for individual product-market entries within a particular business unit—whether services or goods—may vary a good deal on some or all of the four Ps: product, price, promotion, and place of distribution. Within the constraints imposed by the characteristics of the offering and the business's strategy, individual marketing managers usually have a range of strategic options to choose from when developing a marketing plan. The nature of those options, their relative advantages and weaknesses, and the environmental conditions in which each is most appropriate are the focus of the rest of this book.

---

[32]Leavitt, *The Marketing Imagination*, pp. 38–61.

[33]Heskett et al., "Putting the Service-Profit Chain to Work."

SUMMARY

To be implemented successfully, the marketing program for a given product-market entry must be compatible with the internal capabilities, resources, management processes, and procedures of the firm. It should also fit with the corporation's higher-level strategies, particularly the competitive strategy of the entry's business unit.

When formulating a business-level strategy, managers must make recommendations about (1) the SBU's objectives and scope, (2) how resources should be allocated across product-markets and functional departments within the SBU, and (3) which competitive strategy the unit should pursue in attempting to build a sustainable competitive advantage in its product-markets. Decisions about an SBU's scope, objectives, and resource deployments are similar to and should be consistent with those made at the corporate level. However, the major question to be addressed by a business-level strategy is, How are we going to compete within our industry? Thus, an SBU's competitive strategy should take into account the unit's unique strengths and weaknesses relative to competitors and the needs and desires of customers in its target markets.

Researchers have identified general categories of business-unit strategies based on observations of how those SBUs compete within their industries. We combined the classification schemes of Porter and Miles and Snow to arrive at a typology of six different business-level competitive strategies: (1) prospector, (2) differentiated analyzer, (3) low-cost analyzer, (4) differentiated defender, (5) low-cost defender, and (6) reactor.

Businesses pursuing a prospector strategy are primarily concerned with attaining rapid volume growth by developing and introducing new products and by attaining a leading share of new markets. This strategy is particularly appropriate for industries in the introductory or early growth stages of their life cycle.

At the other extreme, defender businesses are primarily concerned with maintaining an already strong position in one or more major market segments in industries where the technology, customer segments, and competitive structure are all relatively well developed, stable, and mature. Their major objective is usually to gain and sustain a substantial return from their businesses. Differentiated defenders try to do this by maintaining an advantage based on either premium product quality or superior customer service. Low-cost defenders seek economies of scale, attempt to minimize unit costs in production and marketing, and compete largely on the basis of low price.

The analyzer strategies fall in between prospectors and defenders. These strategies are most commonly found in industries that are in the late growth or early maturity stages of their life cycles where, although the industry is largely developed, some technological changes, shifts in customers needs, or adjustments in competitive structure are still occurring. Because the analyzer is a hybrid strategy, it is difficult to make many generalizations about its implications for the allocation of resources across functional departments or for the design of marketing programs for individual product-market entries within such businesses.

Reactors are businesses that operate without any well-defined or consistently applied competitive strategy. They react to changing circumstances in an ad hoc, unsystematic way. Consequently, they tend not to perform as well on any dimension as units with more consistent strategies, and it is impossible to draw conclusions about how such businesses are likely to market their products.

Most business units incorporate multiple product-market entries. Although those entries often face different market and competitive situations, their marketing programs are all likely to be influenced and constrained by the SBU's overall competitive strategy.

Successful prospector businesses tend to be competent in, and allocate a relatively large proportion of their resources to, functional areas directly related to new product and market development, such as R&D, product engineering, marketing, sales, and marketing research. Differentiated defenders also spend substantial resources on marketing and sales to maintain a strong product quality or customer service position. But low-cost defenders usually allocate relatively few resources to any of these functions to hold down costs and prices.

The competitive thrust of a business unit's strategy influences and constrains marketing policies and programs, such as the breadth of the product line, pricing policies, and the size of advertising and promotion budgets. Thus, while marketing managers often play a crucial role in formulating the SBU's strategy, that strategy subsequently imposes constraints and direction on the marketer's decisions about the marketing program for a specific product-market entry within the SBU.

Finally, service businesses tend to pursue the same kinds of business-level strategies as goods producers, and those strategies impose the same kinds of influences and constraints on their marketing policies and programs. However, service offerings often have some unique characteristics, including (1) intangibility, (2) perishability, (3) close customer contact, and (4) variability, which can create special marketing and operational challenges.

2 SECTION

Opportunity Analysis

4 CHAPTER

Environmental Analysis

DANGEROUS ROAD AHEAD FOR AMERICA'S AUTOMOTIVE INDUSTRY[1]

By any standards automaking is one of America's largest industries, accounting for directly and indirectly one out of seven jobs. Sales of all vehicles (cars and trucks) for 1997 are estimated at 15.1 million with imports accounting for about 4 million vehicles, mainly from Japan. About three million of the 11 million vehicles produced in the United States and Canada are "transplants"; that is, they are made by foreign-owned factories.

America's Big Three automakers— General Motors, Ford, and Chrysler—after a decade of restructuring, reengineering, and investing billions in new plants combined with favorable economic conditions had record earnings in 1994 and strong aggregate profits in 1995 and 1996. Domination (an 83 percent share) of the rapidly growing light truck market, which includes minivans and off-road vehicles and represents 40 percent of total vehicle sales, contributed strongly to this out-standing profit performance.

The declining value of the yen versus the U.S. dollar (from ¥ 108.95 in June 1996 to ¥ 126.07 in November 1997) has enabled the Japanese to become much more competitive.[2] They have done so not only by reducing their list prices, but also by offering generous incentives and favorable leasing terms. Thus, the drop in the yen's value relative to the dollar has made it difficult for the Big Three to win back the customers they lost in the 1980s and capture a larger share of younger buyers.

The Big Three continue to experience regulatory pressures dealing with pollution, safety, and mileage which challenge current technological capabilities. Coupled with difficult labor relations, rising health care costs, and higher capital demand, these pressures make it difficult to hold the line or prices.

Future industry sales in the United States are expected to grow slowly given the trend of higher prices, relatively slow

---

[1]This case example relies heavily on materials prepared by Robert Schpoont, "Autos and Auto Parts," *Standard & Poor's Industrial Surveys*, January 9, 1997.
[2]*USA Today*, November 14, 1997, p. 7B.

growth in disposable income, and the overall maturation of the automotive market. Another important factor compounding the demand problem is that the industry is producing better-quality cars which has encouraged consumers to postpone the purchase of new cars.

Targeting new markets

The above problems, coupled with the possibility of a further decline in the yen versus the dollar and the increased competition for the U.S. truck market from Japan, has made the Big Three automakers reluctant to invest more locally. Not surprisingly, they are seeking new markets. This is not an easy task given that both the United States and European markets are saturated and that both Japan and South Korea have strong auto industries. This leaves Asia, which represents a highly undeveloped market.[3]

China and India have the biggest potential, but both have undeveloped infrastructures, thus making it years before auto sales could take off there. Despite this handicap and the dangers of investing in China (high inflation rates, widespread corruption, and the unpredictability of its rulers), the Big Three are eager to make "deals."[4] That foreign manufacturers such as Peugeot, Citroen, and Volkswagen have invested billions with tragic results has not slowed their eagerness to invest. General Motors has been the biggest investor—its

Delphi Parts operation has 15 ventures, and it is building a $1.6 billion complex in Shanghai—because it expects car sales to grow 20 percent annually through the year 2000 from sales of 280,000 units in 1996.[5] Ford has less ambitious plans, and Chrysler has decided to withdraw from China at least for the present.

The Big Three also are targeting Southeast Asia—Indonesia, Malaysia, the Philippines, Singapore, Thailand, and Vietnam. The region had sales of fewer than 1.5 million units in 1996, of which Thailand sold 560,000. By 2000 Thailand (the Detroit of Southeast Asia) will have the capacity to produce more cars than the rest of the area combined. Capacity by then is expected to be close to 3 million, but sales are forecasted at only 2 million.

General Motors and Ford hope to each win 10 percent of the Southeast Asian market, although they currently have less than 1 percent. Chrysler is less ambitious and plans to service the region through exports. Penetrating this market will prove difficult because Japan currently controls 80 percent of it. Since Japan has the advantage of local market knowledge, brand name recognition, skilled labor, and distribution networks in place, it will be difficult to get "a piece of the action."[6] But as Alex Taylor wrote, U.S. automakers "must explore new markets and Asia is the biggest of all. They won't exactly be panning for fool's gold, but no one should expect the Comstock Lode anytime soon."[7]

---

[3]Alex Taylor, III, "Danger: Rough Road Ahead," *Fortune,* March 17, 1997, p. 115.

[4]For a discussion of the problems facing China in its quest to become an economic superpower, see Mark Clifford, Dexter Roberts, and Pete Engardis, "Can China Reform Its Economy?" *Business Week,* December 29, 1997, p. 116.

[5]Kathleen Kervin, Dexter Roberts, and Mark Clifford, "GM's New Promised Land," *Business Week,* June 16, 1997, p. 34; and Dexter Roberts, "Where's That Pot of Gold?" *Business Week,* February 3, 1997, p. 54; for a discussion of the growth in China's coastal cities, see Mike Edwards, "Boom Times on the Gold Coast of China," *Atlantic Monthly,* March, 1997, p. 7.

[6]Robert Schpoort, "Autos & Auto Parts"; and Taylor, "Danger: A Rough Road Ahead," p. 116.

[7]Taylor, "Danger: Rough Road Ahead," p. 118.

═══════════════════ **E X H I B I T   4 – 1** ═══════════════════

Building a Corporate Perspective of the Future

> Senior managers are too often preoccupied with downsizing and redesigning core processes, neither of which is a substitute for developing an understanding of the future and its implications for a firm's core strategies. If a company fails to create future markets, then it faces declining margins and profits. To better understand what it takes to be a market leader in the future, managers should answer questions dealing with 5 to 10 years in the future such as, Which customers will you be serving? What channels will you use to service them? Who will be your competitors? What will be the basis of your competitive advantage? Where will your margins come from? and What skills will make you unique?

SOURCE: Gary Hamel and C. K. Prahalad, *Competing for the Future* (Boston: Harvard Business School Press, 1996) pp. 3–5, 18. Reprinted by permission of Harvard Business School Press. © 1996 by the President and Fellows of Harvard College, all rights reserved.

The case of America's automotive industry and the dynamics of change impacting it amply demonstrate the need to analyze trends under way in the macroenvironment. Without doing so, it would not be possible to develop strategic marketing programs that take advantage of the opportunities and minimize the threats in the changing environment of marketing. After all, most strategies derive from changes external to the firm (see Exhibit 4-1 for a discussion of the importance for managers to spend more time on external issues).

For the sake of our discussion, we have divided the macroenvironment into seven major parts: the physical, political/legal, technological, demographic, economic, sociocultural, and competitive. Managers of America's Big Three automakers are experiencing changes of considerable magnitude in all of these areas. To complicate their decision making, these components frequently interact to set off a chain reaction. For example, a problem in the physical environment (pollution) leads to legislation (U.S. Clean Air Act), which stimulates the development of new technologies (catalytic converters and alternative fuels), which in turn impact the economics of the firm and its cost structure.

Each of the seven environmental components will be highlighted in this chapter largely in terms of how the dynamics of change affect marketing strategies and programs. We then discuss the strategic issue management process required to evaluate environmental factors that are important in targeting market segments and in formulating viable strategic marketing programs.

THE PHYSICAL ENVIRONMENT

Beyond the depletion of many of the earth's valuable resources, there are indications that its overall health is declining—deserts are growing while forests are shrinking, lakes are dying, the quality and quantity of groundwater is declining, and temperatures may be rising. One of the more frightening environmental scenarios concerns the buildup of carbon dioxide in the atmosphere resulting from the heavy use of fossil fuels. This carbon dioxide "blanket" traps the sun's radiation, which leads to an increase in the earth's average temperature. While the evidence is increasing that greenhouse gases are changing the climate (airborne carbon dioxide has increased by one-third since the Industrial Revolution and seems to be on its way to doubling), there is considerable disagreement over the details of the warming effects. Still, various concerned groups (e.g., insurance companies) are demanding that governments take strong remedial action, and economists have banded together to argue that their analysis shows that greenhouse emissions can be reduced without seriously hurting U.S. living standards. In early December 1997, more than 160 countries approved an accord to slow global warming by setting emission limits on a country-by-country basis.[8] Among other undesirable eventualities, a rising temperature could cause a melting of polar ice which would cause flooding of coastal plains, shift agriculture to less productive soils, and the infection of nontropical populations with diseases such as malaria, hepatitis, yellow fever, cholera, and meningitis.[9]

Worldwide, inadequate supplies of municipal water have forced European cities to use tertiary sewage treatments to purify water for household use. California has only recently begun to use its reclaimed sewage water for parks, golf courses, and roadside landscaping, but not for drinking.[10] Poor water quality causes Americans to spend $7 billion annually for bottled water and tap water purification. Americans currently drink three times as much bottled water as they did a decade ago.[11]

Pollution problems exist throughout the world—especially in Eastern Europe, China, and the developing countries. Germany is spending billions of marks to clean up eastern Germany, where under Communist rule, forests were blighted, drinking water badly polluted, and the air fouled so much that motorists were forced to use their headlights during the day. China is the world's worst polluter, dumping billions of tons of industrial pollutants into waterways and hundreds of millions of tons of carbon emissions into the atmosphere. It is encouraging to note that pollution regulations are becoming stricter throughout the world, including China, where authorities are considering making serious pollution punishable by death.[12] Recycling programs also are increasing in popularity throughout the world.[13]

Green products as a response to environmental problems

In general, discussion of the physical environment has stressed the threats and penalties facing business throughout the world. But business can do a number of things to turn problems into opportunities. One is to invest in research to find ways to save energy in heating and lighting. Another is to find new energy sources such as low-cost wind farms and hydroelectric projects. Businesses have also found opportunities to develop hundreds of **green products**—products that are environmentally friendly, such as phosphate-free detergents, recycled motor oil, tuna caught without netting dolphins, organic fertilizers, high-efficiency light bulbs, recycled paper, and men's and women's casual clothes made from 100 percent organic cotton and colored with nontoxic dyes.[14]

---

[8]"Science and Technology: Reading the Patterns," *The Economist,* April 1, 1995, p. 65; Gregg Easterbrook, "Greenhouse Common Sense," *U.S. News and World Report,* December 1, 1997, p. 58; "For Kyoto, a Modest Proposal," *The Economist,* November 19, 1997, p. 16; and Traci Watson, "Pack OK'd," *USA Today,* December 11, 1997, p. A1.

[9]George F. Sanderson, "Climate Change: The Threat to Human Health," *The Futurist,* March–April 1992, p. 34.

[10]"California Water—Want Some More?" *The Economist,* October 8, 1994, p. 30.

[11]Carole R. Hedder, "Water Works," *American Demographics,* January 1996, p. 46.

[12]Lii, "Boom at a Glance," *New York Times Magazine,* February 18, 1995, p. 27.

[13]In some countries voluntary recycling programs have been so successful that systems cannot keep up with the supply. See "Austria Has Recycling Problems," *Business Europe,* March 7, 1994, p. 6.

[14]Pat Sloan, "Where-O-Where Can You Get `Green' Garb?" *Advertising Age,* June 5, 1992, p. 3.

Sustainability—a basis for strategy

Despite considerable progress in reducing pollution in the developed nations, the earth continues on an unsustainable course toward that goal given the explosive population and strong economic growth in the developing countries. World population is expected to double to 11 billion by 2020. To provide just the minimum standard of living for such a population would require a tenfold increase in economic activity.[15]

To date, solutions to environmental problems center chiefly on maintaining the status quo. Rarely are they linked to a firm's long-term strategy and the development of technology; thus, most companies fail to recognize the "biggest opportunities in the history of commerce."[16] A large U.S. chemical company is an exception. Its growth strategy is based on "sustainability" and few companies can ignore the conviction that it represents a strategic discontinuity. The firm has moved from pollution control to searching for growth opportunities in environmentally sustainable new technologies and products. Its scientists have focused on designing genetically engineered products that will increase productivity without harming the environment. Three new products are the new leaf potato which defends against potato beetles, BT cotton which kills the cotton bollworm, and a system using herbicides that produces better quality soils and prevents erosion.[17]

THE POLITICAL/LEGAL ENVIRONMENT

Every country has a legislative or **regulatory environment** within which both local and foreign firms must operate. As with any external force, the political/legal environment presents a firm with strategic opportunities as well as threats. Inevitably the business regulations adopted by a country reflect its economic maturity and political philosophy. At the extreme, political risk includes confiscation (seizure without compensation as happened in Iran a few years ago), expropriation (seizure with some compensation), and domestication (requiring transfer of ownership to the host country and local management and sourcing).

Other risks include changes in exchange control (which can take a variety of forms), local content laws, import restrictions, discrimination, taxes, and price controls—all of which usually operate to the advantage of local industry. Clearly, many third world countries present an array of political risks to companies seeking to do business there (see Exhibit 4-2 for a discussion of the risks of investing in China).[18] Controversies over copyright infringement involve the highest stakes. In China, pirate factories, which often are under the protection of senior politicians and high-ranking military officials, engage in counterfeiting items such as video movies, compact disks, computer software, prescription drugs, herbicides, and Rolex watches. Counterfeiting costs U.S. companies an estimated $1 to $2 billion a year.[19]

---

[15]Stuart L. Hart, "Beyond Greening: Strategies for a Sustainable World," *Harvard Business Review,* January–February, 1997, p. 71.

[16]Ibid.

[17]Jean Magrelta, "Growth through Global Sustainability: An Interview with Monsanto's CEO, Robert B. Shapiro," *Harvard Business Review,* January–February 1997, p. 79.

[18]Ever-changing government regulations by the Ukraine has caused Motorola to forgo a $500 million investment in that country. See Matthew Brezinski, "Regulatory Surprises in Ukraine Lead Motorola to Pull Investment," *The Wall Street Journal,* March 25, 1997, p. 27.

[19]Bill Montague, "China Deal Unlikely to Halt Piracy," *USA Today,* June 18, 1996, p. A1.

E X H I B I T 4 – 2

China: A Risky Investment

In but a few years China has emerged as a powerful economic force with the world's largest potential market. Because of its longer-term attractiveness, it has attracted substantial investments by a diverse group of multinational firms despite high inflation rates, widespread corruption, the growing power of the military, and an unsettled political scene. Examples of the poor treatment accorded foreign investors include the eviction of McDonald's from a prime location in Beijing, even though its lease had 17 years to run, Lehman Brothers having to sue two state corporations to pay $100 million for losses in foreign exchange trading, and a group of Japanese, German, and Italian banks begging Beijing to reimburse them for $400 million of defaulted loans made to state enterprises.

SOURCE: Louis Kraar, "The Risks Are Rising in China," *Fortune*, March 6, 1995; see also Pete Engardio and Dexter Roberts, "Rethinking China," *Business Week,* March 4, 1995, p. 57.

Government regulation

The number and intricacies of laws and regulations make it difficult to understand regulatory elements affecting marketing. Most countries have regulations concerning food and drugs, as well as price, products, promotion, and distribution, but these vary considerably in their applicability to marketing. For example, the European Union (EU) is phasing in thousands of rules designed to provide uniform safety, health, and environmental standards for its member countries. These rules favor companies now producing different products for different countries, but some exporters will be required to make costly design changes, to retool substantially, and to add new quality control systems.

It has long been argued that regulations cripple the economy and stifle innovation. This is often true, but the effects are frequently overstated because businesses will strive to find innovative ways to adhere to regulations at less than the anticipated costs. For example, when the U.S. Occupational Safety and Health Administration issued a higher standard for avoiding worker exposure to the toxic chemical formaldehyde, industry costs were expected to be $10 million yearly. However, by modifying the resins and reducing the amount of formaldehyde, costs were negligible. Further, the changes enhanced the global competitiveness of the U.S. foundry supply and equipment industry.[20]

Government deregulation

Government, business, and the general public throughout much of the world have become increasingly aware that overregulation protects inefficiencies, restricts entry by new competitors, and creates inflationary pressures. In the United States, airlines, trucking, railroads, telecommunications, and banking have been deregulated. Markets are also being

---

[20]John Carey and Mary Beth Regan, "Are Regs Bleeding the Economy," *Business Week,* June 17, 1995, p. 75; see also Michael E. Porter and Clas Van der Linde, "Green and Competitive," *Harvard Business Review,* September–October 1995, p. 123. U.S. companies have long insisted they were overregulated. For a discussion of why this may not be true—at least as far as Germany and Japan are concerned—see "To All U.S. Managers Upset by Regulations: Try Germany or Japan," *The Wall Street Journal,* December 14, 1995, p. A5. For a discussion of the merits of using taxes versus regulations to curb pollution, see "Taxes for a Cleaner Planet," *The Economist,* June 28, 1997, p. 84.

liberated in Europe, Asia, and many of the developing countries. Trade barriers are crumbling due to political unrest and technological innovation.

Deregulation has typically affected the structure of the relevant industries as well as lowered prices. For example, in the decade following deregulation of the U.S. airline industry (1978–1985), more than 200 new air carriers entered the market, and prices were an estimated 40 percent cheaper than they would have been under regulation. Also, some 900 monopoly routes were made more competitive.[21] The early actions of firms following deregulation include improving pricing capabilities, finding new ways to differentiate their services, increasing their marketing skills, and conserving capital to maintain flexibility. Later, the strategies of the surviving companies center on fine-tuning their pricing capabilities, preempting competitors through strategic alliances, and further developing their marketing skills.[22]

THE TECHNOLOGICAL ENVIRONMENT

Technology can substantially impact an industry's performance. Consider the effect of genetic engineering on pharmaceuticals, transistors on telecommunications, and plastics on metals. Identifying the commercial potential of technological developments has dramatically accelerated, and the lag between ideas, invention, and commercialization has decreased. In addition to creating new products, technological developments affect all marketing activities, including communication (making available new media or new selling tools), distribution (opening new channels or modifying the operations and performance of existing ones), packaging (use of new materials), and marketing research (monitoring food store sales by means of scanners).

In the past decade or so, an amazing number of new technologies have brought forth products such as video recorders, compact disks, ever-more-powerful and ever-smaller computers, fax machines, new lightweight materials, and highly effective genetically engineered drugs. Technological progress over the next 10 years is predicted to be several times greater than that experienced during the past 10 years; much of it will be spurred by the need to find solutions to our environmental problems. Major technological innovations can be expected in a variety of fields, especially in biology and electronics/ telecommunications.[23]

Trends in biology

The biological revolution is of fairly recent origin, especially that concerning gene therapy about which much has been written. Each cell has some 100,000 genes which, by instructing cells to make proteins, can dictate not only our physical characteristics (e.g., eye color), but our susceptibility to certain diseases. All are expected to be decoded by the year 2003. A single gene can trigger a protein that, if it works like a drug, can lead to the development of a drug worth $500 million annually (e.g., Amgen's anemia-fighting Epogen). Research to discover faulty genes, if successful, can lead to the development of therapeutic

---

[21]Peter R. Dickson, *Marketing Management* (Ft. Worth, Tex.: Dryden Press, 1994), p. 92.

[22]Joel A. Bleeke, "Strategic Choices for Newly Opened Markets," *Harvard Business Review,* September–October 1990, p. 163.

[23]These were among the top technologies in importance ranked by scientists at a leading research institute. Others include those concerned with high-density energy sources (fuel cells), miniaturization (supercomputers that fit into a pocket), and antiaging products (making the process less traumatic), and sensors that can detect diseases at an early stage (lung cancer from breath measurements); see Douglas E. Olesen, "The Top Technologies for the Next 10 Years," *The Futurist,* September–October 1995, p. 9.

treatments by the year 2000 for such diseases as cystic fibrosis and colon cancer which would be worth billions of dollars.[24]

Drug companies around the world are investing vast sums in R&D in their continued search for new problem-solving drugs. Anticipated results in the pharmaceutical and agricultural areas include a number of exciting areas.[25]

- *Pharmaceuticals:* production of human growth hormones to cure dwarfism and prevent muscle wasting, the introduction of powerful genetically engineered vaccines to treat certain kinds of cancers, and replacing defective genes which cause a variety of diseases (e.g., cystic fibrosis). A gene has recently been discovered which holds the promise of successfully treating obesity.[26] Scientists are also making good progress in the development of mass-produced tissue cultures for growing skin (for treating severe burn patients) and other organs (livers). This technology could reduce the need for donated transplants and plastic implants.[27]

- *Agriculture:* production of more disease-resistant livestock and plants, nonpolluting biological pesticides and insecticides, and a solution to the crop losses from salty soil.[28] Farmers are beginning to plant commercial crops of genetically engineered corn, cotton, soybeans, and potatoes. The biotech seeds are targeted at making crops resistant to popular weed killers as well as viruses and fungal diseases. Research may result in customized livestock in terms of growth, nutrition, the ability to withstand difficult environments, and their ability to produce pure human proteins to treat many diseases (e.g., through a herd of cloned Dollys).[29]

Trends in electronics/telecommunications

Electronics have played an important role in our society since the 1950s. They were first used primarily in areas such as radio and television and later added to the development of new products such as digital watches, automatic cameras, video games, and microcomputers and in vehicle emission control, collision avoidance, and destination mapping. Probably nothing has changed the workplace more in recent years than the personal computer, now numbering over 150 million worldwide. By the year 2000 we can expect personal computers and computers in general that will be not only smaller but many times more powerful, will understand verbal and written messages, will be able to access a far greater volume of data, and will provide quality displays.[30] See Exhibit 4-3 for a description of Intel's new supercomputer—which already is outdated.

---

[24]John Carey, Joan O. C. Hamilton, Jullia Flynn, and Geoffery South, "The Gene Kings," *Business Week,* May 8, 1995, p. 72.

[25]For a discussion of the validity of the hype that surrounds gene therapy, see "A Triumph of Hype over Experience," *The Economist,* December 16, 1995, p. 77.

[26]Laura Johnannes, "Scientists Clone Gene Said to Be Curb on Weight," *The Wall Street Journal,* December 29, 1995, p. B6.

[27]"Sowing Cells, Growing Organs," *The Economist,* January 6, 1996, p. 65.

[28]"A Sweeter Life for Crops in Salty Soil," *Business Week,* January 15, 1996, p. 90.

[29]Joseph F. Coates, John B. Mahnffre, and Andy Hines, "The Promise of Genetics," *The Futurist,* September–October 1997, p. 18.

[30]Using a PC as part of a company's internal web system—often called "intranet"—enables workers to share information as they work on projects. Such systems are expanding rapidly in use. See also Alison L. Sprout, "The Internet inside Your Company," *Fortune,* November 27, 1995, p. 161. See Robert D. Hof, "The Race Is On to Simplify," *Business Week,* June 24, 1996, p. 72, for a discussion of the drive by many companies to develop an inexpensive appliance that will make it easy to process vast quantities of data.

E X H I B I T   4 – 3

Present and Future Supercomputers

> Intel's new dream computer will break the barrier at 1.6 trillion calculations per second. The previous record was 281,000 per second. But that's nothing compared to what's likely to happen in the future. By 2005 the rate of calculations per second could increase to 100 and possibly 500 trillion. Such incredibly powerful machines would be especially important in areas such as modeling the atomic makeup of new materials and their performance under a variety of conditions, biological modeling, and simulating the effects of air and car crashes on humans.

SOURCE: Otis Port, "Speed Gets a Whole New Meaning," *Business Week,* April 29, 1996, p. 90. Reprinted with permission © 1996 by McGraw-Hill Companies.

Technology is also changing the nature and scope of the telecommunications industry now called by some the *infocommunications* industry because of the merging of telecommunications, computing, and audiovisual sectors of the economy. The changes are revolutionizing how businesses operate (banks, airlines, retail stores, and marketing research firms), how goods and services as well as ideas are exchanged, and how individuals learn and earn as well as interact with one another. Within a few years we can expect to experience check-free banking, the death of the invoice, and ticketless air travel.

These innovations are the result not only of changes in computing systems but reduced costs in communicating (voice or data) from one point to another. For example, the cost of processing an additional telephone call is so small it might as well be free. And distance is no longer a factor—it costs about the same to make a transatlantic call as one to your next-door neighbor.[31] The following major events are responsible for fueling the information revolution:[32]

- The development of fiber-optic cables in which a single fiber can carry 30,000 messages simultaneously. Such cables can be used by both telephone and cable operators, and they cost less to develop and maintain than copper wire systems.

- The development of storage devices to handle the increasing volume of data required to make the modern corporation competitive. Information about a firm's customers accounts for much of the increase. Over the next several years the information storage market is expected to grow an average of 98 percent a year. By the year 2000 this market will be worth $87.1 billion annually.[33]

- Breakthroughs leading to the use of flexible low-cost wireless transmissions which compared with fixed systems, provide mobility to the user and inexpensive access to homes.

- The development of even more powerful low-cost multimedia chips (microprocessors).

---

[31]"The Death of Distance," *The Economist,* September 30, 1995, p. 5; and Bill Gates, *The Road Ahead* (New York: Viking Penguin, 1995), p. 6.

[32]Ibid.

[33]Audrey Choi, "Storage Devices Take Spotlight in Computer Industry," *The Wall Street Journal,* April 22, 1996, p. B4.

The infocommunications industry annually generates global revenues of trillions of dollars and is growing about twice as fast as the rest of the global economy. It is defined in various ways, including a high-performance computer network, a multimedia network, and as an interactive television network. The digitalization of data has made it likely that a single network can service the needs of the computer, telecommunications, and entertainment industries.[34] The United States has set the year 2000 as the deadline for connecting every school, library, and medical facility. But the cost of such networks is staggering. Japan estimates that the cost of developing a national network to integrate the flow of data will be from $300 to $500 billion.[35] Small wonder that Bill Gates envisions:

". . . a day, not far distant, when you will be able to conduct business, study, explore the world and its cultures, call up any great entertainment, make friends, attend neighborhood markets . . . without leaving your desk or armchair.[36]

THE DEMOGRAPHIC ENVIRONMENT

World population explosion

The world's population in 1996 was 5.77 billion compared with 2.52 billion in 1950. It is expected to grow to 6.09 billion by the year 2000 and 7.47 billion by 2015. Currently some 80 percent of the world's population live in the developing countries, where 95 percent of the increase in population takes place. Africa and Asia represent nearly 90 percent of the increase. Africa's population is expected to double by 2025—from 728 million in 1996 to 1.49 billion, while that of Asia is estimated to grow by 40 percent—from 3.46 billion in 1996 to 4.96 billion. China and India will account for most of this increase. Over the next 30 years Europe is expected to have a declining population. The United States is the only major developed country that is projected to show a population increase—from 265 million (current) to 331 million by 2025.[37]

A major trend is the aging of the world's population caused primarily by declining mortality rates. The developing nations are experiencing dramatic changes in their over-65 age group: A severalfold increase is expected over the next 30 years. Another important global trend is the rapid population shift in the less developed countries from rural to urban areas. By 2025 nearly 60 percent of the population of the less developed countries is expected to be urban compared with 37 percent currently. In contrast, 75 percent of the population of developed countries is currently urban, but this share is expected to grow only very slowly in the future.[38] By the year 2015, an estimated 7 cities will have populations in excess of 20 million; by 2020, some 30 cities will have populations in excess of 8 million and 500 with populations of over 1 million.

---

[34]*World Telecommunications Development Report 1995* (Geneva, Switzerland: International Telecommunication Union, 1995).

[35]Ibid.

[36]Gates, *The Road Ahead,* pp. 4–5.

[37]*Review of Population Trends, Policies, and Programs: Monitoring of World Population Trends and Policies* (New York: United Nations, January 1996).

[38]Ibid.

U.S. Demographics[39]

The U.S. population has grown by 13 million persons since the census in 1990—the largest increase of any developed country—and is expected to grow at about 2 million a year well into the next century. Four major shifts are occurring in the U.S. population: the changing family structure, aging, geographic distribution, and ethnic composition.

Family structure: The traditional husband-dominated, closely-structured family is less and less typical of the American society. Because of divorce (about half of all marriages end in divorce) and remarriage, today's households have evolved into a number of different kinds of households populated by single individuals, adults of the same sex or both sexes (married or not) living together, unmarried adults—related and unrelated living with children—single parent families, and married couples with children. The situation is further complicated since a substantial number of these households have two or more wage earners. These different types of households vary in income and in purchases of various products and services. For example, households with two wage earners are apt to have more than one car and spend more money on eating out.

Aging: Baby boomers (those born between 1949 and 1964), who now constitute nearly 80 million persons, continue to dominate growth in the age groups they pass through en route to old age. And the number of people over 65 has increased by 7.3 percent since 1990 to over 33 million. Those over 85 have increased 18.5 percent to over 3.7 million during this time span. In the years ahead we can expect the over-65 age group to increase substantially, and it will take two workers to support one retiree.[40] As boomers age, they increasingly impact the purchase of goods and services. Households age 45–54 are the single most affluent U.S. consumer segment. For a description of what these households are buying, see Exhibit 4-4.

Geographic Distribution: Immigrants account for nearly one-third of U.S. annual growth and reside mostly in the large metropolitan areas located in California, New York, Texas, Florida, New Jersey, and Illinois. The South and West continue to gain population at the expense of the Midwest and Northeast. California, Texas, and Florida accounted for over half the U.S. growth in the 1980s and the latter two have continued to have strong growth during the 1990s. Yet another trend is the migration of jobs and people to suburban cities—farther and farther from central cities.

Ethnic composition: Another major trend is that the United States is becoming more diverse ethnically. At present 25 percent of the population is composed of racial minorities. The Hispanic population is the fastest-growing segment and is expected to increase from 22.5 million in 1990 to nearly 90 million in 2050, rising from 9 percent to a 22 percent share of the total population. The African-American population is forecasted to double by 2050—from 30.6 to 62.0 million, while Asians will increase from 7.6 million to 41.0 million. Over the next 50 years or so the three groups will account for nearly 50 percent of the total U.S. population. Such growth will further internationalize the United States—especially in major cities such as Los Angeles, Miami, and New York. Products with high ethnic appeal, such as food and clothing, should be in high demand in these areas.

---

[39]This section is based on data contained in the following: Kevin E. Deardorff and Patricia Montgomery, *National Population Trends* (Washington, D.C.: U.S. Census Bureau, June 1996); Carl Haub, "Global and U.S. National Population Trends," *Consequences,* a publication (1995) funded by NOAA, NASA, and NSF produced by Saginaw Valley State University, Michigan 48710; Cheryl Russell, "The Baby Boom Turns 50," *American Demographics,* December 1995, p. 22; Cyndie Miller, "Boomers Come of Old Age," *American Demographics,* January 15, 1996, p. 1; and the *Statistical Abstract of the United States* (Washington, D.C.: U.S. Department of Commerce, 1996). For an interesting discussion on U.S. teenagers as a market, see Peter Zollo, "Talking to Teens," *American Demographics,* November 1995, p. 22.

[40]David Shrigman, "Phoney Wars in Washington," *Fortune,* April 4, 1997, p. 45.

═══════════════════════════ E X H I B I T   4 – 4 ═══════════════════════════

What Boomers Age 45–64 Buy

> As baby-boomers fight aging, they consume large quantities of skin creams, suntan lotions, hair coloring, cosmetics, vitamins, and nutritional supplements. This segment spends more than any other on books, women's clothing, home computers, entertainment, new cars and trucks, and restaurant meals. By 2000 they will account for the largest share of purchasing a majority of most categories of goods and services.

SOURCE: Cheryl Russell, "The Baby Boomers Turn 50," *American Demographics,* December 1995, p. 22.

THE ECONOMIC ENVIRONMENT

Economic performance is generally measured by gross domestic product (GDP), usually on a per capita basis after accounting for inflation. To realistically compare incomes across countries, however, a **purchasing power parity (PPP)** approach must be used that takes into account the cost of a standard basket of products (expressed in U.S. dollars) for each country. Thus, using a PPP analysis helps to compare the relative purchasing power for goods of a given country to what these same goods would cost in the United States. If per capita GDP is calculated on the basis of exchange rates, then Japan has the world's highest average. But the United States has the highest if PPP is used to calculate per capita GDP.[41] *The Economist* has a Big Mac Index which is based on the concept of purchasing power parity; that is, the dollar should buy the same amount in every country. In the United States the nondiscounted price of a Big Mac is $2.42. China's Big Mac is the cheapest at $1.16, and Switzerland's the most expensive at $4.02.[42]

The rich versus the poor nations

Using PPP values typically produces lower GDP per capita income for the wealthier countries and higher ones for the poorer nations. Despite this "leveling," the gap in real GDP (less inflation) has increased between rich and poor countries, mainly because of higher population growth.[43] But PPP does not take into account the subsidies provided by many countries for such essentials as food, utilities, shelter, transportation, education, and medical care, which account for about half of the average household income in developed countries. If these "subsidies" are taken into account, then China, which has an urban population of 400 million, would have a GNP of $2.7 trillion compared with $520 billion without such adjustments.[44]

The world's economic growth continues to increase when measured by total gross national product (GNP). In the years ahead, developing countries are expected to have substantially higher rates of economic growth than developed countries. Asia has experienced

---

[41]See Chip Walker, "The Global Middle Class," *American Demographics,* September 1995, p. 40.

[42]"Big Mac Currencies," *The Economist,* April 12, 1997.

[43]Ibid.

[44]Andrew Marshall Hamaer, "Cashing In on China's Burgeoning Middle Class," *Marketing Management,* Summer 1995, p. 3.

the strongest annual growth—averaging over 8 percent, primarily because of China's explosive growth—and is expected to continue at a 7 percent rate in the near term. In Latin America, Argentina and Brazil are forecasted to continue their strong growth rates while Mexico is experiencing a faster than expected recovery from its economic difficulties. Central Europe will have difficulty avoiding negative growth.[45]

America seems to have regained its competitiveness because of a powerful surge in productivity triggered by low interest rates, flat unit labor costs, low inflation, and heavy capital investments—especially in high-tech equipment. The more open U.S. market has made its companies more competitive compared with Europe and to some extent, Japan.[46]

The United States may experience a slow growth in consumer spending for the next five years—a reversal of recent trends. Growth will come chiefly from the large number of baby boomers moving into their peak earning years (i.e., ages 44–54). This will be offset for the most part by an increase in the number of low-income households entering retirement. Overall the forecast calls for increased spending on personal insurance and pensions, home ownership, appliances, home furnishings, meals at home, utilities, health insurance, entertainment, and education. Expected to decline are expenditures for meals away from home, alcoholic beverages, rental units, apparel, vehicles, gasoline, reading, and tobacco products.[47] A matter of considerable concern is the growing gap between the classes. An average U.S. middle-class household experienced a 4.6 percent decline in its inflation-adjusted annual income over the past 15 years compared with a 7.9 percent increase for the top one-third income group. The richest 5 percent of U.S. families had an increase of 29.1 percent in their annual income.[48]

International trade

Increasingly, countries and many of their industries have become more economically interdependent. Free trade agreements in various stages of completion embrace a high percentage of the industrialized nations, including a single European market between the European Union (EU) and the European Free Trade Association (EFTA) called the European Economic Area (EEA); and the North American Free Trade Agreement (NAFTA) between the United States, Canada, and Mexico, which will eventually embrace most Latin American countries.

The United States has by far the largest **national** market, representing about 25 percent of the total world market for goods and services. This makes the U.S. market a high-priority target for the business firms of most countries, especially those of Japan and Europe. Inevitably the United States is a highly competitive market for many goods and services. Not only is it the biggest importer of goods and services, but also the biggest exporter, with Germany a close second.

Today nearly one-third of all automobiles sold in the United States are of Japanese origin. A large percentage of all television sets, radios, handheld calculators, motorcycles, binoculars, robots, cameras, VCRs, tape players, and digital watches sold in the United States are foreign made. Many U.S. companies are now foreign-owned—for example,

---

[45]*U.S. Trade Outlook* (Columbus, Ohio: Trade Point USA, 1995); see also "Economic Growth: The Poor and the Rich," *The Economist,* May 25, 1996.

[46]Christopher Farrell, Michael J. Mandel, and Joseph Weber, "Riding High," *Business Week,* October 9, 1995, p. 134.

[47]"The Future of Spending," *American Demographics,* January 1995, p. 12.

[48]John Cassidy, "Who Killed the Middle Class?" *The New Yorker,* October 16, 1995, p. 113.

Pillsbury (English), Carnation (Swiss), Firestone (Japanese), and CBS Records (Japanese).

U.S. business firms increasingly compete aggressively for foreign markets. In 1995 sales of the top 10 U.S. exporters totaled over $65 billion.[49] Small companies are increasingly becoming exporters. A recent survey shows that 20 percent of companies with fewer than 150 employees exported goods or services compared with 11 percent in 1992.[50] Even so, the U.S. continues to experience a chronic annual deficit in its merchandise trade account. As we noted earlier in our discussion of the automobile industry, the devaluation of the Japanese yen against the U.S. dollar in 1997 helped Japanese automakers to gain a larger share in the U.S. market, up from 21.2 percent in 1996 to 24.6 percent.[51] Fluctuating exchange rates can significantly change the relative price competitiveness of firms manufacturing in different countries.

THE SOCIOCULTURAL ENVIRONMENT

This environment represents the values, attributes, and general behavior of the individuals in a given society. Compared to economic, political, and technological changes, the sociocultural environment evolves slowly. People grow up in a system of values they tend to carry throughout their lifetimes. Transformations in the structure of society, in its institutions, and in the distribution of wealth occur gradually in democratic countries. Even so, we have in recent years seen a substantial change in individual values, family structure, minority rights, leisure activities, and conservation. These changes have affected the sale of personal consumer products, advertising programs to accommodate more joint decision making, the creation of special marketing programs for minority groups, the popularity of fast-food outlets, and the emergence of more energy-saving, reliable, and longer-lasting products. The declining sales of men's suits bear witness to the informal trend in clothing.[52]

The evolution of individual values

North American society has traditionally been characterized by such values as the Protestant ethic of hard work, thriftiness, and faith in others and in institutions. In the 1960s, however, a new social force emerged that did not entirely share these values. Instead of leaving the destiny of their country in the hands of their elders and institutions, the young—particularly college students—collectively fought for what they perceived to be good causes: civil rights, the end of the Vietnam War, and nonconformism. The young emerged as a new social force—sharing and defending a common set of new values even across national borders. This era is often referred to as the "Age of Us."

More recently, individual values have shifted again, particularly in the younger generation (20–29 years of age) sometimes referred to as generation X.[53] This shift is not

---

[49]"The Top 50 U.S. Exporters," *Fortune,* November 13, 1995, p. 74.

[50]Amy Barrett, "It's A Small (Business) World," *Business Week,* April 17, 1995, p. 96.

[51]Earle Eldridge and Micheline Maynard, "Big Three: Weak Yen Gives Sales Strength to Japan Kabota," *USA Today,* February 6, 1997, p. B1.

[52]Margaret Mannix, "Casual Friday Five Days a Week," *U.S. News and World Report,* August 4, 1997, p. 66.

[53]Early research on this group reported their behavior as being strange and unexplainable—hence the name "generation X" which derived from a novel of that name written by Douglas Copeland (New York: St. Martin's Press, 1991). Subsequent research reveals this stereotype to be highly inaccurate in describing the values and beliefs of this generation.

──────────────── E X H I B I T   4 – 5 ────────────────

Shifting Values in Western Societies

Traditional values	New values
Self-denial ethic	Self-fulfillment ethic
Higher standard of living	Better quality of life
Traditional sex roles	Blurring of sex roles
Accepted definition of success	Individualized definition of success
Traditional family life	Alternative families
Faith in industry, institutions	Self-reliance
Live to work	Work to live
Hero worship	Love of ideas
Expansionism	Pluralism
Patriotism	Less nationalistic
Unparalleled growth	Growing sense of limits
Industrial growth	Information/service growth
Receptivity to technology	Technology orientation

Developed Western societies are gradually moving away from traditional values and toward the emerging new values being embraced on an ever-widening scale, says author Joseph Plummer.

SOURCE: "Changing Values: The New Emphasis on Self-Actualization," *The Futurist,* January–February 1989, p. 15.

surprising given that during their formative years this age group has been exposed to dire predictions about the economic health of the United States, many public scandals, the advent of the knowledge society, the electronic/computer revolution, the changing structure of the American family, and the growing influence of minority groups.

As a consequence of these experiences, members of this generation are greatly concerned with simplifying their lives, obtaining a college education, relations with their families and the opposite sex, and economic security. Their coping includes living at home (particularly men), postponing marriage, and delaying having children. They are realistic and pragmatic about surviving, yet do not define success solely in terms of money. They place considerable emphasis on the family life they missed as children. While generally turned off by big government, they care a great deal about such issues as AIDS, abortion, and the environment.[54] The shifting values in Western societies are listed in Exhibit 4-5.

According to a recent study, a major cultural change is taking place in the United States. About 25 percent of American adults (44 million) live by a new set of values called *cultural creatives*. These distinctive values include ecological sustainability; strong interest in global issues; women's issues such as concerns about marital violence, building caring relationships, and the importance of families; spiritualism and the development of the inner self; and a social conscience that centers on rebuilding and healing society.[55]

---

[54]Material summarized in this section came from "A Trend Analysis Report on Youth," Nachus Ov Realities," 1, no. 1 (New York: BKG Young, n.d.); Chiat/Day, "Notes from the Emerging Media Frontier," *Fame and Flame,* January 6, 1994; "The New Femininity," *Mademoiselles,* Spring 1994; Karen Ritchie, "Marketing to Generation X," *American Demographics,* April 1995, p. 34; Karen Cooperman, "Marketing to Generation X—A Special Report," *Advertising Age,* February 6, 1994, p. 27; John Naisbitt's *Trendletter* 14, no. 9 (April 27, 1995); and Diedre R. Schwieslow, "Sixties Legacy: This Monstrous Bureaucracy," *USA Today,* July 26, 1995, p. 1.

[55]Paul H. Ray, "The Emerging Culture," *American Demographics,* February 1997, p. 29.

The evolution of family structure

The traditional husband-dominated, closely structured family is increasingly less typical of North American society. Children are becoming more autonomous and participate at an earlier age in many family decisions. A more balanced allocation of power between husband and wife has also emerged, in part because of the greater economic independence of more and more women. The absence of working parents from the home has substantially reduced the interactions between family members and family cohesiveness. The increasing divorce rate has made one-parent households more common. All of these factors—as noted earlier—have considerably changed the buying process for many goods, including which family members are involved in the purchase of certain goods.[56]

THE COMPETITIVE ENVIRONMENT[57]

The changes under way in the various components of the macroenvironment converge on the competitive environment, thereby impacting competitive behavior in many industries. There is little doubt that the intensity of competition has increased, as witnessed by the vast array of new and higher quality products and services, the aggressive pricing practices of many companies, the increased number of mergers and acquisitions, the process by which competitors are evaluated, the formulation of competitive strategies, and the use of downsizing to remain competitive. In addition, we find that the nature and scope of many industries has changed dramatically with respect to the number and national origin of the players, the size and scope of the market, the extent to which rivalry between industry members is based on price, and the relative size and power base of industry players.

Our coverage of the competitive environment is limited to a brief discussion of the chief forces that shape its major characteristics and make it so intense. These forces include the globalization of business, the impact of technology on innovation, changing channels of distribution, new business alignments resulting from regulation/deregulation, and reactions to changing social values, attitudes, and lifestyles. Each of these is discussed below.

Globalization of business

An important result of this trend is the effect that increased market size has on the number of competitors and their interaction. Since it takes more resources to be a major global player, the number of players becomes increasingly limited; for example, Federal Express and UPS are the only two major competitors in the $30 billion a year package delivery business.[58] Thus, globalization of any consequence almost always results in a change in an industry's structure which makes it more difficult for competitors to enter the market and for some to survive, especially those which are primarily local operators.

---

[56]For a discussion of the major societal trends that are and will dramatically affect the future of families in the United States and elsewhere, see Joseph F. Coates, "What's Ahead for Families," special report by the World Future Society, Bethesda, Maryland, 1996.

[57]Competition is a major theme that runs throughout this text. In addition to the discussion in this chapter on the subject, subsequent chapters will deal with obtaining and evaluating sources of competitive information (Chapter 5), how industry dynamics and the product life cycle affect competition (Chapter 6), the process by which competitors are evaluated (Chapter 8), and the formulation of competitive strategies (Chapters 9, 10, and 11).

[58]Les Harrison, "The Competitive Edge," *Executive Focus,* January 1996, p. 35.

Impact of technology on innovation

The rate of technological growth—and its complexities—has a strong impact on innovations in the production process and in the development of new and improved products (see the "Technological Environment" earlier in this chapter). Such developments not only give birth to new industries, but can radically change existing ones by requiring new levels of investments in production, R&D, and marketing. It may even change the benefits associated with vertical integration and mergers. In the fast-moving software business, where being first to market and company size (scale effects) are important, mergers and acquisitions have become increasingly popular. Recently Hewlett-Packard has aligned itself with Intel and Microsoft by announcing its use of the former's new Pentium Pro microprocessor and the latter's Windows NT operating systems. This alignment will surely increase the competition for the fast growing, high-end business computer market (worth over $200 billion annually) and threaten the position of Sun, IBM, and Compaq.[59]

Changing channels of distribution

Developments in distribution, especially in retailing, have been numerous and far-reaching. Changes include:

- The rapid growth of general merchandise discount stores with operating costs substantially lower than those of more traditional retailers such as department stores. Wal-Mart, with more than 2,200 U.S. stores and annual sales over $100 billion, has operating expenses of 15.8 percent compared with 33.3 percent for Federated Department Stores. Category Killer Stores in such areas as computers (Computer City), consumer electronics and appliances (Circuit City), drugs (Drug Emporium), office supplies and equipment (Office Depot), and building materials (Home Depot) operate in a similar fashion.
- Direct marketing (worth $600 million in 1995) to consumers by means of telemarketing, direct mail including catalogs, and the Internet have collectively impacted the sales of traditional retailers.[60]
- Growth in vertical marketing systems which integrate producer, wholesaler, and retailer into a unified system designed to achieve lower costs while increasing market power. Such systems have been particularly effective in franchising; for example, fast foods (McDonald's), hotels (Marriott), and soft drinks (Coca-Cola).[61]

The result of the distribution changes given above has caused a shakeout in retailing. For example, hundreds of record stores are closing because of price competition from such giants as Wal-Mart and Circuit City. To compound the problem, consumers can now sample and buy recordings from their home by dialing a toll-free number or by browsing the Internet.[62]

---

[59]Lee Jones, "H-P Aims at High End of Business Computing Market," *The Wall Street Journal,* May 29, 1996, p. B4.

[60]"Telemarketing Cited as Chief Form of Direct Marketing," *Marketing News,* January 1, 1995, p. 9.

[61]Richard Gibson, "McDonald's Accelerates Store Openings in U.S. and Abroad, Pressuring Rivals," *The Wall Street Journal,* January 18, 1996, p. A3.

[62]Jeffrey A. Trachtenberg and Eben Shapiro, "Record-Store Shakeout Rocks Music Industry," *The Wall Street Journal,* February 26, 1996, p. B1.

New business alignments from regulation/deregulation

In recent years U.S. deregulation has affected the airline, trucking, banking, natural gas, electric utilities, and, more recently, the telecommunication industries. In the latter industry legislators have struggled to bring more competition to the local $96 billion annual telephone market which is controlled by the seven Baby Bells. The new legislation will open these markets to competition and, in exchange, permit the Baby Bells to compete in the annual $176 billion long-distance market. The bill will also change the structure of the TV industry. Cable TV operators will be permitted to offer telephone service while telephone companies will be free to provide video services. Clearly, the next decade will see all-out war between industry members, causing prices of telephone services to drop by as much as 70 percent.[63]

Reactions of business to changing values/attitudes/and lifestyles

Changing values, attitudes and lifestyles also can be powerful engines of change as companies compete to take advantage of these trends. For example, increased concern about physical fitness has been responsible for the emergence of new industries concerned with athletic clubs, exercise equipment, specialized jogging and running shoes, and athletic wear which compete against each other and more traditional products and services. Our preoccupation with healthy nutritional foods have led to a host of low-fat, cholesterol-free, and saltless food products. The desire for informality in clothing has practically revolutionized the clothing industry. Men's suits are no longer "in," but slacks and sport shirts are. Concerns for the health of the planet has led to the development of green products that are compatible with the environment and the recycling of certain materials such as paper and metal cans. Safety issues have become sufficiently important so that automakers are taking the initiative in adding safety features such as a second airbag, a safety seat for children, and reinforcement of the driver's side panel.

STRATEGIC ENVIRONMENTAL EVENTS MANAGEMENT

Management needs a system to help it identify, evaluate, and respond to environmental events that may affect the firm's longer-term profitability and market position. One approach uses an **opportunity/threat matrix** to better assess the impact and the timing of an event followed by the development of an appropriate response strategy. This approach is discussed below.

The impact and timing of the event

In any given period, many environmental events that could impact the firm positively or negatively may be detected. Somehow, management must determine the probability of occurrence and the degree of impact (profitability and/or market share) of each event. One relatively simple way to accomplish these tasks is to use a two-by-two dimensional opportunity/threat matrix (see Exhibit 4.6). The example contains four potential environmental events which a large U.S. telecommunications company might have identified as worthy of concern in the mid-1990s. The probability of each occurring by the year 2010 was rated along with the impact on company profitability or market share. Those events likely to have the greatest impact appear in the upper left-hand box. At the very least, such events

---

[63]"Washington's Wake-up Call," *The Economist,* January 20, 1996, p. 61.

E X H I B I T   4 – 6

Opportunity/Threat Matrix for a Telecommunications Company

Level of impact on company*	Probability of occurrence (2010)	
	High	Low
High	4	1
Low	2	3

1. Wireless communications technology will make networks based on fiber and copper wires redundant.
2. Technology will provide for the storage and accessing of vast quantities of data at affordable costs.
3. The prices of large-screen (over 36-inch) digitalized TV sets will be reduced by 50 percent (constant dollars).
4. Telephone companies will emerge as the dominant force in the telecommunications industry as well as the operators of telecommunications systems.

*Profits or market share or both.

should be examined closely, including estimating as precisely as possible their impact on profitability and market share.

The opportunity/threat matrix enables the handling of a large number of events in such a way that management can focus on the most important ones. Thus, management should closely monitor events such as number 4 with a high probability of occurring and a high-level impact. Those with a low probability of occurrence and low impact, such as number 3 in the exhibit, should probably be dropped, at least for the moment. Events with a low probability/high-impact (number 1) should be reexamined less frequently to determine if the impact rating remains basically sound.

Response strategies

A firm's strategy includes both reactive and proactive responses to an environmental event. A **reactive strategy** is undertaken in response to the occurrence of a major event, often in a crisis situation (e.g., the handling of a major oil spill). A **proactive strategy** responds in anticipation of an event occurring. In the early 1990s, for example, the U.S. pharmaceutical industry was threatened with price control legislation which would have a strong negative impact on its profitability. The industry responded by spending millions of dollars on lobbying, advertising, and public relations to emphasize that its R&D saved millions of lives at a cost of only a few cents in each health care dollar. A proactive strategy is usually more desirable than a reactive one because it avoids pressure decisions and enables a firm to perform more in-depth analyses. Further, the greater the lead time, the broader the array of options. Exhibit 4-7 discusses examples of six response strategies that can be fashioned in either reactive or proactive modes.

Ethical issues and the environment

Since there are a variety of ways that business and the environment interact, it is not surprising that firms find it difficult to cope with environmental issues. More and more companies are, however, taking an active role in dealing with the environmental issues that

═══════════════════════════ **E X H I B I T   4 – 7** ═══════════════════════════

Response Strategies to Environmental Issues

1. **Opposition strategy:** The effectiveness of this strategy is limited because environmental factors are largely beyond the control of a firm. In some situations, a firm may, however, try to delay, attenuate, or otherwise influence an environmental force. Lobbying and corporate issue advertising are examples of opposition strategy used by some large firms.

2. **Adaptation strategy:** Adaptations are often compulsory as, for example, is the case with legislation on product specifications, packaging, and labeling. Choices often exist, however, in the type and extent of adaptation. The danger is that if an adaptation strategy is pursued to the extreme, the environment (not management) sets the pace and scope of strategic change.

3. **Offensive strategy:** Such a strategy uses the environmental issue to improve the firm's competitive position. A key environmental issue may have a destabilizing effect on an industry, which may create opportunities for the more aggressive firms. This was the type of strategy used by Merck in its offer to cut its prices to Medicaid programs. Merck's discounts would be 7 to 13 percent less than the company's regular wholesale prices.

4. **Redeployment strategy:** Faced with major environmental issues in one market, a firm may decide to redeploy its resources in other, less-exposed areas. For example, tobacco companies such as Philip Morris and R. J. Reynolds have diversified into other consumer goods because of the environmental pressures concerning the health effects of cigarette smoking.

5. **Contingency strategies:** One such strategy decreases the risk of being exposed to potentially harmful environmental events. For example, a search may be launched for substitutes for raw materials with volatile prices. Another contingency strategy designs alternative courses of action corresponding to the different possible evolutions of the environment. This involves isolating discrete environmental scenarios the firm may have to face in the future and designing appropriate responses for each. For example, in the early 1990s, gasoline-fueled cars were restricted in certain localities (e.g., Los Angeles) and, thus, some automobile companies began experimenting with electric cars and natural gas-powered vehicles.

6. **Passive strategy:** This strategy calls for not responding to an environmental threat or opportunity. For example, in the early days of modern consumerism, some corporations took major public action to oppose their critics—which only provided greater exposure to the issue and worsened their images. A better alternative would have been not to have taken *any* action until performing more complete analyses and formulating an appropriate response.

society faces today. These actions range from to-the-letter compliance with environmental regulations to taking a strong pro-environment stance, which includes abandoning products which are environmentally harmful.

Most companies strive to develop a pro-environment attitude among their employees, customers, and the general public. A substantial majority have ethical codes of behavior to guide their employees on environmental concerns. Many firms support green organizations such as the National Wildlife Federation, the Sierra Club, and the Environmental Defense Fund. Resource conservation and recycling receive considerable support by both consumers and the business community. McDonald's has been particularly active in addressing the problem of disposing of its used plastic and Styrofoam packaging.[64]

Another ethical problem area has to do with treatment of Third World countries. Concern for the residents of such countries has a long history, including especially South Africa's apartheid and, more recently, civil rights in China. U.S. companies have come under severe criticism for contracting with suppliers that use child or prison labor or

---

[64]N. Craig Smith and John A. Quelch, eds., *Ethics in Marketing* (Homewood, Ill.: Richard D. Irwin, 1993), p. 61.

provide an unhealthy working environment; others have been criticized for charging high prices to the residents of developing countries for goods such as pharmaceutical drugs.

Even when business seeks to develop and market green products and to use packaging that facilitates its disposal, problems remain. Part of the problem in the United States is the maze of local, state, and federal laws regulating the disposal of solid waste and the formulation of certain products. What is legal in one state may be illegal in another.

Dealing with environmental problems might seem intractable because of the difficulty in defining the severity of the problem (e.g., the greenhouse effect), let alone in knowing how to solve it (e.g., replenishing underground water supplies). Even when business thinks it has found a solution, it cannot be sure of the long-term versus short-term effects and the extent to which the solution may even be dysfunctional. In some areas, however, the picture is clearer, and a positive response may even be good business.

SUMMARY

An analysis of the firm's external environment is concerned not only with the relevant industry and marketplace but with the environmental trends affecting them. There are seven components of the macroenvironment of importance to marketing: the physical, political/legal, technological, demographic, economic, sociocultural, and competitive. Of these, the demographic, economic, and competitive components are the most pervasive, although all seven are important.

The deteriorating physical environment is rightly a cause of considerable concern, although the severity of the planet's several problems may be somewhat difficult to measure. The political/legal environment in the form of regulation and deregulation is not necessarily negative—opportunities abound, especially in the area of new products.

Technology can have a substantial impact on the performance and competitive structure of an industry. The pace of technological development has been increasing and promises to become even more intensive in the future. Two technologies having a significant influence on the future of our society are electronics/telecommunications and biology.

Changing demographics are one of the best indicators of which markets to target; for example, the growing market of people 45 to 54 years old. Demographics reveal the problems facing the world because of substantial increases in the populations of the developing countries while those of most of the developed countries are declining.

The economic environment—as it relates to per capita GDP, international trade, household expenditures, and exchange rates—reveals a great deal about the ability of certain groups worldwide to buy different products and services, and the competitive strategies of local and multinational businesses.

The slowly evolving sociocultural environment represents the values, attitudes, and behaviors of people in a given society. Some of the more significant trends involve shifts in individual values toward self-realization and fulfillment, recognition of the human rights of diverse populations, changes in family structure, and concern about the environment.

The competitive environment is becoming increasingly intensive because of the changes in the other components of the macroenvironment. The nature and scope of these changes have affected industries in terms of their size, number, and national origin of the players and in terms of competition (i.e., price, product differentiation). The major engines of change are globalization of business, technology, changing channels of distribution, regulation/deregulation, and changing values, attitudes, and lifestyles.

Management needs a process for strategic environmental issues to help it identify key issues, estimate the probability of their happening, evaluate their impact, and formulate a response strategy. The response strategy can adopt one of six modes: opposition, adaptation, offensive action, redeployment, contingency planning, and doing nothing.

Most firms, especially the large ones, have a code of ethics to which they aspire to conform. More and more companies are taking the initiative to participate in pro-environment activities. Many have developed green products designed to be compatible with the physical environment.

5 CHAPTER

Marketing Information

THE MARKETING INFORMATION REVOLUTION

In recent years an increasing number of managers have focused on the consumer in their efforts to gain a competitive advantage in the marketplace. They have done so by building **market-driven** organizations which base their competitive strategy on customer satisfaction. As Robert C. Blattberg and Rashi Glazer noted, "This renewed emphasis on customers . . . represents nothing more than the fulfillment of the age-old marketing concept which was supposed to guide company behavior—find out what the people want and give it to them."[1] But, of course, a customer-focused/market-driven organization cannot be successful unless it develops superior skills in the generation and use of information about its customers and competitors. The value of customer relationships, according to Philip B. Evans and Thomas S. Wurster, "is the proprietary information that they have about their customers and that their customers have about the company and its products. Brands . . . are nothing but the information—real or imagined, intellectual or emotional—that consumers have in their head about a product."[2]

The United States and other highly developed countries are now recognized as being postindustrial societies in which information leading to knowledge—through individuals who have an in-depth grasp of a subject—is their most important resource. The technological revolution, which allowed information to be speedily gathered, processed, and stored—and at lower costs—led to the information age. This revolution has affected all parts of the modern corporation, and none more so than marketing.

In Chapter 1 we noted how the importing of information about the marketplace helped Compaq successfully redesign its product line and develop a new aggressive personality. Also, in Chapter 1 we used Compaq as an example of how information technology can be

---

[1]Robert C. Blattberg and Rashi Glazer, "Marketing in the Information Revolution," in Robert C. Blattberg, Rashi Glazer, and John D. C. Little, eds., *The Marketing Information Revolution* (Boston, Mass.: Harvard Business School Press, 1994), p. 9.

[2]Philip B. Evans and Thomas S. Wurster, "Strategy and the New Economics of Information," *Harvard Business Review*, September–October, 1997, pp. 72–73.

E X H I B I T   5 – 1

Hewlett Packard's Electronic Sales Partner System

> The company's Electronic Sales Partner (ESP) system is designed to help its computer systems salesforce in the sales process. The amount of product knowledge required to help customers solve their problems involving interactions between hardware, software, and communications gear is horrendous—and ever growing. The system includes a variety of information—white papers, sales presentation, technical specs, and cues on external sources—all of which is available worldwide through an Intranet Web. A search engine as well as the facility to easily browse documents by category are included in the system. HP's sales support manager reports that it's the most successful software implementation he's seen in 20 years, with great feedback from submitters and users.

SOURCE: Thomas H. Davenport and Lawrence Prusak, *Working Knowledge* (Boston, Mass: Harvard Business School Press, 1998), pp. xiv, 123–24.

used to define—with considerable precision—micro segments and to provide information about how best to market to them. A more detailed example showing Hewlett Packard (one of America's most admired computer company) appears in Exhibit 5-1.

Information about the marketplace can serve as the basis for a strong competitive advantage. This was certainly the case with the ESP system described in Exhibit 5-1. It was also the case with Wal-Mart's success in "streamlining its supply chain" to get the right goods on the right shelf at the right time, which decreased stockouts, increased turnover, and decreased inventories. The result was lower operating costs and greater sales, and it put Kmart in a catch-up position.[3] Another example is Nike, which "has masterfully employed advertising, endorsements, and microsegmentation of its market to transform sneakers into high-priced fashion goods."[4]

Over time competitors are able to match the advantages resulting from differentiated products and successful cost containment programs. But a company with in-depth knowledge about the marketplace can maintain its superiority by providing a continuous flow of innovative and highly desirable products as well as finding new ways of becoming more efficient. In the long run *only knowledge can provide a company with a sustainable advantage* in the form of giving consumers what they want and doing it better than anybody else!

Each year the average company adds millions of pieces of information to an already huge inventory of marketing information. This information comes from a wide variety of sources, including company records, professional journals, books, census and registration data, industry reports, monographs, publicly circulated reports of individual projects, marketing research, and so on. All one has to do is surf the World Wide Web to get some idea of the diversity of sources.

This chapter focuses on computerized marketing information systems, not on describing marketing data sources. After considering these systems in general, we discuss standardized/commercial marketing information systems, internal database marketing, information systems, marketing research, and marketing-decision support systems. Next, we discuss three separate data sets concerned with the critically important areas of competition, customer satisfaction, and market measures. A discussion of ethical issues concludes

---

[3]Peter G. W. Keen, *The Process Edge* (Boston: Harvard Business School Press, 1997), pp. 7–8.

[4]Evans and Wurster, "Strategy and the New Economics of Information," p. 73.

the chapter. Before discussing these subjects, however, we need to comment on marketing information systems in general.[5]

Marketing managers have long sought ways to gain a better understanding of individual customers so that they could deliver both information and products tailored to their needs. The growing sophistication of information technology made possible the development of computerized customer data banks which used internal and external data to develop and communicate individualized marketing programs. These are being used to make marketing programs more efficient and effective. Efficiency is made possible by means of more detailed information about the consumer, thereby improving the customer targeting process. Effectiveness is improved because database marketing helps the firm to better develop its strategic marketing programs—especially their pricing, communication, and promotion components—based on the targeted consumer's past purchasing behavior.

Blattberg and Unglaub summarized how database marketing can affect strategy:[6]

- By taking into account the lifetime value of a customer.
- By concentrating on selling more to an existing customer.
- By making it possible to develop one-on-one marketing plans.
- By improving both the efficiency and effectiveness of marketing programs.

Marketing systems can and are used by both consumer and industrial goods companies. In Chapter 1 we used Fingerhut as an example of a retailer using its massive consumer data bank to develop personalized catalogs and mail them to customers when they are most likely to buy. At the beginning of this chapter we cited Hewlett-Packard's use of a database designed to help its computer salespersons solve a customer's problems, thereby making a sale.

STANDARDIZED/COMMERCIALIZED MARKETING SYSTEMS

We mentioned at the beginning of the chapter how the Neilsen organization provides syndicated services on the price and sales of merchandise based on point-of-sale (POS) scanner data. Currently, Nielsen (the world's largest research firm with annual sales in excess of $1.3 billion) provides a variety of services based largely on POS data to clients in over 90 countries.[7]

More specifically, Nielsen provides continuous sales (tracking) information on a wide variety of products and brands sold by an array of retailers, including supermarkets, drugstores, mass merchandisers, convenience chains, and supercenters utilizing in-store scanning of universal product codes. This stands in contrast to some 40 years ago, when Nielsen sent auditors with clipboards every two months into a sample of stores located throughout the United States to collect data which would determine the sales of a variety of items.

Nielsen provides at frequent intervals (on a subscription basis) information on the sales of a client's brand(s) (also on competing brands), as well as their prices, store inventories, and in-store merchandising displays—all by type, size, and location of store. Nielsen augments its POS retail service by operating a 40,000 household panel that provides

---

[5]The contents of this section benefited from a discussion of database marketing by Robert C. Blattberg and Lynn C. Unglaub, in Sydney J. Levy, ed., *Winning Marketing Plans* (Chicago: Dartnell Corporation, 1996), chap. 4.

[6]Ibid., p. 50.

[7]Jack C. Totten and Mike Duffy, "Marketing Technology and Consumer Scanning," Sidney J. Levy, ed., *Winning Marketing Plans*.

━━━━━━━━━━━━━━━━━━━ **E X H I B I T   5 – 2** ━━━━━━━━━━━━━━━━━━━

Donnelley's DQI² Consumer Information System

> This powerful consumer data bank offered by Donnelly Marketing of Stamford, Conn. helps to answer a company's targeting questions plus identifying and selecting those individuals and households which fit the desired profiles. DQI² includes consumer data on over 150 million individual U. S. consumers and 90 million U. S. households. It contains over 1,600 demographic, lifestyle, and purchase behavior variables, including age, name, gender of family members, household income, creditworthiness, presence of children, purchasing power, mail responsiveness, and make and age of car. These data can be accessed at any geographical level— including blocks.
>
> Donnelly Marketing offers another interesting data bank (Share Force) comprised of 17 million individuals for which demographic, geographic, and lifestyle data are available. Both of these databases are continuously updated and expanded.

SOURCE: Terry G. Vavra, *Aftermarketing* (Burr Ridge, Ill.: Irwin Professional Publishing, 1992); updated July 1996 from information supplied by Donnelley over the Internet.

continuous detailed purchase information on consumer products. Purchases of each item are recorded via the computer using an electric wand to scan the bar codes of each item, as are the price paid, coupons used, retail outlet involved, and the demographics of the person making the purchase. Nielsen also collects data on household TV viewing, radio listening, and more recently, print media, the demographics of which can be correlated with its consumer panel data, thus providing a single-source service.[8] The new breed of marketing information data banks link a variety of information about the consumer including brand loyalty and the ability to measure the effect of promotion events on brand switching. Such data are also helpful in tracking the sales of new products.

The geodemographic industry offers another important source of information about the consumer. Its data are useful in segmenting the market for consumer goods and services and for providing a way to reach prospects. Claritas's PRIZM (Potential Rating Index for ZIP Markets) service attempts to predict purchasing behavior based on consumer identity and residential location. Originally, census demographics were matched with 36,000 ZIP codes to produce 40 lifestyle segments. More recently, PRIZM classified all U. S. households into 62 demographically and behaviorally distinct clusters (e.g., shotguns and pickups, urban gold coast, pools and patios), each of which is then assigned to one of 15 social groups.

Geodemographic databases have become increasingly sophisticated; the industry now provides four types of data in detail: demographics, geographics (market area, ZIP code, census area, and address), psychographics (social class, values, and lifestyles), and consumer behavior (benefits sought, product usage, loyalty, and attributes of specific products). The massive databases that provide such information are formed by accessing public records and purchasing consumer buying behavior profiles from private companies.[9] For a brief discussion of another massive database supplier, see Exhibit 5-2.[10]

---

[8]The information about Nielsen was obtained via the Internet from the A. C. Nielsen Company in July, 1996. Also, see "Data Wars," *The Economist*, July 22, 1995, p. 62; and Jack Honemichl, "The Top 50 U. S. Research Organizations," *Marketing News*, June 9, 1997.

[9]Information contained in this section comes largely from Jon Goss, "We Know Who You Are and We Know Where You Live: The Instrumental Rationality of Geodemographics," *Economic Geography*, no. 2 (1995), p. 171.

[10]Jonathan D. Barsky, *World-Class Customer Satisfaction* (Burr Ridge, Ill.: Irwin Professional Publishing, 1995), p. 41.

The above discussion highlights only a few of the thousands of databases now available for a wide range of business-related needs. The largest collection of statistics in the United States originates from the U. S. Bureau of the Census. The major uses of census data are in sales forecasting, development of market potentials, construction of sales territories and quotas, store location, and plant locations. Eight censuses cover agriculture, construction, housing, manufacturers, population, retail trade, service industries, and wholesale trade. All are taken every five years, except for population which is mandated every 10 years. In addition, the census publishes data on counties, cities, states, and metropolitan areas.

Considering the billions of dollars spent annually on advertising, it is not surprising that an enormous amount of information is available from a variety of sources. In addition to the Nielsen media data, examples include Arbitron, which measures local TV, cable, and radio audiences; Simmons Market Research Bureau, which reports annually on exposure to TV, radio, newspapers, and magazines as well as product usage, leisure activities, and financial services; Starch, which provides readership measures of advertisements contained in consumer, farm, and business magazines as well as in newspapers; and the Audit Bureau of Circulation, which supplies data on the paid circulation of newspapers and magazines.

Other prominent database services include Dun and Bradstreet, which furnishes credit information on individual firms; T. W. Dodge Corporation, which compiles construction statistics; Moody's Investors Service, which provides detailed financial information on more than 22,000 companies worldwide and 28,000 state and local governments; and the Bureau of Labor Statistics Continuous Consumer Expenditure data based on type of expenditure and household demographics.

Internal marketing database information systems

These systems are based on a variety of information, most of which concerns sales in one form or another. This is especially true with manufactures of industrial products who sell direct and because of the nature of their goods, they cannot benefit from a service of the type Nielsen provides. The data often include additional information about the customer, such as the type of business, size, name of parent company, the demographics of the buyer (purchasing agent), and credit rating. This information can be used to undertake basic analyses such as those relating to products (e.g., which items to abandon), customers (e.g., their level of importance), order size (e.g., what should the minimum order size be?), distribution (e.g., which middlemen are best for the company?), and the performance of individual salesmen.

Direct incentive programs

In recent years retention database marketing information systems have become increasingly popular. The most common type is one that provides a direct incentive to customers for heavy usage. This in turn encourages repeat business, epitomized by the airlines' frequent flier programs which have been around since the 1980s and have spread to a variety of businesses such as hotels, car rentals, book and record clubs, and credit cards. It is important to note that these programs, while offering value, may not of themselves build enduring loyalty because the sponsor must continue to provide a high level of customer satisfaction with its products or services. Exhibit 5-3 provides an example of exclusive clubs that require a membership fee.

The key task facing management in developing successful retention programs is to use the information contained in the database to determine how customers differ and how to develop marketing programs that exploit such differences. American Express has

════════════════════ **E X H I B I T   5 – 3** ════════════════════

Club Membership at a Price

> Open clubs such as frequent flier and other perk programs are very common. Recently, however, some companies are setting up exclusive clubs for which they charge membership dues. The objective is, of course, to retain core customers who are responsible for the largest portion of a company's profits. Limited membership clubs originated in Europe and provide a mixture of benefits. In the United States, Volkswagen charges $25 to join its club, upon which a member receives a T-shirt, road atlas and decal, a phone card, discount offers on travel and recreation as well as on parts and services from local dealers, and the opportunity to apply for a club Visa card with a picture of their own VW on the front. Discounts and benefits are oriented to younger people with active lifestyles, which is the company's target audience.

SOURCE: Ian P. Murphy, "Customers Can Join the Club—But at a Price," *Marketing News*, April 28, 1997, p. 8. Reprinted with permission from American Marketing Association.

customized programs that enable merchants to target customers for their products. For example, an airline-expanding its service to a new city can have AmEx isolate a group of its customers who are frequent travelers to that city. The airline can then target these potential customers with a promotional offer. This kind of service is good for everybody. Marketers can target proven prospects, AmEx customers get products and events tailored to their interests, and AmEx is positioned to complete the transaction with one of its charge cards.[11]

Affinity Clubs

Affinity clubs are another type of retention program that attempts to improve the image a customer has of a company and its brands. For example, relationship marketing at LaQuinta Inns (a large U. S. hotel-motel chain) began like that of many other organizations with a frequent traveler club. LaQuinta sends club members newsletters on hotel events and promotions and special-interest information tailored to the needs and interests of various market segments. One newsletter targeted senior citizens and traveling salespersons—two very important segments for LaQuinta. Dietary, transportation, sightseeing, and other travel information was highlighted for the seniors while professional selling suggestions were included for salespersons. The latter information was also available on audiocassette.[12]

Lost Customer Programs

Lost customer programs, or win-back programs, also are important because a firm will lose, on average, 10 to 15 percent of its customer base annually. Reducing defections is the objective of lost customer programs. But since defections are a function of a great many variables, no company will succeed in obtaining zero defections no matter how hard it tries—hence the need for win-back programs. To develop and execute such programs, a firm must identify defectors, determine why they defected, and develop appropriate win-back programs.[13]

---

[11]Kate Fitzgerald, "Marketers Capture Prospects Using AmEx 'Closed Loop'," *Advertising Age*, October 9, 1996, p. 19.

[12]Barsky, *World-Class Customer Satisfaction*, p. 41.

[13]For an insightful discussion of the importance of learning from failure, see Frederick F. Reichheld, "Learning from Customer Defections," *Harvard Business Review*, March–April 1996, p. 57.

Identifying lost customers is not an easy undertaking, especially for companies that have no direct contact with end-users (it is an easier task for many service organizations and sellers of certain industrial products). To make an identification requires that a lost customer be defined. Too often, businesses define a defector as one that stops buying *all* of its requirements from the firm when in fact the definition should include partial defectors. In addition, it is important to determine the relative importance of individual defectors not only for their loyalty to the firm, but for their total purchases over given periods of time. Only a computerized comprehensive sales data information system can provide these data—especially for multiproduct companies with a large customer base.

Finding out why a customer defected requires that a firm undertake a marketing research project, although the lost customer files should be analyzed to see whether there are any defection patterns by variables such as dates of "defection," geography, types of companies, or kinds of products. Once the reasons for defection are known, the company needs to develop one or more win-back programs, which must be monitored to determine their success.

The future of marketing information systems

It seems clear that technological changes will enable us to process information faster and faster while the costs of processing and communicating large amounts of data will continue to decrease greatly. Thus, more information in more comprehensive form will be captured, processed, and communicated from and to more people and places. Managers will find that inventories can be reduced and just-in-time efforts made more productive. Response time to changes in the marketplace will be reduced substantially. Software systems that facilitate data access and causal analysis will be constantly improved.[14]

For consumer goods, control of the customer will increasingly shift to the retailer instead of to the manufacturer, although the latter will attempt to block such efforts through direct customer contact, exchanging information with retailers, and the development of individualized marketing programs that include the mass customization of their products. Other elements in marketing programs will change, especially price and advertising. As to price, "information technology allows firms . . . to set up a bid/ask price system in which products are essentially auctioned. An auto manufacturer with short production lead times could price as a function of time . . . At present, products are produced, then priced. In the auction market, buyers bid before the product is produced." In advertising, firms that base their strategy on more interaction with their customers will use less traditional media in favor of direct communication based on detailed consumer buying behavior.[15]

MARKETING RESEARCH

Annual marketing research expenditures are probably in the range of $6 to $7 billion for the United States and $12 to $14 billion globally. In 1996, the 50 leading U. S commercial research firms had billings of $5.05 billion of which $2.10 billion came from outside the Untied States.[16] Factors driving significant worldwide expenditure growth are increased

---

[14]Stephan H. Haeckel, "Managing the Information-Intensive Firm of 2001," in Blattberg, Glazer, and Little, eds., *The Marketing Revolution*, pp. 346–47.

[15]Robert C. Blattberg and Rashi Glazer, "Marketing the Information Revolution," in Blattberg, Glazer, and Little, eds. pp. 24–29.

[16]Jack Honomichi, "The Top 50 Research Organizations," *Marketing News*, June 1997.

E X H I B I T   5 – 4

Steps in the Marketing Research Process and Potential Sources of Error

Steps	Potential error
1. Problem formulation	Management identifies the wrong problem or defines it poorly.
2. Determining information needs and data sources	Management fails to identify the specific information needed for decision making or the researcher uses the wrong source.
3. Research design, including questionnaire	Ambiguous questions or poor experimental designs result in invalid responses.
4. Sample design and size	Sample procedures result in the selection of a biased sample.
5. Data collection	Errors are caused by nonrespondents, by poor selection of respondents, by the interviewer, or by the nature of interviewer/respondent interaction.
6. Tabulation and analysis	Errors occur while transforming raw data from questionnaires into research findings.

global competition in products and services, research involved with the building of large data banks, customized studies concerned with consumer behavior, and consumer satisfaction.[17]

The American Marketing Association defines **marketing research** as "the function which links the consumer, customer, and public to the marketer through information—information used to identify and define marketing opportunities and problems; generate, refine, and evaluate marketing actions; monitor marketing performance; and improve understanding of marketing as a process." Thus, by definition marketing research is used to collect and structure the data contained in marketing database information systems. Most large firms have marketing research departments that undertake a variety of studies. Almost all large-size companies do research on their products and markets, including market potential, market share, sales analysis, and forecasting. Consumer companies do more research than industrial companies on new products, advertising, consumer behavior, and merchandising, while the latter do more on business trends, sales analysis, and ecology.

The scope for such research is much broader for firms involved in international marketing research because they are not only concerned with providing data about elements in the marketing plan (e.g., advertising, pricing, distribution), but also with general economic, social, and political information about one or more countries and their infrastructure. We discuss the difficulties of obtaining such data later in this chapter.

Regardless of the type and locale of the marketing research, it is essential that researchers follow the six steps in the research process in order to minimize the magnitude of overall error. A brief discussion of each of the major steps in the research process follows.[18] Exhibit 5-4 lists the steps and the potential sources of error for each.

---

[17]"Data Wars," *The Economist*, pp. 60–61.

[18]For a detailed discussion of research methods and their applicability to marketing problems, see Seymour Sudman and Edward Blair, *Marketing Research; A Problem Solving Approach* (Burr Ridge, Ill.: Irwin/McGraw Hill, 1997).

Problem formulation

In this step, researchers must obtain answers to the questions, "What is the purpose of this study?" and "What are the objectives of the research?" If these questions are not properly answered at the outset, the study is likely to be misdirected and pursue the wrong goals.

Determining information needs and data sources

Once the problem has been formulated, researchers should specify what information and sources they need. This helps determine the relative importance of alternative sources of information and enables the researcher to better structure the research design needed to obtain the desired reliability. Another advantage to this requirement is that it gives a manager insights into the kinds of information obtainable from the research undertaking. This in turn helps prevent unrealistic expectations on the manager's part because only rarely does research provide conclusive evidence leading to the right answer.

Data sources

For each piece of information specified, researchers should seek the most reliable source. Frequently, the best source is not available or cannot be interviewed—for instance, a report on how five-year-old children think and feel about a cereal product. All data derive from sources internal or external to the firm. *Internal data* are generated by departments such as marketing, accounting, and production in the course of their normal operating activities; they are particularly important in the compilation of sales and cost data.

External data consist of *primary* and *secondary* sources. Primary data are collected specifically for the problem at hand and require the firm itself to carry out the steps in the research process or to hire an outside agency to do so. Secondary data are collected by other organizations and usually are not tied directly to the firm's problem, but they have the advantage of saving time and money. However, the data must be compatible with the needs of the specific study even though they're often collected with a different objective in mind. Also, the data may not be current, the units of measurement may not meet the researcher's requirements, or the class intervals may be too broad. For example, the secondary data may use manufacturing establishments instead of companies, or report at 10-year intervals when a more narrowly defined time period is wanted.

Secondary sources include internally generated data, commercial research subscription firms, financial reports, periodicals, the Internet, and government publications. Researchers frequently find themselves swamped by the ever-increasing amounts of information available. The Internet, with its millions of pages of information about companies and their products from sources located all over the world, is rapidly becoming an important secondary source. Admittedly, researchers will find the Internet a crowded and complex environment in which to search for information pertinent to their subject, but its potential for generating useful information should not be ignored.

International differences in information services

There is a scarcity of secondary data in many countries, especially developing ones, and often what is available is out of date and poorly done. The availability and quality of a country's secondary data tend to correlate closely with its degree of economic development; for example, some countries have not taken a census in 25 years or more. Also, it is frequently difficult to compare data from different countries. For instance, wholesalers and retailers are defined in different ways across countries, and data may be available in such broad categories as to be useless. The United States generates by far the most economic and demographic data, although most industrialized countries do a good job.

After locating a possible secondary source, researchers must assess its reliability. They must answer the question, "How good are the data?" If the source specifies the data collection method used, it can serve as the basis for the evaluation. If it does not, researchers are forced to judge the quality of the research on other factors. These include the research sponsor (e.g., the federal government or a trade association), the purpose for which the study was made (e.g., was it self-serving?—the case with many media audience studies), and the methods of data collection (e.g., mail or personal interview).[19]

Research design

After the researcher has found the necessary information and specified the sources, the next step is to determine the research design. The two major research designs are **exploratory research**, which uses secondary data, case studies, and interviews with knowledgeable people, and **conclusive research**, which comprises descriptive and experimental studies.

Exploratory research

Researchers use exploratory research to learn more about the nature and scope of the problem and to investigate the more likely solutions. It is often a preliminary step which is followed by conclusive research that test the relevant findings. Flexibility is the key to the investigation; that is, the investigator is free to pursue ideas as they emerge in the investigation.

There are several ways of undertaking exploratory research. The easiest is to study pertinent secondary data, including reports from research organizations that furnish continuing data. Another is to do in-depth analyses of several cases consisting of organizations or key individuals. By making an intensive study of one or more pertinent organizations, researchers can more easily perceive relationships and understand the why behind them. For example, a company faced with problems in selling through distributors might study two or three cases of its best and poorest distributors to identify and understand their essential differences. Japanese managers frequently use this type of investigation and have done so with considerable success.

More and more large consumer goods firms use focus groups to explore a given subject area. A focus group consists of 6 to 12 consumers from the product or service target audience brought together to discuss a given topic. The discussion is designed to provide insights into some of the complex, subtle aspects of the interaction between consumers and a company's advertising and sales activities. Findings are essentially qualitative, not quantitative, and they characterize, for example, how consumers perceive and react to a company's product or advertising efforts. In recent years the use of focus groups has increased dramatically: nationwide about 2,300 focus group facilities exist and the number is growing. Some researchers see this trend as alarming since many users find focus groups as a relatively inexpensive way to get information about the consumer without understanding focus group limitations, which center in part on its sample size and its representativeness, data distortion caused by the presence of a dominant person, and

[19]Not even the U. S. Bureau of the Census data is immune to the problems of collecting reliable data. For example, the 1990 census failed to count approximately 5 million persons. See John Pierson, "Preparing for 2000, Census Bureau Tests Carrots to Sticks," *The Wall Street Journal*, May 2, 1996, p. B13.

EXHIBIT 5–5

Using Qualitative Research Methods to Learn about Consumer Behavior

> Many, if not most, consumers are unwilling or unable to provide researchers with insights into the whys of their behavior. Qualitative research often uses projective techniques to help overcome this problem. These involve the use of indirect stimuli which are based on the belief that respondents, in answering, will reveal more than if questioned directly. For example, when asked to imagine long-distance carriers as animals, group members described AT&T as a lion, MCI as a snake, and Sprint as a puma. This information was used to help develop an advertising campaign for one of these companies.
>
> Other projective methods include similar questions to the animal one above ("If brand X were a car, what would it be?"), word association ("What brand of detergent comes to your mind first when I mention soft and fluffy clothes?"), sentence completion ("*Fortune* magazine is most liked by . . . ?"), story completion in which respondents are presented with part of a story and asked to finish it, and pictorial devices such as cartoons in which two or more characters are shown in a particular situation and one of the balloons is left open and the respondent is asked to fill it in.

SOURCE: Rebecca Piirto Heath, "The Frontiers of Psychographics," *American Demographics*, July 1996, p. 42. Reprinted with permission © 1996 Cowles Business Media, Ithaca, New York.

---

the difficulty of interpreting the results.[20] See Exhibit 5-5 for a further discussion of qualitative research.

Conclusive research

Researchers use conclusive research to test alternative solutions to a problem. This type of research design can incorporate either descriptive studies or experimental research. **Descriptive studies**, often referred to as *survey research*, are the more commonly used design. Determining the demographic and attitudinal characteristics of heavy purchasers, occasional purchasers, and nonbuyers of a defined product class is one example. Determining the buying process and the role of buying influentials in the purchase of an industrial product is a second example.

Experimental studies have the advantage of permitting the researcher to show cause-and-effect relationships between the variables—something that can only be inferred from descriptive studies. In essence, this type of research design tests a given hypothesis—for example, a new package design that will increase sales—in a setting where all conditions are controlled except the relationship between the new package (the experimental variable) and sales (the dependent variable). Single-source data from Nielsen often enables companies to perform these causal analyses.

The experimental method has some serious disadvantages that limit its usefulness in marketing. First, most experiments can measure only immediate results because respondents typically will not cooperate over long periods of time. Also, experiments are expensive. Further, they use small samples that may not be representative of the national market, and they have difficulty holding all other variables constant. Finally, they can pose severe administrative problems (e.g., getting and maintaining cooperation of the subjects involved), and they can be audited by competitors.

---

[20]Rebecca Piirto Heath, "The Frontiers of Psychographics," *American Demographics*, July 1996, p. 42.

Sample design and size

The sample design determines how respondents are identified and selected. Along with sample size, the design has a strong impact on the cost of the study and the magnitude of error contained in the findings. In any sampling operation, the first problem is to *define the universe* (population) being studied. This is the group that contains all the items that the researcher wants to study—for example, all households in the continental United States. To make our definition of this universe operational, we would have to define *households* in a way by which interviewers could identify them while conducting the study.

A second problem is defining the variables or attributes being studied. Assume that a publisher of college textbooks wanted to determine how college and university faculty members rank the publisher compared with its competitors on attributes such as number of titles, unit sales, readability of its books, and the reputation of its authors. A number of variables here must be defined. For example, are junior colleges to be included under colleges and universities? And are lecturers considered faculty members or graduate assistants? Clearly, even a seemingly simple market study requires precise definitions of the variables.

A third problem is to choose the sample design—the method used to select the sampling units, such as faculty members in our example. Two alternative designs can be used: probability or nonprobability. **Probability sampling** ensures that every unit in the "universe" has a known probability of being selected and is the only method that enables the researcher to measure the reliability of the sample data.

Nonprobability sampling methods do not provide every unit in the universe with a known probability of being included in the sample. Thus, the results cannot be generalized with any degree of certainty to a larger population—the sampling universe. This selection process is not objective; a unit is included because the researcher thinks it should be, because it is convenient, or because a quota of units has been set (e.g., households with a certain total income, a specific race, or family size). But even the use of probability sample has its problems. Minorities and the poor are underrepresented in telephone and mall surveys, and it's becoming increasingly difficult to find respondents who will cooperate in any type of interviewing method. In the developing countries, the problems are more acute because up-to-date telephone and street directories, census tract data, and demographic information are typically unavailable, out of date, or inaccurate.

Data collection

Questioning

The two basic ways of collecting marketing research information are through questioning and observation. **Questioning** is the most common way. Researchers can use it to tackle almost any problem, and problems involving attitudes, knowledge, and buying intentions can be approached only through this method. Also, many behaviors cannot be observed because they do not happen on a planned basis. Imagine trying to observe how people take care of their cars throughout an entire year!

Unfortunately, collecting data through direct questioning has substantial disadvantages. Respondents often refuse to cooperate, they may be unable to remember the information wanted, or they may be biased by the interviewing process and not want to report things that reflect poorly on their intelligence or social position. For a brief discussion of data collection problems in international marketing research, see Exhibit 5-6.

Interviewers must ask whether a question means the same thing to Smith in California as it does to Jones in New York. And does a questionnaire mean the same when the

---

E X H I B I T   5 – 6

Data Collection Problems in Performing International Marketing Research

> Internationally, the researcher faces an array of response problems. Japanese culture favors courtesy, which makes for cooperative respondents, but respondents often say things simply to please the interviewer. In some cultures women are not allowed to talk to a stranger—nor are they permitted to serve as interviewers. Industrial marketing research is hampered in some countries by a desire for secrecy, as well as by the fear that the interviewer may be a tax agent. A respondent's inability, because of little or no education, to understand the questions or articulate answers further complicates data collection.

SOURCE: Vern Terpstra, *International Dimensions of Marketing* (Boston: Kent Publishing, 1988), chap. 4.

---

researcher wants to replicate a research project across different cultures (e.g., Germans versus Greeks?) Questionnaire construction is still more of an art than a science.

Whatever method is selected—telephone or personal interviews—an interviewer often selects the person to interview, asks questions, and records the answers—and errors can occur at each step. The growing concern with privacy in our society and the growing number of telephone and mail intrusions are causing more respondents to refuse to cooperate, thus adding a serious source of potential error because people who agree to participate in a study may not be representative of the population of interest.

Observation

The other method of collecting data is through observation, a process that recognizes and takes note of people, objects, and actions, rather than *asking* for information. While decidedly less popular than interviewing respondents, the use of observation has increased substantially through the development of the universal product code and scanning at supermarket checkout counters and in the home, which facilitates single-source research.

The Japanese rely heavily on observing how consumers behave in stores and, where applicable, how salespeople respond to this behavior. Researchers for Toyota Motor Corporation watched how prospective car buyers inspected cars in Cadillac, Mercedes, and BMW showrooms. They noted what parts of a car were examined, what questions were asked, and even how shoppers were dressed.[21]

A relatively new type of observation research uses the video camera. For example, in a study of the American shopper, a series of video cameras were placed strategically throughout a test store to determine the number of shoppers, the time spent shopping, the number of items shopped, the quantity purchased, the extent to which the store was penetrated, and the specifics of individual sales, including the interaction between the salesperson and the consumer. Such well-known U.S. consumer goods companies as Levi Strauss, McDonald's, Blockbuster, Apple Computer, and Starbucks have used video research to good advantage.[22]

---

[21]Kim Foltz, "New Species Is for Study: Consumers in Action, " *The New York Times*, December 18, 1989, p. D1.

[22]Malcolm Gladwell, "The Science of Shopping," *The New Yorker*, November 4, 1996, pp. 66–67.

Methods of questioning

Information can be gathered by questioning respondents by means of personal interviewers, the telephone, or mail. For years, most marketing research studies were conducted by interviewers in the respondent's home. This is no longer the case in the United States and Canada. Telephone and personal interviews at shopping malls now dominate because they are less expensive and appear to give satisfactory results. Personal interviews in the home, however, remain popular in Europe and in the developing countries.

Nearly half the surveys in the United States and Canada are conducted by telephone largely because, in addition to speed and cost considerations, almost all households have phones. This is largely true for parts of Europe, although considerable variation exists in telephone penetration across countries (e.g., Great Britain versus Portugal). Many households in the developing countries not only have no telephones, but the telephone directories are often hopelessly outdated.

Mail surveys in the developed countries have extremely low rates of return unless the audience is interested in the subject area or has a close tie with the source. In the developing countries, the problems of using mail surveys are substantial due to illiteracy, unreliable mail systems, and the inaccessibility of many respondents living in villages and rural areas.

With over 20 percent of U.S. households on-line—a figure that is growing rapidly—more companies are undertaking interactive marketing research using the World Wide Web. Given that computer users are better educated, more affluent, younger, and more apt to be early adopters than the rest of the population, a large number of companies are interested in reaching them. Most studies use a prerecruited panel of interactive consumers to do on-line surveys or focus interviews. The results are obtained quickly and at low cost. For surveys sample size has little effect on costs. Another advantage is that interactive research enables the use of three-dimensional graphics and virtual reality images for testing packaging designs, advertising, and product concepts.[23] Use of the Internet has reduced dramatically the time and cost of doing international research studies.

The data collection step probably contributes more to the overall data error than any other in the research process. Errors derive from nonresponse by some respondents; selection errors by the interviewer; the way the interviewer stimulates responses from the respondent, including wording of the questions; interpretation and recording of answers; and interviewer cheating. Using the telephone is the best way to control the sample, but even to complete 100 interviews in the United States with randomly selected telephone homes by way of random digit dialing can require several hundred telephone numbers and about 1,000 dialings.

Tabulation and analysis

When the fieldwork is finished, the completed data forms must be processed to yield the information the project was designed to collect. The forms are edited to ensure that the instructions were followed, that all questions were asked or observations made, and that the resulting data are logical and consistent within each form. For the tabulation and analysis function, researchers establish procedures to transform the raw data into the information needed. They must array the data in tabular form, compute percentages and averages, and

---

[23]Ian P. Murphy, "Interactive Research," *Marketing News*, January 20, 1997, p. 1; and Charlie Hamlin, "Market Research and the Wired Consumer," *Marketing News*, June 9, 1997, p. 6. See also, John B. Elmer, "Travel the High-Speed Road to Global Market Research," *Marketing News*, September 23, 1996.

make comparisons between different classes, categories, and groups. Some cases require sophisticated statistical analytical techniques. Researchers working in the international area must have an in-depth understanding of the culture of the marketplace.

COMPETITOR ANALYSIS

Competitor analysis of present and potential key rivals consists mainly of examining their characteristics, objectives, strategies, performance to date, and strengths and weaknesses to gain insights into their future behavior. Managers need to assess the likelihood that each firm will change its strategy in response to dissatisfaction with its present position, changes in the environment, or moves made by other competitors. The evaluation process also helps management better understand its own capabilities as well as a competitor's vulnerability, which can be an important source of opportunities.

Characteristics of the competitor

Managers are concerned with characteristics such as size of sales, profitability, market position or share growth, financial strengths, relation to parent company, domestic compared with foreign coverage, and specialization of their competitors. The trend of a competitor's relative strategic business unit (SBU) and product-market entry sales and market share are of particular interest because—along with profitability data—they reveal the success of a competitor's strategy. When growth (or loss) is substantial over the short term, these data also provide insights into the stresses to which the competitor's organization is being subjected.

Analyzing the financial strengths of key competitors helps evaluate their durability or staying power. This is an especially important characteristic during periods of turmoil and strong competitive pressures. Financial strengths can be assessed on the basis of profitability, margins, cost trends, price/earning ratios, and other performance measures; unfortunately, detailed data may not be available at the level of the SBU. Even so, knowing the financial condition of the parent company helps assess the likelihood of its being able to finance high growth or a period of intense competitive action—especially when the SBU is losing substantial sums.

Along somewhat similar lines, knowing the relation of the SBU to the parent company is particularly important. The unit's assigned role and the parent's performance expectations strongly influence its response profile. Thus, a large and highly successful parent that has assigned an important strategic role to an SBU is likely to respond strongly to any competitive actions it perceives as threatening. Certainly this is true with PepsiCo, which overall has enviable earnings records and expects strong performances from its snack food SBU.

Competitor's objectives

An analysis of a competitor's objectives is important for several reasons. It provides insights into whether the competitor is satisfied with its profitability and current market position and, thus, how likely the competitor is to retain its present strategy. It helps a firm predict how the competition will respond to changes in the environment and a particular strategic move made by a competitor.

Objectives usually include more than simply financial goals. Most also include competitive position (i.e., market share) and qualitative objectives, such as industry leadership in price, product technology, and social responsibility. Managers must know which trade-offs the company will make between these and its economic (i.e., profitability) objectives during times of stress. Some of the more important questions that a firm needs to ask at the business unit level follow:

1. What are the competitor's financial and market position objectives? How are trade-offs made between these objectives, especially short-term versus long-term?
2. What incentive and control systems does the competitive use? How do these affect the manager's response to competitive action?
3. What significant successes or failures has the competitor had recently? Will these affect future behavior? How?
4. Does the competitor have any commitments that may inhibit action? (Commitments may or may not be contractual, and include licensing, debt, and joint ventures.)
5. Does the competitor have any regulatory constraints on its behavior? (This constraint can be inferred, for example, when a large firm is reluctant to respond to the price moves made by a small competitor.)

In addition to the answers to these questions, the parent organization may directly or indirectly impose constraints on the behavior of its SBUs. Thus, the following questions need to be asked at the *corporate level* of the competitor: What are the objectives of the parent company, and how important is the SBU in helping attain these objectives? How successful has the parent been, and how does this affect its reaction to the performance of the SBU? What strategic value does the SBU have in the parent's overall strategy? What is the economic relationship between the SBU and other SBUs?—that is, to what extent do they involve shared costs or complementary products? Does the parent have any regulatory, antitrust, or other constraints outstanding and, if so, how will they affect the actions of the SBU?

Strategy of the competitor's

This component of competitor analysis reviews past and present strategies of each major competitor. Past strategies provide insights into failures and reveal how the firm engineered change, especially in new product-market relationships. Such historical information helps anticipate which elements of marketing mix strategy the competitor might emphasize in the future. Understanding the competitor's current elements of marketing mix strategy is important in assessing its strengths and weaknesses and leads to a better understanding of how the competition will react to opportunities and threats.

Evaluating the success of the competitor

The next step is to evaluate how successful the competitor has been in achieving its objectives and carrying out its strategies. Profitability measures may be difficult to come by when the competitor is part of a large corporate entity, and even more difficult where specific product-market entries are concerned. It is often possible, however, to obtain reliable estimates of sales and market share even at the segment level from a variety of sources including syndicated commercial service organizations such as Nielsen. When viewed especially on a trend basis, these data should give a good indication of how well the competitor is performing currently compared with its performance in prior years.

Another success indicator is the number of times the competitor has failed or succeeded in recent years. The memory of past successes or failures can affect a competitor's confidence for better or worse. In a similar vein, how has the competitor responded over the years to market and industry changes, including strategy moves made by other firms? Was there a response? How quickly? Was it a rational or emotional response? Was it effective?

Competitor's strength and weaknesses

Knowledge of strengths and weaknesses derives to a considerable extent from the previous steps in evaluating competitors. This information is important, especially when tied to the competitor's objectives and strategies. Any evaluation of strengths and weaknesses must take into account the relative importance of the elements of marketing mix strategy required to exploit the situation, Ideally, a firm would take advantage of a competitor's weakness using its own strength.

Competitor's future behavior

Thus far the analysis has had as its objective assessing the competitor's likely future behavior in terms of its objectives and strategies. To develop a response profile for each key competitor, analysts ask the following questions, the answers to which should help a firm decide which competitors to target within each major segment and which strategies to use.

1. How satisfied is the competitor with its current position?
2. How likely is the competitor to change its current strategy? What specific changes will it make in individual strategy elements?
3. How much weight will the competitor put behind such changes?
4. What will be the likely response of other competitors to these moves? How will they impact the competitor initiating the changes?
5. What opportunities does the competitor provide its close rivals? Will these opportunities endure for some time or will they close down shortly?
6. How effective will the competitor be in responding to environmental change, including moves made by competitors? Which events and moves can it respond to well and which poorly? For each event or move, what retaliatory action is most likely?

Obtaining information about competitors

To answer questions like those cited above requires a good deal of information, hereafter referred to as *intelligence,* about present and potential competitors—their past performances, current strategies, and future plans. Intelligence has become a management tool of considerable power, something that Japanese managers have long recognized.

A considerable amount of competitive intelligence can be obtained from public sources such as government and industry publications, press clippings, trade association reports, industry experts, annual reports and 10-K reports to the Securities and Exchange Commission and commercial research firms. In the aggregate it provides reasonably accurate intelligence about a competitor's sales, market share, financial resources, and strategy. As you have read, detailed information about many consumer products, especially packaged food and household items, is available from syndicated sources such as Nielsen. The Internet Global Computer systems make available hundreds of helpful data banks on a great many subjects.

One of the more common forms of competitive intelligence is *reverse engineering*, which involves taking a competitor's product apart in an effort to learn everything about it, including its costs. *Benchmarking* is a similar way to obtain information about competitors. It consists of taking a process or procedure (e.g., order processing), measuring its components in terms of time, cost, and quality, and comparing the results against those of another organization that is clearly managing the same procedure much better. The "other" organization may be a competitor, another department or SBU within the same firm, or a party outside the industry. For example, Xerox benchmarked L. L. Bean, a high-profile retailer with an enviable order fulfillment process. By copying parts of Bean's process, Xerox cut its own warehousing costs 10 percent.[24]

Data confidentiality[25]

Companies are finding it increasingly difficult to keep their highly confidential information—such as that relating to new products—out of the hands of their competitors. The Computer Security Institute in San Francisco estimated that over the past 10 years penetration from outside a firm's confidential files has increased substantially.

Personal computers are by far the biggest contributors to increased security problems. Companies have found it necessary to put their data storehouses on their computers because they have empowered their middle managers to solve problems which require the use of such data, but this access proliferation makes theft relatively easy, especially to insiders. Also, as company computers are increasingly linked to the Internet, theft from outside is made less difficult.

Keeping tabs on competitors—particularly trying to anticipate their future strategic moves and reactions—has become so important that many larger firms have created entire departments to collect and analyze corporate intelligence. They're also getting help from consultants and information vendors who specialize in this area. Some companies prefer to assign the task to specific individuals in their marketing research or corporate planning departments. In addition to collecting and analyzing information from secondary data and the firm's own marketing research studies, competitor intelligence units can obtain information by talking with a competitor's technical and management people at trade shows, companies that do business with competitors (e.g., wholesalers), and former employees of competitors. Sometimes a firm finds that by using a consulting firm, it is even possible to talk directly with present employees of competitors.

CUSTOMER SATISFACTION STUDIES

We have already noted the importance of customer retention to the firm; for example, improving a company's retention rate by 20 percent has the same effect on profits as reducing costs by 10 percent.[26] As products and services become more alike, the ability to satisfy the customer across a variety of activities—of which the product is only one—will become an even greater profit determinant. Measures relating to customer satisfaction as an

[24]Barsky, *World-Class Customer Satisfaction*, chap. 4.

[25]This section is based on information from Milo Geyelin, "Why Many Businesses Can't keep Their Secrets," *The Wall Street Journal*, November 20, 1995, p. B1. See also, Ernest Brode, "This Is the CEO—Get Me the CIA," *The Wall Street Journal*, November 14, 1995, p. A15.

[26]C. Power, "Smart Selling: How Companies Are Winning Over Today's Tougher Customer," *Business Week*, August 3, 1992, p. 46.

early warning of impending problems and as the basis for developing win-back programs are essential.[27]

A multiproduct firm may need customer satisfaction measures for each of its different products, even if they are sold to the same customer. This would be the case if the choice criteria varied substantially between products, especially in terms of expectations about service delivery, repairs, and availability of spare parts. Also, we should note that a firm needs to develop its own satisfaction measures with its various intermediaries (channel members) and major suppliers (advertising agencies).

Developing meaningful measures of customer satisfaction requires the merging of two kinds of measures. The first has to do with an understanding and measurement of the criteria used by customers to evaluate the quality of the firm's relationship with them. Knowing the product/service attributes that constitute the customer's choice criteria as well as the relative importance of each should facilitate this task. Once these attributes are identified, they serve as the basis for developing **expectation measures**. The second type of measurement is concerned with how well the firm is meeting the customer's expectations on individual attributes as well as on an overall basis. Thus, if the choice criteria of a cruise line's target market included attributes such as food, exercise facilities, and entertainment, then a performance measure would be developed for each.

Expectation measures

In most cases the individual attributes on which satisfaction expectations are based are multidimensional. Thus, it is necessary to obtain a measure for each dimension and then weight the results by their relative importance to get an overall measure. Unless this is done, it is impossible to understand the nature and scope of a consumer's expectancy ratings and to take corrective action. This is certainly the case with the cruise line attributes cited above—food (selection/choice, taste, size of portion), exercise facilities (availability/hours open, type of equipment, presence of instructors), and entertainment (availability, type, and participants).

It is difficult to develop *quantitative* expectation measures for some attributes. In those cases the customer can be asked to rate the firm's performance on a given attribute as less than, equal to, or better than the competition. Or the customer is asked to respond using, for example, a 10-point scale where under 5 is unsatisfactory (below expectations), 5-8 is satisfactory (equal to expectations), and 9-10 is considered more than satisfactory (above expectations). Some expectations cannot be met for economic reasons (e.g., 100 percent order fulfillment—no back orders). Then the company should study the process by which the customers derived their expectations. Is the salesperson making unreasonable promises? Is the customer knowledgeable about the causes of stockouts over which the company has no control? Is the customer aware of what substitutes are available for some stockouts? Is it possible the customer is using "unreasonable" expectations as a way of bargaining for certain concessions?

Performance measures

Performance measures gauge how well the company has met the customer's expectation on a given attribute (as well as its dimensions). Of course, overall performance measures are meaningless unless they are compared with the appropriate customer expectation measure.

---

[27]This is not to suggest that consumer complaints are no longer an important source of information about customer satisfaction. Some companies have set up 800-number hot lines to make it easier for consumers to complain to customer service representatives.

========= **E X H I B I T   5 – 7** =========

Olympic Machine: Measuring the Market

> The Olympic Machine Company, with annual sales of more than $400 million, produced turning machines★
> selling for $30,000 on up. A new sales manager noted the lack of information on the market potential of
> individual sales territories, thereby making it difficult to evaluate the performance of individual salespersons as
> well as competitors. Because replacement sales were a significant part of the market, the sales manager felt it
> essential to inventory installed machines by type, age, and manufacturer at the county level. The data could
> then be aggregated to provide information for individual sales territories.
>
> Using a variety of sources, the number of large and small plants, or prospects was determined by *county*.
> The company next measured the average inventory of installed machines by size of plant. It selected a
> probability sample from a list of companies maintained by Dun & Bradstreet and conducted a telephone
> interview with each. Only 6 percent of the respondents refused to cooperate. With a national average
> inventory for each large and small plant and the number of both large and small plants in each county, it was
> possible to project total inventories by type and age of machine by sales territory.

★These are machines which function like a lathe; in other words, they hold a piece of metal and rotate it against a tool that
shapes it.

The results can be negative when performance is less than expected, satisfactory when it is
at least as good as expected, and positive when performance is better than expected.

Performance measures come in a variety of forms. The two most common are *absolute
measures* (e.g., delivery time/number of stockouts) and *scaled measures*. Some companies
use a simple yes or no question such as "Was our delivery satisfactory?" or "Was our salesperson courteous?" Even if a company has factual data about its performance on a given
variable, it needs a customer's rating since, in the final analysis, this is the one that matters.
Where the perceived performance rating is less than the factual performance or considered
unreasonable, the firm should make every effort to change the customer's perception of the
situation.

MARKET POTENTIAL MEASUREMENTS

Market measurements are critical in determining which markets to target, what resources to
allocate to each, and whether the firm's sales performance in each is satisfactory. Exhibit 5-7
describes the research the Olympic Machine Company undertook to determine the attractiveness of its various markets. The firm used inventory data—past sales of turning
machines—as a measure of the sales potential for the machines in each of its sales territories.

Olympic Machine Company next determined market share (column 2 divided by
column 1 in Exhibit 5-8 in each territory. Column 3 in Exhibit 5-8 indicates the variation in
the company's performance (market share) by territory—ranging from 11 percent to 54
percent. When compared to the national average of 26 percent, the company clearly performed below average in territories 2, 3, and 9 while the remaining territories performed
at or above the average.

The number of units over or under the national average can be obtained by subtracting
the territory's share from the industry's average (26 percent) and then multiplying total
industry sales by this figure. For example, territory 2's share deficit is 10 share points (26
percent minus 16 percent) which is used to multiply total industry inventory of 2,545,
thereby yielding a shortage of 254 units. This figure could be made even more meaningful
if converted into sales and gross margin dollars.

E X H I B I T   5 – 8

Inventory of Turning Machines in Place and Olympic's Sales of Turning Machines
by Sales Territories

Market Share

Territory	Territory inventory	Olympic Sales	Sales as Percent of Territory Inventory
1	1,350	440	33%
2	2,545	405	16
3	430	44	11
4	350	99	29
5	822	309	38
6	711	186	27
7	597	207	35
8	3,881	996	26
9	845	193	23
10	179	98	54
Total	11,710	2,977	26%

We learn from the Olympic Machine Company example that data about the sales potential (i.e., attractiveness of different segments) can help in deciding which markets to target and also can serve as the basis for allocating the firm's resources across geographical areas, especially those concerned with salespeople and advertising. This type of analysis does not reveal the competitive structure of a market and the firm's ability to exploit it. For example, territory 2 may have a high potential for the firm, but the competition may be so firmly entrenched that the moneys required to improve the share would be better spent elsewhere. Actually, market responsiveness is a function of not only the potential but of the competitive structure, and the firm's inputs into the market.

To be effective, market potential data must be augmented with other information about the marketplace. For example, one firm obtains the following intelligence about each of its markets.

- Brands in the market and the brand share of each.
- Trend of each major brand's market share over the past several years.
- Amount of money spent by the major brands on advertising now and over the past several years.
- Price structure.
- Distribution structure with particular reference to the leading retail outlets and exclusive distribution franchises.
- Availability and cost of prime-time local station television time.

These data are then combined with the company's sales experience in the market and the data on market potential. The results form the basis for the firm's allocation of its sales resources across its various markets.

Industry sales

In the Olympic Machine Company example, cumulative industry sales were used as an indicator of the market potential for the company's product in each sales territory. Such data are rarely available at the sales territory level except from syndicated research services such as Nielsen or from a company's own marketing research, as was the case with Olympic. Aside from availability, the primary limitation in using industry sales data is its lack of currency. Changes underway in the industry's environment may not be revealed, yet these changes can shift demand and need to be taken into account.

Corollary data

When industry sales are unavailable, corollary data can be used. This method is based on the premise that if one series of data (e.g., industry sales) is closely related to a second series (e.g., number of persons employed), the distribution of the second series by market areas or sales territories can indicate the distribution of the first series in the same market areas.

Single-factor index.   The simplest corollary data method is the **single-factor index**. Researchers use it most successfully when the two items being analyzed have a derived or complementary demand, such as the number of industrial workers and the demand for paper toweling. Population and household income data are often used as single-factor indexes in lieu of corollary sales data. This method makes the assumption that such data explain the relative demand for a given consumer item. For example, if twice as many households are in area A as area B, then analysts reason that area A has twice the potential of area B.

The problem with the corollary data method is the difficulty of determining the degree of correlation between the related series and the sales of the product under investigation. Ideally, determining the fit would call for a comparison of the related series with industry sales. However, if industry sales were available for all areas, there would be no reason to worry about a related series. In addition, it is impossible to validate the usefulness of a related series by comparing it with company sales because the aim is to discover where company sales differ from potentials based on industry sales. For a few products, industry sales are available at the state level and can corroborate the merit of a related series. If the fit is good at the state level, it may be reasonable to assume that the related series is adequate to distribute the potential by lower geographic units.

Multiple-factor indexes.   **Multiple-factor indexes** are a combination of two or more factors to estimate relative market potentials. Individual companies can develop a multi-factor index for their own purposes, or they can use a general index such as the buying power index (BPI) published annually by *Sales and Marketing Management*, which is the best known index of consumer purchasing power in the United States. The BPI combines three factors: retail sales, income, and population, and assigns retail sales a weight of 3; income a weight of 5; and population a weight of 2. Analysts reduce these three factors to percentages of the U.S. total for each county, and weight each percentage. Then they divide the sum of the weighted potentials by 10 (the sum of the weights). The result provides an index of the potential for the county. For example, the buying power index for an area is determined as follows.

$$BPI = 3\,(R) + 5(I) + 2\,(P)$$

where

R = the percentage of total retail sales
I = the percentage of disposable income
P = the percentage of U. S. population.

A general index such as the BPI is not intended to measure the potential for any specific product; therefore, it must be used with care. For example, the BPI would be a poor index on which to base estimates of relative potential for winter clothing because temperature, a major determinant of demand, is not an index factor.

MARKETING-DECISION SUPPORT SYSTEMS (MDSSs)

The marketing-decision support system (MDSS) is a "coordinated collection of data, systems, tools, and techniques with supporting software and hardware by which an organization gathers and interprets relevant information from business and its environment and turns it into a basis for marketing action."[28] It is the final step in the development and use of marketing database information systems that contain—to a grater or lesser extent—the kinds of information discussed in this chapter. The MDSS represents the step through which value is added to the data by facilitating their use and analysis.

How MDSS works

Such a system permits the user to manipulate the data to conduct any desired analysis—from simply adding a set of numbers to a sophisticated statistical analysis. MDSS uses dialogue systems that permit managers to access and explore the databases, using models to generate reports for their specific needs. Managers can query the computer and, based on the answer, ask another question. This can be done at a workstation rather than by means of a computer printout. For example, a marketing manager who notes that sales are down in a given region can ask the computer whether sales for the product type are down; whether the company's brand is losing share and, if so, to which competitors; or whether the decline is confined to a specific type of retailer. Marketing offers considerable opportunities for the use of the MDSS because of its lack of structure in many decision-making situations.

MDSSs are highly flexible and action oriented. They enable managers to follow their instincts in solving a problem and to do so on-line. Serving the needs of different managers, MDSSs are interactive systems designed to facilitate decision making. They do so by providing access to relevant data and statistical models which increase the nature and scope of the manager's analysis.

An increasing number of software programs are available to help managers better plan and control their activities; for example, programs are available to help in segmenting markets, planning sales calls, determining media budgets, and setting prices. Such software is especially important in repetitive situations where management is interested in what would happen if the decision variables are changed (e.g., increasing the value of a coupon from 35 cents to 50 cents). To help in making these analyses, companies like Nielsen are providing subscribers easy access to their data.

The future of MDSSs

A number of reasons explain why some companies have not progressed further in developing more sophisticated systems. A major reason has to do with the risk involved in making a large investment, given the difficulty of estimating the return. A closely related

[28]John D. C. Little, "Decision Support Systems for Marketing Managers," *Journal of Marketing*, Summer 1979, p. 11.

problem is that the success of the marketing-decision support system depends heavily on the decision-making capabilities of the user—"The tools don't make decisions. If you put MDSS in the hands of lousy decision makers, you get lousy decisions."[29] Yet another factor inhibiting the adoption of MDSSs is the long-term nature of most strategic decisions; therefore, the decision maker may not know for several years whether the decision was correct. Further complicating the situation is that many factors beyond the decision maker's control typically influence the outcome. Not surprisingly, many marketers believe that the benefits derived from an MDSS lie more at the short-term operational level than at the strategic level.

Still, there is every reason to believe that an increasing number of companies will adopt more sophisticated MDSSs during the next decade. First, companies are increasingly empowering managers throughout the organization to make bigger, more complex decisions more quickly because of increased environmental dynamics. Thus, the MDSS becomes a critically needed resource, especially because it enables marketers to correlate large quantities of external data related to areas of sales and company decisions such as price and promotion as well as the salesforce. Also, marketing will become increasingly concerned with ever-smaller segments including single customers.

For managers who make decisions with customers at the global level, a MDSS that facilitates group decision making is a growing necessity. These systems enable a group of users in a conference room or in different locations to access and work simultaneously with the same data. Furthermore, interactive personal computer hardware—with greater storage capacity when coupled with a large number of workstations employing user-friendly software—will make MDSSs faster, less expensive, and more convenient. In addition, new software packages will be better able to determine the kinds of responses that can be obtained with particular kinds of inputs; for example, what level of awareness will result from advertising expenditures of X dollars.

ETHICAL ISSUES IN MARKETING INFORMATION SYSTEMS AND MARKETING RESEARCH

New technologies relating to the gathering and use of information about consumers and their behavior, interests, and intentions raise a host of legal and ethical questions. Obviously these new technologies have the potential to harm individuals when such information "is used without their knowledge and/or consent, leading them to be *excluded from* or *included* in activities in such a way that they are harmed economically, psychologically, or physically." Examples include the improper disclosure of a person's credit rating, denying medical insurance based on confidential information, and being placed on target lists for direct mail and telemarketing.[30]

Ethical issues in marketing research stem in large part from the interaction between the researcher and respondents, clients, and the general public. For instance, respondents should not be pressured to participate, should have the right to remain anonymous, and should not be deceived by fake sponsorship. Client issues are concerned with the confidentiality of the research findings and the obligation to strive in all ways to provide

---

[29]Tom Eisenhart, "Where's the Pay-Off?" *Business Marketing*, June 1990, p. 46.

[30]Paul N. Bloom, Robert Adler, and George R. Milne, "Identifying the Legal and Ethical Risks and Costs of Using New Information Technologies to Support Marketing Programs," in Blattberg, Glazer, and Little, eds., *The Marketing Revolution*, p. 294.

unbiased and honest results regardless of client expectations. The public is very much involved when they are exposed to a sales solicitation disguised as a marketing research study or from data obtained from "volunteer surveys" using write-ins or call-ins.

In discussing the reliability and ethical issues involved in marketing research studies, *The Wall Street Journal* noted that many studies "are little more than vehicles for pitching a product or opinion. An examination of hundreds of recent studies indicated that the business of research has become pervaded by bias and distortion."[31] More and more studies are being sponsored by companies or groups with a financial interest in the results. This too often leads to a bias in the way questions are asked.

Because of shortages in time and money, analysts are reducing sample sizes to the point that the margin of error becomes unacceptable when groups are further broken into subgroups, assuming a probability sample was used. In addition to sample size, the way a sampling universe is defined can bias the results. For example, a Chrysler study showing that people preferred its cars to Toyota's used a sample of only 100 respondents in each of two tests, and none owned a foreign car. Thus, they may well have been biased in favor of U. S. cars.[32]

In addition to the problems already noted, firms often use subjective sampling procedures that lead to flawed data analysis or report only the best conclusions. Frequently companies hire researchers whose views on the subject being researched are known to be similar to those of the client. To regulate the marketing research industry, several codes of conduct/ethics have been developed. These include published codes by the American Marketing Association, the American Association for Public Opinion Research, the Marketing Research Association, and the Council of American Survey Research Organizations.

SUMMARY

In recent years more companies have focused on the consumer to gain an advantage in the marketplace. This in turn has required greater knowledge about consumers. The technological revolution which enables vast amounts of data to be gathered, processed, transmitted, and stored has made possible the development of large marketing database information systems that facilitate better decisions on ways to service the consumer. This has benefited marketing research firms such as A. C. Nielsen in their efforts to provide clients with tracking data about their products and those of the competition. These data are commonly referred to as point-of-sale (POS) information and are collected by scanners or wands, that read and record the bar codes of the products purchased.

POS information systems are only one of several types of marketing information systems. Others include those used in direct marketing, prospecting, retention of customer, and winning back lost customers. The information systems used to support these programs can be generated through the use of internal data, external data, or some combination of the two.

Most large companies have their own marketing research departments, and almost all companies do research on products and markets. These and other kinds of research information are collected using a six-step process: (1) formulating the problem (2) determining

---

[31]Cynthia Crossen, "Studies Galore Support Products and Positions, But Are They Reliable?" *The Wall Street Journal*, November 14, 1991, pp. A1, A8.

[32]Ibid., p. A8.

information needs and data sources, (3) specifying the research design, including preparation of the questionnaire, (4) determining the sample design and sample size, (5) collecting data, and (6) performing the tabulation and analysis.

Marketing research is used to collect many different kinds of information, including those concerned with competition, customer satisfaction, and market potentials. The primary use of market potentials lies in the allocation of marketing resources (especially for the salesforce and advertising) across geographical areas. Marketing potentials do not, however, reveal the competitive structure of a market and the firm's ability to exploit it. Some problems inherent in the measurement of market potentials can be alleviated by using relative measures which can be obtained by using the direct data method or the corollary data method. The latter uses multiple factors to estimate the relative value of each segment.

Marketing decision support systems (MDSSs) are integrated collections of data, systems, tools, and techniques with supporting software and hardware that permit the user to manipulate the data to conduct any analysis desired. Managers can query the computer and, based on the answer, ask a follow-up question. While MDSSs have been used primarily by large companies, they are being designed in ways that encourage their use by smaller companies. As more managers are empowered to make decisions, their use—especially in undertaking causal analyses—will spread.

The development of marketing information systems raises many legal and ethical questions because of their potential to harm individuals. Ethical issues in marketing research derive from pressuring respondents to participate, misrepresenting the purpose of the research and its sponsorship, and failure to respect the confidentiality of the information obtained. Researchers should strive to provide unbiased and honest results, including the use of reliable research methods.

6 CHAPTER

Industry Dynamics and Strategic Change

REMARKABLE GROWTH IN THE CREDIT CARD BUSINESS[1]

Given the robust nature of the U.S. economy in recent years it is hardly surprising that financial services companies have experienced strong profit growth. This has been especially the case with credit card operators who have witnessed a substantial increase in the use of general purchase cards at the expense of cash and checks—from 11 percent of all transactions in 1980 to 17 percent in 1995. The era of the credit card has indeed arrived!

A number of reasons explain why the use of such cards has increased, not the least of which are their convenience (in both spending and borrowing) and relative safety (compared with cash). Other reasons include their increased acceptance by retailers, their expanded use in purchasing (and financing) more expensive products (durables) and services (travel and

medical), technology that has made credit card transactions cheaper and faster, and a passive banking industry which for the most part chose not to compete against financial services companies.

Strong marketing efforts, including large advertising expenditures, by credit card companies have also contributed to the increased use of cards. Issuers have been highly competitive in their drive for new customers through the use of low introductory interest charges, charging no annual fees, free balance transfers from another credit card issuer charging higher rates, and offering reward programs that include, for example, the awarding of points that can be redeemed for various goods and services, including free airfares. Some card issuers have added volume by cobranding with major

[1]Stephen Biggar, "Financial Services: Diversified," *Standard & Poor's Industry Surveys,* February 20, 1997; Alan P. Murray, "Debt and 'the' Consumer," *The Journal of the National Association of Business Economics,* April 1997, p. 41; Laurie Hays, "Banks' Marketing Blitz Yields Rash of Defaults," *The Wall Street Journal,* September 25, 1996, p. B1; and "The Cutting Edge," *The Economist,* July 26, 1996, p. 63; and "Debit Cards: Way to Pay," *The Economist,* October 4, 1997, p. 80.

retailers which benefit from a larger sales base financed by a reputable third party. During 1994 and 1995 Americans were deluged by 5 billion direct mail credit card solicitations—the equivalent of 32 invitations for each citizen between 18 and 64 years old.

Card companies are increasingly segmenting their markets and developing special products for them. To accommodate different spending habits, for example, they have issued both gold and platinum cards which permit larger spending limits and outstanding balances. American Express, one of the largest credit card companies, maintains a profile of 450 attributes, including demographics and purchasing patterns, on every cardholder. This information is used to design card enhancements for specific segments such as extra travel insurance for senior citizens. Card companies have also developed affinity cards with organizations such as colleges, fraternities, and professional groups (e.g., doctors and lawyers). Card members use these cards to demonstrate support for the organization involved, which receives a small percentage of the revenue generated.

Despite a favorable economic environment, rising bankruptcies over the past several years have plagued the industry. Bankruptcy filings have increased by about 25 percent since 1990—over one

million are expected for 1997. In 1997 Standard and Poor's reported that bad debts associated with credit cards jumped 78 percent over the **past two years**. If interest rates were to increase only modestly or if the economy was to go into a recession, loan defaults would move up substantially. Among the reasons attributed to the increased number of bankruptcies are the ease with which consumers can file for bankruptcy. Other industry observers, however, blame the industry for encouraging consumers to overspend by making too much credit easily available to consumers with too few financial resources and poor credit histories.

In the past several years the debit card which electronically transfers money from the cardholder's bank account rather than provide credit has proved increasingly popular; in 1996 debit cards in use increased by 53 percent to 61.5 million. Some industry observers think it may overtake the credit card as it has in Great Britain. Banks are particularly anxious to promote the debit card because profits are declining in the crowded credit card market. Banks can charge a retailer 2 percent of the value of the transaction whereas they receive nothing from a cash sale. Processing costs are half that of a check.

STRATEGIC VALUE OF PRODUCT-MARKET EVOLUTION

As illustrated by the credit card component of the financial services industry, products or services and markets are constantly evolving. On the product side, the growing commonality of technology and market knowledge increases the difficulty of maintaining strong product differentiation. Over time, costs per unit tend to decline because of scale and learning effects leading to lower prices, "more for your dollar," or both. On the market side, demand eventually slows, and consumers become more knowledgeable about the product, forming attitudes about the attractiveness of competing brands. And over time, industry structure and rivalry between established companies change as the rapid expansion in the number of different credit cards issued illustrates. Other sectors of the financial services industry have experienced consolidation as the decrease in the number of banking institutions by nearly 40 percent shows.[2]

These evolutionary forces interact to affect not only a market's attractiveness but also the success requirements for a firm's various product-market entries. The management implications of this evolutionary process are as follows:

At the *corporate* and *business unit levels* the firm must generate new products or enter new markets to sustain its profitability over time. Certainly this has been the case with credit card companies. It has also been the case in the beer industry, where overall demand is down, but the sales of micro brews have experienced an average annual growth of 40 percent over the past 10 years. The younger generation finds micro beers particularly attractive.[3]

At the *product level* objectives and strategy change as the product passes through various evolutionary stages as witness the emphasis placed on debit cards by banks. Another example is the PC consumer market which is growing at a slower pace and, according to one industry analyst, will take outsiders with consumer electronics experience to push the market into a new orbit. This may be about to happen since five large Japanese electronics companies (Fuijiton, Hitachi, NEC, Sony, and Toshiba) are targeting the nearly $50 billion U.S. PC market. They view the PC as the pivotal product in the digital age. Sony is offering products with exceptionally high quality audio and video capabilities which are designed to serve as the anchor for an entire household line of electronic products. Toshiba has a product which is a valid PC/TV while others are launching simple and inexpensive units that let consumers surf the Internet on their TV screens.[4]

At the *marketing program level* the evolutionary process typically generates significant changes. For example, as competition heated up in the credit card industry, companies turned to an array of imaginative incentives to gain and hold customers. They also launched unique products such as affinity cards and those which are cobranded with major retailers.

Anticipating change is a very difficult undertaking and requires a systematic framework to help managers better understand the product-market evolutionary process. This is especially the case as more and more markets become internationalized. In this chapter we first discuss the product life cycle, which is a generalized model of the sales history of a given product over a long time. It then discusses the major components of the evolutionary process—the market, the product, and the competitive environment—in an effort to provide a better understanding of the forces at work.

DEFINING PRODUCTS AND MARKETS: THE UNITS OF ANALYSIS

Specifying a framework for understanding product-market evolution—including the product life cycle concept—requires understanding what is meant by a product and a market. This task is made difficult since products and markets can be linked in a variety of ways. For example, Gillette, which has long employed the strategy of introducing its new products in the United States and marketing its older products overseas, several year ago introduced its Sensor Razor in the United States while continuing to market its Platinum

---

[2]In almost all major U.S. industries, the number of major companies is declining. See Michael J. Mandel, Alison Rea, and Cathering Yang, "A Pack of 800 Lb. Gorillas," *Business Week*, February 3, 1997, p. 34.

[3]John Student, "True Brew" *American Demographics*, May 1995, p. 32.

[4]David Kirkpatrick, "Your Next PC May Be Japanese," *Fortune,* October 28, 1996, P. 141.

Plus blade, which was first sold in the United States in 1967, in Pakistan.[5] Some credit card companies market a number of product-market entries consisting of a range of cards targeted at a number of market segments, both in the United States and overseas.

Product definitions

Products can be defined at the industry, product class, product type, and brand level. The problem with using the **industry level** is that it typically includes an array of noncompeting products. For example, are credit cards in the financial services industry in competition with life insurance and mutual funds? In the automotive industry, is a Honda Civic in competition with a BMW? Within the chemical industry, do polymers that substitute for natural materials compete with gasoline additives, dye stuffs, and industrial coatings?

Product class suffers from this same type of problem because the products involved may serve diverse markets; for example, all-purpose credit cards, affinity cards, cobranded cards, and debit cards compete with one another. The more generic the definition of a product class, the higher the aggregation level of products and the more stable the product life-cycle curve. Basic needs change slowly, and the effect of substitution, or *cross elasticity*, is lessened by the level of aggregation used; further, the more the product class is defined by generic need, the less useful it is for strategic planning, which seeks to identify opportunities and threats for specific product-market relationships.

Product types are subsets of a product class and contain items that are technically the same, although they may vary in such aspects as appearance and price. The level assigned to the product component of a product-market life-cycle analysis depends on the breadth of the product-class definition. In the case of credit cards, for example, product types would include regular versus gold versus platinum cards, cobranded cards, affinity cards, and debit cards. For cereals, the product types could be defined as hot or cold (ready-to-eat) cereals. Hot cereals would include at least two subtypes: regular and instant. Cold cereals would include regular, presweetened, natural, and nutritional. Regular could be broken down into such categories as corn flakes, raisin bran and shredded wheat. Other examples of product hierarchies abound, especially when different processing technologies are involved—frozen, canned, fresh, dehydrated, and freeze-dry fruits and vegetables. We have selected the product-type level as our unit of analysis because, while serving different subsets of needs, they are typically close substitutes for one another. The product-type level of aggregation is considerably more sensitive than the other levels to environmental changes that lead to opportunities and threats for individual product-market entries.

Brands, which are at the bottom of the aggregation hierarchy, are also inappropriate units of analysis. Their sales are largely a function of management's strategic decisions, marketing expenditures, and competitive action.

Market definitions

A *market hierarchy* is also a complex one to define because there are numerous ways markets can be arranged. Although firms differ in the levels they target, the trend is toward greater specificity; that is, to target more precisely defined segments at the lower levels in the hierarchy (see Exhibit 6-1). Many smaller firms compete effectively in the credit card business by targeting specific demographic areas, types of retailing, or niche segments that

---

[5]Eric D. Randall, "Gillette Strategy Rides Cutting Edge," *USA Today,* September 16, 1992, p. 3B.

EXHIBIT 6-1

Illustration of a Market Hierarchy for A Consumer Product

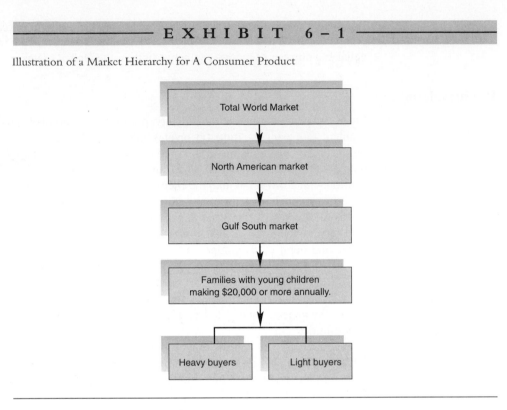

---

are fragmented or ignored by the big players. Several year ago, Johnson & Johnson targeted children aged two to six years old with a special line of Winnie-the-Pooh shampoo products that include Pooh's shampoo, Eeyore's conditioning detangler, Tigger bath bubbles, and Piglet liquid bath. The company uses a thicker formula in the new products than that used in its baby products, and the Winnie-the-Pooh line has a new fruity fragrance.[6]

Like the product hierarchy, product life-cycle curves vary depending on which market level is the basis for defining the target market—the higher the level of aggregation, the more apt the curve is to change slowly.

The product life cycle: an overview

The product life cycle is concerned with the sales history of a product or service. The concept holds that a product's sales change predictably over time and that products go through a series of five distinct stages: introduction, growth, shakeout, maturity, and decline (see Exhibit 6-2). Each of these stages provides distinct opportunities and threats, thereby affecting the firm's strategy as well as its marketing programs. While many new products do not follow this prescribed route because of failure, the concept is extremely valuable in helping management look into the future and better anticipate what changes will need to be made in their strategic marketing programs.

---

[6]Jennifer Lawrence and Pat Sloan, "P&G Heads Shampoo into Preteen Segment with Pert Line Extension," *Advertising Age,* April 26, 1992, p. 3.

═════════════ E X H I B I T 6 – 2 ═════════════

Generalized Product Life Cycle

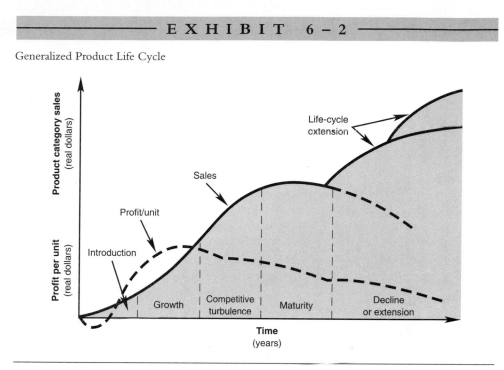

SOURCE: Reprinted by permission from p. 60 of *Analysis for Strategic Marketing Decisions,* by George Day. Copyright © 1986 by West Publishing Company. All rights reserved.

At the beginning (the **introductory stage**), a new product's purchase is limited because members of the target market are insufficiently aware of its existence; further, the product often lacks easy availability. As more people learn about the product and it becomes more readily available, sales increase at a progressively faster rate (the **growth stage**). Growth slows as the number of buyers nears the maximum and repeat sales become increasingly more important than trial sales. As the number of both buyers and their purchases stabilizes, growth becomes largely a function of population growth in the target market. At the end of the growth period—just before the advent of maturity—the **shakeout** or **competitive turbulence** stage occurs. This is characterized by a decreasing growth rate that results in strong price competition, forcing many firms to leave the industry or sell out. The **mature stage** is reached when the net adoption rate holds steady; that is, when adopters approximate dropouts. When the latter begin to exceed new first-time users, the sales rate declines and the product is said to have reached its final or **decline stage.**[7]

Life-cycle curves

Many products do not go through the product life-cycle curve shown in Exhibit 6-2 because a high percentage are aborted after an unsatisfactory introductory period. Other products seem to never die (Scotch whiskey, consumer lending, TVs, automobiles). The

---

[7]For a discussion of the application of the life-cycle concept to almost anything besides products (e.g., the fall of the Berlin Wall, the unification of Europe, and the demise of communism), see Theodore Modes, "Life Cycles," *The Futurist,* September–October, 1994, p. 20.

===== E X H I B I T   6 – 3 =====

More–Common Product Life–Cycle Curves

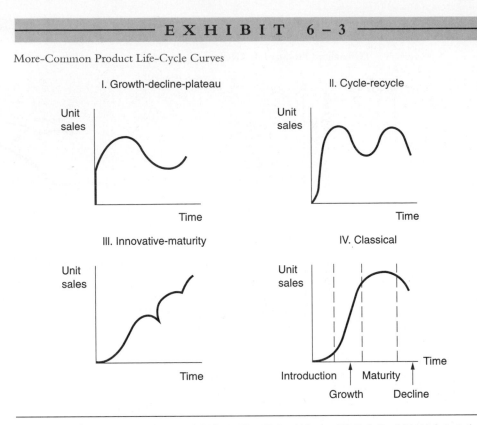

SOURCE: Adopted from J.E. Swan and D.R. Rink, "Effective Use of Industrial Product Life Cycle Trends," in *Marketing in the '80s* (New York: American Marketing Association, 1980), pp. 198–99.

shape of the life-cycle curve varies considerably between and within industries, but is typically described as S-shaped; one study even identified 12 different types of curves.[8]

In general, only one or a very few curves typify an industry (see Exhibit 6-3). The growth-decline plateau is probably the most common because a majority of products are in their mature stage (e.g., most household appliances). This is followed by the cycle/recycle type, which is characteristic of many pharmaceutical products that receive heavy promotions at the outset and again when sales begin to falter. The innovative-maturity curve goes through more than one life cycle because new innovative characteristics as well as new uses are discovered; this is the case with the debit card. A classic illustration of a situation involving several life-cycles is 3M's Scotch tape which initially expanded to a line of colored and patterned items for gift wrapping. Next, 3M added a low-price commercial line followed by a coated type to compete with reflective tape. All of these tapes are still doing very well.[9] The classic S-shaped curve only occurs when the product passes through all stages to its death (e.g., steam engines and many prescription drugs).

---

[8]J.E. Swann and D.R. Rink, "Effective Use of Industrial Life Cycle Trends," in *Marketing in the '80s* (New York: American Marketing Association, 1908), pp. 198–99.

[9]Theodore Levitt, "Exploit the Life Cycle," *Harvard Business Review,* November–December 1963, p. 93.

E X H I B I T   6 – 4

Expected Characteristics and Responses by Major Life-Cycle Stages

Stages in Product Life Cycle

Stage characteristics	Introduction	Growth	Shakeout	Mature	Decline
Market growth rate (constant dollars)	Moderate	High	Leveling off	Insignificant	Negative
Technical change in product design	High	Moderate	Limited	Limited	Limited
Segments	Few	Few to many	Few to many	Few to many	Few
Competitors	Small	Large	Decreasing	Limited	Few
Profitability	Negative	Large	Low	Large for high market-share holders	Low
Firm's normative responses					
Strategic marketing objectives	Stimulate primary demand	Build share	Build share	Hold share	Harvest
Product	Quality improvement	Continue quality improvement	Rationalize	Concentrate on features	No change
Product line	Narrow	Broad	Rationalize	Hold length of line	Reduce length of line
Price	Skimming versus penetration	Reduce	Reduce	Hold or reduce selectively	Reduce
Channels	Selective	Intensive	Intensive	Intensive	Selective
Communications	High	High	High	High to declining	Reduce

Fads—such as troll dolls, pet rocks, and hula hoops—enter suddenly, experience strong and quick enthusiasm, peak early, and enter the decline stage shortly thereafter. Thus, even when successful, the life cycle of fads is unusually short and is typically depicted in the form of an inverted V.[10]

CHARACTERISTICS AND IMPLICATIONS OF PRODUCT LIFE-CYCLE STAGES

The stages of the product life cycle present different opportunities and threats to the firm. By understanding the characteristics of the major stages, a firm can do a better job of setting forth its objectives, formulating its strategies, and developing its action plans (see Exhibit 6-4.) Our discussion here is generalized because we present in later chapters a more comprehensive examination of specific marketing strategy programs and do so for both leaders and followers.

[10]For a discussion of fads and trends, see Martin G. Letscher, "How to Tell Fads from Trends," *American Demographics*, December 1994, p. 38.

Introductory stage

There is a vast difference between pioneering a product class and a product type. The former is more difficult, time-consuming, expensive, and risky, as must have been the case when the telephone was introduced compared with the introduction of the cellular phone or when the credit card was introduced compared with the introduction of the debit card. The introductory period, in particular, is apt to be long—even for relatively simple product classes such as packaged food products. Because product type and subtype entries usually emerge during the late-growth and maturity stages of the product class, they have shorter introductory and growth periods. Once the product is launched, the firm's goal should be to move it through the introductory stage as quickly as possible. Research, engineering, and manufacturing capacity are critical to ensure the availability of quality products. Where service as part of the product is important, the firm must be able to provide it promptly as in postpurchase service and spare-parts availability. For services, trained personnel—especially those who interface with the customer—are critical. The length of the product line should be relatively short to reduce production costs and hold down inventories.

For sophisticated industrial products, the initial market consists mainly of large companies with enough resources to risk adoption, the technical capabilities to objectively evaluate the merits of the new product, and the most to gain if it works out well. To encourage trial and repeat buying, marketers of consumer products use a combination of methods, including heavy demonstration-oriented TV advertising, in-store displays, free samples, coupons, and special introductory prices. A firm also must obtain distribution and ample shelf space to provide product availability—particularly in self-service outlets such as supermarkets.

Marketing mix

The firm's pricing is strongly affected by a variety of factors: the product's value to the end user; how quickly it can be imitated by competitors; the presence of close substitutes; and the effect of price on volume (elasticity) and, in turn, on costs. Basic strategy choices involve skimming and penetration. **Skimming** is designed to obtain as much margin per unit as possible. This enables a company to recover its new product investments more quickly. The skimming strategy is particularly appropriate in niche markets and where consumers are relatively insensitive to price, as was the case in the sale of cellular phones to business executives early in the product life cycle. **Penetration pricing** enables a firm to strive for quick market development and makes sense when there is a steep experience curve (which lowers costs), a large market, and strong potential competition.

The importance of **distribution** and channel intermediaries varies substantially from consumer to industrial goods. The latter are often sold direct, but with few exceptions consumer goods use one or more channel intermediaries. Product availability is particularly important with consumer goods because of the large amount spent on promotion to make consumers aware of the product and to induce usage. Distribution is easier if the company uses the same channels for its other products and has a successful track record with new product introductions.

During the introductory period, promotion expenditures involving advertising and the salesforce are a high percentage of sales, especially for a mass market, small-value type product. For industrial goods, personal selling costs are apt to be much higher than advertising costs.

The communications task at the outset is to build awareness of the new product's uniqueness, which is typically an expensive undertaking. Further, the promotional expenditures (e.g., in-store displays, premiums, coupons, samples, and off-list pricing) required to obtain product availability and trial are substantial. For industrial products, the time required to develop awareness of the product's uniqueness is often extensive because of the number of people in the buying center and the complexity of the buying systems.

Growth stage

This stage starts with a sharp increase in sales. Important product improvements continue in the growth stage, but at a slower rate. Increased brand differentiation occurs primarily in product features. The product line expands to attract new segments. It does so by offering many price levels and different product features. During the latter part of the growth stage, the firm—especially the dominant one—makes every effort to extend the growth stage by adding new segments, lowering costs, improving product quality, adding new features, and trying to increase product usage among present users.

Marketing mix changes

Prices tend to decline during the growth period; for example, the average cost of processing credit card transactions has been dropping substantially each year. In general, the extent of the decline depends on cost-volume relationships, industry concentration, and the volatility of raw material costs. If growth is so strong that it outpaces supply, there is little or no pressure on price; indeed, it may enable sellers to charge premium prices.

During the growth stage, sellers of both industrial and consumer goods strive to build a channel or a direct-sales system that provides maximum product availability and service at the lowest cost. If this can be accomplished, rivals are placed at a disadvantage, even to the extent of being excluded from some markets. This is particularly true of some industrial goods where the number of intermediaries in any one market is limited. A brand must attain some degree of distribution success in advance of the mature stage, because channel members otherwise tend to disinvest in less-successful brands.

Promotion costs (advertising and personal selling) become more concerned with building demand for a company's brand (selective demand) than demand for the product class or type (primary demand). Firms strive to build favorable attitudes toward their brand on the basis of its unique features. Communications are also used to cultivate new segments. Even though promotion costs remain high, they typically decline as a percentage of sales.

Shakeout period

The advent of this period is signaled by a drop in the overall growth rate and is typically marked by substantial price cuts. As weaker competitors exit the market, the stronger firms gain market share. Thus, major changes in the industry's competitive structure occur. In the credit card industry, the market seems to have reached saturation. Over half of all households with an annual income of less than $10,000 have cards—double what it was a few year ago. Issuers are reporting declining incomes and losses; for example, the Bank of New York announced a $350 million addition to its loan loss reserves, earmarked specifically for its credit card portfolio, and both Advanta (a bank specializing in credit cards) and First Chicago have warned that credit card income is falling.[11]

Marketing mix changes

In addition to entering into more direct price competition, firms make every effort to maintain and—if possible, enhance their distribution system. Channel intermediaries use this downturn in industry sales to reduce the number of products carried and, hence, their inventories. Weaker competitors often have to offer their intermediaries substantial

---

[11]See "The Cutting Edge," *The Economist,* July 27, 1996, p. 63; "The Trouble with Credit Cards," *Fortune,* May 26, 1997, p. 28; and Laurel Hayes, "Banks Marketing Blitz Yields Rash of Defaults," *The Wall Street Journal,* September 25, 1996, p. B8.

E X H I B I T   6 – 5

What the Bicycle Industry Needs Is Innovation

> In the early 1980s mountain bikes gave the bicycle industry a much needed boost in sales. But the demand for such bikes has peaked and most firms in the industry are experiencing flat or declining sales. Clearly what the industry needs, and is attempting to do, is reinvent the bike. An attempt to do so via the use of a battery-powered motor to propel the bike failed, but one entrepreneur is working on a foldable bike which weighs less than 3.5 lbs.

Source: "Reinventing the Bicycle," *The Economist,* November 18, 1995, p. 76.

---

inducements to continue stocking all or even part of their line. Promotion costs may increase, particularly for low-share firms, as companies attempt to maintain their distribution by offering buying incentives to consumers. This is particularly the case for sellers of consumer goods.

Mature stage

When sales plateau, the product enters the mature stage, which typically lasts for some time. Most products now on the market are in the mature stage. Stability in terms of demand, technology, and competition characterizes maturity. Strong market leaders, because of lower per unit costs and the lack of any need to expand their facilities, should enjoy strong profits and high positive cash flows. But there is always the possibility of changes in the marketplace, the product, the channels of distribution, the production processes, and the nature and scope of competition. The longer the mature stage lasts, the greater the possibility of change. If a firm does not respond successfully to a major change, it faces a serious problem which may take a long time and considerable resources to solve.

Marketing mix changes

Because of technical maturity, the various brands in the marketplace become more similar; therefore, any significant breakthroughs by R&D or engineering that help to differentiate the **product** or redirect its cost can have a substantial payout (see Exhibit 6-5). One option is to add value to the product that benefits the customer: by improving the ease of use (voice-activated dialing with cellular phones), incorporating labor-saving features, or selling systems rather than single products (adding extended service contracts). American Express has added value by designing card enhancements such as limousine pickup at airports for its platinum cardholders. Increasingly, service becomes a way of differentiating the offering—how long does it take to replace a lost credit card? Promotion expenditures and prices tend to remain stable during the mature stage. But the nature of the former is apt to change; media advertising for consumer goods declines and in-store promotions, including price deals, increase. The price premium attainable by the high-quality producer tends to erode. The effect of experience on costs and prices becomes less. Competition may force prices down, especially when the two leading competitors hold similar shares. For consumer goods, distribution and in-store displays (shelf facings) and effective cost management, become increasingly important.

━━━━━━━━━━━━━━━ E X H I B I T   6 – 6 ━━━━━━━━━━━━━━━

GM Sinks Its Big Boats

General Motors recently announced plans to stop producing its Chevrolet Caprice Classic—a large, rear-wheel drive car that has long been the favorite of police departments and taxis—and its gargantuan Cadillac Fleetwood which is the model of choice for stretch limos and hearses. The factory where all three cars are built will be used to assemble a more trendy line of cars and pickup trucks. In dropping this trio, GM turns their markets over to Ford who had been considering abandoning its big rear-wheel drive Crown Victoria, but who no doubt will reconsider its decision. Not everyone at GM agrees with the company's decision. Some want to continue these models "as is" while others argue for small volume production even if it requires an outside contractor.

SOURCE: Gabriella Stern and Neal Timplin, "GM Turns Away From Cop-car, Limo Markets," *The Wall Street Journal*, May 16, 1995, p. B1. Reprinted with permission of *The Wall Street Journal*, © 1995 Dow Jones & Company, Inc. All rights reserved worldwide.

Decline stage

Eventually most products enter the decline stage which may be gradual (e.g., canned vegetables/hot cereals) or extremely fast (e.g., some prescription drugs). The sales pattern may be one of decline and then petrification as a small residual segment still clings to the use of the product (e.g., tooth powder versus toothpaste). Products enter this stage primarily because of technologically superior substitutes (e.g., jet engines over piston engines) and a shift in consumer tastes, values, and beliefs (e.g., cholesterol-free margarine over butter).

As sales decline, costs increase, and radical efforts are needed to reduce costs and the asset base. Even so, if exit barriers are low, many firms vacate the market, which increases the sales of remaining firms, thereby delaying their exit (see Exhibit 6-6). Stronger firms may even prosper for a time. If the curve is a steep decline followed by a plateau, then some firms can adjust. If the firm is strong in some segments vacated by its competitors, then it may experience a sufficient increase in market share to compensate for loss of sales elsewhere.

Marketing mix changes

Marketing expenditures, especially those associated with *promotion*, usually decrease as a percentage of sales in the decline stage. Prices tend to remain stable if the rate of decline is slow, there are some enduring profitable segments and low exit barriers, customers are weak and fragmented, and there are few single-product competitors. Conversely, aggressive pricing is apt to occur when decline is fast and erratic, there are no strong unique segments, there are high exit barriers a number of large single-product competitors are present, and customers have strong bargaining power. For consumer goods, marketing activity centers on distribution—persuading intermediaries to continue to stock the item even though they may not promote it. For industrial products the problem may center around maintaining the interest of the salesforce in selling the item.

Harvesting or withdrawal has as its objective an increase in cash flow which can be accomplished by milking (i.e., making only the essential investments), internal transfer of assets, and sale of the business or its assets. In any milking operation, management looks for ways to reduce assets, costs, and the number of items in the product line.

─── **E X H I B I T   6 – 7** ───

Relationship of Strategic Market Position Objective, Investment Levels, Profits, and Cash Flow to Individual Stages in the Product Life Cycle

Stage	Strategic market objective	Investments	Profits	Cash flow
Introduction	For both innovators and followers, accelerate overall market growth and product acceptance through awareness, trial, and product availability	Moderate to high for R&D, capacity, working capital, and marketing (sales and advertising)	Highly negative	Highly negative
Growth	Increase competitive position	High to very high	High	Negative
Shakeout	Improve/solidify competitive position	Moderate	Low to moderate	Low to moderate
Mature	Maintain position	Low	High	Moderate

Strategic implications of the product life cycle

The product life-cycle model is a framework that signals the occurrence of opportunities and threats in the marketplace and the industry, thereby helping the business better anticipate change in the product's strategic market objective, its strategy, and its marketing program. By matching the entry's market position objective with the investment level required and the profits and cash flows associated with each stage in the product life-cycle, we can better visualize the interrelationships (see Exhibit 6-7). As would be expected, there is a high correlation between the market and industry characteristics of each stage, the market share objectives, and the level of investment, which, in turn, strongly affects cash flow.

Investment strategy during the introductory and growth stages

Because the introduction of a new product requires large investments, most firms sustain a rather sizable short-term loss. As the product moves into the growth stage, sales increase rapidly; hence, substantial investments continue. Profitability is depressed because facilities have to be built in advance to ensure supply. The firm with the largest share during this period should have the lowest per unit costs due to scale and learning effects. If it chooses to decrease its real price proportionate to the decline in its costs, it dries up the investment incentives of would-be entrants and lower-share competitors. The innovating firm's share is likely to erode substantially during the growth stage. Nevertheless, it must still make large investments because its sales are increasing even though it is losing share. New entrants and low-share sellers are at a substantial disadvantage in this stage. They must not only invest to accommodate market growth but also to gain market share.

Investment strategy during mature and declining stages

As the product enters the mature stage, the larger-share sellers should be able to reap the benefits of their earlier investments. Given that the price is sufficient to keep the higher-cost sellers in business, that growth investments are no longer needed, and that most competitors may no longer be striving to gain share, the leader's profitability and positive cash flow can be substantial. But the leader needs to continue making investments to improve its product and to make its manufacturing, marketing, and physical logistics more efficient. The generalized product life-cycle model portrays a profitability peak during the latter part of the growth stage. But one study of more than 1,000 industrial businesses found that despite declining margins, overall profitability did not decline during maturity mainly because less money was spent on marketing and R&D.[12]

The product life-cycle's major weakness lies in its normative approach to prescribing strategies based on assumptions about the features or characteristics of each stage. It fails to take into account that the product life-cycle is, in reality driven by market forces concerned with the evolution of consumer preferences (the market), technology (the product), and competition (the supply side).[13] Mary Lambkin and George Day argued strongly that greater emphasis on competitive issues helps to better understand the evolution of a product-market. This is especially the case in understanding the dynamics of competitive behavior in evolving market structures.[14] We discuss the three driving forces in the remainder of this chapter.

MARKET EVOLUTION

The product life-cycle concept owes much to the **diffusion of innovation theory**, which seeks to explain adoption of a product or a service over time among a group of potential buyers. Thus, lack of awareness limits early adoption. As word about the product spreads, the product enters the growth stage. When the net adoption rate holds steady, the mature stage is reached; when the rate begins to decline, the product has reached its final or decline stage. Diffusion theory emphasizes not only the behavior of individuals, their demographics, and how they respond to various kinds of communication, but also considers product attributes and the competitive environment as determinants of the adoption rate.

The adoption process

The **adoption process** involves the attitudinal changes experienced by individuals from the time they first hear about a new product, service, or idea until they adopt it. As might be expected, not all individuals respond alike—some tend to adopt early, some late, and some never, as has certainly been the case with the pharmaceuticals. Thus, the market for a new product tends to be segmented over time.

The five stages in the adoption process include awareness, interest, evaluation, trial, and adoption.

1. *Awareness.* In this stage the person is only aware of the existence of the new product and is insufficiently motivated to seek information about it.

2. *Interest.* Here the individual becomes sufficiently interested in the new product but is not yet involved.

---

[12]Hans B. Thorelli and Stephen C. Burnett, "The Nature of Product Life-Cycles for Industrial Goods Businesses," *Journal of Marketing,* Fall 1981, p. 108.

[13]Frederick E. Webster, Jr., *Industrial Marketing Strategy,* (New York: John Wiley & Sons, 1991) p. 128.
[14]Mary Lambkin and George S. Day, "Evolutionary Processes in Competitive Markets beyond the Product Life Cycle," *Journal of Marketing,* July 1989, pp 8–9.

== **E X H I B I T   6 – 8** ==

Slow Adoption of Lifesaving Medical Treatments Costs Lives

> A research study several years ago that focused on heart disease treatments concluded that influential medical experts too often failed to recommend lifesaving treatments until years after clinical data supported their use. The result was that thousands of lives were lost each year because such influentials were not "keeping up" with the increased flow of research results on new remedies. For example, there was sufficient data available by 1973 to reveal that the use of blood clot dissolving drugs would significantly reduce death rates caused by heart attacks. But most "expert reviewers" didn't begin to recommend the use of such drugs until 1986—some 13 years later. According to one medical researcher, 10,000–12,000 lives would have been saved each year if clot dissolves had been widely used.

SOURCE: David Stipp, "Medical Experts Slow to Adopt New Remedies," *The Wall Street Journal,* July 8, 1992, p. B1. Reprinted by permission, © 1992 Dow Jones & Company, Inc. All rights reserved worldwide.

3. *Evaluation.* This is sometimes referred to as the *mental rehearsal stage.* At this point the individual is mentally applying the new product to his or her own use requirements and anticipating the results.

4. *Trial.* Here the individual actually uses the product but, if possible, on a limited basis to minimize risk. Trial is not tantamount to adoption because only if the use experience is satisfactory will the product stand a chance of being adopted.

5. *Adoption.* In this stage the individual not only continues to use the new product but adopts it in lieu of substitutes.

The rate of adoption

If plotted on a cumulative basis, the percentage of people adopting a new product over time resembles an S curve. Although the curve tends to have the same shape regardless of the product involved, the length of time required differs among products, often substantially.

The time dimension is a function of the rate at which people in the target group (those ultimately adopting) move through the five stages in the adoption process. Generally speaking, the speed of the adoption process depends on six factors: (1) the risk—cost of product failure or dissatisfaction or in the case of credit cards the fear of charging too much, (2) the relative advantage over other products (e.g., cards versus checks), (3) the relative simplicity of the new product, (4) its compatibility with previously adopted ideas, (5) the extent to which its trial can be accomplished on a small-scale basis, and (6) the ease with which the central idea of the new product can be communicated.[15] Some new products move quickly through the adoption process (e.g., credit cards, a new toothpaste), while others take years. Clearly risk minimization through guarantees and reliable and prompt service are critical, as is the ability to demonstrate the product's uniqueness in meeting the customer's needs. Source credibility is of course also important. For an interesting, if tragic, example of the importance of speeding up the adoption process, see Exhibit 6-8.

The rate at which a product passes through the adoption process is also a function of the actions taken by the product's supplier. Thus, the diffusion process is faster when there is strong competition among members of the supplier group, when they have favorable

---

[15]Everett M. Rogers, *Diffusion of Innovations* (New York: Free Press, 1983).

═══════════════════════ **E X H I B I T 6 – 9** ═══════════════════════

Size and Characteristics of Individual Adopter Groups

- **Innovators** represent the first 2.5 percent of all individuals who ultimately adopt a new product. They are more venturesome than later adopters, more likely to be receptive to new ideas, and tend to have high incomes which reduce the risk of a loss arising from an early adoption.
- **Early adopters** represent the next 13 to 14 percent who adopt. They are more a part of the local scene, are often opinion leaders, serve as vital links to members of the early majority group (because of their social proximity), and participate more in community organizations than later adopters.
- The **early majority** includes 34 percent of those who adopt. These individuals display less leadership than early adopters, tend to be active in community affairs (thereby gaining respect from their peers), do not like to take unnecessary risks, and want to be sure that a new product will prove successful before they adopt it.
- The **late majority** represents another 34 percent. Frequently, these individuals adopt a new product because they are forced to do so for economic or social reasons. They participate in community activities less than the previous groups and only rarely assume a leadership role.
- **Laggards** comprise the last 16 percent of adopters. They are the most "local" of all adopters. They participate less in community matters than members of the other groups and stubbornly resist change. In some cases their adoption of a product is so late it has already been replaced by another new product.

reputations, and when they allocate substantial sums to R&D (to improve performance) and marketing (to build awareness).[16] The PC and credit card industries would score high on these adoption factors.

Adopter categories

Early adopters differ from later adopters. Using time of adoption as a basis for classifying individuals, five major groups can be distinguished: innovators, early adopters, early majority, late majority, and laggards. (Note that the types of adopters are different from the five stages of adoption just discussed.) Because each category comprises individuals who have similar characteristics and because individuals differ substantially across categories, adopter groups can be considered market segments. Thus, one would use a different set of strategies to market a new product to the early adopter group than to market it to the late majority group. See Exhibit 6-9 for the approximate size and characteristics of each group.[17]

Implications for marketing strategy

The differences cited in the Exhibit 6-9 are important because they help in the development of strategic marketing programs. In organizational markets, suppliers can identify innovative firms by reputation, profitability, size, and the suppliers' experiences in dealing with them. Information alone about the product or service is not usually a sufficient reason

---

[16]Thomas S. Robertson and Hubert Gatignon, "Competitive Effects on Technological Diffusion," *Journal of Marketing,* July 1986, pp. 1–12.

[17]Rogers, *Diffusion of Innovations.* For a discussion of the technology adoption life cycle, see Paul Wiefels, "Change Marketing Tactics as Buyer Attitudes Shift," *Marketing News,* June 9, 1997, p. 10.

to adopt. Commercial sources of information (e.g., salespeople and mass media advertising) are important at the outset, but less commercial and more professional sources are sought to validate the proclaimed merits of the new product, especially during the evaluation stage. Advice from opinion leaders is more critical as a legitimizing agent than as a source of information. A classic study of how doctors reacted to the introduction of a new "miracle drug" found that only 10 percent adopted on the basis of data provided by their initial source of information, indicating that data alone will not cause adoption.[18]

Thus, commercial sources are most important at the awareness stage in the adoption process, while personal influence is most important at the evaluation stage. In the interest stage, both are important. In the trail stage, marketers should attempt to make it relatively easy for a prospect to try a product under conditions that minimize risk. Therefore, strategic marketing programs should accommodate the various stages in the adoption process as well as the different adoption audiences.

PRODUCT EVOLUTION

Our discussion of the diffusion process described the impact of the product and its characteristics on the rate of diffusion; for example, the more complex and expensive the product, the slower this rate. As product characteristics evolve over time, they generate opportunities and threats, which in turn affect product differentiation, which is a key variable in determining the intensity and form of rivalry among existing firms within an industry and the ease of entry into it.

Product differentiation over time

The **profit impact of market strategy (PIMS)** research on competitive strategy has studied how a product-market's characteristics change as the market evolves.[19] As might be expected, product innovations diminish over time. Thus, the sales of new products—those entering the market for the first time—decline as a percentage of total market volume from 10.2 percent during the growth stage of evolution to 5.4 percent during growth maturity, to 3.5 and 3.7 percent during stable maturity and declining maturity, and to 2.8 percent in the decline stage.

Research and development (R&D), expressed as an average percentage of sales, also declines over time. Rates fall from 3.1 percent during the growth period to 2.0 percent during the maturity period and to only 1.2 percent during the decline phase. An important point here is that product R&D declines from 72 percent of total R&D costs during growth to 60 percent during the decline period. Thus, the proportion of the R&D expenditure spent on process (rather than on product) R&D increases over time in an effort to decrease per unit costs as the product matures.

The type and amount of R&D also appear to affect the evolutionary process by increasing the rate and level of diffusion. The more standardized the technology, the higher the diffusion rate. Thus, the more the industry spends on product R&D, the faster stan-

---

[18]Webster, *Industrial Marketing Strategy,* pp. 158–74.

[19]The PIMS program involves data relating to the strategies and financial results of about 3,000 strategic business units from 450 companies (many of which are international) for periods of 2 to 12 years. For more information about PIMS, see Robert Buzzell and Bradley gale, *The PIMS Principles* (New York: Free Press, 1987), chap. 3. This section of our discussion is based largely on Chapter 10 of the book.

dardization is achieved.[20] Assuming that process R&D leads to lower manufacturing costs, which in turn are translated into lower prices, then the more money spent on this activity, the faster the diffusion rate.

An analysis by PIMS indicates that competitors become more alike over time. The index of product differentiation drops substantially (from 51 to 32) from the growth to the decline stage.[21] As the market evolves, more major competitors have similar lines and serve the same types of customers. As would be expected when differentiation declines, so do prices, margins, and return on investment (ROI). According to PIMS, margins drop from 30.5 percent during the growth period to 26.0 percent during stable maturity and to 21.8 percent in the decline stage. The decline in marketing expenditures for consumer goods declines from 14.1 percent in the growth period to 10.9 percent in the decline period. Similar figures for industrial goods are 9.9 percent and 5.9 percent.

PIMS indicates very clearly that as the market moves from one stage of evolution to the next, some strategic marketing program changes are necessary. Thus, in the later evolutionary stages, managers should anticipate more market share stability, fewer new products of any real significance, increased direct competition from chief rivals, and greater price sensitivity.[22]

COMPETITIVE (SUPPLY-SIDE) EVOLUTION

This part of the evolutionary framework is concerned primarily with the effect of evolving industry structures on competitive behavior among firms serving much the same market(s). There seems little doubt that an industry's structural changes affect not only the degree of competitive intensity but also the bases of competition. Industry evolution can best be judged by analyzing an industry's long-term attractiveness, its characteristics, its driving forces, its success determinants, and especially the major competitive forces: present competitors, potential competitors, the bargaining power of suppliers and buyers, and substitute products. First, it is necessary to briefly discuss industry composition and strategic groups.

Industry identification and strategic groups

Industry evolution can best be judged by analyzing those conditions that are responsible for change. However, it is first necessary to define the relevant industry and its strategic groups. Industries comprise firms that produce similar products, but only at a high level of generality as, for example, the various instruments to satisfy the financial needs of a great variety of individuals and organizations. This does not mean that all products in an industry are close substitutes for one another. Different market segments need different benefit bundles—and thus different products. Industry membership alone does not indicate which firms compete with each other nor the extent of rivalry. Much depends on how the industry is defined and the level of aggregation used.

For example, the carbonated soft drink industry produces colas, root beers, ginger ales, and fruit flavors. These products come in diet or regular form, and some are caffeine free.

---

[20]Robertson and Gatignon, "Competitive Effects," pp. 4–6.

[21]The relative superiority of a company's product was determined by asking managers to rate their product's performance in comparison with those of leading competitors on a scale of 1 to 10 for each product attribute. For further information on how this rating takes place, see Buzzell and Gale, *The PIMS Principles,* chaps. 3 and 6.

[22]Buzzell and Gale, *The PIMS Principles,* pp. 204–9.

There are some 50 soda concentrate producing and marketing firms in the United States, but Coca-Cola and PepsiCo dominate the industry with their full lines. A different alignment of products and firms emerges if we add noncarbonated products to our industry definition. This definition adds fruit juices, vegetable juices, and bottled water which are produced by several hundred firms including Campbell Soup, Kraft, General Foods, Del Monte, and Perrier. This level of aggregation is so huge that identifying competitors and analyzing competitive changes simply on industry membership is meaningless.

Much the same can be said of the financial services "macro" industry definition, which would include large finance companies such as General Electric's Capital Services (with assets over $150 billion), international banks with a variety of specialties, and thousands of local banks and thrifts, insurance companies, and specialized credit card companies. Thus, defining the appropriate combination of industry sectors for a product or a group of products is not an easy task.

The identification of strategic groups makes it easier to learn more about the dynamics of an industry. A **strategic group** consists of firms pursuing similar strategies; that is, employing a similar mix of strategy elements. For example, Coke and Pepsi follow much the same strategy with respect to market served, products and product line, price, channels, advertising, in-store promotions, and personal selling; thus they constitute a strategic group. In a similar fashion, a strategic group of credit card companies would likely include American Express, Visa, and MasterCard. A strategic group is analyzed in the hope that the firms comprising it are enough alike to react essentially the same to environmental change. The more common elements used (often in combination) as the basis for identifying strategic groups are market served, products/product line, and distribution.

Industry analysis

A number of questions need to be answered in making an industry analysis. The more important ones are the following:

1. How profitable is the industry likely to be short term? Longer term? An attractive industry plays a large role in determining a firm's strategy—particularly its aggressiveness. An unattractive industry, on the other hand, could lead the firm into withdrawal strategies or an attempt to form an alliance with a competitor.

2. What are the more important industry characteristics? In answering this question, the following factors should be considered: market size and growth rate, number of firms, geographical scope, degree of vertical integration, ease of entry and exit, channels of distribution, customers, technology, and scale/learning effects.

3. What are the industry driving forces? Michael Porter identified a number of driving forces that to a greater or lesser degree are present in the evolution of any industry. These include (1) changes in the market's long-term growth rate, which directly affect investment decisions and intensity of competition; (2) changes in buyer segments, which affect demand and strategic marketing programs; (3) diffusion of proprietary knowledge, which controls both the rate at which products become more alike and the entry of new firms; (4) changes in cost and efficiency, derived from scale and learning effects, which have the potential of making entry more difficult; and (5) changes in government regulations, which can affect entry, costs, bases of competition, and profitability.[23]

---

[23]Michael Porter, *Competitive Strategy* (New York: Free Press, 1980), chap. 3.

═══════════════ E X H I B I T   6 – 1 0 ═══════════════

The Major Forces that Determine Industry Competition

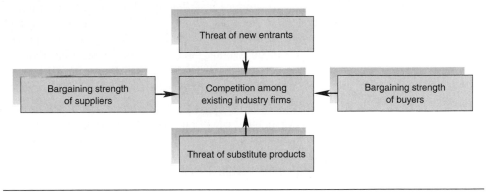

SOURCE: Adapted from Michael E. Porter, "Industry Structure and Competitive Strategy: Keys to Profitability," *Financial Analysts Journal*, July–August 1980, p. 33.

4. What are the essential determinants of success? These are the capabilities a firm must have or be able to achieve in order to be competitive and viable financially. Some of the more common determinants are concerned with the major elements in the marketing mix: product (ability to generate successful new products), price (be a low-cost producer), channels (obtain widespread product availability), and personal selling (ability to service large customers).

Major forces determining industry competition

This subject is closely linked to the section covering industry analysis, but because of its importance we discuss it separately in detail. Five interactive competitive forces determine collectively an industry's long-term attractiveness: present competitors, potential competitors, the bargaining power of suppliers and buyers, and substitute products (see Exhibit 6-10). This mix of forces explains why some industries are consistently more profitable than others and provides further insights into what resources are required and which strategies should be adopted to be successful.[24]

The strength of the individual forces varies from industry to industry and, over time, within the same industry. In the credit card industry, the key forces are present competitors and the threat of new entrants (e.g., banks promoting debit cards) while in the fast-food industry the key forces are present competitors (e.g., Wendy's versus Burger King versus McDonald's), substitute products (e.g., neighborhood delis, salad bars, all-you-can-eat buffet restaurants, and frozen meals), and buyers who are concerned about health and nutrition and who see fast foods as a symbol of a throwaway society.

Present competitors

Rivalry occurs among firms that produce products that are close substitutes for each other—especially when one competitor acts to improve its standing or protect its position. Thus, firms are mutually dependent: What one firm does affects others and vice versa.

---

[24]Ibid., pp. 30–41.

Ordinarily, profitability decreases as rivalry increases. Competition is greater under the following conditions:

- *There is high investment intensity; that is, the amount of fixed and working capital required to produce a dollar of sales is large.* High intensity requires firms to operate at or near capacity as much as possible, thereby putting strong downward pressure on prices when demand slackens. Thus, high investment-intensity businesses are, on average, much less profitable than those with a lower level of investment. Bob Crandall, the CEO of American Airlines, once described the airlines business as being "intensely, vigorously, bitterly, savagely competitive."[25]

- *There are many small firms in an industry or when no dominant firms exist.* In recent years hundreds of pharmaceutical companies have started up, all hoping to produce new wonder drugs. In such crowded segments as neurosciences, inflammatory diseases, and drug delivery, competition is keen, and some companies are considering preemptive steps in an effort to dominate their niches.[26]

- *There is little product differentiation*—for example, major appliances, TV sets, and passenger car tires.

- *There is a high cost to changing suppliers (switching costs)* as would be the case in changing a major computer software system.[27]

Threat of new entrants

A second driving force affecting competition is the threat of new entrants. New competitors add capacity to the industry and, because they need to gain market share, make competition more intense. The threat of new entrants from Japan in the PC industry is a very real concern to present players. Entry is more difficult under the following conditions:

- *When strong economies of scale and learning effects are present,* entry is much more difficult because it takes time to obtain the volume and learning required to yield a low relative cost per unit. If firms already present are vertically integrated, entry becomes more expensive. Also, if the existing firms share their output with related businesses, the problem of overcoming the cost disadvantage is made even more difficult.

- *If the industry has strong capital requirements at the outset.*

- *When strong product differentiation exists.*

- *If gaining distribution is particularly difficult.*

- *If a buyer incurs switching costs in moving from one supplier to another.*

Bargaining strengths of suppliers

The bargaining power of suppliers over firms in an industry is the third major determinant of industry competition. It is exercised largely through increased prices. Its impact can be significant, particularly when a limited number of suppliers service a number of different

---

[25]Windy Zellner, Andrea Rothman, and Eric Schine, "The Airlines Mess," *Business Week,* July 6, 1992.

[26]Vdayan Gupta, "Consolidation in Biotechnology Industry Accelerates," *The Wall Street Journal,* July 27, 1992, p. B2.

[27]Myron Magnet, "Meet the New Revolutionaries," *Fortune,* February 24, 1992, pp. 98–99.

industries. Their power is increased if switching costs and prices of substitutes are high and they can realistically threaten forward integration. Suppliers are especially important when their product is a large part of the buyer's value added, as is the case with metal cans, where the cost of tin plate is over 60 percent of the value added. In recent years the bargaining strength of suppliers in many industries has changed dramatically as more companies seek a partnership (or just-in-time) relationship with their suppliers. What was once an arm's length adversarial relationship has turned into a cooperative one, resulting in lower transaction costs, improved quality derived primarily from using a supplier's technological skills to design and manufacture parts, and decreased transaction time in terms of inventory replenishments.

Bargaining strength of buyers

An industry's customers constantly look for reduced prices, improved product quality, and added services and thus can affect competition within an industry. Buyers play individual suppliers against one another in their efforts to obtain these and other concessions. This is certainly the case with some large retailers in their dealings with many of their suppliers.

The extent to which buyers succeed in their bargaining efforts depends on (1) the extent of buyer concentration when, for example, a few large buyers that account for a large portion of industry sales facilitate gaining concessions; (2) switching costs that reduce the buyer's bargaining power; (3) the threat of backward integration, thereby alleviating the need for the supplier; (4) the product's importance to the performance of the buyer's product—the greater the importance, the lower their bargaining powers; and (5) buyer profitability—if buyers earn low profits and the product is an important part of their costs, then bargaining will be more aggressive.

Threat of substitute products

Substitutes are alternative product types, not brands, that perform essentially the same functions: oleomargarine versus butter, the faxing of documents versus overnight express delivery, and the use of checks instead of a credit card. Substitute products put a ceiling on the profitability of an industry by limiting the price that can be charged, especially when supply exceeds demand. No longer do almost all regular-size beer and soda products use aluminum cans. Today, more companies are turning to containers with new shapes and features in an effort to gain customers. Innovations from plastic, glass, and even steel is threatening aluminum's domination of the $71 billion beverage container market (see Exhibit 6-11).[28]

Changing competition and industry evolution

All five competitive forces just discussed are affected by the passage of time; therefore, their strength varies as the industry passes from its introductory stage to its growth stage and on to maturity, followed by decline. Competitive forces are apt to be weakest during the fast-growth period; thus, there are substantial opportunities for gaining market share. During the shakeout period, competitive forces are at their strongest, and many competitors are forced to exit the industry. During industry maturity, competition typically slackens, but only if the industry leader holds a strong relative share position. An industry will experience more price competition during maturity if the leader holds a weak relative share

---

[28]Stephen Baker and Nicole Harris, "What's Foiling the Aluminum Can?" *Business Week,* October 6, 1997.

════════════ **E X H I B I T   6 – 1 1** ════════════

Steel versus Aluminum in the Automotive Industry

Experimental aluminum cars accelerate faster, shift gears more smoothly and stop more quickly than a steel car—but the latter is sturdier and safer, thereby keeping the competition between the two metals a draw. Steel, which makes up 55 percent of the weight of the average car, is feeling seriously threatened since the car industry is mandated to produce a more fuel-efficient vehicle (getting up to 80 miles per gallon) which meets the consumers' needs for performance and safety—all at a reasonable price. Aluminum has a substantial weight advantage and is easier to mold. Steel, however, is cheaper and easier to recycle and it is safer. Neither industry can afford to ignore competition from plastics. Given the billions of dollars at stake, small wonder that scientists, engineers, and CEOs around the world are spending tens of millions of dollars to increase their share of the materials used to produce a car.

SOURCE: Erle Norton and Gabriella Stern, "Steel and Aluminum Vie over Every Ounce in a Car's Construction," *The Wall Street Journal,* May 9, 1995, p. A1. Reprinted with permission of *The Wall Street Journal,* © 1995 Dow Jones & Company, Inc. All rights reserved worldwide.

position. Kellogg and General Mills hold two-thirds of the U.S. domestic cereal market, but because Kellogg does not hold a dominant relative share, the industry experiences considerable price competition. A decling industry usually witnesses considerable rivalry, the extent of which depends on the strength of the exit barriers and the rate of decline.

Industry evolution and potential competitors

During the early stages of industry evolution, technology is a major entry barrier along with scale economies and product differentiation. Thus, an existing company can take advantage of technology barriers to build sales and customer loyalty. This is what Gillette did with its high-tech Sensor razor and Federal Express did in the overnight express business it created 20 years ago.

As an industry passes through its high-growth period, technology as a barrier to entry declines; witness UPS's entry into the overnight express business formerly dominated by Federal Express. As an industry passes through the shakeout stage and enters maturity, entry barriers increase because firms focus on reducing costs and developing a favorable brand image, both of which constitute entry barriers. When the decline stage is reached, entry is further inhibited by the industry's low profits.

SUMMARY

Firms benefit greatly if they are among the first to identify and take advantage of environmental change. This is especially true when a new product-market is involved. Early entrants tend to attain higher market share and profitability than later entrants. In addition to analyzing the several dimensions of the macroenvironment, firms must also consider the evolution of their product-market entries.

The product life cycle is the traditional model used to explain the evolution of product-market entries. Essentially, it is a generalized model of the sales history of a given product category over a long period. This concept holds that a product's sales change over time in a predictable way and that the product goes through a series of distinct stages. The product life-cycle concept has been used as a framework that, by signaling the timing of opportunities and threats, prescribes the strategies and marketing programs most appropriate for each stage of the cycle. The major weakness of the concept lies in its normative approach to prescribing strategies based on assumptions concerning the features or characteristics of each stage. Hence, a firm must also consider forces relating to the product, the market, and the competitive environment.

Diffusion theory seeks to explain the adoption process for a given product, service, or idea over time and thus relates directly to market evolution. It emphasizes the behavior of individuals, their demographics and how they respond to various kinds of communication. The process is defined as the attitudinal changes experienced by individuals from the time they first hear about a new product until they adopt it. It consists of five stages: awareness, interest, evaluation, trial, and adoption. Adopter categories are innovators, early adopters, early majority, late majority, and laggards. There are substantial demographic differences between early and late adopters.

Product evolution is mainly affected by changes in a firm's product differentiation. PIMS research shows that innovation diminishes over time, based on such measures as new product sales as a percentage of the sales of all firms, R&D expenditures, a switch from product R&D to process R&D, and the percentage change in markets experiencing a major change in technology. As time passes, competitors become more alike with respect to product, the breadth of product line, and the type of customers served.

Competitive environment evolution can best be studied by analyzing industry profitability, the more important industry characteristics, the major industry driving forces, the determinants of success, and especially the interplay of five competitive forces over time: present competitors, potential competitors, bargaining power of buyers and suppliers, and substitute products. The strength of these individual forces varies from industry to industry, and over time within the same industry. Competitive forces are apt to be at their weakest during the fast-growth and mature periods and at their strongest during the shakeout and decline stages. The forces of present and potential competitors are the two most affected by industry revolution.

7 CHAPTER

Market Segmentation and Market Targeting

SEGMENTING THE SPORTS APPAREL MARKET[1]

To find out what consumers wanted in sports apparel, the Council of the Sporting Goods Manufacturers Association commissioned a marketing research study to identify and describe the market's benefit segments. Over a thousand consumers (both men and women) were interviewed in 60 locations using a pretested questionnaire which was developed largely from information obtained from focus groups.

Respondents were asked to rate the importance of a number of characteristics they might consider in the purchase of their sports apparel; for instance, style, fit, fabric, durability, versatility, ease of care, and "made in America." Similar information was obtained for casual activity clothing. Information about each respondent's demographics, lifestyles, expenditures on sports apparel, and media habits was also obtained. The individual

"importance" ratings were clustered into seven benefit segments (see Exhibit 7-1), following which the demographics, spending patterns, and media habits were summarized for each benefit group.

The procedure maximized differences across and similarities within segments based on the degree of their benefit importance. Many of the differences are profiled in Exhibit 7-2. A summary of the lifestyle characteristics of each benefit segment follows, along with those benefits unique to the group; for instance, because all segments considered "comfortable fit" to be very important, it is not considered a unique characteristic of any group.

- The *self-oriented* segment has no unique benefit of any significance. The reasons participants gave for sports participation were

[1]Adapted from a case study of the sports apparel industry presented in Vithala R. Rao and Joel H. Stickel, *The New Science of Marketing* (Chicago: Irwin Professional Publishing, 1995), pp. 297–307. Reprinted with permission.

EXHIBIT 7–1

Sports Apparel Segmentation

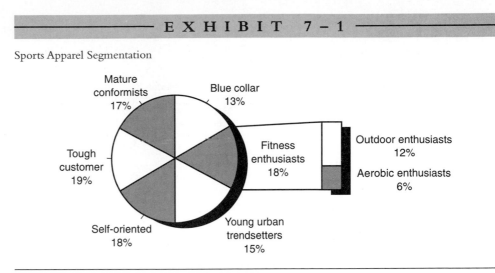

SOURCE: Vithala R. Rao and Joel H. Steckel, *The New Science of Marketing* (Chicago, Ill.: Irwin Professional Publishing, 1995), p. 302. Copyright 1995 by Irwin/McGraw-Hill. Reproduced with permission of the McGraw-Hill Companies.

to attract the opposite sex, experience the feeling of competition, improve their skills, and make new friends.

- *Tough customers,* more than any other group, demand a number of benefits. Tough customers walk for exercise to control their weight. They do not like to be in public unless they look their best, probably because they feel you can tell a lot about a person by the way he or she dresses.

- *Young, urban trendsetters'* most desired primary benefit is that "all their friends have it." They jog, lift weights, play basketball and exercise for the competition it provides. They enjoy spending money on their appearance and are fashion-conscious. They tend to be single and live in urban areas.

- *Blue collars* want versatile sports apparel. They own a higher-than-average amount of outdoor wear and place a high level of emphasis on sports. They lift weights, bowl, fish, and play a lot of football and softball.

- *Mature conformists* tend to be a bit older and favor walking and exercise in general. They feel health is more important than appearance. They are conservative, like to garden, spend time with their spouse, and participate in church and religious activities.

- *Aerobic enthusiasts* are primarily homemakers and participate heavily in aerobics. They are heavy impulse buyers and feel that the way one looks strongly affects the way one feels.

- *Outdoor enthusiasts* are heavy spenders and want sports apparel that is nonbinding, durable, weather resistant, and breathable. They participate in camping, biking, boating, fishing, and weight lifting. They place considerable emphasis on their careers and are down-to-earth thinkers.

The two segments with the greatest growth potential are the *self-orienteds* and *blue-collar jocks.* The first is especially attractive to sports apparel firms because

---

E X H I B I T   7 – 2

Profiles of Sports Apparel Benefits Segments

	Market Segments						
	Self-oriented	Tough customers	Young urban trendsetters	Blue collar	Mature conformists	Aerobic enthusiasts	Outdoor enthusiasts
Male	X		X	X	X		X
Female	X	X	X		X	X	X
Age (mean)	35.0	41.0	33.0	35.0	45.0	38.0	40.0
Percent married	58%	69%	36%	44%	65%	59%	54%
Income (mean) (thousands)	$44.0	$43.0	$40.0	$40.0	$36.0	$45.0	$40.0
Percent of sample	18%	19%	15%	13%	17%	6%	12%
Amount spent past year ($ hundreds)	$76.7	$59.6	$73.0	$71.5	$53.7	$41.7	$75.5
Amount willing to spend next year ($ hundreds)	$85.9	$47.1	$78.3	$79.1	$57.8	$44.1	$73.9
Media							
Television							
Sports	X		X	X			X
Drama						X	
News					X	X	
Talk shows		X					
MTV	X		X	X			
Cartoons		X	X				
Sitcoms		X					
Variety							
Documentaries					X		
Soaps		X					
Magazines							
General sports	X		X	X			X
Women's		X					
General interest		X	X				
TV Guide			X				
African-American			X				
Teen							
Men's lifestyle			X				
Benefits sought	Old	Higher on most	All friends have it	Authentic use	Protects from weather; easy care	Nonbinding; breathable; stretches; practical; need for sport	Nonbinding; durable; protects from weather; breathable

SOURCE: Vithala R. Rao and Joel H. Steckel, *The New Science of Marketing* (Burr Ridge, Ill.: Irwin Professional Publishing, 1995) p. 302. Copyright 1995 Irwin/McGraw-Hill. Reproduced with permission of the McGraw-Hill Companies.

its members anticipate spending more next year. The *mature conformist* segment, however, represents a group growing in size because it will be filled in the not-too-distance future with today's baby boomers.

SEGMENTATION, TARGETING, AND POSITIONING

The sports apparel example illustrates three interrelated marketing concepts—market segmentation, target marketing, and product positioning. **Market segmentation** is the process by which a market is divided into distinct customer subsets of people with similar needs and characteristics that lead them to respond in similar ways to a particular product offering and strategic marketing program. In the sports apparel example, the researchers segmented the market for sports apparel into seven groups according to the benefits each sought from such apparel and the relative importance attached to various choice criteria (e.g., fit, durability, versatility) they might use in deciding which sports apparel brand to buy. Next, they described each segment's demographics, lifestyle, and media habits.

Since few, if any, sports apparel firms could hope to satisfy the needs of all seven segments, each firm would have to decide which segment or segments to target. To do so requires evaluating the relative attractiveness of each segment (size, revenue potential, and growth rate), the benefits sought, and the firm's relative business strengths. This process is called **target marketing.** Finally, **product positioning**—designing product offerings and developing strategic marketing programs which collectively create an enduring competitive advantage in the target market—would need to be undertaken. In the sports apparel example, the study did not provide information on how each segment's respondents perceived the offerings of individual firms. Thus, each firm would have to do its own research before developing its positioning strategy.

These three decisions—market segmentation, market targeting, and positioning—are closely linked and have a strong interdependence. All must be well considered and implemented if the firm is to succeed in managing a given product-market relationship. More often than not, successful companies have been able to finesse this relationship and in so doing distance themselves from their competitors. Consider the following international example.[2]

> In England, Japanese companies have outperformed their British rivals across a range of industries. A major reason for this was that the Japanese were better at managing the segmentation, targeting, and positioning relationships. Thus, only 13 percent of the Japanese firms versus 47 percent of the British were unclear about their target segment of customers and their special needs.
>
> All too often the marketing directors of the British companies remarked that they see their market as being the whole industry and since their products had wide appeal, there was no need to segment the market. As a consequence, the Japanese concentrated their resources in specific high-potential segments while the British tended to spread theirs thinly across the entire market. When British companies did segment, they did so at the lower, cheaper end of the market. This resulted in customers increasingly perceiving the Japanese, in contrast to the British, as offering quality and status.

What is clear from the above example is that however large the firm, its resources are usually limited compared to the number of alternative marketing investments available. Thus, a firm must make choices. For a given market, the marketing investment options are expressed in terms of market segments. Even in the unusual case where a firm can afford to serve all market segments, it must determine the most appropriate allocation of its marketing effort *across* segments.

---

[2]Peter Doyle, "Managing the Marketing Mix," in Michael J. Baker, ed., *The Marketing Book* (Oxford, England: Butterworth-Heinemann, 1992), p. 273.

The remainder of this chapter examines market segmentation and market targeting; Chapter 8 discusses positioning. We have several concerns here: First, we take a closer look at the rationale for segmenting. Next, we examine the various ways to segment consumer and organizational markets. Finally, we discuss the criteria and procedures for evaluating the long-run attractiveness of different segments and the firm's business strengths relative to customer needs and competitors. The outcome of this analysis should make it possible for a manager to decide which segments to target.

RATIONALE FOR MARKET SEGMENTATION

Market segmentation is one, if not the most important, of the strategic concepts business firms and other organizations use today. Indeed, to some the history of marketing in the United States is a history of segmentation.[3] It is based on the premise that markets are rarely homogeneous in benefits wanted, usage rates, and price and promotion elasticities; as a result their response rates to products and marketing programs differ. Variations among markets in product preferences, size and growth in demand, media habits, and competitive structures further affect the differences and response rates. Thus, markets are complex entities which can be defined, or segmented, in a variety of ways. The critical issue for a firm is to find an appropriate segmentation scheme that will facilitate market targeting, product positioning, and the formulation of successful marketing strategies and programs.

A firm has the option of adopting a market aggregation strategy or a segmentation strategy. Most companies adopt the latter. A *market-aggregation strategy* is appropriate when the total market has few differences in customer needs or desires, especially when the product can be standardized. It is also appropriate when it is operationally difficult to develop distinct products or marketing programs to reach different customer segments; that is, not all segmentation schemes can be acted upon. Because customers and their needs are diverse, relatively few product-markets meet these conditions. Even so, some firms have pursued at least a partial aggregation strategy. Lever's 2000 successful multipurpose soap, for example, was designed to appeal to both sexes regardless of the individual's skin condition (dry versus oil), fragrance preferences, and deodorant needs.

Growing importance of segmentation

For several reasons market segmentation has become increasingly important in the development of marketing strategies. First, population growth has slowed, and more product-markets are maturing. This in turn sparks more intense competition as firms seek growth through gains in market share (e.g., the situation in the automobile industry) as well as in an increase in brand extensions (e.g., Mr. Coffee's coffee, Colgate toothbrushes, Visa traveler's checks).

Second, social and economic forces such as expanding disposable incomes, higher educational levels, and more awareness of the world have produced customers with more varied and sophisticated needs, tastes, and lifestyles than ever before. This has led to an outpouring of goods and services that are competing with each other for the opportunity of satisfying some group of consumers.

Third, as we noted from our earlier discussion of marketing information systems, technology has facilitated the trend towards microsegmentation and the use of relationship

---

[3]N. Craig Smith and Elizabeth Cooper-Martin, "Ethics and Target Marketing: The Role of Product Harm and Consumer Vulnerability," *Journal of Marketing,* July 3, 1997, p. 1.

marketing often made operational by the use of telemarketing.[4] This trend has been accelerated in some industries by new technology such as computer-aided design, which has enabled firms to mass customize many products as diverse as designer jeans and cars. For example, many automobile companies are using a flexible production system which can produce different models on the same production line. This enables the company to literally produce cars made to order.[5]

Finally, many marketing organizations have made the implementation of specialized marketing programs easier by broadening and segmenting their own services. For example, new advertising media have sprung up to appeal to narrow-interest groups. These include special-interest magazines, radio programs, and cable TV. Also, a growing number of broad-based magazines (e.g., *Time, Southern Living, Sports Illustrated*) offer advertisers the opportunity to target specific groups of people within their subscription base. This approach relies heavily on ZIP codes and permits businesses to target not only specific regions and cities for their advertising but also selected income groups.

Benefits of market segmentation

In addition to forcing firms to face the realities of the marketplace, segmentation offers the following benefits:

- *It identifies opportunities for new product development.* Often a careful analysis of various segments of potential customers reveals one or more groups whose specific needs and concerns are not being well satisfied by existing competitive offerings. Such uncovered segments may represent attractive opportunities for development of new products or innovative marketing approaches; for example, the laptop computer (see Exhibit 7-3).

- *Segmentation helps in the design of marketing programs that are most effective for reaching homogeneous groups of customers*; for example, the success of Procter & Gamble in marketing several brands of detergents targeted on different segments.

- *It improves the strategic allocation of marketing resources.* The strategic benefits of segmentation are sometimes overlooked. Well-defined segments, when coupled with specific products, serve as potential investment centers for a business. Most successful business strategies are based on market segmentation and a concentration of resources in the more attractive ones. Segmentation should focus on subdividing markets into areas in which investments can gain a long-term competitive advantage.

THE SEGMENTATION PROCESS

There are many ways of dividing a market into segments. As we will note in the following pages, a great number of variables influence consumers in their purchases of different products. The objective of the segmentation process is to divide the market into relative

---

[4]Laurie Hayes, "Using Computers to Divine Who Might Buy a Gas Grill," *The Wall Street Journal,* August 16, 1994, p. B1. The article notes that American Express has a data bank of 500 billion bytes of data describing not only the purchases made since 1991 by 35 million buyers worth some $350 billion but their demographics as well.

[5]Some of the problems of implementing a highly segmented, customized strategy are discussed in Joseph Pine II, Burt Victor, and Andrew C. Boyerton, "Making Mass Customization Work," *Harvard Business Review,* September–October 1993, pp. 108–19.

━━━━━ E X H I B I T   7 – 3 ━━━━━

Forget Hertz and Avis—Enterprise Is the Nation's Biggest Rental Car Enterprise

Founded only 40 years ago, Enterprise owns more cars (310,000) and operates in more locations (2,800) than Hertz. Revenues are over $3 billion worldwide and the company has a 20 percent share of the U.S. car rental business compared with 17 percent for Hertz and 12 percent for Avis. The company's strategy is quite simple. Rather than compete head to head with Hertz and Avis, the company's presence is mainly in the smaller cities where its goal is to provide a spare family car. If your car has been hit, breaks down, or is in for routine maintenance, Enterprise is there for you. It used to be you could borrow your wife's car, but it's no longer available because she works. The company sets up inexpensive rental offices just about everywhere, and employees then develop close relationships with all nearby auto dealerships and body shops in the area to get them to recommend Enterprise cars while their cars are out of circulation. It even sets up shop in some dealer showrooms. These relationships, coupled with relatively low per diem rates and prompt and friendly service, have been responsible for revenues growing 25 to 30 percent annually for the past 11 years.

SOURCE: Brian O'Reilly, "The Rental Car Jocks Who Made Enterprise #1," *Fortune,* October 28, 1996, p. 126. Reprinted with permission.

homogeneous groups of prospective buyers of a product or service with regard to their demands. Ideally, the variances within these individual groups are relatively small compared with the differences between groups. The process also must describe these groups so that members can be readily identified, determine the size/value of each group, and describe the differences between the groups. The segmentation variables used (termed *descriptors*) should facilitate these objectives.

Regardless of which variables are used, most segmentation efforts follow essentially the same process which consists of the following steps.

1. *Selection of meaningful descriptors (variables) in a given market situation.* These can be determined in advance (a priori) or on the basis of the research findings (post hoc). Both of these approaches are valid and are not necessarily mutually exclusive.

   A priori segmentation implies that the firm has enough knowledge about the market to decide in advance the segmentation descriptors. For example, a manager might want to determine in advance how different demographic groups (age, income, education, and sizes of family) varied with respect to their usage of the firm's product as well as their media habits.

   Post hoc segmentation is typically used to determine attitudes, product usage, benefits wanted, and perceptions concerning a given product or service. An example of this type of segmentation is the case study of the sports apparel market which appeared at the beginning of this chapter. Based on interviews with over 1,000 consumers, seven benefit segments were identified following which the demographics, spending patterns, and media habits were determined for each group.

2. *Determination of whether and to what extent there are differences in the dependent (outcome) variable(s)*; for example, differences in benefits sought across the various segments as defined by demographics, product usage, and lifestyle. This involves clustering, which requires the use of data analysis techniques. These range from simple cross tabs to the use of sophisticated techniques such as multivariate analysis that can consider large numbers of variables in the clustering efforts. Some variation of the latter technique was used to cluster the data received from the over 1,000 respondents into seven benefit segments in the sport apparel study. Obviously, one problem in clustering

is to determine the appropriate number of segments—that is, where the differences are sufficiently strong to be actionable by the company.[6]

3. *Evaluation* of the results from step 2 to determine the effectiveness and usefulness of the segment scheme. The following criteria are useful in making this evaluation.

- *Different.* Segments must respond differently to one or more of the marketing (independent) variables; that is, the segments must be clearly distinguishable from all other segments.

- *Identifiable.* It must be possible to clearly identify the customers that inhabit the various segments in order to facilitate the targeting of marketing efforts. This is often referred to as *accessibility.*

- *Adequate size.* There must be sufficient potential customers in each segment to make the company's efforts cost effective. This involves trade-offs between customer homogeneity and scale effects.

- *Measurability.* This involves the use of measurable variables as the basis for segmentation.

- *Compatibility.* The segmentation scheme must be consistent with the company's resources.

The last criteria takes us into target marketing and marketing segmentation strategy which we will discuss later in the chapter.

IDENTIFICATION OF MARKET SEGMENTS

Marketers divide segmentation descriptors into four major categories for consumer and industrial markets: physical descriptors, person- or firm-related behavioral descriptors, product-related behavioral descriptors, and customer-needs descriptors. Increasingly, segments are being defined using a combination of descriptors from these four categories even though this requires the collection of extensive marketing research data and the use of sophisticated statistical methods. Each of these categories is discussed next. See also Exhibit 7-4.

Physical descriptors

These are used mainly to describe consumers (in contrast to organizations) largely on the basis of demographics such as those shown in Exhibit 7-5. Some examples of their use follow:

Age. "Thanks to a demographic trend that is being called *invasion of the stroller people,* babies are hot, both as consumers and marketing tools." There are nearly 24 million children under age 5 in the United States—20 percent more than in 1980. Aside from medical costs, new parents spend, on average, $7,000 during a baby's first year. Revlon has recently entered the skin-care

---

[6]For an excellent example of the numbers problem, see James H. Myers, *Segmentation and Positioning for Strategic Marketing Decisions* (Chicago: American Marketing Association, 1996), p. 21. For a discussion of various techniques used to segment markets, see Chapters 2–5.

EXHIBIT 7-4

Descriptors Used to Segment Consumer and Industrial Markets

Descriptors	Consumer	Industrial
Physical		
Age	X	
Sex	X	
Household life cycle	X	
Income	X	
Occupation/position	X	
Education	X	
Geography	X	X
Event	X	
Race and ethnic origin	X	
Company size		X
Industry (SIC code)		X
General behavioral		
Lifestyle	X	
Social class	X	
Interests		
Purchase structure		X
Buying situation		X
Product-related behavior		
Product usage	X	X
Loyalty	X	X
Purchase predisposition	X	
Innovativeness	X	
Present customers	X	X
Customer needs	X	X

market because of the increasing number of women over 50 who want to make their skin look young again.[7]

Sex. Recently General Motors' Chevrolet division spent considerable money on advertising and events to convince women that its cars are made with them in mind. Chevrolet's efforts recognize that women spend $85 billion annually in buying half of all the new cars bought in the United States.[8]

Household life cycle. Formerly known as family life cycle, this concept has been "modernized" by incorporating nontraditional households such as single-parent and never-married singles households. Essentially it describes the stages in the formation, growth, and decline in a household unit. Each stage differs in its expenditure pattern. Thus, young marrieds are heavy buyers of small appliances, furniture, and linens. With the arrival of children, purchases include insurance, washers and dryers, medical care, and an assortment of child-oriented products. A recent study confirmed that transitions in household situations are related to meaningful changes in spending behavior, but that it is often difficult to relate these changes to the purchase of specific products.[9]

---

[7]See Ellen Newborne, "Marketers Tap Growth Market," *USA Today,* May 8, 1995, p. B1; and Tara Parker-Pope, "For Revlon, Skincare Is the New Frontier," *The Wall Street Journal,* April 9, 1997, p. B1.

[8]Julie Ralston, "Chevy Targets Women," *Advertising Age,* August 7, 1995, p. 24.

[9]Robert E. Wilkes, "Household Life-Cycle Stages, Transitions and Product Expenditures," *Journal of Consumer Research,* June 1995, p. 27.

———— E X H I B I T 7 – 5 ————

Some of the More Commonly Used Demographic Descriptors and Their Categories*

Demographic descriptors	Examples of categories
Age	Under 2, 2–5, 6–11, 12–17, 18–24, 25–34, 35–49, 50–64, or older
Sex	Male, female
Household cycle	Young, single; newly married, no children; youngest child under 6; youngest child 6 or over; older couples with dependent children; older couples without dependent children; older couples retired; older, single
Income	Under $15,000; $15,000–$24,999; $25,000–$74,999, etc.
Occupation	Professional, manager, clerical, sales, supervisor, blue-collar, homemaker, student, unemployed
Education	Some high school, graduated high school, some college, graduated college
Geography	Regions, countries, cities, metropolitan areas, counties, ZIP codes, and blocks
Event	Birthdays, graduations, anniversaries, national holidays, sporting events
Race and ethnic origin	Anglo-Saxon, African American, Italian, Jewish, Scandinavian, Hispanic, Asian

*Others include marital status, home ownership, and presence and age of children.

Income. Higher-income households purchase a disproportionate number of cellular phones, expensive cars, and theater tickets. The circulation and advertising of magazines targeting the rich have increased dramatically in recent years—for example, *The Robb Report,* a monthly magazine whose readers have an average income of $755,000.[10]

Occupation. The sales of certain kinds of products (e.g., work shoes, automobiles, uniforms, and trade magazines) are tied closely to occupational type. The increase in the number of working women has created needs for specialized goods and services, including financial services, business wardrobes, convenience foods, automobiles, and special interest magazines.

Education. There is a strong positive correlation between the level of education and the purchase of travel, books, magazines, insurance, theater tickets, and photographic equipment.

Geography. Different locations vary in their sales potential, growth rates, customer needs, cultures, climates, service needs, and competitive structures as well as purchase rates for a variety of goods. For example, more pickup trucks are sold in the Southwest, more vans in the Northeast, and more high-priced imports in the West. More and more advertisers are taking advantage of geographic media buys, and Uni-marts, Inc., a convenience store operator of over 400 stores, focuses on small towns and rural areas, thereby avoiding big competitors. In its 23-year history, it has yet to record a loss.[11]

Geodemographics. This is an increasingly popular type of segmentation. As discussed in Chapter 5, it attempts to predict consumer behavior by making demographic, psychographic, and consumer purchase information available at the block and ZIP code levels. Claritas' PRIZM service classifies all U.S. households into 62 demographically and behaviorally distinct clusters each of which, in turn, is assigned to one of 15 social groups.[12]

Events. These include a varied set of activities ranging from national holidays, sports, and back-to-school week, to personal events such as birthdays, anniversaries, and weddings. Each requires a specific marketing program.

———————

[10]Anita Sharpe, "Magazines for the Rich Rake in Readers, *The Wall Street Journal,* February 2, 1996, p. B1.

[11]Mora Somassundarm, "Uni-Marts Inc.'s Small Town Strategy for Convenience Stores Is Paying Off," *The Wall Street Journal,* November 20, 1995, p. B5A.

[12]Jon Goss, "We Know Who You Are and We Know Where You Live: The Instrumental Rationality of Geodemographics," *Economic Geography* 71, no. 2 (1995), p. 171.

Race and ethnic origin. More and more companies are targeting ethnic segments by means of specialized marketing programs. Motorola has run separate advertising campaigns for its pagers and cellular phones to African Americans, Asian Americans, and Hispanics. Spiegel and Ebony have combined to produce a direct-mail catalog designed to provide apparel which meets the style, color, and fit needs of African Americans. Sears offers black women a line of clothing called African Village and is planning to market two new labels to minority men and women.[13]

Physical descriptors are also important in the segmentation of industrial markets, which are segmented in two stages. The first, *macrosegmentation,* divides the market according to the characteristics of the buying organization, using descriptors such as geographical location, company size, and industry affiliation (SIC code). The international counterpart of SIC is the trade category code.

The second stage, *microsegmentation,* groups customers by the characteristics of the individuals who influence the purchasing decision (e.g., age, sex, and position within the organization). *International markets* are segmented in a similar hierarchical fashion, starting with countries, followed by groups of individuals or buying organizations.

General behavioral descriptors

These seek to produce a better understanding of how a consumer behaves in the market-place and why. The most common behavioral descriptors in consumer markets are lifestyle (psychographics) and social class.

Lifestyle

Segmentation by lifestyle, or psychographics, groups consumers on the basis of their activities, interests, and opinions. From such information it is possible to infer what types of products and services appeal to a particular group, as well as how best to communicate with individuals in the group. Lifestyle was used to describe the benefit segments for sports apparel. Some credit card companies are using reward programs linked to products that represent a particular lifestyle.[14]

In the international area, Goodyear Tire and Rubber and Ogilvy and Mather, the advertising agency, working separately, have developed several classifications for global lifestyle segments. The Goodyear effort consists of six groups: the prestige buyer, the comfortable conservative, the value shopper, the pretender, the trusting patron, and the bargain hunter. Ogilvy and Mather propose 10 global segments based on its lifestyle characteristics: basic needs, fairer deal, traditional family life, conventional family life, look-at-me, somebody better, real conservatism, young optimist, visible achiever, and socially aware.[15]

Stanford Research Institute (SRI) has developed an improved U.S. segmentation scheme (called VALS2), which builds on the concept of self-orientation and resources for the individual. *Self-orientation* is based on how consumers pursue and acquire products and services that provide satisfaction and shape their identities. In doing so, they are motivated

---

[13] Michael Wilke and Todd Preizan, "Motorola Puts Ethnic Marketing to Work for Cellular Phones, Pagers," *Advertising Age,* June 24, 1996, p. 16; Cyndi Miller, "Catalogers Learn to Take Blacks Seriously," *Marketing News,* March 3, 1995, p. 8; and "Sears to Market New Line of Clothing for Minorities," *Marketing News,* March 17, 1997, p. 6.

[14] Christine Dugas, "Credit Card Companies Tap into Lifestyles," *USA Today,* September 22, 1997, p. 5B.

[15] Salah S. Hassar and Lea P. Katsaris, "Identification of Global Consumer Segments: A Behavioral Framework," *Journal of International Consumer Marketing* 3, no. 2 (1991), p. 16.

by principle, status, and action. Principle-oriented consumers are motivated by abstract and idealized criteria while status-oriented consumers shop for products that demonstrate the consumer's success. Action-oriented consumers are guided by the need for social or physical activity, variety, and risk taking. **Resources** represent all of the psychological, physical, demographic, and material means consumers have to draw on, including education, income, self-confidence, health, eagerness to buy, intelligence, and energy level.

Based on these two dimensions, VALS 2 defines eight segments that exhibit distinctive behavior and decision making: actualizers, fulfillers, achievers, experiencers, believers, strivers, makers, and strugglers. The segments are approximately the same size so that they represent viable market targets. Claritas and similar commercial organizations identify each of their respondents by their VAL type, thereby permitting a cross classification of VAL type with the product usage and personal information collected by these companies. Thus, users can determine what each VAL segment bought, what their media habits are, and similar data. The VAL system has been further developed in Europe and Asia.[16]

Social Class

Every society has its status groupings based largely on similarities in income, education, and occupation. Because researchers have long documented the values of the various classes, it is possible to infer certain behavior concerning a given product. For example, the middle classes tend to place more value on education, family activities, cleanliness, and being up-to-date than do lower class families. In the United States many of the criteria used to define class status seem to some to be no longer applicable as the nation becomes increasingly fragmented into dozens of distinct subcultures, each with its own unique tastes and ambitions.

Interests

Those concerned with hobbies, do-it-yourself activities, sports, travel, health, raising a family, job-related activities, and education are increasingly an important segmentation variable given the emergence of Web communities consisting of people with like interests.[17] The formation of these communities was inevitable given the explosion in the number of people using the World Wide Web—currently up to 40 million from 1 million in 1994. The demographics have also changed; the average age of a user has increased and women now account for 41 percent of the Internet population, up from 21 percent 18 months ago. As these new millions enter cyberspace, they find it a confusing place, given the hundreds of thousands of websites. Inevitably they gravitate to those websites where they can find friends and feel comfortable.

Research shows that if a website doesn't get a surfer's interest in eight seconds, he or she is gone. Even when they stay, the average visit is only seven minutes. But in Internet neighborhoods, providing a way for surfers to chat boosts traffic 50 percent and increases their staying time to a half hour. The ideal community not only focuses on a common interest but encourages lots of communication and interaction.

Garden Escape, Inc., started its website in March 1996 as an on-line nursery but was soon swamped by E-mail inquiries. The company quickly added forums for regional

---

[16] Information provided by the Stanford Research Institute.

[17] See Robert D. Hof, Deanna Browden, and Peter Elstrom, "Internet Communities," *Business Week,* May 5, 1997, p. 65; see also Ian P. Murphy, "Web Communities a Target Marketers' Dream," *Marketing News,* July 7, 1997, p. 2.

gardening usage. Web visitors began spending more time on the site, and sales have increased 40 percent a month. Chat participants spend an average of $100 per order contrasted with $60 from others.

Industrial or firm behavioral descriptors

Purchasing structure and buying situation segmentation descriptors are unique to industrial markets. **Purchasing structure** is the degree to which the purchasing activity is centralized. In such a structure the buyer is likely to consider all transactions with a given supplier on a global basis, emphasizing cost savings and minimal risk. In a decentralized situation, the buyer is apt to be more sensitive to the user's need, emphasize product quality and fast delivery, and be less cost conscious.

The **buying situation** descriptor includes three distinct types of situations: *straight rebuy,* a recurring situation handled on a routine basis; *modified rebuy,* which occurs when some element, such as price or delivery schedules, has changed in a client-supplier relationship; and a *new buying situation,* which may require the gathering of considerable information and an evaluation of alternative suppliers.

Product-related behavioral descriptors

These descriptors reflect the behavior of customers toward a specific product. They include product usage, loyalty, purchase predisposition, and purchase influence, all of which can be used to segment both consumer and industrial markets. **Product usage** is important because in many markets, a small proportion of potential customers makes a high percentage of all purchases. Over the past several years Kraft Foods has focused on both heavy users of its Miracle Whip brand and dual users of mayonnaise and Miracle Whip. The hope is to stimulate greater use of its brand in part by switching mayonnaise users to it.[18] In industrial markets the customers are better known, and heavy users (often called *key accounts*) are easier to identify.

With respect to **loyalty**—reflected by the numbers of successive purchases made over time—current users may vary considerably in their purchases of a given brand or patronage of a particular supplier. In industrial markets, sellers can often observe this directly; in consumer markets, identifying loyal customers requires marketing research.

Consumers hold different predispositions toward the purchase of a product. A market segmentation scheme based on product knowledge (are they aware of it?) and **purchase predisposition** can identify the nonusers who are most likely to become future buyers. For example, knowledgeable nonusers who state intentions to buy, for example, a high-fiber cereal, are the most likely to become future users. Knowledgeable nonusers who do not intend to buy, on the other hand, would probably represent a low potential.

Market segmentation based on sources of **purchase influence** is relevant for both consumer and industrial markets. Many products used by various family members are purchased by the wife, but joint husband-wife decisions are becoming more common. Children's products, prescription drugs, and gifts are clearly influenced by a variety of individuals. In industrial markets several individuals or organizational units with varying degrees of influence participate in the buying center.

---

[18]Judamin Pollack, "Kraft's Miracle Whip Targets Core Consumers with '97 Ado," *Advertising Age,* February 3, 1997, p. 12.

Innovativeness is concerned with how individuals and organizations vary in their capacity and desire to innovate. This is particularly so for the adoption of new products. As we noted in Chapter 6, substantial differences exist between early and late adopters. Thus, each of the various adopter groups (innovators, early adopters, early majority, late majority, and laggards) can be considered a segment. All too frequently **present customers** are not considered as an important segment despite their substantial value over time and ease of identifying. Data about their product usage and loyalty should be evaluated at regular intervals along with their changing demographics.

Customer needs

Customer needs are expressed in **benefits sought** from a particular product or service. Individual customers do not have identical needs and thus attach different degrees of importance to the benefits offered by different products. In the end, the product that provides the best bundle of benefits—given the customer's particular needs—is most likely to be purchased. Schick has launched a new flagship razor called The Schick Protector. Its focus is safety—that of Gilette is "closeness"—because Schick's research shows that this is one of the three attributes men look for in a razor. It plans to target African-American men who often find shaving painful because of a condition that causes skin bumps. Another target is teenagers who are concerned about nicks and cuts.[19]

Because purchasing is a problem-solving process, consumers evaluate product or brand alternatives on the basis of desired characteristics and how valuable each characteristic is to the consumer's **choice criteria.** Marketers therefore can define segments according to these different choice criteria in terms of the presence or absence of certain characteristics and the importance attached to each. Firms typically single out a limited number of benefit segments to target. Thus, for example, different automobile manufacturers have emphasized different benefits over the years, such as safety, reliability, and high mileage in contrast with styling, quickness, and status.

In industrial markets, customers consider relevant benefits that include product performance in different use situations. For example, Cray Computers are bought because they meet the high-speed computational requirements of a small group of customers such as governments, universities, and research labs. Other considerations in the purchase of industrial products and services include on-time delivery, credit terms, economy, spare parts availability, and training.

Note that benefits sought must often be linked to usage situations. There is ample evidence that usage often strongly affects product choice and substitutability. Thus, the appropriateness of product attributes varies across different usage environments. Any attempt to define viable segments must recognize this fact; for example, consumer needs vary in different usage situations for products such as baking soda, furniture chairs and tables, and foods (cheese and Jell-O). Usage can be very important for certain industrial goods; for example, the use of trucks, computer software, and security systems are developed with user segments in mind.

As we move through the range of descriptors—from physical to general behavioral to product-related to customer needs—the implications for the formulation of marketing strategies and programs become more apparent and meaningful. But all the various

---

[19] Mark Maremont, "Close vs. Safe: Rivals Prepare to Market New Razors," *The Wall Street Journal,* September 29, 1997, p. B1.

descriptors are important and are likely to be used to some extent in the segmentation of a given market. Thus, marketers try to define segments using a combination of benefit, behavioral, and physical factors, even though this often requires the collection of market research data and the use of sophisticated statistical analyses.

GLOBAL MARKET SEGMENTATION

The traditional approach to global market segmentation has been to view a country or a group of countries as a single segment made up of all consumers living in that country. This approach is, however, seriously flawed because it relies on country variables rather than consumer behavior, assumes homogeneity *within* the country segment, and ignores the possibility of the existence of homogeneous groups of consumers *across* country segments.[20]

More and more companies are approaching global market segmentation by identifying consumers with similar needs and wants in a range of countries and then grouping them according to their behavior in the marketplace. This international segmentation enables a company to develop reasonably standardized programs which require little change across local markets, thereby resulting in scale economies. There seems to be reasonable agreement that two obvious international segments exist: the global elite and the global teenage segments. The former is targeted by producers of products and services that fit an image of exclusivity (e.g., cellular phones, personal computers, luxury cars, expensive perfumes). The growing number of reasonably affluent groups in Latin America offers considerable potential for a variety of goods, including automobiles, compact disk players, children's clothing, and health and beauty aids.[21]

The global teenage segment assumes a minimum of differences in cultural norms and lifestyles for teenagers across countries. Empirical evidence supports this view for certain kinds of products such as Swatch watches, Sony's line of audio products for children, and Benetton's colorful knitwear. Even in Japan—typed as a homogeneous culture featuring the "Japan First" sentiment—there is considerable evidence that younger generations are becoming more positive about U.S. and European products (see Exhibit 7-6).[22]

Clearly, many global trends are influencing the behavior of consumers, including increased per capita GNP, increased literacy and education, growth in urbanization, greater availability of television, and more travel. Many consumer products are becoming more commonplace (e.g., automobiles, major home appliances, TVs). Thus, the global market for many products can be regarded as in transition. This development will require global marketers to continuously monitor their markets to identify emerging segments.

SERVICE SEGMENTATION

Much of what we have been discussing applies to both products and services. But as Valerie Zeithaml and Mary Jo Bitner have pointed out, there are important differences, the most powerful of which is the need for compatibility in the segments. Because customers are often part of the production and delivery of services, it is important that they be

---

[20]Hassan and Katsaris, "Identification of Global Consumer Segments," p. 16.

[21]Ignacio Galeeran and Jon Berry, "A New World of Consumers," *American Demographics,* March 1995, p. 26.

[22]Marte J. Rhea, Barbara C. Garland, and John C. Crawford, "International Market Segmentation: The U.S.–Japanese Markets," *Journal of International Consumer Marketing* 2, no. 2 (1989), pp. 75–90. See also Robert M. March, *The Honorable Consumer* (London: Pitman, 1990), p. 150.

─────────────────── **E X H I B I T   7 – 6** ───────────────────

World Youths Splurge Mostly on U.S. Goods

> The developing countries are wallowing in teenagers; about 25 percent of their huge populations are in their teens. A surprisingly large percentage prefer American brands—Coke, Nike, McDonald's, Motorola cellular phones, and Levis. This can be explained by the rapid spread of satellite TV delivery and cable TV which use a lot of American programming. Viacom's Network division has more viewers in the developing countries than in the United States. No wonder teenagers around the world have buyer appetites similar to those in California.

SOURCE: Bernard Wysocki, Jr., "In the Emerging World, Many Youths Splurge Mainly on U.S. Goods," *The Wall Street Journal,* June 26, 1997, p. A1. Reprinted by permission of the Wall Street Journal © 1997 Dow Jones & Company, Inc. All rights reserved worldwide.

compatible with each other. For example, a retailer's inventory clearance sale may attract a class of customer incompatible with the store's regular clientele.

A second major difference is that services lend themselves to customization far better than products. This takes place because of the difficulty inherent in standardizing services owing to the role the customer plays in the purchase of services. While this poses problems of "consistency," it also provides an opportunity to customize the service offering to meet the needs of specific groups of customers. This is exactly what many large service firms do (e.g., advertising agencies, travel agencies, banks, and insurance firms).[23]

An alternative approach is to reduce the variability resulting from the contacts between producers and consumers. Theodore Levitt suggested that, where possible, services be "industrialized" to overcome this problem. This can be done in three ways.[24]

1. *Use of hard technologies.* This involves substituting machinery and/or tools for people. Examples include automatic tellers, vending machines, and bank credit cards such as Visa and American Express, that make it easy to grant loans to people.

2. *Use of software technologies.* These technologies are concerned primarily with the systematic improvement of task performance. This approach is not new; for example, use of self-service to replace clerk services in supermarkets. It is the solution used by McDonald's, Pizza Hut, Marriott Hotels, and H&R Block as well as the providers of prepackaged vacation tours, off-the-shelf insurance programs, and payroll deduction savings programs.

3. *Hybrid technologies.* Hybrid technologies use hard equipment in conjunction with planned industrial systems to obtain greater efficiency. Examples include limited-service, fast, low-priced automobile repair businesses that specialize in mufflers and brakes (Midas), and radio-controlled, ready-mix concrete truck routings.

Using much the same reasoning, James H. Gilmore and Joseph Pine II suggested several approaches to successful mass customization of services. These include working with consumers to help determine their needs, identifying the product or service that best meets these needs, and then making a customized collaborative product for them. Examples include health care, financial services, and personal care services. A variation of this approach is to develop a standardized service for everyone but which the user can adapt to

───────────

[23] Valerie A. Zeithaml and Mary Jo Bitner, *Services Marketing* (New York: McGraw-Hill, 1996), pp. 181–89.

[24] Theodore Levitt, *The Marketing Imagination,* (New York: Free Press, 1986), p. 38-39.

his or her needs; for example, interactive computer services. A third way is to combine standard modules; for example, tailored travel tours, physical fitness programs, and software packages.[25]

MARKET ATTRACTIVENESS

Most firms no longer aim a single product and marketing program at the mass market. Instead, they break that market into homogeneous segments on the basis of meaningful differences in the benefits sought by different groups of customers. Then they tailor products and marketing programs to the particular desires and idiosyncrasies of each segment. But not all segments represent equally attractive opportunities for a firm. To prioritize segments by their potential, marketers must evaluate their future attractiveness and their firm's strengths and capabilities relative to the needs and competitive situations of the segments.

Analyzing and prioritizing potential target markets

Rather than allowing each business unit or product manager to develop an approach to evaluate the potential of alternative market segments, it is often better to apply a common analytical framework across segments. With this approach, managers can compare the future potential of different segments, using the same set of criteria, and then prioritize these segments to decide which to target and how resources and marketing efforts should be allocated. One useful analytical framework managers can use for this purpose is the **market attractiveness/business position matrix.** Managers use such models at the corporate level to allocate resources across businesses, or at the business-unit level to assign resources across product-markets. We are concerned here with the second application.

Exhibit 7-7 outlines the steps involved in developing a market attractiveness/business position matrix for analyzing current and potential target markets. Underlying such a matrix is the notion that managers can judge the attractiveness of a market (its profit potential) by examining market, competitive, and environmental factors that may influence profitability. Similarly, they can estimate the strength of the firm's competitive position by looking at the firm's capabilities or shortcomings relative to the needs of the market and the competencies of likely competitors.

The first steps in developing a matrix are to identify the most relevant variables for evaluating alternative market segments and the firm's competitive position regarding them, and to weight each variable in importance. Note, too, that Exhibit 7-7 suggests conducting a forecast of future changes in market attractiveness or competitive position in addition to, but separately from, an assessment of the current situation. This reflects the fact that a decision to target a particular segment is a strategic choice that the firm will have to live with for some time into the future.

Step 1: Select market attractiveness and business strength factors

An evaluation of the attractiveness of a particular market and of the strength of the firm's current or potential competitive position in it builds naturally on the kind of opportunity analysis we have described. Managers can assess both dimensions on the basis of

[25]James H. Gilmore and Joseph Pine II, "The Four Faces of Mass Customization," *Harvard Business Review,* January–February 1997, p. 91; see also Joseph Pine II, *Mass Customization* (Boston: Harvard Business School Press, 1993).

─────────────── E X H I B I T   7 – 7 ───────────────

Steps in Constructing a Market-Attractiveness/Business-Position Matrix for Evaluating Potential Target Markets

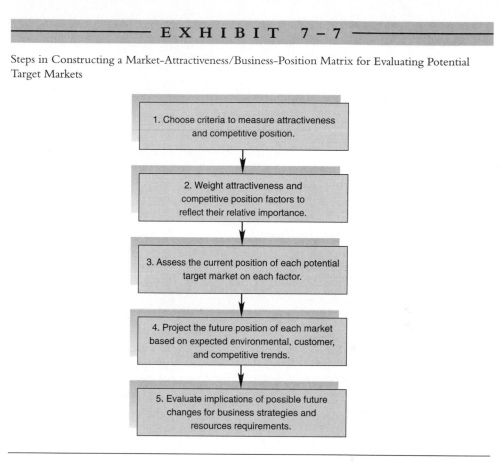

information obtained from analyses of the environment, customer segments, the competitive situations, and market potential estimates.

Factors underlying market attractiveness   As Exhibit 7-8 indicates, managers judge the attractiveness of a current or potential target market on the basis of four broad sets of variables. **Market factors** reflect the characteristics of the customers making up the market in question—the benefits they seek, their satisfaction with current product offerings, their power relative to suppliers—and factors that might shape the market's future volume potential, such as its overall size, growth rate, and the life-cycle stage.

Economic and technological factors examine the capital and technology a firm needs to compete in the market, plus structural variables (e.g., entry and exit barriers) that help shape long-term competitiveness and profit potential. **Competitive factors** measure the number and strengths of existing competitors in the marketplace and consider the possibility of future competitive changes through the appearance of substitute products. Finally, **environmental factors** reflect broad social or political constraints on the firm's ability to compete profitably in a market, such as governmental regulations or special interest groups.

Each of the factors shown in the left-hand column of Exhibit 7-8 can either increase or decrease the attractiveness of a market. Unfortunately, the relationship between a factor and market attractiveness is often complex and varies across industries and business units.

E X H I B I T   7 - 8

Factors Underlying Market Attractiveness and Competitive Position

Market-attractiveness factors	Competitive-position factors
Market/customer factors:	*Market position factors:*
Size (dollars, units)	Relative market share
Market potential	Rate of change in share
Market growth rate	Perceived actual or potential differentiation (quality/service/price)
Stage in life cycle	Breadth of current or planned product line
Diversity of competitive offerings (potential for differentiation)	Company image
Customer loyalty/satisfaction with current offerings	*Economic and technological factors:*
Price elasticity	Relative cost position
Bargaining power of customers	Capacity utilization
Cyclicality/seasonality of demand	Technological position
Economic and technological factors:	Patented technology (product or manufacturing)
Investment intensity	*Capabilities:*
Industry capacity	Management strength and depth
Level and maturity of technology utilization	Financial
Ability to pass through effects of inflation	R&D/product development
Barriers to entry/exit	Manufacturing
Access to raw materials	Marketing
Competitive factors:	Salesforce
Industry structure	Distribution system
Competitive groupings	Labor relations
Substitution threats	Relations with regulators
Perceived differentiation among competitors	*Interactions with other segments:*
Individual competitors' strengths	Market synergies
Environmental factors:	Operating synergies
Regulatory climate	
Degree of social acceptance	

SOURCE: Adapted from George S. Day, *Analysis for Strategic Market Decisions* (St. Paul: West, 1986). pp. 198–99; and Derek F. Abell and John S. Hammond, *Strategic Market Planning Problems and Analytical Approaches* (Englewood Cliffs, N.J.: Prentice Hall, 1979), p. 214.

The first step in evaluating the relative attractiveness of current and potential market segments, then, is to identify the determinants of attractiveness that are appropriate for a given industry from the firm's perspective. One caveat is that the factors used to judge market attractiveness should be relevant to all of the markets considered as possible targets. Such comparability is essential if the aggregate attractiveness scores are to be a valid basis for rank ordering alternative markets.

Factors underlying competitive position/business strengths   The right-hand column in Exhibit 7-8 displays factors managers might use to evaluate the current or potential competitive position of a business within a given target market. Once again, these factors reflect the information discussed in earlier chapters dealing with the customer, industry, and competitor analysis.

The **market position factors** are most appropriate for evaluating markets in which the business is already competing because they reflect the strength of a firm's current share position and product offerings compared with those of existing competitors. *Economic and technological factors* can indicate a business's current or potential competitive advantages or shortcomings in low production costs (capacity use and process technology), or sustainable product differentiation (superior product technology or patent protection). The

E X H I B I T   7 – 9

Examples of Weights and Ratings Accorded Market Attractiveness and Business Strength Factors by Large Packaged Food Company

	Attractiveness		
Factor group	**Weight**	**Rating***	**Total**
Market	50	8	400
Economic/technology	20	9	180
Competition	20	9	180
Environment	10	10	100
Total	100	36	860

Attractiveness rating = $\dfrac{860}{100}$ = 86

	Business strengths		
Factor group	**Weight**	**Rating***	**Total**
Market position	20	9	180
Economic/technology	20	8	160
Capabilities	50	9	450
Interaction with other segments	10	10	100
Total	100	36	890

Business strength rating = $\dfrac{890}{100}$ = 89

*Rating scale = 0–10.

business's **capabilities** might reflect operational strengths or weaknesses relative to competitors, such as a more extensive distribution channel or more limited financial resources to support future growth. Finally, managers should consider the possible positive or negative **interactions across multiple target markets.** Such interactions or synergies result from sharing operational activities and resources across markets (e.g., the use of a common salesforce to cover two or more target markets). Or they can result from the carryover effects of customer perceptions from one market to another. For example, Deere felt that its reputation for quality and reliability in farm equipment would carry over and provide a competitive advantage when it decided to enter the residential lawnmower market.

Step 2: Weigh each attractiveness and business strength factor

A numerical weight is assigned to each factor to indicate its relative importance. For example, the marketing managers of a large food company assigned the weights indicated in Exhibit 7-9. (Note that weights were assigned only to groups of factors although individual factors were taken into account in so doing.)

Steps 3–4: Rate each segment as to its market attractiveness and company strengths

These steps require that each market segment be rated as to its attractiveness and the company's strengths (using a scale of 0 to 10). In the large packaged food products company example (see Exhibit 7-9), the market received an attractiveness rating of 86 and a business strength rating of 89. On the basis of these strong scores, management considered its competitive position to be very strong. Exhibit 7-10 shows a matrix of the

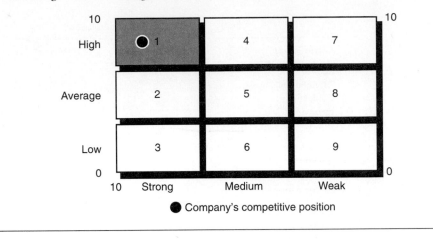

═════════ **E X H I B I T   7 – 1 0** ═════════

Matrix Showing the Competitive Position of a Packaged Food Company in a Given Segment Based on a Matching of Business Strengths and Market Attractiveness

two ratings, which indicates that management should strongly consider making the necessary investment to seek, or maintain, a strong (high-share) position.

Because a firm's capabilities or resources can best be judged by assessing their value relative to the needs of the market and those of major competitors, it is important to undertake the kind of detailed analysis of these competitors—especially with respect to their objectives, strategy, and marketing programs—that we discussed in Chapter 5.

Step 5: Project the future position of a market

Forecasting a market's future is more difficult than assessing its current state. Managers should first determine how the market's attractiveness is likely to change over the next three to five years. The starting point for this assessment is the product-market evolution analysis discussed in Chapter 6, including consideration of possible shifts in customer needs and behavior, the entry or exit of competitors, and changes in their strategies. Managers also must address several broader issues, such as possible changes in product or process technology, shifts in the economic climate, the impact of social or political trends, and shifts in the bargaining power or vertical integration of customers.

Managers must next determine how the competitive position of a business in the market is likely to change, assuming that it responds effectively to projected environmental changes but does not undertake any initiatives requiring a change in basic strategy. The expected changes in both market attractiveness and competitive position can then be plotted on the matrix in the form of a vector (arrow) that reflects the direction and magnitude of the expected changes.

Step 6: Evaluate implications for choosing target markets and allocating resources

Managers should consider a market to be a desirable target only if it is strongly positive on at least one of the two dimensions of market attractiveness and potential competitive position and at least moderately positive on the other. In Exhibit 7-11 this includes markets positioned in any of the three cells in the upper left-hand corner of the matrix. However, a

── E X H I B I T   7 - 1 1 ──

Implications of Alternative Positions within the Market-Attractiveness/Business-Position Matrix for Target Market Selection, Strategic Objectives, and Resource Allocation

	Competitive position		
	Strong	**Medium**	**Weak**
High	DESIRABLE POTENTIAL TARGET Protect position: • Invest to grow at maximum digestible rate • Concentrate on maintaining strength	DESIRABLE POTENTIAL TARGET Invest to build: • Challenge for leadership • Build selectively on strengths • Reinforce vulnerable areas	Build selectively: • Specialize around limited strengths • Seek ways to overcome weaknesses • Withdraw if indications of sustainable growth are lacking
Medium	DESIRABLE POTENTIAL TARGET Build selectively: • Emphasize profitability by increasing productivity • Build up ability to counter competition	Manage for earnings: • Protect existing strengths • Invest to improve position only in areas where risk is low	Limited expansion or harvest: • Look for ways to expand without high risk; otherwise, minimize investment and focus operations
Low	Protect and refocus: • Defend strengths • Seek ways to increase current earnings without speeding market's decline	Manage for earnings: • Protect position • Minimize investment	Divest: • Sell when possible to maximize cash value • Meantime, cut fixed costs and avoid further investment

Market Attractiveness (vertical axis label)

SOURCE: Adapted from George S. Day, *Analysis for Strategic Market Decisions* (St. Paul: West, 1986), p. 204; D. F. Abell and J. S. Hammond, *Strategic Market Planning Problems and Analytical Approaches* (Englewood Cliffs, N.J.: Prentice Hall, 1979); and S. J. Robinson, R. E. Hitchens, and D. P. Wade, "The Directional Policy Matrix: Tool for Strategic Planning," *Long Range Planning* 11 (1978), pp. 8–15.

business may decide to enter a market that currently falls into one of the middle cells under these conditions: (1) managers believe that the market's attractiveness or their competitive strength is likely to improve over the next few years; (2) they see such markets as stepping-stones to entering larger, more attractive markets in the future; or (3) shared costs are present, thereby benefiting another entry.

The market attractiveness/business-position matrix offers general guidance for strategic objectives and allocation of resources for segments currently targeted and suggests which new segments to enter. Exhibit 7-11 also summarizes generic guidelines for strategic objectives and allocations of resources for markets in each of the matrix cells. The general thrust of these guidelines is that managers should concentrate resources in attractive markets where the business is securely positioned, use them to improve a weak competitive position in attractive markets, and disengage from unattractive markets where the firm enjoys no competitive advantage.

TARGETING STRATEGIES

A number of strategies can help guide a manager's choice of target markets. Three of the more common of these are *mass-market, niche-market,* and *growth-market strategies.*

Mass-market strategy

The primary object of the **mass-market strategy** is to capture sufficient volume to gain economies of scale and a cost advantage. This strategy requires substantial resources, including production capacity, and good mass-marketing capabilities. Consequently, it is favored by larger business units or those whose parent corporation provides substantial support. For example, when Honda first entered the U.S. and European motorcycle markets, it targeted the high-volume segment consisting of buyers of low-displacement, low-priced cycles. Honda subsequently used the sales volume and scale economies it achieved in that mass-market segment to help it expand into smaller, more specialized segments of the market.

A business can pursue a mass-market strategy in two ways. First, it can ignore any segment differences and design a single product and marketing program—as Honda did—that will appeal to the largest number of consumers.

A second approach to the mass market is to design separate products and marketing programs for the differing segments. This is often called **differentiated marketing.** For example, Marriott did this with its various hotel chains. Although a differentiated marketing strategy can generate more sales than an undifferentiated strategy, it also increases costs in product design, manufacturing, inventory, and marketing—especially promotion.

Niche-market strategy

The **niche-market strategy** involves serving one or more segments that, while not the largest, consist of substantial numbers of customers seeking somewhat specialized benefits from a product or service. This strategy is designed to avoid direct competition with larger firms that are pursuing the bigger segments. For example, overall coffee consumption is down substantially, but the sales of gourmet coffees have boomed in recent years.

Growth-market strategy

Businesses pursuing a **growth-market strategy** target one or more fast-growth segments, even though they may not currently be very large. This strategy is often favored by smaller competitors to avoid direct confrontations with larger firms while building volume and share for the future. However, growth-market strategy usually requires strong R&D and marketing capabilities to identify and develop products appealing to newly emerging user segments. In addition, a firm should have the resources to finance rapid growth. The problem is that fast growth, if sustained, attracts large competitors. This happened to DEC (Digital Equipment) when IBM entered the minicomputer business. The goal of the defender is to have developed an enduring competitive position by means of superior products, service, distribution, and costs by the time competitors enter.

SELECTING TARGET MARKETS IN THE INTERNATIONAL ARENA

Some companies go international to defend their home position against global competitors that are constantly looking for vulnerability in their competition. This forces a firm to target major developed countries (e.g., the United States, Japan, and some Western European countries). The reasoning behind this strategy is that a global competitor can attack the home market by reducing price, the cost of which is subsidized by profits generated elsewhere in the world. If the defending company is solely a domestic player, it has to respond by cutting price on its entire volume, while the aggressor has to do so on only part of its total sales.

To prevent such attacks or at least minimize their impact, a firm must have the capacity to strike back in markets where the aggressor is vulnerable. For example, Caterpillar, through a joint venture with Mitsubishi Heavy Industries, has for the past 30 years made a substantial investment in Japan to deny their Japanese competitor, Komatsu, strength at home, thereby taking away its profit sanctuary. Had Caterpillar not been successful in doing so, Komatsu would have been able to compete more aggressively with Cat not only in the United States but in other major world markets.[26]

Another reason a firm may go overseas and in so doing target a specific country is to service customers who also are engaged in global expansion. In recent years Japanese automobile companies that have created U.S. manufacturing facilities have encouraged some of their parts suppliers to do the same. Firms also enter overseas markets to earn foreign exchange and, in some cases, their governments subsidize them to do so.

The selection of one or more target countries may be dictated by the availability of an appropriate partner. For example, Kellogg has had a European presence since the 1920s and controls about half the market. General Mills, which is Kellogg's major U.S. competitor, has long wanted to enter the European market, but doing so on its own would have been an extremely expensive undertaking, given Kellogg's high market share. The solution was to enter into a joint venture called Cereal Partners Worldwide with Nestlé, which has no cereals but does have a powerful distribution system.[27] France, Spain, and Portugal constituted the initial target markets for General Mills' Honey Nut Cheerios and Golden Grahams.

With the exception of these strategic special circumstances, the selection of overseas target markets follows essentially the same procedures as that for domestic markets, although given the magnitude of economic, social, and political change, companies are paying considerably more attention to political risk.

ETHICAL ISSUES IN MARKET TARGETING[28]

Over the years marketing managers have experienced a number of ethical problems relating to the selection of target markets. Problems can rise from targeting consumers whose inclusion in the targeted group influences them to make decisions that may not be in their best interest.[29] In other cases exclusion issues are raised because the firm's marketing efforts did not include a particular group.

Inclusion issues

In an effort to simplify advertising messages, advertisers often resort to undesirable stereotypes. These include sex role, race, or age stereotypes. Thus, many people believe that the portrayal of women as sex objects (bikini-clad models in beer ads) and as subordinates to

---

[26] Douglas Lamont, *Winning Worldwide* (Homewood, Ill.: Business One Irwin, 1991), pp. 59–69.

[27] Christopher Knowlton, "Europe Cooks up a Cereal Brawl," *Fortune,* June 3, 1991, p. 175.

[28] The discussion in this section is based largely on N. Craig Smith and John A. Quelch, *Ethics in Marketing* (Burr Ridge, Ill.: Irwin, 1993), pp. 183–95.

[29] Some have argued that advertising $150 sneakers to inner-city teenagers also causes ethical considerations as does the advertising of snack foods and soft drinks to children.

males is dehumanizing and offensive. The increase of reverse sexism, with men shown as sex objects and women as authority figures, has increased much to the dismay of some groups.

In recent years there has been an increase in the targeting of vulnerable groups (often minority groups) for harmful products such as lottery tickets, fast foods, weight-loss products, contraceptives, rental furniture, and financial services such as auto insurance and credit cards. Most extensive, however, has been the criticism of the targeting of alcohol and tobacco products, notably Uptown and Dakota cigarettes and PowerMaster Malt Liquor. In some cases a backlash against such targeting has prompted individual firms and even whole industries to abandon or modify their targeting practices (e.g., some brewers have reduced their marketing programs that target students during spring break) or to emphasize moderation (e.g., responsible drinking). But one can still question the ethics of using sports heroes as role models in the advertising of beer and products that may prove harmful. Indeed, the mass marketing of alcohol and tobacco products in general raises serious ethical questions.

Exclusion issues

The concern with exclusion is not only that certain groups are deprived of products and services but also that they may pay more for those they do receive. Considerable evidence supports the latter claim. A survey in New York City found that food prices are highest in neighborhoods that can least afford it. Low-income shoppers paid 8.8 percent more for their groceries, or $350 a year for a family of four. Further, inner-city stores were on average poorly stocked, had inferior foodstuffs, and offered poor service.[30]

Companies often face the problem of deciding whether to do business with certain groups they would prefer not to serve. For example, insurance companies want only low-risk policyholders, credit card companies only low-risk cardholders, and hospitals only patients with insurance.

SUMMARY

This chapter focused on two interrelated decisions that constitute the first steps toward the formulation of a strategic marketing program for a product-market entry: market segmentation and market targeting. A company must follow either a market-aggregation or a market-segmentation strategy. Market-aggregation strategy is appropriate when most customers have similar needs and desires. When customers are more diverse, a single standardized product and marketing program does not appeal to those who need or want a variety. Segmentation has become increasingly popular because it reflects the realities faced by firms in most markets.

The process of segmentation involves describing the characteristics of customers and identifying the different needs or benefits sought by those customers. To be effective, segments must be clearly identifiable and distinguishable from other segments, and be of adequate size, measurable and compatible. Descriptors are the variables used to explain the differences in product purchases across segments; there are four major categories: physical descriptors, general behavioral, product-related behavioral, and customer needs.

---

[30]Felix M. Freedman, "The Poor Pay More for Food in New York, Survey Finds," *The Wall Street Journal,* April 15, 1991.

The more common descriptors used to segment consumer markets are demographics (age, sex, race, geographic, and education), lifestyle, social class, product usage, product loyalty, and customer needs (benefits wanted). Two segmentation stages are required for industrial goods. The first, *macrosegmentation*, divides the market according to the organizational characteristics of the customer (e.g., product usage and geographical location) while *microsegmentation* groups customers by the characteristics of the individuals who influence the purchasing decision (e.g., purchase influence, loyalty, area of expertise). International segmentation is also a two-stage process, with country selection as the first stage followed by segmentation within the country.

Market targeting uses a market attractiveness/business position matrix as an analytical framework to help managers decide which market segments to target and how to allocate resources and marketing efforts. In applying such a matrix, managers must first identify a relevant set of variables underlying the attractiveness of alternative market segments. This typically involves selecting variables related to four broad sets of factors: market factors, economic and technological factors, competitive factors, and environmental factors. Similarly, managers must select a relevant set of variables to judge a firm's relative competitive position within the market segment. These variables of competitiveness typically include items related to market position factors, economic and technological factors, the capabilities of the business, and interactions or synergies across multiple target markets.

After managers have weighted these factors according to their relative importance, they can rate the attractiveness of alternative market segments and the strength of a firm's competitive position within each of those segments. To validate the ratings of the firm's capabilities, it is important to analyze the major competitors of the firm's product-market entry. They can then test the validity of the combined ratings with a market attractiveness/business position matrix that shows the implications of alternative positions in the matrix. Because a firm or business unit has limited resources, however, it often identifies more attractive potential target markets than it is capable of pursuing. Consequently, a firm must develop a targeting strategy to guide managers' choices of alternative target markets in a manner consistent with corporate objectives, resources, and competitive strengths. The most common targeting strategies include mass-market, niche-market, and growth-market strategies.

Company objectives often influence the selection of target countries. These include the need to protect a firm through the ability to retaliate from competitors who are constantly looking for vulnerability. Another reason is to service customers who have gone overseas; the availability of a partner in a certain venture may be yet another factor influencing country targeting. For many companies, the international targeting problem must consider product strength within a country and geographic expansion. For the most part the emphasis placed on one versus the other depends on the firm's current position relative to competition.

A number of ethical issues are associated with target marketing. These can be classified according to inclusion or exclusion of consumer groups as target markets. Inclusion issues involve the use in advertising of stereotypes (e.g., women as sex objects) and the targeting of minority groups for the sale of such products as tobacco, liquor, and expensive sneakers. Exclusion issues are raised not only when certain groups are deprived of products and services but when they may pay more for those they do receive.

CHAPTER 8

Positioning Decisions

REPOSITIONING FRENCH WINE[1]

French winemakers have launched a three-year campaign in the United States with the objective of repositioning French wine. Traditionally these wines have been positioned as upscale—something you drink when you're dining out at an elegant restaurant serving French cuisine. To broaden the appeal of their wines, French vintners are "trying to make Americans as comfortable with fumé blanc as they are with a Bud." The campaign stresses that French wines can be accessible and affordable, and that there are plenty of such wines between $5 and $15.

Only about 12 percent of American consumers drink wine regularly. To broaden the market the industry has to appeal to more people, especially younger ones. One wine marketer says the industry has only itself to blame for creating an image problem.

For the last 20 years, the wine industry has put up huge barriers to entry. We made people choose red or white, then pick which variety, and then which vineyard. They had to smell it and swirl it to see if it had a good mouth feel . . . The wine industry has this

elitist and sophisticated image that doesn't fit with today's casual society.

The new campaign includes consumer print ads, retail promotions, and a new website. One ad shows a group of young people enjoying some *vin rouge* as they barbecue. The headline reads, "Sizzling things happen in the 'oui' hours" which is a play on the campaign's theme, "Say yes to wines from France" (see Exhibit 8-1). The print media schedule calls for the advertisements to run in *The Wine Spectator* and general interest magazines such as *The New Yorker, Vanity Fair,* and *In Style.*

Retail outlets are targeted in an effort to teach retailers about French wines and encourage them to use the free in-store merchandising materials, including shelf-talkers, case cards, gift bags, and guidebooks. The winemakers' group also has a pocket guide to French wines that consumers can request through an 800 number or through the group's website. The latter includes information on 40 different brands of French wines complete with pictures and prices. Other sections provide data on France's grape-growing regions and how

[1]Based on an article by Cyndee Miller, "Wine for the Brew Crew," *Marketing News,* February 12, 1996, pp. 1–2.

to link wines and foods. Users can even access help in pronouncing *pouilly-fuisse*.

The group reports that so far the campaign has generated a strong response. About 10,000 calls to the toll-free number have been received along with 40,000 hits on the website. And despite exchange rate changes that made the import of French wines more expensive, overall sales in America have increased.

As the campaign launched by the French winemakers illustrates, the success of a product offered to a given target market depends on how well it is positioned within that market segment—that is, how well it performs relative to competitive offerings and the needs of the target audience. The campaign targeted younger consumers and included advertising, in-store promotions, and a new website. Early results suggest that the repositioning efforts succeeded in stimulating some members of the target group to seek out lower-priced French wines because of their quality and ability to enhance the enjoyment from an informal event, but this is hardly conclusive in regard to longer-term profit. **Positioning** (or repositioning), then, is the perceived fit between a particular product and the needs of the target market, and thus the positioning concept must be defined relative to competitive offerings and consumer needs.

Positioning is one of the most important strategic concepts because it is concerned with differentiation. Ries and Trout, who popularized the concept of positioning, view it as a creative undertaking whereby an existing brand in an overcrowded marketplace of similar brands can be given a distinctive position in the minds of targeted prospects. As we shall see later in this chapter, however, the positioning process is concerned with far more than creative communications. While their concept was concerned with an existing brand, it is equally applicable for new products.[2] While typically thought of in relation to the marketing of consumer goods, it has equal value for industrial goods and services and requires essentially the same procedure as for consumer goods.[3]

Positioning has become increasingly important due to the growing maturity of most products coupled with the large number of new products entering the market place each year. It is relatively easy to be successful if your product is demonstrably superior to competitors and you have the resources to exploit the situation. It is much more difficult when there is little difference in any meaningful way between major brands in a given category. This poses a challenging undertaking, yet it is critically important that the firm's positioning efforts succeed.

This chapter is concerned with answering the critical question, "How can a business position its offering so that customers in the target market perceive it as providing the desired benefits, thereby giving it an advantage over current and potential competitors?" The choice of a market position is a strategic decision with implications not only for how the firm's product or service should be designed, but also for detailing the other elements of the strategic marketing program. Each of the marketing mix elements is capable of making a contribution to the positioning of a product.

First, we will discuss the requirements for a successful position. Next, we will cover physical and perceptual positioning followed by a discussion of the steps in the positioning

---

[2] Al Ries and Jack Trout, *Positioning: The Battle for Your Mind* (New York: Warner Books, 1982).

[3] For a discussion of the positioning of industrial goods, see Frederick E. Webster, Jr., *Industrial Marketing Strategy* (New York: John Wiley & Sons, 1991), pp. 102–103.

————— E X H I B I T   8 – 1 —————

An Advertisement aimed at Repositioning French Wines

Courtesy Food and Wines from France, Inc.

process, including the criteria for identifying attractive positions in a given target market and the alternative positioning strategies a business might pursue.

REQUIREMENTS FOR SUCCESSFUL POSITIONING[4]

Because positioning is concerned with differentiating a firm's product or service from those of competitors in a given product category, success depends on the importance consumers attach to the nature and scope of the differentiation. The ideal situation is for a product to

---

[4]For further discussion, see James H. Myers, *Segmentation and Positioning for Strategic Marketing Decisions* (Chicago: American Marketing Association, 1996), pp. 171–74.

be clearly superior in terms of those dimensions or attributes important to targeted consumers; for example, Wal-Mart and IBM in its glory days.

More frequently, companies are successful on the basis of exceeding on one important attribute and having parity on the remaining dimensions. This was the case with Crest toothpaste, which was the first to use a fluoride ingredient, and Federal Express, which pioneered overnight delivery of small packages. Given the growing parity of physical attributes between competitors, more and more companies are attempting to differentiate themselves on the basis of the services attached to the product such as delivery time, repair and maintenance, and credit.

It helps if what is important is also unique, which was certainly the case with the companies cited above. By unique we mean being able to attract the attention of members of the target market in a positive way. If the differentiation is not both important and unique, then firms are forced to rely on advertising that employs endorsements, celebrities, and humor to position their products.

The positioning claim also must be believable if it is to be effective. Ideally, the credibility of the claim can be demonstrated visually in the advertising or by salespersons. Reliable and well-known sources such as *Consumer Report* also can be used to authenticate positioning claims. A critical question is whether the target audience believes the seller can deliver on its claim both short and long term.

Finally, when the above requirements have been met, it is necessary to develop a single positioning "claim" that will capture the importance and uniqueness factors and make them memorable and believable. Positioning claims need to focus on relatively few key benefits in order not to confuse the consumer and dilute the importance of the claim. Glen Urban and his colleagues suggested that the key benefits should be identified in a statement called the **core benefit proposition** which facilitates an identification of essential product features; for example, Tylenol pain reliever is "effective, fast, and long-lasting relief without an upset stomach."[5]

PHYSICAL VERSUS PERCEPTUAL PRODUCT POSITIONING

One way to assess the current position of a product offering relative to competitors is on the basis of how the various offerings compare on some set of objective *physical characteristics.* For example, an article in *The Wall Street Journal* discussed the pending battle between the various brands of behemoth sport utility vehicles (SUVs). It compared Ford's 1996 Expedition with General Motors' Suburban on seating capacity, engine, city mileage, highway mileage, length, and price (see Exhibit 8-2).[6] In many cases a physical product positioning analysis can provide useful information to a marketing manager, particularly in the early stages of identifying and designing new product offerings.

Despite being based primarily on technical instead of market data, physical product positioning can be an essential step in undertaking a strategic marketing analysis. This is especially true with the competitive offerings of many industrial goods and services, which buyers typically evaluate largely on the basis of such characteristics. In addition, it contributes to a better marketing/R&D interface by determining key physical product

---

[5]Glen L. Urban, John R. Hauser, and M. Kiles Dholakia, *Essentials of New Product Management* (Englewood Cliffs, N.J.: Prentice Hall, 1987), p. 22.

[6]Aaron Lucchetti, "Ford's New Expedition Heads into Suburban's Terrain," *The Wall Street Journal,* January 24, 1996, p. B1.

E X H I B I T 8 – 2

1996 Ford Expedition vs. GM Suburban on Selected Number of Physical Dimensions

Feature	Expedition	Suburban
Seating capacity	9	9
Cargo capacity	115 cu. ft.	149.5 cu. ft.
Engine	4.6 liter, V-8	5.7 liter, V-8
City mileage	14 mpg	13 mpg
Highway mileage	18 mpg	17 mpg
Length	204.6 inches	220 inches
Price	$24,000–36,000	$24,682–38,000

SOURCE: Aaron Lucchetti, "Ford's New Expedition Heads into Suburban's Terrain," *The Wall Street Journal,* June 24, 1996, p. B1. Reprinted by permission of the Wall Street Journal, © 1996 Dow Jones & Company, Inc. All rights reserved worldwide.

characteristics, helps define the structure of competition by revealing the degree to which the various brands compete with one another, and may indicate the presence of meaningful product gaps (the lack of products having certain desired physical characteristics) which, in turn, may reveal opportunities for a new product entry.

Limitations of physical positioning

A simple comparison of only the physical dimensions of alternative offerings usually does not provide a complete picture of relative positions because positioning ultimately takes place in customers' minds. Even though a product's physical characteristics, packaging, brand name, price, and ancillary services can be designed to achieve a particular position in the market, customers may attach less importance to some of these characteristics, or perceive them differently from what the firm expects. Also, customers' attitudes toward a product are often based on social or psychological attributes not amenable to objective comparison, such as perceptions of the product's aesthetic appeal, sportiness, or status image. Given the data contained in Exhibit 8-2, one wonders whether Ford would be successful with its new Expedition against GM's Suburban. But we lack information on other attributes, their relative importance, and the psychological dimensions of the two brands and hence cannot draw such a conclusion. Consequently, *perceptual positioning analyses*—whether aimed at discovering opportunities for new product entries or evaluating and adjusting the position of a current offering—are critically important. The remainder of this chapter is concerned with this type of positioning analysis.

Perceptual product positioning

Consumers often know very little about the essential physical attributes of many products, especially those involving the household, and even if they did, they would not understand them well enough to use them as a basis for choosing between competitive offerings. (For the major differences between physical and perceptual product positioning analyses, see Exhibit 8-3). Many consumers do not want to be bothered with information about a product's physical characteristics because they are not buying these physical properties but the benefits they provide. While the physical properties of a product certainly influence the benefits provided, a consumer can typically evaluate a product better on the basis of what

====================== E X H I B I T   8 – 3 ======================

Comparison of Physical and Perceptual Analyses

Physical positioning	Perceptual analyses
• Technical orientation	• Consumer orientation
• Physical characteristics	• Perceptual attributes
• Objective measures	• Perceptual measures
• Data readily available	• Need marketing research
• Physical brand properties	• Perceptual brand positions and positioning intensities
• Large number of dimensions	• Limited number of dimensions
• Represents impact of product specs and price	• Represents impact of products specs and communication
• Direct R&D implications	• R&D implications need to be interpreted

it *does* than what it *is*. Thus, for example, a headache remedy is judged on how quickly it brings relief, a toothpaste on the freshness of breath provided, a beer on its taste, and a vehicle on how comfortably it rides.

The evaluation of many products is subjective because it is influenced by factors other than physical properties, including the way products are presented, our past experiences with them, and the opinion of others. Thus, physically similar products may be perceived as being different because of different histories, names, and advertising campaigns. For example, some people pay considerably more for Bayer aspirin than for an unadvertised private label even though they are essentially the same product.

Dimensions on which consumers perceive competitive offerings

Consumers perceive competitive offerings on various dimensions that can be classified as follows:

- *Simple physically based attributes.* These are directly related to a single physical dimension such as price, quality, power, or size. While there is a direct correspondence between a physical dimension and a perceptual attribute, an analysis of the consumers' perception of products on these attributes may unveil some phenomena of interest to a marketing strategy. For instance, two cars with estimated gasoline mileage of 23.2 and 25.8 miles per gallon may be perceived as having similar gasoline consumption.

- *Complex physically based attributes.* Because of the presence of a large number of physical characteristics, consumers may use composite attributes to evaluate competitive offerings. The development of such summary indicators is usually subjective because of the relative importance attached to different cues. Examples of composite attributes are the efficiency of a computer system, roominess of a car, and a product's or service's being user friendly.

- *Essentially abstract attributes.* Although these perceptual attributes are influenced by physical characteristics, they are not related to them in any direct way. Examples include bodiness of a beer, sexiness of a perfume, quality of a French wine, and prestige of a car. All of these attributes are highly subjective and difficult to relate to physical characteristics other than by experience. Thus, it is difficult to believe that the attempted repositioning of French wines will be very successful because not only have these wines traditionally been thought of as very expensive and an accompaniment to French foods but because of the wide assortment of popular, low-priced American wines.

The importance of perceptual attributes with their subjective components varies across consumers and product classes. Thus, it can be argued that consumers familiar with a given product class are apt to rely more on physical characteristics and less on perceptual attributes than consumers who are less familiar with that product class. It can also be argued that perceptual product positioning is essential for nondurable consumer goods, but less so for consumer durables (e.g. sports utility vehicles) and many industrial goods.

Even though there is considerable truth in these statements, it is important to note that perceptual attributes must be considered the basis for a positioning strategy for most products. One reason is the growing similarity of the physical characteristics of more and more products. This increases the importance of other, largely subjective dimensions; for example, consider how consumers might evaluate the significance of the rugged appearance of an off-road vehicle.

THE POSITIONING PROCESS

Determining the perceived positions of a set of product offerings and evaluating strategies for positioning a new entry or repositioning an existing one involves the steps outlined in Exhibit 8-4. These steps are applicable to any product or service in the international arena regardless of the country involved. This is not to suggest that the determinant product attributes and consumer perceptions of the various competitive offerings will remain constant across countries; rather, they are likely to vary with most products. In any event, after managers have selected a relevant set of competing offerings (Step 1), they must identify a set of critical or determinant product attributes (Step 2).

Step 3 involves collecting information from a sample of customers about their perceptions of the various offerings, and in Step 4 researchers analyze this information to determine the intensity of a product's current position in customers' minds—for example, does it occupy a predominant position?

In Step 5 managers analyze the location of the product's position in the **product space** relative to those of competing products. They then ascertain the customers' most preferred combination of determinant attributes, which requires the collection of further data (Step 6). This allows an examination of the fit between the preferences of a given target segment of customers and the current positions of competitive offerings (Step 7). Finally, in Step 8 managers examine the degree of fit between the positions of competitive products and the preferences of various market segments as a basis for choosing a successful strategy for positioning a new entry or for repositioning an existing product.

A discussion of each of these steps takes up the remainder of this chapter.

Step 1: Identify a relevant set of competitive products

A positioning analysis can take place at the **company, product line, product category,** or **brand levels.** At the product category level, the analysis examines customers' perceptions about types of products they might consider as substitutes to satisfy the same basic need. Suppose, for example, that a company is considering introducing a new instant breakfast drink. The new product would have to compete with other breakfast foods such as bacon, eggs, and cereals. To understand the new product's position in the market, a marketer could

─────────────────────── E X H I B I T   8 – 4 ───────────────────────

Steps in the Positioning Process

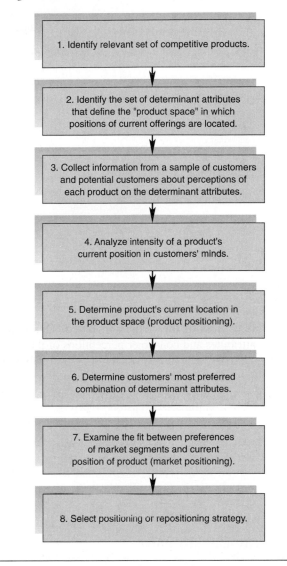

1. Identify relevant set of competitive products.

2. Identify the set of determinant attributes that define the "product space" in which positions of current offerings are located.

3. Collect information from a sample of customers and potential customers about perceptions of each product on the determinant attributes.

4. Analyze intensity of a product's current position in customers' minds.

5. Determine product's current location in the product space (product positioning).

6. Determine customers' most preferred combination of determinant attributes.

7. Examine the fit between preferences of market segments and current position of product (market positioning).

8. Select positioning or repositioning strategy.

use a positioning map that shows the location of the new product compared with that of competing products. Marketing research is necessary to obtain customer perceptions of the new product concept relative to likely substitute products on several critical determinant attributes. The positioning maps enable marketers to determine how their product compares with the competition and the attributes that best describe the entry. Panel A of Exhibit 8-5 shows a product positioning map for a breakfast drink constructed from such information. The two attributes defining the product space were price and convenience of preparation. The proposed new drink occupies a distinctive position because customers perceive it as a comparatively low-cost, convenient breakfast food.

E X H I B I T   8 – 5

Product Category and Brand Positioning

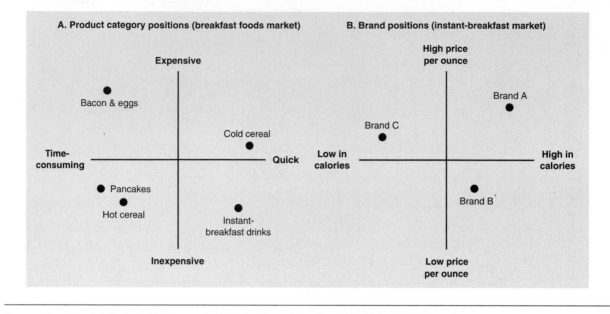

A. Product category positions (breakfast foods market)

B. Brand positions (instant-breakfast market)

SOURCE: Adapted from P. S. Busch and M. J. Houston, *Marketing Strategic Foundations* (Burr Ridge, Ill.: Richard D. Irwin, 1985), p. 430.

Once competitors introduce similar brands into the same product category, a marketer needs to find out how the brand is perceived compared with competitors' brands. Thus, panel B of Exhibit 8-5 shows the results of a positioning analysis conducted at the brand level. It summarizes customer perceptions concerning three existing brands of instant breakfast drinks. Notice, however, that two different attributes define the product space in this analysis: relative price per ounce and calorie content. This brand-level analysis is very useful for helping marketers understand a brand's competitive strengths and weaknesses and for determining whether the brand should be repositioned to differentiate and strengthen its position. The danger in conducting only a brand-level positioning analysis is that it can overlook threats from possible substitutes in other product categories.

Step 2: Identify determinant attributes

Positioning can be based on a variety of attributes—some in the form of surrogates which imply desirable features or benefits as a positioning base. The more common types of bases are discussed briefly below.[7]

- **Features** are often used in physical product positioning and, hence, with industrial products. An example of its use with a consumer good is Jenn-Air's claim that "This is the quietest dishwasher made in America."

- **Benefits,** like features, are directly related to a product. Examples here include Volvo's emphasis on safety and durability and Norelco's promise of a "close and comfortable shave."

---

[7]Adapted from C. Merle Crawford, *New Product Management* (Burr Ridge, Ill.: Richard D. Irwin, 1996), p. 348.

- **Usage** includes **end use** (If you've got it in the kitchen, it probably goes with PORK"—a versatility claim); **demographic** ("Just because kids will be kids doesn't mean you can't have knock-down, gorgeous floors"—Congoleum); and **psychographic** or **behavioral** (Ellesse positioning itself as the producer of a fashionable upscale active wear line); and **popularity** (Hertz as the biggest rental car company in the world).

- **Parentage** includes who makes it (bottled by a French vintner; "At Fidelity, you're not just buying a fund, a stock, or a bond—you're buying a better way to manage it"), and prior products ("Buying a car is like getting married. It's a good idea to know the family first"—followed by a picture of the ancestors of the Mercedes Benz S class model).

- **Manufacturing process** is often the subject of a firm's positioning efforts. An example is Jaeger-LeCoultre's statement about its watches—"We know it's perfect, but we take another 1,000 hours just to be sure."

- **Ingredients** as a positioning concept is illustrated by some clothing manufacturers claiming that their sports shirts are made only of pure cotton.

- **Endorsements** are of two types—those by experts ("Discover why over 5,000 American doctors and medical professionals prescribe this Swedish mattress—Tempor-Pedic) and those by emulation—Michael Jordan wearing Nike shoes.

- **Comparison** with a competitor's product is commonplace ("Tests prove Pedigree is more nutritious than IAMS, costs less than IAMS, and tastes great, too"—Pedigree Mealtime).

- **Proenvironment** positioning seeks to portray a company as a good citizen ("Because we recycle over 100 million plastic bottles a year, landfills can be filled with other things, like land, for instance"—Phillips Petroleum).

- **Product** class—when freeze-dry coffee was introduced as a new and different product type compared with regular or instant coffees.

- **Price/quality**—Wal-Mart has successfully positioned itself as the lowest price seller of quality household products.

- **Country or geographic area** (French wines, Russian vodka).

Theoretically consumers can use many attributes to evaluate products or brands, but the number of features or benefits actually influencing a consumer's choice is typically small. Obviously, the more variables used in positioning a given product, the greater the chance of confusion and even disbelief on the part of the consumer. In any event, it is critical that the positioning effort be kept as simple as possible and that complexity be avoided at all costs.[8]

In using one or more attributes as the basis of a brand's positioning effort, it is important to recognize that the degree of importance attached to these attributes typically varies across customers. For example, whether a hotel offers 24-hour room service may be an attribute that some consumers might use in evaluating hotels, but most would be unlikely to attach much importance to it when deciding which hotel chain to patronize. Further, even an important attribute may not greatly influence a consumer's preference if all the alternative brands are perceived to be about equal on that dimension. Deposit safety is an important attribute to consider when choosing a bank, but most consumers perceive all

[8]Jack Trout, *The New Positioning,* (New York: McGraw-Hill, 1996), chap. 3.

banks to be about equally safe. Consequently, deposit safety is not a **determinant attribute:** It does not play a major role in helping customers to differentiate between the alternatives and determine which bank they prefer.

Marketers therefore should rely primarily on determinant attributes in defining the product space in a positioning analysis. The question is, How can a marketer find out which product dimensions are determinant attributes? The answer depends on the analytical technique the marketer uses. Choosing an appropriate statistical technique (the next step in the planning process) can help the marketer determine which of the important attributes are truly determinant in guiding customers' choices.

Step 3: Determine consumers' perceptions

Marketers use several techniques to construct perceptual maps. The two main technologies to collect and analyze customers' perceptions about the competitive positioning of alternative products or brands are **multidimensional scaling (MDS)** and **discriminate analysis.** The analyst must first identify the salient attributes consumers use to evaluate products or services in the category under investigation. The discriminate analysis program then determines the consumers' perceptual dimensions on the basis of which attributes best discriminate among brands. This technique is excellent for producing perceptual positioning maps because it permits the researcher to analyze the differences between products or brands using several variables (descriptive ratings based on several attributes) simultaneously.

MDS requires the selection of specific products or brands for consumers to judge on the basis of their similarity to one another. Thus, a paired comparison basis using 15 products would mean judging 105 pairs, and for 20 products 190 pairs. The degree of similarity of each pair is rated on a 10-point scale. Two or more brands can be compared on the basis of no criteria or on as many dimensions as desired. The trouble is that the comparisons have to be on a one-by-one basis. Thus, using eight dimensions of attributes and 15 products would require a rating by each respondent of $115 \times 8 = 920$ pairs! This poses an enormous burden on respondents and makes the computer output data difficult to use. James Myers also noted that another difficulty occurs when even one brand from the set is added or subtracted, which "can change the final solution and configuration on the map."[9]

Step 4: Analyze the intensity of a product's current position

The position of a brand may not exist in the minds of consumers or may vary in intensity. Often the awareness set for a given product class is three or fewer brands even though the number of available brands is greater than 20. Thus, many if not most brands have little or no position in the minds of many consumers. For example, in the last 10 or so years more than 200 new soft drinks have been introduced, most of which went unnoticed by consumers.

A brand that is not known by a consumer cannot, by definition, occupy a position in that consumer's mind. Thus, the first step in acquiring an intense position for a brand is to build brand awareness. In doing so, the brand needs to be strongly associated with several

---

[9] Myers, *Segmentation and Positioning,* p. 207. For a discussion and examples relating not only to discriminate analysis and multidimensional scaling but also to factor analysis, correspondence analysis, and laddering, see Myers, chapters 7–11.

concepts relating to the purchase decision. An intense position is best obtained by developing a strong relationship between a brand and a limited number of attributes.[10]

Marketing opportunities to gain positioning intensity

In situations where one or a limited number of brands dominate a product class (or type) in the minds of consumers, the main opportunity for competitors lies in obtaining a profitable position within a market segment not dominated by a leading brand. Competing head-on against the leaders on the basis of attributes appropriated by larger competitors is not likely to be effective.

A better option is to concentrate on an attribute prized by members of a given market segment. Thus, Ford, having targeted women and young families, positioned its Windstar minivan primarily on the basis of safety and cargo (the most of any minivan). Introduced in the spring of 1994, Windstar's attributes, coupled with a successful advertising campaign, enabled Ford's Windstar to compete effectively against the leading minivan seller, Dodge Caravan.[11]

Constraints imposed by an intense position

Although marketers should seek an intense position for their brands, they must keep in mind that attaining such a position imposes some constraints on future strategies. First, if shifts in the market environment cause customers to reduce the importance they attach to a current determinant attribute, marketers may have difficulty repositioning a brand with an intensely perceived position on that attribute. This is the problem the French wine industry faces. It remains to be seen whether the industry will be successful in its attempt to reposition French wines so that they are appropriate for both the upper end of the market—its present position—and younger wine drinkers who favor less expensive wines to serve in less formal settings. Repositioning could threaten to alienate part or all of the product's present users regardless of success with its newly targeted group. Indeed, the wine industry's very success in its repositioning efforts could ensure that it will lose its present group of users.

Second, an existing intense position could be diluted as a result of consolidation. For example, British Leyland was formed through a series of mergers involving a number of British car manufacturers. For years the company did not have a clear identity because it was new and distributed a variety of brands, including Rover, Triumph, and Austin-Morris. Indeed, most Europeans had difficulty recalling spontaneously any British car manufacturer after once-strong brand names such as Austin and Morris lost their identity and meaning.

Third, another danger concerning an intensely positioned brand is the temptation of marketers to overexploit that position by using the brand name on line extensions and new products. The danger is that the new products may not fit the original positioning, thus diluting the brand's strong image. For example, how many travelers know the difference between Holiday Inn, Holiday Inn Express, Holiday Inn Select, and Holiday Inn Garden Court?[12]

---

[10]David A. Aaker, *Managing Brand Equity* (New York: Free Press, 1991), pp. 109–79. BSN, Europe's third-largest food company, opted to rename itself after its best-known brand (Danone) because its BSN name received a low name recognition rating among housewives around the world. See "BSN Who?" *The Economist,* May 14, 1994, p. 70.

[11]Steve Lyons, "The Marketing 100—Ford Windstar," *Advertising Age,* June 26, 1995, p. S-27.

[12] Bruce Orwall, "Multiplying Hotel Brands Puzzle Travelers," *The Wall Street Journal,* April 17, 1996, p. B1.

E X H I B I T 8 – 6

Perceptual Map of Women's Clothing Retailers in Washington, D.C.

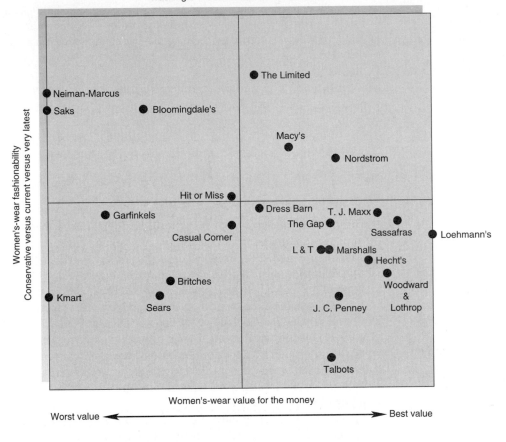

Washington 1990 Women's fashion market

Women's-wear fashionability
Conservative versus current versus very latest

- The Limited
- Neiman-Marcus
- Saks
- Bloomingdale's
- Macy's
- Nordstrom
- Hit or Miss
- Dress Barn
- T. J. Maxx
- Garfinkels
- The Gap
- Sassafras
- Loehmann's
- Casual Corner
- L & T Marshalls
- Hecht's
- Britches
- Woodward & Lothrop
- Kmart
- Sears
- J. C. Penney
- Talbots

Women's-wear value for the money

Worst value ◄——————————————► Best value

SOURCE: Adapted from Douglas Tigert and Stephen Arnold, "Nordstrom: How Good Are They?" *Babson College Retailing Research Reports,* September 1990, as shown in Michael Levy and Barton A. Weitz, *Retailing Management* (Burr Ridge, Ill.: Richard D. Irwin, 1992), p. 205.

Step 5: Analyze the product's current position

How does a marketer know if a brand occupies a strong position on a particular attribute? The only way to find out is to collect information through marketing research and analyze it using the techniques discussed in Step 3. Exhibit 8-6 provides an example of what can be done with such information; it shows the results of a Babson College study that portrays how a sample of consumers positioned a number of women's clothing retailers in the Washington, D. C., area.[13] Respondents rated the various stores on the two determinant attributes of value and fashionability. Some stores (e.g., Nordstrom and Kmart) occupy

---

[13]Douglas Tigert and Stephen Arnold, "Nordstrom: How Good Are They?" *Babson College Retailing Research Reports,* September 1990.

relatively distant positions from one another, indicating that consumers perceive them as being very different. Other stores occupy positions comparable to one another (e.g., Neiman-Marcus and Saks) and thus are considered relatively alike. This means that the intensity of competition between these stores is likely to be considerably greater than that for stores occupying widely divergent positions.[14]

The store positioning shown in Exhibit 8-6 also provides useful information about possible opportunities for the launching of a new store or the repositioning of an existing one. Positioning for a new store could be done by examining the positioning map for empty spaces (i.e., competitive gaps) where no existing store is currently located. There is such a gap in the upper-right-hand quadrant of the "value/fashionability" map. This gap may represent an opportunity for developing a new entry or repositioning an old one that is perceived to offer greater fashionability than Nordstrom but at a lower price. Of course, such gaps may exist simply because a particular position is either (1) impossible for any brand to attain due to technical constraints or (2) undesirable since there are few prospective customers for a brand with that particular set of attributes.

Limitations of product positioning analysis

The analysis depicted in Exhibit 8-6 is usually referred to as *product positioning* because it indicates how customers position alternative products or brands relative to one another. The problem with this analysis, however, is that it does not tell the marketer which positions are most appealing to customers.[15] Thus, there is no way to determine whether there is a market for a new brand or store that locates in an "open" position or whether customers in different market segments prefer brands with different attributes and positions. To solve such problems, marketers need to measure customers' preferences and locate them in the product space along with their perceptions of the positions of existing brands. This is called a *market positioning analysis.*

Step 6: Determine consumers' preferred combination of attributes

There are several ways analysts can measure customer preferences and include them in a positioning analysis. For instance, survey respondents can be asked to think of the ideal product or brand within a product category—a hypothetical brand possessing the perfect combination of attributes (from the customer's viewpoint). Respondents could then rate their ideal product and existing products on a number of attributes. An alternative approach is to ask respondents to not only judge the degree of similarity between pairs of existing brands but to also indicate their degree of preference for each. In either case the analyst, using the appropriate statistical techniques, can locate the respondents' ideal points relative to the positions of the various existing brands on the product space map.

Whichever approach is used, the results will look something like Exhibit 8-7, which shows a hypothetical cluster of ideal points for one segment of women's clothing consumers. As a group, this segment would seem to prefer Nordstrom over any other women's clothing retailer on the map. There are, however, several reasons why not all customers in this segment are likely to prefer Nordstrom. First, the ideal points of some customers are actually closer to Macy's than Nordstrom. Second, customers whose ideal point is

---

[14] Michael Levy and Barton A. Weitz, *Retailing Management* (Homewood, Ill.: Irwin, 1992), p. 205.

[15] The attractiveness of existing brands can be inferred from current sales volumes and market shares. The position occupied by the share leader is obviously more appealing to a greater number of customers than the positions occupied by lesser brands.

—— E X H I B I T   8 – 7 ——

Perceptual Map of Women's Clothing Retailers in Washington, D.C. Showing the Ideal Points of a Segment of Consumers

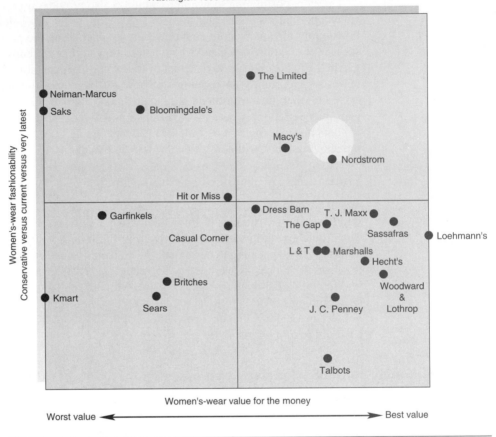

Washington 1990 women's fashion market

SOURCE: Adapted from Douglas Tigert and Stephen Arnold, "Nordstrom: How Good Are They?" *Babson College Retailing Research Reports,* September 1990.

equidistant between the two stores may be relatively indifferent in their choice of which store to patronize. Finally, customers sometimes may patronize stores somewhat farther away from their ideal—particularly when buying nondurable goods or services—to assess the qualities of new stores, to reassess older stores from time to time, or just for the sake of variety.

Step 7: Define market positioning and market segmentation

An important criterion for defining market segments is the difference in the benefits sought by different customers. Because differences between customers' ideal points reflect variations in the benefits they seek, a market positioning analysis can simultaneously identify distinct market segments as well as the perceived positions of different brands. When

---

E X H I B I T   8 – 8

Perceptual Map of Women's Clothing Retailers in Washington, D.C., Showing Five Segments Based on Ideal Points

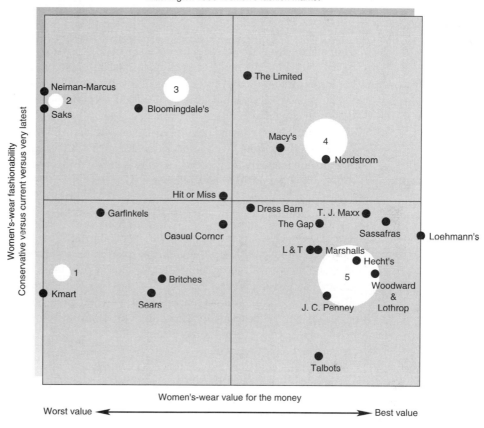

Washington 1990 Women's fashion market

Women's-wear fashionability
Conservative versus current versus very latest

The Limited

Neiman-Marcus
2
Saks   3   Bloomingdale's

Macy's   4   Nordstrom

Hit or Miss

Garfinkels   Dress Barn   T. J. Maxx
                         The Gap   Sassafras   Loehmann's
Casual Corner
                                         L & T   Marshalls
                                                          Hecht's
1   Britches   5
Kmart   Woodward &
         Sears   J. C. Penney   Lothrop

                         Talbots

Women's-wear value for the money

Worst value ◄─────────────────────────► Best value

SOURCE: Adapted from Douglas Tigert and Stephen Arnold, "Nordstrom: How Good Are They?" *Babson College Retailing Research Reports*, September 1990.

customers' ideal points cluster in two or more locations on the product space map, the analyst can consider each cluster a distinct market segment.[16] For analytical purposes, each cluster is represented by a circle that encloses most of the ideal points for that segment; the size of the circle reflects the relative proportion of customers within a particular segment.

Exhibit 8-8 groups the sample of Washington, D.C., respondents into five distinct segments on the basis of clusters of ideal points. Segment 5 contains the largest proportion of

---

[16]When using preference data to define market segments, however, the analyst also should collect information about customers' demographic characteristics, lifestyle, product usage, and other potential segmentation variables. This enables the analyst to develop a more complete picture of the differences between benefit segments. Such information can be useful for developing advertising appeals, selecting media, focusing personal selling efforts, and designing many of the other elements of a marketing program that can be effective in appealing to a particular segment.

customers; segment 1, the smallest.[17] By examining the preferences of customers in different segments together with their perceptions of the positions of existing brands, analysts can learn much about (1) the competitive strength of different brands in different segments, (2) the intensity of the rivalry between brands in a given segment, and (3) the opportunities for gaining a differentiated position within a specific target segment.

Step 8: Select positioning strategies

The final decision about where to position a new brand or reposition an existing one should be based on both the market targeting analysis discussed in Chapter 7 and the results of a market positioning analysis. The position chosen should match the preferences of a particular market segment and should take into account the current positions of competing brands. It should also reflect the current and *future* attractiveness of the target market (its size, expected growth, and environmental constraints) and the relative strengths and weaknesses of competitors. Such information, together with an analysis of the costs required to acquire and maintain these positions, allows an assessment of the economic implications of different market positioning strategies.

Sales potential of market positions

The sales level of a brand is affected by many things, some of which are controlled by the firm (e.g., product, price, promotion, and distribution) and some that are not (e.g., competitive activities and the environment's evolution). All of these influence elements of the consumer's purchasing process, such as awareness, purchase intent, and search for the product. The **purchase intent share** represents the percentage of consumers who intend to buy a specific brand before actually searching for it. It is one of the most important indicators of the likely success of a given product and integrates all the factors that influence the perceived qualities of a product.

Analysts can estimate the purchase intent share a brand could acquire in a segment, assuming a certain positioning strategy, from the positions of existing brands and the preferences of consumers in the segments. In a perceptual map obtained by means of multidimensional scaling, the purchase intent is related to the inverse of the distance of the brand's position from the ideal point.

The estimation of the sales potential of two positions is illustrated in Exhibits 8-9 and 8-10 and is based on the distance between a brand's position and the ideal points. Two segments are considered, with the size of the second being about half the size of the first. The overall market is currently dominated by three brands—E, H, and B, with brands E and B strongly positioned in segment 1 and H in segment 2. The firm owning brand B is considering the introduction of a new brand and, as a first step, evaluates the marketing potential of two positions, X and Y. They correspond to a reinforcement of the firm's position in segment 1 and a penetration of segment 2, respectively.

The estimates made in Exhibit 8-10 assume that the new brand—X or Y—will obtain adequate awareness and distribution. Brand X is expected to gain a 17.3 purchase intent

---

[17]The size of the individual circles in Exhibit 8-8 is fictitious and designed for illustrative purposes only. The map shows five distinct preference segments but only one set of perceived product positions. The implication is that consumers in this sample were similar in the way they perceived existing brands but different in the product attributes they preferred. This is the most common situation; customers tend to vary more in the benefits they seek than in how they perceive available products or brands. Sometimes, however, various segments may perceive the positions of existing brands quite differently, even using different determinant attributes in assessing these positions. Under such circumstances, a marketer should construct a separate market positioning map for each segment.

— E X H I B I T   8 - 9 —

Perceptual Map of Sales Potential for Two Positions

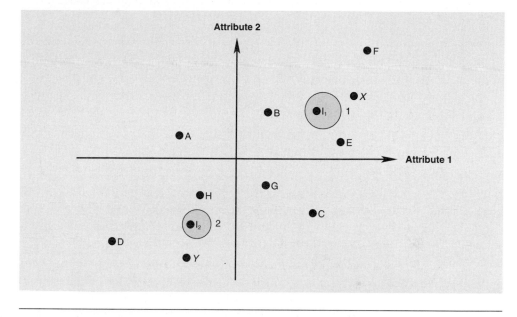

NOTE: Circles identify ideal points 1 and 2.

share, of which about one-third would come from the cannibalization of brand B. The firm's total purchase intent share is expected to increase from 17.5 percent to 30.8 percent. Brand Y would cannibalize brand B less, but the expected purchase intent share of Y is only 10.9 percent because of the smaller size of segment 2 and the strong position of brand H in this segment. The expected increase in total purchase intent share would be greater for brand X than Y despite its higher degree of cannibalization.

Evaluations of the sales potential of alternative positions also should consider the more pertinent market dynamics. These include:

- *Growth of market segments.* The current sales potential of a position close to the ideal point may be limited. If the segment's growth rate is higher than the market growth rate, the cumulative sales potential of this segment may be substantial.

- *Evolution of segments' ideal points.* If at all possible, brands should be positioned on the evolutionary path of a segment's ideal point to enjoy an increasing market share.

- *Changes in positioning intensity.* If an existing brand has a low positioning intensity and a favorable position in a segment, the firm marketing this brand should try to increase its positioning intensity, thereby increasing the brand's penetration and market share.

- *Evolution of existing brands' positions.* The shifts in the positions of existing brands may be difficult to predict, but their evolution can often be anticipated. For example, in recent years Chrysler has emphasized greater styling in its cars.

E X H I B I T   8 – 1 0

Illustration of Purchase of Intent Shares before and after Introduction of New Product (in Percent)

		A	B	C	D	E	F	G	H	X or Y
					Existing brands					New brand
Current	Segment 1	3.9	24.0	6.4	1.3	38.1	12.2	9.6	4.4	—
	Segment 2	11.1	4.5	5.9	14.0	2.9	1.4	10.3	49.9	—
	Total	6.3	17.5	6.2	5.5	26.4	8.6	9.8	19.6	—
With X	Segment 1	2.9	18.0	4.8	1.0	28.6	9.2	7.2	3.3	25.0
	Segment 2	10.9	4.4	5.8	13.7	2.9	1.4	10.1	48.9	1.9
	Total	5.6	13.5	5.1	5.2	20.0	6.6	8.2	18.5	17.3
With Y	Segment 1	3.8	23.4	6.3	1.3	37.2	11.9	9.4	4.3	2.4
	Segment 2	8.0	3.3	4.2	10.1	2.1	1.0	7.4	36.0	27.8
	Total	5.2	16.7	5.6	4.2	25.5	8.3	8.7	14.9	10.9

- *Emerging attributes.* The long-term sales potential of a brand will be affected not only by its position on the current determinant attributes but by its position on emerging attributes For example, in the last decade, the increasing importance of caloric content in food has had a significant impact on the sales potential of brands in the product class.

- *Development of new segments.* The number of consumers with similar needs distinct from the rest of the market may increase to the point where some firms consider these consumers a separate segment. The emergence of new segments will create new opportunities but may also weaken the sales potential of existing brands.

- *Introduction of new brands.* The introduction of new brands by competitors is often unpredictable. The analysis of a product space from a competitor's point of view gives an indication of moves that competitors might make.

Market-positioning strategies

Formulating a market-positioning strategy consists of selecting and defining a market position the firm plans to occupy in reaching its marketing objectives. This requires estimates of the economic potential of alternative positions, which are based largely on analysis of the sales potential of each position and the investments required to occupy the targeted position. The seven market-positioning strategies described below are relevant to a large number of situations.

1. *Monosegment positioning.* As the name suggests, monosegment positioning involves developing a product and marketing program tailored to the preferences of a single market segment. Successful implementation of this strategy would give the brand an obvious advantage within the target segment but would not generate many sales from customers in other segments. This strategy is best used with mass marketing.

2. *Multisegment positioning.* This consists of positioning a product so as to attract consumers from different segments. This is an attractive strategy because it provides higher economies of scale, requires smaller investments, and avoids dispersion of managerial attention. It is particularly appropriate when individual segments are small, as is generally the case in the early stages of a product's life cycle.

3. *Standby positioning.* It may not be in the best economic interest of a firm to switch from a multisegment positioning strategy to a monosegment strategy—assuming the use of several brands, each positioned to serve the needs of only one segment—even if it increases total market share. In such a case the firm may decide to implement a monosegment positioning strategy *only* when forced to do so. To minimize response time the firm prepares a standby plan specifying the products and their attributes as well as details of the marketing programs that would be used to position the new product.

4. *Imitative positioning.* This is essentially the same as a head-on strategy where a new brand targets a position similar to that of an existing successful brand. It may be an appropriate strategy if the imitative firm has a distinctive advantage beyond positioning, such as better access to channels of distribution, a more effective salesforce, or substantially more money to spend on promotion, including "price deals."

5. *Anticipatory positioning.* A firm may position a new brand in anticipation of the evolution of a segment's needs. This is particularly appropriate when the new brand is not expected to have a fast acceptance, and market share will build as the needs of consumers become increasingly aligned with the benefits being offered. At its best, this strategy enables a firm to preempt a market position that may have a substantial long-term potential. At its worst, it may cause a firm to face a difficult economic situation for an extended period, if the needs of a segment do not evolve as expected.

6. *Adaptive positioning.* This consists of periodically repositioning a brand to follow the evolution of the segment's needs.

7. *Defensive positioning.* When a firm occupies a strong position in a market segment with a single brand, it is vulnerable to imitative positioning strategies. The firm may preempt competitive strategies by introducing an additional brand in a similar position for the same segment. This will reduce immediate profitability but it may allow the firm to better protect itself against competitors in the long term. For example, Procter and Gamble has seven brands of laundry detergents, such as Tide and Bold, several of which occupy similar positions in the minds of consumers.

Positioning of services

While typically thought of in relation to the marketing of consumer products, it should be clear from the discussion here that positioning has equal value for services that require essentially the same procedure as consumer goods. Because services are characterized by their intangibility, perishability, consumer participation in their delivery, and the simultaneous nature of their production and consumption, they are—when compared with products—more difficult for consumers to understand, to compare with competing services, to predict in terms of their performance, and, therefore, more difficult for marketers to position.

These characteristics inhibit the development of a new service, particularly during the concept, market testing, and commercialization stages. Once developed, the inability to describe in meaningful ways the key service characteristics makes it difficult to communicate with employees and customers. Professional services and those consumed over time (e.g., cruises, hospitalization) make the transfer of information even more difficult.

Valarie Zeithaml and Mary Jo Bitner proposed the use of a service blueprint to help solve the communication problems. The goal of such a map is to accurately portray "the service system so that the different people involved in providing it can understand and deal with it objectively regardless of their roles or their individual points of view . . . A service blueprint visually displays the service by simultaneously depicting the process of service delivery. It provides a way to break a service down into its logical components and to depict the steps or tasks in the process, the means by which the tasks are accomplished, and the evidence of service as the customer experiences it." The key components of such a map are the customer's actions, the "onstage" contact employee actions, and the support processes.[18]

SUMMARY

Positioning seeks to maximize a product's performance relative to competitive offerings and the needs (benefits sought) of one or more targeted market segments. There are two types of positioning—one based on the physical product, the other on the market's perception of the product. Physical product positioning depends primarily on technical versus market data, but it still represents an important step in the formulation and implementation of marketing strategy because it facilitates the interface between marketing and R&D, forces management to discriminate between selected physical characteristics, helps in identifying key competitors, and may reveal important product gaps.

Physical product positioning is flawed by its failure to explicitly consider the consumer. Consumers know very little about the physical characteristics of many products, and even if they did, they would not understand them well enough to use them as a basis for selecting one brand over another. Indeed, what consumers perceive in a product has various dimensions that can be classified as simple physically based attributes, such as miles per gallon; complex physically based attributes, such as user-friendliness; or essentially abstract attributes such as prestige.

To determine which positioning strategy to adopt, a firm must proceed through the eight steps in the positioning process. These are (1) identify a relevant set of competitive products, (2) identify the set of determinant attributes that define the product space in which positions of current offerings are located, (3) collect data from a sample of customers and potential customers about perceptions of each product on the determinant attributes, (4) analyze the intensity of a product's current position in the customers' minds, (5) determine the product's current location in the product space (product positioning), (6) determine customers' most preferred combination of determinant attributes, (7) examine the fit between preferences of market segments and the current position of the product (market positioning), and (8) select a positioning or repositioning strategy which should reflect *future* potential of various positions. Relevant to many market situations are common strategies such as monosegment, multiple segment, standby, imitative,

---

[18] Valarie A. Zeithaml, and Mary Jo Bitner, *Services Marketing* (New York: McGraw-Hill, 1996), pp. 277–78. See also pp. 278–87 for a discussion of the step-by-step process by which a map is developed and for examples of service blueprints.

anticipatory, adaptive, and defensive positioning. Because services are characterized by their intangibility, perishability, consumer participation in their delivery, and the simultaneous nature of their production and consumption, they are—when compared to products—more difficult for consumers to understand, to compare against competing services, to predict in terms of their performance, and therefore more difficult to position successfully.

3 SECTION

Formulating Marketing Strategies

9 CHAPTER

Marketing Strategies for New Market Entries

ILLINOIS TOOL WORKS: NEW NUTS AND BOLTS TO FILL MANY NICHES[1]

Unglamorous and low profile, Illinois Tool Works (ITW) makes a diverse array of products that typically are attached to, embedded in, or wrapped around somebody else's goods. It manufactures nails, screws, bolts, strapping, wrapping, valves, capacitors, filters, and adhesives as well as the tools and machines to apply them.

Long known for superior engineering—and premium prices—in recent years the Chicago conglomerate has managed to develop and implement more cost-efficient manufacturing methods, become more price-competitive, and aggressively expand its global presence. More important, the firm has been extraordinarily innovative in a variety of mundane product areas. It is the inventor and world's largest producer of plastic safety buckles, a leading supplier of fasteners to General Motors, the inventor of the plastic loops that hold six-packs

together, the maker of Zip-Pak resealable food packages, and the producer of painting equipment for Toyota's auto plants. ITW holds 2,400 active U.S. patents, but the firm is so decentralized—and has been so prolific—that nobody at corporate headquarters can come up with an exact tally of how many products it makes.

How can a $5 billion company manage such diversity, reduce costs, and generate a constant stream of new products all at the same time? As we shall see in Chapter 12, the firm's organization structure and management policies have a lot to do with it. For one thing, the company is highly decentralized. Lower-level managers are given a great deal of authority to identify and pursue new products or new markets. This helps the firm maintain close contact and relationships with its many customers. And when engineers and marketers in one

[1]This example is based on material found in Ronald Henkoff, "The Ultimate Nuts & Bolts Co.," *Fortune*, July 16, 1990, pp. 70–73; and I. Jeanne Dugan, Alison Rea, and Joseph Weber, "The Best Performers," *Business Week*, March 24, 1997, pp. 80–90.

division develop and commercialize a successful new product, the company often spins off the product and the personnel as a new division. Consequently, ITW now has about 360 separate divisions or business units, each with its own marketing, R&D, and manufacturing operations. Most of these units are quite small and nimble, usually accounting for less than $50 million in annual sales. Amazingly, ITW's world headquarters in Chicago is run with only 100 people.

While the company's divisions develop hundreds of new products every year, many are variations of existing products which are redesigned for new applications in new market segments. For instance, in the mid-1980's an ITW researcher invented a durable safety-rated plastic buckle for a customer who makes life jackets. Now, the firm sells millions of dollars of buckles designed for backpacks, bicycle helmets, pet collars, and many other applications.

ITW is often the pioneer in developing new product-markets, but it does not always end up as the market share leader as those product categories mature. Instead, it tends to focus on—and often dominates—smaller niche markets where competition is less intense and profit margins are higher. As one ITW manager says, "We try to sell where our competitors aren't."

Although, the company is not the market share leader in all of its many businesses, its revenue growth and profitability over the last decade have been among the best in the United States. The firm has consistently been first or second among the most admired firms in the metal products industry on *Fortune's* annual survey, and it ranked 30th on *Business Week's* list of top performing companies for 1996, with $486 million in profit and a 39 percent return to shareholders.

STRATEGIC ISSUES CONCERNING NEW PRODUCT ENTRIES

The success of Illinois Tool Works illustrates several important points about new product and market development. First, both sales growth and cost cutting can help improve profits. But while it is often easier to cut costs in the short term, revenue growth—particularly growth generated by the development of innovative new products—can have a bigger impact on a firm's profitability and shareholder value over the long-haul. This point is confirmed by a study of 847 large corporations conducted by Mercer Management Consulting. The authors found that the compound annual growth rate in the market value of companies that achieved higher-than-average profit growth but lower revenue growth than their industry's average—companies that increased profits mostly by cutting costs—was 11.6 percent from 1989 to 1992. By contrast, companies that achieved higher-than-average profits as the result of higher-than-average revenue growth saw their market value jump at an annual rate double that—23.5 percent.[2]

Illinois Tool Works' history also illustrates that new product introductions can involve products that differ in their degree of newness from the perspective of the company and its customers. Some of the products developed by the firm, such as the first plastic safety-rated buckle, were new innovations in the eyes of both the company and its customers. But while

[2]These results are reported in Myron Magnet, "Let's Go for Growth," *Fortune*, March 7, 1994, pp. 60–72.

many of the products ITW develops for new applications—like buckles designed especially for bicycle helmets or pet collars—are new to the customers in those target niches, they are old hat to the company.

This chapter examines marketing strategies and programs appropriate for developing markets for offerings that are *new to the target customers*. Our primary focus is on programs used by the *pioneer* firm—or first entrant—into a particular product-market. Of course, later entrants also face difficulties when developing and introducing their own versions of a product. But given that the challenge facing such *followers* is essentially to capture market share in the face of established competitors, we will postpone our discussion of marketing programs appropriate for later entrants until Chapter 10, where we examine share-building strategies.

Finally, ITW's experience shows that the pioneer in a new product category does not always end up as the market share leader in that category as it matures. In ITW's case this was due to its strategy of avoiding competition by focusing on specialized niche markets, but in other cases followers may have captured a larger share by offering better products or lower prices. This leads to an interesting strategic question: Is it usually better for a firm to bear the high costs and risks of being the pioneer in developing a new product in hopes of establishing and maintaining a profitable position as the market grows, or to be a follower that watches for possible design or marketing mistakes by the pioneer before joining the fray with its own entry? Before discussing the specific marketing programs that might be adopted by pioneers or followers, we first examine the conditions where pioneer and follower strategies each have the greatest probability of long-term success.

HOW NEW IS "NEW"?

A survey of the new product development practices of 700 U.S. corporations conducted by the consulting firm of Booz, Allen & Hamilton found that the products introduced by those firms over a five-year period were not all equally new. The study identified six categories of new products based on their degree of newness as perceived by both the company introducing them and the customers in the target market. These categories are discussed here and diagrammed in Exhibit 9-1, which also indicates the percentage of new entries falling in each category. Notice that only 10 percent of all new product introductions fell into the new-to-the-world category.[3]

- *New-to-the-world products* (10 percent)—True innovations that are new to the firm and create an entirely new market.

- *New product lines* (20 percent)—A product category that is new for the company introducing it but is not new to customers in the target market because of the existence of one or more competitive brands.

- *Additions to existing product lines* (26 percent)—New items that supplement a firm's established product line. These items may be moderately new to both the

---

[3]*New Products Management for the 1980s* (New York: Booz, Allen & Hamilton, 1982). More recent studies, though focusing on smaller samples of new products, suggest that the relative proportions of new-to-the-world versus less innovative product introductions have not changed substantially over the years. For example, see Eric M. Olson, Orville C. Walker, Jr., and Robert W. Ruekert, "Organizing for Effective New Product Development: The Moderating Role of Product Innovativeness," *Journal of Marketing*, January 1995, pp. 48–62.

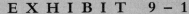

E X H I B I T   9 – 1

Categories of New Products Defined According to Their Degree of Newness to the Company and Customers in the Target Market

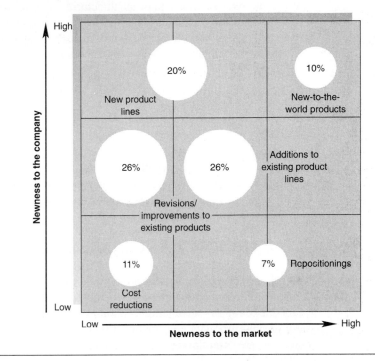

SOURCE: New Products Management for the 1980s (New York: Booz, Allen & Hamilton, 1982), p. 8.

firm and the customers in its established product-markets. They also may serve to expand the market segments appealed to by the line.

· *Improvements in or revisions of existing products* (26 percent)—Items providing improved performance or greater perceived value brought out to replace existing products. These items may present moderately new marketing and production challenges to the firm, but unless they represent a technologically new generation of products, customers are likely to perceive them as similar to the products they replace.

· *Repositionings* (7 percent)—Existing products that are targeted at new applications and new market segments.

· *Cost reductions* (11 percent)—Product modifications providing similar performance at a lower cost.

A product's degree of newness to the company, its target customers, or both help determine the amount of complexity and uncertainty involved in the engineering, operations, and marketing tasks necessary to make it a successful new entry. It also contributes to the amount of risk inherent in those tasks. Introducing a product that is new to both the firm and to target customers requires the greatest expenditure of effort and resources. It also involves the greatest amount of uncertainty and risk of failure due to the lack of information and experience with the technology and the target customers.

Products that are new to target customers but not to the firm (e.g., line extensions or modifications aimed at new customer segments or repositionings of existing products) are often not very innovative in design or manufacturing requirements, but they may present a great deal of marketing uncertainty. The marketing challenge here—as with new-to-the-world products—is to build **primary demand**, making target customers aware of the product and convincing them to adopt it. This is the marketing problem we investigate in this chapter.

Finally, products that are new to the company but not to the market (e.g., new product lines, line extensions, product modifications, and cost reductions) often present fewer challenges for R&D and product engineering. The company can study and learn from earlier designs or competitors' products. However, these products can present major challenges for process engineering, production scheduling, quality control, and inventory management. Once such a product is introduced into the market, the primary marketing objective becomes one of building **selective demand**: capturing market share and convincing customers that the new offering is better than existing competitive products. We discuss marketing programs a firm might use to accomplish these objectives in Chapter 10.

OBJECTIVES OF NEW PRODUCT AND MARKET DEVELOPMENT

The primary objective of most new product and market development efforts is to secure future volume and profit growth. This objective has become even more crucial in recent years due to rapidly advancing technology and more intense global competition. A steady flow of new products and the development of new markets, including those in foreign countries, are essential for the continued growth of most firms.

The ITW case illustrates, however, that individual development projects may also accomplish a variety of other strategic objectives. When asked what strategic role was served by their most successful recent new entry, the respondents in the Booz, Allen & Hamilton survey mentioned eight different strategic objectives. Exhibit 9-2 lists these objectives and the percentage of respondents that mentioned each one. The exhibit also indicates which objectives focused on external concerns (e.g., defending market share) and which were driven by a desire to improve or build upon the firm's internal strengths. Most respondents indicated their new entry helped accomplish more than one objective.

Exhibit 9-3 shows that different types of new entries are appropriate for achieving different strategic objectives. For example, if the objective is to establish a foothold in or preempt a new market segment, the firm must introduce a product that is new to that market, although it may not be entirely new to the company. On the other hand, if the objective is to improve cash flow by adding another cash generator, simple line extensions or product modifications—particularly those that reduce unit costs—may do the trick.

A business's objectives for its new entries influence the kind of entry strategy it should pursue and the marketing and other functional programs needed to implement that strategy. For instance, if a business is pursuing a prospector strategy and its objectives are to maintain a position as a product innovator and to establish footholds in a variety of new product-markets, it should attempt to be the pioneer in as many of those markets as possible. As we saw in Chapter 3, successful implementation of such a strategy requires the business to be competent in and devote substantial resources to R&D, product engineering, marketing, and marketing research.

On the other hand, if the business is concerned primarily with defending an already strong market share position in its industry, it may prefer to be a follower. Usually entering

━━━━━━━━━━━━━━━━━━━━━ **E X H I B I T   9 – 2** ━━━━━━━━━━━━━━━━━━━━━

Strategic Objectives Attained by Successful New Market Entries

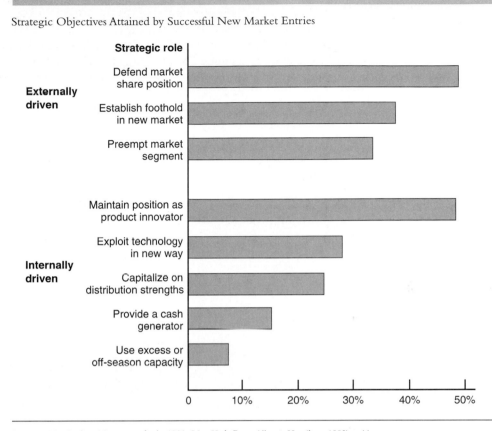

SOURCE: *New Products Management for the 1980s* (New York: Booz, Allen & Hamilton, 1982), p. 11.

new product-markets only after an innovator, a follower relies on superior quality, better customer service, or lower prices to offset the pioneer's early lead. This strategy usually requires fewer investments in R&D and product development, but marketing and sales still are critical in implementing it effectively. A more detailed comparison of these alternative new market entry strategies is the focus of the next section of this chapter.

MARKET ENTRY STRATEGIES: PIONEERS VERSUS FOLLOWERS

Even though IBM is viewed as one of the world's premier high-tech companies, it usually has not been a pioneer in the sense of being the first to enter new markets. For example, IBM did not enter the personal computer (PC) market until after several other firms, including Apple and Tandy, had already established substantial sales volumes. But as a follower, IBM developed an improved product design offering superior performance. It also had vast financial resources to support extensive advertising and promotional efforts, as well as an established reputation for reliability and customer service. Consequently, IBM was able to capture a commanding share of the PC market within a year of its entry.

Of course, in view of IBM's struggles during the 1990s one might ask whether the firm would have been better off pursuing a more innovative prospector strategy in at least some

---

EXHIBIT 9 – 3

Types of New Market Entries Appropriate for Different Strategic Objectives

Objective	New entry
Maintain position as a product innovator	New-to-the-world products; improvements or revisions to existing products
Defend a current market-share position	Improvements or revisions to existing products; additions to existing product line; cost reductions
Establish a foothold in a future new market; preempt a market segment	New-to-the-world products; additions to existing product line; repositionings
Exploit technology in a new way	New-to-the-world products; new product line; additions to or revision of existing product line
Capitalize on distribution strengths	New-to-the-world products; new product line; additions to or revisions of existing product line
Provide a cash generator	Additions to or revisions of existing product line; repositionings; cost reductions
Use excess or off-season capacity	New-to-the-world product; new product line

---

of its businesses. On the other hand, some of the pioneering firms in the computer industry, such as Commodore and Apple, have not fared so well in the marketplace either. The important strategic question, then, is which of the two entry approaches—being the pioneer or a fast follower—*usually* makes the most sense? Or do both entry strategies have particular advantages under different sets of conditions?

Pioneer strategy

Although they take the greatest risks and probably experience more failures than their more conservative competitors, conventional wisdom holds that successful pioneers are handsomely rewarded. It is assumed that competitive advantages inherent in being the first to enter a new product-market can be sustained through the growth stage and into the maturity stage of the product life cycle, resulting in a strong share position and substantial returns.

Some of the potential sources of competitive advantage available to pioneers are briefly summarized in Exhibit 9-4 and discussed below.[4]

1. *First choice of market segments and positions.* The pioneer has the opportunity to develop a product offering with attributes most important to the largest segment of customers, or to promote the importance of attributes that favor its brand. Thus, the pioneer's brand can become the standard of reference customers use to evaluate other brands. This can make it more difficult for followers with me-too products to convince existing customers that their new brands are superior to the older and more familiar pioneer. If the pioneer has successfully tied its offering to the choice criteria of the

---

[4]For a more extensive review of the potential competitive advantages of being a first-mover, and the controllable and uncontrollable forces that influence a firm's ability to capitalize on those potential advantages, see Roger A. Kerin, P. Rajan Varadarajan, and Robert A. Peterson, "First-Mover Advantage: A Synthesis, Conceptual Framework, and Research Propositions," *Journal of Marketing*, October 1992, pp. 33–52.

=== E X H I B I T   9 – 4 ===

Potential Advantages of Pioneer and Follower Strategies

Pioneer	Follower
• Economies of scale and experience. • High switching costs for early adopters. • Ability to define the rules of the game. • Distribution advantage. • Influence on consumer choice criteria and attitudes. • Possibility of preempting scarce resources.	• Ability to take advantage of pioneer's positioning mistakes. • Ability to take advantage of pioneer's product mistakes. • Ability to take advantage of pioneer's marketing mistakes. • Ability to take advantage of pioneer's limited resources. • Ability to take advantage of the latest technology.

largest group of customers, it also becomes more difficult for followers to differentiate their offerings in ways that are attractive to the mass-market segment. They may have to target a smaller peripheral segment or niche instead.

2. *Ability to define the rules of the game.* The pioneer's actions on such variables as product quality, price, distribution, warranties, postsale service, and promotional appeals and budgets set standards that subsequent competitors must meet or beat. If the pioneer sets those standards high enough, it can raise the costs of entry and perhaps preempt some potential competitors.[5]

3. *Distribution advantages.* The pioneer has the most options in designing a distribution channel to bring the new product to market. This is particularly important for industrial goods where, if the pioneer exercises its options well and with dispatch, it should end up with a network of the best distributors. This can exclude later entrants from some markets. Distributors are often reluctant to take on second or third brands. This is especially true when the product is technically complex and the distributor must carry large inventories of the product and spare parts and invest in specialized training and service.

  For consumer packaged goods, it is more difficult to slow the entry of later competitors by preempting distribution alternatives. Nevertheless, the pioneer still has the advantage of attaining more shelf facings at the outset of the growth stage. By quickly expanding its product line following an initial success, the pioneer can appropriate still more shelf space, thereby making the challenge faced by followers even more difficult.

4. *Economies of scale and experience.* Being first means the pioneer can gain accumulated volume and experience and thereby lower per unit costs at a faster rate than followers. This advantage is particularly pronounced when the product is technically sophisticated and involves high development costs or when its life cycle is likely to be short with sales increasing rapidly during the introduction and early growth stages.

[5]Thomas S. Gruca and D. Sudharshan, "A Framework for Entry Deterrence Strategy: The Competitive Environment, Choices, and Consequences," *Journal of Marketing*, July 1995, pp. 44–55.

As we shall see later, the pioneer can deploy these cost advantages in a number of ways to protect its early lead against followers. One strategy is to lower price, which can discourage followers from entering the market because it raises the volume necessary for them to break even. Or the pioneer might invest its savings in additional marketing efforts to expand its penetration of the market, such as heavier advertising, a larger sales force, or continuing product improvements or line extensions.

5. *High switching costs for early adopters.* Customers who are early to adopt a pioneer's new product may be reluctant to change suppliers when competitive products appear. This is particularly true for industrial goods, where the costs of switching suppliers can be high. Compatible equipment and spare parts, investments in employee training, and the risks of lower product quality or customer service make it easier for the pioneer to retain its early customers over time.

   In some cases, however, switching costs can work against the pioneer and in favor of followers. A pioneer may have trouble converting customers to a new technology if they must bear high switching costs to abandon their old way of doing things. Pioneers in the manufacture of ethanol, for instance, had a difficult time convincing car owners to modify their engines to be able to use ethanol instead of gasoline. Once the pioneer has persuaded early adopters to change technologies, however, their costs of switching to a follower's brand within the new product category may be relatively low.

6. *Possibility of preempting scarce resources and suppliers.* The pioneer may be able to negotiate favorable deals with suppliers who are eager for new business or who do not appreciate the size of the opportunity for their raw materials or component parts. If later entrants subsequently find those materials and components in short supply, they may be constrained from expanding as fast as they might like or be forced to pay premium prices.

Not all pioneers capitalize on their potential advantages

Some evidence suggests that the above advantages can help pioneers to gain and maintain a competitive edge in new markets. For instance, researchers have found that surviving pioneers hold a significantly larger average market share when their industries reach maturity than firms that were either fast followers or late entrants in the product category.[6]

On the other hand, some pioneers fail. They either abandon the product category, go out of business, or get acquired before their industry matures. One recent study, which took these failed pioneers into account and averaged their performances with those of the more successful survivors, found that overall pioneers did not perform as well over the long haul as followers.[7]

Of course, volume and market share are not the only dimensions in which success can be measured. Unfortunately, there is little evidence concerning the effect of the timing of a firm's entry into a new market on its ultimate profitability in that market or the value generated for shareholders.[8]

---

[6]For example, see William T. Robinson, "Market Pioneering and Sustainable Market Share Advantages in Industrial Goods Manufacturing Industries," working paper, Purdue University, 1984; Robert D. Buzzell and Bradley T. Gale, *The PIMS Principles: Linking Strategy to Performance* (New York: Free Press, 1987), p. 183; and David M. Szymanski, Lisa C. Troy, and Sundar G. Bharadwaj, "Order of Entry and Business Performance: An Empirical Synthesis and Reexamination," *Journal of Marketing*, October 1995, pp. 17–33.

[7]Peter N. Golder and Gerard J. Tellis, "Pioneer Advantage: Marketing Logic or Marketing Legend," *Journal of Marketing Research*, May 1993, pp. 158–70.

[8]Marvin B. Lieberman and David B. Montgomery, "First-Mover Advantages," *Strategic Management Journal* 9 (1988), pp. 41–59; and Michael J. Moore, William Boulding, and Ronald C. Goodstein, "Pioneering and Market Share: Is Entry Time Endogenous and Does It Matter?" *Journal of Marketing*, February 1991, pp. 97–104.

In view of the mixed research evidence, then, it seems reasonable to conclude that while a pioneer may have some *potential* competitive advantages, not all pioneers are successful at capitalizing on them. Some fail during the introductory or shakeout stages of their industries' life cycles. And those that survive may lack the resources to keep up with rapid growth or the competencies needed to maintain their early lead in the face of onslaughts by strong followers.

Follower strategy

In many cases a firm becomes a follower by default. It is simply beaten to a new product-market by a quicker competitor. But even when a company has the capability of being the first mover, the previous observations suggest there may be some advantages to letting other firms go first into a product-market. Let the pioneer shoulder the initial risks while the followers observe the pioneer's shortcomings and mistakes. Possible advantages of such a follower strategy are briefly summarized in Exhibit 9-4 and discussed here.

1. *Ability to take advantage of the pioneer's positioning mistakes.* If the pioneer misjudges the preferences and purchase criteria of the mass-market segment or attempts to satisfy two or more segments at once, it is vulnerable to the introduction of more precisely positioned products by a follower. By tailoring its offerings to each distinct segment, the follower(s) can successfully encircle the pioneer.

2. *Ability to take advantage of the pioneer's product mistakes.* If the pioneer's initial product has technical limitations or design flaws, the follower can benefit by overcoming these weaknesses. Even when the pioneering product is technically satisfactory, a follower may gain an advantage through product enhancements. For example, Compaq captured a substantial share of the commercial PC market by developing faster and more portable versions of IBM's original machine.

3. *Ability to take advantage of the pioneer's marketing mistakes.* If the pioneer makes any marketing mistakes in introducing a new entry, it opens opportunities for later entrants. This observation is closely related to the first two points, yet goes beyond product positioning and design to the actual execution of the pioneer's marketing program. For example, the pioneer may fail to attain adequate distribution, spend too little on introductory advertising, or use ineffective promotional appeals to communicate the product's benefits. A follower can observe these mistakes, design a marketing program to overcome them, and successfully compete head-to-head with the pioneer.

4. *Ability to take advantage of the latest technology.* In industries characterized by rapid technological advances, followers can possibly introduce products based on a superior, second-generation technology and thereby gain an advantage over the pioneer. And the pioneer may have difficulty reacting quickly to such advances if it is heavily committed to an earlier technology. Consumer popularity of the newer VHS format, for instance, gave followers in the videocassette recorder market an advantage over pioneer Sony, which was locked into the less popular Beta format.

5. *Ability to take advantage of the pioneer's limited resources.* If the pioneer has limited resources for production facilities or marketing programs or fails to commit sufficient resources to its new entry, followers willing and able to outspend the pioneer experience few enduring constraints.

Determinants of success for pioneers and followers

Our discussion suggests that a pioneering firm stands the best chance for long-term success in market-share leadership and profitability when (1) the new product-market is insulated from the entry of competitors, at least for a while, by strong patent protection, proprietary technology (such as a unique production process), or substantial investment requirements; or (2) the firm has sufficient size, resources, and competencies to take full advantage of its pioneering position and preserve it in the face of later competitive entries. Indeed, some recent evidence suggests that not only do organizational competencies such as R&D and marketing skills affect a firm's success as a pioneer, they may also influence the company's decision about whether to be a pioneer in the first place. Firms that lack the competencies necessary to sustain a first-mover advantage may be more likely to wait for another company to take the lead and enter the market later.[9]

Polaroid Corporation is a pioneer that profited from the first kind of situation. Strong patent protection enabled the firm to grow from an entrepreneurial start-up to a $1.6 billion company with little direct competition. Kodak, the only firm that attempted to challenge Polaroid in the instant photography business, dropped out of the industry after losing a patent infringement suit in 1985. Consequently, Polaroid could grow and profit by introducing a steady but narrowly focused stream of product improvements and by supporting those products with only modest advertising and promotion. However, the firm's insulated market situation led it to focus largely on the instant photography business rather than expanding into other technologies or product-markets. As a result, the firm's primary concern now is that instant photography is declining as consumers shift their purchases to products based on newer technologies, such as video recorders and digital cameras.

McDonald's is an example of a pioneer that has succeeded by aggressively building on the foundations of its early advantage. Although the firm started small as a single hamburger restaurant, it used the franchise system of distribution to rapidly expand the number of McDonald's outlets with minimal cash investment. That expansion plus stringent quality and cost controls, relatively low prices made possible by experience curve effects, heavy advertising expenditures, and product-line expansion aimed at specific market segments (e.g., Egg McMuffin for the breakfast crowd) have all enabled the firm to maintain a commanding share of the fast-food hamburger industry.

On the other hand, a follower will most likely succeed when there are few legal, technological, or financial barriers to inhibit entry and when it has sufficient resources or competencies to overwhelm the pioneer's early advantage. For example, given Procter & Gamble's well-established brand name and superior advertising and promotional resources, the company was able to quickly take the market share lead away from pioneer Minnetonka, Inc., in the plaque-fighting toothpaste market with a reformulated version of Crest.

A study conducted across a broad range of industries in the PIMS database supports these observations.[10] The findings are briefly summarized in Exhibit 9-5. The author found that regardless of the industry involved, pioneers able to maintain their preeminent position well into the market's growth stage had supported their early entry with the following marketing strategy elements:

- *Large entry scale.* Successful pioneers had sufficient capacity, or could expand quickly enough, to pursue a mass-market targeting strategy, usually on a national rather than a local or regional basis. Thus they could expand their volume quickly and achieve the benefits of experience curve effects before major competitors could confront them.

---

[9]Moore, Boulding, and Goodstein, "Pioneering and Market Share."

[10]Mary L. Coyle, "Competition in Developing Markets: The Impact of Order of Entry," unpublished doctoral dissertation, University of Toronto, 1986; See also Kerin, Varadarajan, and Peterson, "First-Mover Advantage."

━━━━━━━━━━━━━━━━━ **E X H I B I T 9 – 5** ━━━━━━━━━━━━━━━━━

Marketing Strategy Elements Pursued by Successful Pioneers, Fast Followers, and Late Entrants

These marketers . . .	are characterized by one or more of these strategy elements:
Successful pioneers	• Large entry scale • Broad product line • High product quality • Heavy promotional expenditures

Successful fast followers	• Larger entry scale than the pioneer
	• Leapfrogging the pioneer with superior:
	   Product technology
	   Product quality
	   Customer service

Successful late entrants	• Focus on peripheral target markets or niches

- *Broad product line.* Successful pioneers also quickly add line extensions or modifications to their initial product to tailor their offerings to specific market segments. This helps reduce their vulnerability to later entrants who might differentiate themselves by targeting one or more peripheral markets.

- *High product quality.* Successful pioneers offer a high-quality, well-designed product from the beginning, thus removing one potential differential advantage for later followers. Competent engineering, thorough product and market testing before commercialization, and good quality control during the production process are all important to the continued success of pioneers.

- *Heavy promotional expenditures.* Characterizing the marketing programs of pioneers who continue to be successful are relatively high advertising and promotional expenditures as a percentage of sales. Initially the promotion helps to stimulate awareness and primary demand for the new product category, build volume, and reduce unit costs. Later, this promotion focuses on building selective demand for the pioneer's brand and reinforcing loyalty as new competitors enter.

The same study found that the most successful fast followers tend to have the resources to enter the new market on a larger scale than the pioneer. Consequently, they can quickly reduce their unit costs and offer lower prices than incumbent competitors. Some fast followers achieve success, however, by leapfrogging earlier entrants by offering a product with more sophisticated technology, better quality, or superior service (like IBM in the PC market). As mentioned, followers in high-tech industries have the potential advantage of being able to use the second generation of technology to develop products technically superior to those of the pioneer. As we shall see in Chapter 10, however, the success of such a leapfrog strategy depends heavily on the speed and effectiveness of the follower's product development process.[11]

Finally, the study found that some late followers also achieve substantial profits by avoiding direct confrontation with established competitors and targeting peripheral

[11]Ralph E. Gomory, "From the 'Ladder of Science' to the Product Development Cycle," *Harvard Business Review*, November–December 1989, pp. 99–105.

markets. They offer products tailored to the needs of smaller market niches and support them with high levels of customer service.

A more detailed discussion of the marketing strategies appropriate for followers is presented in the next chapter. Followers typically enter a market after it has entered the growth stage of its life cycle, and they start with low market shares relative to the more established pioneer. Consequently, the next chapter's examination of strategies for low-share competitors in growth markets is relevant to both fast followers and late entrants. The remainder of this chapter concentrates only on the strategic marketing programs that pioneers in new product-markets might successfully pursue.

STRATEGIC MARKETING PROGRAMS FOR PIONEERS

The preceding discussion suggests that the ultimate success of a pioneering strategy depends on (1) the nature of the demand and potential competitive situation the pioneer encounters in the market and (2) the pioneer's ability to design and support an effective marketing program. The outcome of such a strategy also depends on how the pioneer defines *success*—in other words, the objectives it seeks to achieve. Thus a pioneer might choose from one of three different types of marketing strategies geared to achieving different purposes in different market environments: mass-market penetration, niche penetration, or skimming and early withdrawal. Exhibit 9-6 summarizes the circumstances favoring the use of each strategy. Keep in mind, however, that while conditions may be suited to a given strategy, they do not guarantee its success. Much still depends on how effectively the strategy is implemented. Also, it is highly unlikely that all the listed conditions will exist simultaneously in any product-market.

Mass-market penetration

The ultimate objective of a **mass-market penetration** strategy is to capture and maintain a commanding share of the total market of the new product. Thus, the critical marketing task is to get as many potential customers as possible to adopt the new product quickly to drive down unit costs and build a large contingent of loyal customers before competitors enter the market. As Exhibit 9-6 suggests, this task is often easier to accomplish when the market is relatively homogeneous and the diffusion process is short. When most potential customers have similar needs and preferences, the firm does not need to develop many product modifications or line extensions to capture a large share of the total market. In addition, when customers adopt the new product quickly, it is easier for the pioneer to build a large base of loyal adopters before competitors enter.

Strategies of mass-market penetration also tend to be most successful when barriers inhibit or delay the entry of competitors, thus allowing the pioneer more time to build volume, lower unit costs, and gain loyal customers. These entry barriers can result from a number of factors, including patent protection for the pioneer's technology, limited sources or availability of crucial materials or components parts, or a complex production process requiring substantial development effort or investment requirements.

Finally, a mass-market penetration strategy makes most sense when future competition is unlikely to be very intense. This is the case when few firms have the competencies necessary to compete in the new product category, or when most potential competitors lack the resources needed to enter the market on a major scale.

Successful implementation of a mass-market penetration strategy requires several different competencies, including product engineering and marketing skills and the financial and organizational resources necessary to expand capacity in advance of demand. In some

======================= E X H I B I T   9 – 6 =======================

Situations Favoring Alternative Marketing Strategies for New Product Pioneers

	Alternative marketing strategies		
	Mass-market penetration	**Niche penetration**	**Skimming and early withdrawal**
Market characteristics	• Large potential demand • Homogeneous customers • Short diffusion process	• Large potential demand • Fragmented market • Short adoption process	• Limited potential demand • Long adoption process • Demand is price inelastic
Product characteristics	• Product technology patentable or difficult to copy • Limited sources of supply • Complex production process	• Product technology offers little patent protection • Many sources of supply • Relatively simple production process	• Product technology offers little patent protection • Many sources of supply • Relatively simple production process
Competitor characteristics	• Few potential competitors • Potential competitors have limited resources and competencies	• Many potential competitors • Some potential competitors have substantial resources and competencies	• Many potential competitors • Some potential competitors have substantial resources and competencies
Firm characteristics	• Strong product engineering skills • Strong marketing skills and resources • Sufficient financial and organizational resources to build capacity in advance of growth in demand	• Limited product engineering skills and resources • Limited marketing skills and resources • Insufficient financial or organizational resources to build capacity in advance of growing demand	• Strong basic R&D and new product development skills • Good sales and promotional skills • Limited financial or organizational resources to commit to building capacity in advance of growth in demand

cases, though, a smaller firm with limited resources can successfully employ a mass-market penetration strategy if the market has a protracted adoption process and slow initial growth. Slow growth can delay competitive entry because fewer competitors are attracted to a market with questionable future growth. This allows the pioneer more time to expand capacity. For example, while Medtronic introduced heart pacemakers in 1960, it took nearly a decade for cardiologists to embrace the new technology in large numbers. Consequently, even though Medtronic was a small entrepreneurial firm, it could keep pace with the slow rate of volume growth and expand its capacity and product line sufficiently to maintain a leading position in the pacemaker industry.[12]

Niche penetration

Even when a new product-market expands quickly, however, it may still be possible for a small firm with limited resources to be a successful pioneer. In such cases, though, the firm must define success in a more limited way. Instead of pursuing the objective of capturing

---

[12]David H. Gobeli and William Rudelius, "Managing Innovation: Lessons from the Cardiac-Pacing Industry," *Sloan Management Review*, Summer 1985, pp. 29–43.

and sustaining a leading share of the entire market, it may make more sense for such firms to focus their efforts on a single market segment. This **niche penetration** strategy can help the smaller pioneer gain the biggest bang for its limited bucks and avoid future direct confrontations with bigger competitors.

As Exhibit 9-6 suggests, a niche penetration strategy is most appropriate when the new market is expected to grow quickly and there are a number of different benefit or application segments to appeal to. It is particularly attractive when there are few barriers to the entry of major competitors and when the pioneer has only limited resources and competencies to defend any advantage it gains through early entry.

Illinois Tool Works is a good example of this strategy. While the firm develops a great many new products, most are rather low tech and easy for competitors to copy. Also, many of the firm's markets are heterogeneous and fragmented, involving a variety of different applications and benefit segments. Consequently, ITW seldom sets out to dominate entire product categories. Instead, it tends to focus on smaller market niches where competition is less intense and it can command higher prices and profit margins.

Some pioneers may intend to pursue a mass-market penetration strategy when introducing a new product or service but end up implementing a niche penetration strategy instead. This is particularly likely when the new market grows faster or is more fragmented than the pioneer expects. Facing such a situation, a pioneer with limited resources may decide to concentrate on holding its leading position in one or a few segments rather than spreading itself too thin developing unique line extensions and marketing programs for many different markets or going deep into debt to finance rapid expansion.

For example, Progressive—a property and casualty insurer that was one of America's fastest-growing companies during the late 1980s and early 1990s—prospered by developing insurance policies for high-risk drivers. It succeeded by developing an extensive database on the personalities, lifestyles, and driving habits of various high-risk groups. Then, by differentiating between, for instance, bartenders and rock musicians, the firm priced policies to match the underwriting risk. But Progressive ran into trouble after a plunge into trucking and transportation insurance. "We thought we were better than we really were," says CEO Peter H. Lewis. "We jumped into new markets and put on too much business too fast—our organization and support systems couldn't handle it." To get back on track the firm refocused its efforts on its original market niche and put its more aggressive expansion program on hold, at least for a while.[13]

Skimming and early withdrawal

Even when a firm has the resources and competencies necessary to sustain a leading position in a new product-market, it may choose not to. Competition is usually inevitable; and prices and margins trend to drop dramatically after followers enter the market. Therefore, some pioneers opt to pursue a **skimming** strategy while planning an early withdrawal from the market. This involves setting a high price and engaging in only limited introductory advertising and promotion to maximize per unit profits and recover the product's development costs as quickly as possible. At the same time the firm may work to develop new applications for its technology or the next generation of more advanced technology. Then when competitors enter the market and margins fall, the firm is ready to cannibalize its own product with one based on new technology or to move into new segments of the market.

---

[13]William E. Sheeline, "Avoiding Growth's Perils," *Fortune,* August 13, 1990, pp. 55–58.

─────────────────── **E X H I B I T   9 – 7** ───────────────────

3M's Skimming Strategy in the Casting Tape Market

3M developed the first water–activated synthetic casting tape to set broken bones in 1980, but by 1982 eight other companies had brought out copycat products. 3M's R&D people retreated to their labs and developed and tested 140 new versions in a variety of fabrics. In 1983 the firm dropped the old product and introduced a technically superior version that was stronger and easier to use and commanded a premium price.

SOURCE: Christopher Knowlton, "What America Makes Best," *Fortune*, March 28, 1988, p. 45.

The 3M Company is a master of the skimming strategy. According to one 3M manager, "We hit fast, price high [full economic value of the product to the user], and get the heck out when the me-too products pour in." The new markets pioneered by the company are often smaller ones of $20 million to $50 million; and the firm may dominate them for only about three years or so. By then it is ready to launch the next generation of new technology or to move the old technology into new applications. An example of 3M's approach is described in Exhibit 9-7.

Skimming and early withdrawal might be employed by either small or large firms. But it is critical that the company have good R&D and product development skills so it can produce a constant stream of new products or new applications to replace older ones as they attract heavy competition. Also, because a firm pursuing this kind of strategy plans to remain in a market only for a short term, it is most appropriate when there are few barriers to entry, the product is expected to diffuse rapidly, and the pioneer lacks the capacity or other resources necessary to defend a leading share position over the long haul.

Objectives of alternative pioneer strategies

Exhibit 9-8 outlines both the long-term and short-term strategic objectives on which pioneers should focus in pursuing mass-market, niche penetration, or skimming strategies. The ultimate long-term objective of a mass-market penetration strategy is to maximize ROI. But to accomplish this, the firm must seek in the intermediate term to gain and hold a leading share of the new product-market throughout its growth and perhaps to even preempt competitors from entering the market. Thus, the short-term objective should be to maximize the number of customers adopting the new product as quickly as possible.

The short-, intermediate-, and long-term objectives of a niche penetration strategy are largely the same as those of a mass-market penetration strategy. The one essential difference is that a firm pursuing a niche strategy tries to capture and maintain a leading share of a more narrowly focused market segment rather than diffusing its limited resources across the entire market.

Finally, since businesses pursuing a skimming strategy usually expect to leave the market eventually, they have no long-term objectives. Therefore, their intermediate-term objective is to maximize returns before competitors enter the market. When increasing competition begins to reduce profit margins, firms pursuing this strategy typically license the product to another firm, introduce a new generation of products, or move to other markets or product categories. Thus, the short-term objective should be to gain as much volume as possible while simultaneously maintaining high margins to recoup development expenses and to generate profits quickly.

═══════════════════════ E X H I B I T   9 – 8 ═══════════════════════

Objectives of Strategic Marketing Programs for Pioneers

	Alternative strategic marketing programs		
Strategic objectives	**Mass-market penetration**	**Niche penetration**	**Skimming; early withdrawal**
Short-term objectives	• Maximize number of triers and adopters in total market; invest heavily to build future volume and share	• Maximize number of triers and adopters in target segment; limited investment to build volume and share in chosen niche	• Obtain as many adopters as possible with limited investment; maintain high margins to recoup product development and commercialization costs as soon as possible
Intermediate-term objectives	• Attempt to preempt competition; maintain leading share position even if some sacrifice of margins is necessary in short term as new competitors enter	• Maintain leading share position in target segment even if some sacrifice of short-term margins is necessary	• Maximize ROI; withdraw from market when increasing competition puts downward pressure on margins
Long-term objectives	• Maximize ROI	• Maximize ROI	• Withdraw

Marketing program components for a mass-market penetration strategy

As mentioned, the short-term objective of a mass-market penetration strategy is to maximize the number of customers adopting the firm's new product as quickly as possible. This requires a marketing program focused on (1) aggressively building product awareness and motivation to buy among a broad cross section of potential customers and (2) making it as easy as possible for those customers to try the new product on the assumption that they will try it, like it, develop loyalty, and make repeat purchases. Exhibit 9-9 outlines a number of marketing program activities in each of the four Ps that might help increase customers' awareness and willingness to buy or improve their ability to try the product. This is by no means an exhaustive list, nor do we mean to imply that a successful pioneer must necessarily engage in all of the listed activities. Marketing managers must develop programs combining activities that fit both the objectives of a mass-market penetration strategy and the specific market and potential competitive conditions the new product faces.

Increasing customers' awareness and willingness to buy

Obviously, heavy expenditures on advertising, introductory promotions such as sampling and couponing, and personal selling efforts can all increase awareness of a new product or service among potential customers. This is the critical first step in the adoption process for a new entry. The relative importance of these promotional tools varies, however, depending on the nature of the product and the number of potential customers. For instance, personal selling efforts are often the most critical component of the promotional mix for highly technical industrial products with a limited potential customer base. Media advertising and sales promotion are usually more useful for building awareness and primary demand for a new consumer good among customers in the mass market. In either case, when designing a mass-market penetration marketing program, firms should broadly focus promotional

─── E X H I B I T 9 – 9 ───

Components of Strategic Marketing Programs for Pioneers

Strategic objectives and tasks	Alternative strategic marketing programs		
	Mass-market penetration	Niche penetration	Skimming; early withdrawal
Increase customers' awareness and willingness to buy	• Heavy advertising to generate awareness among customers in mass market	• Heavy advertising directed at target segment to generate awareness	• Limited advertising to generate awareness, particularly among least price-sensitive early adopters
	• Extensive salesforce efforts to win new adopters	• Extensive salesforce efforts focused on potential customers in target segment	• Extensive salesforce efforts, particularly focused on largest potential adopters
	• Extensive introductory sales promotions to induce trial (sampling, couponing, quantity discounts)	• Extensive introductory sales promotions to induce trial, but focused on target segment	• Limited use, if any, of introductory sales promotions
	• Quickly expand offerings to appeal to multiple segments	• Additional product development limited to improvements to increase appeal to target segment	• Little, if any, additional development within the product category
	• Offer free trial, liberal return, or extended warranty policies to reduce customers' perceived risk	• Offer free trial, liberal return, or extended warranty policies to reduce target customers' perceived risk	• Offer free trial, liberal return, or extended warranty policies to reduce target customers' perceived risk
Increase customers's ability to buy	• Penetration pricing; or bring out lower-priced versions in anticipation of competitive entries	• Penetration pricing, or bring out lower-priced versions in anticipation of competitive entries	• Skimming pricing
	• Extended credit terms to encourage initial purchases	• Extended credit terms to encourage initial purchases	• Extended credit terms to encourage initial purchases
	• Heavy use of trade promotions aimed at gaining extensive distribution	• Trade promotions aimed at gaining distribution pertinent for reaching target segment	• Limited use of trade promotions
	• Offer engineering, installation, and training services to increase new product's compatibility with customers' current operations	• Offer engineering installation, and training services to increase new product's compatibility with customers' current operations	• Offer limited engineering, installation, and services as necessary to overcome customers' objections

efforts to expose and attract as many potential customers as possible before competitors show up.

Firms might also attempt to increase customers' willingness to buy their products by reducing the risk associated with buying something new. This can be done by letting customers try the product without obligation, as when car dealers allow potential customers to test-drive a new model, or by committing to liberal return or extended warranty policies for the product. When Lee Iacocca took over Chrysler, for instance, he decreed that all new car models should be introduced with the longest warranty in the industry to overcome the low-quality image of Chrysler products.

Finally, a firm committed to mass-market penetration might also broaden its product offerings to increase its appeal to as many market segments as possible. This helps reduce its vulnerability to later entrants who could focus on specific market niches. Firms can accomplish such market expansion through the rapid introduction of line extensions, additional package sizes, or product modifications targeted at new applications and market segments. Illinois Tool Works, for example, rapidly increased sales of its plastic safety buckle by modifying it for use with a variety of products, such as bicycle helmets, backpacks, and pet collars.

Increasing customers' ability to buy

For customers to adopt a new product and develop loyalty toward it, they must be aware of the item and be motivated to buy. But they must also have the wherewithal to purchase it. Thus, to capture as many customers in as short a time as possible, it usually makes sense for a firm pursuing mass-market penetration to keep prices low (penetration pricing) and perhaps offer liberal financing arrangements or easy credit terms during the introductory period.

Another factor that can inhibit customers' ability to buy is a lack of product availability within the distribution system. Thus, extensive personal selling and trade promotions aimed at gaining adequate distribution are usually a critical part of a mass-market penetration marketing program. Such efforts should take place before the start of promotional campaigns to ensure that the product is available as soon as customers are motivated to buy it.

A highly technical new product's incompatibility with other related products or systems currently used can also inhibit customers' purchases. It can result in high switching costs for a potential adopter. The pioneer might reduce those costs by designing the product to be as compatible as possible with related equipment. It might also offer engineering services to help make the new product more compatible with existing operations, provide free installation assistance, and conduct training programs for the customer's employees.

Additional considerations for pioneering global markets

Whether the product-market a pioneer is trying to penetrate is domestic or foreign, many of the marketing tasks appropriate for increasing potential customers' awareness, willingness, and ability to buy the new product or service are largely the same. Of course, some of the tactical aspects of the pioneer's strategic marketing program (e.g., specific product features, promotional appeals, or distribution channels) may have to be adjusted to fit different cultural, legal, or economic circumstances across national borders. In order for Bausch & Lomb to develop the Chinese market for contact lenses, for instance, it first had to develop an extensive training program for the country's opticians and build a network of retail outlets; these actions were not necessary in more developed markets.

Unless the firm already has an economic presence in a country via the manufacture or marketing of other products or services, however, a potential global pioneer faces at least one additional question: What mode of entry is most appropriate? There are three basic mechanisms for entering a foreign market: exporting through agents (e.g., using local manufacturers' representatives or distributors), contractual agreements (e.g., licensing or franchise arrangements with local firms), and direct investment.

Exporting is the simplest way to enter a foreign market because it involves the least commitment and risk. It can be direct or indirect. The latter relies on the expertise of domestic international middlemen: **export merchants**, who buy the product and sell it overseas for their own account; **export agents**, who sell on a commission basis; and **cooperative organizations**, which export for several producers—especially those selling farm products. Direct exporting uses foreign-based distributors and agents or operating units (i.e., branches or subsidiaries) set up in the foreign country.

Contractual entry modes are nonequity arrangements which involve the transfer of technology or skills to an entity in a foreign country. In **licensing,** a firm offers the right to use its intangible assets (e.g., technology, know-how, patents, company name, trademarks) in exchange for royalties or some other form of payment. Licensing is less flexible and provides less control than exporting. Further, if the contract is terminated, the licensor may have developed a competitor. It is appropriate, however, when the market is unstable or difficult to penetrate.

Franchising grants the right to use the company's name, trademarks, and technology. Also, the franchisee typically receives help in setting up the franchise. It is an especially attractive way for service firms to penetrate foreign markets at low cost and to couple their skills with local knowledge and entrepreneurial spirit. Host countries are reasonably receptive to this type of exporting since it involves local ownership. U. S. companies have largely pioneered franchising—especially such fast-food companies as McDonald's, Pizza Hut, Burger King, and Kentucky Fried Chicken. In recent years foreign franchisers have entered the United States—largely from Canada, Great Britain, and Japan—in a variety of fields, including food, shoe repair, leather furniture, and wall cleaning.[14]

Other contractual entry modes include **contract manufacturing**, which involves sourcing a product from a manufacturer located in a foreign country for sale there or elsewhere (e.g., auto parts, clothes, and furniture). Contract manufacturing is most attractive when the local market is too small to warrant making an investment, export entry is blocked, and a quality licensee is not available. A **turnkey construction contract** requires the contractor to have the project up and operating before releasing it to the owner. **Coproduction** involves a company's providing technical know-how and components in return for a share of the output which it must sell. **Countertrade** transactions include barter (direct exchange of goods—hams for aircraft), compensation packages (cash and local goods), counterpurchase (delayed sale of bartered goods to enable the local buyer to sell the goods), and a **buyback arrangement** in which the products being sold are used to produce other goods.

Overseas direct investment can be implemented in two ways: joint ventures or sole ownership. **Joint ventures** involve a joint ownership arrangement (e.g., one between a U.S. firm and one in the host country) to produce or market goods in a foreign country. Today, joint ventures are commonplace because they avoid quotas and import taxes and satisfy government demands to produce locally. They also have the advantage of sharing investment costs and gaining local marketing expertise. For example, Motorola had difficulty penetrating the Japanese market until it formed an alliance with Toshiba to set up a joint chip-making venture. In addition, Toshiba provided Motorola with marketing help.

A **sole ownership** investment entry strategy involves setting up a production facility in a foreign country. Direct investment usually allows the parent organization to retain total control of the overseas operation and avoids the problems of shared management and loss of

[14]Jerry A. Tannenbaum, "Foreign Franchisers Entering U.S. in Greater Numbers," *The Wall Street Journal,* June 11, 1990, p. B2.

flexibility. This strategy is particularly appropriate when the politics of the situation require a dedicated local facility. Firms using a direct investment strategy extensively include General Motors, Procter & Gamble, General Foods, Hewlett-Packard, and General Electric.

Exporting has the advantage of lowering the financial risk for a pioneer entering an unfamiliar foreign market. Unfortunately, such arrangements also afford a pioneer relatively little control over the marketing and distribution of its product or service—activities that are critical for winning customer awareness and loyalty in a new market. At the other extreme, investing in a wholly owned subsidiary typically makes little sense until it becomes clear that the pioneering product will win customer acceptance. Consequently, intermediate modes of entry, such as licensing or forming a joint venture with a local firm in the host country, tend to be the preferred means of developing global markets for new products. Joint ventures are particularly appropriate in this regard because they avoid quotas and import restrictions or taxes, and they allow a pioneer to share financial risks while gaining local marketing expertise.[15] Thus Bausch & Lomb established a joint venture with Beijing Optical as a basis for building contact lens factories in China and for gaining access to Chinese opticians.

Marketing program components for a niche penetration strategy

Because the objectives of a niche penetration strategy are similar to but more narrowly focused than those of a mass-market strategy, the marketing program elements are also likely to be similar under the two strategies. Obviously, however, a niche penetrator should keep its marketing efforts clearly focused on the target segment to gain as much impact as possible from its limited resources. This point is clearly evident in the outline of program components in Exhibit 9-9. For example, while a niche strategy calls for the same advertising, sales promotion, personal selling, and trade promotion activities as a mass-market program, the former should use more selective media, call schedules, and channel designs to precisely direct those activities toward the target segment.

Marketing program components for a skimming strategy

As Exhibit 9-9 suggests, one major difference between a skimming strategy and a mass-market strategy involves pricing policies. A relatively high price is appropriate for a skimming strategy to increase margins and revenues, even though some price-sensitive customers may be reluctant to adopt the product at that price.[16] This also suggests that introductory promotional programs might best focus on customer groups who are least sensitive to price and most likely to be early adopters of the new product. This can help hold down promotion costs and avoid wasting marketing efforts on less profitable market segments. Thus, in many consumer goods businesses, skimming strategies focus on relatively upscale customers because they are often more likely to be early adopters and less sensitive to price.

Another critical element of a skimming strategy is the nature of a firm's continuing product development efforts. A pioneer that plans to leave a market when competitors enter should not devote much effort to expanding its product line through line extensions or mul-

---

[15]Franklin R. Root, *Entry Strategy for International Markets* (Lexington, Mass.: D. C. Heath, 1987); see also Jeremy Main, "Making Global Alliances Work," *Fortune*, December 17, 1990, pp. 121–26.

[16]This assumes that demand is relatively price inelastic. In markets where price elasticity is high, a skimming price strategy may lead to lower total revenues due to its dampening effect on total demand.

tiple package sizes. Instead, it should concentrate on the next generation of technology or on identifying new application segments—in other words, preparing its avenue of escape from the market.

Now that we have examined some strategies a pioneer might follow in entering a new market, we are left with two important strategic questions. The pioneer is by definition the early share leader in the new market; hence the first question is, What adjustments in strategy might be necessary for the pioneer to maintain its leading share position after competitors arrive on the scene? The second is, What strategies might followers adopt to take business away from the early leader and increase their relative share position as the market grows? These two strategic issues are the focus of the next chapter.

SUMMARY

Not all new products are equally new. Only about 10 percent of the new product introductions made by U.S. companies involve new-to-the-world products. Many new entries, such as line extensions or modifications, are new to the customers in the target market but are relatively familiar to the company. Other new entries, like new product lines, extensions of an existing line, or cost reductions, may be quite new to the company but not to the target customers. The firm that introduces products new to the target market must build primary demand by making potential customers aware of the new product and stimulating their willingness and ability to buy.

The primary objective of most new market entries is to secure future volume and profit growth for the firm. However, individual market development efforts often accomplish a variety of secondary objectives as well: maintaining the firm's position as a product innovator, defending a current market-share position in an industry, establishing a foothold in a future new market, preempting a market segment, or exploiting technology in a new way. Top management must clearly specify the new market entry objectives for each strategic business unit (SBU). If a prospector SBU's new entry objectives are to maintain a position as a product innovator and establish footholds in many new markets, for example, its most appropriate new entry strategy is to be the *pioneer*, or first entrant, in as many new product-markets as possible. But if a SBU is primarily concerned with defending a strong market-share position in its industry, it might adopt a *follower* strategy whereby it enters new product-markets later and relies on superior product quality, better customer service, or lower prices to offset the pioneer's early lead.

New market entry strategies of both pioneer and follower offer unique potential sources of competitive advantage. A pioneering strategy is most likely to lead to long-term share leadership and profitability when the new market is insulated from the entry of competitors by patent protection for the pioneer's product, proprietary technology, or other barriers or when the pioneer has sufficient marketing resources and competence to maintain its early lead in the face of competitive attacks. Pioneers are most likely to maintain their early market-share lead when they can enter the new market on a large scale, quickly add line extensions, offer and sustain high product quality, and support their product introduction with heavy promotional expenditures. Followers are most successful when they can enter the market on a larger scale and attain lower per unit costs than the pioneer or when they can leapfrog the pioneer by offering a superior product or better service.

Alternative strategic marketing programs that are appropriate for a pioneer include a *mass-market penetration* strategy, a *niche penetration* strategy, or a *skimming* strategy. A mass-market penetration strategy aims at getting as many potential customers as possible to try the new product and develop brand loyalty before competitors can enter. The pioneer must maximize customers' awareness of the new product and attempt to increase their willingness and ability to buy. Because the necessary actions require substantial resources, a mass-market strategy is most appropriate for larger businesses or when barriers slow competitive entry.

Pioneers with limited resources are better off adopting a niche penetration strategy. The marketing objectives and actions involved in a niche strategy are similar to those of mass-market penetration, but they focus on a smaller segment of customers where fewer resources are needed to defend the pioneer's early lead.

Finally, some technological leaders, particularly those pursuing a prospector business strategy, may prefer to enter many new markets, attain as much profit as possible before competitors enter, and then withdraw as competition increases and margins erode. A skimming strategy incorporating relatively high prices and low marketing expenditures is appropriate for such businesses.

10

CHAPTER

Strategies for Growth Markets

J & J'S VISTAKON: A CHALLENGER CAPTURES THE LEADING SHARE OF THE CONTACT LENS MARKET[1]

Bausch & Lomb, one of the pioneers in the development of soft contact lenses, is no longer the share leader in the global contact lens market. That position was captured by an upstart challenger: Vistakon, a subsidiary of Johnson and Johnson (J&J).

In 1983 Vistakon was only a minor player in the contact lens business, generating $20 million in annual sales primarily from a specialty product designed for people with astigmatism. Then Vistakon's president got a tip from a salesperson working at another J&J subsidiary about a Copenhagen ophthalmologist who had conceived a way of manufacturing inexpensive disposable contact lenses. Vistakon quickly bought the rights to the new technology, assembled a management team to oversee development, and invested heavily

in a state-of-the-art facility in Florida capable of manufacturing lenses at a cost of less than $2.50 a pair—one-tenth the cost of other soft contacts. At that price the lenses could be worn a week or two and thrown away, thus reducing the need for cleaning and maintenance.

By the summer of 1987 the new lenses—given the brand name Acuvue—were ready for test-marketing. In less than a year they were rolled out across the United States with a high-visibility advertising campaign. However, Vistakon also needed to market the product to eye doctors and opticians who feared they would lose money if disposable lens users didn't come back for checkups and new lenses. Consequently, the firm decided to sell its lenses only through eye specialists, not even by prescription in pharmacies,

---

[1] This case example is based on information found in Brian O'Reilly, "J&J Is on a Roll," *Fortune,* December 26, 1994, pp. 178–92; and Michael Treacy and Fred Wiersema, "How Market Leaders Keep Their Edge," *Fortune.* February 6, 1995, pp. 88–98: and *Johnson & Johnson 1996 Annual Report,* found on the company's website at www.jnj.com

and in packs with just a few months' worth at a time. When competitors challenged the safety of the lenses, Vistakon quickly responded by distributing data via Federal Express refuting the charges to 17,000 eye-care professionals, thereby generating additional confidence and goodwill among its channel partners.

Because Vistakon and its parent Johnson & Johnson were willing to adopt an innovative new technology and to make substantial investments in manufacturing facilities and marketing programs, the firm was able to leapfrog over its more established rivals, including Bausch & Lomb.

Caught off guard, the competition never caught up. Within three years the firm had captured 25 percent of the U.S. contact lens market. And by 1994 Acuvue sales had reached nearly half a billion dollars, and Vistakon had become the domestic market-share leader.

In recent years the company has expanded its product line to include both higher-performance 1-Day Acuvue lenses, and more economical Surevue 2-week replacement lenses. It has also extended its distribution coverage to more than 70 countries, enabling it to become the number one supplier of contact lenses in the world.

STRATEGIC ISSUES IN GROWTH MARKETS

Bausch & Lomb's experience in the contact lens market, where increasingly intense competition eroded the pioneer's market-share position and its profitability, is common. As we discussed in Chapter 6, product-markets in the growth stage of their life cycles are usually characterized by the entry of many competitive followers. Both conventional wisdom and the various portfolio models suggest there are advantages in quickly entering—and investing heavily to build share in—growth markets. But a market is neither inherently attractive or unattractive simply because it promises rapid future growth. Managers must consider how the market and competitive situations are likely to evolve and whether their firms can exploit the rapid growth opportunities to establish a competitive advantage. The next section of this chapter examines both the opportunities and competitive risks often found in growing product-markets.

The primary objective of the early share leader, usually the market pioneer, in a growth market is **share maintenance**. From a marketing perspective the firm must accomplish two important tasks: (1) retain repeat or replacement business from its existing customers, and (2) continue to capture the major portion of sales to the growing number of new customers entering the market for the first time. The leader might use any of several marketing strategies to accomplish these objectives. It might try to build on its early scale and experience advantages to achieve low-cost production and reduce its prices. Alternatively, the leader might focus on rapid product improvements, expand its product line to appeal to newly emerging segments, or increase its marketing and sales efforts. The third section of this chapter explores marketing strategies—both defensive and offensive—that leaders might use to maintain market share in the face of market growth and increasing competition.

A challenger's strategic objective in a growth market is usually to build its share by expanding its sales faster than the overall market growth rate. Firms do this by stealing existing customers away from the leader or other competitors, capturing a larger share of new customers than the market leader, or both. Once again, challengers might use a number of strategies to accomplish these objectives. These include developing a superior product technology, as Vistakon did with great success; differentiating through rapid product innovations, line extensions, or customer service; offering lower prices; or focusing on market niches where the leader is not well established. The fourth section details these and other **share-growth** strategies that market challengers use under different conditions.

The success of a firm's strategy during the growth stage is a critical determinant of its ability to reap profits, or even survive, as a product-market moves toward maturity. Unfortunately, the growth stage is often short; and increasingly rapid technological change and market fragmentation are causing it to become even shorter in many industries.[2] This shortening of the growth stage concerns many firms—particularly late entrants or those who fail to acquire a substantial market share—because as growth slows during the transition to maturity, there is often a shakeout of marginal competitors. Thus, when choosing marketing strategies for competing in a growing product-market, managers should keep one eye on building a competitive advantage that the business can sustain as growth slows and the market matures.

OPPORTUNITIES AND RISKS IN GROWTH MARKETS[3]

Why are followers attracted to rapidly growing markets? Conventional wisdom suggests such markets present attractive opportunities for future profits because

- It is easier to gain share when a market is growing.
- Share gains are worth more in a growth market than in a mature market.
- Price competition is likely to be less intense.
- Early participation in a growth market is necessary to make sure that the firm keeps pace with the technology.

While generally valid, each of these premises may be seriously misleading for a particular business in a specific situation. Many followers attracted to a market by its rapid growth rate are likely to be shaken out later when growth slows because either the preceding premises did not hold or they could not exploit growth advantages sufficiently to build a sustainable competitive position. By understanding the limitations of the assumptions about growth markets and the conditions under which they are most likely to hold, a manager can make better decisions about entering a market and the kind of marketing strategy likely to be most effective in doing so.

Gaining share is easier

The premise that it is easier for a business to increase its share in a growing market is based on two arguments. First, there may be many potential new users who have no established brand loyalties or supplier commitments and who may have different needs or preferences than earlier adopters. Thus there may be gaps or undeveloped segments in the market. It is

---

[2]Neil Gross, Peter Coy, and Otis Port, "The Technology Paradox," *Business Week,* March 6, 1995, pp. 76–84.

[3]For a more extensive discussion of the potential opportunities and pitfalls of rapidly growing markets, see David A. Aaker and George S. Day, "The Perils of High-Growth Markets," *Strategic Management Journal* 7 (1986), pp. 409–21; and Myron Magnet, "Let's Go for Growth," *Fortune,* March 7, 1994, pp. 60–72.

easier, then, for a new competitor to attract those potential new users than to convert customers in a mature market. Second, established competitors are less likely to react aggressively to market-share erosion as long as their sales continue to grow at a satisfactory rate.

There is some truth to the first argument. It usually is easier for a new entrant to attract first-time users than to take business away from entrenched competitors. To take full advantage of the situation, however, the new entrant must be able to develop a product offering that new customers perceive as more attractive than other alternatives, and it must have the marketing resources and competence to effectively persuade them of that fact. This can be difficult, especially when the pioneer has had months or years to influence potential customers' decision criteria and preferences.[4]

The notion that established competitors are less likely to react to share losses so long as their revenues are growing at an acceptable rate is more tenuous. It overlooks the fact that those competitors may have higher expectations for increased revenues when the market itself is growing. Capital investments and annual operating budgets are usually tied to those sales expectations; therefore, competitors are likely to react aggressively when sales fall below expected levels whether or not their absolute volumes continue to grow. This is particularly true given that increased competition will likely erode the leader's relative market share even though its volume may continue to increase. As illustrated by the hypothetical example in Exhibit 10-1, the leader's market share might drop from a high of 100 percent at the beginning of the growth stage to 50 percent by the maturity stage, even though the firm's absolute volume shows steady growth.

Industry leaders often react forcefully when their sales growth falls below industry levels and their relative market share begins to decline. For example, IBM's objective for the PC market during the 1980s was to equal or exceed the growth rate for the overall market. Thus, when the entry of lower-priced IBM clones and Apple's new Macintosh knocked IBM's sales growth below the industry rate and reduced its relative market share in the middle of the decade, IBM took aggressive action, such as reducing prices and introducing the more technically advanced PS/2 line, even though the firm's absolute sales volume was still increasing.

Share gains are worth more

The premise that share gains are more valuable when the market is growing stems from the expectation that the earnings produced by each share point continue to expand as the market expands. The implicit assumption in this argument, of course, is that the business can hold its relative share as the market grows. The validity of such an assumption depends on a number of factors, including the following:

- *Future changes in technology or other key success factors.* If the rules of the game change, the competencies a firm relied on to capture share may no longer be adequate to maintain that share. For instance, Sony was the pioneer and early share leader in the videocassette recorder industry with its Betamax technology. But Matsushita's longer-playing and lower-priced VHS format equipment ultimately proved much more popular with consumers, captured a commanding portion of the market, and dethroned Sony as industry leader.

---

[4]Gregory S. Carpenter and Kent Nakamoto, "Consumer Preference Formation and Pioneering Advantage," *Journal of Marketing Research,* August 1989, pp. 285–98.

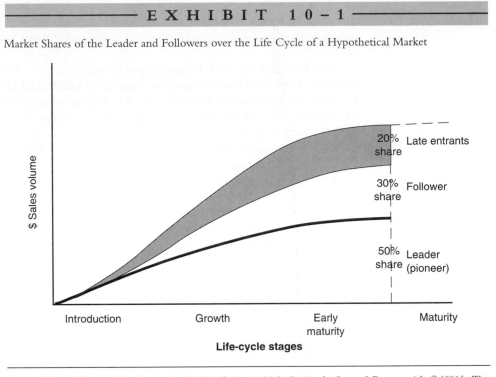

EXHIBIT 10-1

Market Shares of the Leader and Followers over the Life Cycle of a Hypothetical Market

SOURCE: Reprinted by permission from p. 60 of *Analysis for Strategic Market Decisions* by George S. Day; copyright © 1986 by West Publishing Company. All rights reserved.

- *Future competitive structure of the industry.* The number of firms that ultimately decide to compete for a share of the market may turn out to be larger than the early entrants anticipate, particularly if there are few barriers to entry. The sheer weight of numbers can make it difficult for any single competitor to maintain a substantial relative share of the total market.

- *Future fragmentation of the market.* As the market expands, it may fragment into numerous small segments, particularly if potential customers have relatively heterogeneous functional, distribution, or service needs. When such fragmentation occurs, the market in which a given competitor competes may shrink as segments splinter away.

In addition to these possible changes in future market conditions, a firm's ability to hold its early gains in market share also depends on how it obtained them. If a firm captures share through short-term promotions or price cuts that competitors can easily match and that may tarnish its image among customers, its gains may be short-lived.

Price competition is likely to be less intense

In many rapidly growing markets demand exceeds supply. The market exerts little pressure on prices initially; the excess demand may even support a price premium. Thus, early entry provides a good opportunity for a firm to recover its initial product development and commercialization investment relatively quickly. New customers may also be willing to pay a premium for technical service as they learn how to make full use of the new product. In contrast, as the market matures and customers gain more experience, the premium a firm can charge without losing market share slowly shrinks; it may eventually disappear entirely.[5]

However, this scenario does not hold true in every developing product-market. If there are few barriers to entry or if the adoption process is protracted and new customers enter the market slowly, demand may not exceed supply—at least not for very long. Also, the pioneer, or one of the earliest followers, might adopt a penetration strategy and set its initial prices relatively low to move quickly down the experience curve and discourage other potential competitors from entering the market.

Early entry is necessary to maintain technical expertise

In high-tech industries early involvement in new product categories may be critical for staying abreast of technology. The early experience gained in developing the first generation of products and in helping customers apply the new technology can put the firm in a strong position for developing the next generation of superior products. Later entrants, lacking such customer contact and production and R&D experience, are likely to be at a disadvantage.

There is substantial wisdom in these arguments. Sometimes, however, an early commitment to a specific technology can turn out to be a liability. This is particularly true when multiple unrelated technologies might serve a market or when a newly emerging technology might replace the current one. Once a firm is committed to one technology, adopting a new one can be difficult. Management is often reluctant to abandon a technology in which it has made substantial investments, and it might worry that a rapid shift to a new technology will upset present customers. As a result, early commitment to a technology has become increasingly problematic because of more rapid rates of technological change. This problem is dramatically illustrated by the experience of Medtronic, Inc., as described in Exhibit 10-2.

GROWTH-MARKET STRATEGIES FOR MARKET LEADERS

For the share leader in a growing market, of course, the question of the relative advantages versus risks of market entry is moot. The leader is typically the pioneer, or at least one of the first entrants, who developed the product-market in the first place. Its strategic objective is to maintain its leading relative share in the face of increasing competition as the market expands. Share maintenance may not seem like a very aggressive objective because it implies the business is merely trying to stay even rather than forge ahead. But two important facts must be kept in mind. First, the dynamics of a growth market—including the increasing number of competitors, the fragmentation of market segments, and the threat of product innovation from within and outside the industry—make maintaining an early lead in relative market share very difficult. The continuing need for investment to finance growth, the likely negative cash flows that result, and the threat of governmental antitrust action can make it even more difficult. For example, 31 percent of the 877 market-share leaders in the PIMS database experienced losses in relative share, as shown in Exhibit 10-3. Note, too, that leaders are especially likely to suffer this fate when their market shares are very large.

---

[5]Irwin Gross, "Insights from Pricing Research," *Pricing Practices and Strategies* (New York: Conference Board, 1979). In some rapidly evolving high-tech markets, price premiums can disappear *very* quickly, as pointed out in Gross, Coy, and Port, "Technology Paradox."

═══════════ **E X H I B I T 1 0 – 2** ═══════════

Medtronic's Commitment to an Old Technology Cost It Sales and Market Share

> The dangers inherent in being overly committed to an early technology are demonstrated by Medtronic, Inc., the pioneer in the cardiac pacemaker industry. Medtronic was reluctant to switch to a new lithium-based technology that enabled pacemakers to work much longer before being replaced. As a result, several Medtronic employees left the company and founded Cardiac Pacemakers Inc. to produce and market the new lithium-based product. They quickly captured nearly 20 percent of the total market. And Medtronic saw its share of the cardiac pacemaker market fall rapidly from nearly 70 percent to 40 percent.

SOURCE: Daniel H. Gobeli and William Rudelius, "Managing Innovation: Insights from the Cardiac-Pacing Industry," *Sloan Management Review*, Summer 1985, pp. 29–43. Reprinted with permission. Copyright 1985 by Sloan Management Review Association. All rights reserved.

Second, a firm can maintain its current share position in a growth market only if its sales volume continues to grow at a rate equal to that of the overall market, enabling the firm to stay even in *absolute* market share. It may, however, be able to maintain a *relative* share lead even if its volume growth is less than the industry's.

Marketing objectives for share leaders

Share maintenance for a market leader involves two important marketing objectives. First, the firm must *retain its current customers*, ensuring that those customers remain brand loyal when making repeat or replacement purchases. This is particularly critical for firms in consumer nondurable, service, and industrial materials and components industries, where a substantial portion of total sales volume consists of repeat purchases. Second, the firm must *stimulate selective demand among later adopters* to ensure that it captures a large share of the continuing growth in industry sales.

In some cases a market leader might pursue a third objective of stimulating primary demand to help speed up overall market growth. This can be particularly important in product-markets where the adoption process is protracted because of the technical sophistication of the new product or high switching costs for potential customers.

The market leader is the logical firm to stimulate market growth in such situations; it has the most to gain from increased volume, assuming, of course, that it can maintain its relative share of that volume. However, expanding total demand—by promoting new uses for the product or stimulating existing customers' usage and repeat purchase rates—is often more critical near the end of the growth and early in the maturity stages of a product's life cycle. Consequently, we discuss marketing actions appropriate to this objective in the next chapter.

Marketing actions and strategies to achieve share-maintenance objectives

A business might take a variety of marketing actions to maintain a leading share position in a growing market. Exhibit 10-4 outlines a lengthy, though by no means exhaustive, list of such actions and their specific marketing objectives. Because share maintenance involves multiple objectives, and different marketing actions may be needed to achieve each one, a strategic marketing program usually integrates a mix of the actions outlined in the exhibit.

Not all of the actions summarized in Exhibit 10-4 are consistent with one another. It would be unusual, for instance, for a business to invest heavily in new product

EXHIBIT 10 – 3

The Proportion of Market Leaders in the PIMS Database Who Lost Market Share, by Size of Their Initial Share

Leader's initial market share	Percent losing share
Under 20%	16%
20–29	24
30–39	34
40–49	41
Over 50	45
All leaders	31

SOURCE: Adapted with permission of The Free Press, an imprint of Simon & Schuster Inc. from *The PIMS Principles: Linking Strategy to Performance* by Robert D. Buzzell and Bradley T. Gale. Copyright © 1987 by The Free Press.

improvements and promotion to enhance its product's high-quality image and simultaneously slash prices, unless it was trying to drive out weaker competitors in the short run with an eye on higher profits in the future. Thus, the activities outlined in Exhibit 10–4 cluster into five internally consistent strategies that a market leader might employ, singly or in combination, to maintain its leading share position: a **fortress** or **position defense strategy**, a **flanker strategy**, a **confrontation strategy**, a **market expansion** or **mobile strategy**, and a **contraction** or **strategic withdrawal strategy**. Exhibit 10-5 diagrams this set of strategies. It is consistent with what a number of military strategists and some marketing authorities have identified as common defensive strategies.[6] However, to think of them as strictly defensive can be misleading. Companies can use some of these strategies offensively to preempt expected future actions by potential competitors. Or they can use them to capture an even larger share of future new customers.

Exhibit 10-6 summarizes the primary objectives that each of the five share-maintenance strategies focuses upon. Of course, the strategy, or combination of strategies, most appropriate for a particular product-market depends on (1) the market's size and its customers' characteristics; (2) the number and relative strengths of competitors or potential competitors; and (3) the leader's own resources and competencies. We examine these issues along with the marketing actions appropriate for implementing each strategy in the following sections.

Fortress, or position defense, strategy

The basic defensive strategy is to continually strengthen a strongly held current position: to build an impregnable fortress capable of repelling attacks by current or future competitors. This strategy is nearly always at least a part of a leader's share-maintenance efforts. By shoring up an already strong position, the firm can improve the satisfaction of current customers while increasing the attractiveness of its offering to new customers with needs and characteristics similar to those of earlier adopters.

---

[6]For a detailed discussion of these strategies in a military context, see Carl von Clausewitz, *On War* (London: Routledge and Kegan Paul, 1908); and B. H. Liddell-Hart, *Strategy* (New York: Praeger, 1967). For a related discussion of the application of such strategies in a business setting, see Philip Kotler and Ravi Singh Achrol, "Marketing Warfare in the 1980s," *Journal of Business Strategy*, Winter 1981, pp 30–41.

═══════════════ E X H I B I T   1 0 – 4 ═══════════════

Marketing Actions to Achieve Share-Maintenance Objectives

Marketing objectives	Possible marketing actions
Retain current customers by:	
• Maintaining/improving satisfaction and loyalty	• Increase attention to quality control as output expands. • Continue product modification and improvement efforts to increase customer benefits and/or reduce costs. • Focus advertising on stimulation of selective demand; stress product's superior features and benefits; reminder advertising. • Increase salesforce's servicing of current accounts; consider formation of national or key account representatives for major customers; consider replacing independent manufacturers' reps with company salespeople. • Expand postsale service capabilities; develop or expand company's own service force, or develop training programs for distributors' and dealers' service people; expand parts inventory; consider development of customer service hotline.
• Encourage/simplify repeat purchase	• Expand production capacity in advance of increasing demand to avoid stockouts. • Improve inventory control and logistics systems to reduce delivery times. • Continue to build distribution channels; use periodic trade promotions to gain more extensive retail coverage and maintain shelf facings; strengthen relationships with strongest distributors/dealers. • Consider negotiating long-term requirements contracts with major customers. • Consider developing automatic reorder systems for major customers. • Consider logistical alliances with major customers.
• Reduce attractiveness of switching	• Develop a second brand or product line with features or price more appealing to a specific segment of current customers (*flanker strategy*). • Develop multiple line extensions or brand offerings targeted to the needs of several user segments in the market (*market expansion, mobile strategy*). • Meet or beat lower prices or heavier promotional efforts by competitors—or try to preempt such efforts by potential competitors—when necessary to retain customers and when lower unit costs allow (*confrontation strategy*).
Stimulate selective demand among later adopters by:	
• Head-to-head positioning against competitive offerings or potential offerings	• Develop a second brand or product line with features or price more appealing to a specific segment of potential customers (*flanker strategy*). • Make product modifications or improvements to match or beat superior competitive offerings (*confrontation strategy*). • Meet or beat lower prices or heavier promotional efforts by competitors when necessary to retain customers and when lower unit costs allow (*confrontation strategy*). • When resources are limited relative to competitor's, consider withdrawing from smaller or slower-growing segments to focus product development and promotional efforts on higher-potential segments threatened by competitor (*contraction or strategic withdrawal strategy*).
• Differentiated positioning against competitive offerings or potential offerings	• Develop multiple line extensions or brand offerings targeted to the needs of various potential user applications or geographical segments within the market (*market expansion or mobile strategy*). • Build unique distribution channels to more effectively reach specific segments of potential customers (*market expansion or mobile strategy*). • Design multiple advertising and/or sales promotion campaigns targeted at specific segments of potential customers (*market expansion or mobile strategy*).

E X H I B I T   1 0 – 5

Strategic Choices for Share Leaders in Growth Markets

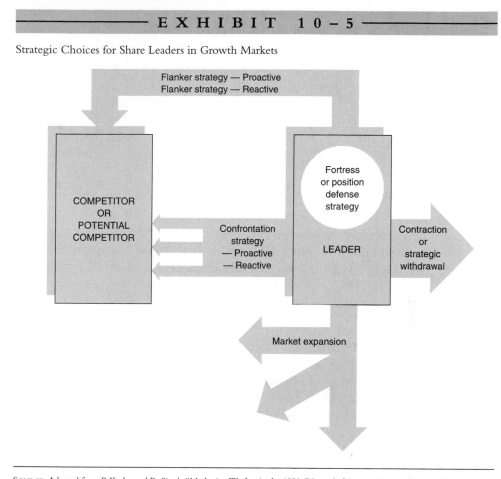

SOURCE: Adapted from P. Kotler and R. Singh, "Marketing Warfare in the 1980s," *Journal of Business Strategy*, Winter 1981, pp. 30–41.

Strengthening the firm's current position makes particularly good sense when the target market is relatively homogeneous—that is, when both current and potential customers have similar needs and desires—and when the leader's offering already enjoys a high level of awareness and preference among those customers and potential customers. Obviously, too, such a strategy is likely to be most effective when the leader has substantial competencies and resources in the areas crucial for strengthening customer awareness, preference, and satisfaction (e.g., R&D, marketing, and customer service) and when competitors do not have sufficient competencies or resources in those functions to mount a direct challenge. Indeed, in some homogeneous markets where competition is weak and fragmented, a well-implemented position defense strategy may be all that is needed for share maintenance.

Most of the marketing actions listed in Exhibit 10-4 as relevant for retaining current customers might be incorporated into a position defense strategy. Anything the business can do to improve customer satisfaction and loyalty and encourage and simplify repeat purchasing should help the firm protect its current customer base and make its offering more attractive

---
E X H I B I T   1 0 – 6

Marketing Objectives of Share–Maintenance Strategies in Growth Markets

		Share maintenance strategies		
Fortress or position defense	**Flanker**	**Confrontation**	**Market expansion**	**Contraction or strategic withdrawal**
Increase satisfaction, loyalty, and repeat purchase among current customers by building on existing strengths; appeal to late adopters with same attributes and benefits offered to early adopters.	Protect against loss of specific segment of current customers by developing a second entry that covers a weakness in original offering; improve ability to attract new customers with specific needs or purchase criteria different from those of early adopters.	Protect against loss of share among current customers by meeting or beating a head-to-head competitive offering; improve ability to win new customers who might otherwise be attracted to competitor's offering.	Increase ability to attract new customers by developing new product offerings or line extensions aimed at a variety of new applications and user segments; improve ability to retain current customers as market fragments.	Increase ability to attract new customers in selected high-growth segments by focusing offerings and resources on those segments; withdraw from smaller or slower-growing segments to conserve resources.

to new customers. Some of the specific actions appropriate for accomplishing these two objectives are now discussed in more detail.

Actions to improve customer satisfaction and loyalty   The rapid expansion of output necessary to keep up with a growth market often can lead to quality control problems for the market leader. As new plants, equipment, and personnel are quickly brought on-line, bugs can suddenly appear in the production process. Thus, the leader must pay particular attention to quality control during this phase. Most customers have only limited, if any, positive past experiences with the new brand to offset their disappointment when a purchase does not live up to expectations.

Perhaps the most obvious way a leader can strengthen its position is to continue to modify and improve its product. This can reduce the opportunities for competitors to differentiate their products by designing in features or performance levels the leader does not offer. A leader might also try to reduce unit costs to discourage low-price competition.

A leader should take steps to improve not only the physical product but customers' perceptions of it as well. As competitors enter or prepare to enter the market, the leader's advertising and sales promotion emphasis should shift from stimulating primary demand to building selective demand for the company's brand. This usually involves creating appeals that emphasize the brand's superior features and benefits. While the leader may continue sales promotion efforts aimed at stimulating trial among later adopters, some of those efforts might be shifted toward encouraging repeat purchases among existing customers. For instance, it might include cents-off coupons inside the package to give customers a price break on their next purchases of the brand.

For industrial goods, some salesforce efforts should shift from prospecting for new accounts to servicing existing customers. Firms that relied on independent manufacturers' representatives to introduce their new product might consider replacing them with company salespeople to increase the customer service orientation of their sales efforts.

Firms whose own salespeople introduced the product might reorganize their salesforces into specialized groups focused on major industries or user segments. Or they might assign key account representatives, or cross-functional account teams, to service their largest customers.

Finally, a leader can strengthen its position as the market grows by giving increased attention to postsale service. Rapid growth in demand can not only outstrip a firm's ability to produce a high-quality product, it can also overload the firm's ability to service customers. Obviously, this can lead to a loss of existing customers as well as negative word-of-mouth that might inhibit the firm's ability to attract new users. Thus, the growth phase often requires increased investments to expand the firm's parts inventory and hire and train service personnel and dealers.

Actions to encourage and simplify repeat purchasing   One of the most critical actions a leader must take to ensure that customers continue buying its product is to maximize its availability. It must reduce stockouts on retail store shelves or shorten delivery times for industrial goods. To do this, the firm must invest in plant and equipment to expand capacity in advance of demand, and it must implement adequate inventory control and logistics systems to provide a steady flow of goods through the distribution system. The firm should also continue to build its distribution channels.

Some market leaders, particularly in industrial goods markets, can take more proactive steps to turn their major customers into captives and help guarantee future purchases. For example, a firm might negotiate requirements contracts or guaranteed price agreements with its customers to ensure future purchases, or it might tie them into a computerized reorder system or logistical alliance. For instance, Procter & Gamble has formed alliances with major supermarket chains, such as Kroger, to develop a restocking system called continuous product replenishment. Sales information from Kroger's checkout scanners is sent directly to P & G's computers, which figure out automatically when to replenish each product and schedule deliveries direct to each store. This paperless exchange minimizes mistakes and billbacks, minimizes inventory, decreases out-of-stocks, and improves cash flow.[7]

One authority estimated that U.S. organizations purchase $500 billion worth of goods and services electronically each year, and the adoption of such systems is growing rapidly.[8] Although to the present such systems have been adopted most widely by manufacturers of relatively standardized consumer products, many industrial goods manufacturers are also developing computerized reordering systems. This is particularly true for firms that customize their products to a customer's order. By having orders sent directly to its computer, the supplier can quickly organize production schedules, speed up the production process, and minimize finished goods inventories.[9]

Building long-term relationships with customers.   From the customer's viewpoint, computerized ordering is more convenient, flexible, and less time-consuming than placing an order through a salesperson. From the supplier's perspective, linking established customers to a dedicated reorder system can help "tie" those customers to the firm, increase their

---

[7]Bill Saporito, "Behind the Tumult At P&G," *Fortune*, March 7, 1994, pp. 74–82.

[8]John W. Verity, "Invoice? What's An Invoice?" *Business Week*, June 10, 1996, pp. 110–12.

[9]Joseph B. Fuller, James O'Conor, and Richard Rawlinson, "Tailored Logistics: The Next Advantage," *Harvard Business Review*, May–June, 1993, pp. 87–98.

satisfaction and loyalty, and thereby help maintain the company's market share over time.[10] But building long-term relationships with loyal customers often involves more than merely linking computer systems and sharing inventory data. Suppliers also may customize their products or services to meet the special needs of a particular customer, or include major customers as active participants in new product development or product improvement projects.

The importance of trust   Such complex relationships involve not only a great deal of cooperation between the parties but also require a great deal of *mutual trust*. Before making a substantial investment to produce a specialized product that no other customers may want, for example, a supplier must trust the buyer to continue purchasing an adequate volume for a sufficient period of time to enable the firm to recoup that investment. Similarly, before the buyer agrees to concentrate all its purchases of that product with a single supplier, it must trust that firm to continue supplying a quality product that meets specifications at a competitive price. In other words, both parties must trust each other to avoid opportunistic behaviors that would advance their own short-term self-interest at their partner's expense.[11]

Conditions favoring trust and commitment   While mutual trust is important for the development and maintenance of long-term commitments between suppliers and their organizational customers, it is not always easy to develop. First, trust tends to build slowly over time.[12] Thus, the parties must have some history of satisfying experiences with one another to provide a foundation for trust. It also helps if each party brings an established reputation for fair dealing within its industry.[13]

From the customer's perspective, a firm is more likely to trust and develop a long-term commitment to a supplier when that supplier makes dedicated, customer-specific investments, such as developing customized products for individual customers. Such investments send a powerful signal about the vendor's credibility and commitment to the relationship since the assets are not easily deployable elsewhere.

On the other hand, in markets characterized by complex and uncertain technical environments—such as those where competing technologies are emerging simultaneously, as in the networking software industry—customers are less likely to develop a long-term orientation toward a single supplier. Because firms in such circumstances cannot tell which supplier's technology will eventually win out as the industry standard, they are more likely to keep their options open by spreading their purchases across multiple suppliers if it is economically feasible to do so.[14]

---

[10]Sang-Lin Han, David T. Wilson, and Shirish P. Dant, "Buyer-Supplier Relationships Today," *Industrial Marketing Management* 22 (1993), pp. 331–38. See also Robert S. Duboff and Lori Underhill Sherer, "Customized Customer Loyalty, " *Marketing Management*, Summer 1997, pp. 21–27.

[11]Robert M. Morgan and Shelby D. Hunt, "The Commitment-Trust Theory of Relationship Marketing," *Journal of Marketing* 58 (July 1994), pp. 20–38.

[12]F. Robert Dwyer, Paul H. Schurr, and Sejo Oh, "Developing Buyer-Seller Relationships," *Journal of Marketing* 51 (April 1987), pp. 11–27.

[13]Shankar Ganesan, "Determinants of Long-Term Orientation in Buyer-Seller Relationships," *Journal of Marketing* 58 (April 1994), pp 1–19.

[14] Ibid.; see also Jan B. Heide and George John, "Alliances in Industrial Purchasing: The Determinants of Joint Action in Buyer-Supplier Relationships," *Journal of Marketing Research* 27 (February 1990), pp. 24–36.

Flanker strategy

One shortcoming of a fortress strategy is that a challenger might simply choose to bypass the leader's fortress and try to capture territory where the leader has not yet established a strong presence. This can represent a particular threat when the market is fragmented into major segments with different needs and preferences and the leader's current brand does not meet the needs of one or more of those segments. A competitor with sufficient resources and competencies can develop a differentiated product offering to appeal to the segment where the leader is weak and thereby capture a substantial share of the overall market.

To defend against an attack directed at a weakness in its current offering (its exposed flank), a leader might develop a second brand (a flanker or fighting brand) to compete directly against the challenger's offering. This might involve trading up, where the leader develops a high-quality brand offered at a higher price to appeal to the prestige segment of the market. Honda did this with the development of the Acura. The new brand not only penetrated the higher-priced segment of the market, it also helped Honda hold on to former Accord owners who were beginning to trade up to more expensive European brands as they got older and earned higher incomes.

More commonly, though, a flanker brand is a lower-quality product designed to appeal to a low-price segment to protect the leader's primary brand from direct price competition. Pillsbury's premium-quality Hungry Jack brand holds the major share of the refrigerated biscuit dough market; however, a substantial number of consumers prefer to pay less for a somewhat lower-quality biscuit. Rather than conceding that low-price segment to competitors or reducing Hungry Jack prices and margins in an attempt to attract price-sensitive consumers, Pillsbury introduced Ballard, a low-priced flanker brand.

A flanker strategy is *always* used in conjunction with a position defense strategy. The leader simultaneously strengthens its primary brand while introducing a flanker to compete in segments where the primary brand is vulnerable. This suggests that a flanker strategy is only appropriate when the firm has sufficient resources to develop and fully support two or more entries. After all, a flanker is of little value if it is so lightly supported that a competitor can easily wipe it out.

Finally, a flanker strategy can be either proactive or reactive. The leader might introduce a flanker in anticipation of a competitor's entry either to establish a strong position before the competitor arrives or to dissuade the competitor from entering. In some cases, however, the leader does not recognize the severity of the threat until a competitor has already begun to enjoy a measure of success. Pillsbury did not develop its Ballard brand, for instance, until after a number of low-priced regional private labels began capturing significant chunks of the market.

Confrontation strategy

Suppose a competitor chooses to attack the leader head-to-head and attempts to steal customers in the leader's main target market. If the leader has established a strong position and attained a high level of preference and loyalty among customers and the trade, it may be able to sit back and wait for the competitor to fail. In many cases, though, the leader's brand is not strong enough to withstand a frontal assault from a well-funded, competent competitor. Even mighty IBM, for instance, lost 20 market-share points in the commercial PC market during the mid-1980s to competitors like Compaq—whose machines cost about the same but offered features or performance levels that were better—and to the clones who offered IBM-compatible machines at much lower prices.

In such situations, the leader may have no choice but to confront the competitive threat directly. If the leader's competitive intelligence is good, it may decide to move proactively and change its marketing program before a suspected competitive challenge occurs. A confrontational strategy, though, is more commonly reactive. The leader usually decides to meet or beat the attractive features of a competitor's offering—by making product improvements, increasing promotional efforts, or lowering prices—only after the challenger's success has become obvious.

Simply meeting the improved features or lower price of a challenger, however, does nothing to reestablish a sustainable competitive advantage for the leader. And a confrontation based largely on lowering prices creates an additional problem of shrinking margins for all concerned.[15] Unless decreased prices generate substantial new industry volume and the leader's production costs fall with that increasing volume, the leader may be better off responding to price threats with increased promotion or product improvements while trying to maintain its profit margins. Evidence also suggests that in product-markets with high repeat purchase rates or a protracted diffusion process, the leader may be wise to adopt a penetration pricing policy in the first place. This would strengthen its share position and may preempt low-price competitors from entering.[16]

The leader can avoid the problems of a confrontation strategy by reestablishing the competitive advantage eroded by challengers' frontal attacks. But this typically requires additional investments in process improvements aimed at reducing unit costs, improvements in product quality or customer service, or even the development of the next generation of improved products to offer customers greater value for their dollars.

Market expansion or mobile strategy

A market expansion or mobile strategy is a more aggressive and proactive version of the flanker strategy. Here the leader defends its relative market share by establishing positions in a number of different market segments. This strategy's primary objective is to capture a large share of new customer groups who may prefer something different than the firm's initial offering, protecting the firm from future competitive threats from a number of different directions. Such a strategy is particularly appropriate in fragmented markets if the leader has the resources to undertake multiple product development and marketing efforts.

The most obvious way a leader can implement a market expansion strategy is to develop line extensions, new brands, or even alternative product forms utilizing similar technologies to appeal to multiple market segments. For instance, although Pillsbury holds a strong position in the refrigerated biscuit dough category, biscuit consumption is concentrated among older, more traditional consumers in the South. To expand its total market, gain increased experience curve effects, and protect its overall technological lead, Pillsbury developed a variety of other product forms that use the same refrigerated dough technology and production facilities but appeal to different customer segments. The expanded line includes crescent rolls, Danish rolls, and soft breadsticks.

A less expensive way to appeal to a variety of customer segments is to retain the basic product but vary other elements of the marketing program to make it relatively more attractive to specific users. Thus, a leader might create specialized salesforces to deal with the unique concerns of different user groups. Or it might offer different ancillary services

---

[15]Thomas T. Nagle, "Managing Price Competition," *Marketing Management* 2 (Spring 1993), pp. 36–45; see also George E. Cressman, Jr., "Snatching Defeat from the Jaws of Victory: Why Do Good Managers Make Bad Pricing Decisions?" *Marketing Management*, Summer 1997, pp. 9–19.

[16]Robert J. Dolan and Abel P. Jewland, "Experience Curves and Dynamic Demand Models: Implications for Optimal Pricing Strategy," *Journal of Marketing*, Winter 1981, p. 52.

to different types of customers or tailor sales promotion efforts to different segments. Thus performing arts groups often promote reduced ticket prices, transportation services, and other inducements to attract senior citizens and students to matinee performances.

Contraction or strategic withdrawal

In some highly fragmented markets, a leader may be unable to defend itself adequately in all segments. This is particularly likely when newly emerging competitors have more resources than the leader. The firm may then have to reduce or abandon its efforts in some segments to focus on areas where it enjoys the greatest relative advantages or that have the greatest potential for future growth. Even some very large firms may decide that certain segments are not profitable enough to continue pursuing. For example, IBM made an early attempt to capture the low end of the home hobbyist market for personal computers with the introduction of the PC Jr. But the firm eventually abandoned that effort to concentrate on the more lucrative commercial and education segments.

SHARE-GROWTH STRATEGIES FOR FOLLOWERS

Marketing objectives for followers

Not all late entrants to a growing product-market have illusions about eventually surpassing the leader and capturing a dominant market share. Some competitors, particularly those with limited resources and competencies, may simply seek to build a small but profitable business within a specialized segment of the larger market that earlier entrants have overlooked. As we have seen, this kind of niche strategy is one of the few entry options that small, late entrants can pursue with a reasonable degree of success. If a firm can successfully build a profitable business in a small segment while avoiding direct competition with larger competitors, it can often survive the shakeout period near the end of the growth stage and remain profitable throughout the maturity stage.

On the other hand, many followers—particularly larger firms entering a product-market shortly after the pioneer—have more grandiose objectives. They often seek to displace the leader or at least to become a powerful competitor within the total market. Thus, their major marketing objective is to attain *share growth*, and the size of the increased relative share such challengers seek is usually substantial. For instance, although it was a later entrant into the personal computer wars, Compaq competed aggressively to become the share leader in the global commercial PC market.

Marketing actions and strategies to achieve share growth

A challenger with visions of taking over the leading share position in an industry has two basic strategic options, each involving somewhat different marketing objectives and actions. Where the share leader and perhaps some other early followers have already penetrated a large portion of the potential market, a challenger may have no choice but to steal away some of the repeat purchase or replacement demand from the competitors' current customers. As Exhibit 10-7 indicates, the challenger can attempt this through marketing activities that give it an advantage in a head-to-head confrontation with a target competitor. Or it can attempt to leapfrog over the leader by developing a new generation of products with enough benefits to induce customers to trade in their existing brand for a new one. Secondarily, such actions may also help the challenger attract a larger share of late adopters in the mass market.

EXHIBIT 10–7

Marketing Actions to Achieve Share-Growth Objectives

Marketing objectives	Possible marketing actions

Capture repeat/replacement purchases from current customers of the leader or other target competitor by:
• Head-to-head positioning against competitor's offering in primary target market
	• Develop products with features and/or performance levels superior to those of the target competitor.
	• Draw on superior product design, process engineering, and supplier relationships to achieve lower unit costs.
	• Set prices below target competitor's for comparable level of quality or performance, but only if low-cost position is achieved.
	• Outspend the target competitor on promotion aimed at stimulating selective demand:
	    Comparative advertising appeals directed at gaining a more favorable positioning than the target competitor's brand enjoys among customers in the mass market.
	    Sales promotions to encourage trial if offering's quality or performance is perceptively better than target competitor's, or induce brand switching.
	    Build more extensive and/or better-trained salesforce than target competitor's.
	• Outspend the target competitor on trade promotion to attain more extensive retail coverage, better shelf space, and/or representation by the best distributors/dealers.
	• Outperform the target competitor on customer service:
	    Develop superior production scheduling, inventory control, and logistics systems to minimize delivery times and stockouts.
	    Develop superior postsales service capabilities; build a more extensive company service force, or provide better training programs for distributor/dealer service people than target competitor.
	• If resources are limited, engage in one or more of the preceding actions (such as an advertising blitz or sales or trade promotions) on a sporadic basis in selected territories (*guerrilla attack strategy*).

• Technological differentiation from target competitor's offering in its primary target market	• Develop a new generation of products based on different technology that offers superior performance or additional benefits desired by current and potential customers in the mass market (*leapfrog strategy*).

If the market is relatively early in the growth phase and no previous entrant has captured a commanding share of potential customers, the challenger can focus on *attracting a larger share of potential new customers* who enter the market for the first time. This may also be a viable option when the overall market is heterogeneous and fragmented and the current share leader has established a strong position in only one or a few segments. In either case, the primary marketing activities for increasing share via this approach should aim at *differentiating* the challenger's offering from those of existing competitors by making it more appealing to new customers in untapped or underdeveloped segments of the market.

Once again, the list of possible marketing actions for challengers (see Exhibit 10-7) is not exhaustive; and it contains actions that do not always fit well together. The activities that do fit tend to cluster into five internally consistent strategies that a challenger might use singly or in combination to secure growth in its relative market share. As Exhibit 10-8 indicates, these five share-growth strategies are *frontal attack, leapfrog strategy, flanking attack, encirclement,* and *guerrilla attack.* Many of these strategies are mirror images of the share-maintenance strategies discussed earlier.

continued

Marketing objectives	Possible marketing actions
	• Build awareness, preference, and replacement demand through heavy introductory promotion:
	Comparative advertising stressing product's superiority.
	Sales promotions to stimulate trial or encourage switching.
	Extensive, well-trained salesforce; heavy use of product demonstrations in sales presentations.
	• Build adequate distribution through trade promotions and dealer training programs.
Stimulate selective demand among later adopters by:	
• Head-to-head positioning against target competitor's offering in established market segments	• See preceding actions.
• Differentiated positioning focused on untapped or underdeveloped segments	• Develop a differentiated brand or product line with unique features or price that is more appealing to a major segment of potential customers whose needs are not met by existing offerings (*flanking strategy*).
	<div align="center">or</div>
	• Develop multiple line extensions or brand offerings with features or prices targeted to the unique needs and preferences of several smaller potential applications or regional segments (*encirclement strategy*).
	• Design advertising, personal selling, and/or sales promotion campaigns that address specific interests and concerns of potential customers in one or multiple underdeveloped segments to stimulate selective demand.
	• Build unique distribution channels to more effectively reach potential customers in one or multiple underdeveloped segments.
	• Design service programs to reduce the perceived risks of trial and/or solve the unique problems faced by potential customers in one or multiple underdeveloped segments (for example, systems engineering, installation, operator training, or extended warranties).

Exhibit 10-9 summarizes the marketing objectives that each of the five share-growth strategies attempts to accomplish. Once again, however, the specific strategy—or combination of strategies—that is best for a particular challenger depends on market characteristics, the existing competitors' current positions and strengths, and the challenger's own resources and competencies. We examine these issues, and the marketing actions appropriate for each strategy, below.

Deciding whom to attack

When more than one competitor is already established in the market, a challenger must decide which competitor, if any, to target. There are several options:

> • *Attack the market-share leader within its primary target market.* As we shall see, this typically involves either a *frontal assault* or an attempt to *leapfrog* the leader through the development of superior technology or product design. It may seem logical to try to win customers away from the competitor with the most customers

---

EXHIBIT 10 – 8

Strategic Choices for Challengers in Growth Markets

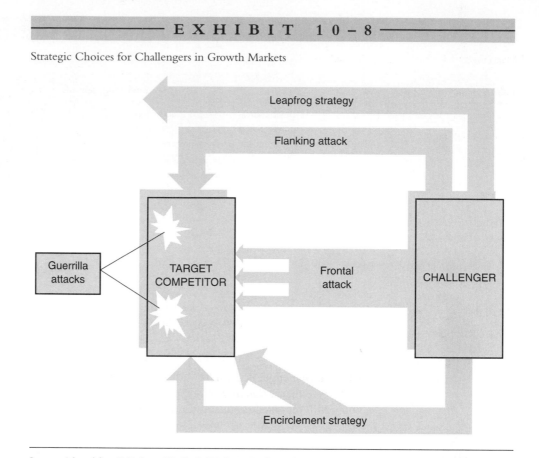

Source: Adapted from P. Kotler and R. Singh, "Marketing Warfare in the 1980s." Reprinted with permission from *Journal of Business Strategy*, Winter 1981, pp. 30–41. Copyright © Warren, Gorham & Lambert, Inc., 210 South Street, Boston, MA 02111. All rights reserved.

to lose, but this can be a dangerous strategy unless the challenger has superior resources and competencies that can be converted into a sustainable advantage. In some cases, however, a smaller challenger may be able to avoid disastrous retaliation by confronting the leader only occasionally in limited geographic territories through a series of *guerrilla attacks*.

- *Attack another follower who has an established position within a major market segment.* This also usually involves a *frontal assault*, but it may be easier for the challenger to gain a sustainable advantage if the target competitor is not as well established as the market leader in the minds and buying habits of customers.

- *Attack one or more smaller competitors who have only limited resources.* Because smaller competitors usually hold only a small share of the total market, this may seem like an inefficient way to attain substantial share increases. But by focusing on several small regional competitors one at a time, a challenger can sometimes achieve major gains without inviting retaliation from stronger firms. For example, by first challenging and ultimately acquiring a series of smaller regional manufacturers, Borden managed to capture the leading share of the fragmented domestic pasta market.

E X H I B I T   1 0 – 9

Marketing Objectives of Share-Growth Strategies

Share-growth strategies

Frontal attack	Leapfrog	Flank attack	Encirclement	Guerrilla attack
Capture substantial repeat/replacement purchases from target competitor's current customers; attract new customers among later adopters by offering lower price or more attractive features.	Induce current customers in mass market to replace their current brand with superior new offering; attract new customers by providing enhanced benefits.	Attract substantial share of new customers in one or more major segments where customer's needs are different from those of early adopters in the mass market.	Attract a substantial share of new customers in a variety of smaller, specialized segments where customers' needs or preferences differ from those of early adopters in the mass market.	Capture a modest share of repeat/replacement purchases in several market segments or territories; attract a share of new customers in a number of existing segments.

- *Avoid direct attacks on any established competitor.* In fragmented markets in which the leader or other major competitors are not currently satisfying one or more segments, a challenger is often best advised to "hit 'em where they ain't." This usually involves either a *flanking* or an *encirclement* strategy, with the challenger developing differentiated product offerings targeted at one large or several smaller segments in which no competitor currently holds a strong position.

Deciding which competitor to attack necessitates a comparison of relative strengths and weaknesses, a critical first step in developing an effective share-growth strategy. It can also help limit the scope of the battlefield, a particularly important consideration for challengers with limited resources.

Frontal attack strategy

Where the market for a product category is relatively homogeneous, with few untapped segments and at least one well-established competitor, a follower wanting to capture an increased market share may have little choice but to tackle a major competitor head-on. Such an approach is most likely to succeed when most existing customers do not have strong brand preferences or loyalties and when the challenger's resources and competencies—particularly in marketing—are greater than the target competitor's. But even superior resources are no guarantee of success if the challenger's assault merely imitates the target competitor's offering.

To successfully implement a frontal attack, a challenger should seek one or more ways to achieve a sustainable advantage over the target competitor. As discussed earlier, such an advantage is usually based on attaining lower costs or a differentiated position in the market. If the challenger has a cost advantage, it can cut prices to lure away the target competitor's customers (as a number of the clone manufacturers did to IBM in the commercial PC market) or it can maintain a similar price but engage in more extensive promotion.

Challenging a leader solely on the basis of low price is a highway to disaster, however, unless the challenger really does have a sustainable cost advantage. Otherwise, the leader might simply match the lower prices until the challenger is driven from the market. The problem is that initially a challenger is often at a cost *disadvantage* because of the experience curve effects established competitors have accumulated. The challenger must have offsetting advantages like superior production technology, established relations with low-cost suppliers, the ability to share production facilities or marketing efforts across multiple SBUs, or other sources of synergy before a low-price assault makes sense.

A similar caveat applies to frontal assaults based solely on heftier promotional budgets. Unless the target competitor's resources are substantially more limited than the challenger's, it can retaliate against any attempt to win away customers through more extensive advertising or attractive sales and trade promotions.

One possible exception to this limitation of greater promotional effort is the use of a more extensive and better-trained salesforce to gain a competitive advantage. A knowledgeable salesperson's technical advice and problem-solving abilities can add additional value to a firm's product offering, particularly in newly developing high-tech industries.

In general, the best way for a challenger to effectively implement a frontal attack is to find a way to provide customers with better *value* than its target competitor; by offering superior product features or service at a comparable price, similar quality and performance at a lower price, or both. For instance, Compaq has gained ground in the race for share leadership in the global PC market by being the first company to offer prices below $1,000 for its most basic machines while simultaneously investing in R&D, product development activities, and acquisitions aimed at producing a continuing stream of product and service improvements to appeal to more technically demanding market segments.[17]

Variables that might limit the target competitor's willingness or ability to retaliate can also improve the chances for successful frontal attack. For example, a competitor with a reputation for high product quality may be loath to cut prices in response to a lower-priced challenger for fear of cheapening its brand's image. And a competitor pursuing high ROI or cash flow objectives may be reluctant to increase its promotion or R&D expenditures in the short run to fend off an attack.[18]

Leapfrog strategy

A challenger stands the best chance of attracting repeat or replacement purchases from a competitor's current customers when it can offer a product that is attractively differentiated from the competitor's offerings. The odds of success might be even greater if the challenger can offer a far superior product based on advanced technology or a more sophisticated design. This is the essence of a leapfrog strategy, which attempts to gain a significant advantage over the existing competition by introducing a new generation of products that significantly outperform or offer more desirable customer benefits than existing brands. For example, Vistakon's development of low-cost disposable lenses enabled it to capture a leading share of the global contact lens market.

In addition, such a strategy often inhibits quick retaliation by established competitors. Firms that have achieved some success with one technology—or that have committed substantial resources to plant and equipment dedicated to a current product—may be reluctant to switch to a new one because of the large investments involved or a fear of disrupting current customers.

---

[17]Gary McWilliams, Ira Sager, Paul C. Judge, and Peter Burrows, "Power Play: How the Compaq-Digital Deal Will Reshape the Entire World of Computers," *Business Week*, February 9, 1998, pp. 90–97.

[18]For a more extensive discussion of factors that can limit a leader's willingness or ability to retaliate against a direct attack, see Michael E. Porter, *Competitive Advantage* (New York: Free Press, 1985), chap. 15.

On the other hand, a leapfrog strategy is not viable for all challengers. To be successful, the challenger must have technology superior to that of established competitors as well as the product and process engineering capabilities to turn that technology into an appealing product. Also, the challenger must have the marketing resources to effectively promote its new offering and convince customers already committed to an earlier technology that the new product offers sufficient benefits to justify the costs of switching. Vistakon reduced such problems by limiting the distribution of its disposable lenses to eye care professionals and relying on them to prescribe the lenses for patients who might benefit from their unique advantages.

Unfortunately, a leapfrog strategy is harder to implement in durable goods industries where customers engage in replacement purchases less frequently. To speed up the replacement process in such markets, the challenger may have to offer substantial trade-in allowances or develop sales promotion or customer service programs aimed at reducing switching costs. For industrial goods, the offer of systems engineering services or product features that help potential customers integrate the new technology with their existing equipment and processes can encourage them to switch suppliers.

Flanking and encirclement strategies

The military historian B. H. Liddell-Hart, after analyzing battles ranging from the Greek Wars to World War I, determined that only 6 out of 280 victories were the result of a frontal attack.[19] He concluded that it is usually wiser to avoid attacking an established adversary's point of strength and to focus instead on an area of weakness in the adversary's defenses. This is the basic premise behind flanking and encirclement strategies. They both seek to avoid direct confrontations by focusing on market segments whose needs are not being satisfied by existing brands and where no current competitor has a strongly held position.

Flank attack A flank attack is appropriate when the market can be broken into two or more large segments, when the leader and/or other major competitors hold a strong position in the primary segment, and when no existing brand fully satisfies the needs of customers in at least one other segment. A challenger may be able to capture a significant share of the total market by concentrating primarily on one large untapped segment. This usually involves developing product features or services tailored to the needs and preferences of the targeted customers, together with appropriate promotional and pricing policies to quickly build selective demand. Japanese auto companies, for instance, first penetrated the U.S. car market by focusing on the low-price segment, where domestic manufacturers' offerings were limited. Domestic automobile manufacturers were relatively unconcerned by this flanking action at first. They failed to retaliate very aggressively because the Japanese were pursuing a segment they considered to be rather small and unprofitable. History proved them wrong.

In some cases a successful flank attack need not involve unique product features. Instead, a challenger can sometimes meet the special needs of an untapped segment by providing specially designed customer services or distribution channels. One major reason for the success of L'eggs pantyhose, for instance, was that it was the first brand to be distributed through an extensive channel of convenience goods retailers, such as grocery and drugstores, instead of more fashionable department and clothing stores. The greater

[19]Liddell-Hart, *Strategy*, p.163.

═══════════════ E X H I B I T   1 0 – 1 0 ═══════════════

A Small Citrus-Juice Co-Op Squeezes Big Rivals

> When a little-known farmers' cooperative called Citrus World Inc. started to market its own brand of pasteurized orange juice, it looked like an improbable player in the $3 billion juice market. Citrus World, an 800-employee operation in rural Florida, was up against a couple of established giants: Seagram Co., owner of the Tropicana brand, and Coca-Cola Co., with its Minute Maid line.
>
> But Citrus World knew exactly what to do: Squeeze that folksy image for all it was worth. To sell its Florida's Natural brand, it ordered TV commercials featuring sunburned farmers gulping down juice. In one ad, growers holding boxes of oranges hold a "stockholders' meeting" in the back of a truck. Other workers cut "overhead" by chopping a branch from an orange tree.
>
> Thanks to catchy ads, a quality product, and aggressive pricing, Citrus World has made a splash. In 1995 Florida's Natural knocked Minute Maid out of the number 2 spot in the rapidly growing market for "premium," or pasteurized, not-from-concentrate orange juice, and the brand experienced a larger percentage sales increase than Tropicana. While Citrus World attacked its larger rivals' exposed flanks, in part, by offering lower prices, its success also demonstrates that a substantial segment of consumers prefers to deal with what they perceive to be small, "underdog" companies.

SOURCE: Yumiko Ono, "A Pulp Tale: Juice Co-op Squeezes Big Rivals," *The Wall Street Journal*, January 30, 1996, p. 81. Reprinted with permission.

shopping convenience provided by this new distribution channel appealed strongly to the growing segment of working women.

Sometimes, a successful flank attack can be based solely on intangible differences. For instance, a challenger may appeal to an untapped customer segment with a more appealing brand image developed by means of unique product design or creative promotional appeals. The success of the small citrus farmers' cooperative described in Exhibit 10-10 illustrates this.

Encirclement   An encirclement strategy involves targeting several smaller untapped or underdeveloped segments in the market simultaneously. The idea is to surround the leader's brand with a variety of offerings aimed at several peripheral segments. This strategy makes the most sense when the market is fragmented into many different application segments or geographical regions with somewhat unique needs or tastes.

Once again, this strategy usually involves developing a varied line of products with features tailored to the needs of different segments. Thus, while Compaq has frontally assaulted IBM and other major competitors by offering similar products at lower prices, it also launched an encirclement strategy aimed at developing and promoting different product offerings for distinct segments in the fragmenting PC market. In the early 1990s, for instance, Compaq introduced its Presario line with user-friendly features such as factory-installed software to appeal to technophobes, and the lower-priced Prolinea line to attract more price-sensitive customers. More recently, the firm has developed powerful servers for the commercial market, and it acquired Digital Equipment Corporation to help strengthen its ability to offer consulting services and customized computer systems to large organizational customers.[20]

[20]McWilliams, et al., "Power Play."

E X H I B I T   1 0 – 1 1

The Guerrilla Attack on AT&T

Kitchen phones across the United States are sprouting little stickers with official-looking five-digit codes and slogans like "Dial & Save." They are evidence of a sneakily successful marketing campaign that has taken a $900 million bite out of AT&T and its major long-distance rivals. The stickers arrive in direct mail promotions by resellers of phone service known as *dial-around companies*. A customer can punch in the five-digit code when making a long-distance call and save from 10 to 50 percent over the undiscounted rates of the major long-distance companies.

Dial-around companies are mostly small, privately held firms that buy long-distance capacity in bulk from telephone giants and resell it at cut rates, routing calls through the switching equipment of other companies or their own. Their services are marketed under a variety of different brand names and promoted largely through direct mail campaigns. The mailings are usually targeted at customers whom AT&T and its rivals tend to neglect, such as older people. These consumers are often bargain hunters, yet typically they don't use the phone enough to qualify for most long-distance savings plans.

How did dial-arounds gain so much ground without provoking a counter-attack from AT&T? First, they focused on customers that the bigger firms did not deem very important or profitable. Second, many small companies were involved so it was hard for AT&T to retaliate against them individually. But as the volume of business of the dial-around companies continued to increase, the firm was eventually forced to react against them as a group. The firm instituted its One Rate plan, promising residential customers calls anywhere, anytime for 15 cents a minute. Nevertheless, with some dial-around firms touting rates as low as 9.5 cents a minute, they may continue to ambush the industry leaders.

SOURCE: Henry Goldblatt, "The Guerrilla Attack on AT&T," *Fortune*, November 25, 1996, pp. 126–27.

Guerrilla attack

When well-established competitors already cover all major segments of the market and the challenger's resources are relatively limited, flanking, encirclement, or all-out frontal attacks may be impossible. In such cases, the challenger may be reduced to making a series of surprise raids against its more established competitors. To avoid massive retaliation, the challenger should use guerrilla attacks sporadically, perhaps in limited geographic areas where the target competitor is not particularly well entrenched.

A challenger can choose from a variety of means for carrying out guerrilla attacks. These include sales promotion efforts (e.g., coupon drops and merchandising deals), local advertising blitzes, and even legal action. Short-term price reductions through sales promotion campaigns are a particularly favored guerrilla tactic in consumer goods markets. They can target specific customer groups in limited geographic areas; they can be implemented quickly; and they are often difficult for a larger competitor to respond to because that firm's higher share level means that a given discount will cost it more in absolute dollars.[21] For similar reasons, carefully targeted direct mail campaigns can also be an effective guerrilla tactic, as illustrated by the dial-around companies described in Exhibit 10-11.

In some cases the ultimate objective of a series of guerrilla attacks is not so much for the challenger to build its own share as it is to prevent a powerful leader from further expanding its share or engaging in aggressive actions to which it would be costly for the followers to respond. Lawsuits brought against the leader by several smaller competitors over a range of activities can effectively slow down the leader's expansionist tendencies by diverting some of its resources and attention.

---

[21] A. L. Stern, "New Marketing Game: Stealing Customers," *Dun's Business Month*, February 1985, pp. 48–50.

―――― E X H I B I T   1 0 – 1 2 ――――

Strategic Changes Made by Challengers That Gained or Lost Market Share

Strategic changes	Share-gaining challengers	Share-losing challengers
Relative product quality scores	+1.8	−0.6
New products as a percentage of sales	+0.1	−0.5
Relative price	+0.3	+0.2
Marketing expenditures (adjusted for market growth)		
Salesforce	+9.0%	−8.0%
Advertising		
Consumer products	+13.0%	−9.0%
Industrial products	−1.0	−14.0
Promotion		
Consumer products	+13.0%	−5.0%
Industrial products	+7.0	−10.0

SOURCE: Adapted with permission of The Free Press, an imprint of Simon & Schuster Inc. from *The PIMS Principles: Linking Strategy to Performance* by Robert D. Buzzell and Bradley T. Gale. Copyright ©1987 by The Free Press.

Empirical evidence

Several empirical studies conducted with the PIMS database provide empirical support for many of the managerial prescriptions discussed.[22] These studies compare businesses that achieved high market shares during the growth stage of the product life cycle, or that increased their market shares over time, with low-share businesses. As shown in Exhibit 10-12, the marketing programs and activities of businesses that successfully increased market share differed from their less successful counterparts in the following ways:

- Businesses that increased the quality of their products relative to those of competitors achieved greater share increases than businesses whose product quality remained constant or declined.

- Share-gaining businesses typically developed and added more new products, line extensions, or product modifications than share-losing businesses.

- Share-gaining businesses tended to increase their marketing expenditures faster than the rate of market growth. Increases in both salesforce and sales promotion expenditures were effective for producing share gains in both consumer and industrial goods businesses. Increased advertising expenditures were effective for producing share gains primarily in consumer goods businesses.

- Surprisingly, there was little difference in the relative prices charged between firms that gained and those that lost market share.

---

[22]Robert D. Buzzell and Frederik D. Wiersema, "Successful Share-Building Strategies," *Harvard Business Review*. January–February 1981, pp. 135–43; Carl R. Anderson and Carl P. Zeithaml, "Stages in the Product Life Cycle, Business Strategy, and Business Performance," *Academy of Management Journal*, March 1984, pp. 5–25; and Robert D. Buzzell and Bradley T. Gale, *The PIMS Principles: Linking Strategy to Performance* (New York: Free Press, 1987), chap. 9.

These findings are consistent with many of our earlier observations. For instance, they underline the folly of launching a frontal attack solely on the basis of lower price. Unless the challenger has substantially lower unit costs or the leader is inhibited from cutting its own prices for some reason, the challenger's price cuts are likely to be retaliated against and will therefore generate few new customers. On the other hand, frontal, leapfrog, flanking, or encirclement attacks based on product improvements tailored to specific segments are more likely to succeed, particularly when the challenger supports those attacks with substantial promotional efforts.

Regardless of the strategies pursued by market leaders and challengers during a product-market's growth stage, the competitive situation often changes as the market matures and its growth rate slows. In the next chapter we examine the environmental changes that occur as a market matures and the marketing strategies that firms might use to adapt to those changes.

SUMMARY

Both conventional wisdom and the various portfolio models suggest that firms gain advantages by quickly entering, and investing heavily to build share in, growth markets. Among the premises on which the early, aggressive pursuit of growing markets is based are (1) it is easier to gain share when a market is growing, (2) share gains are worth more when total volume is expanding rather than stable, (3) price competition is likely to be less intense in growing markets because demand often exceeds supply, and (4) early experience gained in developing products and applications for a growth market can give a firm the technical expertise needed to keep up with advancing technology.

Although true in general, each of these premises is not always valid for every firm in every situation. Thus, a market does not always represent an attractive opportunity for a business simply because it promises rapid future growth. Managers must consider how the market and competitive situations are likely to evolve and whether their firms can exploit the market's rapid growth to establish a sustainable competitive advantage.

The primary strategic objective of the early share leader, typically the market pioneer, in a growth market is *share maintenance*. From a marketing view, the firm must accomplish two important tasks: (1) retain repeat or replacement business from its existing customers and (2) continue to capture the major portion of sales to the growing number of new customers entering the market for the first time. Among the marketing strategies a firm might use singly or in combination to maintain a leading share position are (1) a fortress or position defense strategy, (2) a flanker strategy, (3) a confrontation strategy, (4) a market expansion or mobile strategy, and (5) a contraction or strategic withdrawal strategy.

A challenger's strategic objective in a growth market is usually to *build its share* by expanding its sales faster than the overall market growth rate. It can accomplish this by stealing existing customers away from other competitors, capturing a larger share of new customers than the market leader, or both. Possible share-growth strategies include (1) a frontal attack, (2) a leapfrog strategy, (3) a flanking attack, (4) encirclement, and (5) guerrilla attacks.

11

CHAPTER

Strategies for Mature and Declining Markets

JOHNSON CONTROLS: MAKING MONEY IN MATURE MARKETS[1]

Jim Keyes, CEO of Johnson Controls in Glendale, Wisconsin, appears to deserve your condolences. After all, his conglomerate's success and future survival depend heavily on four product categories that have experienced little or no growth in recent years. Johnson Controls makes batteries and seats for cars, heating and cooling systems for office buildings and schools, and plastic beverage bottles.

But Keyes isn't looking for sympathy. Instead, he has developed a successful three-pronged strategy for making money in these mature markets. His strategy involves (1) acquiring weaker competitors to gain market share and remove excess capacity, (2) fattening profit margins by improving operating efficiencies, and (3) gaining additional revenue through the development of new technologies, product offerings, and services.

A strong balance sheet and a long-term perspective help Johnson build market share through the acquisition of competitors. In some cases the company has used such acquisitions to expand its product offerings in one of its established target markets. For instance, the firm spent $167 million to buy Pan Am's World Services division, a facility management operation that does everything from mow the lawn to run the cafeteria. That acquisition, together with some new products and services developed internally, helped Johnson grow from just a manufacturer of heating and cooling systems for new buildings into a full-service facilities operator. Johnson can now manage a client's entire building while offering highly customized heating and cooling systems and controls that save money. This combination of custom products

---

[1]This case example is based on material found in Rick Tetzeli, "Mining Money in Mature Markets," *Fortune*, March 22, 1993, pp. 77–80; the *Johnson Controls, Inc. 1997 Annual Report* (Milwaukee, Wis.: Johnson Controls, 1998); and the Johnson Controls website at www.jci.com

and full service has not only increased Johnson's revenues in the commercial real estate market, but also has generated higher operating profit margins.

In other businesses Johnson has combined the economies of scale generated through savvy acquisitions with process reengineering to push down operating costs. For example, the firm has captured a 40 percent share of the U. S. market for outsourced automotive seats—and has begun to win a commanding share of the European market as well—by supplying successful lines like the Jeep Grand Cherokee. Says Tom Donoughe, the Chrysler engineer in charge of the interior of the company's Neon compact car, "Johnson is able to completely integrate the design, development, and manufacture of the seats"—and do it for less than the auto companies could.

Product development based on new technology is another way that Johnson has managed to increase sales to current customers as well as penetrating new market segments. Until recently, for instance, only glass bottles could safely handle certain fruit juices, including cranberry and apple, that are poured into containers when they are hot. But Johnson's R & D people are among the leaders in developing blow-molded plastic bottles that don't shrivel at high temperatures. Consequently, the firm is winning substantial business from new customers such as Ocean Spray and Gatorade.

Despite the maturity of its markets, Johnson's three-pronged strategy is paying off. The firm doubled its sales and profits during the first half of the 1990s. In the firm's 1997 fiscal year, sales advanced 21 percent to nearly $11.5 billion, profits rose 17 percent to $261 million, and the firm produced a 16 percent return on shareholders' equity. For an update on the company's recent performance, visit its website at *www.jci.com.*

STRATEGIC ISSUES IN MATURE AND DECLINING MARKETS

Many managers, particularly those in marketing, seem obsessed with growth. Their objectives tend to emphasize annual increases in sales volume, market share, or both. But the biggest challenge for many managers in developed nations in future years will be making money in markets that grow slowly, if at all. The majority of product-markets in those nations are in the mature or decline stages of their life cycles. And as accelerating rates of technological and social change continue to shorten such life cycles, today's innovations will move from growth to maturity—and ultimately to decline—ever faster.

However, the situation is not always as depressing as it sounds, as Johnson Controls' performance confirms. In many cases managers can find opportunities to earn substantial profits and even increase volume in mature and declining markets.

Issues during the transition to market maturity

A period of competitive turbulence almost always accompanies the transition from market growth to maturity in an industry. This period often begins after approximately half the potential customers have adopted the product and the rate of sales growth starts to decline. As the growth rate slows, many competitors tend to overestimate future sales volume and consequently end up developing too much production capacity. Competition becomes more intense as firms battle to increase sales volume to cover their high fixed costs and maintain profitability. As a result, such transition periods are commonly accompanied by a **shakeout**, during which weaker businesses fail, withdraw from the industry, or are acquired by other firms—as has happened to some of Johnson Controls' competitors in the U. S. and European automotive seat and battery industries. The shakeout period is pivotal in influencing a brand's continued survival and the strength of its competitive position during the later maturity and decline stages of the life cycle. The next section of this chapter examines some common strategic traps that can threaten a firm's survival during an industry shakeout.

Issues in mature markets

Businesses that survive the shakeout face new challenges as market growth stagnates. As a market matures, total volume stabilizes; replacement purchases rather than first-time buyers account for the vast majority of that volume. A primary marketing objective of all competitors in mature markets, therefore, is simply to hold their existing customers—to sustain a meaningful competitive advantage that will help ensure the continued satisfaction and loyalty of those customers. Thus a product's financial success during the mature life cycle stage depends heavily on the firm's ability to achieve and sustain a lower delivered cost or some perceived product quality or customer service superiority.

Some firms tend to passively defend mature products while using the bulk of the revenues produced by those items to develop and aggressively market new products with more growth potential. This can be shortsighted, however. All segments of a market and all brands in an industry do not necessarily reach maturity at the same time. Aging brands like Jell-O, Johnson's baby shampoo, and Arm & Hammer baking soda experienced sales revivals in recent years because of creative marketing strategies. Thus, a share leader in a mature industry might build upon a cost or product differentiation advantage and pursue a marketing strategy aimed at increasing volume by promoting new uses for an old product or by encouraging current customers to buy and use the product more often. A later section of this chapter examines basic business strategies necessary for survival in mature markets and marketing strategies a firm might use to extend a brand's sales and profits.

Issues in declining markets

Eventually, technological advances, changing customer demographics, tastes, or lifestyles, and development of substitutes result in declining demand for most product forms and brands. As a product starts to decline, managers face the critical question of whether to divest or liquidate the business. Unfortunately, firms sometimes support dying products too long at the expense of current profitability and the aggressive pursuit of future breadwinners.

An appropriate marketing strategy can, however, produce substantial sales and profits even in a declining market. If few exit barriers exist, an industry leader might attempt to increase market share via aggressive pricing or promotion policies aimed at driving out weaker competitors. Or it might try to consolidate the industry by acquiring weaker brands and reducing overhead by eliminating excess capacity and duplicate marketing programs. Alternatively, a firm might decide to harvest a mature product by maximizing cash flow and profit over the product's remaining life. The last section of this chapter discusses specific marketing strategies for gaining the greatest possible returns from products approaching the end of their life cycle.

————————————————— **E X H I B I T   1 1 – 1** —————————————————

The Transition or Shakeout Stage of the Generalized Product Life Cycle

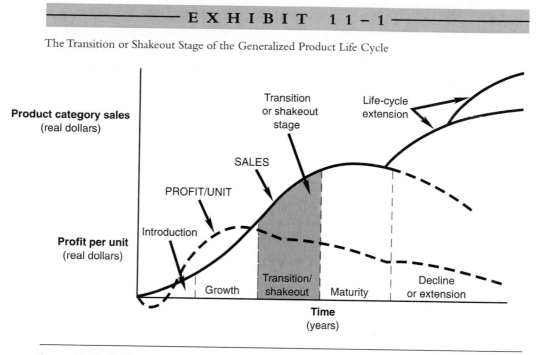

Source: Reprinted with permission from p. 60 of *Analysis for Strategic Market Decisions*, by George S. Day, copyright © 1986 by West Publishing Company. All rights reserved.

SHAKEOUT: THE TRANSITION FROM MARKET GROWTH TO MATURITY

Characteristics of the transition period

The transition from growth to maturity typically begins when the market is still growing but the rate of growth starts to decline, as shown in Exhibit 11-1. This declining growth either sparks or occurs simultaneously with other changes in the market and competitive environment. Such changes include the appearance of excess capacity, increased intensity of competition, increased difficulty of maintaining product differentiation, worsening distribution problems, and growing pressures on costs and profits. Weaker members of the industry often fail or are acquired by larger competitors during this shakeout stage.

Excess capacity

During a market's growth stage, manufacturers must usually invest heavily in new plants, equipment, and personnel to keep up with increasing demand. Some competitors fail to anticipate the transition from growth to maturity, however, and their expansion plans eventually overshoot market demand. Thus, excess production capacity often develops at the end of the growth stage. This leads to an intense struggle for market share as firms seek increased volume to hold down unit costs and maintain profit margins.

More intense competition

The intensified battle for increased volume and market share at this stage often leads to price reductions and increased selling and promotional efforts. Firms modify products to appeal to more specialized user segments, make deals to produce for private labels, and take other actions that lower per unit revenues, increase R&D and marketing costs, and put pressure on profit margins.

Difficulty of maintaining differentiation

As an industry's technology matures, the better and more popular designs tend to become industry standards, and the physical differences among brands become less substantial. The popularity of the VHS format among video cassette recorder customers, for example, eventually made it the industry standard, and Sony's alternative Beta format disappeared from the market. This decline in differentiation across brands often leads to a weakening of brand preference among consumers and makes it more difficult for even the market leaders to command premium prices for their products.[2] Such problems have been magnified in recent years as consumers have become more demanding and more willing to objectively evaluate alternatives rather than rely on past loyalty.[3]

Diminishing product differentiation can also increase costs as firms seek differentiation in other ways, such as through improved service. As the products and prices offered by competing suppliers become more similar, many purchasing agents become increasingly concerned with service and its impact on their firm's costs. For instance, they may demand a higher level of delivery reliability (as in just-in-time deliveries) to help reduce their cost of capital tied up in inventory.

Distribution problems

During an industry's transition from growth to maturity, channel members often become more assertive in ways particularly detrimental to smaller-share competitors. As sales growth slows, for example, retailers may reduce the number of brands they carry to reduce inventory costs and space requirements. Much the same can happen at the wholesale/distributor level. Because any reduction in product availability has serious repercussions for a manufacturer, low-share firms often must offer additional trade incentives simply to hold their distribution coverage during this period.

Pressures on prices and profits

Prices typically decrease and margins get squeezed during shakeout, which increases the industry's instability and volatility. Given their higher per unit costs, smaller-share businesses often operate at a loss during transition. Some are ultimately forced to leave the industry. This is particularly likely with commodity-type products, when few unique market niches exist in which the firm can maintain a competitive advantage and when heavy investments in fixed assets are required and experience curve effects are high.

Firms that enter the transition period with high relative market shares are more likely to survive. Even these firms may experience a severe drop in profits, however. As the shakeout proceeds, the shares held by firms exiting the industry pass to the surviving firms, increasing their volumes and lowering per unit costs. This does not necessarily mean,

---

[2]Neil Gross, Peter Coy, and Otis Port, "The Technology Paradox," *Business Week*, March 6, 1995, pp. 76–84.

[3]Rahul Jacob, "Beyond Quality and Value," *Fortune*, Special Issue, Fall–Winter, 1993, pp. 8–11.

——————————————— E X H I B I T   1 1 – 2 ———————————————

Common Strategic Traps Firms Can Fall into during the Shakeout Period

1. Failure to anticipate transition from growth to maturity.
   - Firms may make overly optimistic forecasts of future sales volume.
   - As a result, they expand too rapidly and production capacity overshoots demand as growth slows.
   - Their excess capacity leads to higher costs per unit.
   - Consequently, they must cut prices or increase promotion in an attempt to increase their volume.
2. No clear competitive advantage as growth slows.
   - Many firms can succeed without a strong competitive advantage during periods of rapid growth.
   - However, firms that do not have the lowest costs or a superior offering in terms of product quality or service can have difficulty sustaining their market share and volume as growth slows and competition intensifies.
3. Assumption that an early advantage will insulate the firm from price or service competition.
   - In many cases, technological differentials become smaller as more competitors enter and initiate product improvements as an industry approaches maturity.
   - If customers perceive that the quality of competing brands has become more equal, they are likely to attach greater importance to price or service differences.
   - Failure to detect such trends can cause an early leader to be complacent and slow to respond to competitive threats.
4. Sacrificing market share in favor of short-run profit.
   - A firm may cut marketing or R&D budgets or forgo other expenditures in order to maintain its historical level of profitability even though industry profits tend to fall during the transition period.
   - This can cause long-run erosion of market share and further increases in unit costs as the industry matures.

though, that the leaders' market shares remain stable after shakeout. One study indicates that larger firms tend to lose share during market maturity because they fail to maintain their cost advantage.[4] We will discuss this danger in more detail later in this chapter.

Strategic traps during the transition period

A business's ability to survive the transition from market growth to maturity also depends to a great extent on whether it can avoid some common strategic traps.[5] Four such traps are summarized in Exhibit 11-2.

The most obvious trap is simply the failure to recognize the events signaling the beginning of the shakeout period. The best way to minimize the impact of slowing growth is to accurately forecast the slowdown in sales and hold the firm's production capacity to a sustainable level. For both industrial and consumer durable goods markets, models can forecast when replacement sales will begin to outweigh first-time purchases, a common signal that a market is beginning to mature.[6] But in consumer nondurable markets—particularly those where growth slows because of shifting consumer preferences or the

---

[4]Robert D. Buzzell, "Are There 'Natural' Market Structures?" *Journal of Marketing*, Winter 1981, pp. 42–51.

[5]For a more detailed discussion of these traps, see Michael E. Porter, *Competitive Strategy* (New York: Free Press, 1980), pp. 247–49.

[6]Fareena Sultan, John U. Farley, and Donald R. Lehmann, "A Meta-Analysis of Applications of Diffusion Models," *Journal of Marketing Research*, Febrauary 1990, pp. 70–77.

emergence of substitute products—the start of the transition period can be nearly impossible to predict.

A second strategic trap is for a business to get caught in the middle during the transition period without a clear strategic advantage. A business may survive and prosper during the growth stage even though it has neither differentiated its offering from competitors nor attained the lowest-cost position in its industry. But during the transition period, such is not the case.

A third trap is the failure to recognize the declining importance of product differentiation and the increasing importance of price or service. Businesses that have built their success on technological superiority or other forms of product differentiation often disdain aggressive pricing or marketing practices even though such differentiation typically erodes as markets mature.[7] As a result, such firms may delay meeting their more aggressive competitors head-on and end up losing market share.

Why should a firm not put off responding to the more aggressive pricing or marketing actions of its competitors? Because doing so may lead to a fourth trap—giving up market share too easily in favor of short-run profit. Many businesses try to maintain the profitability of the recent past as markets enter the transition period. They usually do this at the expense of market share or by forgoing marketing, R&D, and other investments crucial for maintaining future market position. While some smaller firms with limited resources may have no choice, this tendency can be seriously shortsighted, particularly if economies of scale are crucial for the business's continued success during market maturity.

BUSINESS STRATEGIES FOR MATURE MARKETS

The maturity phase of an industry's life cycle is often depicted as one of stability characterized by few changes in the market shares of leading competitors and steady prices. The industry leaders, because of their low per unit costs and little need to make any further investments, enjoy high profits and positive cash flows. These cash flows are harvested and diverted to other strategic business units (SBUs) or products in the firm's portfolio that promise greater future growth.

Unfortunately, this conventional scenario provides an overly simplistic description of the situation businesses face in most mature markets. For one thing, it is not always easy to tell when a market has reached maturity. Variations in brands, marketing programs, and customer groups can mean that different brands and market segments reach maturity at different times.

Further, as the maturity stage progresses, a variety of threats and opportunities can disrupt an industry's stability. Shifts in customer needs or preferences, product substitutes, increased raw material costs, changes in government regulations, or factors such as the entry of low-cost foreign producers or mergers and acquisitions can threaten individual competitors and even throw the entire industry into early decline. Consider, for example, the competitive position of Timex, a brand that dominated the low-price segment of the U.S. watch market in the 1970s. First the appearance of imported digital watches and later a shift in consumer preferences toward more fashionable and prestigious brands buffeted the firm and eroded its market share.

---

[7]Ming Jer Chen and Ian C. MacMillan, "Nonresponse and Delayed Response to Competitive Moves: The Roles of Competitor Dependence and Action Irreversibility," *Academy of Management Journal* 35 (1992), pp. 539–70; and Hubert Gatignon, Eric Anderson, and Kristiaan Helsen, "Competitive Reactions to Market Entry: Explaining Interfirm Differences," *Journal of Marketing Research*, February 1989, pp. 44–55.

On the positive side, such changes can also open new growth opportunities in mature industries. Product improvements (such as the development of high-fiber nutritional cereals), advances in process technology (e.g., the creation of minimills for steel production), falling raw materials costs, increased prices for close substitutes, or environmental changes (such as the increased demand for storm windows in the energy crisis of the 1970s and early 1980s) can all provide opportunities for a firm to dramatically increase its sales and profits. An entire industry can even experience a period of renewed growth.

Discontinuities during industry maturity suggest that it is dangerously shortsighted for a firm to simply milk its cash cows. Even industry followers can substantially improve volume, share, and profitability during industry maturity if they can adjust their marketing objectives and programs to fit the new opportunities that arise.[8] Thus success in mature markets requires two sets of strategic actions: (1) the development of a well-implemented business strategy to sustain a competitive advantage and (2) flexible and creative marketing programs geared to pursue growth or profit opportunities as conditions change in specific product-markets.

Strategies for maintaining competitive advantage

As discussed in Chapter 3, both *analyzer* and *defender strategies* may be appropriate for units with a leading, or at least a profitable, share of one or more major segments in a mature industry. Analyzers and defenders are both concerned with maintaining a strong share position in established product-markets. But analyzers also do some product and market development to avoid being leapfrogged by competitors with more advanced products or being left behind in new application segments. On the other hand, defenders may initiate some product improvements or line extensions to protect and strengthen their position in existing markets, but they spend relatively little on new product R&D. Thus, an analyzer strategy is most appropriate for developed industries that are still experiencing some technological change and may have opportunities for continued growth, such as the computer and commercial aircraft industries. The defender strategy works best in industries where the basic technology is not very complex or is unlikely to change dramatically in the short run, as in the food industry.

Both analyzers and defenders can attempt to sustain a competitive advantage in established product-markets through *differentiation* of their product offering (either on the basis of superior quality or service) or by maintaining a *low-cost* position. Evidence suggests the ability to maintain either a strongly differentiated or a low-cost position continues to be a critical determinant of success throughout both the transition and the maturity stages. One study examined the competitive strategies pursued by the two leading firms (in terms of return on investment) in eight mature industries characterized by slow growth and intense competition. In each industry the two leading firms offered either the lowest relative delivered cost or high relative product differentiation.[9] Similarly, Michael Treacy and Fred Wiersema observed that market leaders tend to pursue one of three strategic disciplines. They either stress operational excellence, which

[8]Cathy Anterasian and Lynn W. Phillips, "Discontinuities, Value Delivery, and the Share-Returns Association: A Re-Examination of the 'Share-Causes-Profits' Controversy," distributed working paper, Marketing Science Institute, (Cambridge, Mass., April 1988; see also Robert Jacobson, "Distinguishing among Competing Theories of the Market Share Effect," *Journal of Marketing*, October 1988, pp. 68–80.

[9]William K. Hall, "Survival Strategies in a Hostile Environment," *Harvard Business Review*, September–October 1980, pp. 75–85.

—————————— E X H I B I T   1 1 – 3 ——————————

Three Strategic Disciplines of Market Leaders and the Traits of Businesses That Implement Them Effectively

	Disciplines		
Company traits	**Operational excellence**	**Product leadership**	**Customer intimacy**
Core business processes	Sharpen distribution systems and provide no-hassle service	Nurture ideas, translate them into products, and market them skillfully	Provide solutions and help customers run their businesses
Structure	Has strong, central authority and a finite level of empowerment	Acts in an ad hoc, organic, loosely knit, and ever-changing way	Pushes empowerment close to customer contact
Management systems	Maintain standard operating procedures	Reward individuals' innovative capacity and new product success	Measure the cost of providing service and of maintaining customer loyalty
Culture	Acts predictably and believes "one size fits all"	Experiments and thinks "out-of-the-box"	Is flexible and thinks "have it your way"

SOURCE: Michael Treacy, Fred Wiersema, "How Market Leaders Keep Their Edge," *Fortune*, February 6, 1995, p. 96. Excerpted from *The Discipliine of Market Leaders*, © 1996 by Michael Treacy, Fred Wiersema and CSC Index, Inc. Reprinted by permission of Addison Wesley Longman.

typically translates into lower costs, or they differentiate themselves through product leadership or customer intimacy and superior service.[10] These three disciplines are summarized in Exhibit 11-3 along with some of the traits of businesses that are able to implement them effectively.

Generally, it is difficult for a single business to pursue both low-cost and differentiation strategies at the same time. For instance, businesses taking the low-cost approach typically compete primarily by offering the lowest prices in the industry. Such prices allow little room for the firm to make the investments or cover the costs inherent in maintaining superior product quality, performance, or service over time.

It is important to keep in mind, however, that pursuit of a low-cost strategy does not mean that a business can ignore the delivery of desirable benefits to the customer. Similarly, customers will not pay an unlimited price premium for superior quality or service, no matter how superior it is. In both consumer and commercial markets customers seek good *value* for their money—either a solid, no-frills product or service at an outstanding price, or an offering whose higher price is justified by the superior benefits it delivers on one or more dimensions.[11] Thus, even low-cost producers should continually seek ways to improve the quality and performance of their offerings within the financial constraints of their competitive strategy. And even differentiated defenders should continually work to improve efficiency without sacrificing product quality or performance. The critical strategic questions, then, are How can a business continue to differentiate its offerings and justify a premium price as its market matures and becomes more competitive? and How can businesses—particularly those pursuing low-cost strategies—continue to reduce their costs and improve their efficiency as their markets mature?

———————

[10]Michael Treacy and Fred Wiersema, *The Discipline of Market Leaders* (Reading, Mass.: Addison-Wesley, 1995).

[11]Jacob, "Beyond Quality and Value," pp. 8–11.

E X H I B I T   1 1 – 4

Dimensions of Product Quality

• Performance	How well does the washing machine wash clothes?
• Durability	How long will the lawn mower last?
• Conformance with specifications	What is the incidence of product defects?
• Features	Does an airline flight offer a movie and dinner?
• Reliability	Will each visit to a restaurant result in consistent quality?
	What percentage of the time will a product perform satisfactorily?
• Serviceability	Is the product easy to service?
	Is the service system efficient, competent, and convenient?
• Fit and finish	Does the product look and feel like a quality product?
• Brand name	Is this a name that customers associate with quality?
	What is the brand's image?

SOURCE: Adapted from "What Does 'Product Quality' Really Mean?" by David A. Garvin, *Sloan Management Review*, Fall 1984, pp. 25–43. Copyright © 1984 by the Sloan Management Review Association. All rights reserved. Used by permission of the publisher.

Methods of differentiation

At the most basic level, a business can attempt to differentiate its offering from competitors' by offering either superior product quality, superior service, or both. The problem is that *quality* and *service* may be defined in a variety of different ways by different customers.

Dimensions of product quality[12]

To maintain a competitive advantage in product quality, a firm must understand what dimensions customers perceive to underlie differences across products within a given category. One authority has identified eight such dimensions of product quality. These are summarized in Exhibit 11-4 and discussed here.

European manufacturers of prestige automobiles, such as Mercedes-Benz and Porsche, have emphasized the first dimension of product quality—**functional performance**. These automakers have designed cars that provide excellent performance on attributes such as handling, acceleration, and comfort. Volvo, on the other hand, has emphasized and aggressively promoted a different quality dimension—**durability** (and the related attribute of safety). A third quality dimension, **conformance to specifications**, or the absence of defects, has been a major focus of Japanese automakers. Until recent years U.S. automakers relied heavily on broad product lines and a wide **variety of features**, both standard and optional, to offset their shortcomings on some of the other quality dimensions.

The **reliability** quality dimension can refer to the consistency of performance from purchase to purchase or to a product's uptime, the percentage of time that it can perform satisfactorily over its life. Tandem Computers has maintained a competitive advantage based

---

[12]The following discussion is based on material found in David A. Garvin, "What Does 'Product Quality' Really Mean?" *Sloan Management Review*, Fall 1984, pp. 25–43; and David A. Aaker, *Strategic Market Management*, 2nd ed. (New York: John Wiley & Sons, 1988), chap. 11.

on reliability by designing computers with several processors that work in tandem, so that if one fails, the only impact is the slowing of low-priority tasks. IBM cannot match Tandem's reliability because of its commitment to an operating system not easily adapted to the multiple-processor concept. Consequently, Tandem has maintained a strong position in market segments consisting of large-scale computer users—such as financial institutions and large retailers—for whom system downtime is particularly undesirable.

The quality dimension of **serviceability** refers to a customer's ability to obtain prompt and competent service when the product does break down. For example, Caterpillar Tractor has long differentiated itself with a parts and service organization dedicated to providing "24-hour parts service anywhere in the world."

Many of these quality dimensions can be difficult for customers to evaluate, particularly for consumer products. As a result, consumers often generalize from quality dimensions that are more visual or qualitative. Thus, the **fit and finish** dimension can help convince consumers that a product is of high quality. They tend to perceive attractive and well-designed products as generally high in quality, as witnessed by the success of the Krups line of small appliances. Similarly, the **quality reputation of the brand name**, and the promotional activities that sustain that reputation, can strongly influence consumers' perceptions of a product's quality. Indeed, a brand's quality reputation together with psychological factors such as name recognition and loyalty substantially determine a brand's *equity*—the perceived value customers associate with a particular brand name and its logo or symbol.[13]

In many cases, too, the value customers attach to a particular brand is at least partly determined by the sensory experiences they derive from the attractiveness of the product's design, packaging, graphics, and advertising and promotional materials. For example, although Absolut Vodka was a late entrant into the U.S. market for imported vodka, it has managed to capture a 60 percent share of a market characterized by little physical differentiation across brands. Absolut's simple but unique bottle and logo, its creative and trendy advertising campaign, and its association with cultural events (e.g., *Esquire's* Absolut Story writing contest) have provided superior sensory value for consumers. Therefore, a growing number of firms are paying greater attention to the **aesthetics** of their products and marketing programs.[14]

Thus, to successfully pursue a differentiation strategy based on product quality, managers must understand what dimensions or cues their firm's potential customers use to judge quality. They also should pay particular attention to some of the less concrete, but more visible, sensory and symbolic attributes of the product.

Dimensions of service quality

Customers also judge the quality of the service they receive on multiple dimensions. A number of such dimensions of perceived service quality have been identified by a series of studies conducted across industries as diverse as retail banking and appliance repair. Five of those dimensions are listed and briefly defined in Exhibit 11-5.[15]

---

[13]For a more extensive discussion of brand equity, see David A. Aaker, *Brand Equity* (New York: Free Press, 1991); and Kevin L. Keller, "Conceptualizing, Measuring, and Managing Customer-Based Brand Equity," *Journal of Marketing*, January 1993, pp. 1–22.

[14]Bernd Schmitt and Alex Simonson, *Marketing Aesthetics: The Strategic Management of Brands, Identity, and Image* (New York: Free Press, 1997).

[15]Valarie A. Zeithaml, A. Parasuraman, and Leonard L. Berry, *Delivering Quality Service: Balancing Customer Perceptions and Expectations* (New York: Free Press, 1990); see also Valarie A. Zeithaml and Mary Jo Bitner, *Services Marketing* (New York: McGraw-Hill, 1996).

─────── E X H I B I T   1 1 − 5 ───────

Dimensions of Service Quality

• Tangibles	Appearance of physical facilities, equipment, personnel, and communications materials
• Reliability	Ability to perform the promised service dependably and accurately
• Responsiveness	Willingness to help customers and provide prompt service
• Assurance	Knowledge and courtesy of employees and their ability to convey trust and confidence
• Empathy	Caring, individualized attention the firm provides its customers

SOURCE: Valarie A. Zeithaml, A. Parasuraman, and Leonard L. Berry, *Delivering Quality Service: Balancing Customer Perceptions and Expectations* (New York: Free Press, 1990), p. 26. Reprinted with permission.

The quality dimensions listed in Exhibit 11-5 apply specifically to service businesses, but most of them are also relevant for judging the service component of a product offering. This pertains to both the objective performance dimensions of the service delivery system—such as its **reliability** and **responsiveness**—as well as to elements of the performance of service personnel, such as their **empathy** and level of **assurance**.

The results of a number of surveys suggest that customers perceive all five dimensions of service quality to be very important regardless of the kind of service being evaluated. As Exhibit 11-6 indicates, customers of four different kinds of services gave reliability, responsiveness, assurance, and empathy mean importance ratings of more than 9 on a 10-point scale. And though the mean ratings for tangibles were somewhat lower in comparison, they still fell toward the upper end of the scale, ranging from 7.14 to 8.56.

The same respondents were also asked which of the five dimensions they would choose as the most critical in their assessment of service quality. Their responses (see Exhibit 11-6) suggest that reliability is the most important aspect of service quality to the greatest number of customers. The key to a differentiation strategy based on providing superior service, then, is to meet or exceed target customers' service quality expectations and to do it more consistently than competitors. The problem is that sometimes managers underestimate the level of those customer expectations, and sometimes those expectations can be unrealistically high. Therefore, a firm needs to clearly identify target customers' desires with respect to service quality and clearly define and communicate what level of service they intend to deliver. When this is done, customers have a more realistic idea of what to expect and are less likely to be disappointed with the service they receive.

Improving customer perceptions of service quality

The major factors that determine a customer's expectations and perceptions concerning service quality—and five gaps that can lead to dissatisfaction with service delivery—are outlined in Exhibit 11-7 and discussed next.

1. *Gap between the customer's expectations and the marketer's perceptions.* Managers do not always have an accurate understanding of what customers want or how they will evaluate a firm's service efforts. The first step in providing good service, then, is to collect information—through customer surveys, evaluations of customer complaints, or other methods—to determine which service attributes customers consider important.

EXHIBIT 11–6

Perceived Importance of Service Quality Dimensions in Four Different Industries

	Mean importance rating on 10-point scale*	Percentage of respondents indicating dimension is most important
Credit card customers (*n* = 187)		
Tangibles	7.43	0.6
Reliability	9.45	48.6
Responsiveness	9.37	19.8
Assurance	9.25	17.5
Empathy	9.09	13.6
Repair and maintenance customers (*n* = 183)		
Tangibles	8.48	1.2
Reliability	9.64	57.2
Responsiveness	9.54	19.9
Assurance	9.62	12.0
Empathy	9.30	9.6
Long-distance telephone customers (*n* = 184)		
Tangibles	7.14	0.6
Reliability	9.67	60.6
Responsiveness	9.57	16.0
Assurance	9.29	12.6
Empathy	9.25	10.3
Bank customers (*n* = 177)		
Tangibles	8.56	1.1
Reliability	9.44	42.1
Responsiveness	9.34	18.0
Assurance	9.18	13.6
Empathy	9.30	25.1

*Scale ranges from 1 (not at all important) to 10 (extremely important).

SOURCE: Reprinted with permission of The Free Press, a division of Macmillan, Inc. from *Delivering Quality Service: Balancing Customer Perceptions and Expectations* by Valarie A. Zeithaml, A. Parasuraman, and Leonard L. Berry. Copyright © 1990 by The Free Press.

2. *Gap between management perceptions and service quality specifications.* Even when management has a clear understanding of what customers want, that understanding might not get translated into effective operating standards. A firm's policies concerning customer service may be unclear, poorly communicated to employees, or haphazardly enforced. Unless a firm's employees know what the company's service policies are and believe that management is seriously committed to those standards, their performance is likely to fall short of desired levels.

3. *Gap between service quality specifications and service delivery.* Lip service by management is not enough to produce high-quality service. High standards must be backed by the programs, resources, and rewards necessary to enable and encourage employees to deliver good service. Employees must be provided with the training, equipment, and time necessary to deliver good service. Their service performance must be measured and evaluated. And good performance must be rewarded by making it part of the criteria for pay raises or promotions, or by other more direct inducements, in order to motivate the additional effort good service requires.

— E X H I B I T   1 1 – 7 —

Determinants of Perceived Service Quality

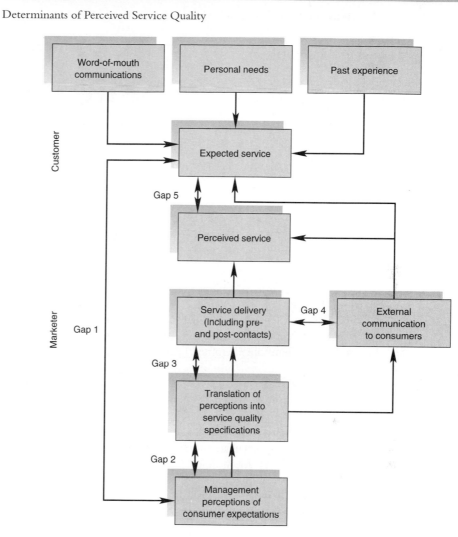

SOURCE: Reprinted with permission from A. Parasuraman, Valarie A. Zeithaml, and Leonard L. Berry, "A Conceptual Model of Service Quality and Its Implications for Future Research," *Journal of Marketing*, Fall 1985, p. 44. Published by the American Marketing Association.

4. *Gap between service delivery and external communications.* Even good service performance may disappoint some customers if the firm's marketing communications cause them to have unrealistically high expectations. If the photographs in a vacation resort's advertising and brochures make the rooms look more spacious and luxurious than they really are, for instance, first-time customers are likely to be disappointed no matter how clean or well-tended those rooms are kept by the resort's staff.

5. *Gap between perceived service and expected service.* This results when management fails to close one or more of the other four gaps. It is this difference between a customer's expectations and his or her actual experience with the firm that leads to dissatisfaction.

E X H I B I T   1 1 – 8

Hertz's Program for Excellent Customer Service

> No. 1 has been trying harder, and as a result Hertz tops all five categories in the Zagat survey of car rental customers. Hertz's secret: the #1 Club Gold program. Pay $50 a year to become a member, and skip endless late-night lines at rental counters. Just call up to reserve your car, hop on the courtesy airport bus when you arrive at your destination, tell the driver your last name, and get dropped off in front of your auto. You'll know it's yours because your surname is in glowing lights above it. Since the bus driver radios ahead, Hertz starts your car up and turns on the a.c. or heat, depending on the temperature. Show the gate attendant your driver's license, and off you go. Says Boston Consulting Group VP, Gary Curtis, who travels a lot: "This is the best thing that ever happened to rental cars."

SOURCE: Reprinted with permission from "Companies That Serve You Best," by Patricia Sellers, *Fortune*, May 31, 1993, p. 76. © 1993 Time, Inc. All rights reserved.

This discussion suggests a number of actions management can take to close the possible gaps and improve customer satisfaction with a company's service. An example of how such actions can be translated into a successful service program that satisfies customers is provided by Hertz's #1 Club Gold program, (see Exhibit 11-8). Achieving and sustaining such high levels of service quality can present some difficult implementation problems, however, because it often involves the coordination of efforts of many different employees from different functional departments and organizational levels. Some of these coordination problems are examined later in Chapter 12.

Methods for maintaining a low-cost position

Moving down the experience curve is the most commonly discussed method for achieving and sustaining a low-cost position in an industry. But a firm does not necessarily need a large relative market share to implement a low-cost strategy. The small clone manufacturers in the PC industry, for instance, found other ways to hold their costs well below those of the industry leaders. Other means for obtaining a sustainable cost advantage include producing a no-frills product, creating an innovative product design, finding cheaper raw materials, automating production, developing low-cost distribution channels, and reducing overhead.[16]

A no-frills product

A direct approach to obtaining a low-cost position involves simply removing all frills and extras from the basic product or service. Thus, Suzuki cars, warehouse furniture stores, legal services clinics, and grocery stores selling canned goods out of crates all offer lower costs and prices than their competitors. This lower production cost is often sustainable because established differentiated competitors find it difficult to stop offering features and services their customers have come to expect. However, those established firms may lower their own prices in the short run—even to the point of suffering losses—in an attempt to drive out a no-frills competitor that poses a serious threat. This was the response of the major airlines to inroads made by People Express. Thus, a firm considering a no-frills strategy needs the resources to withstand a possible price war.

---

[16]For a more detailed discussion of these and other approaches for lowering costs, see Aaker, *Strategic Market Management*, chap. 12.

Innovative product design

A simplified product design and standardized component parts can also lead to cost advantages. In the office copier industry, for instance, Japanese firms overcame substantial entry barriers by designing extremely simple copiers with a fraction of the number of parts in the design used by market-leading Xerox.

Cheaper raw materials

A firm with the foresight to acquire or the creativity to find a way to use relatively cheap raw materials can also gain a sustainable cost advantage. For example, Fort Howard Paper achieved an advantage by being the only major papermaker to rely exclusively on recycled pulp. While the finished product was not so high in quality as paper from virgin wood, Fort Howard's lower cost gave it a competitive edge in the price-sensitive commercial market for toilet paper and other similar products used in hotels, restaurants, and office buildings.

Innovative production processes

Although low-cost defender businesses typically spend little on *product R&D*, they often continue to devote substantial sums to *process R&D*. Innovations in the production process, including the development of automated or computer-controlled processes, can help them sustain cost advantages over competitors.

In some labor-intensive industries a business can achieve a cost advantage, at least in the short term, by gaining access to inexpensive labor. This is usually achieved by moving all or part of the production process to countries with low wage rates, such as Taiwan, Korea, or Mexico. Unfortunately, such moves are relatively easy to emulate, possibly making this kind of cost advantage unsustainable.

Low-cost distribution

When distribution accounts for a relatively high proportion of a product's total delivered cost, a firm might gain a substantial advantage by developing lower-cost alternative channels. Typically, this involves eliminating, or shifting to the customer, some of the functions performed by traditional channels in return for a lower price. In the PC hardware and software industries, for example, mail-order discounters can offer lower prices because they have fewer fixed costs than the retail stores with which they compete. However, they also do not provide as much technical advice or postsale service to their customers.

Reductions in overhead

Successfully sustaining a low-cost strategy requires that the firm pare and control its major overhead costs as quickly as possible as its industry matures. Indeed, many U. S. companies learned this lesson the hard way during the 1980s when high costs of old plants, labor, and large inventories left them vulnerable to more efficient foreign competitors and to corporate raiders.

Business strategy and performance

Analyzer and especially defender businesses are mostly concerned with protecting their existing positions in one or more mature market segments and maximizing profitability over the remaining life of those product-markets. Thus, financial dimensions of performance, such as return on investment and cash flow, are usually of greater interest to such businesses than more growth-oriented dimensions like volume increases or new product success. Businesses can achieve such financial objectives by either successfully differentiating their offerings or by maintaining a low-cost position.

While the primary emphasis in many businesses during the early 1990s was on improving efficiency through downsizing and reengineering,[17] there is substantial evidence that firms with superior quality goods and services also obtain higher returns on investment than businesses with average or below-average quality offerings.[18] The lesson to be learned is that the choice between a differentiation or a low-cost strategy is probably not the critical determinant of success in mature markets. What is critical is that a business *continually work to improve the value* of its offerings—either by improving product or service quality, reducing costs, or some combination—as a basis for maintaining its customer base as its markets mature and become increasingly competitive.

Measuring customer satisfaction

To gain the knowledge necessary to continually improve the value of their offerings to target customers, firms must understand how satisfied existing and potential customers are with their current offerings. This focus on customer satisfaction has become increasingly important as more firms question whether all attempts to improve the *absolute* quality of their products and services generate sufficient additional sales and profits to justify their cost. This growing concern with the economic "return on quality" has motivated firms to ask which dimensions of product or service quality are most important to customers, and which dimensions customers might be willing to sacrifice for lower prices. For instance, United Parcel Service (UPS) recently discovered that many of its customers wanted more time to interact with the company's drivers in order to seek advice on their shipping problems, and they were willing to put up with slightly slower delivery times in return. Consequently, UPS now allows its drivers an additional 30 minutes a day to spend at their discretion to strengthen ties with customers and perhaps bring in new sales.[19]

As the diagram in Exhibit 11-7 indicates, useful measures of customer satisfaction should examine both (1) customers' **expectations and preferences** concerning the various dimensions of product and service quality (e.g., product performance, features, reliability, on-time delivery, competence of service personnel) and (2) their **perceptions** concerning how well the firm is meeting those expectations. Any gaps where customer expectations exceed their recent experiences may indicate fruitful areas for the firm to work at improving customer value and satisfaction. Of course, such measurements must be made periodically to determine whether the actions taken have actually been effective.[20]

Improving customer retention

Maintaining the loyalty of existing customers is crucial for improving a business's profitability as markets mature. Exhibit 11-9 shows that loyal customers become more profitable over time. The firm not only avoids the high costs of acquiring a new customer, but

---

[17]Ronald Henkoff, "Getting Beyond Downsizing," *Fortune*, January 10, 1994, pp. 58–64.

[18]Robert Jacobson and David A. Aaker, "The Strategic Role of Product Quality," *Journal of Marketing*, October 1987, pp. 31–44.

[19]David Greising, "Quality: How to Make It Pay," *Business Week*, August 8, 1994, pp. 54–59.

[20]For a discussion of various approaches to measuring customer satisfaction, see J. Joseph Cronin and Steven A. Taylor, "Measuring Service Quality: A Reexamination and Extension," *Journal of Marketing*, July 1992, pp. 55–68; and Susan J. Devlin and H. K. Dong, "Service Quality from the Customers' Perspective," *Marketing Research* 6 (1994), pp. 5–13.

════════════════ E X H I B I T   1 1 – 9 ════════════════

Sources of Increased Profit from Loyal Customers

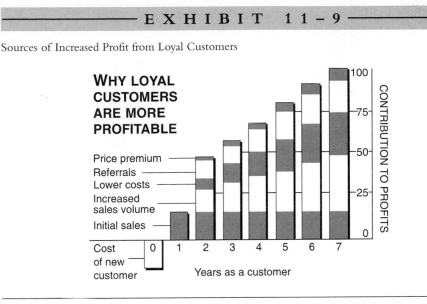

SOURCE: Rahul Jacob, "Why Some Customers Are More Equal Than Others," *Fortune*, September 19, 1994, p. 220.

it typically benefits because loyal customers (1) tend to concentrate their purchases, thus leading to larger volumes and lower selling and distribution costs, (2) provide positive word-of-mouth and customer referrals, and (3) may be willing to pay premium prices for the value they receive.[21]

Periodic measurement of customer satisfaction is important, then, because a dissatisfied customer is unlikely to remain loyal to a company over time. Unfortunately, however, the corollary is not always true: Customers who describe themselves as satisfied are not necessarily loyal. Indeed, one author estimated that 60 to 80 percent of customer defectors in most businesses said they were "satisfied" or "very satisfied" on the last customer survey before their defection.[22] In the interim, perhaps, competitors improved their offerings, the customer's requirements changed, or other environmental factors shifted. The point is that businesses that measure customer satisfaction should be commended—but urged not to stop there. Satisfaction measures need to be supplemented with examinations of customer *behavior*, such as measures of the annual retention rate, frequency of purchases, and the percentage of a customer's total purchases captured by the firm.

Most important, defecting customers should be studied in detail to discover *why* the firm failed to provide sufficient value to retain their loyalty. Such failures often provide more valuable information than satisfaction measures because they stand out as a clear, understandable message telling the organization exactly where improvements are needed. The MicroScan division of Baxter Diagnostics, Inc., provides a good example of the intelligent use of such defector analysis (see Exhibit 11-10).

---

[21]Frederick F. Reichheld, "Loyalty and the Renaissance of Marketing," *Marketing Management* 2 (1994), pp. 10–21; see also Robert S. Duboff and Lori Underhill Sherer, "Customized Customer Loyalty," *Marketing Management*, Summer 1997, pp. 21–27.

[22]Reichheld, "Loyalty and the Renaissance of Marketing," pp. 10–21.

━━━━━━━━━━━━ E X H I B I T   1 1 – 1 0 ━━━━━━━━━━━━

Microscan Examines Defectors to Improve Customer Loyalty

> The MicroScan division of Baxter Diagnostics, Inc., makes instruments used by medical laboratories to identify microbes in patient cultures. In 1990 MicroScan was neck-and-neck with Vitek Systems, Inc., for market leadership, but its management knew they would have to do better to win the race. The firm analyzed its customer base, highlighting accounts that had been lost as well as those that remained active but showed a declining volume of testing. MicroScan interviewed all the lost customers and a large portion of the "decliners," probing deeply for the causes underlying their change in behavior. They found that such customers had concerns about the company's instrument features, reliability, and responsiveness to their problems.
>
> In response, MicroScan's management shifted R&D priorities to address specific shortcomings its lost customers had identified, such as test accuracy and time-to-result. It also redesigned customer service protocols to ensure that immediate attention was given to equipment faults and delivery problems. As a result, MicroScan's sales began to improve and it established a clear market-share lead within two years.

SOURCE: Frederick F. Reichheld, "Loyalty and the Renaissance of Marketing," *Marketing Management* 2 (1994), pp. 10–21. Reprinted with permission.

As MicroScan's experience shows, improving customer loyalty is crucial for maintaining market share and profitability as markets mature. We point out next, however, that simply holding onto current customers may not be the only relevant objective in many mature markets.

MARKETING STRATEGIES FOR MATURE MARKETS

Strategies for maintaining current market share

Since markets can remain in the maturity stage for decades, milking or harvesting mature product-markets by maximizing short-run profits makes little sense. Pursuing such an objective typically involves substantial cuts in marketing and R&D expenses, which can lead to premature losses of volume and market share and lower profits in the longer term. The business should strive during the early years of market maturity to maximize the flow of profits over the remaining life of the product-market. Thus, the most critical marketing objective is to maintain and protect the business's market share. In a mature market where few new customers buy the product for the first time, the business must continue to win its share of repeat purchases from existing customers.

In Chapter 10 we discussed a number of marketing strategies that businesses might use to maintain their market share in growth markets. Many of those same strategies continue to be relevant for holding onto customers as markets mature, particularly for firms that survived the shakeout period with a relatively strong share position. The most obvious strategy for such share leaders is simply to continue strengthening their position through a *fortress defense*. Recall that such a strategy involves two sets of marketing actions: those aimed at improving customer satisfaction and loyalty, and those intended to encourage and simplify repeat purchasing. Actions like those discussed earlier for improving the quality of a firm's offering and for reducing costs suggest ways to increase customer satisfaction and loyalty. Similarly, improvements to service quality (e.g., just-in-time delivery arrangements or computerized reordering systems) can help encourage repeat purchases.

Since markets often become more fragmented as they grow and mature, share leaders also may have to expand their product lines or add one or more *flanker* brands to protect their position against competitive inroads. Thus, Johnson Controls strengthened its position in the commercial facilities management arena by expanding its array of services through a combination of acquisitions and continued internal development.

Small-share competitors also can earn substantial profits in a mature market. To do so, however, it is often wise for them to focus on strategies that avoid prolonged direct confrontations with larger share leaders. A *niche strategy* can be particularly effective when the target segment is too small to appeal to larger competitors or when the smaller firm can establish a strong differential advantage or brand preference in the segment. For instance, with only thirty-six hotels worldwide the Four Seasons chain is a small player in the lodging industry. But by focusing on the high end of the business travel market, the chain has grown and prospered. The chain's hotels differentiate themselves by offering a wide range of amenities (e.g., free overnight shoe shining) that are important to business travelers. Thus, while they charge relatively high prices, they are also seen as delivering good value and rank first in the *Business Travel News* survey of customer satisfaction.[23]

Strategies for extending volume growth

Market maturity is defined by a flattening of the growth rate. In some instances growth slows for structural reasons, such as the emergence of substitute products or a shift in customer preferences. Marketers can do little to revitalize the market under such conditions. But in some cases a market only *appears* to be mature because of the limitations of current marketing programs, such as target segments that are too narrowly defined or limited product offerings. Here more innovative or aggressive marketing strategies might successfully extend the market's life cycle into a period of renewed growth. Thus, stimulating additional volume growth can be an important secondary objective under such circumstances, particularly for industry share leaders because they often can capture a relatively large share of any additional volume generated.

A firm might pursue several different marketing strategies either singly or in combination to squeeze additional volume from a mature market. These include an *increased penetration strategy*, an *extended use strategy*, and a *market expansion strategy*. Exhibit 11-11 summarizes the environmental situations where each of these strategies is most appropriate and the objectives each is best suited for accomplishing. Exhibit 11-12 outlines some specific marketing actions a firm might employ to implement each of the strategies, as discussed in more detail in the following paragraphs.

Increased penetration strategy

The total sales volume produced by a target segment of customers is a function of (1) the number of potential customers in the segment, (2) the product's penetration of that segment, that is, the proportion of potential customers who actually use the product, and (3) the average frequency with which customers consume the product and make another purchase. Where usage frequency is quite high among current customers but only a relatively small portion of all potential users actually buy the product, a firm might aim at increasing market penetration. This is an appropriate strategy for an industry's share leader because

---

[23]Patricia Sellers, "Companies That Serve You Best," *Fortune*, May 31, 1993, p. 80.

E X H I B I T   1 1 – 1 1

Situational Determinants of Appropriate Marketing Objectives and Strategies for
Extending Growth in Mature Markets

	Growth extension strategies		
Situational variables	**Increased penetration**	**Extended use**	**Market expansion**
Primary objective	Increase the proportion of users by converting current nonusers in one or more major market segments.	Increase the amount of product used by the average customer by increasing frequency of use or developing new ways to use the product.	Expand the number of potential customers by targeting underdeveloped geographic areas or applications segments.
Market characteristics	Relatively low penetration in one or more segments (i.e., low percentage of potential users have adopted the product).	Relatively high penetration but low frequency of use in one or more major segments; product used in only limited ways or for special occasions.	Relatively heterogeneous market with a variety of segments; some geographic areas, including foreign countries, with low penetration; some product applications underdeveloped.
Competitors characteristics	Competitors hold relatively small market shares; limited resources or competencies make it unlikely they will steal a significant portion of converted nonusers.	Competitors hold relatively small market shares; limited resources or competencies make it unlikely their brands will be purchased for newly developed uses.	Competitors hold relatively small market shares; have insufficient resources or competencies to preempt underdeveloped geographic areas or applications segments.
Firm's characteristics	A market share leader in the industry; has R&D and marketing competencies to produce product modifications or line extensions; has promotional resources to stimulate primary demand among current nonusers.	A market share leader in the industry; has marketing competencies and resources to develop and promote new uses.	A market share leader in the industry; has marketing and distribution competencies and resources to develop new global markets or applications segments.

such firms can more likely gain and retain a substantial share of new customers than smaller firms with less well-known brands.

The secret to a successful increased penetration strategy lies in discovering why nonusers are uninterested in the product. Very often the product does not offer sufficient value from the potential customer's point of view to justify the effort or expense involved in buying and using it. One obvious solution to such a problem is to enhance the product's value to potential customers by adding features or benefits, usually by means of line extensions.

Another way to add value to a product is to develop and sell integrated systems that help improve the basic product's performance or ease of use. For instance, instead of simply selling control mechanisms for heating and cooling systems, Johnson Controls offers integrated facilities management programs designed to lower the total costs of operating a commercial building.

A firm may also enhance a product's value by offering services that improve its performance or ease of use for the potential customer. Because it is unlikely that people who do not know how to knit will ever buy yarn or knitting needles, for example, most yarn shops offer free knitting lessons.

E X H I B I T   1 1 – 1 2

Possible Marketing Actions for Accomplishing Growth Extension Objectives

Marketing strategy and objectives	Possible marketing actions

Increased penetration
Convert current nonusers in target segment into users.
	• Enhance product's value by adding features, benefits, or services.
	• Enhance product's value by including it in the design of integrated systems.
	• Stimulate additional primary demand through promotional efforts stressing new features or benefits:
	    Advertising through selective media aimed at the target segment.
	    Sales promotions directed at stimulating trial among current nonusers (e.g., tie-ins with other products).
	    Some sales efforts redirected toward new account generation, perhaps by assigning some sales personnel as account development reps or by offering incentives for new account sales.
	• Improve product's availability by developing innovative distribution systems.

Extended use
Increase frequency of use among current users.
	• Move storage of the product closer to the point of end use by offering additional package sizes or designs.
	• Encourage larger-volume purchases (for nonperishable products):
	    Offer quantity discounts.
	    Offer consumer promotions to stimulate volume purchases or more frequent use (e.g., multipack deals, frequent flier programs).
	• Reminder advertising stressing basic product benefits for a variety of usage occasions.

Encourage a wider variety of uses among current users.	• Develop line extensions suitable for additional uses or applications. • Develop and promote new uses, applications, or recipes for the basic product. Include information about new applications/recipes on package. Develop extended use advertising campaign, particularly with print media. Communicate new application ideas through sales presentations to current customers. • Encourage new uses through sales promotions (e.g., tie-ins with complementary products).
Market expansion Develop differentiated positioning focused on untapped or underdeveloped segments.	• Develop a differentiated flanker brand or product line with unique features or price that is more appealing to a segment of potential customers whose needs are not met by existing offerings. or • Develop multiple line extensions or brand offerings with features or prices targeted to the unique needs and preferences of several smaller potential applications or regional segments. • Consider producing for private labels. • Design advertising, personal selling, and/or sales promotion campaigns that address specific interests and concerns of potential customers in one or multiple underdeveloped segments to stimulate selective demand. • Build unique distribution channels to more effectively reach potential customers in one or multiple underdeveloped segments. • Design service programs to reduce the perceived risks of trial and/or solve the unique problems faced by potential customers in one or multiple underdeveloped segments (e.g., systems engineering, installation, operator training, extended warranties). • Enter global markets where product category is in an earlier stage of its life cycle.

Product modifications or line extensions will not, however, attract nonusers unless the enhanced benefits are effectively promoted. For industrial goods, this may mean redirecting some sales efforts toward nonusers. The firm may offer additional incentives for new account sales or assign specific salespeople to call on targeted nonusers and convert them into new customers. For consumer goods, some combination of advertising to stimulate primary demand in the target segment and sales promotions to encourage trial, such as free samples or tie-in promotions with complementary products that nonusers currently buy, can be effective.

Finally, some potential customers may be having trouble finding the product because of limited distribution, or the product's benefits may simply be too modest to justify much purchasing effort. In such cases, expanding distribution or developing more convenient and accessible channels may help expand market penetration. For example, few travelers are so leery of flying that they would go through the effort of calling an insurance agent to buy an accident policy for a single flight. But the sales of such policies are greatly increased by making them conveniently available through vending machines in airport terminals.

Extended use strategy

Some years ago, the manager of General Foods' Cool Whip frozen dessert topping discovered through marketing research that nearly three-fourths of all households used the product, but the average consumer used it only four times per year and served it on only 7 percent of all toppable desserts. In situations of good market penetration but low frequency of use, an extended use strategy may effectively increase volume. This was particularly true in the Cool Whip case; the relatively large and homogeneous target market consisted for the most part of a single mass-market segment. Also, General Foods held nearly a two-thirds share of the frozen topping market, and it had the marketing resources and competencies to capture most of the additional volume that an extended use strategy might generate.

One effective approach for stimulating increased frequency of use is to move product inventories closer to the point of use. This approach works particularly well with low-involvement consumer goods. Marketers know that most consumers are unlikely to expend any additional time or effort to obtain such products when they are ready to use them. If there is no Cool Whip in the refrigerator when the consumer is preparing dessert, for instance, he or she is unlikely to run to the store immediately and will probably serve the dessert without topping.

One obvious way to move inventory closer to the point of consumption is to offer larger package sizes. The more customers buy at one time, the less likely they are to be out of stock when a usage opportunity arises. This approach can backfire, though, for a perishable product or one that consumers perceive to be an impulse indulgence. Thus, many super-premium ice creams, such as Häagen-Dazs, are sold in small pint containers; most consumers want to avoid the temptation of having large quantities of such a high-calorie indulgence too readily available.

The design of a package can also help increase use frequency by making the product more convenient or easy to use. Examples include single-serving packages of Jell-O pudding to pack in lunches, packages of paper cups that include a convenient dispenser, and frozen-food packages that can go directly into a microwave oven.

Various sales promotion programs also help move inventories of a product closer to the point of use by encouraging larger volume purchases. Marketers commonly offer quantity discounts for this purpose in selling industrial goods. For consumer products, multi-item discounts or two-for-one deals serve the same purpose. Promotional programs also encourage greater frequency of use and increase customer loyalty in many service industries. Consider, for instance, the frequent flier programs offered by major airlines.

Sometimes the product's characteristics inhibit customers from using it more frequently. If marketers can change those characteristics, such as difficulty of preparation or high caloric content, a new line extension might encourage customers to use more of the product or to use it more often. Microwave waffles and low-calorie salad dressings are examples of such line extensions. For industrial goods, however, firms may have to develop new technology to overcome a product's limitations for some applications. Thus Johnson Controls is working to develop plastic containers that will not shrivel when filled with hot liquids as a means of expanding its potential market.

Finally, advertising can sometimes effectively increase use frequency by simply reminding customers to use the product more often. For instance, General Foods conducted a reminder campaign for Jell-O pudding that featured Bill Cosby asking, "When was the last time you served pudding, Mom?"

Another approach for extending use among current customers involves finding and promoting new functional uses for the product. Jell-O gelatin is a classic example, having generated substantial new sales volume over the years by promoting the use of Jell-O as an ingredient in salads, pie fillings, and other dishes.

Firms promote new ways to use a product through a variety of methods. For industrial products, firms send technical advisories about new applications to the salesforce to present to their customers during regular sales calls. For consumer products, new use suggestions or recipes may be included on the package or in an advertising campaign. Sales promotions, such as including cents-off coupons in ads featuring a new recipe, encourage customers to try a new application. To reduce costs, two or more manufacturers of complementary products sometimes cooperate in running such promotions. A recent ad promoting a simple Italian dinner, for instance, featured coupons for Kraft's Parmesan cheese, Pillsbury's Soft Breadsticks, and Campbell's Prego spaghetti sauce.

In some cases slightly modified line extensions might encourage customers to use the product in different ways. Thus, Kraft introduced a jalapeño-flavored Cheese-Whiz in a microwavable container and promoted the product as an easy-to-prepare topping for nachos.

Market expansion strategy

In a mature industry with a fragmented and heterogeneous market where some segments are less well developed than others, a market expansion strategy may generate substantial additional volume growth. Such a strategy aims at gaining new customers by targeting new or underdeveloped geographic markets (either regional or foreign) or new customer segments. Once again, share leaders tend to be best suited for implementing this strategy. But even smaller competitors can employ such a strategy successfully if they focus on relatively small or specialized market niches.

Pursuing market expansion by strengthening a firm's position in new or underdeveloped **domestic geographic markets** can lead to experience curve benefits and operating synergies. The firm can rely on largely the same expertise and technology, and perhaps even the same production and distribution facilities, it has already developed. Unfortunately, domestic geographic expansion is often not viable in a mature industry because the share leaders usually have attained national market coverage. Smaller regional competitors, on the other hand, might consider domestic geographic expansion a means for improving their volume and share position. However, such a move risks retaliation from the large national brands and entrenched regional competitors in the prospective new territory.

To get around the retaliation problem, a regional producer might try to expand by acquiring small producers in other regions. This can be a viable option when (1) the low profitability of some regional producers enables the acquiring firm to buy their assets for less than the replacement cost of the capacity involved, and (2) synergies gained by combining regional operations and the infusion of resources from the acquiring firm can improve the effectiveness and profitability of the acquired producers. For example, Heileman Brewing Company grew from the 31st largest brewer of beer in the mid-1960s to the fourth largest by the mid-1980s through the acquisition of nearly 30 regional brands. Heileman took control of strong regional brands such as Old Style, Carling, and Rainier, but because it had no dominant national brand it avoided antitrust opposition to its acquisition program. After acquisition, Heileman maintained the identity of each brand, increased its advertising budget, and expanded its distribution by incorporating it into the firm's distribution system in other regions. As a result, Heileman achieved a strong earnings record for two decades.

In a different approach to domestic market expansion, the firm identifies and develops entirely **new customer** or **application segments**. Sometimes the firm can effectively reach new customer segments by simply expanding the distribution system without changing the product's characteristics or the other marketing mix elements. A sporting goods manufacturer that sells its products to consumers through retail stores, for instance, might expand into the commercial market consisting of schools and amateur and professional sports teams by establishing a direct salesforce. In most instances, though, developing new market segments requires modifying the product to make it more suitable for the application or to provide more of the benefits desired by customers in the new segment.

One final possibility for domestic market expansion is to produce **private-label brands** for large retailers such as Sears or Safeway. Firms whose own brands hold relatively weak positions and who have excess production capacity find this a particularly attractive option. Private labeling allows such firms to gain access to established customer segments without making substantial marketing expenditures, thus increasing the firm's volume and lowering its per unit costs. However, because private labels typically compete with low prices and their sponsors usually have strong bargaining power, producing for private labels is often an unprofitable option unless a manufacturer already has a relatively low-cost position in the industry. It can also be a risky strategy, particularly for the smaller firm, because reliance on one or a few large private-label customers can result in drastic volume reductions and unit cost increases should those customers decide to switch suppliers.

Expansion into global markets

For firms with leading positions in mature domestic markets, less developed markets in foreign countries often present attractive opportunities for geographic expansion. As discussed in Chapter 9, firms can enter foreign markets in a variety of ways, from simply relying on import agents to developing joint ventures to establishing wholly owned subsidiaries, as Johnson Controls did by acquiring an automotive seat manufacturer in Europe. Regardles of which mode of entry a firm chooses, however, two important strategic questions remain to be answered: (1) which countries to pursue first, and (2) whether the various elements of the firm's marketing program should be standardized across countries or adapted to local conditions.

Global expansion routes   Firms can follow a number of different routes when pursuing global expansion.[24] By *route* we mean the sequence or order in which the firm enters global markets. Japanese companies provide illustrations of different global expansion paths. The

---

[24]The following discussion of sequential strategies is based largely on material found in Somkid Jatusripitak, Liam Fahey, and Philip Kotler, "Strategic Global Marketing: Lessons from the Japanese," *Columbia Journal of World Business*, Spring 1985, pp. 47–53.

most common expansion route involves moving from Japan to developing countries to developed countries. They used this path, for example, with automobiles (Toyota), consumer electronics (National), watches (Seiko), cameras (Minolta), and home appliances, steel, and petrochemicals. This routing reduced manufacturing costs and enabled them to gain marketing experience. In penetrating the U. S. market, the Japanese obtained further economies of scale and gained recognition for their products, which made penetration of European markets easier.

This sequential strategy succeeded: By the early 1970s, 60 percent of Japanese exports went to developed countries—more than half to the United States. Japanese motorcycles, watches, and cameras dominate Europe. Its cars have been able to gain a respectable share in most European countries.

A second type of *expansion path* has been used primarily for high-tech products such as computers and semiconductors. For the Japanese it consists of first securing their home market and then targeting developed countries. Japan largely ignored developing countries in this strategy because of their small demand for high-tech products. When demand increased to a point where developing countries became "interesting," Japanese producers quickly entered and established strong market positions through the use of price cuts of up to 50 percent.

Standardization versus adaptation of the marketing mix To what extent can firms standardize the elements of their marketing plans as they attempt to expand into foreign markets? In general, pressures for more standardization have been greatest in the areas of product design, packaging, and brand strategy because of potential economies of scale and experience. Distribution channels tend to be somewhat less standardized because of national differences in the types and operating methods of available wholesalers and retailers. Pricing decisions tend to vary substantially across countries because of local differences in manufacturing and marketing costs, taxes and regulations, the prices of competing products, and so forth. Similarly, cultural and language differences frequently require firms to adapt advertising messages to local markets, and media allocations often vary owing to differences in availability and quality.

Product strategy Producing a standardized "world" product is not easy. The same product may be used under different conditions—and for different reasons—in different countries. Therefore, marketing research and competitor analysis are usually necessary in each national market to determine how much standardization is feasible.

A firm has three basic options relative to the level of standardization of its product's physical dimensions.

1. *Market the same product to all countries.* This strategy requires that the physical product sold in each country be the same except for labeling and the language used in the product manuals. It is appropriate when customer needs are essentially the same across national boundaries. Under such conditions, a firm is able to offer a quality product at a relatively low cost due to scale effects.

2. *Adapt the product to local conditions.* This strategy keeps the physical product essentially the same across countries while allowing minor adaptations that represent only a small percentage of total costs, such as variations in voltage, packaging, or product aesthetics. Examples include computers, copiers, cars, calculators and motorcycles. Similary, P&G varied the formulation of its Cheer detergent in Japan to accommodate differences in the way the Japanese wash clothes.

3. *Develop a country-specific product.* In this strategy the physical product is substantially altered to accommodate differences in customer preferences and behavior across countries or groups of countries. This strategy is often used with products that are subject to wide cultural differences, such as packaged food and personal care items.

Pricing   Firms typically find it hard to adopt a standardized global pricing strategy because of different transporation costs; fluctuating and different exchange rates; variation in competition, market demand, or strategic objectives (e.g., volume versus profits); different governmental tax policies or legal regulations; and other factors such as differences in channels of distribution and global buyers who demand equal price treatment regardless of location.

In some cases firms attempt to minimize such adjustments by adopting a global pricing policy similar to an FOB (free on board) origin policy in the domestic market. They charge the same price around the world and require each customer to absorb all freight and import duties. This kind of policy has the obvious virtue of simplicity but fails to take into account variations in local demand or competitive conditions.

Other firms charge a transer price to their various branches or subsidiaries but then give their country managers wide latitude to charge their customers whatever price they think is most appropriate. Although sensitive to variations in local conditions, this policy may lead to arbitrage involving the transshipment of goods across countries when price differences exceed the freight-and-duty costs separating markets.

For these reasons most firms follow an intermediate approach to global pricing. First corporate management establishes an acceptable range of prices. Local managers are then given the flexibility to select the price within that range that is best suited to local demand and competitive conditions, though their decisions are often subject to review by top management. Thus, a firm might permit a high price in a country where its product had a strong competitive position and high perceived value but settle for a lower penetration price in less established markets.

Countertrade   An additional pricing problem often arises when a firm sells to customers in developing economies that may lack sufficient hard currency to pay for their purchases. Such customers may offer items other than money as payment. While companies dislike such deals, it is often in their best interest to facilitate them through a set of activities known as **countertrade**, which can take a variety of forms (see Exhibit 11-13).

Distribution channels   While performing similar functions, wholesalers around the world vary a great deal in size, margins, and the quality of service they provide for suppliers and customers. A broad generalization is that the less developed a country, the smaller its wholesalers and the more fragmented its wholesale distribution channels. Similarly, retailers vary substantially across countries because of differences in cultural, economic, and political environments. Once again, a country's retail structure is generally a function of its level of economic development; stores tend to increase in size and sophistication as a nation's per capita GNP increases. In recent years retailing in the developed nations of Europe and Asia has been following an evolutionary path similar to the one evidenced in the United States, moving toward larger stores, longer hours, and greater use of automation (e.g., the use of checkout scanners). These nations are also experiencing rapid growth in discounters and direct marketing operations.[25]

---

[25]For examples, see Emily Thorton, "Revolution in Japanese Retailing," *Fortune*, February 7, 1994, p. 140; Paula Dwyer, Karen Lowery Miller, Stewart Toy, and Patrick Oster, "Shop Til You Drop Hits Europe," *Business Week*, November 29, 1993, p. 54; and "Europe's Discount Dogfights," *The Economist*, May 8, 1993, p. 69.

--- **E X H I B I T   1 1 – 1 3** ---

Global Countertrade

> Countertrade, which ocurs in international transactions where the potential customer lacks sufficient hard currency to pay for a purchase, can take a variety of forms:
>
> • *Barter.* Barter involves the direct exchange of goods with no money and no third party involved. For instance, a German firm might agree to build a steel plant in Mexico in exchange for a given amount of Mexican oil.
>
> • *Compensation deals.* Here the seller agrees to take some percentage of the payment in cash and the rest in goods, as when Boeing sells airplanes to Brazil for 70 percent cash and an agreed-upon number of tons of coffee.
>
> • *Buyback arrangements.* Under such arrangements a seller offers a plant, equipment, or technical expertise to a customer and agrees to accept as partial payment products manufactured with the equipment or training supplied. For example, a U.S. chemical company built a plant for an Indian company in return for some cash and a volume of chemicals to be made in the plant.
>
> • *Offsets.* The seller is compensated in cash but agrees to spend a substantial amount of that cash with the customer or its government over a stated period. For instance, Pepsi sells its cola syrup to Russia for rubles and agrees to buy Russian vodka at a given rate for sale in the United States.

SOURCE: Adapted from Stephen S. Cohen and John Zysman, "Countertrade, Offsets, Barter, and Buybacks." *California Management Review*, Winter 1986, pp. 41–56.

Although the problems encountered by a manufacturer in establishing and maintaining a channel system overseas are similar to those experienced domestically, there are some important differences:

1. The kind of channel needed may not be available because of the country's low level of economic development (e.g., a lack of refrigeration) or the presence of only state-controlled intermediaries.

2. Existing distributors have already been appropriated by other manufacturers (particularly local ones) by mean of various arrangements, including financial, and the exclusive use of private labels. This has often been the case in Japan.

3. Control is yet another problem. An international marketer will almost always use a variety of channel systems to penetrate and service its various markets, no two of which are identical. The problems of controlling this varied set of distribution systems are so numerous that many companies use a contractual entry mode (licensing or franchising) whenever possible to facilitate control.

4. It is hard to maintain interest in a manufacturer's product because of the number of intermediaries involved—a situation often found in developing countries and where the brand name is relatively unknown. Consequently, a higher percentage of the advertising budget is spent communicating with the various channels than is typically the case in the United States.

Despite these problems, international wholesalers have not only increased in number but also have become more adept at fulfilling their functions. Even so, the establishment and maintenance of an effective and efficient overseas distribution network remains one of the biggest challenges the international marketer faces.

Promotion   The issues of whether to adopt a standardized promotional strategy (particularly advertising) or a local one has been much debated in recent years. The benefits of standardization derive primarily from scale economies in production and the use of international media. Localization advocates, on the other hand, argue that it is extremely difficult to standardize the elements of the promotional mix because prospective customers live in very different social, economic, and political environments. For example, the impact of local culture is clearly evident in the way consumers in different countries respond to communications based on humor, sexual appeals, and nonverbal imagery.[26]

Today, most advertisers appear to have concluded that it is best to "plan globally, act locally." In other words, start with a standard product positioning and key benefits to be communicated, and then adapt creative elements of the promotional message to fit local cultures when it is advantageous to do so. For example, Procter & Gamble's advertisement in the United States for its all-in-one shampoo featured a woman slamming a locker door in a gym. This scene was considered too confrontational for Thailand, so a new, softer ad was developed that preserved the essential theme of convenience.[27]

While most media types are available throughout the world, print has been used most frequently because all countries have newspapers (some of which are national or regional in scope) and most have magazines that circulate nationally. The use of television has been inhibited until recently by limited programming, government regulations restricting the amount of advertising, and other constraints. These conditions are changing rapidly, however, and heavy use of broadcast, cable, and satellite TV networks as advertising media in most countries seems assured in the future.

One of the most critical decisions facing firms expanding their marketing efforts into other countries is how to organize their personal selling efforts across national boundaries. While globalization obviously adds complexity to the problem, the basic questions to be answered are the same as those faced in domestic markets. First, should the firm use independent agents or hire its own salesforce in a foreign country? If the firm decides on the latter, a second question arises: Should the salesforce be organized geographically, by product line, by type of customer, or in some other way?

A recent survey of 14 large multinational corporations examined their sales management practices across 135 subsidiaries in 45 countries.[28] The result showed that about 25 percent used agents either alone or in cooperation with company salespeople (about one-third of all firms used manufacturers' representatives in the United States). Firms selling complex high-tech products like computers and pharmaceuticals were likely to employ their own salesforce. About half the sample of subsidiaries used geographic territories to organize their selling efforts within a given country. The rest used more specialized structures with different salespeople assigned to specific products and/or customer types, especially when selling a broad line of complex products in highly developed countries.

Services   Because of the characteristics of services (intangibility, perishability, amount of customer contact, and quality variability), many do not require the same physical export distribution channels as manufactured goods.[29] Some services are embodied in a good,

---

[26]Rita Martenson, "International Advertising in Cross-Cultural Environments," *Journal of International Consumer Marketing* 1 (1989), p. 7; and Dora L. Alden, Wayne D. Hoyer, and Chol Lee, "Identifying Global and Culture-Specific Dimensions of Humor in Advertising: A Multinational Approach," *Journal of Marketing*, April 1993, pp. 44–64.

[27]Ashish Banerjee, "Global Campaigns Don't Work; Multinationals Do," *Advertising Age*, April 18, 1994; see also Matthew Agrawn, "Review of a 40-Year Debate in International Advertising," *International Marketing Review* 12 (1996), p. 2.

[28]John S. Hill and Richard R. Still, "Organizing the Overseas Sales Force: How Multinationals Do It," *Journal of Personal Selling and Sales Management*, Spring 1990, pp. 57–66.

[29]For a discussion of the extent to which consumers are involved in service marketing across countries, see Lee D. Dahringer, Charles D. Frame, Oliver Yaw, and Janet McCall-Kennedy, "Consumer Involvement in Services: An International Evaluation," *Journal of International Consumer Marketing* 3 (1991), pp. 61–77.

thereby making them easier to export. For example, America's pop culture can easily be exported in the form of novels, CDs, tapes, and TV programs. Much the same can be said of some business services such as data processing, consulting services, and certain banking services (e.g., those provided by automatic teller machines). Such services can use not only exporting but franchising, licensing, direct investment, and joint ventures.

Other services such as airline travel, hotels, tourism, food, entertainment, and medical and legal services require that production and consumption occur simultaneously; thus, these are not suitable for export. However, they can be internationalized by means of franchising, licensing, and direct investment. Increasingly, internationally minded service companies are facing a complex array of trade barriers ranging from exclusion to certification of selected professionals (e.g., lawyers) rendering services.

STRATEGIES FOR DECLINING MARKETS

Most products eventually enter a decline phase in their life cycles. As sales decline, excess capacity once again develops. As the remaining competitors fight to hold volume in the face of falling sales, industry profits erode. Consequently, conventional wisdom suggests that firms should either divest declining products quickly or harvest them to maximize short-term profits. However, not all markets decline in the same way or at the same speed, nor do all firms have the same competitive strengths and weaknesses within those markets. Therefore, as in most other situations, the relative attractiveness of the declining product-market and the business's competitive position within it should dictate the appropriate strategy.

Relative attractiveness of declining markets

Although U. S. high school enrollment declined by about 2 million students from its peak in 1976 through the end of the 1980s, Jostens, Inc.—the leading manufacturer of class rings and other school merchandise—achieved annual increases in revenues and profits every year during that period. One reason for the firm's success was that it saw the market decline coming and prepared for it by improving the efficiency of its operations and developing marketing programs that were effective at persuading a larger proportion of students to buy class rings.[30]

Jostens experience shows that some declining product-markets can offer attractive opportunities well into the future, at least for one or a few strong competitors. In other product-markets, particularly those where decline is the result of customers switching to a new technology (e.g., more students buying personal computers instead of portable typewriters), the potential for continued profits during the decline stage is more bleak.

Three sets of factors help determine the strategic attractiveness of declining product-markets: *conditions of demand*, including the rate and certainty of future declines in volume; *exit barriers*, or the ease with which weaker competitors can leave the market; and factors affecting the *intensity of future competitive rivalry* within the market.[31] The impact of these variables on the attractiveness of declining market environments is summarized in Exhibit 11-14 and discussed next.

---

[30]Jaclyn Fierman, "How To Make Money in Mature Markets," *Fortune*, November 25, 1985, p. 47.

[31]Katherine Rudie Harrigan and Michael E. Porter, "End-Game Strategies for Declining Industries," *Harvard Business Review*, July–August 1983, pp. 111–20; see also Katherine Rudie Harrigan, *Strategies for Declining Businesses* (Lexington, Mass.: D.C. Heath, 1980).

E X H I B I T   1 1 – 1 4

Factors Affecting the Attractiveness of Declining Markets

	Environmental attractiveness	
	Hospitable	**Inhospitable**
Conditions of demand		
Speed of decline	Very slow	Rapid or erratic
Certainty of decline	100% certain predictable patterns	Great uncertainty, erratic patterns
Pockets of enduring demand	Several or major ones	No niches
Product differentiation	Brand loyalty	Commonditylike products
Price stability	Stable, price premiums attainable	Very unstable, pricing below costs
Exit barriers		
Reinvestment requirements	None	High, often mandatory and involving capital assets
Excess capacity	Little	Substantial
Asset age	Mostly old assets	Sizable new assets and old ones not retired
Resale markets for assets	Easy to convert or sell	No markets available, substantial costs to retire
Shared facilities	Few; freestanding plants	Substantial and interconnected with important businesses
Vertical integration	Little	Substantial
Single-product competitors	None	Several large companies
Rivalry determinants		
Customer industries	Fragmented, weak	Strong bargaining power
Customer switching costs	High	Minimal
Diseconomies of scale	None	Substantial penalty
Dissimilar strategic groups	Few	Several in same target markets

SOURCE: Kathryn Rudie Harrigan and Michael E. Porter, "End-Game Strategies for Declining Industries," *Harvard Business Review,* July–August 1983, p. 117. Reprinted by permission of *Harvard Business Review.* Copyright 1983 by the President and Fellows of Harvard College, all rights reserved.

Conditions of demand

Demand in a product-market declines for a number of reasons. Technological advances produce substitute products (e.g., electronic calculators for slide rules), often with higher quality or lower cost. Demographic shifts lead to a shrinking target market (e.g., baby foods). Customers' needs, tastes, or lifestyles change—consider the falling consumption of beef. Finally, the cost of inputs or complementary products rises and shrinks demand, as happened a few years ago when rising gasoline prices reduced sales of recreational vehicles.

The cause of a decline in demand can affect both the rate and the predictability of that decline. A fall in sales because of a demographic shift, for instance, is likely to be gradual, whereas the switch to a technically superior substitute can be abrupt. Similarly, the fall in demand as customers switch to a better substitute is predictable, while a decline in sales caused by a change in tastes is not.

As Exhibit 11-14 indicates, both the rate and certainty of sales decline are demand characteristics that affect a market's attractiveness. A slow and gradual decline allows an orderly withdrawal of weaker competitors. Overcapacity does not become excessive and lead to predatory competitive behavior, and the competitors who remain are more likely to make profits than in a quick or erratic decline. Also, when most industry managers believe market decline is predictable and certain, reduction of capacity is more likely to be orderly than when they feel substantial uncertainty about whether demand might level off or even become revitalized.

Of course, not all segments of a market decline at the same time or at the same rate. The number and size of enduring niches or pockets of demand and the customer purchase behavior within them also influence the continuing attractiveness of the market. When the demand pockets are large or numerous and the customers in those niches are brand loyal and relatively insensitive to price, competitors with large shares and differentiated products can continue to make substantial profits. For example, even though the market for cigars shrank for years, there continued to be a sizable number of smokers who bought premium-quality cigars. Those firms with well-established positions at the premium end of the cigar industry continued to earn above-average returns, and have recently benefitted from a resurgence in cigar sales.

Exit barriers

The higher the exit barriers, the less hospitable a product-market will be during the decline phase of its life cycle. When weaker competitors find it hard to leave a product-market as demand falls, excess capacity develops and firms engage in aggressive pricing or promotional efforts to try to prop up their volume and hold down unit costs. Thus, exit barriers lead to competitive volatility.

Once again, Exhibit 11-14 indicates that a variety of factors influence the ease with which businesses can exit an industry. One critical consideration involves the amount of highly specialized assets. Assets unique to a given business are difficult to divest because of their low liquidation value. The only potential buyers for such assets are other firms who would use them for a similar purpose, which is unlikely in a declining industry. Thus, the firm may have little choice but to remain in the business or to sell the assets for their scrap value. This option is particularly unattractive when the assets are relatively new and not fully depreciated.

Another major exit barrier occurs when the assets or resources of the declining business intertwine with the firm's other business units, either through shared facilities and programs or through vertical integration. Exit from the declining business might shut down shared production facilities, lower salesforce commissions, damage customer relations, and increase unit costs in the firm's other businesses to a point that damages their profitability.

Emotional factors also can act as exit barriers. Managers often feel reluctant to admit failure by divesting a business even though it no longer produces acceptable returns. This is especially true when the business played an important role in the firm's history and it houses a large number of senior managers.

Intensity of future competitive rivalry

Even when substantial pockets of continuing demand remain within a declining business, it may not be wise for a firm to pursue them in the face of future intense competitive rivalry. In addition to exit barriers, other factors also affect the ability of the remaining firms to avoid intense price competition and maintain reasonable margins: size and bargaining power of the customers who continue to buy the product; customers' ability to switch to substitute products or to alternative suppliers; and any potential diseconomies of scale involved in capturing an increased share of the remaining volume.

Divestment or liquidation?

When the market environment in a declining industry is unattractive or a business has a relatively weak competitive position, the firm may recover more of its investment by selling the business in the early stages of decline rather than later. The earlier the business is sold, the more uncertain potential buyers are likely to be about the future direction of demand in the industry and thus the more likely that a willing buyer can be found. Thus, Raytheon sold its vacuum-tube business in the early 1960s even though transistors had just begun replacing tubes in radios and TV sets and there was still a strong replacement demand for tubes. By moving early, the firm achieved a much higher liquidation value than companies that tried to unload their tube-making facilities in the 1970s when the industry was clearly in its twilight years.[32]

Of course, a firm that divests early runs the risk that its forecast of the industry's future may be wrong. Also, quick divestment may not be possible if a firm faces high exit barriers, such as interdependencies across business units or customer expectations of continued product availability. By planning early for departure, however, a firm may be able to reduce some of those barriers before the liquidation is necessary.

Marketing strategies for remaining competitors

Conventional wisdom suggests that a business remaining in a declining product-market should pursue a harvesting strategy aimed at maximizing its cash flow in the short run. But such businesses also have other strategic options. They might attempt to maintain their position as the market declines, improve their position to become the profitable survivor, or focus efforts on one or more remaining demand pockets or market niches. Once again, the appropriateness of these strategies depends on factors affecting the attractiveness of the declining market and on the business's competitive strengths and weaknesses. Exhibit 11-15 summarizes the situational determinants of the appropriateness of each strategy. Some of the marketing actions a firm might take to implement them are discussed here and listed in Exhibit 11-16.

Harvesting strategy

The objective of a harvesting or milking strategy is to generate cash quickly by maximizing cash flow over a relatively short term. This typically involves avoiding any additional investment in the business, greatly reducing operating (including marketing) expenses, and perhaps raising prices. Since the firm usually expects to ultimately divest or abandon the business, some loss of sales and market share during the pursuit of this strategy is likely. The trick is to hold the business's volume and share declines to a relatively slow and steady rate. A precipitous and premature loss of share would limit the total amount of cash the business could generate during the market's decline.

A harvesting strategy is most appropriate for a firm holding a relatively strong competitive position in the market at the start of the decline and a cadre of current customers likely to continue buying the brand even after marketing support is reduced. Such a strategy also works best when the market's decline is inevitable but likely to occur at a relatively slow and steady rate and when rivalry among remaining competitors is not likely to be very

---

[32]Harrigan and Porter, "End-Game Strategies," p. 114.

E X H I B I T   1 1 – 1 5

Situational Determinants of Appropriate Marketing Objectives and Strategies for Declining Markets

| Situational variables | Strategies for declining markets | | | |
	Harvesting	Maintenance	Profitable survivor	Niche
Primary objective	Maximize short-term cash flow; maintain or increase margins even at the expense of a slow decline in market share.	Maintain share in short term as market declines, even if margins must be sacrificed.	Increase share of the declining market with an eye to future profits; encourage weaker competitors to exit.	Focus on strengthening position in one or a few relatively substantial segments with potential for future profits.
Market characteristics	Future market decline is certain but likely to occur at a slow and steady rate.	Market has experienced recent declines, but future direction and attractiveness are currently hard to predict.	Future market decline is certain but likely to occur at a slow and steady rate; substantial pockets of demand will continue to exist.	Overall market may decline quickly, but one or more segments will remain as demand pockets or decay slowly.
Competitor characteristics	Few strong competitors, low exist barriers; future rivalry not likely to be instense.	Few strong competitors, but intensity of future rivalry is hard to predict.	Few strong competitors; exit barriers are low or can be reduced by firm's intervention.	One or more strong competitors in mass market, but not in the target segment.
Firm's characteristics	Has a leading share position; has a substantial proportion of loyal customers who are likely to continue buying brand even if marketing support is reduced.	Has a leading share of the market and a relatively strong competitive position.	Has a leading share of the market and a strong competitive position; has superior resources or competencies necessary to encourage competitors to exit or to acquire them.	Has a sustainable competitive advantage in target segment, but overall resources may be limited.

intense. Such conditions help enable the business to maintain adequate price levels and profit margins as volume gradually falls.

Implementing a harvesting strategy means avoiding any additional long-term investments in plants, equipment, or R&D. It also necessitates substantial cuts in operating expenditures for marketing activities which often means that the firm should greatly reduce the number of models or package sizes in its product line in order to reduce inventory and manufacturing costs.

The business should improve the efficiency of sales and distribution. For instance, an industrial goods manufacturer might service its smaller accounts through telemarketing rather than a field salesforce or assign its smaller customers to agent intermediaries. For consumer goods the business might move to more selective distribution by concentrating its efforts on the larger retail chains.

The firm would likely reduce advertising and promotion expenditures, usually to the minimum level necessary to retain adequate distribution. Finally, the business should attempt to maintain or perhaps even increase its price levels to increase margins.

=========== E X H I B I T   1 1 – 1 6 ===========

Possible Marketing Actions Appropriate for Different Strategies in Declining Markets

Marketing strategy and objectives	Possible marketing actions

Harvesting strategy
Maximize short-term cash flow: maintain or increase margins even at the expense of market share decline.
	• Eliminate R&D expenditures and capital investments related to the business.
	• Reduce marketing and sales budgets.
	    Greatly reduce or eliminate advertising and sales promotion expenditures, with the possible exception of periodic reminder advertising targeted at current customers.
	    Reduce trade promotions to minimum level necessary to prevent rapid loss of distribution coverage.
	    Focus salesforce efforts on attaining repeat purchases from current customers.
	• Seek ways to reduce production costs, even at the expense of slow erosion in product quality.
	• Raise price if necessary to maintain margins.

Maintenance strategy Maintain market share for the short term, even at the expense of margins.	• Continue product and process R&D expenditures in short term aimed at maintaining or improving product quality. • Continue maintenance levels of advertising and sales promotion targeted at current users. • Continue trade promotion at levels sufficient to avoid any reduction in distribution coverage. • Focus salesforce efforts on attaining repeat purchases from current users. • Lower prices if necessary to maintain share, even at the expense of reduced margins.

Profitable survivor strategy
Increase share of the declining market; encourage weaker competitors to exit.
	• Signal competitors that firm intends to remain in industry and pursue an increased share.
	    Maintain or increase advertising and sales promotion budgets.
	    Maintain or increase distribution coverage through aggressive trade promotion.
	    Focus some salesforce effort on winning away competitors' customers.
	    Continue product and process R&D to seek product improvements or cost reductions.
	• Consider introducing line extensions to appeal to remaining demand segments.
	• Lower prices if necessary to increase share, even at the expense of short-term margins.
	• Consider agreements to produce replacement parts or private labels for smaller competitors considering getting out of production.

Niche strategy Strengthen share position in one or a few segments with potential for continued profit.	• Continue product and process R&D aimed at product improvements or modifications that will appeal to target segment(s). • Consider producing for private labels in order to maintain volume and hold down unit costs. • Focus advertising, sales promotion, and personal selling campaigns on customers in target segment(s); stress appeals of greatest importance to those customers. • Maintain distribution channels appropriate for reaching target segment; seek unique channel arrangements to more effectively reach customers in target segment(s). • Design service programs that address unique concerns/problems of customers in the target segment(s).

Maintenance strategy

In markets where future volume trends are highly uncertain, a business with a leading share position might consider pursuing a strategy aimed at maintaining its market share, at least until the market's future becomes more predictable. In such a maintenance strategy the business continues to pursue the same strategy that brought it success during the market's mature stage. This approach often results in reduced margins and profits in the short term, though, because firms usually must reduce prices or increase marketing expenditures to hold share in the face of declining industry volume. Thus, a firm should consider share maintenance an interim strategy. Once it becomes clear that the market will continue to decline, the business should switch to a different strategy that will provide better cash flows and return on investment over the market's remaining life.

Profitable survivor strategy

An aggressive alternative for a business with a strong share position and a sustainable competitive advantage in a declining product-market is to invest enough to increase its share position and establish itself as the industry leader for the remainder of the market's decline. This kind of strategy makes the most sense when the firm expects a gradual decline in market demand or when substantial pockets of continuing demand are likely well into the future. It is also an attractive strategy when a firm's declining business is closely intertwined with other SBUs through shared facilities and programs or common customer segments.

A strong competitor can often improve its share position in a declining market at relatively low cost because other competitors may be harvesting their businesses or preparing to exit. The key to the success of such a strategy is to encourage other competitors to leave the market early. Once the firm has achieved a strong and unchallenged position, it can switch to a harvesting strategy and reap substantial profits over the remaining life of the product-market.

A firm might encourage smaller competitors to abandon the industry by being visible and explicit about its commitment to become the leading survivor. It should aggressively seek increased market share, either by cutting prices or by increasing advertising and promotion expenditures. It might also introduce line extensions aimed at remaining pockets of demand to make it more difficult for smaller competitors to find profitable niches. Finally, the firm might act to reduce its competitors' exit barriers, making it easier for them to leave the industry. This could involve taking over competitors' long-term contracts, agreeing to supply spare parts, service their products in the field, or provide them with components or private-label products. For instance, large regional bakeries have encouraged grocery chains to abandon their own bakery operations by supplying them with private-label baked goods.

The ultimate way to remove competitors' exit barriers is to purchase their operations and either improve their efficiency or remove them from the industry to avoid excess capacity. With continued decline in industry sales a certainty, smaller competitors may be forced to sell their assets at a book value price low enough for the survivor to reap high returns on its investment, as Heileman Brewing Company did on its acquisitions of smaller regional brewers during the 1970s and 1980s.

Niche strategy

Even when most segments of an industry are expected to decline rapidly, a niche strategy may still be viable if one or more substantial segments will either remain as stable pockets of demand or decay slowly. The business pursuing this strategy should have a strong competitive position in the target segment or be able to build a sustainable competitive advantage relatively quickly to preempt competitors. This is one strategy that even smaller competitors can sometimes pursue successfully because they can focus the required assets and resources on a limited portion of the total market. The marketing actions a business might take to strengthen and preserve its position in a target niche are similar to those discussed earlier concerning niche strategies in mature markets.

SUMMARY

An industry's transition from growth to maturity begins when approximately half the potential customers have adopted the product and, while sales are still growing, the rate of growth begins to decline. As growth slows, some competitors are likely to find themselves with excess production capacity. Other changes in the competitive environment, including a reduction in the degree of differentiation across brands and increased difficulty in maintaining adequate distribution, occur at about the same time. As a result, competition becomes more intense with firms cutting prices or increasing their marketing expenditures as they battle to increase volume, cover high fixed costs, and maintain profitability. This transition is usually accompanied by a shakeout as weaker competitors fail or leave the industry.

Success during the maturity stage of a product-market's life cycle requires two sets of strategic actions. First, managers should work to maintain and strengthen either the differentiation of the firm's offerings on quality or service dimensions or its position as a low-cost competitor within the industry. The second strategic consideration during the maturity stage is to develop meaningful marketing objectives and a marketing strategy appropriate for achieving them. Since maturity can last for many years, the most critical marketing objective is to maintain and protect the business's market share. For share leaders, some variation of the fortress defense, confrontation, or flanker strategies are often appropriate for achieving that objective. Smaller competitors, on the other hand, may have to rely on a niche strategy to hold their position.

Since different market segments may mature at different times and environmental conditions can change over the mature phase of a product's life, firms often find opportunities to extend the growth of seemingly mature product-markets. Thus, an important secondary objective for firms in many mature markets is to stimulate additional volume growth. Among the marketing strategies firms might use to accomplish that objective are an increased penetration strategy, an extended use strategy, or a market expansion strategy focused on developing either new geographic territories, including global markets, or new application segments.

Conventional wisdom suggests that declining products should be divested or harvested to maximize short-term profits. However, some declining product-markets remain attractive enough to justify more aggressive marketing strategies. The attractiveness of these markets is determined by three sets of factors: (1) conditions of demand, including the rate and certainty of future declines in volume; (2) exit barriers, or the ease with which weaker competitors can leave the market; and (3) factors affecting the intensity of future competitive rivalry. When a declining product-market is judged to offer continuing opportunities for profitable sales, managers might consider one of several strategic alternatives to divestment or harvesting. Those alternative strategies include a maintenance strategy, a profitable survivor strategy, and a niche strategy.

4 SECTION

IMPLEMENTATION AND CONTROL

CHAPTER 12

Implementing Business and Marketing Strategies

HEWLETT-PACKARD: A MUCH ADMIRED COMPANY![1]

Only a few years ago Hewlett-Packard (H-P) was in the doldrums and seemed headed for trouble. Now it is the most admired computer company in the United States. HP's annual revenues in 1996 were $38.4 billion, net profit $2.6 billion, and return on equity 20.3 percent. Revenues and profits for the first nine months of 1997 were excellent. A primary reason for this turnaround is that management runs the company as a conglomerate of small ventures, each responsible for its own success.

No H-P division employs more than 1,500 people (worldwide employment is over 100,000) and each division has no more than two levels between the highest and lowest levels. This makes it easier to respond to the dynamics of the market place. Also, division executives are granted great freedom because they can reinvest the capital their businesses generate.

The company's strategy, unlike that of its competitors, emphasizes "preemptive self-destruction and renewal.[2] This means a willingness to cannibalize present products to ensure the future—or as they say in Silicon Valley, "it's better to eat your lunch before someone else eats it for you." No H-P division is immune to competition from another division.

H-P has been uniquely successful in developing new and successful products. More than half of its sales in 1995 were

---

[1]"The Metamorphosis of Hewlett-Packard," *The Economist*, June 19, 1993, p. 67; Alan Deutschman, "How H-P Continues to Grow and Grow," *Fortune*, May 2, 1994, p. 90; Kevin Manley, "Giant Goes from Stodgy to Nimble," *USA Today*, May 18, 1994, p. B1; Wendy Zellner, "The Go-Go Goliaths," *Business Week*, February 13, 1995, p. 64; Brian Gillooly, "H-P's New Course," *Information Week*, March 20, 1995, cover story; Hewlett-Packard, *Annual Report, 1996*; "Performer of the Year—Hewlett Packard," *Forbes*, January 1, 1996; Anne B. Fisher, "America's Most Admired Companies," *Fortune*, March 4, 1996; "The 431 Best and the Worst," *Fortune*, March 3, 1997, p. 71; Stratford Sherman, "Secrets of H-P's 'Muddled' Team," *Fortune*, March 18, 1996.

[2]Deutschman, "How H-P Continues to Grow and Grow," p. 90.

from products introduced during the past two years. To accomplish such an "outpouring" H-P has relied heavily on the use of teams operating in an open and informal environment. The personal computer (PC) division, for example, was reorganized into small teams, each focused on a market segment, to develop each component of a new computer simultaneously, thereby reducing the time to develop the new product by two-thirds.

H-P also uses teams in its sales programs. Each team builds an information database on the leading prospects in each industry (including their data processing budget) and proceeds to develop an account sales strategy. A team member is designated as the development manager responsible for building a close relationship with the account's key decision

makers. This person also decides which prospects to invite to H-P's offices for a day-long presentation covering how the company's capabilities can solve their problems. A senior vice president who is the CEO's deputy spends 40 to 50 percent of his time listening to customers. In 1996 H-P's direct salesforce was rated the best in the United States for the third time in the past five years.[3]

These changes have made H-P into a highly flexible technology company driven by its customers. Despite its huge size, it has many more parts "than an Erector set. Pull one piece off, bolt a couple others together, and—voila! The company can quickly change and attack any emerging market." In this sense, "it's more like a biological system than a company."[4]

ISSUES IN THE IMPLEMENTATION OF BUSINESS AND MARKETING STRATEGIES

The recent changes at Hewlett-Packard illustrate that the success of a business is determined by two aspects of strategic fit. First, its competitive and marketing strategy must fit the needs and constraints of the external environment. Second, the business must be able to effectively implement that strategy through its internal structure, policies, procedures, and resources. When it cannot effectively implement its chosen strategy—even if the strategy is appropriate in the circumstances—trouble will ensue. Worse, management may conclude the strategy was inappropriate, switch to a less desirable one, and ultimately depress performance of the business even further. On the one hand, excellent execution may offset the negative effects of a poorly conceived strategy; on the other hand, good implementation of the wrong strategy can speed the business along the road to failure.

In this chapter we discuss the subject of organizational fit: the fit between the strategies of a business and the organizational structures, policies, processes, and plans necessary to implement those strategies. Four major sets of internal variables affect a business's ability to implement particular strategies:

1. The fit between the marketing strategies pursued in individual product-markets and the firm's higher-level corporate and business strategies.

2. Administrative relationships between the strategic business unit (SBU) and corporate headquarters.

[3]H-P's Third Quarter Report, 1997, p. 3.
[4]Manley, "Giant Goes from Stodgy to Nimble," pp. B1–B2.

3. The SBU's organization structure and coordination mechanisms, including variables such as the technical competence of the various functional departments within the SBU, the manner in which resources are allocated across functions, and the mechanisms used to coordinate and resolve conflicts between the departments.

4. The contents of a marketing action plan for each product-market entry.

These four sets of variables serve as the framework for organizing the remainder of this chapter. Before beginning our discussion, we should note that the dynamics of global markets coupled with strong competition make for opportunities that demand a rapid response. This in turn requires highly adaptive organizations—like that of H-P—that can quickly analyze the marketplace, formulate a response strategy, and develop an appropriate plan of action. Thus in recent years high-level executives have tried to find ways to simplify their organizational structures and procedures.

These restructuring efforts are mirrored in good part by the transition of H-P to a highly decentralized, market-oriented company where the consumer comes first. These efforts also include a reduction in the number of organizational levels; recognition that processes hold the key to developing a core competency; the use of joint ventures and strategic alliances; attempts to develop innovative, entrepreneurial managers; the use of self-managing "empowered" teams, emphasizing the notion of "pay for performance"; and greater leeway for the SBU managers to run their own business.

RELATIONSHIPS BETWEEN BUSINESS AND MARKETING STRATEGIES

As discussed in an earlier chapter, generic business-level strategies define how an SBU intends to compete in its industry by setting a general direction for the types of markets to target, the way to compete in those markets, and the objectives to pursue. These in turn strongly influence the general policies of an SBU concerning marketing elements such as relative product quality, service levels, price, and promotional intensity as well as its organizational structure, processes, and annual marketing plan. Exhibit 12-1 itemizes the appropriate marketing policies and strategies for each of the four business strategies: prospector, analyzer, differentiated defender, and low-cost defender.

ADMINISTRATIVE RELATIONSHIPS AND STRATEGY IMPLEMENTATION

The administrative relationships between the unit and corporate headquarters influence the ability of SBU managers, including its marketing personnel, to implement specific competitive and marketing strategies successfully. This section will discuss three aspects of the corporate business unit relationship that can affect the SBU's success in implementing a particular competitive strategy:

1. The degree of autonomy provided each business unit manager.

2. The degree to which the business unit shares functional programs and facilities with other units.

3. The manner in which the corporation evaluates and rewards the performance of its SBU managers.

───────────────── **E X H I B I T   1 2 – 1** ─────────────────

The Fit between Business Strategies and Marketing Programs

Appropriate marketing policies and strategies	Business Strategies			
	Prospector	Analyzer	Differentiated defender	Low-cost defender
Product and service policies	Broad, technically sophisticated product lines; moderate to high quality and levels of service, especially sales engineering services.	Moderately broad and technically sophisticated product lines; service levels and quality indeterminant.	Relatively narrow but high quality and technically sophisticated product lines; high quality and levels of service.	Narrow, less technically sophisticated product lines; relatively low levels of quality and service.
Price policy	Relatively high prices.	Relatively high prices.	Relatively high prices.	Relatively low to competitive prices.
Distribution policies	Little forward vertical integration; relatively high trade promotion expenses as a percent of sales.	Degree of forward vertical integration indeterminant; moderate to high trade promotion expenses as a percent of sales.	Relatively high degree of forward vertical integration; low trade promotion expenses as a percent of sales.	Degree of forward vertical integration indeterminant; low trade promotion expenses as a percent of sales.
Promotion policies	High advertising, sales promotion, and salesforce expenditures as a percent of sales.	Moderate advertising and sales promotion expenditures as a percent of sales; salesforce expenditures indeterminant.	Relatively low advertising and sales promotion expenditures as a percent of sales; high salesforce expenditures as a percent of sales.	Low advertising, sales promotion, and salesforce expenditures as a percent of sales.
Common marketing strategies	Mass-market penetration; niche penetration; skimming and early withdrawal; market expansion; encirclement.	Flanker strategy; market expansion; leapfrog strategy; encirclement.	Fortress defense; confrontation; flanker strategy; increased penetration; extended use; market expansion; profitable survivor strategy; maintenance strategy; niche strategy.	Fortress defense; confrontation; profitable survivor strategy; maintenance strategy; niche strategy; harvesting strategy.

Exhibit 12–2 summarizes how these variables relate to the successful implementation of different business strategies. We do not include analyzer strategies in our discussion because they incorporate some elements of both prospector and defender strategies. The administrative arrangements appropriate for implementing an analyzer strategy typically

EXHIBIT 12 – 2

Adminstrative Factors Related to the Successful Implementation of Business Strategies

Administrative factor	Types of Business Strategy		
	Prospector	Differentiated defender	Low-cost defender
SBU autonomy	Relatively high level	Moderate level	Relatively low level
Shared programs and synergy	Relatively little synergy—few shared programs	Little synergy in areas central to differentiation—shared programs elsewhere	High level of synergy and shared programs
Evaluation and reward systems	High incentives based on sales and share growth	High incentives based on profits or ROI	High incentives based on profits or ROI

fall somewhere between those best suited for the other two types. To simplify the following discussion we focus only on the prospector, differentiated defender, and low-cost defender strategies.

Business-unit autonomy

Prospector business units like many of those at Hewlett-Packard are likely to perform better on the critical dimensions of new product success and increased volume and market share when organizational decision making is relatively decentralized and the SBU's managers have substantial autonomy. There are several reasons for this. First, more decentralized decision making allows the managers closest to the market to make more major decisions on their own. Second, greater autonomy enables the SBU's managers to be more flexible and adaptable; it frees them from the restrictions of standard procedures imposed from above, allows them to make decisions with fewer consultations and participants, and disperses power. All of these help produce quicker and more innovative responses to environmental opportunities—something H-P has been able to accomplish successfully.

On the other hand, low-cost defender SBUs perform better on ROI and cash flow by giving their managers relatively little autonomy. For a low-cost strategy to succeed, managers must relentlessly pursue cost economies and productivity improvements. Such efficiencies are more likely to be attained when decision making and control are relatively centralized.

The relationship between autonomy and the ROI performance of differentiated defenders is more difficult to predict. On the one hand, such businesses defend existing positions in established markets and their primary objective is ROI rather than volume growth. Thus, the increased efficiency and tighter control associated with relatively low autonomy should lead to better performance. On the other hand, such businesses can maintain profitability only if they continue to differentiate themselves by offering superior products and services. As customers' wants change and new competitive threats emerge, the greater flexibility and market focus associated with greater autonomy may allow these businesses to more successfully maintain their differentiated positions and higher levels of ROI over time. These arguments suggest that the relationship between autonomy and performance for differentiated defenders may be mediated by the level of stability in their environments and by the proportion of offensive or proactive marketing strategies they employ. Units operating in relatively unstable environments and pursuing more proactive marketing programs (e.g., extended use or market expansion strategies) are likely to perform better when they have greater autonomy.

Shared programs and facilities

Firms face a trade-off when designing strategic business units. An SBU should be large enough to afford critical resources and to operate on an efficient scale, but it should not be so large that its market scope is too broad or that it is inflexible and therefore cannot respond to its unique market opportunities. Some firms attempt to avoid this trade-off between efficiency and adaptability by designing relatively small, narrowly focused business units (as H-P does), but then having two or more units share functional programs or facilities, such as common manufacturing plants, R&D programs, or a single salesforce.

Sharing resources poses a particular problem for prospector business units.[5] Suppose, for instance, that a business wants to introduce a new product but shares a manufacturing plant and salesforce with other SBUs. The business would have to negotiate a production schedule for the new product, and it may not be able to produce adequate quantities as quickly as needed if other units sharing the plant are trying to maintain sufficient volumes of their own products. It also may be difficult to train salespeople on the new product or to motivate them to reduce the time spent on established products in order to push the new item. When Frito-Lay introduced Grandma's soft cookies, for instance, they relied on their 10,000 salty-snack route salespeople to get supermarket shelf space for the new line. However, because those salespeople were paid a commission based on their total sales revenue, they were reluctant to take time away from their profitable salty-snack lines to sell the new cookies. The resulting lack of strong sales support contributed to Grandma's failure to capture a sustainable share of the packaged cookie market.

One exception to this generalization may be sharing sales and distribution programs across consumer packaged goods SBUs. In such cases a prospector's new product may have an easier time obtaining retailer support and shelf space if it is represented by salespeople who also sell established brands to the same retail outlets. For prospectors producing consumer durable or industrial goods, however, functional independence generally facilitates good performance, which certainly has been the case with H-P.

On the other hand, the increased efficiencies gained through sharing functional programs and facilities often boost the ROI performance of low-cost defender SBUs. Also, the inflexibility inherent in sharing is usually not a major problem for such businesses because their markets and technologies tend to be mature and relatively stable. Thus, Heinz, the cost leader in a number of food categories, uses a single salesforce, representing a wide variety of products from different business units to make calls on supermarkets.

The impact of shared programs on the performance of differentiated defenders is more difficult to predict because they must often modify their products and marketing programs in response to changing market conditions to maintain their competitive advantage over time. Thus, greater functional independence in areas directly related to the SBU's differential advantage (e.g., R&D, sales, and marketing) tends to be positively associated with the long-run ROI performance of such businesses. But greater sharing of facilities and programs in less crucial functional areas, such as manufacturing or distribution, also may help improve efficiency and short-term ROI levels.

---

[5] Robert W. Ruekert and Orville C. Walker, Jr., "The Sharing of Marketing Resources across Strategic Business Units: The Effect of Strategy on Performance," in *Review of Marketing* 1990 (Chicago: American Marketing Association, 1990).

Evaluation and reward systems

SBU managers are often motivated to achieve their planned objectives by bonuses or other financial incentives tied to their unit's performance. Since these managers often remain in one position for only three to five years, such evaluation and reward systems encourage them to concentrate on short-term returns and adopt policies that may discourage innovation, the acceptance of risk, and the aggressive pursuit of growth for future returns.[6]

In recent years an increasing number of U.S. firms have adopted some form of a pay-for-performance compensation scheme. Some do it for individuals who meet specific goals, others on the basis of performance of small groups, and still others on the performance of the SBU or the company as a whole. But most companies admit that such programs are difficult to implement.[7] A growing number of companies are using **economic value added (EVA)** which determines whether a business is earning more than its cost of capital. This measure is designed to show managers whether they are creating shareholder wealth. Thus, EVA makes managers more concerned about stockholder value and capital expenditures.[8] Many companies have shifted their executive pay from cash bonuses to stock options, but given a bull market coupled with large option grants and easy performance standards, executive pay has soared—many would say gotten out of hand. In 1996 the average total compensation of CEOs increased 54 percent over the previous year—to $5.7 million. This was 209 times that of a factory worker who received only a 3 percent increase.[9]

Many high-level U.S. executives receive some kind of a long-term performance incentive tied to stock price performance, options, direct stock awards, and so on.[10] This is not the case in Japan and continental Europe. In addition, U.S. executives are paid much more than their counterparts abroad. The CEO of a very large Japanese firm earns 17 times what the average Japanese worker does. In France and Germany this ratio is 24, while in the United States it is 109. One reason why managers in various countries are rewarded differently is that the nature and scope of their jobs differ, especially in Japan where greater reliance is placed on consensus and bottom-up planning. Also, long-term growth is often considered more important than return to stockholders.[11]

ORGANIZATIONAL STRUCTURE, PROCESSES, AND STRATEGY IMPLEMENTATION

Different strategies emphasize different ways to gain a competitive advantage. Thus, a given functional area may be key to the success of one type of strategy but less critical for others. For instance, competence in new product R&D is critical for the success of a prospector business (e.g., H-P) but less so for a low-cost defender.

---

[6] Bernard J. Jaworski, "Toward a Theory of Marketing Control: Environmental Context, Control Types, and Consequences," *Journal of Marketing*, July 1988, pp. 23–39.

[7] John Byrne, "Deliver or Else," *Business Week*, March 27, 1995, p. 36; and Peter Nulty, "Incentive Pay Can Be Crippling," *Fortune*, November 3, 1995, p. 135.

[8] Justin Martin, "Eli Lilly Is Making Shareholders Rich. How? By Linking Pay to EVA," *Fortune*, December 9, 1996, p. 173.

[9] Jennifer Reingold, "Executive Pay," *Business Week*, April 21, 1997.

[10] For a discussion about how such salaries and perquisites are determined, see Jennifer Reese, "Dueling for Dollars," *Stanford Business School Magazine*, March 1995, p. 2.

[11] Paul Milgram and John Roberts, "Pay, Perks, and Parachutes," *Stanford Business School Magazine*, June 1992, p. 18.

E X H I B I T   1 2 – 3

Organizational and Interfunctional Factors Related to the Successful Implementation of Business Strategies

	Type of business strategy		
Organizational factor	**Prospector**	**Differentiated defender**	**Low-cost defender**
Functional competencies of the SBU	SBU will perform best on critical volume and share-growth dimensions when its functional strengths include marketing, sales, product R&D, and engineering.	SBU will perform best on critical ROI dimension when its functional strengths include sales, financial management and control, and those functions related to its differential advantage (e.g., marketing, product R&D).	SBU will perform best on critical ROI and cash flow dimensions when its functional strengths include process engineering, production, distribution, and financial management and control.
Resource allocation across functions	SBU will perform best on volume and share growth dimensions when percentage of sales spent on marketing, sales, and product R&D are high and when gross fixed assets per employee and percent of capacity utilization are low relative to competitors'.	SBU will perform best on the ROI dimension when percentage of sales spent on the salesforce, gross fixed assets per employee, percent of capacity utilization, and percentage of sales devoted to other functions related to the SBU's differential advantage are high relative to competitors'.	SBU will perform best on ROI and cash flow dimensions when marketing, sales, and product R&D expenses are low, but process R&D, fixed assets per employee, and percentage of capacity utilization are high relative to competitors'.
Decision-making influence and participation	SBU will perform best on volume and share-growth dimensions when managers from marketing, sales, product R&D, and engineering have substantial influence on unit's business and marketing strategy decisions.	SBU will perform best on ROI dimension when financial managers, controller, and managers of functions related to unit's differential advantage have substantial influence on business and marketing strategy decisions.	SBU will perform best on ROI and cash flow when controller, financial, and production managers have substantial influence on business and marketing strategy decisions.

(continues)

Successful implementation of a given strategy, then, is more likely when the business has the **functional competencies** demanded by its strategy and supports them with substantial **resources** relative to competitors, is **organized** suitably for its technical, market, and competitive environment, and has developed appropriate **mechanisms** for coordinating efforts and resolving conflicts across functional departments. Exhibit 12–3 summarizes the relationships between these organizational structure and process variables and the performance of different generic business strategies.

Functional competencies and resource allocation

Competence in activities relating to marketing, sales, product R&D, and engineering is critical to the success of prospector businesses because those functions play pivotal roles in new product and market development and thus must be supported with budgets set at a

EXHIBIT 12–3

Concluded

Organizational factor	Type of business strategy		
	Prospector	Differentiated defender	Low-cost defender
SBU's organization structure	SBU will perform best on volume and share-growth dimensions when structure has low levels of formalization and centralization, but high level of specialization.	SBU will perform best on ROI dimension when structure has moderate levels of formalization, centralization, and specialization.	SBU will perform best on ROI and cash flow dimensions when structure has high levels of formalization and centralization, but low level of specialization.
Functional coordination and conflict resolution	SBU will experience high levels of interfunctional conflict; SBU will perform best on volume and share-growth dimensions when participative resolution mechanisms are used (e.g., product teams).	SBU will experience moderate levels of interfunctional conflict; SBU will perform best on ROI dimension when resolution is participative for issues related to differential advantage, but hierarchical for others (e.g., product managers, product improvement teams).	SBU will experience low levels of interfunctional conflict; SBU will perform best on ROI and cash flow dimensions when conflict resolution mechanisms are hierarchical (e.g., functional organization).

SOURCE: Adapted from Orville C. Walker, Jr., and Robert W. Rueckert, "Marketing's Role in the Implementation of Business Strategies," *Journal of Marketing*, July 1987, p. 31. Reprinted by permission from the American Marketing Association.

larger percentage of sales than their competitors. Because marketing, sales, and R&D managers are closest to the changes occurring in the market, competitive, and technological environments of a business, they should be given considerable authority in making strategic decisions. This argues that bottom-up strategic planning systems are particularly well suited to prospector businesses operating in unstable environments. Success here is positively affected by the extent to which customer orientation is an integral part of the unit's corporate culture.

In low-cost defender businesses, on the other hand, the functional areas most directly related to operating efficiency—such as financial management and control, production, process R&D, and distribution or logistics—play the most crucial roles in enabling the SBU to attain good ROI performance. Because differentiated defenders need to attain high returns on their established products, functional areas related to efficiency are also critical for their success. Similarly, such units also seek to improve efficiency by investing in process R&D, making needed capital investments, and maintaining a high level of capacity utilization. But because they must also maintain their differential advantage over time, functional departments related to the source of that advantage—the salesforce and product R&D for SBUs with a technical product advantage, or marketing and distribution for SBUs with a customer service advantage—are also critical for the unit's continued success.

Additional considerations for service organizations

Given that service organizations pursue the same kinds of business-level competitive strategies as goods producers, they must meet the same functional and resource requirements to implement those strategies effectively. However, service organizations—and manufacturers that provide high levels of customer service as part of their product offering—often need some additional functional competencies because of the unique problems involved in delivering quality service.

This is particularly true for services involving high customer contact. Because the sale, production, and delivery of such services occur almost simultaneously, close coordination between operations, sales, and marketing is crucial. Also, because many different employees may be involved in producing and delivering the service (e.g., when thousands of different cooks prepare Big Macs at McDonald's outlets around the world), production planning and standardization are needed to reduce variations in quality from one transaction to the next. Similarly, detailed policies and procedures for dealing with customers are necessary to reduce variability in customer treatment across employees. All of this suggests that human resource management—particularly the activities of employee selection, training, motivation, and evaluation—is an important adjunct to the production and marketing efforts of high-contact service organizations.

Competence in human resource development is more crucial for service businesses pursuing prospector strategies—and perhaps also for defenders and analyzers who differentiate their offerings on the basis of good service—than for those focused primarily on efficiency and low cost. In prospector service organizations employees often play a critical role in identifying potential new service offerings and in introducing them to potential customers. Consequently, the effective implementation of such a strategy requires employees with superior communication and social skills and necessitates frequent employee retraining and performance feedback. For instance, banks pursuing a prospector strategy not only have more branches and engage in more market scanning, advertising, and new service development than those with other types of competitive strategies, but they also devote more effort to screening potential employees and providing training and support after they are hired.[12]

ORGANIZATIONAL STRUCTURES

Three structural variables—formalization, centralization, and specialization—are important in shaping both an SBU's and its marketing department's performance within the context of a given competitive strategy. **Formalization** is the degree to which formal rules and standard policies and procedures govern decisions and working relationships. **Centralization** refers to the location of decision authority and control within an organization's hierarchy. In highly centralized SBUs or marketing departments, only one or a few top managers hold most decision-making authority. In more decentralized units, middle- and lower-level managers have more autonomy and participate in a wider range of decisions. Finally, **specialization** refers to the division of tasks and activities across positions within the organizational unit. A highly specialized marketing department, for instance, has a large number of specialists (e.g., market researchers, advertising managers, and sales promotion managers) who perform a narrowly defined set of activities, often as consultants to product managers.

Highly structured business units and marketing departments are unlikely to be very innovative or quick to adapt to changing environmental circumstance. Adaptiveness and

[12]David O. McKee, P. Rajan Varadarajan, and William M. Pride, "Strategic Adaptability and Firm Performance: A Market-Contingent Perspective," *Journal of Marketing*, July 1989, p. 18. For a discussion of recent developments in the implementation of strategies for service organizations, see James L. Heskett, W. Earl Sasser, Jr., and Christopher W. L. Hart, *Implementing Strategy: Service Breakthroughs: Changing the Rules of the Game* (Cambridge, Mass.: The Mac Group, n.d.).

innovativeness are enhanced when (1) decision-making authority is decentralized, (2) managerial discretion and informal coordination mechanisms replace rigid rules and policies, and (3) more specialists are present. Thus, prospector business units and their marketing departments are more likely to perform better when they are decentralized, have little formalization, and are highly specialized, as is the case with H-P.

Differentiated defenders perform best when their organizational structures incorporate moderate levels of formalization, centralization, and specialization. Those departments most directly related to the source of a differentiated defender's competitive advantage (sales, marketing, and R&D), however, should be less highly structured than those more crucial for the efficiency of the unit's operations (production and logistics).

Several common organizational designs incorporate differences in both the structural variables—formalization, centralization, and specialization—and in the mechanisms for resolving interfunctional conflicts. These include (1) functional, (2) product management, (3) market management, and (4) various types of matrix organizational designs, usually involving cross-functional teams.

Functional organizations

The functional form of organization is the simplest and most bureaucratic design. At the SBU level, managers of each functional department, such as production or marketing, report to the general manager. Within the marketing department managers of specific marketing activity areas, such as sales, advertising, or marketing research, report to the marketing vice president or director. At each level the top manager coordinates the activities of all the functional areas reporting to him or her, often with heavy reliance on standard rules and operating procedures. This is the most centralized and formalized organizational form and relies primarily on hierarchical mechanisms for resolving conflicts across functional areas. Also, because top managers perform their coordination activities across all product-markets in the SBU, there is little specialization by product or customer type.

These characteristics make the functional form simple, efficient, and particularly suitable for companies operating in stable and slow-growth industries where the environments are predictable. Thus, the form is appropriate for low-cost defender SBUs attempting to maximize their efficiency and profitability in mature or declining industries. For example, Ingersol-Rand, a low-cost manufacturer of low-tech air compressors and air-driven tools such as jackhammers, uses a functional structure.

Product management organizations

The simple functional form of organization is inadequate for an SBU with many product-market entries. A single manager finds it difficult to stay abreast of functional activities across a variety of different product-markets or to coordinate them efficiently. One common means of dealing with this problem is to adopt a product management organization structure. As Exhibit 12–4 illustrates, this form adds an additional layer of managers to the marketing department, usually called product managers, brand managers, or marketing managers, each of whom has the responsibility to plan and manage the marketing programs and to coordinate the activities of other functional departments for a specific product or product line.

A product management structure decentralizes decision making while increasing the amount of product specialization within the SBU. If the product managers have substantial autonomy to develop their own marketing plans and programs, this structure can also decrease the formalization within the business. Finally, although the product managers are

---

E X H I B I T   1 2 – 4

A Marketing Department with a Product Management Organization

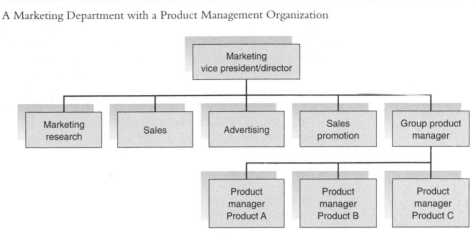

responsible for obtaining cooperation from other functional areas both within and outside the marketing department, they have no formal authority over these areas. They must rely on persuasion and compromise—in other words, more participative methods—to overcome conflicts and objections when coordinating functional activities. These factors make the product management form of organization less bureaucratic than the functional structure. It is more appropriate, then, for businesses pursuing differentiated defender and analyzer strategies, particularly when they operate in industries with complex and relatively unstable market and competitive environments. Exhibit 12-5 discusses why the Ford Motor Company's Ford division opted for brand management.

When a firm targets a number of different brands at different market segments, a product management organization typically includes one or more "group" or "category" marketing managers on the level immediately above the product managers. The marketing managers allocate resources across brands. Category management also provides an opportunity for the involvement of more experienced managers in brand management, particularly in coordinating pricing and other marketing efforts.[13]

Product management organizations have a number of advantages, including the ability to identify and react more quickly to the threats and opportunities individual product-market entries face; improved coordination of functional activities within and across product-markets; and increased attention to smaller product-market entries that might be neglected in a functional organization. Consequently, about 85 percent of all consumer goods manufacturers use some form of product management organization, including the use of market managers (Exhibit 12-6 describes this type of organization).

Despite its advantages, a product management organization has its shortcomings. The major one is the difficulty of obtaining the cooperation necessary to develop and implement effective programs for a particular product since the product manager has little direct authority. Also, the environment facing product managers is changing drastically.

---

[13]Michael J. Zenor, "The Profit Benefits of Category Management," *Journal of Marketing Research*, May 1994, p. 202.

=============== **E X H I B I T   1 2 – 5** ===============

Ford Opts for Brand Management

> Ford Motor Company's Ford division has joined the company's Lincoln-Mercury division and General
> Motors in adopting brand management. Driving this trend is the intense global competition which demands
> more distinctive products aimed at sharply defined segments and the need to react faster to changes in the
> market place. Both companies copy the organizations of such packaged household goods companies as Procter
> & Gamble in making a single executive responsible for all aspects relating to the marketing of a given brand.
>
> The new Ford marketing organization means that the company will no longer distinguish organizationally
> between cars and trucks because consumers cross-shop these vehicles. Ford has named five brand managers,
> each of whom will have marketing responsibility for a group of vehicles as follows:
>
> Youthful vehicles—Aspire, Escort, Contour, and Ranger
> Family vehicles—Taurus, Crown Victoria, and Windstar and Aerostar minivans
> Sporting cars—Mustang, Probe, and Thunderbird
> Expressive cars—Bronco, Explorer, and Expedition
> Tough vehicles—F-Series pickups and the Econoline and Club Wagon vans
>
> Ford's brand managers will work closely with the company's global marketing plans unit which in turn will
> work with five global vehicle development centers to design products. Brand managers at General Motors, on
> the other hand, work directly with the engineer who oversees product design (called a vehicle line executive).

SOURCE: Raymond Serafin, "Ford Puts Brands in the Driver's Seat," *Advertising Age*, October 8, 1995, p. 3; Raymond Serafin, "Why
GM Opted for Brand Management," *Advertising Age*, October 23, 1995, p. 3; and Raymond Serafin, "Ford Taps Insiders as Brand
Manager," *Advertising Age*, January 1, 1996, p. 3.

Competition is becoming globalized, markets are more open, the dynamics of change have
become more intense, and technology is creating new products and cost savings as well as
independent and timely knowledge about the marketplace.

In addition to the above shortcoming is the increase in the power of distributors at the
expense of manufacturers, which is due in no small part to the distributors' ability to
control information about the marketplace. Brands, too, are increasingly being thought of
as key business drivers that require the support of the entire organization; little wonder that
there have been changes in the brand manager's role in the organization. Some companies
have responded by elevating brand management to a higher level in the organization,
broadening its responsibilities to include not only traditional areas but also customer
service, distribution, sales, and finance.[14]

Other firms have adopted a more radical approach by using teams to administer certain
processes such as order fulfillment and new product development, both of which cut across
traditional lines of responsibility (see Exhibit 12-7). Because of the growing use of these
two organizational dynamics—process management and multifunctional teams—they are
discussed at some length below.

Process improvement[15]

The dynamics of the marketplace have forced companies to respond more quickly to their
opportunities and threats. To do so companies are struggling to develop an entrepreneurial
culture in which "customers count for everything. Time is of the essence. Markets are

---

[14]Alan J. Bergstrom, "Brand Management Poised for Change," *Marketing News*, July 7, 1997, p. 5.

[15]We are indebted for the contents of this section to Peter G. W. Keen, *The Process Edge* (Boston: Harvard
Business School Press, 1997), chap. 1.

—————————————— **E X H I B I T   1 2 – 6** ——————————————

Market Management Organizations

> In some industries an SBU may market a product or service to a large number of different markets where
> customers have very different requirements. Thus, banks and metals companies typically have industry
> specialists. Many use account managers to handle the sales and servicing of all the firm's products to a large
> account such as Wal-Mart. Some use a combination of product and regional market management organization
> structure. The former has the overall responsibility for planning and implementing a national marketing
> program for the product, but regional market managers are given authority and a budget to work with
> salespeople to develop promotional programs geared to a particular user segment or geographic market. This
> kind of decentralization or regionalization has become popular with consumer goods companies that need to
> cope with the growing power of regional retail chains.

unforgiving."[16] The essential instrument of change is the firm's business processes which
serve as the basis for developing a sustainable competitive advantage.[17]

If a firm can respond to opportunities and threats through a dramatic process
improvement, it can often obtain a leadership position in its industry; for example, Hewlett-
Packard was able to turn out new products successfully and in record times to satisfy its
customers' needs. Wal-Mart was able to shorten dramatically the process by which store
inventories are replenished. Information technology that lowers coordination costs and
makes possible new and more effective processes has been and is playing a major role in
such breakthrough process improvements.

Considerable difference of opinion exists concerning how many *major* processes most
firms have; generally the number is less than 20, not counting subprocesses. Peter Keen
suggested dividing a firm's processes into four categories to simplify the determination of
which are most important.[18] These are:

1. An *identity* process serves to differentiate the firm and its products from competitors and
   explains the company's (product) success; for example, it defines the firm's offerings in
   terms of benefits provided to specific audience groups. H-P's success in terms of its
   ability to solve its customers' computer problems by way of imaginative new products
   resulted from an identity process. Most unusual successes or failures involve identity
   processes.

2. *Priority* processes determine how well identity processes are carried out. Thus, their
   effectiveness is critical to the success of the firm. Priority processes for H-P are those
   that have to do with the gathering of information from customers about their need for
   new products with certain features.

3. *Background* processes support daily operations such as accounting, payroll, and administration of employee benefits. They are probably the most numerous type of process
   and, as such, have been singled out for study and reform. While necessary, background
   processes rarely generate much value to the firm.

---

[16] Thomas A. Stewart, "The Search for the Organization of Tomorrow," *Fortune*, May 18, 1992, p. 93.

[17] Samuel E. Blucker, "The Virtual Organization," *The Futurist*, March–April 1994, p. 9; Edward A. Gargan,
"Virtual Companies Thrive, Let Others Do the Work," *Arkansas Democrat-Gazette*, July 25, 1994, p. 60; and
Alan Deutschman, "The Managing Wisdom of High-Tech Superstars," *Fortune*, October 17, 1994, p. 197.

[18] Keen, *The Process Edge*, chapters 2 and 3.

—————————— **E X H I B I T   1 2 – 7** ——————————

Using Teams to Get the Job Done

Pillsbury (the U.S. subsidiary of Great Britain's Grand Metropolitan Group) has replaced its traditional
marketing department with multiple discipline teams centered around a product group (e.g., pizza snacks).
Each involves managers from marketing, sales, and production. Lever Brothers has restructured in a similar
fashion. It has reorganized its marketing and sales departments into a series of business groups and set up a
separate customer development team responsible for retailer relations across all the several SBU brands.

SOURCE: "Death of the Brand Manager," *The Economist*, April 9, 1994, p. 67.

4. *Mandated* processes are those that the firm is required by law to undertake; for example,
filing income tax returns. These are typically liability processes that generate a negative
economic value.

The future of the firm depends on how well it manages its identity and priority processes, both of which depend heavily on marketing for their success. While important operationally, the other two types can contribute only in the sense of efficiency.

To determine the worth of a business process, we need to estimate how much capital is
tied up in the process and, after deducting the cost of capital, the extent to which it generates a positive cash flow. If the process returns more than it costs, it adds value to the firm
and is an asset. If it costs more than it returns, it drains cash and is a liability. For more
information concerning the economic value added model (EVA), see the discussion in
Chapter 2.[19]

Managing processes makes the organization essentially horizontal—flat (few layers)
and lean compared to a vertical or hierarchical model. Thus, executive positions will no
longer be defined in terms of managing a group of functionally oriented people; instead,
executives will be concerned with a process that strongly emphasizes the importance of
customer satisfaction.[20] Process management is quite different from the management of a
function. First, it uses external objectives—for example, customer satisfaction over simple
revenues. Second, people with different skills are grouped to undertake a complete piece of
work; their work is done simultaneously, not in sequence. Third, information flows directly
to where it is used. Thus, if a firm has a problem upstream, it can deal with the people
directly involved rather than someone at corporate headquarters.

Self-management teams

More and more companies are using such teams to perform a variety of tasks. Typically
they are *self-directed* and based on the concept of *empowerment*—that those doing the
work should have the means to achieve the common goal (e.g., Hewlett-Packard). Such
teams have been used in marketing to develop new products, manage order fulfillment,
and handle customer sales and service. In some teams, the work is continuous so team

---

[19]For a discussion of EVA and ways of enhancing process value, see Keen, *The Process Edge*, chapters 4–7.

[20]Rahul Jacob, "The Struggle to Create an Organization for the 21st Century," *Fortune*, April 3, 1995, p. 90; and
Thomas A. Stewart, "Planning a Career in a World without Managers," *Fortune*, March 20, 1995, p. 72.

membership is full time and ongoing (as in customer sales and service) while others are project oriented and membership is temporary (as in new product development).

There is an obvious link between process management and the use of teams. Because major processes typically cut across functional lines of authority, they are best managed by teams made up of members with different functional areas of expertise. This is particularly true in today's turbulent environment which demands fast and innovative responses requiring the talents of several people.

A successful team is one that uses information technology to access data, analyze it, and communicate it to others. Such technology

> makes it possible to integrate the various functions that make up the process. It opens up the boundaries so that pooled knowledge can be brought to bear on complex, time-critical issues. Everyone involved in the work process can have access to the same information and can therefore work together to serve customer needs.[21]

In the future many companies will use teams as the basis for collaborative networks that link thousands of people. These networks enable businesses to form and dissolve relations quickly and bring the needed resources to bear on an opportunity or a threat regardless of who owns them.[22] For example, AT&T linked Japan's Marubeni Trading Company with Matsushita Electric Industrial Company to jump-start the manufacture of its Safari Notebook Computer, which was designed by Henry Dreyfuss Associates.[23] Advanced tele-conferencing systems make it possible for network members to interact even though they are widely separated in space. With a click of a computer mouse, such systems enable a face-to-face meeting between interested parties located thousands of miles apart to take place.[24] However, not all collaborative networks are successful, especially those involving **joint ventures**. At its best, partnering is a difficult and demanding undertaking that requires considerable managerial skills as well as a great deal of trust. A major difficulty—especially for those involving companies from different parts of the world—is that "they cannot be controlled by formal systems, but require a dense web of interpersonal connections and internal infrastructures that enhance learning."[25] U.S. companies are poor at handling this kind of situation. Asian companies are best, with the Europeans somewhere in between.

Organizational design and the international company[26]

An organization's complexity increases, often dramatically, as it "goes international" and especially so when overseas sales as a percent of total sales increases. The issue is essentially one of deciding what organizational design is best for developing and implementing

---

[21]Don Manki, Susan G. Cohen, and Tora K. Bikson, *Teams and Technology* (Boston: Harvard Business School Press, 1996), p. 9.

[22]Samuel E. Blucker, "The Virtual Organization," *The Futurist*, March–April, 1994, p. 9; Edward A. Gargan, "Virtual Companies Thrive, Let Others Do the Work," *Arkansas Democrat-Gazette*, July 25, 1994, p. 60; and Alan Deutschman, "The Managing Wisdom of High-Tech Superstars," *Fortune*, October 17, 1994, p. 197.

[23]John A. Byrne, Richard Brandt, and Otis Port, "The Virtual Corporation," *Business Week*, February 8, 1993, p. 98.

[24]Leon Jaroff, "Age of the Road Warrior," *Time*, Spring, 1995, p. 36.

[25]Rosabeth Moss Kanter, "Collaborative Advantage: The Art of Alliance," *Harvard Business Review*, July–August 1994, p. 97.

[26]The discussion that follows draws heavily from Michael R. Czinkota, Pietra Rivali, and Idkka A. Ronkausen, *International Business* (New York: Dryden Press, 1992), pp. 536–45.

worldwide strategies while simultaneously maintaining flexibility in individual markets.[27] In evaluating the several types of international organizational structures discussed in this section, keep in mind two things: "First, . . . innovation is the key to success. An organization which relies on one culture for its ideas and treats foreign subsidiaries as dumb production-colonies might as well hire subcontractors."[28] Second, technology is slowly making the world smaller.

Little or no formal organization

Early on in a firm's international involvement, the structure ranges between the domestic organization handling international transactions to a separate export department. The latter may be tied to the marketing department or may be a freestanding functional department in its own right.

An international division

To avoid having international customers discriminated against in comparison with domestic customers, an international division is often established to house all international activities, most of which relate to marketing. Manufacturing, engineering, finance, and R&D typically remain in their previous form to take advantage of scale effects. This type organization serves best with a limited number of products that lack cultural sensitivity— for example, basic types such as chemicals, metals, and industrial machinery.

Japanese firms have emphasized low-cost manufacturing coupled with quality assurance as the essence of their international competitive strategy. Both of these require strong centralized control and thus the use of an export-based organizational structure. In recent years Japanese firms have become more interested in global structures based on products or areas.[29]

Global structures

There are a variety of global types, the simplest of which replicates the firm's basic functional departments. Thus, a global company using the functional type organization would have vice presidents around the world in manufacturing, marketing, and finance—all reporting to the president.

By far the most common global structure is one based on **products**, which translates into giving SBUs worldwide control over their product lines. The main advantages of this type of structure are the economies derived from centralizing manufacturing activities and the ability to respond quickly to product-related problems originating in overseas markets. Marketing is localized at the country or regional level.

The **area** structure is another popular global organizational type, one that is especially appropriate when considerable variance exists across markets in product acceptance and marketing activities. Firms typically organize on a regional basis (e.g., North America, Latin America, Far East, Middle East, and Africa) with a central staff that coordinates worldwide planning and control activities.

---

[27] For a discussion of what CEOs from large U.S. companies think "being global" means, see Martha T. Moore, "New Breed CEO Markets Locally—Worldwide," *USA Today*, February 8, 1996, p. B1.

[28]The Discreet Charm of the Multicultural Multinational," *The Economist*, July 30, 1994, p. 57.

[29]Christopher A. Bartlett and Sumantra Ghoshal, *Transnational Management* (Burr Ridge, Ill.: Irwin 1992), p. 520.

Some companies use a hybrid organization that combines some aspects of the functional, product, or area types of structure. The **global matrix** is one such attempt. It has individual business managers reporting to both area and functional groups, or area managers reporting to business and functional groups, thereby enabling the company to balance the need for centralized efficiency and to respond to local needs. However, the dual reporting sets up conflicts and slows the management process to such an extent that many companies, including Dow and Citicorp, have returned to more traditional organizational designs.[30]

Decision making and organizational structure

Organization structures can be centralized or decentralized in terms of decision making. In the latter, controls are relatively simple and relations between subsidiaries and headquarters mainly financial. The logic here is that local management is closest to the market and can respond quickly to change. But multinationals faced with strong global competition require more centralization, which calls for headquarters to provide the overall strategy that subsidiaries (country units) can implement within a range agreed upon with headquarters.[31]

Culture plays an important role in organizational design and decision making. For example, Americans believe that an organization with few hierarchical levels can be successful while many European and Asian managers disagree. Also, most American managers believe that the primary role of a manager is to help subordinates solve problems and not simply answer questions, while most French managers disagree strongly with this view because they see managers as "experts" who must answer questions as a way of maintaining their credibility.[32]

MARKETING ACTION PLANS

Despite the ritualistic overtones that accompany the preparation of any formal written plan, most firms believe "unless all the key elements of a plan are written down . . . there will always be loopholes for ambiguity or misunderstanding of strategies and objectives, or of assigned responsibilities for taking action."[33] Thus, preparation of written plans is a key step in ensuring the effective execution of a strategy because the plans spell out what actions are to be taken, when, and by whom.

Preparing the action plan

Each functional department within a business—and perhaps even different areas within a functional department (e.g., sales and marketing research within the marketing department)—prepares an annual plan detailing its intended role in carrying out the business's strategy. Our concern here, however, is with the annual marketing plan for a specific product-market entry, which may well be the most important undertaking of a product or market manager. Much of this book has focused on the planning process, the decisions

---

[30]Ibid.

[31]Czinkota et al, *International Business*, p. 545.

[32]Nancy J. Adler, *International Dimensions of Organizational Behavior* (Boston: PWS Kent Publishing, 1991), chap. 2.

[33]David S. Hopkins, *The Marketing Plan* (New York: Conference Board, 1981). p. 2

that a firm must make when formulating a marketing strategy and its various components, the development of strategic marketing plans, and the analytical tools managers can use in reaching those decisions. Consequently, we will say little here about the processes or procedures involved in putting together a marketing plan. Instead, our focus is on what should be included in the plan and how its content should be organized and presented to best ensure that the strategy for a product-market entry will be effectively carried out.

Before discussing each of the major components of a marketing plan, it is important to note that its success depends largely on "agreements" made with other corporate departments (e.g., production, engineering, and R&D) and a variety of marketing units—especially those concerned with sales, advertising, promotions, and marketing research. By using the experience of others (as consultants) in preparing action programs (e.g., in-store promotions), a planner not only benefits from the expertise of specialists, but also increases their buying into the overall marketing plan, thereby increasing the likelihood of its success.

Action programs should reflect agreements made with other departments and marketing units concerning their responsibilities over the planning period for the product. For example, if a special sale is to take place in a given month, the production department must commit to making sufficient product available and to the use of a special package; the promotion group must agree to develop in-store displays and have them available for use by the salesforce; the salesforce in turn must allocate the time necessary to prepare and carry out the in-store work; and so on. Thus, the annual plan serves as a means of allocating the firm's resources and a way of assigning responsibility for its implementation.

Planning meetings are typically held about six months before the start of a firm's next financial year. These meetings are attended by representatives from the other major functional areas, by top management, the product manager (who coordinates the planning session) and representatives from marketing units such as sales, advertising, research, and promotion. Those present critique the proposed marketing plan for a given product. Several months later, unless major problems are encountered, the revised plan is renewed and finalized.[34]

Marketing plans across companies vary a good deal in content and organization. In general, however, most marketing plans are developed annually—some industrial products, especially heavy equipment, have longer durations—and follow a format similar to that summarized in Exhibit 12–8 and discussed below. To illustrate the kinds of information that might be included in each section of a marketing plan, the contents of an annual marketing plan for Pillsbury refrigerated bread dough are summarized in Exhibit 12-9.[35]

Sections of a typical marketing plan

Analysis of the current situation[36]

This section of the marketing plan summarizes relevant background information drawn from a detailed analysis of target customers, competitors, and macro environmental variables. It also reviews the recent performance of the product on variables such as sales volume, margin, and profit contribution. This information provides the foundation for

---

[34] Donald R. Lehmann and Russell S. Winer, *Product Management* (Burr Ridge, Ill.: Irwin, 1994), pp. 28–29.

[35] While this example is based on the material contained in an actual marketing plan for a Pillsbury product, the name of the brand and some of the specific numbers included in this example have been disguised to protect proprietary information.

[36] This section has benefited from Arthur A. Thompson, Jr., and A. J. Strickland III, *Crafting and Implementing Strategy* (Burr Ridge, Ill.: Irwin, 1995), chap. 4.

——— **E X H I B I T   1 2 – 8** ———

Contents of an Annual Marketing Plan

Section	Content
I. Executive summary	Presents a short overview of the issues, objectives, strategy, and actions incorporated in the plan and their expected outcomes for quick management review.
II. Current situation	Summarizes relevant background information on the market, competition, past performance of the product and the various elements of its marketing program (e.g., distribution, promotion, etc.), and trends in the macroenvironment.
III. Key issues	Identifies the main opportunities and threats to the product that the plan must deal with in the coming year and the relative strengths and weaknesses of the product and business unit that must be taken into account in facing those issues.
IV. Objectives	Specifies the goals to be accomplished in terms of sales volume, market share, and profit.
V. Marketing strategy	Summarizes the overall strategic approach that will be used to meet the plan's objectives.
VI. Action plans	This is the most critical section of the annual plan for helping to ensure effective implementation and coordination of activities across functional departments. It specifies • What specific actions are to be taken. • Who is responsible for each action. • When the action will be engaged in. • How much will be budgeted for each action.
VII. Projected profit-and-loss statement	Presents the expected financial payoff from the plan.
VIII. Controls	Discusses how the plan's progress will be monitored; may present contingency plans to be used if performance falls below expectations or the situation changes.

identifying the key issues—the threats and opportunities—the product will face in the coming year.

Market situation Here data are presented on the target market. Total market size and growth trends should be discussed, along with any variations across geographic regions or other market segments. Marketing research information might also be presented concerning customer perceptions (e.g., awareness of the brand) and buying behavior trends (e.g., market penetration, repeat purchase rate, heavy versus light users). For example, information about the market situation presented in the plan for Pillsbury's refrigerated bread dough (RBD) unit includes not only data about the size of the total market for dinner breadstuffs and Pillsbury's market share, but also the low penetration and use frequency of RBD products among potential users (see Exhibit 12-9).

Competitive situation This section of the marketing plan identifies and describes the product's major competitors in terms of size, market share, product quality, marketing strategies, and other relevant factions. It also should discuss the likelihood that other potential competitors will enter the market in the near future and the possible impact of

---

E X H I B I T   1 2 – 9

Summary of an Annual Marketing Plan for a Refrigerated Bread Dough Product

I. Analysis of current situation
  A. Market situation
    • The total U.S. market for dinner breadstuffs is enormous, amounting to about 10.5 billion servings per year.
    • Specialty breads, such as whole grain breads, are growing in popularity, largely at the expense of traditional white breads.
    • Pillsbury's share of the total dinner breadstuffs market, accounted for by several brands, including Crescent rolls as well as refrigerated bread dough, is small, amounting to only about 2% of the total dollar volume.
    • Since its introduction several years ago, refrigerated bread dough (RBD) has been able to achieve only low levels of penetration (only about 15% of all households have used the product) and use frequency (nearly two-thirds of the product's volume comes from light users who buy only one or two cans per year).
    • RBD consumption is concentrated in the northern states and during the fall and winter months (about 75 percent of volume is achieved from September through February).
    • Marketing research results suggest consumers believe RBD is relatively expensive in terms of price/value compared to alternative forms of dinner breadstuffs.
  B. Competitive situation
    • RBD's share of the total dinner breadstuffs category is likely to remain low because of the wide variety of competing choices available to consumers.
    • The largest proportion of volume within the category is captured by ready-to-eat breads and rolls produced by supermarket chains and regional bakeries and distributed through retail grocery stores.
    • RBD's major competition within the refrigerated dough category comes from other Pillsbury products, such as Crescent rolls and Soft Breadsticks.
    • There are currently no other national competitors in the refrigerated bread dough category; but Merico, a small regional producer, was recently acquired by a major national food manufacturer. Evidence suggests Merico may be preparing to introduce a competing product line into national distribution at a price about 10 percent lower than Pillsbury's.
  C. Macroenvironmental situation
    • Changes in American eating habits may pose future problems for dinner breadstuffs in general and for RBD in particular:
      –More meals are being eaten away from home, and this trend is likely to continue.
      –People are eating fewer starchy foods.
      –While total volume of dinner breadstuffs did not fall during the early 1990s, neither did it keep pace with population growth.
    • Increasing numbers of women working outside the home, and the resulting desire for convenience, may reduce consumers' willingness to wait 30 minutes while RBD bakes, even though the dough is already prepared.
    • Because RBD does not use yeast as a leavening agent, Food and Drug Administration regulations prohibit the company from referring to it as "bread" in advertising or package copy, even though the finished product looks, smells, and tastes like bread.
  D. Past product performance
    • While sales volume in units increased only slightly during the past, dollar volume increased by 24 percent due to a price increase taken early in the year.
    • The improvement to gross margin was even greater than the price increase due to an improvement in manufacturing costs.
    • The improvement in gross margin, however, was not sufficient to produce a positive net margin due to high advertising and sales promotion expenditures aimed at stimulating primary demand and increasing market penetration of RBD.
    • Consequently, while RBD has shown improvement over the last year, it was still unable to make a positive contribution to overhead and profit.

II. Key issues
  A. Threats
    • Lack of growth in the dinner breadstuffs category suggests the market is mature and may decline in the future.
    • The large variety of alternatives available to consumers suggests it may be impossible for RBD to substantially increase its share of the total market.
    • Potential entry of a new, lower-priced competitor poses a threat to RBD's existing share and may result in lower margins if RBD responds by reducing its price.

EXHIBIT 12-9

Continued

    B. Opportunities
- The largest percentage of RBD volume accounted for by light users suggests an opportunity of increasing volume among current users by stimulating frequency of use.
- Trends toward increased consumption of specialty breads suggests possible line extensions, such as whole wheat or other whole grain flavors.

    C. Strengths
- RBD has a strong distribution base, with shelf facings in nearly 90 percent of available retail outlets.
- RBD sales have proved responsive to sales promotion efforts (such as cents-off coupons), primarily by increasing purchases among existing users.
- The fact that most consumers who try RBD make repeat purchases indicates a high level of customer satisfaction.

    D. Weaknesses
- RBD sales have proved unresponsive to advertising. Attempts to stimulate primary demand have not been able to increase market penetration.
- Consumer concerns about RBD's price/value place limits on ability to take future price increases.

III. Objectives
    A. Financial objectives
- Achieve a positive contribution to overhead and profit of $4 million in current year.
- Reach the target level of an average of 20 percent return on investment over the next five years.

    B. Marketing objectives
- Maintain market share and net sales revenues at previous year's levels.
- Maintain current levels of retail distribution coverage.
- Reduce marketing expenditures sufficiently to achieve profit contribution objective.
- Identify viable opportunities for future volume and profit expansion.

IV. Marketing strategy
- Pursue a maintenance strategy aimed at holding or slightly increasing RBD volume and market share primarily by stimulating increased frequency of use among current users.
- Reduce advertising aimed at stimulation of primary demand/penetration and reduce manufacturing costs in order to achieve profit contribution objective.
- Initiate development and test marketing of possible line extensions to identify opportunities for future volume expansion.

V. Marketing action plans
- Improve the perceived price/value of RBD by maintaining current suggested retail price at least through the peak selling season (February). Review the competitive situation and the brand's profit performance in March to assess the desirability of a price increase at that time.
- Work with production to identify and implement cost savings opportunities that will reduce manufacturing costs by 5 percent without compromising product quality.
- Maintain retail distribution coverage with two trade promotion discount offers totaling $855,000; one offered in October–November to support peak season inventories, and another offered in February–March to maintain inventories as volume slows.
- Reduce advertising to a maintenance level of 1,100 gross ratings points during the peak sales period of September to March. Focus copy on maintaining awareness among current users.
- Encourage greater frequency of use among current users through three sales promotion events, with a total budget of $748,000, that will stimulate immediate purchase:
  - One free-standing insert (FSI) coupon for 15 cents off next purchase to appear in newspaper on September 19.
  - One tear-off offer (buy three, get one free) placed in retailers' shelves during November.
  - A $1 refund with proof of purchase offer placed in women's service books (e.g., women's magazines like *Good Housekeeping*) during March.

EXHIBIT 12-10

Historical and Projected Financial Performance of Refrigerated Bread Dough Product

Variable	Last Year	This Year	Percent change	Next Year	Percent change
Sales volume (cases in 000s)	2,290	2,350	+3%	2,300	(2%)
Net sales ($000s)	$17,078	$21,165	+24	$21,182	0
Gross margin ($000s)	$ 6,522	$10,787	+65	$11,430	+5
Gross margin/net sales	38%	51%	—	54%	—
Advertising and sales promotion ($000s)	$11,609	$12,492	+6	$ 6,100	(51)
Advertising and sales promotion/gross margin	178%	116%	—	53%	—
Net Margin ($000s)	(5,087)	(1,725)	—	$ 5,330	—
Net margin/net sales	—	—	—	25%	—
Product contribution ($000s)	$(6,342)	$(3,740)	—	$ 4,017	—

their entry on the product's competitive position. Note, for instance, that while other Pillsbury brands are the primary competitors of RBD in the refrigerated dough category, the potential entry of a new low-cost competitor could dramatically change the competitive situation.

Macroenvironmental situation   This section describes broad environmental occurrences or trends that may have a bearing on the product's future. The issues mentioned here include any relevant economic, technological, political/legal, or social/cultural changes. As Exhibit 12-9 indicates, a possible threat to future demand for Pillsbury's RBD is posed by lifestyle trends that lead people to eat more meals away from home and increased desires for convenience.

Past product performance   This part of the situation analysis discusses the product's performance on sales volume, margins, marketing expenditures, and profit contributions for several recent years. This information is usually presented in the form of a table, such as the one for RBD shown in Exhibit 12-10. The table indicates that even though RBD showed an improvement in gross margin due in part to reduced manufacturing costs, high advertising and sales expenditures prevented the product from making a positive contribution to overhead and profit.

The data contained in Exhibit 12-9 do not answer the question of whether the company's RBD prices and costs are competitive. This kind of information is critical because the product's market position is jeopardized if its costs are not kept in line. This is especially true with commodity-type products, but even when products are differentiated it is essential that a company maintain costs at competitive levels and that any price premium it charges provide a corresponding benefit to buyers.

The best way to determine a firm's relative cost position is to use the **value chain concept** which identifies "the activities, functions, and business processes that have to be performed in designing, producing, marketing, delivering and supporting a product or service.[37] The chain of value-creating activities starts with raw materials and continues

---

[37] Michael E. Porter, *Competitive Advantage* (New York: Free Press, 1985), chaps. 2 and 3; Robin Cooper and Robert S. Kaplan, "Measure Costs Right: Make the Right Decisions," *Harvard Business Review*, September–October 1988), pp. 96–103; and John K. Nrahk and Vijay Govindarajan, *Strategic Cost Measurement* (New York: Free Press, 1993), especially chaps. 2–6 and 10.

through parts and components production, manufacturing and assembly, wholesale distribution, and retailing to the ultimate end user of the product or service.[38] As would be expected, developing estimates for each item in the value chain is a difficult and time-consuming undertaking, especially for estimating competitor's costs. Even so, it is well worth the effort.

Key issues

After analyzing the current situation, the product manager must identify the most important issues facing the product in the coming year. These issues typically represent either threats to the future market or financial performance of the product or opportunities to improve those performances. This section also should highlight any special strengths of the product or weaknesses that must be overcome in responding to future threats and opportunities. Some of the key threats and opportunities faced by Pillsbury's RBD, together with the product's major strengths and weaknesses, are summarized in Section II of Exhibit 12-9.

Objectives

Information about the current situation, the product's recent performance, and the key issues to be addressed now serve as the basis for setting specific objectives for the coming year. Two types of objectives need to be specified. **Financial objectives** provide goals for the overall performance of the brand and should reflect the objectives for the SBU as a whole and its competitive strategy. Those financial goals must then be converted into **marketing objectives** that specify the changes in customer behavior and levels of performance of various marketing program elements necessary to reach the product's financial objectives.

The major financial and marketing objectives for Pillsbury's RBD are summarized in Section III of Exhibit 12-9. Sales volume and market share are not expected to increase, but the product is expected to make a $4 million contribution to overhead and profit through additional cost reductions.

Marketing strategy

Because there may be a number of different ways to achieve the objectives specified in the preceding section, the manager must now specify the overall marketing strategy to be pursued. It is likely to be one, or a combination of several, of the strategies discussed earlier. Keep in mind that the marketing strategy selected must not only fit the situation and the objectives faced by the product, but also be consistent with the overall competitive strategy of the business unit.

The RBD product manager recommends that a **maintenance strategy** be pursued. The intense competitve situation, uncertainty over the possible entry of Merico, and the past inability of primary-demand advertising to increase market penetration all suggest that it would be difficult to expand RBD's market by simply doing more of the same. Consequently, the recommended strategy seeks to maintain or slightly increase RBD volume and share primarily by stimulating repeat purchases among current customers. Reductions in advertising expenditures and continued improvements in manufacturing costs will be relied upon to help the brand achieve its profit contribution objective. In

---

[38] Thompson and Strickland, *Crafting and Implementing Strategy*, p. 97.

addition, it is recommended that development and test marketing of several line extensions (e.g., whole wheat and a French-style loaf) be initiated in an attempt to identify viable opportunities for future volume expansion.

Action plans

The action plan is the most crucial part of the annual marketing plan for ensuring proper execution. Here the specific actions necessary to implement the strategy for the product are listed, together with a clear statement of who is responsible for each action, when it will be done, and how much is to be spent on each activity. Of course, actions requiring the cooperation of other functional departments should be included, but only after the product manager has contacted the departments involved, worked out any potential conflicts, and received assurances of support.

Some of the action programs specified for RBD are outlined in Section V of Exhibit 12-9. It is also common practice to display the relative timing of the various actions in the form of an events calendar detailing when each action is scheduled for the coming year.

Projected profit-and-loss statement

The action plan includes a supporting budget that is essentially a projected profit-and-loss statement. On the revenue side, it forecasts next year's sales volume in units and dollars. On the expense side, it reflects manufacturing, distribution, and marketing costs associated with the planned actions. This budget is then presented to higher levels of management for review and possible modification. Once approved, the product's budget serves as a basis for the plans and resource allocation decisions of other functional departments within the SBU, such as manufacturing and purchasing, as well as other marketing units (e.g., marketing research). The projected financial results of RBD's annual plan are summarized in the "next year" column of Exhibit 12-10.

SUMMARY

For a business to be successful it must not only have competitive and marketing strategies that fit the demands of the external market and competitive environment, it must also implement those strategies effectively. The business's internal structure, resources, policies, procedures, and plans must fit the demands of its strategies. This chapter examined four aspects of organizational fit that are critical for effective implementation: (1) the compatibility of strategies at different levels within the business, (2) the administrative relationships between the SBU and corporate headquarters, (3) the organization structure of the SBU and its interfunctional coordination mechanisms, and (4) annual marketing plans that detail the specific actions necessary to execute strategy in each of the SBU's product-markets.

Both the broad marketing policies guiding the development of marketing plans for individual product-markets and the specific marketing strategies pursued within those product-markets should be consistent with the SBU's overall competitive strategy. Thus higher-level strategies and policy decisions often place some constraints on a manager's freedom of action in designing a marketing program for an individual product-market entry.

Administrative relationships between an SBU and its corporate headquarters can influence its ability to implement different business and marketing strategies. Prospector businesses perform best when their managers have substantial autonomy to make independent decisions, when SBUs share few functional programs or facilities, and when evaluation and reward systems are primarily based on growth dimensions of performance such as increases in sales volume or market share. On the other hand, low-cost defender businesses perform best when their managers are relatively tightly controlled, when SBUs substantially share functional programs and facilities, and when evaluation and reward systems focus primarily on financial dimensions of performance.

The SBU's organizational structure and the processes it uses to coordinate functional activities and resolve conflicts across departments also influence its ability to implement different strategies. Prospector businesses perform best when their structures feature low centralization and formalization, high specialization, and participative methods of inter-functional coordination and conflict resolution. Consequently, matrix forms of organizational design, such as interfunctional product teams or product and market management structures, are particularly well suited to such businesses. At the other extreme, low-cost defenders perform best when their structures provide high centralization and formalization, relatively little specialization, and hierarchical methods of coordination. Highly structured and bureaucratic organizational designs, such as those organized along functional lines, are most appropriate for businesses pursuing low-cost defender strategies.

While the product management form of organization is most commonly used, especially in consumer products businesses, it is especially appropriate for businesses pursuing differentiated defender and analyzer strategies. The environment facing product managers is changing because consumers are buying more on price, competition is becoming more international, private labels are increasing in numbers and quality, and the power of distributors is becoming greater because of their control over critical market data. Brand equity is also becoming more important. Organization design will increasingly have to accommodate the management of processes versus functions and the use of empowered self-management teams.

Finally, a detailed annual marketing plan for each product-market entry within the business unit facilitates strategy implementation. Such plans should contain (1) an executive summary, (2) a discussion of the current market and competitive situation and the product's past performance, (3) a summary of the key issues facing the product, (4) the objectives for the coming year, (5) the overall marketing strategy, (6) action plans detailing the specific activities involved in carrying out the strategy, (7) a projected profit-and-loss statement, and (8) a summary of how the business will monitor and control the plan's performance. A detailed set of action plans is particularly crucial for effective implementation because it describes exactly what is to be done, by whom, when, and how much is to be spent on each activity.

CHAPTER 13

Controlling Marketing Strategies and Programs

CONTROLS PAY OFF AT WAL-MART[1]

Wal-Mart is a discount general merchandise retailer with sales of nearly $105 billion and net income of over $3 billion in fiscal 1997. Founded only 35 years ago, it is the largest and most profitable retailer in the United States, and one of its most admired companies. Over the past decade it has continuously ranked as one of the best companies in return on stockholders' equity.

At the end of fiscal 1997 the company operated 2,209 Wal-Mart stores of which 249 were outside the United States, mostly in Mexico and Canada; 370 supercenters—a combination supermarket and general merchandise store—with 26 outside the United States; and 476 Sam's Clubs, with 37 outside the United States.

Management has an aggressive plan for store growth in fiscal 1998: 50 Wal-Mart stores, 120–125 supercenters, and 10 Sam's Clubs.

In only five years Wal-Mart's international division has grown to earn more than $5 billion in sales and currently is operating at a profit. The company has more than 50,000 sales associates (employees) in over 300 locations outside of the United States. The company plan in 1998 is to add 50 to 60 new stores in the seven countries it already serves.

A major reason for Wal-Mart's success is its ability to control costs. In 1997 it was able to hold its operating, selling, and general administrative costs to 16 percent of sales. This is substantially below that of

[1]Sam Walton, *Sam Walton: Made in America* (New York: Doubleday, 1992), pp. 85–86, 118, 212–27; David Smith, "One Step Ahead," *Arkansas Gazette*, September 30, 1991, pp. 7–9; Bill Saporito, "What Sam Walton Taught America," *Fortune*, May 4, 1992, p. 104; Patricia Sellers, "Can Wal-Mart Get Back the Magic," *Fortune*, April 29, 1996, p. 130; D. R. Stewart, "Wal-Mart Set to Open in China," *Arkansas Democrat-Gazette*, August 8, 1996, p. B1; "My Wal-Mart 'tis of Three," *The Economist*, November 23, 1996, p. 27; Wal-Mart's 1997 *Annual Report*; and Lois Flowers, "Wal-Mart Plans 120–125 New Supercenters in '98," *Arkansas Democrat-Gazette*, October 8, 1997, p. D1.

its major competitors and explains, in part, the company's excellent profitability record.

In the 1960s, when he had only 10 stores, Sam Walton realized he couldn't expand successfully unless he could capture the information needed to control his operations. He became, according to one competitor, the best utilizer of control information in the industry. By the late 1970s Wal-Mart was using a storewide computer-driven information system that linked stores, distribution centers, and suppliers. K-mart did not start to use a similar system until the early 1990s.[2]

In the late 1980s Sam Walton tapped David Glass to take over as CEO. More than anyone, Glass has successfully engineered the development of Wal-Mart's advanced distribution and merchandise-tracking systems which were needed to handle the enormous sales increases as the company's stores spread throughout the United States. "Wal-Mart's incomparable systems are a secret of its success—the unadvertised contributor to the stock's 46.8 percent average annual return during the decade before Sam's death."[3]

Today the company can convert information into action almost immediately. To do so requires a massive investment (nearly $1 billion) in computer and satellite systems that collectively generate the largest civilian database of its kind in the world. The company's annual technology and communication budget is $500 million and a staff of 1,200 is employed. In addition to automated replenishment, the system provides up-to-the-minute sales of any item by region, district, and store. By looking at the computer screens in the satellite room, a manager can see sys-temwide data such as the day's sales as they happen, the number of stolen bank cards retrieved that day, whether the seven-second credit card approval system is working properly, and the number of customer transactions completed that day.

Wal-Mart's philosophy has always been that its executives should spend part of their time in the field visiting with associates and customers. Thus, they board the company's prop planes in Bentonville, Arkansas, on Monday of each week and return on Friday and Saturday to share their findings with headquarters personnel and prepare for a series of merchandise meetings. These are no-holds-barred sessions concerned with moving merchandise. For example, in one meeting it was suggested that Wal-Mart was missing a great business opportunity in street-hockey gear—part of the roller blade craze. Others agreed, and within a few minutes appropriate action had been taken, including the development of an eight-foot long display section.[4] This decision was communicated to all store managers by the following morning at the latest using Wal-Mart's computer-driven communications system.

By merging state-of-the-art computer communication technology with hands-on management, Wal-Mart has developed its distribution system to the point where stores should never be out of stock. Doing this better than its rivals has resulted in substantially more sales per square foot than competitors and hence a faster stock turn over. This means less borrowing to carry less inventory and thus lower interest payments—several hundred million dollars less than its nearest competitor. Wal-Mart's lost sales due to stock-outs are minimized.

---

[2]For a discussion of K-mart's new centralized replenishment system, see "Remote Control," *The Economist*, May 29, 1993, p. 90.

[3]Sellers, "Can Wal-Mart Get Back the Magic," p. 132.

[4]Bill Saporito, "A Week Aboard the Wal-Mart Express," *Fortune*, August 24, 1992, p. 77.

As the Wal-Mart example demonstrates, a well-functioning control and reappraisal system is critical to the success of a business. To be successful, this system should be well integrated with other steps in the marketing management process: setting objectives, formulating strategies, and implementing a plan of action. A control system monitors the extent to which a firm is achieving its objectives. When it is not, the firm determines whether the reason lies in the environment, the strategies employed, the action plans, the way the plans are implemented, or some combination thereof. Thus control and reappraisal is diagnostic, serving to start the marketing management process anew.

Control processes differ at each level in the organization. Thus, corporate management is concerned with how well its various SBUs are performing relative to the opportunities and threats each faces and the resources given them. Control here would be strategic. At the SBU level concern is primarily with the unit's own strategy, especially as it pertains to its individual segments and product-market entries. We will concentrate mainly on this organizational level because it constitutes the bulk of any control system.

In this chapter we first discuss the control process and then examine strategic controls. Next, we discuss controls pertaining to individual product-market entries, particularly with their competitive position, their adherence to plan (including budget and share determinants), and the efficiency with which marketing manages its resources. The chapter ends with a discussion of global marketing control, marketing audits, and contingency planning.

THE CONTROL PROCESS

Regardless of the level of the organization involved, the control process is essentially the same. It consists of setting performance standards, specifying and obtaining feedback data, evaluating that data, and taking corrective action (see Exhibit 13–1).The first three steps depend on the kinds of marketing information generated from a variety of sources (see Chapter 5). Although staff is largely responsible for generating the control data, the line organization administers the control process. Certainly, this is the case with Wal-Mart, as can be seen in the involvement of regional vice presidents, district managers, store managers, and department heads in obtaining and processing control data as well as taking corrective action.

Setting standards of performance

Standards of performance derive largely from the objectives and strategies set forth at the SBU and individual product-market entry level. They generate a series of performance expectations for profitability (return on equity or return on assets managed), market share (both absolute and relative), and sales. At the product-market level, standards of performance are strongly correlated with the marketing mix and include (for a consumer product) sales and market-share determinants such as percentage of effective distribution, relative shelf facings, awareness, consumers' attitude change toward a given product attribute, customer satisfaction, and the extent of price parity, and, increasingly, customer satisfaction, including brand loyalty. Finally, budget line items having to do with expenses such as the salesforce and advertising (cost of a specific campaign) serve as cost controls and standards of performance.

Without a reasonable set of performance standards, managers cannot know what results are being obtained, the extent to which they are satisfactory, or whether or not they are satisfactory. Performance standards for services differ in the use of more measures concerned

---

E X H I B I T   1 3 – 1

The Control Process

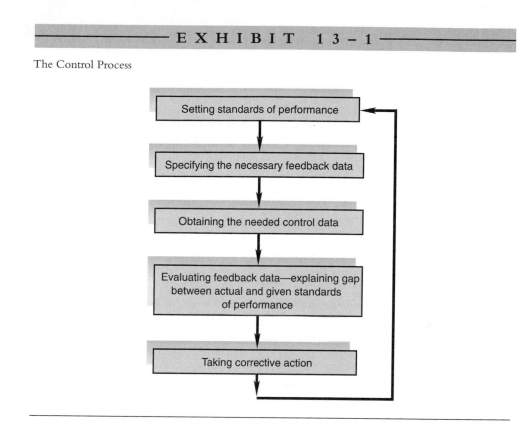

---

with the development of awareness and attitudes about the firm and its services, the extent to which the firm's resources are used (the load factor), the ways in which the service provider interfaces with a prospective customer, and the results of the interface. Performance-based control measures are often tied to the compensation of those individuals responsible for attaining the specified goals. Such a system can cause actions to be taken which over the short term may help attain the desired goals, but may be detrimental to the firm in the long term (see Exhibit 13-2).

Recent years have witnessed a shift from the use of primarily financial-based performance measures to the treatment of them as part of a broader array of measures. While the use of nonfinancial measures is not new, giving them equal or greater status is. Thus, an increasing number of companies is turning to measures which they believe better reflect how their managers think about what decision areas drive the firm's success (e.g., customer satisfaction, product quality, market share, and new product development)—see Exhibit 13-3. If the firm has set enhanced shareholder value as its ultimate objective, then it needs to change from the traditional ROI concept to one that involves the use of a valuation model that focuses on the future cash flow trend which is discounted at an appropriate discount rate adjusted for risk.[5]

The increasing use of cross-functional teams empowered to manage such processes as order fulfillment, major accounts, and new product introductions has required the

---

[5]Frances V. McCrory and Peter G. Gerstberger, "The New Math of Performance Measurements," *Journal of Business Strategy*, March–April 1992, pp. 33–38.

━━━━━━━━━━━━━━━ E X H I B I T   1 3 – 2 ━━━━━━━━━━━━━━━

Blind Ambition at Bausch & Lomb

> Bausch & Lomb, a large international firm known for its Ray-Ban sunglasses, contact lens, and a wide array of eyewear products, has recently experienced serious financial problems. The emphasis on achieving double-digit annual profit growth caused managers to use short-term tactics that would wound the company seriously over the long term. One favorite action was to give customers unusually long payment terms and threaten to fire distributors unless they took on large quantities of unwanted merchandise. They also shipped goods before they were ordered and booked them as sales.
>
> According to some executives, division heads might receive a small bonus if they fell even 10 percent short of yearly earning targets while an overage was handsomely rewarded. A small weight was assigned to assets such as receivables and inventories, but apparently division heads could miss the assigned asset objectives substantially and still get a big bonus. Customer satisfaction was given a small importance rating.

SOURCE: Mark Maremont and Gail DeGeorge, "Blind Amibition," *Business Week,* October 23, 1995, p. 78.

development of a new set of imaginative control measures. In a similar vein, Robert Simons believes that more and more managers are facing the problem of how to exercise control in organizational settings that require flexibility, innovation, and creativity. Employees are being asked to use initiative in servicing customer needs and seizing opportunities, yet in so doing they may take actions that expose the company to substantial risk.[6]

To be of any value, performance standards must be measurable and tied to specific time periods, particularly when they concern a management compensation system. Generally, control systems at the product-market level operate on a monthly, quarterly, and annual basis, with the monthly and quarterly data cumulated to present a current picture and to facilitate comparison with prior years. In recent years the trend has been for control systems to operate over shorter periods—weekly and even daily—and for control data to be more readily available. Wal-Mart's inventory control system, for example, provides instantaneous up-to-date data. Strategic control tends to operate over longer periods of time.

Of particular importance is whether the business unit as a whole and its individual product-market entries have set forth milestone achievement measures. In a three-year strategy plan, for example, an SBU might have 12-month milestones such as annual sales of $100 million, profits of $20 million, and a return on assets managed of 14.5 percent. At the product-market entry level, milestones include measures such as product sales by segments, marginal contributions, and operating margins. At the marketing functional area level, examples of milestone measures for a consumer good are level of awareness, trial, and repeat purchases (i.e., brand loyalty) among members of the target audience, reduction in marketing costs as percent of sales, and percent of stores stocking the product (weighted by sales).

In recent years, major U. S. companies such as AT&T, DuPont, Ford, GM, IBM, and Motorola have used a new type of performance measure: **benchmarking**. This means that the firm's performance in a given area is compared with the performance of other companies. Thus Wal-Mart regularly compares itself with its competitors on merchandise assortment, service quality, and stockouts. In setting up its overseas operations, Wal-Mart studied international pioneers like McDonald's and Ford Motor Company to learn everything it could on a wide range of subjects including control, organizational structures, and

───────────

[6]Robert Simons, "Control in an Age of Empowerment," *Harvard Business Review*, March–April 1995, p. 81.

═══════════════════════ **E X H I B I T   1 3 – 3** ═══════════════════════

The Corporate Scorecard: Helping Business Navigate Through a Hostile Environment

A corporate scorecard is a complex model that keeps track of the variables that need to be managed to reach the final destination of *profitable growth*. It keeps track of such things as financial progress, customer satisfaction, time to market for new products, and employee satisfaction. The assumption is that if you manage the "key profit" drivers, the bottom-line results will take care of themselves. This contrasts with management by the financial measures which simply tell you where you've been—they don't tell you where you're going or what your potential is.

A major advantage is that the scorecard results can be distributed throughout a company's computer network, thereby letting managers organizationwide use the same data when discussing problems or opportunities. For example, if the scorecard shows that the time required to fill an order is increasing, then the managers from such areas as sales, purchasing, manufacturing, and order processing can discuss the problem using the same basic data.

Those who focus on financial measures argue that you need to first know how much value each activity contributes to overall profits. What, for example, is the cost of gaining or losing a customer? What is the lifetime value of a customer? In essence, what the advocates of using financial measures are suggesting is that you start with financial measures and then proceed with the scorecard ones.

SOURCE: Joel Krutzman, "Is Your Company Off Course? Now You Can Find Out Why," *Fortune*, February 17, 1997, p. 128.

partnering.[7] The comparison does not have to be with companies in the same industry; for example, Xerox benchmarked its order filling/shipping performance against L. L. Bean, the mail order retailer catering to the outdoor set, which has a well-deserved reputation for fulfilling orders quickly and accurately. A visit to Bean's warehouse revealed that they could "pick and pack" items three times as fast as Xerox.[8] Hospitals also are learning from Wal-Mart how to better control their inventories.[9]

Profitability analysis

Regardless of the organizational level, control involves some form of profitability analysis. In brief, **profitability analysis** requires that analysts determine the costs associated with specific marketing activities to find out the profitability of different market segments, products, customer accounts, and distribution channels (intermediaries). Wal-Mart does this at the departmental and individual store levels as well as for individual lines of goods within a department. Increasingly managers are attempting to obtain profitability measures for individual products by market segments.

Profitability is probably the single most important measure of performance, but it has limitations: (1) Many objectives can best be measured in nonfinancial terms (e.g., maintaining market share); (2) profit is a short-term measure and can be manipulated by taking actions that may prove dysfunctional in the longer term (e.g., reducing R&D expenses); (3) profits can be affected by factors over which management has no control (e.g., the weather).

---

[7]Wendy Zeller, Louisa Shepard, Ian Katz, and David Lindorf, "Wal-Mart Spoken Here," *Business Week*, June 23, 1997.

[8]Jeremy Mann, "How to Steal the Best Ideas Around," *Fortune*, October 19, 1992, p. 102.

[9]Rhonda L. Rundle, "Hospital Cost Cutters Push Use of Scanners to Track Inventories," *The Wall Street Journal*, June 10, 1997, p. A1.

EXHIBIT 13–4

Finding Product or Entry Profitability with Full Costing and Marginal Contributions Methods (in $000s)

	Full costing	Marginal contribution
Net sales	$5,400	$5,400
Less: Cost of goods sold—includes direct costs (labor, material, and production overhead)★	3,800	3,800
Gross margin	$1,600	$1,600
Expenses		
Salesforce—includes direct costs (commissions) plus indirect costs (sales expenses, sales management overhead)†	510	450
Advertising—includes direct costs (media, production) plus indirect costs (management overhead)	215	185
Physical logistics—includes direct costs (transportation) plus indirect costs (order processing, warehousing costs)	225	190
Occupancy—includes direct costs (telephone) plus indirect costs (heat/air, insurance, taxes, building maintenance)	100	25
Management overhead—includes direct costs (product/brand manager and staff) plus indirect costs (salaries, expenses, occupancy costs of SBU's general management group)	180	100
Total	$1,230	$ 950
Profit before taxes	$ 370	
Contribution to fixed costs and profits		$ 650

★Production facilities dedicated to a single product.

† Multiproduct salesforce.

Analysts can use direct or full costing in determining the profitability of a product or market segment. In **full costing**, analysts assign both direct (or variable) and indirect costs to the unit of analysis. **Indirect costs** involve certain fixed joint costs that cannot be linked directly to a single unit of analysis. For example, the costs of occupancy, general management, and the management of the salesforce are all indirect costs for a multiproduct company. Managers who use full costing argue that only by allocating all costs to a product or a market can they obtain an accurate picture of its value.

Direct costing involves the use of contribution accounting. Those favoring the **contribution margin** approach argue that there is really no accurate way to assign indirect costs. Further, because indirect costs are mostly fixed, a product or a market may make a contribution to profits even if it shows a loss. Thus, even though the company must eventually absorb its overhead costs, the contribution method clearly indicates what is gained by adding or dropping a product or a customer. Exhibit 13-4 shows an example of full and direct costing. The difference in the results obtained is substantial—$370,000 using full costing compared with $650,000 in the contribution method.

Contribution analysis is helpful in determining the yield derived from the application of additional resources (e.g., to certain sales territories). Using the data in Exhibit 13-5, we can answer the question, "How much additional profit would result from a marginal increase in sales of $300,000, assuming the gross margin remains at 19.62 percent and the

E X H I B I T   1 3 – 5

Effect of $300,000 Increase in Sales Resulting from Increased Sales Commissions and Expenses of $35,000 (using same data as in Exhibit 13-4)

Net sales	$5,700
Less: direct costs (29.62%)	4,012
	$1,688
Expenses	
Sales commissions and expenses	485
Advertising	185
Physical logistics	190
Occupancy	25
Management	100
	$ 985
Contribution to overhead and profits	$ 703
Increase in profit (before tax) = $703 – $650 = $53	

only cost is $35,000 more in sales commissions and expenses?" As Exhibit 13-5 shows, the answer is a profit increase before taxes of $53,000.

Customer satisfaction

So far we have been discussing performance measures in essentially financial terms. But financial terms are insufficient because they fail to recognize the importance of customer satisfaction, which is an important driving force of the firm's market share and profitability. As products and services become more alike in an already highly competitive marketplace, the ability to satisfy the customer across a variety of activities (of which the product is only one) will become an even greater determinant of success. Thus measures relating to customer preferences and satisfaction are essential as an early warning of impending problems and opportunities.

A multiproduct firm will need customer satisfaction measures for each of its different products even if they are sold to the same customer. This would especially be true if the choice criteria varied substantially between products, particularly in terms of expectations regarding service—delivery, repairs, and availability of spare parts. Also, a firm needs to develop its own satisfaction measures with its various intermediaries (channel members) and major suppliers (advertising agencies).

As we discussed in Chapter 5, developing a meaningful measure of customer satisfaction requires the merging of two kinds of measures. The first has to do with an understanding and measurement of the criteria used by customers to evaluate the quality of the firm's relationship with them. Knowing the product/service attributes that constitute the customer's choice criteria as well as the relative importance of each should facilitate this task. These attributes were developed during the process in which the firm identifies the target market for its product-market entries. Once these attributes are identified, they serve as the basis for developing **expectation measures.**

The second type of measurement is concerned with how well the firm is meeting the customer's expectations on an individual attribute as well as on an overall basis. Thus, if the choice criteria of a cruise line's target market included such attributes as food, exercise facilities, and entertainment, then a **performance measure** would be developed for each

━━━━━━━━━━━━━━━━━━━━━━ **E X H I B I T   1 3 – 6** ━━━━━━━━━━━━━━━━━━━━

Wal-Mart Uses Marketing Research to Maintain Price Image

Wal-Mart makes every effort to keep its regular everyday prices lower than competitors' on a set of critical products. These "image items" are thought to be the basis of a customer's perception of how expensive a store is. Every few weeks Wal-Mart undertakes research to determine the prices charged by its major competitors for these same items. The company then makes sure that Wal-Mart has the lowest price. Even management staff—including Sam Walton when he was alive—have been known to do comparison shopping.

attribute. By weighting these by the relative importance of each, an overall performance measure can be obtained. These two measures collectively serve as the basis for evaluating the company's performance on customer satisfaction.

In recent years more top level executives are visiting their major accounts (both end-use customers and intermediaries) to learn firsthand how to better serve them. These visits frequently result in joint projects (inventory reductions) designed to reduce the costs incurred by both parties in the sale of a given set of products.[10]

Specifying and obtaining feedback data

Once a company has established its financial and nonfinancial performance standards, its next step is to develop a system that provides usable and timely feedback on actual performance. In most cases someone must gather and process considerable data to obtain the performance measures, especially at the product-market level. Analysts obtain feedback data from a variety of sources, including company accounting records and syndicated marketing information services such as A. C. Nielsen. The sales invoice is the basic internal source of data because it provides a detailed record of each transaction. Invoices are the basis for measuring profitability, sales, and various budget items. They also provide data for the analysis of the geographic distribution of sales and customer accounts by type and size. Special procedures have to be set up to collect the data needed to obtain feedback on the performance of nonfinancial measures.

Another source—typically the most expensive and time consuming—involves undertaking one or more marketing research projects to obtain needed information. In-house research projects are apt to take longer and ultimately to be more expensive than an outside syndicated service. However, there may be no alternative to in-house marketing research for determining customer awareness and attitude changes and obtaining data on customer service. Exhibit 13-6 shows how Wal-Mart uses marketing research to help maintain its low-price image. A third source, discussed earlier, involves the use of executives to gather information from their personal visits with customers.

Evaluating feedback data

Management evaluates feedback data to find out whether there is any deviation from the plan and, if so, why. Wal-Mart does this several ways, including sending its regional vice presidents into the field on a regular basis to learn firsthand what's going on.

───────────

[10]Carl Quintanilla, "More Top Executives Are Hitting the Road," *The Wall Street Journal*, January 12, 1996, p.B1.

Typically managers use a wide range of information to determine what the company's performance *should* have been under the actual market conditions that existed when the plan was executed. In some cases this information can be obtained in measured form; examples include a shift in personal disposable income (available from government sources), a change in the demand for a given product type (obtained in the process of measuring market share), the impact of a new brand on market share (reported by a commercial source), or a change in price by a major competitor. Often, however, the explanation rests on inferences drawn from generalized data; this would be the case, for example, in attributing poor sales performance to an improvement in a competitor's salesforce.

Taking corrective action

The last step in the control process concerns prescribing the action needed to correct the situation. At Wal-Mart this is partly accomplished at its weekly congress where managers decide how to solve selected problems. Successful corrective action depends on how well managers carry out the evaluation step. When linkages between inputs and outputs are clear, managers can presume a causal relationship and specify appropriate action. For example, assume that an advertising schedule specified how often to air a given TV message with the objective of changing attitudes about a given product attribute. If the attitude change did not occur, remedial action would start with an evaluation of the firm's advertising effort, particularly the advertising message and how frequently it was broadcast.

In most cases , however, it is difficult to identify the cause of the problem. Almost always an interactive effect exists between the input variables as well as with the environment. There is also the problem of delayed responses and carryover effects. For example, advertisers can rarely separate the effects of the message, media, frequency of exposure, and competitive responses in an attempt to determine advertising effects. Even if a company could determine the cause of a problem, it faces the difficulty of prescribing the appropriate action to take. Most control systems are "based on the assumption that corrective action is known should significant variations arise. Unfortunately, marketing is not at a stage where performance deviations can be corrected with certainty."[11]

Sometimes the situation is so serious (e.g., shipping time lags competition by 30 percent) that radical change is needed. To more and more business managers this means rethinking and redesigning the relevant business processes. A business process uses a variety of activities to create an output that is of value to a customer. For example, the order-filling process exists only to deliver the goods to a customer in good condition and in the time promised.

Sometimes the outcome is greater or better than management had planned (e.g., when sales and market share exceed the schedule). In these cases marketers still need an evaluation to find out why such a variance occurred. Perhaps a more favorable environment evolved because demand was greater than expected and a major competitor failed to take advantage of it. Or perhaps the advertising message was more effective than expected. These different explanations would call for different marketing responses to keep what had been obtained and to exploit the favorable situation.

---

[11]Bernard J. Jaworski, "Toward a Theory of Marketing Control: Environmental Context, Control Types, and Consequences," *Journal of Marketing*, July 1988, p. 24.

══════════════ **E X H I B I T   1 3 – 7** ══════════════

Examples of Questions A Strategic Control System Should Be Able to Answer

1. What changes in the environment have negatively affected the current strategy (e.g., interest rates, government controls, or price changes in substitute products)?
2. What changes have major competitors made in their objectives and strategies?
3. What changes have occurred in the industry in such attributes as capacity, entry barriers, substitute products?
4. What new opportunities or threats have derived from changes in the environment, competitors' strategies, or the nature of the industry?
5. What changes have occurred in the industry's key success factors?
6. To what extent is the firm's current strategy consistent with the preceeding changes?

STRATEGIC CONTROL

Strategic control is concerned with monitoring and evaluating a firm's SBU-level strategies. Such a system is difficult to implement because there is usually a substantial amount of time between strategy formulation and when a strategy takes hold and results are evident. Since both the external and internal environments are constantly evolving, strategic control must provide some way of changing the firm's thrust if new information about the environment and/or the firm's performance so dictates. Inevitably, much of this intermediate assessment is based on information about the marketplace and the results obtained from the firm's marketing plan. Exhibit 13-7 shows the type of questions that a strategic control system should be able to answer.

Identifying key variables

To implement strategic control a company must identify the key variables to monitor, which are major assumptions (i.e., planning premises) in formulating the strategy. The key variables to monitor are of two types—those concerned with external forces and those concerned with the effects of certain actions taken by the firm to implement the strategy. Examples of the former include changes in the external environment, as those associated with long-term demand, the advent of new technology, a change in governmental legislation, and actions by a competitor. Examples of the latter types (actions by the firm) include the firm's advertising efforts to change attitudes and in-store merchandising activities designed to improve product availability. Deciding exactly which variables to monitor is a company-specific decision; in general, it should focus on those variables most likely to affect the company's future position within its industry group.

Tracking and monitoring

The next step is to specify what information or measures are needed on each of the key variables to determine whether the implementation of the strategic plan is on schedule— and if not, why. A firm can use the control plan as an early-warning system as well as a diagnostic tool. If, for example, a firm has made certain assumptions about the rate of increase for market demand, it should monitor industry sales regularly. If it has made assumptions about advertising and its effect on attitudes, it should use measures of

━━━━━━━━━━━━━━━━━━ E X H I B I T   1 3 – 8 ━━━━━━━━━━━━━━━━━━

Variance Decomposition Analysis

Market volume variance	= actual (50,000,000) less planned (40,000,000) total market units × planned market share (50%) = planned unit contribution (20¢) = $1,000,000
Company volume variance	= actual (22,000,000) less planned (20,000,000) units sold × planned unit contribution (20¢) = $400,000
Company share variance	= actual (44%) less planned (50%) × actual total units (50,000,000) × planned unit contribution (20¢) = $600,000
Contribution unit variance	= actual (17.73¢) less planned (20¢) unit contribution × actual unit sales = –$5,000,000
Total variance	= market volume variance ($1,000,000) + company volume variance ($400,000) + company share variance (–$600,000) + contribution unit variance (–$500,000) = $300,000

SOURCE: James M. Hulbert and Norman E. Toy, "A Strategic Framework for Marketing Control," *Journal of Marketing*, April 1977, pp. 12–20. Reprinted by permission of the American Marketing Association.

awareness, trial, and repeat buying. In any event, a firm must closely examine relevancy, accuracy, and cost of obtaining the needed measures.

Strategy reassessment

Strategy can be reassessed at periodic intervals—usually, quarterly or annually—when a firm evaluates its performance to date along with major changes in the external environment. The control system can alert management of a significant change in its external or internal environments. This involves setting triggers to signal the need to reassess the viability of the firm's strategy. This subject will be discussed in the section on contingency planning later in this chapter.

Competitive position control

James Hulbert and Norman Toy proposed a strategic framework for marketing control that evelutes marketing performance and includes **variance decomposition**, which attempts to isolate the causes for the deviation from plan. For instance, assume an unfavorable contribution variance of $100,000. This could develop from either the difference between planned (20 million) and actual (22 million) units sold and/or contribution per unit (20 cents planned and 17.73 cents actual). The former could be due to difference between planned (40 million units) and actual (50 million) market size and market share (50% planned and 44% actual). Thus, the potential sources of the $100,000 variance are the difference between planned and actual market size, market share, and price per unit. The variance decomposition of each of the three variables is shown in Exhibit 13-8.

The conclusions of the analysis showed:[12]

1. The favorable volume variance of $400,000 was caused by two larger variances, which canceled each other out—one positive ($1,000,000) and one negative ($600,000), but

────────────

[12]James M. Hulbert and Norman E. Toy, "A Strategy Framework for Marketing Control," *Journal of Marketing*, April 1977, p. 20.

neither desirable. By not achieving the planned share of market, the firm lost $600,000 in profit contribution. The loss of market share may have been caused by poor planning or execution or both.

2. The $1 million positive contribution variance more than compensated for the unfavorable share variance ($600,000) because the market turned out to be much larger than forecasted. This represents a forecasting error.

3. The danger signal, strategywise, is clear—as the largest competitor the company lost market share in a fast-growth market.

4. The final variance component is the unfavorable price variance of -$500,000, which, less the company volume variance ($400,000) = $100,000 (contribution variance).

To what extent did the lower price level expand the total market? Was the failure to hold the price at the planned level a failure in tactics or planning, that is, inaccurate forecasting?

The major benefit of the variance decomposition analysis is that it identifies areas where problems may exist. However, determining the factors that caused the favorable or unfavorable variances requires additional information coupled with the skills of an experienced manager.

PRODUCT-MARKET ENTRY CONTROL

These control systems are designed to ensure that the company achieves the sales, profits, and other objectives set forth in its annual product-market entry action plans. In the aggregate, these plans represent the SBU's short-term planning efforts which specify how resources will be allocated across products and markets. These entry plans include a line-item budget and detail the actions required of each organizational unit both inside and outside the marketing department to attain certain financial and competitive position objectives. In this section we discuss budget analysis, sales/share determinants, sales analysis, and adherence to plan control.

Sales/share determinants

Sales and market share have a number of primary determinants. For a consumer product these include effective distribution, relative price, attitude maintenance or change toward one or more salient product characteristics relative to those of the competition, and shelf facings, and time requirements for order fulfillment. These in turn are a function of secondary determinants such as the number and frequency of sales calls, trade deals, and the effectiveness of the advertising message with a given reach and frequency schedule. An analysis of the share determinants should provide insights into presumed linkages between the firm's inputs and outputs; for example, the number and frequency of sales calls and effective distribution. This in turn leads to a better understanding of the firm's marketing efficiency as it relates to certain activities. Is the salesforce making as many calls per day as expected and the right number of calls on target accounts to obtain a certain level of distribution?

Marketing research is usually required to ascertain the extent to which determinants are being attained. For example, consistently having a lower price on the same product relative to major competitors is an important determinant of sales. As with Wal-Mart, interviewers would need to shop the targeted stores to obtain the desired price data.

Sales analysis

A sales analysis involves breaking down aggregate sales data into categories such as products, end-user customers, channel intermediaries, sales territories, and order size. The objective of a sales analysis is to find areas of strength and weakness; for example, products producing the greatest and least volume, customers accounting for the majority of revenue, and salespeople and territories performing the best and the worst.

Sales analysis recognizes that aggregate sales and cost data often mask the real situation. Thus, it not only helps to evaluate and control marketing efforts, but helps management better formulate objectives and strategies, and administer such nonmarketing activities as production planning, inventory management, and facilities planning.

An important decision in designing the firm's sales analysis system concerns which units of analysis to use. Most companies assemble data in the following groupings:

- Geographical areas—regions, counties, and sales territories.
- Product, package size, and grade.
- Customer—by type and size.
- Channel intermediary—such as type and/or size of retailer.
- Method of sale—mail, phone, channel, or direct.
- Size of order—less than $10, $10–25, and so on.

These breakdowns are not mutually exclusive. Most firms perform sales analysis hierarchically: for example, by county within a larger sales region. Further, they usually combine product and account breakdowns with a geographical one; for example, the purchase of product X by large accounts located in sales territory Y, which is part of region A. Only by conducting sales analysis using a combination of breakdowns can analysts be sure that they have made every attempt to locate the opportunities and problems facing their firms.

Sales analysis by territory

The first step in a sales territory analysis is to decide which geographical control unit to use. The county is the typical choice since it can be combined into larger units such as sales territories. The county also represents a geographical area for which a great deal of data are available, such as population, employment, income, and retail sales. Analysts can compare actual sales (derived from company invoices) by county against a standard such as a sales quota that takes into account factors such as market potential and last year's sales adjusted for inflation. They can then single out territories that fall below standard for special attention. Is competition unusually strong? Has less selling effort been expended there? Is the salesforce weak? Studies dealing with such questions as these help a company improve its weak areas and exploit its stronger ones.

Exhibit 13–9 illustrates a sales territory analysis. It shows that only one territory out of seven exceeded its 1997 quota or standard of performance—and this was only by $18,112. The other six territories accounted for a total of $394,685 under quota. This assumes that the quotas were reasonably accurate. Territory 3 alone accounted for 55 percent of the total loss. The sales and the size of the quota in this territory suggest the need for further breakdowns, especially by accounts and products. Such breakdowns may reveal that the firm needs to allocate more selling resources to this territory. In any event, the company needs to improve its sales primarily in territories 3 and 5. If it can reach its potential there, overall sales would increase by $301,911, assuming that the quotas set are valid.

─── **E X H I B I T   1 3 – 9** ───

Sales Analysis Based on Selected Sales Territories

Sales territory	Salesperson	(1) Company sales 1997	(2) Sales quota 1997	(3) Overage, underage	(4) Percentage of potential performance
1	Barlow	$552,630	$585,206	−$32,576	94%
2	Burrows	470,912	452,800	+18,112	104
3	White	763,215	981,441	−218,226	77
4	Finch	287,184	297,000	−9,816	96
5	Brown	380,747	464,432	−83,685	82
6	Roberts	494,120	531,311	−37,191	93
7	Macini	316,592	329,783	−13,191	96

Without a standard against which to compare results, the conclusions would be much different. Thus, if only company sales were considered (column 1), White would be the best salesperson and Finch the worst. But using sales quotas as a performance standard, White was not the best but the worst salesperson with a 77 percent rating.

Sales analysis by product

Over time, a company's product line tends to become overcrowded and less profitable unless management takes strong and continuous action to eliminate items that are no longer profitable. By eliminating weak products and concentrating on strong ones, a company can increase its profits substantially. Before deciding which products to abandon, however, management must study variables such as market-share trends, contribution margins, scale effects, and the extent to which a product is complementary with other items in the line.

A product sales analysis is particularly helpful when combined with account size and sales territory data. Using such an analysis, managers can often pinpoint substantial opportunities and develop specific tactics to take advantage of them. For example, one analysis revealed that the sales of one of its highest-margin products were down in all of the firm's New England sales territories. Further investigation showed that a regional producer was aggressively promoting a recently modified product with reduced prices. An analysis of the competing product revealed questionable reliability under certain operation conditions. The salesforce used this information to turn the sales problem around.

Sales analysis by order size

Sales analysis by order size may identify which dollar-size orders are unprofitable. For example, if some customers frequently place small orders that require salesforce attention and need to be processed, order picked, and shipped, a problem of some importance exists.

Analysis by order size locates products, sales territories, and customer types and sizes where small orders prevail. This kind of analysis may lead to setting a minimum order size, charging extra for small orders, training sales reps to develop larger orders, or dropping some accounts. For example, a needlework product's distributor found that 28 percent of its orders nationwide were $10 or less. Its analysis further revealed that the average cost of servicing such orders was $12.82 and that the company did not break even until the dollar order size reached $20. Based on these findings, the company installed a $35 minimum order, charged a special handling fee of $7.50 on all orders below $35, and alerted its field sales reps and telephone salespeople to the problem. As a result, the company increased its profits substantially.

Sales analysis by customer

Analysts use procedures similar to those described earlier to analyze sales by customers. Such analyses typically show that a relatively small percentage of customers accounts for a large percentage of sales. For example, the needlework products distributor found that 13 percent of its accounts represented 67 percent of its total sales. Frequently, a study of sales calls shows that the salesforce spends a disproportionate amount of its time with the small accounts. Shifting some of this effort to the larger accounts may well increase sales.

Adherence to plan control

Budgets are a vital part of the firm's planning and control activities because they project revenues and expenses for a given time period. They provide the basis for a continuous evaluation and comparison of what was planned with what actually happened. In this sense budgeted revenues and profits serve as objectives against which to measure performance in sales, profits, and actual costs.

Budget analysis requires that managers continuously monitor marketing-expense ratios to make sure that the company does not overspend in its effort to reach its objectives. They also evaluate the magnitude and pattern of deviations from the target ratios. Managers of the various marketing units also have their own control measures. For example, advertising managers track advertising costs per 1,000 target audience buyers per media vehicle, print ad readership, size, and composition of TV audiences, and attitude change. Sales managers typically track the number of calls per salesperson, costs per call, sales per call, and new accounts. The major marketing expenses are those linked to marketing research, brand management, sales salaries, sales expenses, media advertising, consumer promotions, trade promotions, and publicity. Before taking corrective action on any expenses which might be out of line, managers may need to disaggregate the data to help isolate the problem. For example, if total commissions as a percent of sales are out of line, analysts need to study them by each sales territory and product to determine exactly where the problem lies.

GLOBAL MARKETING CONTROL

Maintaining control over global marketing activities is more difficult for companies than domestic marketing, primarily because of the number of countries involved, each of which presents a unique set of opportunities and threats. This makes it difficult to monitor simultaneously a variety of environments and prescribe corrective action for individual countries. Differences in language and customs, accentuated by distance, further compound the control problem. Exhibit 13-10 discusses how Wal-Mart controls its global efforts.

Most global companies use essentially the same format for their control systems in both domestic and foreign operations. The difference would be in the frequency and extent of detail in reports which would vary according to the subsidiary's size and environmental uncertainties. The great advantage of a single system is that it facilitates comparisons between operating units and communications between home office and local managers. On

---
E X H I B I T   1 3 - 1 0

Controlling Wal-Mart's Fast-Growing Global Business

> In less than five years, Wal-Mart's international division has grown to more than 300 stores in six countries with more than $5 billion in sales. The company continues to invest substantial sums in both Mexico and Canada—nearly $2 billion is budgeted for fiscal 1998. Based on what it has learned from its mistakes and successes, Wal-Mart's overseas blueprint calls for a somewhat different kind of Wal-Mart store in each country. The hope is to create autonomous units run by local managers who will handle the buying, training, and accounting activities.
>
> Wal-Mart's home office in Bentonville, Arkansas, will develop new technology and plot overall strategy. A key element in Wal-Mart's success to the presesnt lies in the export of its information systems and its concern for the consumer. Foreign suppliers are finding it necessary to upgrade their information systems if they want to be Wal-Mart suppliers.

SOURCE: Wendy Zellner, Louisa Shepard, Ian Katz, and David Lindorf, "Wal-Mart Spoken Here," *Business Week*, June 23, 1997, p. 138. Reprinted with permission by McGraw-Hill Companies.

the surface the use of electronic data interchange should simplify performance evaluation across countries, but while this is true of budget control, it leaves much to be desired in terms of understanding the reasons for any deviations.[13]

The extent of control exercised over an overseas subsidiary is largely a function of its size; differences in the environment, including its stability, and the extent to which the company employs a standardized rather than a localized strategy. The larger a company's international operation, the greater the likelihood that staff personnel specializing in control activities will be on site, making the control system more elaborate and precise in its operation. Small overseas operations tend to involve fewer specialists and a less intensive control system.

Another factor affecting the control system is the extent to which environmental differences exist. Ordinarily, the greater the differences between the home country and the foreign subsidiary, the more decision-making authority is delegated. Large multinationals compensate for these differences by clustering countries with similar environments into regions that have sufficient revenues to permit the use of a headquarters staff. When considerable environmental instability is present, it is difficult to employ a formal control system; the tendency is to delegate to local management the authority to make certain kinds of decisions without review and approval by the home office.

A third major factor affecting the international control system is the extent to which a firm uses a standardized strategy. The more standardized the strategy, especially with respect to the product, the greater the degree of control exercised over many activities, including purchasing raw materials and determining components, manufacturing, and quality specifications. Ordinarily, control over marketing activities is less stringent than it is with manufacturing. Other factors also affect control: the success of the subsidiary (the greater the success, the less the home office interference) and the physical distance separating the home office and the subsidiary (the greater the distance, the less frequently the subsidiary will be visited). Rapidly improving voice and data communication systems throughout the world have greatly improved the effectiveness of global managers, but many managers still feel strongly that the personal touch is important not only for control purposes but to improve customer satisfaction.

---

[13]Warren J. Keegan, *Global Marketing Management* (Englewood Cliffs, NJ: Prentice Hall, 1989), chap 4.

========== E X H I B I T   1 3 – 1 1 A ==========

Non-Value-Adding Work Contents in a Hewlett-Packard Sales Region

Process	Percentage
Planning	0%
Product promotion	16
Customer search	28
Selling	35
Post-sales operation	62
Control	35
Total	35

THE MARKETING AUDIT

Because of the growing importance of the nonvalue-adding work audit and of its importance to marketing, we discuss it before describing the more traditional types of marketing audits.[14] This audit is based on activity management which requires that work be measured on the basis of its value to the customer. To determine the nature and scope of all nonvalue-adding work throughout the business requires that work be categorized by means of a concept known as the "value-chain." This links a set of value-creating activities starting with the procurement of raw materials and ending with delivery and servicing of the final end-use product. Processes are used to group certain activities which in the aggregate form the **value chain**. Clearly, marketing personnel are actively involved in these processes as evidenced by the role of marketing in the order/delivery cycle and new product development.

An activity is an identifiable step in this chain that can be measured for its costs and value contribution to the enduser. On average, an estimated 200 to 300 activities are cost drivers and about 20 percent account for a majority of total costs. It is not enough for a work activity to be relevant—it must also be of high quality which means being done correctly the first time. Failure to do so is costly and may lead to serious problems throughout the value chain (e.g., an out-of-stock condition can affect production, purchasing, order processing, shipping, accounting, and debt collection).

The results of using activity-based mangement successfully to help eliminate nonvalue-adding work can be significant. U.S. companies that undertake these audits report that no less than 20 percent of their work adds no value to customers—and some report as high as 50 percent or more.

Hewlett-Packard conducted an audit to determine the amount of nonvalue-adding work in one of its sales regions in the United Kingdom. The work of the region was broken down into six key processes; each process was then further broken down into its various activities. The percentage of nonvalue-adding work for each process is shown in Exhibit 13-11A, while Exhibit 13-11B shows the percentage of waste in 10 specific activities. These findings led to cost reductions that contributed significantly to improved profits at H-P, especially in the United Kingdom.

---

[14]We are indebted for the contents of this section to Tony Hope and Jeremy Hope, *Transforming the Bottom Line* (Boston: Harvard Business School Press, 1996), chaps. 3 and 5.

=========== E X H I B I T   1 3 – 1 1 B ===========

Non-Value-Adding Work by Problem/Activity

Problem activity	Percentage
Incorrect deliveries	76%
Ineffective negotiations	31
Poor order processing	45
Incorrect quotations	43
Inconsequential demonstrations	66
Incorrect configurations	53
Ineffective relationship building	42
Wasted time with partners	41
Wasted traveling time	24
Ineffective communications	39

The "traditional" marketing audit is growing in popularity, especially with firms whose many SBUs differ in their market orientation. These audits are both a control and planning activity that involves a comprehensive review of the firm's total marketing efforts cutting across all products and business units. Thus, marketing audits are broader in scope and cover longer time horizons than sales and profitability analysis.

Our concern here is the individual SBU level where an audit covers both the SBU's objectives and strategy and its plan of action for each product-market entry. It provides an assessment of each SBU's current overall competitve position along with that of its individual product-market entries. It requires an analysis of each of the marketing-mix elements and how well they are being implemented in support of each entry. Finally, the audit must take into account the environmental changes that can afffect the SBU's strategy and product-market action programs.[15]

Types of audits

Marketing audits are normally conducted for the SBU's marketing environment, objectives and strategy, planning and control systems, organization, productivity, and individual marketing activities such as sales and advertising. These areas are shown in Exhibit 13-12 with examples of the kinds of questions that need to be answered. They serve as the basis for the discussion that follows.

- The **marketing environment audit** requires an analysis of the firm's present and future environment with respect to its demographic/economic, technological, political, social, and competitive components. The intent is to identify the more significant trends to see how they affect the firm's customers, competitors, channel intermediaries, and suppliers (see Exhibit 13-13).

- The **objectives and strategy audit** calls for an assessment of how appropriate the company's objectives and strategies are, given current major environmental trends and any changes in the firm's resources.

---

[15]Eric N. Berkowitz, Roger A. Kerin, Steven W. Hartley, and William Rudelius, *Marketing* (Burr Ridge, Ill.: Irwin, 1994), pp. 630–32.

========= **E X H I B I T   1 3 – 1 2** =========

Major Areas Covered in Marketing Audit and Questions Concerning Each for a Consumer
Goods Company

Audit area	Examples of questions to be answered
Marketing environment	What opportunities and/or threats derive from the firm's present and future environment; that is, what technological, political, and social trends are significant? How will these trends affect the firm's target markets, competitors, and channel intermediaries? Which opportunities/threats emerge from within the firm?
Objectives and strategy	How logical are the company's objectives, given the more significant opportunities/threats and its relative resources? How valid is the firm's strategy, given the anticipated environment, including the actions of competitors?
Planning and control system	Does the firm have adequate and timely information about consumers' satisfaction with its products? With the actions of competitors? With the services of intermediaries?
Organization	Does the organization structure fit the evolving needs of the marketplace? Can it handle the planning needed at the individual product/brand level? Do good relations exist between sales and merchandising?
Marketing productivity	How profitable are each of the firm's products/brands? How effective are each of its major marketing activities?
Marketing functions	How well does the product line meet the line's objectives? How well do the products/brands meet the needs of the target markets? Does pricing reflect cross elasticities, experience effects, and relative costs? Is the product readily available? What is the level of retail stockouts? What percentage of large stores carries the firm's in-store displays? Is the salesforce large enough? Is the firm spending enough on advertising?

- The units **planning and control system audit** evaluates the adequacy of the systems that develop a firm's product-market entry action plans and the control and reappraisal process. The audit also evaluates a firm's new-product development procedures.

- The **organization audit** deals with a firm's overall structure, how the marketing department is organized and the extent of synergy between the various marketing units.

- The **marketing productivity audit** evaluates the profitability of a company's individual products, markets (including sales territories), and key accounts. It also studies the cost effectiveness of the various marketing activities.

- The **marketing functions audit** examines in depth how adequately a firm handles each of the marketing-mix elements. Questions relating to the *product* concern the attainability of the present product-line objectives, the extent to which individual products fit the needs of the target markets, and whether the product line should be expanded or contracted. *Price* questions have to do with price elasticity, experience effects, relative costs, the actions of major competitors, and consumers' perceptions of the relationship between a product's price and its value. *Distribution* questions center on coverage, functions performed, and cost effectiveness. Questions about *advertising* focus on advertising objectives and strategies, media schedules, and the

---

E X H I B I T   1 3 – 1 3

Measuring Environmental Progress

> Recently Arthur D. Little, the consulting firm, developed an Environmental Performance Index for Northern Telecom in Canada. The index grades, among other things, air and water releases, fines and compliables, energy consumption, and remediation versus stated goals. Northern Telecom wanted—and got—a single indicator to show employees, customers, and others how well the company was performing environmentally. The index sets the determinants, weights them by importance, and sets a benchmark of 100. Thus, a score of 125 would mean improvement while an 80 would represent a decline.

SOURCE: "A Green Gauge," *The Wall Street Journal*, July 13, 1995, p. A1. Reprinted by permission of *The Wall Street Journal*, © 1995 Dow Jones & Company, Inc. All rights reserved worldwide.

procedures used to develop advertising messages. The audit of the salesforce covers its objectives, role, size, coverage, organization, and duties in addition to the quality of its selection, training, motivation, compensation, and control activities.

· A company's **ethical audit** evaluates the extent to which the company engages in ethical and socially responsible marketing. This audit goes well beyond monitoring to make sure that a firm is well within the law in its market behavior. If a company has a written code of ethics, then the main purpose of this audit is to make certain that it is disseminated, understood, and practiced.

· The **product manager audit**—especially in consumer goods companies—seeks to determine whether product managers are channeling their efforts in the best ways possible. Product managers are queried on what they're doing rather than on what they ought to be doing. They are also asked to rate the extent to which various support units were helpful.[16]

CONTINGENCY PLANNING

Because all strategies and the action plans designed to implement them are based on assumptions about the future, they are subject to considerable risk. Too often, assumptions are regarded as facts and little attention is paid to what action or actions can be taken if any of the assumptions turn out to be wrong.

Managers, therefore, follow a contingency planning process that includes the elements shown in Exhibit 13-14: identifying critical assumptions; assigning probabilities of being right about the assumptions; ranking the importance of the assumptions; tracking and monitoring the action plan; setting the triggers that will activate the contingency plan; and specifying alternative response options. We discuss these steps briefly below.

Identifying critical assumptions

Because not all assumptions can be tracked—there are simply too many—contingency plans must cover only the more important ones. Assumptions based on events beyond the control of the individual firm but which strongly impact the entry's strategic objectives are

---

[16]John A. Quelsh, Paul W. Farris, and James M. Oliver, "The Product Manager Audit," *Harvard Business Review*, March–April 1987, p. 30. These authors concluded that product managers spend too much time on routine matters such as promotion execution and too little on product design and development.

E X H I B I T   1 3 – 1 4

The Contingency Planning Process

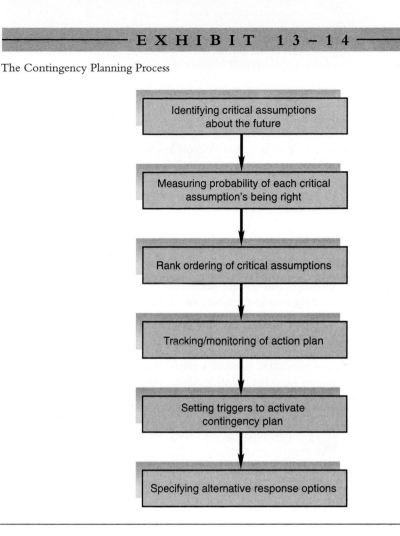

Identifying critical assumptions
about the future

Measuring probability of each critical
assumption's being right

Rank ordering of critical assumptions

Tracking/monitoring of action plan

Setting triggers to activate
contingency plan

Specifying alternative response options

---

particularly important. For example, assumptions about the rate of market growth coupled with the entry's market share will strongly affect the entry's profitability objectives. The effect of a wrong assumption here can be either good or bad; the contingency plan must be prepared to handle both. If the market grows at a rate faster than expected, then the question of how to respond needs to be considered. Too often contingency plans focus only on the downside.

Another uncontrollable event that can strongly affect sales and profit is competitive action. This is particularly true with a new entry (when a competitor responds with its own new product), although it also can apply to more mature products (competitor's advertising is increased). Assumptions about industry price levels must be examined in depth because any price deterioration can quickly erode margins and profits.

Assumptions about the effects of certain actions taken by the firm to attain its strategic objectives also need to be considered in depth. Examples include the firm's advertising objectives, which are based on assumptions about an improvement or maintenance of consumer attitudes toward the product's characteristics compared with competing brands; or the moneys allocated to merchandising to improve the product's availability. Futher, once the targeted levels of the various primary objectives are reached, assumptions can be made about what will happen to sales and share.

Assigning probabilties

This step consists of assigning the probabilities of being right to the critical assumptions. These probabilities must be considered in terms of the consequences of being wrong. Thus, assumptions that have a low probability of being wrong and could strongly affect the firm need to be considered in depth (e.g., gas shortages or high prices or the demand for luxury automobiles).

Rank ordering the critical assumptions

If assumptions are categorized on the basis of their importance, the extent to which they are controllable, and the confidence management has in them, then the basis for rank ordering the assumptions and drafting the contingency plan has been set forth. Ordinarily, these criteria will have screened out those assumptions that need not be included—those with a low impact on objectives and those which are highly unlikely to occur. Assumptions that relate to uncontrollable events should, however, be monitored if they strongly affect the entry's strategic objective because a firm can react to them. For example, if the assumption about the rate of market growth is wrong, then a firm can either slow or increase its investments in plant construction.

Tracking and monitoring

The next step is to specify what information or measures are needed to determine whether the implementation of the action plan is on schedule and, if not, why. Therefore, the contingency plan is an early-warning system as well as a diagnostic tool. If, for example, a firm has made certain assumptions about the rate of increase in market demand, then it would monitor industry sales on a regular basis. If assumptions have been made about advertising and its effect on attitudes, then measures of awareness, trial, and repeat buying are likely to be used. In any event, relevancy, accuracy, and cost of obtaining the needed measures must be examined in depth. Some of the information needed in the contingency plan might have been specified in the control plan, in which case it is already available.

Activating the contingency plan

This step involves setting the "triggers" to activate the contingency plan. It requires a specification of both the level at which an alert will be called and the combination of events that must occur before the firm reacts. If, for example, total industry sales were 10 percent less than expected for a single month, this would not be likely to trigger a response, whereas a 25 percent drop would. Or a firm may decide the triggering would occur only after three successive months in which a difference of 10 percent occurred. Triggers must, therefore, be defined precisely and responsibility assigned for putting the contingency plan into operation.

Specifying response options

Actually, the term *contingency plan* is somewhat misleading. It implies that the firm knows in advance exactly how it will respond if one or more of its assumptions go awry. This implication is unrealistic because there are a great many ways for critical assumptions to turn out wrong. To compound the problem, the firm's preplanned specific responses can be difficult to implement, depending upon the situation and how it develops. This can lead to a set of responses that builds in intensity. Thus, most firms develop a set of *optional* responses that are not detailed to any great extent, in an effort to provide flexibility and ensure further study of the forces that caused the alert.

SUMMARY

Marketing control and reappraisal is the final step in the marketing strategy process. It is necessary if the company is to operate profitably; and yet many, if not most, companies have poor control procedures. Much of the problem is a failure to set measurable objectives; when coupled with a weak plan of action, this failure makes it almost impossible to set up an effective control system. Different control processes correspond to the organizational levels involved. Regardless of level, the control process sets standards of performance, specifies and obtains feedback data, evaluates it, and takes corrective action. Increasingly, managers are using both financial and nonfinancial performance standards. The latter include customer satisfaction, time to market for new products, and the order-fulfillment measures.

Control typically involves some form of profitability analysis. In these analyses managers determine the costs associated with specific marketing activities to find out the profitability of such units of analysis as different market segments, products, customer accounts, and channel intermediaries. In performing their investigations, analysts have the option of using direct or full costing to determine the unit's profitability. In full costing, they assign both direct and indirect costs. Direct costing uses contribution accounting and is favored by those who argue that there is no really accurate way to assign indirect costs.

It is imperative that measures pertaining to customer satisfaction be obtained. Developing such measures requires that company performance be linked to customer expectations. Because customer satisfaction involves a number of variables, determining how well the company has performed is not an easy task.

Strategic control is concerned with the opportunities and threats pertaining to each SBU and their product-market entries and with the strategies adopted to exploit them. A strategic control system provides data to help answer questions about changes in the environment, strategies of major competitors, and the maturity of the industry. From these answers marketers can identify new opportunities and threats and determine whether the current strategy is still viable.

Product-market entry control is concerned with the product's competitive position, its sales/share determinants, and sales analyses. The first has to do with such key parameters as market share, market size, and market growth. It is important to determine whether any deviation from plan is caused by errors in forecasting or errors in management. Control systems are concerned primarily with the extent to which the plan is adhered to.

Sales analysis involves disaggregating sales data into breakdowns such as those related to products, end-user customers, channel intermediaries, sales territories, and order size and comparing the results with a standard. The objective of such analyses is to find strengths and weaknesses in products, territories, and customers accounting for the bulk of revenues.

The marketing audit is the mechanism by which corporate management evaluates the company's total marketing effort. Of critical importance is the nonvalue-adding work audit. Other audits include those concerned with an SBU's objectives, strategy, plan of action, and personnel. It provides an assessment of each SBU's present competitive position and insights into its marketing strengths and weaknesses.

Control over a firm's international operations is a difficult undertaking largely because of the number of different environments present. The extent of control exercised over overseas units varies, depending on the units' size, whether a standardized or a localized marketing strategy is used, and the extent of environmental differences, coupled with the magnitude of risk present.

Contingency planning consists of identifying and assessing the relative importance of assumptions about the future, assigning probabilities about which is correct, rank ordering the critical assumptions, tracking the plan, specifying the triggers to activate the contingency plan, and specifying alternative responses.

A MARKETING STRATEGY SIMULATION

Calgolia Inc.

CALGOLIA, INC.

A Strategic Approach to International Marketing

PART I: INTERNATIONAL MARKETING AT CALGOLIA

"Welcome to Calgolia Europe, Miss Retchi. We are all very much looking forward to working with you." As the doors of the lift slid open, Sylvia Retchi stepped out to shake the outstretched hand of the speaker, Jeremy Fanshawe-Browne, VP of Calgolia Europe and her new boss. "Thank you, Jeremy," she replied, "I'm sure we're all going to get along just fine."

Until recently, Sylvia had been marketing manager at Calgolia USA, the domestic division of Calgolia Inc., a highly successful multinational U.S. consumer goods company, headquartered in Cincinnati, Ohio. She had worked there since earning her MBA at a prominent East Coast business school and was considered one of the company's brightest stars. Placed by her superiors on a fast promotion track, she had quickly climbed up the ranks of the marketing division and, for the last two years, had been responsible for one of Calgolia's core brands throughout North America.

She enjoyed the challenge of managing a product in a variety of markets and understanding the different mindsets of consumers in California and Oklahoma, Quebec and New Hampshire. A move to Europe never entered her mind until her boss offered her the job of European Marketing Manager, based in London but responsible for five of Calgolia's European subsidiaries. She would report to the VP for Europe, Jeremy Fanshawe-Browne.

At first, Sylvia was not too enthusiastic about a job that seemed so far from her home base. "I don't know anything about Europe," she protested. "I just now have a handle on

---

Note: This case was developed by Jean-Claude Larréché, Alfred H. Heineken Professor of Marketing at INSEAD. It is based on actual business situations and is intended to illustrate strategic issues in international marketing. Calgolia Inc. is a fictitious name. The case was written with the editorial assistance of Delphine Parmenter and Charlotte Butler. The Gamar3 simulation was designed by Jean-Claude Larréché and developed at Strat*X under the direction of Rémi Triolet.

the differences between Montreal and Minnesota; working with these guys will be like being on another planet. I can just imagine what they will be like, an old-fashioned lot who are used to women making tea for them, not being in charge." But her boss stressed what a great opportunity it was for her, to bring some American marketing know-how to the European subsidiaries, besides furthering her career. "After you've done this," he said, "you'll be right at the top of the division. No one else will have your breadth of experience. Think what that will mean."

As he had explained, Sylvia's appointment marked an important step in Calgolia's plans to strengthen the international marketing function of its European subsidiaries. Although the company had operations in 43 countries worldwide and marketed brands in 14 product categories, it was thought for some time that a lack of knowledge about the European markets among Calgolia's top management in Cincinnati had been handicapping the success of its global expansion plans. In Europe, marketing planning had, to a large extent, been left to national initiatives, and every year back at Calgolia European headquarters, the annual marketing plans had simply been pieced together from the proposals of local brand managers.

The results were less than satisfactory and after much debate, management decided to send one of its young, up-and-coming managers to try to bring a greater degree of coordination to the European marketing effort, in line with the more global U.S. approach. Sylvia would start working with five subsidiaries, those in the United Kingdom, France, Germany, Italy, and Poland. These five had been specially selected from among all of the Calgolia Europe subsidiaries because they represented a broad range of European markets in which various international issues could be tested.

If Sylvia was not enthusiastic about the move, her arrival was awaited with some trepidation by her European colleagues. When Jeremy Fanshawe-Browne broke the news of her appointment to the marketing directors of the European subsidiaries, there was much shaking of heads. It was a pity, was the unspoken thought, that the new European marketing director wasn't one of them, someone they knew and who was familiar with the culture. They all visualized what this American would be like: a feminist who would talk a lot of incomprehensible American jargon and insist that everything was just like this in Cincinnati. None of them were quite sure how to deal with her.

However, both Sylvia and the Europeans were pleasantly surprised by their first impressions. True, Sylvia noted, Jeremy Fanshawe-Browne looked to be the typical old-fashioned Englishman she had seen portrayed in films, and some of the remarks made by the Italians and French during lunch would not have been made back home, but otherwise they all seemed friendly enough. She would reserve judgment until later. It was June 1997.

Three months after her arrival, Sylvia reviewed the first drafts of the 1998 marketing plans in the quarterly strategy meeting attended by the five marketing directors. She pointed out that while the inputs from each individual subsidiary demonstrated a thorough understanding of local markets, the plans overemphasized promotional activities and advertising schedules, expensively tailored to each country. As she explained crisply, a more coherent global strategy was needed.

Marketing Planning Procedures

Every year, an annual marketing budget was set for each brand in each country. In the past, these budgets had been determined through a long drawn-out process. Local brand managers made proposals that were then consolidated first at the country and then at the Europe-wide level, adjustments being negotiated at each stage until a final agreement was reached. Inevitably, this resulted in fragmentation along country lines of the budget for a given product category, and a lack of any pan-European, let alone global, product perspective.

Sylvia further suspected that this "bottom-up" approach resulted in overspending on well-established brands and underspending on younger brands with higher growth potential. While reluctant to interfere with local management, she felt that in the future, Calgolia European headquarters should play a greater role in determining the annual brand marketing budgets. After some discussion, her European colleagues were persuaded to agree to this. Sylvia was also convinced that substantial financial gains might be made by issuing more explicit guidelines on both the international allocation of marketing funds and the degree of local adaptation of marketing activities.

In establishing these guidelines, her main concern was the long-term objective of maximizing shareholder value, measured by the share price of Calgolia Inc. listed on the New York Stock Exchange (NYSE). For the European part of Calgolia and for planning purposes, however, the long-term valuation of the firm could only be estimated by the net present value of the expected future stream of cash flows. Sylvia pinpointed three key drivers of future cash flow generation: global market share, global revenue growth, and profitability. And while remaining attentive to the long-term objective of shareholder value, she would not forget the importance of satisfactory short-term profitability.

Developing a Global Marketing Strategy

Sylvia set out to develop a 10-year global marketing strategy that would maximize Calgolia Europe's long-term shareholder value. The year was well under way and there was confidence among the local Calgolia marketing departments that the global sales budget for 1997 would be achieved. The authorized global marketing budget for 1998 was set at $45 million, and total consumer and trade marketing expenditures in all countries for all product categories could not exceed that sum.

The Calgolia Product/Country Portfolio

Calgolia Inc.'s international operations were organized around both market and product dimensions. The major product categories in Calgolia's European portfolio were Ovadols, Squazols, and Trigols. All three were frequently purchased consumer goods, distributed mainly through mass retailers.

These products were all marketed in the five industrialized countries for which Sylvia was responsible. At that time, Poland was the only one not to be a member of the European Union (EU), but it was expected to be among the next batch of countries soon allowed to enter. However, as Sylvia soon realized, the situation she had to deal with was quite complex, as the five countries differed by size, economic and political situation, historical links with Calgolia, competitive environment, and so on, all of which made their marketing potential highly individual.

Germany was the largest country, with 81 million inhabitants, followed by the United Kingdom, Italy, and France, all approximately the same size with populations of around 57 million, and finally Poland with 38 million. As might be expected, given the countries' history and highly industrialized status, income levels were high in Germany; medium in the United Kingdom, France, and Italy; but low in Poland. Trade concentration for the product categories in which Calgolia was present was high in the United Kingdom, medium in France and Germany, and low in Italy and Poland.

Calgolia Inc. had long been established in the U.K., French, and German markets, in which it had been investing since the 1950s. In fact, Calgolia's first European venture had been in the United Kingdom shortly after the end of World War II, hence the decision to locate Calgolia Europe in London. In Germany, Calgolia's position in the old eastern part of the country was weaker than in the richer western part. Since German reunification, Calgolia had been investing heavily to try to establish a stronger foothold in these less-advanced markets. Apart from this and thanks to its long presence, Calgolia had built up a strong overall position in these three markets where its brands were well-known and where the company had a good reputation for high-quality products.

In the competitive arena, however, there were important differences among the three countries. Six international (including Calgolia) and three local firms competed in the stable U.K. market, whereas in Germany, where the market was consolidating, there was greater local competition (six firms) as against only two other internationals. The less-stable French market was contested by seven local firms and four internationals (including Calgolia). Overall, Calgolia was number two in the U.K. and German markets where its largest competitor had market shares of 15 percent and 17 percent respectively. In France, the company trailed slightly in fourth position overall, and its largest competitor had a 15 percent market share. Price pressures were high in France and the United Kingdom, medium in Germany.

Although the Italian and Polish markets were both described as dormant, and price pressures there were low, the two markets were otherwise quite different. Italy had been a recent entry and Calgolia had so far made little impact there. Local competition, represented by nine firms, was fierce but only one other international firm was present. Overall, Calgolia ranked number three in Italy, and its largest competitor had a 16 percent market share. In Poland, by contrast, where it had invested strongly since the fall of the Berlin Wall and was ahead of the pack, Calgolia had established an excellent reputation and was number one in a market served by 12 local firms and only one other international rival. Its nearest competitor trailed with only a 10 percent market share.

Customers in the French and U.K. markets were by far the most sophisticated and the least price sensitive. Those in Italy and Poland were less knowledgeable about international product quality standards, with German customers occupying a position midway among all five. These last three markets were moderately price sensitive. In 1997, Poland offered the best growth opportunities followed by Germany and Italy. France and the United Kingdom had the lowest growth prospects of the five.

For the products on offer in these markets, the International Product Report provided essential data on the size, growth, and market share in late 1997 for each of the three product categories in the five different countries (see Exhibit 1).

In 1997, Squazols had the largest market share followed by Ovadols and Trigols. Squazols, the company's newest category, showed the best growth rate, projected to be double that of Ovadols. Of the other two product categories, Ovadols, once Calgolia's core business, was now a mature category with little international growth potential and Trigols, Calgolia's second-oldest product category, commanded moderate global growth.

Calgolia held a fairly strong position vis-à-vis its European competitors. In 1997, only three other international firms offered Squazols but, given the rapid growth of this category, Sylvia anticipated that competition would intensify. For the time being, Calgolia was the global leader in this promising market, with its nearest competitor holding a 15 percent share. Ovadols competed directly with products from five international firms and held the number two position worldwide in the category, to the market leader's 17 percent share. Trigols, which had a weak market share in most countries, occupied fourth position worldwide. Its largest competitor had a 13 percent market share.

EXHIBIT 1

International Product Category Report—Ovadols

Country Name	Results for Period 0 Market Size						Forecast for Period 1 Market Share	
	KU	K$	%U	%$	Average Price ($)	Market Growth %U	Market Size KU	Market Growth %U
U.K.	393	121,288	12.3	12.3	309.0	6.0	431	9.9
Poland	158	47,627	17.0	17.0	301.0	16.2	182	15.3
France	197	62,739	10.6	10.6	319.0	8.1	221	12.6
Germany	284	94,449	16.0	16.0	332.0	11.1	310	9.0
Italy	244	82,813	14.4	14.4	340.0	9.1	265	8.9
Total	**1,275**	**408,916**	**13.8**	**13.9**	**320.6**	**9.3**	**1,410**	**10.6**

International Product Category Report—Squazols

Country Name	Results for Period 0 Market Size						Forecast for Period 1 Market Share	
	KU	K$	%U	%$	Average Price ($)	Market Growth %U	Market Size KU	Market Growth %U
U.K.	511	63,377	19.1	19.1	124.0	15.5	613	20.0
Poland	251	28,914	21.7	21.7	115.2	26.5	320	27.7
France	303	40,008	15.0	15.0	132.0	17.7	346.	14.2
Germany	409	56,482	19.5	19.5	138.0	21.0	504	23.1
Italy	306	44,372	19.8	19.8	145.2	18.8	366	19.7
Total	**1,780**	**233,153**	**18.9**	**18.9**	**131.0**	**19.3**	**2,150**	**20.8**

International Product Category Report—Trigols

Country Name	Results for Period 0 Market Size						Forecast for Period 1 Market Share	
	KU	K$	%U	%$	Average Price ($)	Market Growth %U	Market Size KU	Market Growth %U
U.K.	424	80,829	6.9	6.9	190.8	10.3	480	13.3
Poland	213	38,642	9.3	9.3	181.8	20.8	266	25.2
France	238	48,832	6.2	6.2	205.2	12.4	258	8.5
Germany	296	62,705	8.1	8.1	211.8	15.5	331	11.8
Italy	271	59,745	7.6	7.6	220.2	13.4	315	16.2
Total	**1,442**	**290,752**	**7.5**	**7.5**	**201.7**	**13.8**	**1,650**	**14.5**

For planning purposes, Sylvia made a tentative forecast of market growth rates for the five countries and their three major product categories for the years 1998–2007 (see Exhibit 2). To her European marketing colleagues, she emphasized that the numbers were hypothetical since many external factors, as well as the firm's actions, could either foster or hinder the development of these markets.

EXHIBIT 2

Expected Average Annual Market Growth Rates 1998–2007

| Country | Product Category | | |
	Ovadols	Squazols	Trigols
United Kingdom	1%	9%	7%
Poland	10%	17%	14%
France	6%	13%	9%
Germany	8%	16%	12%
Italy	7%	14%	11%
Average	**6%**	**14%**	**10%**

Allocation of Marketing Resources

The allocation of marketing resources, the most crucial aspect of any international marketing strategy, was generally attributed by product category for a given country. Calgolia called these OMUs (operational market units), and each OMU was the responsibility of a local category manager, reporting to the subsidiary marketing director. In her initial analysis, Sylvia considered 15 such OMUs, reflecting the firm's presence in three product categories and five countries, as described earlier.

Three types of marketing resources were available to support Calgolia's position in a given market: management time (a fixed cost not charged to the unit), consumer marketing expenditure, and trade marketing expenditure. Management time related to managerial resources available at European HQ to help the local subsidiaries, which consisted of staff in various functions, including development, operations, and marketing. Any HQ managerial assistance called upon by a subsidiary was expected to improve the quality—and hence, the effectiveness—of its local activities.

Consumer marketing expenditure financed activities aimed directly at the final consumer. Generally, the largest proportion was absorbed by media advertising in order to build consumer awareness, create interest, and encourage trial. Consumer marketing was generally most effective in the launch or early growth stages of a product's introduction, while improvements in product quality, price, or distribution influenced repeat purchases.

Trade marketing expenditure targeted distributors, especially mass merchandisers. Such expenditures funded a wide variety of marketing tactics such as personal selling, cooperative advertising, the purchase of shelf space, promotional discounts, and in-store displays—all aimed at making the product available to consumers in more-favorable conditions than did the competition. An important concern for Calgolia was to achieve wide distribution coverage so that consumers could easily find their products in local stores. Broad distribution was particularly difficult to achieve for new products like Squazols and for products with a weak market share such as Trigols.

For the coming year, Sylvia had to guide the allocation of management time, as well as consumer and trade marketing expenditures, among the 15 OMUs. Calgolia evaluated the financial performance of its product categories, and of the marketing departments of its subsidiaries, on the basis of their contribution after marketing (CAM). The CAM was calculated as contribution before marketing (CBM) minus consumer and trade marketing expenditure; CBM was obtained by subtracting total variable costs from revenues.

════════════════════════ E X H I B I T   3 ════════════════════════

1997 Projected Income Statement—Ovadols

Item	Unit	Total	U.K.	Poland	France	Germany	Italy
Volume sold	U	176,613	48,133	26,902	20,906	45,533	35,140
Price	$	321.1	309.0	301.0	319.0	332.0	340.0
Revenues	K$	56,704	14,873	8,097	6,669	15,117	11,947
Unit variable cost	$	127.0	127.0	127.0	127.0	127.0	127.0
Total variable cost	K$	−22,430	−6,113	−3,417	−2,655	−5,783	−4,463
CBM	K$	34,274	8,760	4,681	4,014	9,334	7,485
Consumer marketing	K$	−8,300	−2,600	−1,000	−1,300	−1,800	−1,600
Trade marketing	K$	−4,600	−1,400	−600	−700	−1,000	−900
CAM	**K$**	**21,374**	**4,760**	**3,081**	**2,014**	**6,534**	**4,985**

1997 Projected Income Statement—Squazols

Item	Unit	Total	U.K.	Poland	France	Germany	Italy
Volume sold	U	337,266	97,369	54,392	45,387	79,687	60,432
Price	$	130.8	124.0	115.2	132.0	138.0	145.2
Revenues	K$	44,102	12,074	6,266	5,991	10,997	8,775
Unit variable cost	$	41.8	41.8	41.8	41.8	41.8	41.8
Total variable cost	K$	−14,098	−4,070	−2,274	−1,897	−3,331	−2,526
CBM	K$	30,004	8,004	3,992	4,094	7,666	6,249
Consumer marketing	K$	−7,000	−2,000	−1,000	−1,200	−1,600	−1,200
Trade marketing	K$	−4,200	−1,200	−600	−700	−1,000	−700
CAM	**K$**	**18,804**	**4,804**	**2,392**	**2,194**	**5,066**	**4,349**

1997 Projected Income Statement—Trigols

Item	Unit	Total	U.K.	Poland	France	Germany	Italy
Volume sold	U	108,482	29,259	19,826	14,835	24,062	20,501
Price	$	201.3	190.8	181.8	205.2	211.8	220.2
Revenues	K$	21,842	5,583	3,604	3,044	5,096	4,514
Unit variable cost	$	67.2	67.2	67.2	67.2	67.2	67.2
Total variable cost	K$	−7,290	−1,966	−1,332	-997	−1,617	−1,378
CBM	K$	14,552	3,616	2,272	2,047	3,479	3,137
Consumer marketing	K$	−5,600	−1,600	−800	−900	−1,200	−1,100
Trade marketing	K$	−2,700	−800	−400	−400	−600	−500
CAM	**K$**	**6,252**	**1,216**	**1,072**	**747**	**1,679**	**1,537**

Sylvia considered the impact of these marketing expenditures on the firm's overall profitability. She then carefully examined the income statements by product category (see Exhibit 3). In 1997, the division of marketing expenditure between consumer and trade marketing was approximately the same for Ovadols, Squazols, and Trigols. Sylvia had also established that although HQ staff devoted about an equal amount of time to each of the three product categories, nearly half of Calgolia's revenues and CAM were generated by the Ovadol product category. Squazols were also a strong contributor but Trigol's contribution was minimal. Although both Ovadols and Squazols obtained marketing resources proportional to their revenue contribution, Trigols appeared to receive a higher portion of marketing resources than was justified by its level of revenues.

Standardization versus Local Adaptation

Aside from the allocation of marketing resources, another issue currently dividing Calgolia was the extent to which marketing strategies should be standardized. Traditionally, local subsidiaries had enjoyed a high degree of autonomy, but recently, under pressure from the U.S. parent company, support for standardization had grown. The champions of global standardization invariably cited cost benefits, simplified management processes, and a faster response to market changes, while defenders of local adaptation—most of the European managers—claimed that since the marketing environments and customer development were so varied, it was preferable to match the firm's marketing offering to the specific conditions of each country.

Sylvia pinpointed three components that could be adapted or standardized: product specifications, consumer marketing, and trade marketing. Adapting product specifications involved making product and packaging changes to appeal to local consumers, but this could represent an increase in variable costs as high as 30 percent. Similarly, consumer or trade marketing programs could be adapted by developing country-specific advertising copy, promotional schemes, or merchandising tools. However, since the total marketing budget was fixed, the cost of such adaptations reduced the funds available to market the product effectively.

Developed after World War II during an era of international decentralization, Ovadols still benefited in 1997 from the highest level of local adaptation. On the other hand, Squazols, the most recent category, had the highest level of global product standardization. The treatment of Trigols represented a halfway stage between the two extreme poles.

Pricing Decisions

Calgolia's international marketing department could either set a standard price for a given product in all countries or allow each country to set different prices with respect to local conditions. In 1997, the price variation between countries was 12–23 percent, depending on the product category. However, Sylvia anticipated a downward pressure on prices for Ovadols and Squazols in most countries, while Trigol prices were expected to remain stable.

There was a risk that parallel trading could take place when the same product was available at significantly different prices in different countries. Potentially, wholesalers could buy vast quantities in the low-price location and export them to a high-price country, where they would then compete with Calgolia's local subsidiary. For this reason, Sylvia felt that prices should vary by no more than 30 percent between countries. Antidumping regulations also forbade selling below the base unit variable cost, which was $100 for Ovadols, $40 for Squazols, and $60 for Trigols.

International Market Surveys

Before deciding on the degree of local adaptation or standardization for product specifications, pricing, and consumer and trade marketing, Sylvia examined the results of the market research she had recently received. Calgolia collected market information for each product

─────────── **E X H I B I T   4** ───────────

1997 Consumer Satisfaction with Product Specifications

Product Category	Satisfaction Index (0–100)					
	Average	U.K.	Poland	France	Germany	Italy
Ovadols	89	90	88	91	89	89
Squazols	83	86	79	84	81	87
Trigols	79	82	81	78	80	76
Overall average	**84**	**86**	**83**	**84**	**84**	**84**

1997 Consumer Satisfaction with Price

Product Category	Satisfaction Index (0–100)					
	Average	U.K.	Poland	France	Germany	Italy
Ovadols	41	38	47	39	40	41
Squazols	45	43	60	42	41	39
Trigols	38	37	45	40	34	34
Overall average	**41**	**39**	**51**	**40**	**39**	**38**

1997 Effectiveness of Consumer Marketing

Product Category	Satisfaction Index (0–100)					
	Average	U.K.	Poland	France	Germany	Italy
Ovadols	70	65	87	57	84	58
Squazols	61	55	75	55	70	52
Trigols	37	31	45	33	44	32
Overall average	**56**	**50**	**69**	**48**	**66**	**47**

1997 Effectiveness of Trade Marketing

Product Category	Satisfaction Index (0–100)					
	Average	U.K.	Poland	France	Germany	Italy
Ovadols	43	42	36	44	39	56
Squazols	62	62	46	61	58	82
Trigols	45	49	38	42	44	54
Overall average	**50**	**51**	**40**	**49**	**47**	**64**

category in each country on a regular basis. The use of a standard format allowed comparisons to be made over time and across different products and countries.

Two studies measured consumer satisfaction with product specifications and pricing (see Exhibit 4). It was found that a higher level of local product adaptation generally increased consumer satisfaction with the product, and a lower price usually boosted consumer satisfaction with pricing. However, it was not clear whether or not the benefits of these actions outweighed their cost.

Two other studies tracked the effectiveness of consumer and trade marketing (see Exhibit 4). For consumer marketing, a single index took into account various factors such as brand awareness, the perception of key product dimensions, and trial rate. The variables pooled for the trade marketing index related to professional buyers' perceptions of product quality and supplier service, as well as distributors' margins. An increase in consumer or trade marketing spending was expected to result in a higher effectiveness rating for the relevant marketing tool.

Sylvia observed that although consumers in all five countries appeared to be particularly satisfied with product specifications for Ovadols, satisfaction with the other two products was also high. However, on the whole, consumer satisfaction with the different product categories' pricing policies was low across the five countries, except for Squazols, which rated quite highly in Poland. Consumer marketing actions for Ovadols seemed to be very effective in Poland and Germany, although less so in the other three countries. Squazols also scored better in Poland and Germany on consumer marketing effectiveness, whereas Trigols trailed badly in all five markets. Of the three product categories, trade demand was highest for Squazols, followed by Ovadols (medium), and Trigols (low). Sylvia was therefore pleased to note that Squazols had the best average rating for trade marketing effectiveness, scoring particularly highly in Italy. However, she saw considerable scope for improvement for the other two product categories.

Where to Invest Marketing Resources?

Investment decisions for a given operational market unit had to take a number of considerations into account. These included the objectives for an OMU in the firm's overall portfolio, for instance in terms of growth versus profitability; the sensitivity of sales and market share to the type of investment being considered; the effectiveness of the proposed instrument relative to alternatives; and the appropriateness of investing in this particular OMU as opposed to another. Investing higher levels of marketing resources in an OMU would generally increase sales and market share. However, because the effects of most marketing instruments had a time lag, their impact was rarely fully apparent in the same year. Finally, the positive impact of an investment on sales did not automatically imply a positive impact on short-term contribution, long-term profitability, or shareholder value.

Sylvia determined that her first task should be to establish some priorities between the three product categories. She also put a question mark against whether or not the United Kingdom, France, Germany, Italy, and Poland warranted the same level of marketing expenditure. A further objective, she decided, would be to establish some pricing guidelines and a corporate policy on the issue of adaptation versus globalization, although she knew that many other factors could influence the effectiveness of marketing activities.

As Jeremy Fanshawe-Browne and the marketing directors from the five countries studied Sylvia's list of questions and priorities, they finally began to understand the complexity of the marketing resource allocation challenge that Calgolia faced and its implications for the firm's global results. "These Yanks from Cincinnati can sometimes be helpful!" Smiling at her, the Italian director voiced the thought that had occurred to them all over the past two months. Memphis born and bred, Sylvia at first had been shocked by the European habit of referring to every American as a "Yank"—no matter where in the United States they came from. But now, she was getting used to it and realized it was meant as a compliment rather than an insult. "Well, thank you," she said. "I appreciate your confidence in me. Now, let's try to develop together what should be the general lines of a European Marketing Strategy for Calgolia."

PART II: THE GAMAR3 SIMULATION

From past experience Sylvia knew that certain software tools, available from specialist suppliers, could be very valuable in helping to formulate business decisions. She therefore commissioned, soon after her arrival in London, the development of a software model that would simulate Calgolia's marketing environment. This simulation was designed to test alternative international marketing strategies with special emphasis on two key issues: the allocation of resources and the degree of local adaptation. It was given the name GAMAR, standing for Global Allocation of Marketing Resources. Marketing staff at both Calgolia European headquarters and at the local level contributed to determining the parameters used in the model. These were based on a combination of industry data, routine market surveys, ad hoc research studies, and managerial judgment. Initially tested against historic data, the model proved capable of replicating past conditions satisfactorily after several iterations. At the end of September, Sylvia finally approved the third version of the simulation, Gamar3, in time to help her finalize the 1997 marketing plans.

In designing the Gamar3 simulation, a number of assumptions and simplifications had been made. Focused on strategic marketing issues, the model did not explicitly incorporate financial, manufacturing, or personnel aspects of international business. Financial data were expressed in a single currency, the U.S. dollar (commonly used to consolidate international figures) and assumed that exchange rates between local currencies and the U.S. dollar remained constant over the course of the simulation. It was assumed that the same product was available at the same cost in all countries. The unit variable cost of a product included all relevant costs, except for marketing expenditure, which was considered separately. Sourcing, capital investments, inventories, working capital, and other cash flow dimensions were not represented in the simulation.

The purpose of the simulation was to help formulate and test specific international marketing strategies for Calgolia Europe's key countries and product categories. For the purpose of the simulation, Calgolia's country and product portfolio was simplified. The scope of the model accounted for the bulk of Calgolia's European business and was limited to the firm's three main product categories (Ovadols, Squazols, and Trigols) and five countries (the United Kingdom, France, Germany, Italy, and Poland). Each of the three products came in a variety of sizes and packages, representing a significant number of SKUs (stock-keeping units). However, to simplify the software, the simulation considered only each product category as a whole.

Although the Gamar3 simulation incorporated the reactions of competing firms, for the sake of simplicity, competitors' responses were not detailed but treated at the aggregate level. Their impact was implicit in the market response to the firm's actions.

Sylvia was very pleased with the Gamar3 software, its realism and its user-friendliness. All options were available with the click of a button on any screen (see Exhibit 5). The instructions provided by the software developers were concise (see Appendix A) and the Help facility was very useful in obtaining online information on any aspect of the simulation. The Gamar3 software was composed of four modules—Decisions, Results, Analysis, and Simulation—all accessible by clicking on the corresponding button in the top left-hand corner of any screen.

The Gamar3 Simulation Module

The first step in using the Gamar3 simulation was to "create" a simulated firm that would be used to investigate a number of alternative strategies. It was possible to choose any name for the firm, write a short reminder note of what it was about, and choose between

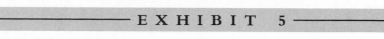

E X H I B I T   5

Gamar3—The Introduction Screen

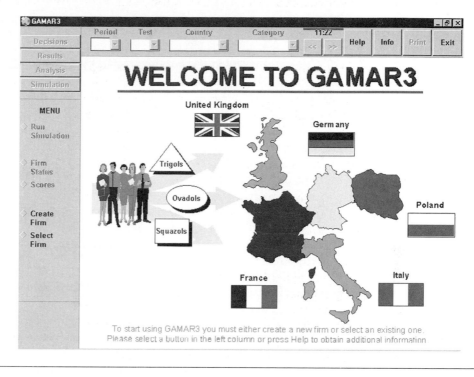

four levels of difficulty (see Exhibit 6). These four levels corresponded to different combinations of countries and product categories, as follows:

Difficulty Level	Product Categories	Countries
Basic	Ovadols	United Kingdom
		Poland
Intermediate	Ovadols	United Kingdom
	Squazols	Poland
Advanced	Ovadols	United Kingdom
	Squazols	Poland
		France
		Germany
Expert	Ovadols	United Kingdom
	Squazols	Poland
	Trigols	France
		Germany
		Italy

——— E X H I B I T   6 ———

Gamar3—The Creation of a New Simulated Firm

Sylvia readily appreciated the possibility of starting with a basic international scenario with only one product category and two countries as different economically as the United Kingdom and Poland. Progressively mastering higher levels of difficulty was, she discovered, a good exercise before using the "Expert" level, which corresponded to her real situation with three product categories and five countries. While seeing the benefits of this gradual approach, she could also envision some of her more internationally seasoned colleagues jumping directly to the "Expert" level, but this she didn't really mind as long as they were able to use it effectively.

The simulation module also gave users the choice of selecting a previously created firm, reviewing the scores obtained in the past, and actually running the simulation model. A typical use of the software was to make decisions for Period 1 of the planning horizon (1998) and then run the simulation. This would provide the simulated results for Period 1 based on the decisions made for that period. Users could then make decisions for Period 2 (1999) and generate the projected results for that period, and so on until the 10th period of the planning horizon (2007). For any given period, the software also allowed testing up to 10 sets of decisions.

The Gamar3 Decisions Module

Using the Gamar3 software, decisions could be made about management resources, consumer marketing expenditures, trade marketing expenditures, product specifications, and pricing. The model simulated the way the market and the competition would react to a specific set of decisions and projected the impact of these decisions on a number of dimensions. These included revenues and share price, as well as measures of consumer satisfaction, marketing effectiveness, and forecasted market trends. Decisions and results covered a 12-month period, and the simulation could be run for 10 successive periods, representing a 10-year time span. The Gamar3 Decision Form gave an overview of all the decisions to be made for the three product categories and five countries (see Appendix B).

Three types of marketing resources—management time, consumer marketing, and trade marketing expenditures—needed to be allocated across the 15 OMUs included in the Gamar3 model. Under the simulation, Sylvia could allot these three types to a given market to be used for a given product category. The European HQ managerial resources called "Management Time" were represented by a pool of 360 man-months. Allocating a greater proportion of this resource to a given OMU meant that it would receive not only more management attention but also more expertise.

The European marketing budget covered consumer and trade marketing expenditures. For 1998, or Period 1 of the simulation, this was set at $45 million. Further into the simulation, the European marketing budget authorized for any subsequent period would depend on the contribution achieved in the previous period. Improved financial results would generally lead to a higher spending authorization, but the budget would always be above a $45 million floor, while never exceeding a ceiling of $150 million.

Consumer marketing expenditures were allocated to each country by product category. Similarly, trade marketing expenditures were fed into the simulation for each country by product category. Both these investments were expressed in thousands of dollars, with the maximum expenditure for any single OMU set at $15 million.

Sylvia had asked the software developers to incorporate a special tool to assist in establishing a resource allocation strategy. Instead of individual values being entered for each product in each country, allocation guidelines could be expressed as a percentage to specify how resources should be distributed across both product categories and different countries. Consumer marketing spending could also be expressed as a ratio of total marketing expenditure, and any remaining marketing resources would be attributed to trade marketing. All decisions concerning management time and consumer and trade marketing then followed from these strategic attributions (see Exhibit 7).

In the Gamar3 simulation, the price of each product category could be set either country by country or as a standard price across all countries. Furthermore, the software made it easy to test the market implications of standardizing prices across all five countries or, conversely, adapting product pricing to local competitive conditions. Year after year, global price increases or decreases for a single product category could be entered as a percentage of last period prices in such a manner as to affect all five countries. The pricing decision screen highlighted this feature (see Exhibit 8).

The Gamar3 simulation made it possible to establish the degree of local adaptation for product specifications, consumer marketing, and trade marketing for each product category. The level could be set on a scale from 0 (total standardization) to 100 (total local adaptation). The higher the number, the greater the degree of local adaptation. In the case of maximum local adaptation, local managers were free to make all the modifications they deemed necessary. With total standardization, the specifications were identical in all countries.

This feature enabled Sylvia and the local marketing managers to decide on the degree of adaptation for product specifications and consumer and trade marketing, and to test their impact on corporate profitability. She knew that high levels of product adaptation increased the unit variable cost of the product, while adapting consumer or trade marketing activities reduced the budget available for media spending. Sylvia tested the efficacy of her

---

E X H I B I T   7

Gamar3—Defining a Resources Allocation Strategy

GAMAR3 - EXPERT3

| Period | Test | Country | Category | 11:28 |

Decisions Period 1 Test 1   Help Info Print Exit

Resu ... Zoom Out

Analy

Simula

This decision box will help you define your resources allocation strategy. (marketing budget and management time). Please follow the four steps explained below.

1. Specify which percentage of your total budget you want to spend this period.

2. Specify how the resources will be distributed across product categories.

3. Specify how the resources will be distributed across countries.
   Note that the same country distribution rules are used for all product categories.

4. Specify for each product category which percentage of the resources you want to spend on consumer marketing. The remaining part will be spent on trade marketing.

% of Total Budget Spent: 72

Distribution on Product Categories:	Ovadols	Squazols	Trigols	Total
	40	35	25	100

Distribution on Countries:	U-K	Poland	France	Germany	Italy	Total
	30	14	16	22	18	100

Ratio Cons. Mktg / Total Mktg (%):	Ovadols	Squazols	Trigols
	64	62	67

Total
6 200
2 800
3 400
4 600
3 900
20 900
32 400
45 000

✓ OK   ✗ Cancel

Reset to default decisions

---

adaptation decisions by examining their impact on consumer satisfaction and marketing effectiveness. In the end, the degree of local adaptation would have to take into account consumer needs, cost efficiencies, and organizational issues.

The Gamar3 Results Module

To provide a concise overview of Calgolia Europe's health at any given point in time, the Gamar3 simulation produced a global scorecard displaying four corporate performance indicators: share price index, global market share, global revenues, and contribution after marketing (see Exhibit 9). The share price index, set arbitrarily at 1000 at the end of Period 0, measured shareholder value for Calgolia Europe. This index was influenced by a number of factors such as revenues, profitability, and market trends, and not only reflected past results, but also anticipated future performance. The other indicators—global market share, global revenues, and contribution after marketing—consolidated all Calgolia's product categories and country operations. Based on these key indicators, corporate management authorized a level of marketing expenditures for the following period. This authorized marketing budget was indicated at the bottom of the global scorecard table.

Each screen of the Gamar3 Results module also offered the possibility to display graphs on the evolution of various dimensions. This was obtained by clicking on the box at the left of the selected item and then by clicking on the "Zoom Out" button. The graph was

———————————————— E X H I B I T   8 ————————————————

Gamar3—Global Price Changes

displayed below the corresponding table (see Exhibit 10). To display the graph or table on the full screen could easily be done by clicking on the "Zoom In" button in its top right-hand corner.

The Gamar3 simulation generated income statements for each OMU to help evaluate the financial performance of both its product categories and the marketing departments of its subsidiaries. The income statement could be presented by country or by product category. The "volume sold" item indicated the quantity sold in a given period in thousands of units (KU). This represented a tangible measure of the market's response to the firm's actions with regard to pricing decisions and consumer or trade marketing expenditures. The variable costs per unit were specific to a given product and, in line with Calgolia's international sourcing and accounting policies, remained the same in all countries. As long as production remained standardized, the impact of volume on variable costs was negligible. The unit variable cost of a product changed only according to the degree of local adaptation to the product specifications.

The four market studies reproduced by the simulation estimated consumer satisfaction and effectiveness ratings on a scale from 0 to 100. The first two studies analyzed levels of consumer satisfaction with product specifications and pricing, ranging from total dissatisfaction (0), to total satisfaction (100). Two other studies tracked the effectiveness of consumer and trade marketing, where a rating of 100 reflected the highest possible effectiveness and 0 indicated complete ineffectiveness. Consumer satisfaction and effectiveness

―――――――――――――― **E X H I B I T   9** ――――――――――――――

Gamar3—The Global Scorecard

GAMAR3 - STATUQUO										_ ⊡ ✕
	Period	Test	Country	Category	11:30					
Decisions	10 ▾	1 ▾	▾	▾	<<	>>	Help	Info	Print	Exit
Results	GLOBAL RESULTS									Zoom Out
Analysis										
Simulation										

MENU

◆ Global Scorecard
◇ Income Statement
◇ Product Satisfact.
◇ Price Satisfact.
◇ Cons. mktg Effectiv.
◇ Trade mktg Effectiv.
◇ Category Report
◇ Decision Overview

GLOBAL SCORECARD				
Item	Unit	Period 9	Period 10	% Change
Share price index	Base 1000	976	994	1.9
Global market share	%$	5.8	5.6	-3.3
Global revenues	K$	121 716	123 848	1.8
Contribution after marketing	K$	45 815	47 226	3.1
Authorized marketing budget	K$	45 000	45 000	0.0

ratings were estimated from the marketing decisions. These international market surveys were essential to understanding the impact of the marketing program.

The product report provided information on market size, share, prices, and growth for past periods. It also forecast market size and growth for the coming period.

The Gamar3 Analysis Module

This module provided five summary screens relating to the market, the firm's position, the profit structure, key performance indicators (KPIs), and a growth/share matrix.

The Market Analysis page presented the size, growth rate, and average price for each market in which Calgolia was present. The page on Calgolia's Marketing Position showed the overall marketing results—market share, revenues, and contribution after marketing, together with key decisions. The page on Profit Structure highlighted the key components of the firm's profit statement: revenues, CBM, consumer marketing, trade marketing, and CAM. These elements were available both in dollars or as a percentage of revenues. For all these three pages, the information was accessible by product category, by country, or for each product category in each country.

The page on KPIs tracked the impact of specific decisions. In addition to overall results such as market share, revenues, and CAM, it presented each marketing decision together with a related indicator: price with the price satisfaction index; product adaptation with the

EXHIBIT 10

Gamar3—Displaying Graphs

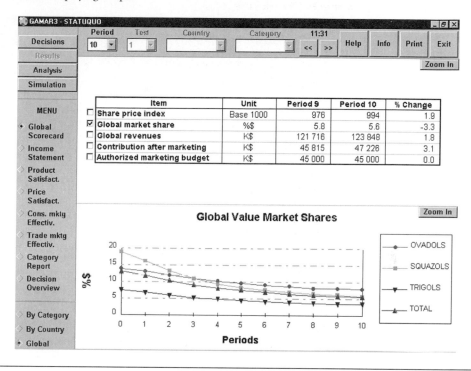

product satisfaction index; consumer marketing budget and adaptation with the consumer marketing effectiveness index; and trade marketing budget and adaptation with the trade marketing effectiveness index.

The last component of the analysis module was the Growth/Share Matrix, built into the Gamar3 simulation to provide a rapid assessment of Calgolia's portfolio. This simple business decision support tool was inspired by those developed by several consulting firms to help corporations cope with the strategic issue of allocating resources between a multitude of business units. In the Gamar3 software, the horizontal axis—market share—was a simplified representation of the unit's strength, and the vertical axis—defined as market growth—was a simplified representation of the OMU's market attractiveness. Each of Calgolia's OMUs was plotted as a circle in the matrix. The area of the circle was proportional to the total sales of the corresponding unit (see Exhibit 11).

Taken together, the various pages of this analysis module provided summary information of greatest relevance to help Sylvia and the local marketing managers in establishing guidelines to allocate marketing resources between Calgolia's 15 OMUs.

The European Marketing Workshop

Sylvia had already familiarized herself with the simulation, starting initially at the Basic level of difficulty with one product category (Ovadols) in two countries (the United Kingdom and Poland). Emboldened by the ease with which she could project different

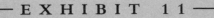

E X H I B I T　　1 1

Gamar3—The Growth/Share Matrix

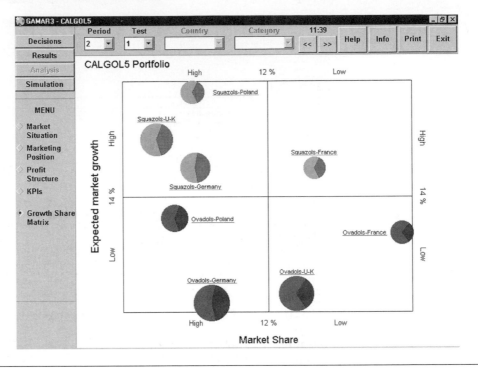

results, she had gone up through the Intermediate and Advanced levels relatively easily. She had also tested a number of strategies at the Expert level and been able to demonstrate that the current situation could be improved. "This is just terrific," she said to herself. "Using this will finally help convince all those doubting local managers of the need for more-integrated and more-effective international marketing strategies."

Sylvia had invited the marketing managers of the five subsidiaries simulated in the Gamar3 model to participate in a two-day workshop in order to finalize the main lines of the 1998–2000 European marketing strategy. They were going to spend a good part of the first day in reaching agreement on a desirable 10-year scenario using the Gamar3 simulation. All participants in the workshop had been given a copy of the software package 10 days earlier and had had the chance to try their own preferred strategies. As Sylvia drove along the narrow roads of Buckinghamshire toward the workshop venue in Marlow, she was confident that this was going to be the kind of meeting where real progress would be made toward transforming Calgolia into a more effective global marketing company.

APPENDIX A

Instructions for Using the Gamar3 Software

1. **Installing the Gamar3 software on your PC.** The Gamar3 software requires a PC operating under the Windows 3.1 or Windows 95 environment. To install the software on your PC, follow the simple instructions on the Gamar3 diskette.

2. **Getting started with the Gamar3 software.** Access the software by double-clicking on the Gamar3 icon appearing in the Windows program manager. An introductory screen will appear giving general information about the Gamar3 simulation and its developers. Click on the Start Gamar3 button, and a screen will then appear showing the Gamar3 map. Create a firm by clicking on the corresponding button in the left-hand menu and then specifying a name up to eight characters long. Your results will be automatically saved under this name. You can create several firms with different names. You can always access data files of firms previously created by clicking the Select Firm button on the left-hand side of the screen.

3. **Understanding the format of a Gamar3 screen.** Each Gamar3 screen is composed of four parts, three of which contain command buttons that can be activated by clicking on them with the mouse when they appear in black (see Exhibit 5). When a button appears as a grey shadow, this means that it is not accessible at this point in time. The four parts are

   • The Master Menu, located on the top left-hand corner. This is composed of four buttons corresponding to the modules of the software: Decisions (to enter your decisions for a given period), Results (to obtain the results of a given simulation run), Analysis (to display summary corporate performance tables), and Simulation (to run the simulation, create new firms, and compare different tests).

   • The Sub-Menus, located in the left-hand column, contain the options available for each of the four modules of the software, and change as you click on different items in the Master Menu.

- The Top Line allows you to specify key parameters (Period number, Test number, Country, Category) and gives you access to common options (Help, Information, Print, and Exit). You will find the Help facility particularly useful at the beginning, until you become familiar with the software operation.
- The Center Screen can contain, in the Decisions and Results modules, a table of numbers, a graph, or both simultaneously. The graphs show the evolution of key variables from Period 0 to present. When only the table or the graph is present, click on the Zoom Out button to obtain both simultaneously. To have a larger representation of the table or graph, click on the corresponding Zoom In button.

4. **Entering decisions.** You can access the decision entry component of the software by clicking on the Decisions button in the top left-hand corner. The menu in the left column allows you to access each type of decision directly. Each table provides you with a reminder of the decisions for the previous period. The software also automatically replicates last period's decisions as default decisions for the current period. You may enter new decisions by simply writing over them, or you may revert to the default decisions at any time by clicking on the corresponding button. As you enter new decisions, the corresponding percentage change is displayed in the right-hand side column. The two buttons in the lower left-hand corner allow you to check for possible errors and warnings, and to display an overview of your decisions. The Decision Overview screen presents a summary of your decisions by product, by country, or on a global basis.

5. **Errors and warnings.** Check this screen before running the simulation. It alerts you to errors and oversights. An error must be corrected before running the simulation. If constraints such as budgets or price limits are violated, the simulation will not run and you will be asked to make the appropriate corrections. A warning, on the other hand, only alerts you to an oversight or a potential problem.

6. **Running the simulation.** Clicking on the Simulation button in the top left-hand corner gives access to the simulation interface module. The menu for this section includes the creation and selection of firms as described in the "Getting started" paragraph above, the display of the firm's status, and the best scores achieved in the tests made during the current period. To run the simulation, click on the Run Simulation button in the menu. The simulation will run based on your decisions, and you will have access to the results.

7. **Test runs.** Once you have run the simulation for a given period, you may change your decisions and rerun the simulation for the same period. In this way, you may test different courses of action for a given period; you are allowed a maximum of 10 such tests for each period. To compare different test runs, view the Best Scores Obtained screen in the simulation module. This gives a summary of your previous test runs within the current period, ranked by decreasing importance of the share price index.

8. **Displaying results.** Results can be obtained by clicking on the corresponding button on the top left-hand corner. When a firm is created, the results correspond to Period 0. Although the displayed results normally correspond to the last simulation run, you can access the results of previous periods and tests by changing the parameters in the top line of the screen. You can access different parts of the Company Report through the menu in the left column, or by turning the pages through the forward and backward arrows in the top line. When you are satisfied with your results, or if you have reached the limit of 10 tests, you should enter your decisions for the next period.

9. **Analyzing the situation.** In the Analysis module of the software, the table presented summarizes the current results in terms of Market Situation, Marketing Position, Profit Structure, and Key Performance Indicators. The menu in the left-hand column allows you to directly access each type of table. You may also examine the information for past periods by changing the Period parameter in the top line, as described above. The graphic representation of the Portfolio tool may also be accessed in this module.

10. **Leaving Gamar3.** When you have finished using the Gamar3 simulation, you can exit by clicking on the Exit button in the top right-hand corner. Any simulated firm that you have created, and any tests you have made, will still be accessible in a later use of the software.

B APPENDIX

Gamar3—The Decision Form

OVADOLS	Management time (man-months)	Consumer marketing (K$)	Trade marketing (K$)	Price ($)	Local adaptation (0=none, 100=total)
U.K.					Product specs.
Poland					Consumer marketing
France					Trade marketing
Germany					
Italy					

SQUAZOLS	Management time (man-months)	Consumer marketing (K$)	Trade marketing (K$)	Price ($)	Local adaptation (0=none, 100=total)
U.K.					Product specs.
Poland					Consumer marketing
France					Trade marketing
Germany					
Italy					

TRIGOLS	Management time (man-months)	Consumer marketing (K$)	Trade marketing (K$)	Price ($)	Local adaptation (0=none, 100=total)
U.K.					Product specs.
Poland					Consumer marketing
France					Trade marketing
Germany					
Italy					

Name Index

Subject Index